# ADVANCED RESEARCH STUDIES IN COMMERCE AND MANAGEMENT

# ADVANCED RESEARCH STUDIES IN COMMERCE AND MANAGEMENT

**DR A VIJAYAKUMAR**

**MD PUBLICATIONS PVT LTD**
**NEW DELHI**
**www.mdppl.com**

*Published by* :

**MD Publications Pvt Ltd**
"MD House", 11, Darya Ganj,
New Delhi - 110 002
Phone : +91-11-45355555
E-mail : contact@mdppl.com
Website: www.mdppl.com

**ISBN** : 978-81-7533-371-0

Published and Printed by Mr. Pranav Gupta on behalf of **MD Publications Pvt Ltd** at Mohit Enterprises, Delhi.

# PREFACE

Research is the systematic effort to gain new knowledge. The new knowledge to be gained out of research relates basically to business, their marketing activities, finances, personal, productivity and profitability performance in general, as well as their interface with government in their social setting and their environment. It is a well recognized fact that there exists a wide time gap in the research being done getting published in journals and in books. It is difficult for most people to consult professional and academic research oriented journals regularly. The benefits which the society may derive from such research remain untapped and the findings based on hard labour and serious efforts of researchers decorate the columns of professional and academic research journals which in turn either pile dust in some obscure corners of the libraries or decorate the offices of senior professors.

To fill this gap, I have attempted to include all my advanced research articles of interest published in well known journals in India and abroad. This book contains 27 research articles focusing nine important areas in the field of commerce and management. The book contains a comprehensive analysis in the areas of corporate profitability, corporate liquidity, EVA and MVA, production, working capital, capital structure, Assessment of financial health, productivity and financial competitiveness etc., so as to help readers develop the skill to understand, analyze and interpret financial problems and to improve the profitability of the concerns by taking prudent final decisions. Further in order to cater to the needs of research scholars, teachers and financial executives, the subject matter in the book has been treated in a conceptual-cum-analytical manner.

The book is useful for practicing managers, financial executives working in the various government organization, business executives, and students of M.Com, MBA, MFC and other professional examinations. Further, this book is special interest of Ph.D and M.Phil. scholars of various universities, colleges and research institutions. I earnestly hope that it would serve its purpose and meet the market needs. However, I would gratefully welcome suggestions and feedback from college's students and practitioners. Any constructive criticism will doubted help me greatly to enhance my research capability.

I am thankful to all my co-authors, the editors of various journals, management of Erode Arts and Science College, Principal , my colleagues, research scholars , family members and friends for their help and support in the completion of this book. I also extend my profound thanks to Mr Pranav Gupta, Director, MD Publications Pvt Ltd, New Delhi, for giving a shape to my ideas by publishing this book in a record time. I look forward for constructive suggestions from readers.

**Dr A VIJAYA KUMAR**

# CONTENTS

# PART - I

# ANALYSIS OF CORPORATE PROFITABILITY

# 1

# An Empirical Analysis of Factors Associated with the Profitability

## The Case of Indian Automobile Firms

### INTRODUCTION

The study of how and why firms attain profitability levels has been the main pre-occupation of Industrial organization economists for the last four decades. Many of the theoretical and empirical developments on the determination of corporate profitability emanate from traditional price theory and the Structure-Conduct-Performance (SCP) paradigm of the modern industrial organization literature. This latter framework was initiated by the Harvard economist Bain (1956), utilizing much of the earlier work of Clark (1940) and Mason (1949). Beyond Bain, over 20 years, a considerable research was undertaken examining the relationship between firm structure and profitability. In determining factors influencing performance diversity, literature dealing with such work suggests that industrial performance and performance differences among firms can be explained as arising from various characteristics; those which are industry specific (collusion hypothesis) and those which are firm-specific (Efficient market hypothesis). (Capon, Farley & Hoenig, 1990).

Industrial organization economists point to industry effects (i.e., concentration levels, industry growth) using the structure – conduct – performance model (SCP) as the main factor determining firm profitability. (Demsetz, 1973; Peltzman,1977; Scherer, 1980; Porter 1981). On the other hand, the resource-based view (Wernerfelt, 1984; Barney, 1991; Peteraf, 1993) suggests that the explanation for the existence of more or less profitable firms within the same industry must be found in the internal factors of each company (for example, market share, firm size, skill level etc.). These firm-effect factors favour the achievement and maintenance of competitive advantages of each firm, which eventually lead to different profitability levels among firms belonging to the same industry (Amato & Wilder, 1990).

Many studies are found testing these competing hypotheses and the results concludes with general mixed opinions. In the market Structure-Conduct-Performance (SCP) literature, the most important hypotheses, appear to fall in to six categories (Bothwell, Cooley and Hall, 1984) which can be characterized as follows: seller's concentration may affect Profit-Monopoly power, conferred by high degrees of seller concentration, may cause high rates of return (Bain, 1951); High entry barriers may also affect profits positively (Mann, 1966; Weiss, 1963; Comanor and Wilson, 1967; Qualls, 1979); Absolute or relative firm size may also explain profits. (Demsetz, 1973; Peltzman, 1977; Gale, 1972; Shephered, 1972); Risk differentials may be another variable affecting profitability differences (Stigler, 1963; Fisher and Hall, 1967; Cootner and Holland, 1970); Advertising Intensity also explaining profits (Bloch, 1974) and Growth also affects the profits (Brozen's 1971).

Actually profitability is a highly sensitive economic variable which is affected by a host of factors operating through a variety of ways. Some of them affect the product prices and quantities; some affect the cost of production while others make changes in capital stock, size, market share and growth of the firm. All such factors ultimately make the profitability of the firm to vary. It is difficult to build a theory of profitability which accounts for all such factors. Because of this difficulty, it is quite natural to analyze the variations in profitability by taking the partial approach, that is, to find the effect of certain major variables, ignoring the implications of other left out independent variables at a time. Hence, in this study the relationship between size, growth, liquidity, leverage, age, persistence of profitability, capital - output ratio, market share and profitability has been made.

## VARIABLES SPECIFICATIONS AND EMPIRICAL MODEL

In order to explain the profitability of the firms in Indian automobile industry, the various factors discussed above, have been taken together. This is achieved by developing a similar empirical framework used by Peter H. Grinyer and Peter Mc kiernan (1991), Jim Nugent (1998), Sumit K. Majumdar (1997), Bala Ramasamy *et al.*, (2005), Abdussalam Mahmoud Abu-Tapanjeh (2006) and Grace Tola Olutunla and Tomola Marshal Obamuyi (2008). The analysis of data employs the use of correlation and a multiple regression model that consists of factors associated with profitability of firms in Indian automobile industry.

The basic model consists of a multiple regression of profitability on a set of independent variables. The dependent variables of the regression model is return on assets (which is defined as, Gross profit as percentage on total assets) which relates the profitability to the asset base. This study investigates the effect of size, growth, liquidity, leverage, age, persistency of profitability, capital-output ratio and market share on firms' profitability. The current study use correlation analysis to identify the association between profitability and the independent variables, as well as regression analysis to estimate the causal relationship. The researcher considered the following regression model.

$$\mathbf{PR_{it} = \beta_0 + \beta_1 (Size)_{it} + \beta_2 (Growth)_{it} + \beta_3 (Liquidity)_{it} + \beta_4 (Leverage)_{it} + \beta_5 (Age)_{it} + \beta_6 (Past\ profitability)_{it} + \beta_7 (Capital\text{-}output\ ratio)_{it} + \beta_8 (Market\ share)_{it} + e_{it}}$$

Where,

| | | |
|---|---|---|
| PR | – | Measures the firm profitability with gross profit as a percentage of total assets for the firm (i) in the year (t) |
| Size | – | Natural logarithm of firm's sales for firm (i) in the year (t) |
| Growth | – | Growth of firm's sales for firm (i) in the year (t) |
| Liquidity | – | Measures cash conversion cycle for the firm (i) in the year (t) |
| Leverage | – | Measures with debt to equity for firm (i) in the year (t) |
| Age | – | Natural logarithms of the firm's age for firm (i) in the year (t) |
| Past Profitability | – | One year lagged profitability for the firm (i) in the year (t) |
| Capital-output ratio | – | Measures the ratio of total capital to total sales for firm (i) in the year (t) |
| Market share | – | Measures the ratio of sales to total industry sales for firm (i) in the year (t) |
| $\beta_0$ | – | Constant term for the firm (i) in the year (t) |
| $\beta_1, \beta_2$..... | – | Regression co-efficient |

e – Disturbance term for the firm (i) in the year (t).

Table 1.1 below summarizes the definition, theoretical predicted signs and a-priori hypotheses were formulated, which were to be tested.

**TABLE 1.1**

**PROXY VARIABLES DEFINITION AND PREDICTED RELATIONSHIPS**

| Proxy variables | Definitions | Predicted Sign | a-priori hypotheses |
|---|---|---|---|
| Size | Natural logarithm of firm's sales | +/- | $P_1$/Size > 0 |
| Growth | Growth of firm's sales | +/- | $P_1$/GS > 0 |
| Liquidity | Cash conversion cycle | +/- | $P_1$/CCC < 0 |
| Leverage | Debt to equity ratio | - | $P_1$/Lev < 0 |
| Age | Age of firm from the starting year | + | $P_1$/Age > 0 |
| Past profitability | One year lagged profitability | + | $P_1$/Past Profitability>0 |
| Capital-output ratio | Ratio of total capital to total sales | +/- | $P_1$/Capital output <0 |
| Market share | Ratio of sales to total industry sales | + | $P_1$/Market share > 0 |

## ANALYSIS AND DISCUSSION

This section describes descriptive statistics summary, correlation, regression analysis and discussion of results.

## DESCRIPTIVE STATISTICS AND ANALYSIS

Descriptive statistics includes the mean, standard deviation, minimum, and maximum, standard error of mean, kurtosis and skewness for the period 1996-2009. The data contains about 20 automobile firms for 216 firm-years observations. Table show that there are negative values at minimum values i.e., some firms have operated with losses during the study period.

Table 1.2 contains descriptive statistics of the variables used in this study. The table reveals that profit rate ranges between -189.39 per cent to 1638.92 per cent with mean of 22.29 per cent and a standard deviation 105.3. The same applies to growth, liquidity, leverage, past profitability capital-output ratio and market share, which show that the standard deviation is more than the mean. This implies that there is a high variations in the firm's mean. The table also reveals that profit rate, growth, leverage, age, past profitability, capital-output ratio and market share have a positive skewness, which indicates that the scores are clustered to the left at the low values. As for size and liquidity have a negative skewness indicating clustering of scores are at the high and as for the kurtosis statistic, all variables except for market share show a positive kurtosis suggesting that the distribution has pecked or clustered in the centre, with long thin tails.

## CORRELATION ANALYSIS

A correlation analysis was performed to verify a possible association between and among the variables, in order to test whether there is any linear correlation between and among the variables. Collinearity explains the dependence of one variable to other. When variables are highly correlated they both express essentially the same information. Table 1.3 reports the Pearson correlation coefficients of all the variables employed in the study. Simple correlations among the variables that are reported in Table 1.3 are quite low. The largest reported value (-.58) was between market share and size. In this respect, Kennedy (1985) suggests that correlation values below 0.80 do not pose a potential multicollinearity problem. Hence, the performance variables used in this study do not seem to pose a serious multicollinearity problem and this allows for standard interpretation of the regression coefficients.

## DISCUSSION OF RESULTS

Using pooled regression technique, the study ran the regression of the profitability on the firm structure variables like size, growth, liquidity, leverages, age, past profitability, capital-output ratio and market share with aim to investigate whether these variables have significant explanatory powers. The estimated results are reported in Table 1.4.

It can be observed from the table that the estimated value of the R-Square is 0.90 for whole automobile industry, 0.98 commercial vehicles sector, 0.97 for passenger cars and multi-utility vehicles sector and 0.93 for two and three wheelers sectors. This implies that more than 90 percent of the variation in profitability of the firms is jointly determined by the said variables. The value of F-statistic indicates that the overall model is good. The Durbin-Watson statistic is also close to 2 which imply that the successive values of estimated residuals are not dependent on each other. This means that there is evidence to accept that there is no auto correlation problem in the estimated model.

Regarding the significance of individual variables, the empirical results shows that size has statistically significant effect on profitability in the Indian Automobile Industry. However, in the overall pooled sample, firm size showed significant negative relation with profitability in the Indian Automobile Industry. This is consistent with the findings of Singh and Whittington (1968) and contradictory to the findings of Samuels and Smith (1968), who postulated positive relationship between size and profitability. The sector wise analysis showed that the size had a significant positive relationship with profitability in case of commercial vehicles and passenger cars and multiutility vehicles sector. This could be due to the changes in output either because of increased demand or reduction of costs. On the other hand, there was a significant negative relationship reported between size and profitability in the two and three wheelers sector. This was due to the reasons that larger firms can lead to organizational inefficiencies, higher bureaucratization and concept of x-inefficiency. X-inefficiency is a measure of the degree to which costs are higher than they need to be. X-inefficiency reasons that general managerial or technological inefficiency in larger firms cause higher production costs which end up in reductions in the bottom line i.e., profit rates decline. Among the various firms selected for the study, some firms showed positive relationships while others not so.

Table 1.4 also showed the results of regression of profitability fitted on growth of sales in all the selected firms, three sectors and whole industry. It is evident from the table that there was a significant variation in the regression co-efficient relating profitability to growth of sales between firms. Further, there is a positive relationship between the two variables (growth and profitability) except Hyundai Motors Ltd under passenger cars and multi-utility vehicles and Kinetic Motor Company Ltd, Hero Honda Motors Ltd and Majestic Auto Ltd under two and three wheeler sector. These results are consistent with the results of Singh and Whittington (1968), who also found positive relationship between growth and profitability in their study. This was due to increased motivation among employees who expect greater gains in the future, gains resulting from greater company size.

Consistent with Deloof (2003), Reheman and Nasr (2007), Garcia-Teruel and Martinez-Solano (2007) and David M. Mathuva, a negative relationship exists between the liquidity (cash conversion cycle) and profitability of selected automobile firms, three sectors and whole automobile industry. This was due to the fact that minimizing the investment in current assets can help in boosting profits. This ensures the liquid cash is not maintained in the business for long and that it is use to generate profits for the firm. These results suggest that managers can create value for their shareholder by reducing the number of days of the cash conversion cycle to its minimum.

Regarding the significance of the leverage, the empirical results presented in Table 1.4 showed that the majority of the Indian automobile firms, profitability are negatively significantly associated with the leverage. This piece of evidence is in line with Pecking Order Theory which postulates a negative correlation between the profitability and leverage. This is consist with the findings of Rajan and Zingales (1995), that is, higher profitable firms uses less debt. There are other evidence for this relationship such as informational asymmetry, high costs of external resources and inefficiency of the market. However, this piece of evidence is in contrast to the Static Trade-off Theory that states that more profitable firms have lower expected bankruptcy costs and higher tax benefits. Despite this, Scooters India Ltd under two and three wheelers sector continue to enjoy such large profit margins that firms using higher proportion of debt in their capital structure were still more profitable than firms using lower proportion of debt.

It is also apparent from Table 1.4 that firm age has significant effects on profitability. Perhaps, it is one of the strongest determinants of profitability in all the selected automobile firms. The co-efficient of the age of firms carries a positive sign, support our a priori expectation. This indicates that older firms to be more profitable because managing the licensing process yields significant experience in pre-empting market capacities, which can then yield superior profitability because of market capture. However, apart from profitability arising from market pre-emption activities, through superior management of the licensing process, firms also become more profitable because of several strategic or operational reasons, one of which is that they are able to tap in to the relevant customer segment and provide differentiated products that meet demand. All though, this results is consistent with the work of Stanger

(2000), Stanger (2000) argues that the relationship should be positive, since older firms are more likely to have attained diminishing costs of production over some range of sales and hence be able to operate more economically and efficiently than recently established ones. However, the study by Hannan and Free man (1989) suggest that older firms are more resistant to change in a competitive environment and newer technologies which may, as a result of the need to operate in an age-old standardized manner, leave older firms progressively outdated and lead to organization failure.

As far as past profitability's relation with profitability of the selected firm of Indian automobile industry is concerned, there was a significant positive relation during the years 1996-2009 as well as for the pooled sample. This indicates positive influences on profitability, confirming our hypothesis. This result conforms to the conclusions of Singh and Whittington (1968). Table 1.4 also showed that the co-efficient of capital-output ratio supported our hypothesis, suggesting positive relationship between increased capital-output ratio and profitability. This result is consistent with the work of Hurdle (1974). Further, regression results suggest that market share is the most important determinant of profitability. The corresponding positive co-efficient suggests that selected Indian automobile firms have increased their profitability by increasing their market share.

## POLICY IMPLICATIONS

It has been often argued that larger firms in an industry are relatively more efficient than the smaller ones. If this is not so, then why does a firm aspire to be larger and larger; and if this is so, then how do smaller and larger firms co-exist in the same industry. Every business is normally encountered with risks and uncertainties; bigger the firm it is expected to be stronger to face such risky and uncertain situations. Moreover a big firm because of its control over the market can buy up the best sites with location advantages, the superior technology, R&D and best professional experts. However, the findings of the study showed that "law of proportional effect" does not hold in the selected Indian automobile firms. While relatively bigger firms perform better in commercial vehicles and passenger cars and multiutility vehicles sector, the opposite hold true in two and three wheeler sector and the whole industry. These findings should be useful to the managerial authorities to decide on the extent to which firm size needs to be monitored and controlled.

Based on the empirical results obtained in this study, it is concluded that there is tendency of positive relationship between profitability and growth. Also the extent of this positive relationship is different in different firms, depending upon their ability and willingness to grow, which may further depend upon their factors like extent of monopoly power, growth of demand, market share, better labour relations and other managerial conditions etc.. Further, the analysis of liquidity and profitability have identified critical management practices and are expected to assist managers in identifying areas where they might improve the financial performance of their operation. The results have provided owner-managers with information regarding the basic financial management practices used by their peers and their peers' attitudes towards these practices. Firms are capable of gaining sustainable competitive advantage by means of effective and efficient utilization of the resources of the organization through a careful reduction of the cash conversion cycle to its minimum. Therefore, managers can create profits for their companies by handling correctly the cash conversion cycle and keeping each different component (accounts receivables, accounts payables and inventory) to an optimum level. The relationship between leverage and profitability showed that the successful selection and use of the debt-to-equity ratio is one of the key elements of the firm's financial strategy.

The study is mainly of theoretical interest, as it examines size, growth, liquidity, leverage, age and profitability of firms and their inter-relationships. However, the empirical results obtained from the analysis of data are of importance to the owners and managers, interested in the growth and profitability of the firms. The policy of increasing total assets or sales with a view to increase profitability may not be rewarding in all cases. Therefore, such policies have to be carefully examined in view of the findings of this study, so that these may not lead to over-capitalization and ultimately reduce profitability. From the point of view of the economy, significant relationship between size and profitability supports the policy of liberalization, initiated in the Indian Economy since 1991. The study suggests that this policy of liberalization should further be strengthened.

## CONCLUSION

The study has contributed to our knowledge on the series of factors associated with the profitability of selected firms in the Indian Automobile Industry. The primary aim of this study was to test the postulated hypotheses and to provide evidence with respect to the impact of firm structure to firm profitability, by examining such major factors as firm size, growth, liquidity, leverage, age, post profitability, market share and capital-output ratio. The study employed regression model in order to test the hypotheses, using profitability measured by the Rate of Return on Assets (PR) along with other independent variables using sample of 20 automobile firms in India. The results demonstrate that firm size and growth are important determinants of profitability in the Indian automobile industry and a positive relationship between profitability and firm size and growth. Further, the results suggest that liquidity and leverage had a negative impact on profitability. Referring the firm as a variable affecting the profitability, the study shows significant result which implied that firm age affect the profitability of a firm. Further more, this study has found empirical evidence that past profitability, capital-output ratio and market share are important determinants of profitability in the Indian automobile Industry. These principal findings can be summarized as in Table 1.5.

In conclusion, these finding have an interesting policy implications, which may add to the ongoing debate on the issue of firm structure and the firm profitability relations. The empirical findings of this study suggest that firm structure emerges as important factor affecting profitability. However, the results indicate that some of the independent variable considered in this study has weak impacts on profitability. These findings should be useful to the management authorities to decide on the extent to which firm structure needs to be monitored and controlled. The validity and the generalization of the conclusions mentioned are pending future research in other industries or sectors that ratifies or refutes them.

## REFERENCES

1. Amato, L and Wilder, R.P. (1990). "Firm and industry effects in industrial Economics", *Southern Economic Journal*, Vol. 50, pp.93-105.
2. Bain, J. (1956). "Barriers to new competition", Harvard University Press:Cambridge, M.A
3. Barney, J. (1991). "Firm Resources and Sustained Competitive Advantage", *Journal of Management*, Vol. 17, pp. 99-120.
4. Bothwell, J.L., Cooley, T.F and Hall, T.E. (1984). "A new view of the Market Structure-Performance Debate", *Journal of Industrial Economic*, Vol. 32, pp. 397- 417.
5. Brozen, Y. (1970). "Bains Concentration and Rates of Return Revisited", *Journal of Law and Economics*, Vol. 14, pp. 351- 369.
6. Clark, J.M. (1940). "Toward a Concept of Workable Competition", *American Economic Review*, Vol. 30.
7. Comanor, W.S and T.A Wilson (1967). "Advertising, Market Structure and Performance", *Review of*

*Economics and Statistics*, Vol. 49, pp. 423-40.

8. Capon, N., Farley, J., and Hoenig, H. (1990). "Determinants of financial performance: A Meta Analysis", *Management Science*, pp.1143-1159.
9. Demsetz, H. (1973). "Industry, Market Rivalry and Public Policy", *Journal of Law and Economics*, Vol. 16, pp. 1-10.
10. Garcia – Teruel P.J., and Martinez – Solano P.M. (2007). "Effects of working capital management on SME Profitability", *International Journal of Managerial Finance*, Vol.3, pp.164-177.
11. Gale, Bradley, T. (1972). "Market share and Rate of return", *Review of Economics*, Vol. 54, pp. 412-23.
12. Hurdle, G.J. (1974). "Leverage Risk and Market Structure and Profitability", *Review of Economics and Statistics*, Vol. 56, pp. 478-85.
13. Mathuva,D.(2009). "The influence of working capital management components on profitability: A Survey on Kenyan Listed Firms", *Research Journal of Business Management*, Vol.3, pp.1-11.
14. Marc Deloof (2003). "Does working capital management affect profitability of Belgian Firms?", *Journal of Business Finance and Accounting*, Vol.30 (3-4), pp. 573-88.
15. Mason, E.S. (1949). "The Current State of the Monopoly Problem in the US", *Harvard Law Review*, Vol. 62, pp.1265-1285.
16. Mann, H.M. (1966). "Seller Concentration, Barriers to Entry and Rates of return in Thirty Industries, 1950-1960", *Review of Economics and Statistics*, Vol. 48, pp.296-307.
17. Peltzman, S. (1977). "The Gains and Losses from Industrial Concentration", *Journal of Law and Economics*, Vol. 20, pp. 229-263.
18. Porter, M. (1981). "The Contributions of Industrial Organisation to Strategic Management", *Academy of Management Review*, Vol. 6, pp. 609-620.
19. Peteraf, M. (1993). "The Cornerstones of Competitive advantage: A Resource-based view", *Strategic*

*Management Journal*, Vol. 14, pp. 179-191.

20. Qualls, P.D (1979). "Market Structure and Cyclical Flexibility of Price-Cost Margins", *The Journal of Business*, Vol. 52, pp. 305-25.
21. Rajan, R., and Zingales, L. (2000). "The firm as a dedicated hierarchy, a theory of the origins and growth of firms", NBER working paper no. W7546.
22. Raheman, A., and M. Nasr (2007). "Working capital management and profitability: case of Pakistani firms", *International Review of Business Research*, Vol.3 (2), pp. 275-96.
23. Scherer, F. (1980). "Industrial Market Structure and Economic Performance (2nd ed) Chicago: Rand-McNally.
24. Shephered, W.G. (1972). "Elements of Market Structure", *Review of Economics and Statistics*, Vol. 54, pp. 25-38.
25. Stigler, G.J. (1963). "Capital and Rates of returns in Manufacturing Industries", Princeton University Press, Princeton
26. Samuels, J. M. and Smyth, D.J. (1968). "Profits, Variability of Profits and Firm size," *Economica*, Vol. 35, pp. 127-139
27. Singh, Ajit and Whittington, G. (1968). "Growth, Profitability and Valuation", Cambridge University Press.
28. Vijayakumar, A. and Kadirvel, S. (2003). "Profitability and size of the firm in Indian Minerals and Metals industry", *The Management Accountant*, pp. 816-821.
29. Weiss, L. W (1963). "Average Concentration Ratios and Industrial Firms", *Journal of Industrial Economics*, Vol. 11, pp. 237-54.

## TABLE 1.2

## DESCRIPTIVE STATISTICS OF INDEPENDENT AND DEPENDENT VARIABLES

**20 Indian Automobile Firms-1996-2009 – 216 Firm-year observations (N = 216)**

| Variables | Mean ± SD | Standard Error of Mean | Median | Minimum | Maximum | Kurtosis | Skew ness |
|---|---|---|---|---|---|---|---|
| PR | 22.29 ± 105.3 | 6.62 | 14.58 | -189.39 | 1638.92 | 222.83 | 14.44 |
| Ln sales (size) | 6.90 ± 1.70 | 0.11 | 6.86 | 0.92 | 10.39 | 0.01 | -0.27 |
| Growth | 10.60 ± 36.83 | 2.32 | 10.13 | -97.62 | 356.66 | 31.46 | 3.48 |
| Liquidity (CCC) | 29.90 ± 65.81 | 4.14 | 19.07 | -225.76 | 312.03 | 5.58 | -.18 |
| Leverage | 1.40 ± 3.18 | 0.20 | 0.71 | 0 | 41.37 | 106.68 | 9.18 |
| Age | 0.06 ± 0.02 | 0.001 | 0.06 | 0.02 | 0.19 | 5.38 | 1.62 |
| Post profitability | 18.67 ± 130.38 | 8.23 | 15.82 | -1190.08 | 1638.92 | 124.98 | 4.51 |
| Capital-output ratio | 1.07 ± 130.38 | 0.44 | 0.26 | -1.89 | 79.78 | 111.18 | 10.40 |
| Market share | 2.05 ± 2.85 | 0.18 | 0.12 | 0.01 | 9.66 | -0.08 | 1.14 |

PR-Profit rate on total assets; Ln Sales-Natural logarithm of sales (Proxy for size); Growth-Sales Growth; CCC-Cash Conversion Cycle (proxy for liquidity); Leverage – Debt/ Equity; Age-Ratio of Depreciation of fixed assets; Past Profitability- Profitability for previous year; Capital-Output Ratio – Ratio of total capital to total sales; Market Share – Ratio of sales to total industry sales.

***Source:*** Computed

## TABLE 1.3

## CORRELATION MATRIX

| | PR | Ln Sales | Growth | Liquidity | Leverage | Age | Past profitability | Capital output ratio | Market share |
|---|---|---|---|---|---|---|---|---|---|
| PR | 1.00 | | | | | | | | |
| Ln Sales | 0.04 | 1.00 | | | | | | | |
| Growth | 0.03 | 0.18 | 1.00 | | | | | | |
| Liquidity | -0.09 | -0.11 | -05.05 | 1.00 | | | | | |
| Leverage | -0.003 | -0.09 | -0.01 | 0.02 | 1.00 | | | | |
| Age | 0.04 | 0.29 | -0.03 | 0.08 | -0.05 | 1.00 | | | |
| Past profitability | 0.02 | 0.05 | 0.001 | 0.005 | -0.01 | 0.34 | 1.00 | | |
| Capital output ratio | 0.02 | 0.31 | 0.005 | -0.02 | -0.03 | 0.04 | 0.003 | 1.00 | |
| Market share | 0.10 | -.58 | -0.05 | -0.05 | 0.11 | -0.28 | -0.11 | 0.06 | 1.00 |

PR-Profit rate on total assets; Ln Sales-Natural logarithm of sales (Proxy for size); Growth-Sales Growth; CCC-Cash Conversion Cycle (proxy for liquidity); Leverage – Debt/ Equity; Age-Ratio of Depreciation of fixed assets; Past Profitability- Profitability for previous year; Capital-Output Ratio – Ratio of total capital to total sales; Market Share – Ratio of sales to total industry sales.

***Source :*** Computed

## TABLE 1.5

## FINDING ON FIRM STRUCTURE VARIABLES AND PROFITABILITY RELATIONSHIPS

| ***Firm Structure* Variables** | ***Measure of Performance on Profitability*** |
|---|---|
| Size of Firm | Larger firms are more Profitable (+) |
| Growth | Positive effects of growth on profitability |
| Liquidity | Negative relationship between profitability and liquidity (-) |
| Leverage | Positive effect with operating leverage (-) |
| Age | Older firms are more profitable (+) |
| Past profitability | Positively affect profitability (+) |
| Capital – output ratio | Positive association with the profitability |
| Market Share | Increased market share leads to improved profitability |

***Source:*** Empirical results of the study

## TABLE 1.4

## REGRESSION ANALYSIS FOR OTHER FACTORS AFFECTING PROFITABILITY

[PR = $\beta_0$ + $\beta_1$ Size + $\beta_2$ Growth + $\beta_3$ Liquidity + $\beta_4$ Leverage + $\beta_5$ Age + $\beta_6$ Past Profitability + $\beta_7$ Capital Output Ratio + $\beta_8$ Market Share]

| *Particulars* | *Constant* | *Size* | *Growth* | *Liquidity* | *Leverage* | *Age* | *Past Profitability* | *Capital Output Ratio* | *Market Share* | *$R^2$* | *Adj $R^2$* | *F Value* | *DW* |
|---|---|---|---|---|---|---|---|---|---|---|---|---|---|
| Ashok Leyland Ltd | 87.97 | 7.71 | 0.07 | -0.03 | -16.53 | 96.77 | 0.67 | 44.13 | 54.01 | 0.99 | 0.97 | 56.38* | 1.94 |
| | | (3.94)* | (2.58)** | (3.41)* | (2.47)*** | (3.56)* | (1.68) | (1.75) | (4.20)* | | | | |
| Tata Motors Ltd | 36.87 | 0.89 | 0.05 | -0.05 | -33.09 | 3.56 | 0.43 | 15.49 | 94.63 | 0.99 | 0.97 | 57.98* | 2.01 |
| | | (3.07)** | (3.57)* | (0.83) | (4.01)* | (3.84)* | (2.19)*** | (3.91)* | (2.61)** | | | | |
| Bajaj Tempo Ltd | -828.66 | -183.1 | 3.34 | -1.65 | -160.9 | 112.4 | 4.93 | 257.1 | 13.40 | 0.88 | 0.81 | 28.20* | 1.97 |
| | | (3.60)* | (2.29)** | (2.69)*** | (2.22)*** | (1.44) | (2.13)*** | (0.93) | (2.79)** | | | | |
| Eicher Motors Ltd | 103.17 | 14.41 | 0.15 | -0.02 | -37.38 | 87.34 | 0.02 | 87.19 | 2.80 | 0.94 | 0.89 | 7.84** | 1.33 |
| | | (3.69)* | (1.32) | (4.07)* | (2.67)*** | (3.88)* | (3.07)** | (2.21)*** | (2.56)*** | | | | |
| Swaraj Mazdar Ltd | 32.59 | 20.33 | 0.08 | -0.12 | -1.21 | 166.14 | 0.17 | 226.1 | 16.77 | 0.81 | 0.79 | 12.2* | 1.98 |
| | | (3.12)** | (4.08)* | (3.19)** | (1.16) | (4.15)* | (0.37) | (4.26)* | (0.89) | | | | |
| **Commercial Vehicles** | **23.07** | **0.55** | **0.05** | **-0.03** | **-10.75** | **3.34** | **0.19** | **7.26** | **8.53** | **0.98** | **0.95** | **26.77*** | **2.01** |
| | | **(3.37)*** | **(2.46)***** | **(2.45)***** | **(3.90)*** | **(1.68)** | **(2.68)**** | **(2.48)**** | **(0.72)** | | | | |
| Hindustan Motors Ltd | -138.74 | 13.67 | 0.16 | -0.01 | -3.36 | 780.0 | 0.04 | 69.72 | 2.96 | 0.86 | 0.81 | 18.26* | 1.80 |
| | | (3.63)* | (2.70)** | (0.01) | (3.34)* | (1.62) | (4.08)* | (3.57)* | (0.35) | | | | |
| Mahindra and Mahindra Ltd | 73.25 | 4.49 | 0.01 | -0.12 | -26.15 | 109.37 | 0.52 | 62.44 | 145.01 | 0.97 | 0.91 | 16.69* | 2.03 |
| | | (3.41)* | (3.02)** | (4.39)* | (2.64)** | (3.26)* | (1.64) | (2.64)** | (3.23)* | | | | |
| Maruti Udyog Ltd | 257.71 | 13.58 | 0.14 | -0.45 | -75.09 | 93.65 | 0.20 | 195.78 | 19.95 | 0.99 | 0.96 | 41.15* | 1.99 |
| | | (4.14)* | (2.86)** | (1.81) | (4.60)* | (1.02) | (2.32)*** | (5.79)* | (3.25)* | | | | |

## TABLE 1.4 (CONTINUED...)

## REGRESSION ANALYSIS FOR OTHER FACTORS AFFECTING PROFITABILITY

[PR = $\beta_0$ + $\beta_1$ Size + $\beta_2$ Growth + $\beta_3$ Liquidity + $\beta_4$ Leverage + $\beta_5$ Age + $\beta_6$ Past Profitability + $\beta_7$ Capital Output Ratio + $\beta_8$ Market Share]

| *Particulars* | *Constant* | *Size* | *Growth* | *Liquidity* | *Leverage* | *Age* | *Past Profitability* | *Capital Output Ratio* | *Market Share* | *$R^2$* | *Adj $R^2$* | *F Value* | *DW* |
|---|---|---|---|---|---|---|---|---|---|---|---|---|---|
| Hyundai Motors | 0.11 | 8.01<br>(7.41)* | -0.01<br>(4.03)* | -9.33<br>(3.97)* | -45.03<br>(8.11)* | 101.33<br>(2.72)* | 0.17<br>(1.20) | 0.90<br>(4.44)* | 8.0<br>(5.81)* | 0.99 | 0.97 | 56.32* | 1.96 |
| Honda Siel Ltd | 0.04 | 2.26<br>(4.19)* | 0.32<br>(3.17)** | 0.22<br>(2.86)** | -38.49<br>(3.98)* | 199.95<br>(1.25) | 0.41<br>(4.36)* | 26.80<br>(2.29)*** | 1.14<br>(3.65)* | 0.93 | 0.88 | 6.24** | 1.72 |
| Ford India Ltd | -0.25 | 9.79<br>(3.48)* | 0.16<br>(3.08)** | -0.55<br>(4.15)* | -7.15<br>(1.12) | 916.67<br>(3.37)* | 0.83<br>(5.48)* | 129.11<br>(3.53)* | 17.46<br>(1.41) | 0.83 | 0.76 | 8.62** | 1.65 |
| **Passenger cars and Multi-utility Vehicles** | **86.33** | **6.54<br>(2.13)***** | **0.08<br>(3.09)**** | **-0.12<br>(4.77)*** | **-12.79<br>(2.50)***** | **102.14<br>(1.19)** | **0.47<br>(2.42)***** | **23.19<br>(3.38)*** | **26.91<br>(0.51)** | **0.97** | **0.90** | **14.54*** | **1.98** |
| Bajaj Auto Ltd | -82.17 | 12.56<br>(3.92)* | 0.01<br>(4.09)* | -0.22<br>(2.36)*** | -7.70<br>(3.22)** | 30.14<br>(0.26) | 0.48<br>(2.64)** | -16.82<br>(1.99) | 21.89<br>(4.42)* | 0.96 | 0.89 | 11.07** | 1.92 |
| LML Ltd | 178.86 | 24.34<br>(0.65) | 0.39<br>(2 79)** | -1.27<br>(2.59)*** | -14.90<br>(5.93)* | 286.65<br>(6.45)* | 1.53<br>(2.32)*** | 128.90<br>(3.91)* | 6.50<br>(1.56) | 0.97 | 0.90 | 14.39* | 1.75 |
| Maharashtra Scooters Ltd | -17.06 | 1.47<br>(4.24)* | 0.08<br>(3.67)* | -0.08<br>(2.96)** | -161.12<br>(3.61)* | 126.80<br>(0.41) | 0.18<br>(2.43)*** | 0.02<br>(0.06) | 0.37<br>(2.44)*** | 0.80 | 0.72 | 12.00* | 1.52 |
| TVS Motor Company Ltd | 83.88 | -11.49<br>(3.56)* | 0.04<br>(4.17)* | -0.48<br>(3.10)** | -28.50<br>(2.86)** | 196.64<br>(4.78)* | 0.24<br>(2.73)** | 115.27<br>(0.75) | 48.31<br>(1.49) | 0.93 | 0.89 | 6.66** | 1.81 |
| Kinetic Motor Company Ltd | -4711.76 | -923.72<br>(4.52)* | -9.49<br>(3.83)* | -3.61<br>(3.28)* | -5.51<br>(0.17) | 371.18<br>(3.54)* | 0.48<br>(4.68)* | 290.42<br>(3.68)* | 7.18<br>(1.18) | 0.98 | 0.94 | 24.75* | 1.86 |

## TABLE 1.4 (CONTINUED...)

## REGRESSION ANALYSIS FOR OTHER FACTORS AFFECTING PROFITABILITY

[PR = $\beta_0 + \beta_1$ Size + $\beta_2$ Growth + $\beta_3$ Liquidity + $\beta_4$ Leverage + $\beta_5$ Age + $\beta_6$ Past Profitability + $\beta_7$ Capital Output Ratio + $\beta_8$ Market Share]

| *Particulars* | *Constant* | *Size* | *Growth* | *Liquidity* | *Leverage* | *Age* | *Past Profitability* | *Capital Output Ratio* | *Market Share* | *$R^2$* | *Adj $R^2$* | *F Value* | *DW* |
|---|---|---|---|---|---|---|---|---|---|---|---|---|---|
| Hero Honda Motors Ltd | 247.99 | 36.06<br>(3.33)* | -0.32<br>(2.55)** | -0.64<br>(2.35)*** | -41.92<br>(4.52)* | 179.26<br>(2.47)*** | 0.16<br>(0.82) | -209.98<br>(3.99)* | 79.12<br>(4.45)* | 0.99 | 0.96 | 35.41* | 1.66 |
| Kinetic Engineering Ltd | -65.06 | 7.38<br>(6.02)* | 0.54<br>(3.01)* | -0.14<br>(2.28)*** | -0.42<br>(3.60)* | 339.54<br>(4.51)* | 0.71<br>(3.15)** | 11.24<br>(2.95)** | 3.15<br>(1.76) | 0.95 | 0.86 | 10.21** | 1.45 |
| Majestic Auto Ltd | 14.98 | -9.34<br>(4.03)* | -0.04<br>(3.65)* | -0.03<br>(0.27) | -6.11<br>(3.91)* | 971.39<br>(3.80)* | 0.08<br>(0.22) | 73.54<br>(3.51)* | 2.45<br>(2.11)*** | 0.92 | 0.81 | 5.51** | 1.37 |
| Scooters India Ltd | 804.21 | -162.5<br>(3.52)* | 1.23<br>(2.47)*** | -0.53<br>(2.33)*** | 40.15<br>(1.58) | 556.58<br>(4.39)* | 0.01<br>(0.04) | 4.52<br>(3.43)* | 2.67<br>(1.12) | 0.92 | 0.86 | 5.68** | 1.25 |
| **Two & Three Wheelers** | **194.82** | **-14.88<br>(2.95)**** | **0.23<br>(2.80)**** | **-0.44<br>(3.67)*** | **-19.68<br>(2.73)**** | **520.54<br>(2.78)**** | **0.20<br>(3.41)*** | **22.98<br>(4.46)*** | **33.52<br>(0.59)** | **0.93** | **0.89** | **6.78*** | **1.88** |
| **Whole Industry** | **19.54** | **-0.46<br>(4.50)*** | **0.06<br>(2.13)***** | **-0.04<br>(3.75)*** | **-6.91<br>(1.80)** | **146.73<br>(3.96)*** | **0.56<br>(2.96)**** | **20.39<br>(2.09)***** | – | **0.90** | **0.85** | **6.54**** | **1.68** |

**Notes:** PR – Profit rate on total assets; Size-Natural logarithm of sales (proxy for size); Growth – Sales Growth; Liquidity – Cash Conversion Cycle (proxy for liquidity); Leverage – Debt/Equity; Age – Ratio of depreciation of fixed assets; Past Profitability – Profitability for previous year; Capital out put ratio – Ratio of total capital to total sales; Market share – Ratio of sales to total industry sales.

***Source :*** Computed

# 2

# An Empirical Study of Firm Structure and Profitability Relationship

## The Case of Indian Automobile Firms

### INTRODUCTION

The study of how and why firms attain profitability levels has been the main pre-occupation of Industrial organization economists for the last four decades. Many of the theoretical and empirical developments on the determination of corporate profitability emanate from traditional price theory and the Structure-Conduct-Performance (SCP) paradigm of the modern industrial organization literature. This latter framework was initiated by the Harvard economist Bain (1956), utilizing much of the earlier work of Clark (1940) and Mason (1949). Beyond Bain, over 20 years, a considerable research was undertaken examining the relationship between firm structure and profitability. In determining factors influencing performance diversity, literature dealing with such work suggests that industrial performance and performance differences among firms can be explained as arising from various characteristics; those which are industry specific (collusion hypothesis) and those which are firm-specific (Efficient market hypothesis). (Capon, Farley and Hoenig, 1990).

Industrial organization economists point to industry effects (i.e., concentration levels, industry growth) using the structure – conduct – performance model (SCP) as the main factor determining firm profitability. (Demsetz, 1973; Peltzman,1977; Scherer, 1980; Porter 1981). On the other hand, the resource-based view (Wernerfelt, 1984; Barney, 1991; Peteraf, 1993) suggests that the explanation for the existence of more or less profitable firms within the same industry must be found in the internal factors of each company (for example, market share, firm size, skill level etc.). These firm-effect factors favour the achievement and maintenance of competitive advantages of each firm, which eventually lead to different profitability levels among firms belonging to the same industry (Amato and Wilder, 1990).

Many studies are found testing these competing hypotheses and the results concludes with general mixed opinions. In the market Structure-Conduct-Performance (SCP) literature, the most important hypotheses, appear to fall in to six categories (Bothwell, Cooley and Hall, 1984) which can be characterized as follows: seller's concentration may affect Profit-Monopoly power, conferred by high degrees of seller concentration, may cause high rates of return (Bain, 1951); High entry barriers may also affect profits positively (Mann, 1966; Weiss, 1963; Comanor and Wilson, 1967; Qualls, 1979); Absolute or relative firm size may also explain profits. (Demsetz, 1973; Peltzman, 1977; Gale, 1972; Shephered, 1972); Risk differentials may be another variable affecting profitability differences (Stigler, 1963; Fisher and Hall, 1967; Cootner and Holland, 1970); Advertising Intensity also explaining prcfits (Bloch, 1974) and Growth also affects the profits (Brozen's 1971).

Actually profitability is a highly sensitive economic variable which is affected by a host of factors operating through a variety of ways. Some of them affect the product prices and quantities; some affect the cost of production while others make changes in capital stock, size, market share and growth of the firm. All such factors ultimately make the profitability of the firm to vary. It is difficult to build a theory of profitability which accounts for all such factors. Because of this difficulty, it is quite natural to analyze the variations in profitability by taking the partial approach, that is, to find the effect of certain major variables, ignoring the implications of other left out independent variables at a time. Hence, in this study the relationship between size, growth, liquidity, leverage, age, persistence of profitability, capital - output ratio, market share and profitability has been made.

## SIZE AND PROFITABILITY

Economic Theory prescribes that increasing firm size allows for incremental advantages because the size of the firm enables it to raise the barriers of entry to potential entrants as well as leverage on the economies of scale to attain higher profitability. Key features of a large firm are its diverse capabilities, the abilities to exploit economies of scale and scope and the formalization of procedures. These characteristics allow larger firms to generate superior performance relative to smaller firms (Penrose, 1959). Baumol (1959) viewed that the larger firm may be in a position to earn a higher rate of return on its investment than the smaller firms because it has all options of a smaller firm open to it and in addition can undertake projects which are of large scale and are denied to smaller firms. On the other hand, larger firms can lead to increased co-ordination requirements, which in turn, make the managerial task more difficult leading to organizational inefficiencies and lower profit rates (Downs, 1967). Further, it has been suggested that increased size tends to be associated with higher bureaucratization (Besanko et al., 2004; and Ahuja and Majumdar, 1998). Another plausible argument to justify the possibility of a negative firm size-profitability relationship can be found in the concept of x-inefficiencies (Leibenstein, 1976).

A good number of researchers had investigated the relationship between firm size and profitability. Among the pioneering studies conducted in this field is attributed to Hall and Weiss (1967) showed that firm size exhibit a positive relationship with profitability. The results of Marcus (1969) study showed that firm size influences profitability in some, but not all industries. Amato and Wilder (1985) also conveyed that the relationship between firm size and profitability may be positive for some firm size ranges and negative for others. The studies by Berk (1997), Michaelas et al., (1999), Hall et al., (2000), Cassar and Holmes (2003), Darko Tipuric (2002), Leledakis et al., (2004), Vijayakumar and Kathirvel (2003) and Renu Luthra and Mishra (2004) showed the positive relationship between the firm size and profitability. On the other hand, studies by Capon et al.,(1990), Rajan and Zingales (2000), Goddard Tavakoli and Wilson (2005), Bala Ramasamy et al., (2005)., Abdussalam Mahomoud Abu-Tapanjeh (2006), Kuldip Kaur (1998) and Abdul Rahaman Ammal (2003) postulated negative relationship between firm size and profitability. Thus, from this theoretical background, the researcher advances the following hypothesis.

**$H_0$: Firm size positively affects profitability.**

## GROWTH AND PROFITABILITY

The relationship between growth and profitability is of considerable interest both from theoretical and practical point of view. Basic economic theory, assuming inverted u-shape cost curves, implies that firms grow until they have reached the size where average variable cost is at minimum (Besanko et al., 2004). In that range, increased size would, ceteris paribus, be associated with improved profitability. By contrast, according to the strategy school theory not only static economies of scale in production, but experience curve effects pertaining to all aspects of the firm's operations can be the basis of cost advantages. This leads to a positive relationship between market share and profitability. However, even in the supportive literature it is observed that growth does not always enhance profits. Growth beyond minimum efficient scale is associated with unknown or reversed effect on profitability, and pursuing growth in low growth markets or by increasing sales for products with low initial market share is no guaranteed recipe for financial success.

Marris (1964) was the first to develop a rigorous model to analyze the growth and profits of firms. According to Marris model, a firm's ability to shift the demand and supply functions (growth-profit frontier) depends on the environment in which it operates. According to Greiner (1972), the relationship between company growth and profitability can be positive or negative. The empirical studies conducted by Fenny and Rogers (1999), Debashish Rai and Debashish Sur (2001), Maninder S.Sarkaria and Shergil (2004), Zeiton and Tian (2007), Martin Hovey (2007), Fulbag Singh and Monica Mogla (2008) and Ahmed Arif Karim Almazari (2009) found evidence that growth had a positive impact on profitability. On the other hand, studies by Hoy et al., (1992), Kaen and Baumann (2003), Abuzar and Ejelly (2004), Long Chan and Xinlei Zhao (2005) and Elodos Mathew Punnoose (2008) postulated negative relationship between growth and profitability. In summary, the empirical evidence on the relationship between growth and profitability is inconclusive. From the above reviews, the researcher concludes that most of the studies support the general notion that there is a positive relationship between growth and profitability. In order to test this general notion, the researcher postulates the following hypothesis.

**$H_0$: Firms growth positively affects profitability.**

## LIQUIDITY AND PROFITABILITY

Promoters of Capital Theory share the axiom that profitability and liquidity comprise the salient calbeit frequently conflicting goals of working capital management. The conflict arises because the maximization of firm's returns could seriously threaten the liquidity and on the other hand, the pursuit of liquidity has a tendency to dilute returns. The crucial part in managing its liquidity in day-to day operations to ensure its smooth running and meets its obligations (Eljelly, 2004). Yet, this is not a simple task since managers must make sure that business operation is running in efficient and profitable manner. There are possibilities of mismatch of current assets and current liabilities during this process. If this happens and firm's manager cannot manage it properly then it will affect firm's profitability.

According to the existing literature on the relationship between liquidity and profitability, in a study by Kamath (1989) found liquidity affects profitability negatively. The other studies, Deloof (2003), Lazaridis and Tryfonidis (2006), Eljelly (2004), Raheman and Nasr (2007), Garcia-Teruel and Martinez-Solano (2007), Mathuva (2009), Falope and Ajilore (2009) and Amarjit Gill, Nahum Biger and Neil Mathur (2010) empirically examined the relationship between profitability and liquidity showed that there exists a significant and negative relationship between them. However, the study conducted by Katerina Lyroudi and Lazoridis (2000), Bardia (2004) and D.Sur, J. Biswas and Ganguly, P. (2001) found that there was positive relationship between liquidity and profitability. From the above reviews, the researcher concludes the most of the studies support the general notion that there is a negative relationship between liquidity and profitability. In order to test this general notion, the researcher postulates the following hypothesis.

**$H_0$: Firms liquidity negatively affects profitability**

## LEVERAGES AND PROFITABILITY

The debate of optimal capital structure has been the focal point of the finance literature for previous several decades. According to Finance Theory, the capital structure do affects firm's cost of capital and consequently financial performance. The pioneering paper published in 1958 by Merton Miller and Franco Modigliani provides the conditions under which a firm's financing decisions do not affect its value. Due to the reflection on MM theorem, the issue of capital structure has generated unforeseen interest among financial researchers. The two most significant theories that aim to explain the relationship between capital structure and the market value of the firm are Pecking Order Theory (POT) and Static-Trade-off Theory (STT). The POT implies that profitable companies would usually not opt for debt financing for their new projects because of the availability of sizeable amounts of internal funds. However, as per STT, profitable companies would give preference to the use of debt financing in view of the attraction of tax shield benefit available on borrowed funds. Thus, STT predicts that there would be a direct relationship between profitability and leverage, while POT expects the opposite i.e., inverse relationship between them.

The available literature on leverages and profitability depicts a great deal of theoretical controversies. Nikolaos P. Eriotis (2000), Zhang et al., (2002), Bevan and Danbolt (2004), Tong and Green (2005), Fraser et al., (2006), Martin Hovey (2007) and Gabriela Michalea and Raluca Antal (2009), their findings suggest that firms follow a pecking order and also reported a negative relationship between profitability and leverage. On the other hand in accordance with trade-off theory in opposite relationship may be envisaged. Various researchers have analyzed different types of trade-offs between capital structure and corporate taxes (Modigliani and Millar, 1963), personal taxes (De Angelo and

Masulis, 1980), Bankruptcy costs (Titman 1984), agency costs (Myers, 1977) and information asymmetry (Myers and Majlof, 1984). The stated rational is when firms are profitable they prefer debt to benefit from the tax shield. The underlying supposition dictates positive relationship between leverage and profitability. Thus, from this theoretical background, the researcher advances the following hypothesis:

**$H_0$: There is a positive relationship between leverages and profitability**

## AGE

Age of the firm can also be important determinant of profitability. Older the firm more may be the profitability of the firm, because experience and efficiency in the production process may decrease costs of production. So, it is expect positive relationship between age and profitability of the firm. However, in a situation of rapid technological progress, older firms may be less profitable as compared to the new ones, if they do not renovate their plants. With respect to the impact of age, one stream of research suggests that older firms are more experienced, have enjoyed the benefits of learning, are not prone to the liabilities of newness, and can, therefore, enjoy superior performance. (Stinchcombe, 1965; Chittenden *et al.*, 1996; Hall et al., 2000; Michaelas et al., 1999). Another stream of research, however, suggests that older firms are prone to inertia, and the bureaucratic ossification that goes along with age; thus, they are unlikely to have the flexibility to make rapid adjustments to changing circumstances and are likely to lose out in the performance stakes to younger, and more agile, firms. (Marshall, 1920). Hence, theory is equivocal. Thus, according to this literature and in order to verify the same results for the Indian automobile firms, the researcher postulates the following hypothesis.

**$H_0$: Firm age positively affects Profitability**

## PERSISTENCY OF PROFITABILITY

The hypothesis that the level of future profitability of a company will reflect its past profitability is one of appealing simplicity. It is also obvious potential value to the task of prediction. It is not, however, so satisfactory from an explanatory point of view, because it merely states that profitability is what it is and tends to remain what it is. Ideally, the economist would like to know why profitability is what it is. If he knows why it is what it is, then changes in profitability can be explained by changes in the factor which determine the level of profitability, any persistency of profitability can be explained by the persistency of these factors. This gives us a clue to the explanatory value of the relationship between past and future profitability.

The past performance of a firm acts as a guide to the future. It is true that the progress of a concern is determined not only by its past history, but by its future operations. However, the future cannot be analyzed; it is only on expectation, and any such expectation, would not be dependable unless based on the past experience. So, Past Profitability ($P_{t-1}$) may have the relevance as a determinant of current profitability. If profitability depends on the quality of the firm's management or on the monopoly power which the firm enjoys, or on both of these factors, one should expect to find some persistency in the profitability of firms over successive years (Singh and Whittington, 1968). Since, there is usually some continuity of good management and of monopoly power, so we expect that profitability in the previous year will determine the profitability in the current year. But, if profitability in the previous year is purely a chance phenomenon, then it may not affect the profitability in the current year. Thus, according to the above reviews and discussions, the researcher proposes the following hypothesis.

**$H_0$: Past profitability positively affects profitability**

## CAPITAL-OUTPUT RATIO

Capital-output ratio indicates the extent to which a firm is capital intensive in nature. Firms that are capital intensive in nature requiring large quantity of capital, may turn towards the cheapest source of finance have a tendency to show stable profits because these firms are less risky one and financial institutions can lead more reliability to these firms's while lending money (Hurdle, 1974). But, Scherer (1970) found just the opposite results and said that capital intensive firms are more risky in nature, because, they may involve themselves in price cutting operations, thus making profitability more variable. According to Ferri and Jones (1980) also, future earnings of a firm will be more variable by the use of fixed assets. So, one can't expect a definite relationship between these two variables. Based on this argument, the researcher postulates the following hypothesis.

**$H_0$: Capital-output ratio associates positively with profitability.**

## MARKET SHARE OF THE FIRM

Profitability of a firm also depends upon its market share i.e., the share of the particular firm in the total sales of that industry. Obviously, if the firm can increase its market share, it can expect more profitability as latter is a direction function of its sales i.e., if it can increase its sales in the market, it will have more profitability. Further, large market share in general is expected to yield high profitability, (i) by giving the firm a share based product differentiation advantages, (ii) by providing opportunities to this firm to operate in oligopolistic group for some joint strategies and increase in its bargaining power, and (iii) by allowing the firm to take advantages of economies of scale. Richard Mancke (1974), B.T Gale (1972), Shephered (1972), Phillips (1972), Day (1973), Hurdle (1974) and Khalilzadeh Shirazi (1974) have affirmed the positive and significant relationship between profitability and market share. Thus, according to this literature, the researcher postulates the following hypothesis.

**$H_0$: Market share positively affects profitability.**

## VARIABLES SPECIFICATIONS AND EMPIRICAL MODEL

In order to explain the profitability of the firms in Indian automobile industry, the various factors discussed above, have been taken together. This is achieved by developing a similar empirical framework used by Peter H. Grinyer and Peter Mc kiernan (1991), Jim Nugent (1998), Sumit K. Majumdar (1997), Bala Ramasamy et al., (2005), Abdussalam Mahmoud Abu-Tapanjeh (2006) and Grace Tola Olutunla and Tomola Marshal Obamuyi (2008). The analysis of data employs the use of correlation and a multiple regression model that consists of factors associated with profitability of firms in Indian automobile industry.

The basic model consists of a multiple regression of profitability on a set of independent variables. The dependent variables of the regression model is return on assets (which is defined as, Gross profit as percentage on total assets) which relates the profitability to the asset base. This study investigates the effect of size, growth, liquidity, leverage, age, persistency of profitability, capital-output ratio and market share on firms' profitability. The current study use correlation analysis to identify the association between profitability and the independent variables, as well as regression analysis to estimate the causal relationship. The researcher considered the following regression model.

$$\mathbf{PR_{it} = \beta_0 + \beta_1 (Size)_{it} + \beta_2 (Growth)_{it} + \beta_3 (Liquidity)_{it} + \beta_4 (Leverage)_{it} + \beta_5 (Age)_{it} + \beta_6 (Past\ profitability)_{it} + \beta_7 (Capital\text{-}output\ ratio)_{it} + \beta_8 (Market\ share)_{it} + e_{it}}$$

Where,

PR – Measures the firm profitability with gross profit as a percentage of total

| | | |
|---|---|---|
| | | assets for the firm (i) in the year (t) |
| Size | – | Natural logarithm of firm's sales for firm (i) in the year (t) |
| Growth | – | Growth of firm's sales for firm (i) in the year (t) |
| Liquidity | – | Measures cash conversion cycle for the firm (i) in the year (t) |
| Leverage | – | Measures with debt to equity for firm (i) in the year (t) |
| Age | – | Natural logarithms of the firm's age for firm (i) in the year (t) |
| Past Profitability | – | One year lagged profitability for the firm (i) in the year (t) |
| Capital-output ratio | – | Measures the ratio of total capital to total sales for firm (i) in the year (t) |
| Market share | – | Measures the ratio of sales to total industry sales for firm (i) in the year (t) |
| $\beta_0$ | – | Constant term for the firm (i) in the year (t) |
| $\beta_1, \beta_2 .....$ | – | Regression co-efficient |
| e | – | Disturbance term for the firm (i) in the year (t). |

Table 2.1 below summarizes the definition, theoretical predicted signs and a-priori hypotheses were formulated, which were to be tested.

## TABLE 2.1
## PROXY VARIABLES DEFINITION AND PREDICTED RELATIONSHIPS

| Proxy variables | Definitions | Predicted sign | a-priori hypotheses |
|---|---|---|---|
| Size | Natural logarithm of firm's sales | +/- | $P_1$/Size > 0 |
| Growth | Growth of firm's sales | +/- | $P_1$/GS > 0 |
| Liquidity | Cash conversion cycle | +/- | $P_1$/CCC < 0 |
| Leverage | Debt to equity ratio | - | $P_1$/Lev < 0 |
| Age | Age of firm from the starting year | + | $P_1$/Age > 0 |
| Past profitability | One year lagged profitability | + | $P_1$/Past Profitability>0 |
| Capital-output ratio | Ratio of total capital to total sales | +/- | $P_1$/Capital output <0 |
| Market share | Ratio of sales to total industry sales | + | $P_1$/Market share >0 |

## ANALYSIS AND DISCUSSION

This section describes descriptive statistics summary, correlation, regression analysis and discussion of results.

## DESCRIPTIVE STATISTICS AND ANALYSIS

Descriptive statistics includes the mean, standard deviation, minimum, and maximum, standard error of mean, kurtosis and skewness for the period 1996-2009. The data contains about 20 automobile firms for 216 firm-years observations. Table show that there are negative values at minimum values i.e., some firms have operated with losses during the study period.

Table 2.2 contains descriptive statistics of the variables used in this study. The table reveals that profit rate ranges between -189.39 per cent to 1638.92 per cent with mean of 22.29 per cent and a standard deviation 105.3. The same applies to growth, liquidity, leverage, past profitability capital-output ratio and market share, which show that the standard deviation is more than the mean. This implies that there is a high variations in the firm's mean. The table also reveals that profit rate, growth, leverage, age, past profitability, capital-output ratio and market share have a positive skewness, which indicates that the scores are clustered to the left at the low values. As for size and liquidity have a negative skewness indicating clustering of scores are at the high and as for the kurtosis statistic, all variables except for market share show a positive kurtosis suggesting that the distribution has pecked or clustered in the centre, with long thin tails.

## CORRELATION ANALYSIS

A correlation analysis was performed to verify a possible association between and among the variables, in order to test whether there is any linear correlation between and among the variables. Collinearity explains the dependence of one variable to other. When variables are highly correlated they both express essentially the same information. Table 2.3 reports the Pearson correlation coefficients of all the variables employed in the study. Simple correlations among the variables that are reported in Table 2.3 are quite low. The largest reported value (-0.58) was between market share and size. In this respect, Kennedy (1985) suggests that correlation values below 0.80 do not pose a potential multicollinearity problem. Hence, the performance variables used in this study do not seem to pose a serious multicollinearity problem and this allows for standard interpretation of the regression coefficients.

## DISCUSSION OF RESULTS

Using pooled regression technique, the study ran the regression of the profitability on the firm structure variables like size, growth, liquidity, leverages, age, past profitability, capital-output ratio and market share with aim to investigate whether these variables have significant explanatory powers. The estimated results are reported in Table 2.4.

It can be observed from the table that the estimated value of the R-Square is 0.90 for whole automobile industry, 0.98 commercial vehicles sector, 0.97 for passenger cars and multi-utility vehicles sector and 0.93 for two and three wheelers sectors. This implies that more than 90 percent of the variation in profitability of the firms is jointly determined by the said variables. The value of F-statistic indicates that the overall model is good. The Durbin-Watson statistic is also close to 2 which imply that the successive values of estimated residuals are not dependent on each other. This means that there is evidence to accept that there is no auto correlation problem in the estimated model.

Regarding the significance of individual variables, the empirical results shows that size has statistically significant effect on profitability in the Indian Automobile Industry. However, in the overall pooled sample, firm size showed significant negative relation with profitability in the Indian Automobile Industry. This is consistent with the findings of Singh and Whittington (1968) and contradictory to the findings of Samuels and Smith (1968), who postulated positive relationship between size and profitability. The sector wise analysis showed that the size had a significant positive relationship with profitability in case of commercial vehicles and passenger cars and multiutility vehicles sector. This could be due to the changes in output either because of increased demand or reduction of costs. On the other hand, there was a significant negative relationship reported between size and profitability in the two and three wheelers sector. This was due to the reasons that larger firms can lead to organizational inefficiencies, higher bureaucratization and concept of x-inefficiency. X-inefficiency is a measure of the degree to which costs are higher than they need to be. X-inefficiency reasons that general managerial or technological inefficiency in larger firms cause higher production costs which end up in reductions in the bottom line i.e., profit rates decline. Among the various firms selected for the study, some firms showed positive relationships while others not so.

Table 2.4 also showed the results of regression of profitability fitted on growth of sales in all the selected firms, three sectors and whole industry. It is evident from the table that there was a significant variation in the regression co-efficient relating profitability to growth of sales between firms. Further, there is a positive relationship between the two variables (growth and profitability) except Hyundai Motors Ltd under passenger cars and multi-utility vehicles and Kinetic Motor Company Ltd, Hero Honda Motors Ltd and Majestic Auto Ltd under two and three wheeler sector. These results are consistent with the results of Singh and Whittington (1968), who also found positive relationship between growth and profitability in their study. This was due to increased motivation among employees who expect greater gains in the future, gains resulting from greater company size.

Consistent with Deloof (2003), Reheman and Nasr (2007), Garcia-Teruel and Martinez-Solano (2007) and David M. Mathuva, a negative relationship exists between the liquidity (cash conversion cycle) and profitability of selected automobile firms, three sectors and whole automobile industry. This was due to the fact that minimizing the investment in current assets can help in boosting profits. This ensures the liquid cash is not maintained in the business for long and that it is use to generate profits for the firm. These results suggest that managers can create value for their shareholder by reducing the number of days of the cash conversion cycle to its minimum.

Regarding the significance of the leverage, the empirical results presented in Table 4 showed that the majority of the Indian automobile firms, profitability are negatively significantly associated with the leverage. This piece of evidence is in line with Pecking Order Theory which postulates a negative correlation between the profitability and leverage. This finding is consist with the findings of Rajan and Zingales (1995), that is, higher profitable firms uses less debt. There are other evidence for this relationship such as informational asymmetry, high costs of external resources and inefficiency of the market. However, this piece of evidence is in contrast to the Static Trade-off Theory that states that more profitable firms have lower expected bankruptcy costs and higher tax benefits. Despite this, Scooters India Ltd under two and three wheelers sector continue to enjoy such large profit margins that firms using higher proportion of debt in their capital structure were still more profitable than firms using lower proportion of debt.

It is also apparent from Table 2.4 that firm age has significant effects on profitability. Perhaps, it is one of the strongest determinants of profitability in all the selected automobile firms. The co-efficient of the age of firms carries a positive sign, support our a priori expectation. This indicates that older firms to be more profitable because managing the licensing process yields significant experience in pre-empting market capacities, which can then yield superior profitability because of market capture. However, apart from profitability arising from market pre-emption activities, through superior management of the licensing process, firms also become more profitable because of several strategic or operational reasons, one of which is that they are able to tap in to the relevant customer segment and provide differentiated products that meet demand. All though, this results is consistent with the work of Stanger (2000), Stanger (2000) argues that the relationship should be positive, since older firms are more likely to have attained diminishing costs of production over some range of sales and hence be able to operate more economically and efficiently than recently established ones. However, the study by Hannan and Free man (1989) suggest that older firms are more resistant to change in a competitive environment and newer technologies which may, as a result of the need to operate in an age-old standardized manner, leave older firms progressively outdated and lead to organization failure.

As far as past profitability's relation with profitability of the selected firm of Indian automobile industry is concerned, there was a significant positive relation during the years 1996-2009 as well as for the pooled sample. This indicates positive influences on profitability, confirming our hypothesis. This result conforms to the conclusions of Singh and Whittington (1968). Table 2.4 also showed that the co-efficient of capital-output ratio supported our hypothesis, suggesting positive relationship between increased capital-output ratio and profitability. This result is consistent with the work of Hurdle (1974). Further, regression results suggest that market share is the most important determinant of profitability. The corresponding positive co-efficient suggests that selected Indian automobile firms have increased their profitability by increasing their market share.

## POLICY IMPLICATIONS

It has been often argued that larger firms in an industry are relatively more efficient than the smaller ones. If this is not so, then why does a firm aspire to be larger and larger; and if this is so, then how do smaller and larger firms co-exist in the same industry. Every business is normally encountered with risks and uncertainties; bigger the firm it is expected to be stronger to face such risky and uncertain situations. Moreover a big firm because of its control over the market can buy up the best sites with location advantages, the superior technology, R&D and best professional experts. However, the findings of the study showed that "law of proportional effect" does not hold in the selected Indian automobile firms. While relatively bigger firms perform better in commercial vehicles and passenger cars and multiutility vehicles sector, the opposite hold true in two and three wheeler sector and the whole industry. These findings should be useful to the managerial authorities to decide on the extent to which firm size needs to be monitored and controlled.

Based on the empirical results obtained in this study, it is concluded that there is tendency of positive relationship between profitability and growth. Also the extent of this positive relationship is different in different firms, depending upon their ability and willingness to grow, which may further depend upon their factors like extent of monopoly power, growth of demand, market share, better labour relations and other managerial conditions etc.. Further, the analyze of liquidity and profitability have identified critical management practices and are expected to assist managers in identifying areas where they might improve the financial performance of their operation. The results have provided owner-managers with information regarding the basic financial management practices used by their peers and their peers' attitudes towards these practices. Firms are capable of gaining sustainable competitive advantage by means of effective and efficient utilization of the resources of the organization through a careful reduction of the cash conversion cycle to its minimum. Therefore, managers can create profits for their companies by handling correctly the cash conversion cycle and keeping each different component (accounts receivables, accounts payables and inventory) to an optimum level. The relationship between leverage and profitability showed that the successful selection and use of the debt-to-equity ratio is one of the key elements of the firm's financial strategy.

The study is mainly of theoretical interest, as it examines size, growth, liquidity, leverage, age and profitability of firms and their inter-relationships. However, the empirical results obtained from the analysis of data are of importance to the owners and managers, interested in the growth and profitability of the firms. The policy of increasing total assets or sales with a view to increase profitability may not be rewarding in all cases. Therefore, such policies have to be carefully examined in view of the findings of this study, so that these may not lead to over-capitalization and ultimately reduce profitability. From the point of view of the economy, significant relationship between size and profitability supports the policy of liberalization, initiated in the Indian Economy since 1991. The study suggests that this policy of liberalization should further be strengthened.

## CONCLUSION

The study has contributed to our knowledge on the series of factors associated with the profitability of selected firms in the Indian Automobile Industry. The primary aim of this study was to test the postulated hypotheses and to provide evidence with respect to the impact of firm structure to firm profitability, by examining such major factors as firm size, growth, liquidity, leverage, age, post profitability, market share and capital-output ratio. The study employed regression model in order to test the hypotheses, using profitability measured by the Rate of Return on Assets (PR) along with other independent variables using sample of 20 automobile firms in India. The results demonstrate that firm size and growth are important determinants of profitability in the Indian automobile industry and a positive relationship between profitability and firm size and growth. Further, the results suggest that liquidity and leverage had a negative impact on profitability. Referring the firm as a variable affecting the profitability, the study shows significant result which implied that firm age affect the profitability of a firm. Further more, this study has found empirical evidence that past profitability, capital-output ratio and market share are important determinants of profitability in the Indian automobile Industry. These principal findings can be summarized as in Table 2.5.

In conclusion, these finding have an interesting policy implications, which may add to the ongoing debate on the issue of firm structure and the firm profitability relations. The empirical findings of this study suggest that firm structure emerges as important factor affecting profitability. However, the results indicate that some of the independent variable considered in this study has weak impacts on profitability. These findings should be useful to the management authorities to decide on the extent to which firm structure needs to be monitored and controlled. The validity and the generalization of the conclusions mentioned are pending future research in other industries or sectors that ratifies or refutes them.

## REFERENCES

1. Abduraham, A., Hanna, A.S., Nordheim, E.V. and Russell, J.S., (2003). "Indicator variable model of firms size-profitability relationship of Electrical contractors using financial and economic data", *Journal of Construction Engineering and Management*@ASCE

2. Ahmed Arif Karim A'lmazari, (2009). "Analysing profitability ratios of the Jordanian Phosphate Mines company (2001 – 2007)", *Journal of Accounting and Finance*, Vol.23 (1), pp. 268-276.

3. Abuzar, M.A. and Eljelly (2004). "Liquidity – Profitability tradeoff: An empirical investigation in an emerging market", *International Journal of Commerce and Management*, Vol.14 (2), pp. 48-61.

4. Amato, L and Wilder, R.P. (1990). "Firm and industry effects in industrial Economics", *Southern Economic Journal*, Vol. 50, pp.93-105.

5. Abdussalam Mahmound Abu-Tapanjeh (2006). "An empirical study of firm structure and profitability relationship: The case of Jordan", *Journal of Economic and Administrative Sciences*, Vol.22 (1), pp.41-59.

6. Amarjit Gill., Nahum Biger., and Neil Mathur (2010). "The Relationship between Working capital management and Profitability: Evidence from the United States", *Business and Economics Journal*, Vol.10, pp.1-9.

7. Berk, J.B. (1997). "Does size really matter?", *Financial analysts journal*, Vol.53, pp.12-18.

8. Bevan, A.A. and J. Danbolt (2004). "Testing for inconsistencies in the estimation of UK capital

structure determinants", *Applied Financial Economics*, Vol. 14 (1), pp. 55-56

9. Bardia, S.C. (2004). "Liquidity Management: A case study of Steel Authority of India Ltd", *The Management Accountant*, pp. 463-67.
10. Baumol, W.J. (1959). "Business Behaviour, Value and Growth", New York: MacMillan.
11. Besanko, D., Dranovc, D., Shanlcy, M., and Schaefer, S. (2004). "Economics of Strategy", Hoboken, N.J: John Wiley & Sons.
12. Bala Ramasamy, Darryl Ong and Matthew C.H. Yeung. (2005). "Firm size, ownership and performance in the Malaysian Palm Oil Industry", *Accounting and Finance*, Vol.1, pp. 81-104.
13. Bain, J. (1956). "Barriers to new competition", Harvard University Press:Cambridge,M.A
14. Barney, J. (1991). "Firm Resources and Sustained Competitive Advantage", *Journal of Management*, Vol. 17, pp. 99-120.
15. Bothwell, J.L., Cooley, T.F and Hall, T.E. (1984). "A new view of the Market Structure-Performance Debate", *Journal of Industrial Economic*, Vol. 32, pp. 397-417.
16. Bain, J.S. (1951). "Relation of Profit Rate to Industry Concentration American Manufacturing, 1936-1940", *Quarterly Journal of Economics*, Vol. 65, pp. 293-324.
17. Brozen, Y. (1970). "Bains Concentration and Rates of Return Revisited", *Journal of Law and Economics*, Vol. 14, pp. 351-369.
18. Clark, J.M. (1940). "Toward a Concept of Workable Competition", *American Economic Review*, Vol. 30.
19. Comanor, W.S and T.A Wilson (1967). "Advertising, Market Structure and Performance", *Review of Economics and Statistics*, Vol. 49, pp. 423-40.
20. Chittenden, F., Hall, G., and Hutchinson, P. (1996). "Small Firm Growth, Access to Capital Markets and

Financial Structure: Review of Issues and Empirical Investigation", *Small Business Economics,* Vol. 8(1), pp. 59-67.

21. Cassar, G., and Holmes (2003). "Capital structure and financing of SMEs: Australian evidence", *Accounting and Finance Journal,* Vol.43 (2), pp.123-147.
22. Capon, N., Farley, J., and Hoenig, H. (1990). "Determinants of financial performance: A Meta Analysis", *Management Science,* pp.1143-1159.
23. DarkoTipuric (2002). "Is there relationship between firm size and profitability?", *Journal Zagreb International Review of Economics and Business,* Vol.5, Conference Issue, pp. 139-154.
24. Debashish Rai and Debashish Sur, (2001). "Profitability analysis of Indian Food products Industry: A Case study of Cadbury India Ltd", *The Management Accountant,* Vol.36 (6), pp. 407-412.
25. Debasish Sur, Joydeep Biswas and Prasenjit Ganguly (2001). "Liquidity Management in Indian Private Sector Enterprises- A case study of Indian Primary Aluminium Industry", *Indian Journal of Accounting,* Vol. XXXII, pp. 8-14.
26. Downs, A. (1976). "Inside Bureaucracy", Boston: Little, Brown & Co.,
27. De Angelo and Masulis (1980). "Optimal capital structure under corporate and personal taxation", *Journal of Financial Economics,* Vol.8.
28. Demsetz, H. (1973). "Industry, Market Rivalry and Public Policy", *Journal of Law and Economics,* Vol. 16, pp. 1-10.
29. Day, C.L. (1973). "Changes in Rates of Return: A Cross Section Study", *Oxford Bulletin of Economics and Statistics,* Vol. 35, pp.135-52.
30. Eljelly, A. (2004). "Liquidity-Profitability Trade off: An empirical investigation in an emerging market", *International Journal of Commerce and Management,* Vol.14 (2), pp. 48-61.

31. Eldos Mathew Punnoose (2008). "A profitability analysis of Business group firms vs. Individual firms in the Indian Electrical Machine manufacturing industry", *The ICFAI Journal of Management Research*, Vol.2 (1), pp. 52-76.

32. Falope,O.I., and Ajilore,O.I (2009). "Working capital management and corporate profitability: Evidence from panel data analysis of selected quoted companies in Nigeria", *Research Journal of Business Management*, Vol.3, pp.73-84.

33. Fraser, D.R., H. Zhang and C. Derashid (2006). "Capital structure and political patronage: the case of Malaysia", *Journal of Banking and Finance*, Vol.30 (4), pp.1291-1308.

34. Fulbag Singh and Monica Mogla (2008). "Impact of Mergers on profitability of Acquiring Companies", *ICFAI University Journal of Mergers and Acquisitions*, Vol.5 (2), pp. 60-76.

35. Garcia – Teruel P.J., and Martinez – Solano P.M. (2007). "Effects of working capital management on SME Profitability", *International Journal of Managerial Finance*, Vol.3, pp.164-177.

36. Gabriela Michalca and Raluca Antal (2009). "An empirical investigation of the Trade-off and pecking order hypotheses on Romanian Market", The XIII International conference" *Applied stochastic models and data analysis*, held at Vilnius, Lithuania on June 2009.

37. Goutam Ahuja and Sumit K. Majumdar (1998). "An Assessment of the performance of Indian State- Owned Enterprises", *Journal of Productivity Analysis*, Vol.9 (2), pp.113-132.

38. Greiner, L.E. (1972). "Evolutions and revolutions as organization growth", *Harvard Business Review*, Vol.50 (4), pp.37-46.

39. Goddard Tavakoli and Wilson (2005). "Determinants of profitability in European manufacturing and service", evidence from Dynamic Panel Model, *Applied Financial Economics*, Vol.15, pp.1269-1282.

40. Gale, Bradley, T. (1972). "Market share and Rate of return", *Review of Economics*, Vol. 54, pp. 412-23.

41. Grace Tola Olutunla and Tomola Marshal Obamuyi (2008). "An Empirical Analysis of Factors Associated with the Profitability of Small and Medium Enterprises in Nigeria", *American Journal of Business Management*, Vol. 2(X), pp.195-200.

42. Hall, G., Hutchinson, P., and Michael, M. (2000). "Industry effects on the determinants of unquoted SME capital structure", *International Journal of the Economics of Business*, Vol.7 (3), pp.297-312.

43. Hoy, F., Mc Dougall, P.P., D'Souza, D.E. (1992). "Strategies and environments of high-growth firms", In D.L Sexton and J.D Kasarda (eds). The State of the Art of Entrepreneurship Boston: PWS - Kent, pp. 341-357.

44. Hall, M. and Weiss, L. (1967). "Firms Size and Profitability", *The Review of Economics and Statistics*, Vol. 49, pp.319-331.

45. Hurdle, G.J. (1974). "Leverage Risk and Market Structure and Profitability", *Review of Economics and Statistics*, Vol. 56, pp. 478-85.

46. Ioannis Lazaridis and Dimitrios Tryfonidis (2006). "Relationship between working capital management and profitability of listed companies in the Athens Stock Exchange", *Journal of Financial Management and Analysis*, Vol.19 (1), pp 25-26.

47. Jim Nugent (1998). "Corporate Profitability in Ireland: Overview and determinants",*Journal of the Statistical and Social Inquiry Society of Ireland*, Vol.XXVIII Part I.

48. Kuldip kaur (1998). "Size, Growth and Profitability of firms in India-An Empirical Investigation", *Finance India*, Vol. XII (2), pp. 455-457.

49. Kean, Fred R. and Hans Baumann (2003). "Firm size, Employees and Profitability in U.S Manufacturing Industries", http://ssrn.com/sol./paper.c? Abstract id=899615.

50. Kamath, R. (1989). "How useful are common liquidity measures?" *Journal of Cash Management*, pp.24-28.
51. Katerina Lyroudi and Jhon Lazaridis (2000). "The cash conversion cycle and liquidity analysis of the food industry in Greece", *http:/papers.ssrn.com/paper.fat?* abstract-id = 236175.
52. Khalilzadeh-Shirazi, Javed (1974). "Market Structure and Price-Cost Margins in UK Manufacturing Industries", *The Review of Economics and Statistics*, Vol. 56, pp. 67-74.
53. Leledakis, G., Davidson, I., and Smith, J. (2004). "Does firm size predict stock returns?: Evidence from the London stock exchange", EFMA, 2004 Basel Meetings Paper.
54. Leibenstein, H. (1976). "Beyond Economic Man", Cambridge, MA: Harward University Press.
55. Long Chan and Xinlei Zhao, (2005). "Profitability Mean reversion of leverage ratios and capital structure choices". JEL classification; G32 website
56. Marcus Matityahu (1969). "Profitability and size of firms", *Review of Economics and Statistics*, Vol. 51, pp. 104-107.
57. Martin Hovey (2007). "Leverage, profitability and ownership structures of listed firms in China", 20th Australian Finance and Banking Conference paper, University of Southern Queensland.
58. Marris, R. (1964). The Economic Theory of Managerial Capitalism, London, MacMillan.
59. Mathuva,D.(2009). "The influence of working capital management components on profitability: A Survey on Kenyan Listed Firms", *Research Journal of Business Management*, Vol.3, pp.1-11.
60. Modigliani and Miller (1963). "Taxes and the cost of capital: a correction", *American Economic Review*, Vol.53.
61. Meyer, J.W., and Rowan, B. (1977). "Institutionalised Organisation: Formal Structures as Myth and Ceremony", *American Journal of Sociology*, Vol.83 (2), pp.340-363.

62. Michaelas, N., Chittenden, F., and Poutziouris, P. (1999). "Financial policy and capital structure choice in U.K SMEs: Empirical evidence from company panel data", *Small Business Economics Journal,* Vol.12 (2), pp.113-130.

63. Marc Deloof (2003). "Does working capital management affect profitability of Belgian Firms?", *Journal of Business Finance and Accounting,* Vol.30 (3-4), pp. 573-88.

64. Maninder S. Sarkaria and Shergil U.S. (2004). "Market structure and financial performance – An Indian Evidence with enhanced controls", Ph.D thesis submitted to the Guru Nanak Dev University.

65. Myers, S., and Majluf, N. (1984). "Corporate financing and investment decisions when firm have information investors do not have", *Journal of Financial Economics,* Vol.13, pp.187-222.

66. Mason, E.S. (1949). "The Current State of the Monopoly Problem in the US", *Harvard Law Review,* Vol. 62, pp.1265-1285.

67. Mann, H.M. (1966). "Seller Concentration, Barriers to Entry and Rates of return in Thirty Industries, 1950-1960", *Review of Economics and Statistics,* Vol. 48, pp.296-307.

68. Marshall, A. (1920). "Principles of Economics", 8th Edition, London: Macmillan.

69. Nikolaos P. Eriotis (2000). "Profit margin and capital structure: an empirical relationship", *The Journal of Applied Business Research,* Vol. 18(2), pp.85-88.

70. Peltzman, S. (1977). "The Gains and Losses from Industrial Concentration", *Journal of Law and Economics,* Vol. 20, pp. 229-263.

71. Porter, M. (1981). "The Contributions of Industrial Organisation to Strategic Management", *Academy of Management Review,* Vol. 6, pp. 609-620.

72. Peteraf, M. (1993). "The Cornerstones of Competitive advantage: A Resource-based view", *Strategic Management Journal,* Vol. 14, pp. 179-191.

73. Phillips, A. (1972). "An Econometric Study of Price-Fixing, Market Structure and Performance in British Industry in the Early 1950s. In K. Cowling, (ed), *Market Structure and Corporate Behaviour*, Gray-Mills, London.
74. Peter H. Grinyer and Peter Mc Kiernan (1991). "The Determinants of Corporate Profitability in the UK Electrical Engineering Industry", *British Journal of Management*, Vol. 2, pp. 17-32.
75. Penrose, E.T. (1959). "The Theory of Growth of the Firm", Oxford: Basil Blackwell.
76. Qualls, P.D (1979). "Market Structure and Cyclical Flexibility of Price-Cost Margins", *The Journal of Business*, Vol. 52, pp. 305-25.
77. Renu Luthra, Vaishampayan and Dheeraj Misra (2004). "Profitability and Size: A study of small scale industries in Uttar Pradesh", *The Icfaian Journal of Management Research*, pp. 28-37.
78. Rajan, R., and Zingales, L. (2000). "The firm as a dedicated hierarchy, a theory of the origins and growth of firms", NBER working paper no. W7546.
79. Raheman, A., and M. Nasr (2007). "Working capital management and profitability: case of Pakistani firms", *International Review of Business Research*, Vol.3 (2), pp.275-96.
80. Scherer, F. (1980). "Industrial Market Structure and Economic Performance (2nd ed) Chicago: Rand-McNally.
81. Shephered, W.G. (1972). "Elements of Market Structure", *Review of Economics and Statistics*, Vol. 54, pp. 25-38.
82. Stigler, G.J. (1963). "Capital and Rates of returns in Manufacturing Industries". Princeton University Press, Princeton.
83. Stinchcombe, A.L. (1956). "Social Structure and Organisations, in J.G. March, ed, *Handbook of Organisations*, Chicago: Rand-McNally.
84. Sumit K. Majumdar (1997). "The Impact of Size and Age on Firm-level Performance: Some Evidence from India",

*Review of Industrial Organisation*, Vol. 12, pp. 231-241.

85. Samuels, J. M. and Smyth, D.J. (1968). "Profits, Variability of Profits and Firm size," *Economica*, Vol. 35, pp. 127-139
86. Singh, Ajit and Whittington, G. (1968). "Growth, Profitability and Valuation", Cambridge University Press.
87. Simon Feeny and Mark Rogers (1999). "The performance of large private Australian enterprises", Melbourne Institute of Applied Economic and Social Research, The University of Melbourne, Working paper No: 2/99.
88. Tong, G. and C.J. Green (2005). "Pecking order or Trade off hypothesis? Evidence on the capital structure of Chinese companies", *Applied Economics*, Vol.37 (19), pp.2179-2189.
89. Titman, Sheridan (1984). "The effect of capital structure on a firm's liquidation decision", *Journal of Financial Economics*, Vol.13, pp.1371- 1375.
90. Vijayakumar, A. and Kadirvel, S. (2003). "Profitability and size of the firm in Indian Minerals and Metals industry", *The Management Accountant*, pp. 816-821.
91. Weiss, L. W (1963). "Average Concentration Ratios and Industrial Firms", *Journal of Industrial Economics*, Vol. 11, pp. 237-54.
92. Zeiton and Tian (2007). "Does ownership affect a firm's performance and default risk in Jordan corporate governance", Vol.7 (1), pp. 66-82.
93. Zhang, A., Y. Zhang and R. Zhao (2002). "Profitability and productivity of Chinese industrial firms: measurement and ownership implications", *China Economic Review*, Vol.13 (1), pp.65-88.

### TABLE 2.2

## DESCRIPTIVE STATISTICS OF INDEPENDENT AND DEPENDENT VARIABLES

**20 Indian Automobile Firms-1996-2009 – 216 Firm-year observations (N = 216)**

| Variables | Mean ± SD | Standard Error of Mean | Median | Minimum | Maximum | Kurtosis | Skew ness |
|---|---|---|---|---|---|---|---|
| PR | 22.29 ± 105.3 | 6.62 | 14.58 | -189.39 | 1638.92 | 222.83 | 14.44 |
| Ln sales (size) | 6.90 ± 1.70 | 0.11 | 6.86 | 0.92 | 10.39 | 0.01 | -0.27 |
| Growth | 10.60 ± 36.83 | 2.32 | 10.13 | -97.62 | 356.66 | 31.46 | 3.48 |
| Liquidity (CCC) | 29.90 ± 65.81 | 4.14 | 19.07 | -225.76 | 312.03 | 5.58 | -.18 |
| Leverage | 1.40 ± 3.18 | 0.20 | 0.71 | 0 | 41.37 | 106.68 | 9.18 |
| Age | 0.06 ± 0.02 | 0.001 | 0.06 | 0.02 | 0.19 | 5.38 | 1.62 |
| Post profitability | 18.67 ± 130.38 | 8.23 | 15.82 | -1190.08 | 1638.92 | 124.98 | 4.51 |
| Capital-output ratio | 1.07 ± 130.38 | 0.44 | 0.26 | -1.89 | 79.78 | 111.18 | 10.40 |
| Market share | 2.05 ± 2.85 | 0.18 | 0.12 | 0.01 | 9.66 | -0.08 | 1.14 |

PR-Profit rate on total assets; Ln Sales-Natural logarithm of sales (Proxy for size); Growth-Sales Growth; CCC-Cash Conversion Cycle (proxy for liquidity); Leverage – Debt/ Equity; Age-Ratio of Depreciation of fixed assets; Past Profitability- Profitability for previous year; Capital-Output Ratio – Ratio of total capital to total sales; Market Share – Ratio of sales to total industry sales.

***Source:*** Computed

## TABLE 2.3

## CORRELATION MATRIX

| | PR | Ln Sales | Growth | Liquidity | Leverage | Age | Past profitability | Capital output ratio | Market share |
|---|---|---|---|---|---|---|---|---|---|
| PR | 1.00 | | | | | | | | |
| Ln Sales | 0.04 | 1.00 | | | | | | | |
| Growth | 0.03 | 0.18 | 1.00 | | | | | | |
| Liquidity | -0.09 | -0.11 | -05.05 | 1.00 | | | | | |
| Leverage | -0.003 | -0.09 | -0.01 | 0.02 | 1.00 | | | | |
| Age | 0.04 | 0.29 | -0.03 | 0.08 | -0.05 | 1.00 | | | |
| Past profitability | 0.02 | 0.05 | 0.001 | 0.005 | -0.01 | 0.34 | 1.00 | | |
| Capital output ratio | 0.02 | 0.31 | 0.005 | -0.02 | -0.03 | 0.04 | 0.003 | 1.00 | |
| Market share | 0.10 | -.58 | -0.05 | -0.05 | 0.11 | -0.28 | -0.11 | 0.06 | 1.00 |

PR-Profit rate on total assets; Ln Sales-Natural logarithm of sales (Proxy for size); Growth-Sales Growth; CCC-Cash Conversion Cycle (proxy for liquidity); Leverage – Debt/ Equity; Age-Ratio of Depreciation of fixed assets; Past Profitability- Profitability for previous year; Capital-Output Ratio – Ratio of total capital to total sales; Market Share – Ratio of sales to total industry sales.

***Source :*** Computed

**TABLE 2.5**

**FINDING ON FIRM STRUCTURE VARIABLES AND PROFITABILITY RELATIONSHIPS**

| ***Firm Structure* Variables** | ***Measure of Performance on Profitability*** |
|---|---|
| Size of Firm | Larger firms are more Profitable (+) |
| Growth | Positive effects of growth on profitability |
| Liquidity | Negative relationship between profitability and liquidity (-) |
| Leverage | Positive effect with operating leverage (-) |
| Age | Older firms are more profitable (+) |
| Past profitability | Positively affect profitability (+) |
| Capital – output ratio | Positive association with the profitability |
| Market Share | Increased market share leads to improved profitability. |

***Source:*** Empirical results of the study

## TABLE 2.4

## REGRESSION ANALYSIS FOR OTHER FACTORS AFFECTING PROFITABILITY

[PR = $\beta_0$ + $\beta_1$ Size + $\beta_2$ Growth + $\beta_3$ Liquidity + $\beta_4$ Leverage + $\beta_5$ Age + $\beta_6$ Past Profitability + $\beta_7$ Capital Output Ratio + $\beta_8$ Market Share]

| *Particulars* | *Constant* | *Size* | *Growth* | *Liquidity* | *Leverage* | *Age* | *Past Profitability* | *Capital Output Ratio* | *Market Share* | $R^2$ | *Adj* $R^2$ | *F Value* | *DW* |
|---|---|---|---|---|---|---|---|---|---|---|---|---|---|
| Ashok Leyland Ltd | 87.97 | 7.71<br>(3.94)* | 0.07<br>(2.58)** | -0.03<br>(3.41)* | -16.53<br>(2.47)*** | 96.77<br>(3.56)* | 0.67<br>(1.68) | 44.13<br>(1.75) | 54.01<br>(4.20)* | 0.99 | 0.97 | 56.38* | 1.94 |
| Tata Motors Ltd | 36.87 | 0.89<br>(3.07)** | 0.05<br>(3.57)* | -0.05<br>(0.83) | -33.09<br>(4.01)* | 3.56<br>(3.84)* | 0.43<br>(2.19)*** | 15.49<br>(3.91)* | 94.63<br>(2.61)** | 0.99 | 0.97 | 57.98* | 2.01 |
| Bajaj Tempo Ltd | -828.66 | -183.1<br>(3.60)* | 3.34<br>(2.29)** | -1.65<br>(2.69)*** | -160.9<br>(2.22)*** | 112.4<br>(1.44) | 4.93<br>(2.13)*** | 257.1<br>(0.93) | 13.40<br>(2.79)** | 0.88 | 0.81 | 28.20* | 1.97 |
| Eicher Motors Ltd | 103.17 | 14.41<br>(3.69)* | 0.15<br>(1.32) | -0.02<br>(4.07)* | -37.38<br>(2.67)*** | 87.34<br>(3.88)* | 0.02<br>(3.07)** | 87.19<br>(2.21)*** | 2.80<br>(2.56)*** | 0.94 | 0.89 | 7.84** | 1.33 |
| Swaraj Mazdar Ltd | 32.59 | 20.33<br>(3.12)** | 0.08<br>(4.08)* | -0.12<br>(3.19)** | -1.21<br>(1.16) | 166.14<br>(4.15)* | 0.17<br>(0.37) | 226.1<br>(4.26)* | 16.77<br>(0.89) | 0.81 | 0.79 | 12.2* | 1.98 |
| **Commercial Vehicles** | **23.07** | **0.55**<br>**(3.37)*** | **0.05**<br>**(2.46)***** | **-0.03**<br>**(2.45)***** | **-10.75**<br>**(3.90)*** | **3.34**<br>**(1.68)** | **0.19**<br>**(2.68)**** | **7.26**<br>**(2.48)**** | **8.53**<br>**(0.72)** | **0.98** | **0.95** | **26.77*** | **2.01** |
| Hindustan Motors Ltd | -138.74 | 13.67<br>(3.63)* | 0.16<br>(2.70)** | -0.01<br>(0.01) | -3.36<br>(3.34)* | 780.0<br>(1.62) | 0.04<br>(4.08)* | 69.72<br>(3.57)* | 2.96<br>(0.35) | 0.86 | 0.81 | 18.26* | 1.80 |
| Mahindra and Mahindra Ltd | 73.25 | 4.49<br>(3.41)* | 0.01<br>(3.02)** | -0.12<br>(4.39)* | -26.15<br>(2.64)** | 109.37<br>(3.26)* | 0.52<br>(1.64) | 62.44<br>(2.64)** | 145.01<br>(3.23)* | 0.97 | 0.91 | 16.69* | 2.03 |
| Maruti Udyog Ltd | 257.71 | 13.58<br>(4.14)* | 0.14<br>(2.86)** | -0.45<br>(1.81) | -75.09<br>(4.60)* | 93.65<br>(1.02) | 0.20<br>(2.32)*** | 195.78<br>(5.79)* | 19.95<br>(3.25)* | 0.99 | 0.96 | 41.15* | 1.99 |

## TABLE 2.4 (CONTINUED...)

## REGRESSION ANALYSIS FOR OTHER FACTORS AFFECTING PROFITABILITY

[PR = $\beta_0 + \beta_1$ Size + $\beta_2$ Growth + $\beta_3$ Liquidity + $\beta_4$ Leverage + $\beta_5$ Age + $\beta_6$ Past Profitability + $\beta_7$ Capital Output Ratio + $\beta_8$ Market Share]

| *Particulars* | *Constant* | *Size* | *Growth* | *Liquidity* | *Leverage* | *Age* | *Past Profitability* | *Capital Output Ratio* | *Market Share* | *$R^2$* | *Adj $R^2$* | *F Value* | *DW* |
|---|---|---|---|---|---|---|---|---|---|---|---|---|---|
| Hyundai Motors | 0.11 | 8.01 (7.41)* | -0.01 (4.03)* | -9.33 (3.97)* | -45.03 (8.11)* | 101.33 (2.72)* | 0.17 (1.20) | 0.90 (4.44)* | 8.0 (5.81)* | 0.99 | 0.97 | 56.32* | 1.96 |
| Honda Siel Ltd | 0.04 | 2.26 (4.19)* | 0.32 (3.17)** | 0.22 (2.86)** | -38.49 (3.98)* | 199.95 (1.25) | 0.41 (4.36)* | 26.80 (2.29)*** | 1.14 (3.65)* | 0.93 | 0.88 | 6.24** | 1.72 |
| Ford India Ltd | -0.25 | 9.79 (3.48)* | 0.16 (3.08)** | -0.55 (4.15)* | -7.15 (1.12) | 916.67 (3.37)* | 0.83 (5.48)* | 129.11 (3.53)* | 17.46 (1.41) | 0.83 | 0.76 | 8.62** | 1.65 |
| **Passenger cars and Multi-utility Vehicles** | **86.33** | **6.54 (2.13)*** ** | **0.08 (3.09)*** * | **-0.12 (4.77)*** | **-12.79 (2.50)*** ** | **102.14 (1.19)** | **0.47 (2.42)*** ** | **23.19 (3.38)*** | **26.91 (0.51)** | **0.97** | **0.90** | **14.54*** | **1.98** |
| Bajaj Auto Ltd | -82.17 | 12.56 (3.92)* | 0.01 (4.09)* | -0.22 (2.36)*** | -7.70 (3.22)** | 30.14 (0.26) | 0.48 (2.64)** | -16.82 (1.99) | 21.89 (4.42)* | 0.96 | 0.89 | 11.07** | 1.92 |
| LML Ltd | 178.86 | 24.34 (0.65) | 0.39 (2.79)** | -1.27 (2.59)*** | -14.90 (5.93)* | 286.65 (6.45)* | 1.53 (2.32)*** | 128.90 (3.91)* | 6.50 (1.56) | 0.97 | 0.90 | 14.39* | 1.75 |
| Maharashtra Scooters Ltd | -17.06 | 1.47 (4.24)* | 0.08 (3.67)* | -0.08 (2.96)** | -161.12 (3.61)* | 126.80 (0.41) | 0.18 (2.43)*** | 0.02 (0.06) | 0.37 (2.44)*** | 0.80 | 0.72 | 12.00* | 1.52 |
| TVS Motor Company Ltd | 83.88 | -11.49 (3.56)* | 0.04 (4.17)* | -0.48 (3.10)** | -28.50 (2.86)** | 196.64 (4.78)* | 0.24 (2.73)** | 115.27 (0.75) | 48.31 (1.49) | 0.93 | 0.89 | 6.66** | 1.81 |
| Kinetic Motor Company Ltd | -4711.76 | -923.72 (4.52)* | -9.49 (3.83)* | -3.61 (3.28)* | -5.51 (0.17) | 371.18 (3.54)* | 0.48 (4.68)* | 290.42 (3.68)* | 7.18 (1.18) | 0.98 | 0.94 | 24.75* | 1.86 |

## TABLE 2.4 (CONTINUED...)

## REGRESSION ANALYSIS FOR OTHER FACTORS AFFECTING PROFITABILITY

[PR = $\beta_0$ + $\beta_1$ Size + $\beta_2$ Growth + $\beta_3$ Liquidity + $\beta_4$ Leverage + $\beta_5$ Age + $\beta_6$ Past Profitability + $\beta_7$ Capital Output Ratio + $\beta_8$ Market Share]

| *Particulars* | *Constant* | *Size* | *Growth* | *Liquidity* | *Leverage* | *Age* | *Past Profitability* | *Capital Output Ratio* | *Market Share* | *$R^2$* | *Adj $R^2$* | *F Value* | *DW* |
|---|---|---|---|---|---|---|---|---|---|---|---|---|---|
| Hero Honda Motors Ltd | 247.99 | 36.06 | -0.32 | -0.64 | -41.92 | 179.26 | 0.16 | -209.98 | 79.12 | 0.99 | 0.96 | 35.41* | 1.66 |
| | | (3.33)* | (2.55)** | (2.35)*** | (4.52)* | (2.47)*** | (0.82) | (3.99)* | (4.45)* | | | | |
| Kinetic Engineering Ltd | -65.06 | 7.38 | 0.54 | -0.14 | -0.42 | 339.54 | 0.71 | 11.24 | 3.15 | 0.95 | 0.86 | 10.21** | 1.45 |
| | | (6.02)* | (3.01)* | (2.28)*** | (3.60)* | (4.51)* | (3.15)** | (2.95)** | (1.76) | | | | |
| Majestic Auto Ltd | 14.98 | -9.34 | -0.04 | -0.03 | -6.11 | 971.39 | 0.08 | 73.54 | 2.45 | 0.92 | 0.81 | 5.51** | 1.37 |
| | | (4.03)* | (3.65)* | (0.27) | (3.91)* | (3.80)* | (0.22) | (3.51)* | (2.11)*** | | | | |
| Scooters India Ltd | 804.21 | -162.5 | 1.23 | -0.53 | 40.15 | 556.58 | 0.01 | 4.52 | 2.67 | 0.92 | 0.86 | 5.68** | 1.25 |
| | | (3.52)* | (2.47)*** | (2.33)*** | (1.58) | (4.39)* | (0.04) | (3.43)* | (1.12) | | | | |
| **Two & Three Wheelers** | **194.82** | **-14.88** | **0.23** | **-0.44** | **-19.68** | **520.54** | **0.20** | **22.98** | **33.52** | **0.93** | **0.89** | **6.78*** | **1.88** |
| | | **(2.95)**** | **(2.80)**** | **(3.67)*** | **(2.73)**** | **(2.78)**** | **(3.41)*** | **(4.46)*** | **(0.59)** | | | | |
| **Whole Industry** | **19.54** | **-0.46** | **0.06** | **-0.04** | **-6.91** | **146.73** | **0.56** | **20.39** | – | **0.90** | **0.85** | **6.54**** | **1.68** |
| | | **(4.50)*** | **(2.13)***** | **(3.75)*** | **(1.80)** | **(3.96)*** | **(2.96)**** | **(2.09)***** | | | | | |

**Notes:** PR – Profit rate on total assets; Size-Natural logarithm of sales (proxy for size); Growth – Sales Growth; Liquidity – Cash Conversion Cycle (proxy for liquidity); Leverage – Debt/Equity; Age – Ratio of depreciation of fixed assets; Past Profitability – Profitability for previous year; Capital out put ratio – Ratio of total capital to total sales; Market share – Ratio of sales to total industry sales.

***Source*** : Computed

# 3

# Determinants of Corporate Dividend in India

## A Study of PSU's

Every investment is made on the expectation and assumption that it will yield some returns. Equity investment is not an exception to this. Every equity investor anticipates a good rate of return in the form of dividend to be declared by the company. So, every company pays higher attention in formulating its own dividend policy. Dividend decision is one of the most important decisions in the field of Financial Management. Dividend policy determines the relationship between a company and the capital market. Payment of dividend enhances the market price of the shares thereby increasing the wealth of the shareholders. Payment of dividend conveys to shareholders the information relating to the profitability of the firm. Economic studies generally show that the dividends act as booster of the shareholder's confidence signaling that the company is being managed well and its future is safe.

A dividend policy must permit the distribution of regular dividend at gradually increasing pace. The desirable aim of all the companies should be the establishment of a stable dividend rate because it aids in raising additional capital, enhances reputation and increases the value of securities. Thus, deciding how much of the current earnings are to be distributed or retained is a major financial decision for a company.

## STATEMENT OF THE PROBLEM

The Sugar Industry in India is one of the oldest industries but has great relevance in the context of the global economy even today. The industry has been facing an unpleasant period. The India Sugar Industry suffers from excessive consumer protectionism, leading to an unwarranted increase in its cost of production primarily due to political decisions leading occasionally to sharp increases in the cost of sugar, thus reducing the competitive edge.

Furthermore, Government policies hitherto have encouraged the establishment of low capacity and uneconomic sugar plants. These policies proceeded despite advice to the inventory by many experts. Under the present sugar policy, sugar factories have to surrender part of their production to the government (presently 30%) at prices about 20% below the cost of production all levy sugar for distribution to the consumers through the Public distribution System.

Besides this, many controls and regulations on the sugar industry right from the purchase of sugarcane to the sale of sugar and by-products have had a telling impact on the economic standing of the industry. The pricing policy for sugarcane is also not free from laws. Unfortunately, in recent years fixing ɔf sugarcane prices has become a political issue based on the populist perceptions of the ruling and opposition parties. This is a direct consequence of the dual authority being exercised by the Central Government and State Government in case price fixing. The Central

Government fixes the statutory minimum Price (SMP) which is used for the computation of the price of levy sugar. However, the actual cane price paid by the sugar mills is the one announced by the State Government, known as the SAP- the State Advised Price. The normal tendency on the start of the State Government is to raise the cane price beyond the economic level to appease the number of farmers involved. Till now, no firm decision has been taken owing to its politically sensitive nature.

All the above problems have been adversely affecting the profitability of the sugar companies. For public limited companies, a fall in the level of profitability destabilizes their dividend payment schedule. Lintner (1956) observes that the financial decisions of corporations are predominantly dividend – oriented and firms pay primary importance to dividends rather than retained earnings. Is this true in the Indian Sugar Industry? To which – dividends or retained earnings-do the companies pay primary importance? Do the companies belonging to sugar industry maintain an increasing steam of dividend? What has been the trend in the dividend payment by the Sugar Industry? Further, an attempt has also been made to study the factors that influence the dividend policy of the Sugar Industry.

## REVIEW OF EMPIRICAL WORKS

A number of studies have been carried out to examine, retained earnings and dividends. The pioneering works are mostly carried out by American researchers. The nature of the studies, objectives with which they have been carried out and the results are briefly summarized in the following paragraphs. Lintmer, John (1956) conducted study on the 'Distribution of Earnings of Corporations among Dividends, Retained Earnings and Taxes'. Twenty-eight American Corporations were chosen for the purpose of the study. He found that the corporations followed a fixed target pay out ratio. The rate of dividends was adjusted along with the increase in the level of earnings. Current year's earnings and previous year's dividend were found to be associated with current year's dividend. He also ascertained that the financial decisions of the corporations were predominantly dividend oriented.

Darling (1957)[2] proceeded on the work of Lintmer. Darling introduced depreciation and change in volume of sales in the place of previous year's dividend. Depreciation was introduced because it represented undistributed cash and change in sales was introduced to represent the need for working capital. His study revealed that depreciation has a positive influence on the amount of dividend. Inverse correlation existed between dividend and growth in sales.

The impact of investment demand on the amount of dividend distribute was examined by Smith (1963)[3]. He added one more variable namely 'Demand for investment' to Lintner's model and found that corporate savings and investment demand were closely associated. He came to the conclusion that dividend decision was only residual.

Purnanandam and Hanumantha Rao (1966)[4] in their study entitled "Corporate Dividends and Target Payout Ratios in the Indian Cotton Textile Industry: 1946-63" attempted estimate the long run desired dividend payment ratios in the Indian Cotton Textile Industry using the Lintner's Dividend Model. The data were taken from several issues of 'Investor's Encyclopedia.' published by Messer. Kothari & Sons, Madras. The two variables that appeared in the study were dividends excluding the issues of bonus shares and net profits during a particular period without the intercept term 'a'. A sample of 50 and net textile companies was chosen for the study. The results indicated that the weights attached to profit as well as lagged dividend were high in case of homogenous equation (model without intercept term 'a') as compared to non-homogeneous equation (model with intercept term 'a'). The target payout ratios as well as the reaction coefficients were higher in the case of homogeneous equation. Their study revealed that a larger volume of dividend was paid by the Textile Industry.

Smith, Deith (1971)[3], carried out a study entitled "Increasing Stream Steam Hypothesis of corporate dividend policy. He attempted to clarify the empirical side of corporate dividend policy by postulating and testing an alternative hypothesis of it, i.e. increasing Stream Hypothesis of corporate dividend policy. A large sample of 900 firms was chosen for the study. A period of 19 years from 1948-1967 was considered for the purpose of the study. The findings of the study supported the increasing stream hypothesis that forms avoid dividend cuts in favour of uninterrupted stream of non-decreasing dividend payments to common shareholders.

In India, Rao and Sarma (1971) [6] carried out a study titled "Dividends and Retained Earnings of Public and Private Limited Companies in India: 1955-56 to 1965-66-'An Econometric Analysis'. The objectives of the study were to enquire into the determinants of dividends of public and private limited companies, to estimate short-run marginal propensity to pay dividend, short-run marginal propensity to saw and the long-run desired payout and savings ratios. The study covered period of 11 years from 1955-56 to 1965-66 in respect of two categories of companies viz., (i) Non-financial and Non-Government companies with a paid-up capital of more than Rs.5 lakh and (ii) medium and large private limited companies. The Basic Lintner model was employed in the study. The results of the study indicated that there were variations in the suitability of the models employed. While the model with cash flow variable fitted well for industries like cotton textiles, iron and steel, paper products and electricity generation and supply, the model with depreciation and net profit, introduced separately, was found to well explain the dividend behaviour of Jute and textiles and Engineering Industries. Further it was also found that the payout ratio widely different among the selected industry groups. The study also revealed that in the case of sugar industry, the substitution of cash flow variable in place of current profits in the basic Lintner model has not improved the explanatory power of the equation as reflected in Adjusted $R^2$. The standard error is lower in the case of the basic Lintner model and hence this model may be preferred for the sugar industry.

Dhameja (1972)[7] in his study entitled Dividend Behaviour in Indian paper industry –1950-65; A Statistical Test', examined the statistical significance of various factors influencing dividend policy in Indian Paper Industry. The variables used were net profit, previous year dividend, weighed average of past profits, depreciation cash flow earnings (net and gross), change in sales, accumulated reserves and provision for tax. The tools used and study were linear multiple regression and coefficient of determination. He concluded that the increase in profit did not result in an equivalent increase in dividend and vice – versa. Dividend determination was influenced by the past year's profit and fluctuations in the earnings did have much influence on dividend. Fluctuations in dividend determinations were influenced by current year's earnings while change in sales had a positive influence on dividend. Further it was ascertained from the study that lagged dividend was directly associated with current year dividend.

In the another study Krishnamurthy and Sastry (1971)[8] made an attempt to examine the dividend behavior of public limited companies based on the data available in the Reserve Bank of India Bulletin. The study period was from 1960 to1970 covering 11 years. They extended Linters model with additional variables to these companies. These variables included cash flow; changed cash flow; investment expenditure and flow of debt. They found that basic Linters model was more appropriate in explaining the dividend behaviour.

Kumar and Khurana (1984) made an attempt to find out the factors influencing the dividend policy of selected Indian Industries. Their study entitled, 'Determinants of Corporate Dividend in India' had two main objectives. They were, (i) to find out the most important factors, which influence increase in dividend and (ii) to ascertain factors, which have a bearing in reduction of dividend. They selected 65 manufacturing companies whose shares were listed in the Bombay Stock Exchange and conducted personal interview with the managements of the selected companies. Their study period covered five years from 1979-1983. They found that whenever the companies increased dividends; they took three factors into account. The factors were (i) increase in net profit after tax, (ii) better liquidity position and (iii) better reserve position. Of these three, the first one was considered to be the most important factor. Three factors, namely (i) reduction in profits after tax, (ii) poor liquidity position and (iii) expansion programmed were considered to be pertinent factors for decrease and non-payment of dividends. Of these three factors, priority was assigned to reduction in profits.

Agarwal (1986) [9], carried out a study entitled, 'Corporate Investment and Financial Behaviour - An Econometric Analysis of Indian Automobile Industry'. Their study period was 20 years from 1959-60 to 1978-79. The Basis Lintner model was used for examining the dividend behaviour of the selected seven units belonging to the Automobile Industry. To the Lintner's model, he added four more variables namely change in sales, liquidity. How of external funds and total investment. It was found that current year's profit was the most important factor, which decided the payment of dividend. The other variables were not found to significantly influence the payment of dividend

Mittal (1992) [10], in his study entitled 'Determinants of Corporate Retained Earnings' examined whether the decisions of retained earnings was a primary decisions variable or residual one. The data had been collected from the Stock Exchange Official Directory, Bombay for 10 years from 1980 – 81 to 1989 – 90 regarding 23 large public limited textile companies in the private sector. Coefficient of variation had been calculated to examine whether retention of earnings was a primary or residual variable. The results of the study revealed that the retained earnings decision was a residual one since there were low variations in the dividends paid and large variations in retained earnings in textile companies.

Kevin (1992) [11] carried out a study titled 'Dividend Policy'. An analysis of Some Determinants'. He examined whether private sector companies in India strive for stability in their dividend payment and how far the dividend pattern of private sector companies in India was consistent with their earnings pattern. A sample of 650 Private Sector companies was chosen and the data were collected from the 'First-ever Computerized Survey of the Top 650 Private Sector Companies' by the Commerce Research Bureau in 1986. Regression Analysis was used in the study and the variables considered were (i) dividend, (ii) net profit, (iii) operating profit, (iv) net assets and (v) net sales. The results of the study revealed that no consistent covariation between dividend payment and *** The companies generally wanted to maintain stable dividend payment and *** that divided stability was the primary determinant of Dividend policy and profitability was only of secondary importance in the sense that companies strove to maintain stable dividends in spite of fluctuations in earnings. It was concluded that the dividend policy was not a passive residual but an active decision variable.

Bhat, Ramesh and Pandey (1994) [12] in their study titled'. Dividend Decision: A Study of 'Managers' perceptions' attempted to find out how the managers perceive the question of dividend payment and retention. A questionnaire was sent to 450 companies and was addressed to finance directors. Thirty-one questionnaires were received, of which 28 were found usable for analysis. The results of the study revealed that the ranking of determinants of Dividend was (i) current earnings,(ii) patterns of past dividends, (iii) increasing equity base and expected future earnings, (iv) liquidity and (v) preference of companies to maintain their dividend policy even if they do not have internally available cash. Moreover, analysis of manager's responses showed that they favoured the view that dividend policy influence the share price i.e., higher the dividend payout, higher would the price of equity per share. The study also revealed that investors in high tax brackets were attracted to shares having low dividend yield and investors in low tax brackets were attracted to shares having high dividend yield.

Mahesh Chand Gang, Saroj Nagpal and Verma (1996) [13] examined the factors affecting payment of dividend in the textile industry in India using ratio analysis. Their study entitled, 'Factors Determining Dividend Payments in textile Industry in India' covered a period of ten years from 1980-81 to 1989-90 and included 44 joint stock companies from the textile industry except jute textiles. Four classifications of rations had been made viz.,(i) capital structure ratios, (ii) liquidity ratios, (iii) profitability ratios and (iv) dividend practices ratios.

The results of the study revealed that capital structure; liquidity and profitability seemed to be the factors determining the dividend payments in the sample companies. With improved capital base, liquidity and profitability, dividend payments increase. Dividend payments have also been on the higher side in the diversified group. In the case of associated group, capital structure, liquidity and profitability position is better and the dividend payments are better.

In their study entitled, 'Dividend Policy of Private Sector Enterprises-A Case study of Engineering Industry', Jain and Khera (1996) [14] examined the dividend policy pursued by the corporate firms affiliated to the engineering industry and liked into its impact on the value of corporate firms. The data for the study has been collected from the "The Stock Exchange Official Directory" of the Bombay Stock Exchange pertaining to General engineering, and from the responses of the financial managers of the engineering corporate firms. The study covered a period from 1981-1991. Forty - one firms were chosen as the sample for the study. Earnings per share, dividend per share, and market price per share, total assets, equity capital, debentures, long term loans, net profit and profit retained, depreciation, net cash earnings, and dividend payout ratios were some of the variables used. It was concluded that the private sector engineering corporate firms by and large tended to practice stable dividend policy. They seemed to be following an approach akin to Lintner's model. Dividend was generally found to be an active decision variable affecting the valuation of the firm whereas decision relating to retention occupied second position. It was also observed that higher growth firms have lower dividend payout ratios as such firms had greater profitable investment opportunities needing more financial resources. Further, with announcements of bonus and right issues along with increase or no decrease in cash dividend has an appreciably favorable impact on the price of the share of the firms.

In a study entitled, 'Dividend Policy and Practices in Select Corporate Firms of India and South – East Asia: A Comparative Study', Jain and Manoj Kumar (1997) examined and compared dividend policies and practices of 96 corporate firms in India and three companies in South-East Asia. The study covered a period of twelve years i.e., 1994- 1995. The data had been collected from a variety of sources, viz, Bombay Stock Exchange Official Directory, Reserve Bank of India Bulletins, Kothari Economic Guide, and Business Magazines like Business India etc. From the study, it was found that sample firms preferred a stable dividend policy. Retained earnings constituted an important source of funds for Indian firms. Sample corporate firm seemed to follow a policy of paying less than 45 per cent of net earnings to equity shareholders during the twelve-year period (1984-1995). Corporate firms in India had a tendency to pay relatively less a dividend compared to South – East Asian companies. Majority of the companies (66 per cent) in India followed stable dividend policy. Indian Corporate firms found Retained Earning as higher significant source than their counter parts in the South-East Asian Region.

## METHODOLOGY

The official stock exchange Directory published by the Bombay Stock Exchange, Mumbai, and furnished data for all the listed companies listed amount to 67. From this, lists of companies that have provided continuous data for a period of 12 years have been short-listed first. From this list, 16 companies have been chosen randomly. The data required for the study is secondary in nature. The main source of data for the present study is the official stock exchange Directory, published by the Bombay Stock Exchange, Mumbai. Apart from, Mumbai maintained by center for monitoring Indian Economy, Mumbai and Data provided in www.indianinfoline.com have also been used.

The data collected has been analysed through simple average, co-efficient of variation, Analysis of variance (ANOVA) and multiple regression. Determinants of dividends have been studies through multiple regression analysis. For this purpose, the following regression equation has been framed.

$$\mathbf{DPS_t = a + b_1\,NS_t + b_2\,INT_t + b_3\,DEP_t + b_4\,PROV_t + b_5\,NPT_t + b_6\,NPT_{t+1} + b_7\,NPT_{t-1} + b_8\,DPS_{t-1} + b_9\,REPSt_{-1} + b_{10}\,LIQ_t + b_{11}\,INGB_{t+1} + e}$$

Where

| | | |
|---|---|---|
| $DPS_t$ | = | Current year's Dividend per share |
| a | = | constant |
| $NS_t$ | = | current year's Sales |
| $DEP_t$ | = | current year's Depreciation |
| $PROV_t$ | = | current year's Provision for Tax |
| $NPT_t$ | = | current year's Net Profit |
| $NPT_{t+1}$ | = | subsequent year's Net Profit |
| $NPT_{t-1}$ | = | previous year's Net Profit |
| $DPS_{t-1}$ | = | previous year's dividend per share |

$REPS_{t-1}$ = previous year's Retained Earnings per share
$LIQ_t$ = current year's Liquidity Ratio
$INGB_{t+1}$ = Subsequent year's increase in Gross block
e = Error Term

The regression co-efficients are tested for their significance through the 't' values. The significance of $R^2$ has been tested through 'F' statistic. The levels of significance chosen are 1% and 5%.

## TRENDS IN CORPORATE DIVIDENDS

It has been found by Smith, Keith V (1971) that corporations follow a policy of increasing the level of dividend over the years. In a study titled "Increasing Stream Hypothesis of Corporate Dividend Policy", he proposes a hypothesis that corporations are oriented towards increase in the rate of dividend. Based on the methodology of Smith, Keith V, an attempt is made here to ascertain the behaviour of dividend of the companies belonging to the Indian Sugar Industry.

The average amounts of earnings dividends as well as the growth rate in dividends of all the selected companies belonging to the Sugar industry are shown in Table 3.1. It can be seen from the table that the mean amount of earnings has ranged between Rs. 1.58 and to Rs. 49.55. The mean amount of dividends has ranged between Rs. 0.08 and to Rs. 4.00. The growth rate of dividend is positive in five selected sugar industries during the study period. Among these, the highest growth rate of dividend observed in Vishnu sugar Mills Limited, followed by Balrampur Chini Mills Limited, Ravalgaon Sugar Farm Limited, Bajaj Hindustan Limited and Bannariamman Sugars Limited. In all other selected sugar mills, the growth rate of dividend is negative during the study period. The average DPS of Sugar Industry is Rs. 2.54 during the study period. Further, the oversell mean growth rate of sugar industry has been worked out as 8.20.

In order to ascertain whether the mean values of dividends per share have differed among the companies, Analysis of Variance (ANOVA) test has been performed and the results are presented in Table 3.2. In this industry, the calculated F value is greater than its table value at 1% level. Hence it is inferred that there is a significant difference among the companies of this industry.

## DETERMINANTS OF DIVIDENDS

Dividend policy has remained one of the most researched areas of study in the field of finance. Many researchers have made attempts to examine the factories that determine the dividend policy of firms. An attempt is made in this part to ascertain the factors that influence the dividend policy of the Indian Sugar Industry. Correlation analysis has been carried out to find out the factors that are correlated with dividends. Dividends are influence by factors like net sales, net profit previous year dividends, retained earnings etc., correlation analysis has been carried out in order to test the association between the selected eleven independent variables and dividend per share and presented in Table 3.3. If the calculated correlation value between any variable and dividend per share is greater than its table value at one percent level then it is inferred that there exists a highly significant correlation between these two variables.

It is found that all the eleven variables namely, net sales, interest, depreciation, provision for tax, current year's net profit subsequent year's net profit, previous year's dividend per share, previous year's retained, earnings per share, liquidity, subsequent year's increase in Gross Block are significantly associated with dividend per share of the current year. All the eleven variables are positively associated with dividends and the relationship is found to be highly significant.

In order to find out the influence of the selected variables on the amount of dividends distributed, Multiple Regression has been carried out. The dividends have been regressed on the selected variables. The results of the analysis are discussed for the sugar industry, as a whole. Table 4 summaries the values of regression co-efficient. Only three variables, namely net profit for the current year, previous year dividend per share and liquidity ratio are found to be significantly associated with the level of dividends distributed.

The regression co-efficient between dividend per share of the current year ($DPS^1$) and net profit of the current year ($NPT^1$) amounts to 0.0143 indicating that the profit is positively related with dividend per share. This indicates that an increase of one rupee in net profit will enhance the amount of dividend per share by Rs. 0.014, keeping the other variables constant. It can also be seen from the table that the influence of previous year dividend is positive and significant at one percent level. The contribution of pervious year dividend per share to current year dividend per share is 0.6848. This indicates that one percent of increase in previous year dividend enhances the current year dividend by Rs. 0.68.

Generally, there exists an inverse relationship between dividends paid and the liquid ratio. If the dividend paid increases, the liquidity position decreases and vice versa. It can be seen from the table that the regression coefficient between liquidity and dividend per share amounts to 0.2225 and is positively related with dividend per share which is significant at 5 percent level. The nature of this relationship is strange. The overall contribution of all the eleven variables is found out by calculating $R^2$ value. The value of $R^2$ amounts to 0.7241. This indicates that the contribution of all these eleven variables significance through 'F' test and has been found to be highly significant.

It has been found that of the eleven variables, only two are found to have significant influence on dividend per share. In order to identify the most significant factors that influence the level of dividend per share, stepwise regression has been performed and the results were presented in Table 3.5. It is evident from the table that previous year's dividend contribution was 62.95 percent. It can also be seen that total contribution from dividend 62.95 percent to 70.29 percent. The total $R^2$ value inclusive of eleven independent variables between these two regression equations is only variables which are not included in the stepwise regression equation.

## CONCLUSION

It is found that all the variables selected are significantly and positively associated with dividend per share of the current year. Three variables namely current year's net profit, previous year's dividend and liquidity have significant influence on dividend distributed. Thus, dividend payment has become almost compulsory for every firm as the share holders are looking for short-term and periodical returns on their investments. The present study has also revealed that companies attach primary importance to dividends and they prefer a stable or increasing trend in dividend payments.

## REFERENCES

1. Lintner J. (1956), 'Distribution of Income of Corporations Among Dividends, Retained Earnings and Taxes', *American Economic Review*, pp: 97-113
2. Darling P.G, (1957), 'The Influence of Expectations and Liquidity on Dividend Policy', Journal of Political Economy, (June), pp: 209-224, Cited in Braj Kishore, (1980), 'Corporate Internal Finance: A Study of Overall Trends and retentions', *Vikalpa*, Vol. 5, No. 3. (July), p.194.
3. Smith David C, (1963), 'Corporate Savings Behaviour', *Canadian Journal of Economics and Political science*, Vol. 29, No. 3, (Aug), pp: 297-130 Darling P. G, Op. cit., p.195.
4. Purananandam J and Hanumautha Rao K. S, (1966),

'Corporate Dividends and Target Payout Ratios in the Indian Cotton Textile Industries 1946-63'. *The Journal of Industrial Economics*, Vol. XV, No. 1, pp: 38-43.

5. Smith Keith V, (1971), 'Increasing Stream Hypothesis of Corporate Dividend Policy' California Management Review, 14(fall). PP: 56-64, in Geerge N. Engter, Managerial Finance- Cases and Readings,(ed) .
6. Rao G.N and Sarma Y.S.R. (1971), 'Dividends and Retained Earnings of Public and Private Limited companies in India, 1955-56. An Econometric Analysis', Reserve Bank of India Bulletin, Vol. 25, No. 6, (June), pp: 860-873.
7. Dhameja N.L,(1972), 'Dividend Behaviour in Indian Paper Industry 1950-65: A Statistical Test', *Indian Economic Journal*, Vol. XIX, No.3, pp:432-442.
8. Krishnamurthy K and Sastry D., (1971), 'Some Aspects of Corporate Behaviour in India: A Cross Sectional Analysis of Investments. Dividends and External Finance for the Chemical industry: 1966-67', Indian Economic Review, (Oct), Cited in Braj Kishore, op.cit.,p.198.
9. Agarwal R.N. (1987), 'Corporate Investment and Financing Behaviour-An Econometric Analysis of Indian Automobile Industry', Delhi, Commonwealth Publishers. pp: 73-90.
10. Mittal R.K. (1992), Determinants of Corporate Retained Earnings'. *Indian Management*, Vol. 31, No. 3, pp. 35-38
11. Kevin S, (1992), Dividend Policy: An Analysis of Some Determinants', *Finance India*, Vol. VI, No. 2, pp. 11-20.
12. Bhat Ramesh and I.M. Pandey, (1994), Dividend Decision: A Study of Managers Perceptions', Decision, Vol. 21, Nos. 1&2, pp: 67-86.
13. Mahesh Chand Garg, Saroj Nagpal and Verma H.l, (1996), Factors Determining Dividend Payments in Textile Industry in India', Vol. X, No.1, pp: 144-156.
14. Jain P.K and Khera B.N, (1996), Dividend of policy of Private Sector Enterprises A Case study of Engineering

Industry', *Journal of Accounting and Finance*, Vol. X, No. 2, (Sept), pp: 221-243.

15. Jain P.K and Manoj Kumar, (1996), Dividend Policy and Practices in Select corporate Firms of Indian and South-East Asia: A Comparative study', *Vision*, Vol. I (2), (July-December), pp: 11-20.

**TABLE 3.1**

## TRENDS IN CORPORATE DIVIDENDS (1989 - 2000)

| Company Name | EPS Mean Value(Rs.) | DPS Mean Value(Rs.) | Growth Rate (%) |
|---|---|---|---|
| Revalgaon Sugar Farm Limited | 49.55 | 4.00 | 6.81 |
| Balrampur Chini Mills Limited | 27.65 | 3.96 | 11.83 |
| Vishnu Sugar Mills Limited | 66.44 | 3.27 | 23.03 |
| New India Sugar Mills Limited | 20.20 | 3.18 | -0.92 |
| Bannariamman Sugars Limited | 10.61 | 2.27 | 2.00 |
| Andhra Sugars Limited | 7.25 | 2.14 | -6.12 |
| Oudh Sugar Mills Limited | 7.37 | 2.11 | -1.87 |
| Kesar Enterprises Limited | 5.91 | 1.84 | -8.81 |
| Sakthi Sugars Limted | 6.43 | 1.77 | -7.61 |
| Bajaj Hindusthan Limited | -1.20 | 1.43 | 5.15 |
| Dhampur Sugar Mills Limited | 19.14 | 1.40 | -1.4 |
| Bhopal Sugar Industrues Limited | -8.34 | 1.08 | -5.72 |
| Ponni Sugars and Chemicals Limited | 1.58 | 1.05 | -7.70 |
| United Provinces Sugar Company Limited | 10.54 | 0.55 | -0.51 |
| India Sugars and Refineries Limited | -3.28 | 0.33 | - |
| Behlapur Industries Limited | -0.15 | 0.08 | - |
| Average | | **2.54** | **8.20** |

**EPS** - Earnings per Share
**DPS** - Dividend per Share

***Source:*** Computed

## TABLE 3.2

## DIFFERENCE IN MEAN DIVIDEND PER SHARE (ANOVA)

| Source | D. F | S. S | M. S | F Value |
|---|---|---|---|---|
| Between Companies | 1549.55 | 262.164.00 | 17.486.81 | 10.82* |
| Error | 176 | 284.35 | 1.62 | |
| **Total** | **191** | **546.51** | | |

* - Significant at 1% level
***Source*** : Computed

## TABLE 3.3

## FACTORS ASSOCIATED WITH DIVIDEND

| Factors | Correltaion Coefficient(r) | Coefficient of Determination ($R^2$) |
|---|---|---|
| Current Year's Sales ($NS_t$) | 0.45* | 0.20 |
| Current Year's Interest ($INT_t$) | 0.31* | 0.09 |
| Current Year's Deprecation ($DEP_t$) | 0.33* | 0.11 |
| Current Year's Provision for tax ($PROV_t$) | 0.30* | 0.09 |
| Current Year's Net Profit($NPT_t$) | 0.53* | 0.28 |
| Subsequent Year's Net Profit ($SNP_{t+1}$) | 0.44* | 0.19 |
| Previous Year's dividend Per Share ($NPT_{t-1}$) | 0.49* | 0.24 |
| Previous Year's Retained Earnings Per Share ($REPS_{t-1}$) | 0.79* | 0.63 |
| Current Year's Liquidity Ratio($LIQ_t$) | 0.46* | 0.21 |
| Subsequent Year's increase in Gross Block ($INGB_{t+1}$) | 0.33* | 0.11 |
| | 0.24* | 0.06 |

* Signification at 1% level. ***Source :*** Computed

## TABLE 3.4

## FACTORS INFLUENCING DIVIDEND

| Variables | Regression Coefficient | Standard Error | Value |
|---|---|---|---|
| $NS_T$ | 0.0002 | 0.0005 | 0.472 |
| $INT_t$ | 0.0029 | 0.0058 | 0.502 |
| $DEP_t$ | -0.0044 | 0.0110 | -0.397 |
| $PROV_t$ | 0.0103 | 0.0142 | 0.727 |
| $NPT_t$ | 0.0143* | 0.0039 | 3.631 |
| $NPT_{t+1}$ | 0.034 | 0.0037 | 0.914 |
| $NPT_{t-1}$ | 0.0648 | 0.0971 | 0.667 |
| $DPS_{t-1}$ | 0.6848* | 0.1134 | 6.038 |
| $REPS_{t-1}$ | -0.0691 | 0.0972 | -0.710 |
| $LIQ_t$ | 0.2225* | 0.1627 | 1.677 |
| $INGB_{t+1}$ | 0.0005 | 0.0007 | 0.716 |

Constant : -0.1181 Ad; $R^2$ : 0.07036

$R^2$ : 0.7241* F Value : 35.316*

* : Significant at 1% level ** : Significant at 5% level

***Source :*** Computed

## TABLE 3.5

## PROMINENTLY ASSOCIATED VARIABLES WITH DIVIDEND

| Step | Constant | $DPS_{t-1}$ | $NPT_t$ | $R^2$ |
|---|---|---|---|---|
| 1 | 0.2083 | 0.9168 | - | 0.6265 |
| 2 | 0.1998 | 0.7991 | 0.0167 | 0.7029 |

***Source :*** Computed

# 4

# Linkage Between Corporate Growth, Liquidity and Profitability

## An Empirical Analysis

When the study of growth is undertaken in terms of systematic influences which may affect growth, rather than regarding the growth as a wholly chance phenomenon, then the most important systematic influence on growth, is that of profitability. Thus the relationship between growth and profitability is of considerable interest both from theoretical and practical points of view. As far the theoretical point of view is concerned, the traditional neo-classical theory of the firm is not very helpful in this respect. Under its usual assumption of perfect competition in all markets, given technology, etc., firm may grow only in order to achieve the 'optimum size' at which they maximize profits. Therefore in equilibrium when all firms are at their optimum size, there will be no relationship at all between the profitability and growth of firms, simply because no firm will grow further.

If, for some reason, some or all firms are not in equilibrium at any moment of time, and are assumed to be moving towards equilibrium, there may well emerge some relationship between profitability and growth on a cross section basis.

Other aspects of relationship between growth and profitability; not only does growth depend on profitability, but profitability itself is a function of growth. There are certain costs involved in the growth which increase as the growth rate increases, thereby reducing profitability. The costs of growth arise mainly from the expenses of obtaining a larger share of existing markets and of increasing rates of diversification for growth, because of increasing resistance from the rival firms and partly due to managerial constraints to the growth of the firm. So it is also due to the conflict between profitability and growth that sometime a relatively high growth rate may not be profitable for the firm in the sense of profit maximization because growth means increase in supply which may mean lower price even lower than the price maximization price. Therefore, the relationship between the growth and profitability may be negative beyond certain growth rate; i.e. the higher the growth the lower the level of profitability of the firm. If this negative relationship between the two exists, it is possible in principle that it may be so strong as to completely outweigh the tendency for positive association between growth and profitability.

Further, it is also argued that growth displays a favourable impact on its profitability except for the samples of bigger firms. It might be argued that smaller firms, being more flexible, tend to take chance more readily than their bigger rivals. It may also be that smaller firms can profitably exploit chances by expanding sales at unreduced prices. A firm's rate of growth depends both on its ability to grow and on its willingness to grow. Its ability to finance growth is closely related to its achieved profitability. The higher the level of its profitability, the more it would be in a position to grow from retained profits. Furthermore, a high 'level of achieved profitability' will be taken by potential investors as a strong indication and the further level of profitability will be high, so that the firm will be able to make new issues on favourable terms. This correspondence between a high ability to grow and 'high level of achieved profitability' is particularly close when growth is measured in terms of the long term finance (i.e. net assets) of the business.

However, a firm's willingness to grow does not depend so directly on its profitability. Profitability does provide an incentive for growth, but there are other factors such as the state of competition, the nature of management, the state of demand and the technological opportunities. For example, for the same profitability, a firm operating in an industry with a buoyant demand may be expected to grow more, by retaining profits or raising new issues, than the firm which operates in an industry with less buoyant demand. Similarly, a firm which is run by a growth oriented management may be expected to grow more than a firm, with the same level of profitability, which is run by a profit maximizing owner manager. In the same way it is possible that there are companies in which there is competition amongst the leading firms to increase their relative market shares, so that they have to grow at a faster rate for the same level of profitability than firms in a less competitive industry.

Further, the factors affecting the willingness to grow may be different for large firms as opposed to small firms in the same industry. In particular, a large firm is usually more diversified and may produce a range of products which could be classified as belonging to more than one industry, so that the firm's willingness to grow will probably be influenced by conditions in a range of companies rather than a single industry. Due to these reasons, the nature of the relationship between profitability and growth for these (large) management dominated firms may be different from that for the smaller sized firms.

In an expanding economy, we could expect a positive association between growth and profitability of firms, because profits provide the ability to grow. However, the factors affecting the willingness to grow are such that these are likely to vary between different companies. These are also likely to vary within the same industry at different points of time, e.g. as demand for the product of the industry changes. This means that the magnitude and the precise form of the positive association between profitability and growth will be different in different companies at a particular time and in the same industry at different times. To sum up, the above considerations suggest that we can expect, in general, a positive or negative association between growth and profitability. Furthermore, the nature and form of this relationship may vary between firms of different sizes, between companies and over time for the same industry. One of the purposes of this article is to examine the extent and significance of these differences for the companies under study.

Liquidity and profitability are two important aspects of corporate business life. Liquidity measures the ability of a company to honour all the maturing obligations. No firm can endure without liquidity. Profitability is the rate of return on company's investment. An unwarranted high investment in current assets would reduce this rate of return. Working capital management has thus, because a basic and broad aspect of adjudicating the performance of a corporate entity. It is, therefore, essential to maintain an adequate degree of liquidity for smooth running of the business operations. The liquidity should be neither excessive nor inadequate. Excessive liquidity indicates accumulation of idle funds which do not earn any profit for the firm and inadequate liquidity not only adversely affects the credit worthiness of the firm but also disrupts the production process and impedes its earning capacity to great extent.

Conventionally, almost all the textbooks pertaining to the financial management and working capital management apparently stress on inverse relationship between liquidity and profitability. The most common measure of liquidity is current ratio and of profitability is return on capital employed. A high current ratio indicates a larger investment in current assets which means a low rate of return on investment for the firm, as excess investment in current asset will not gross enough return. A low current ratio indicates a smaller investment in current assets which means a high rate of return on investment for the firm, as no idle investment is tied up in current assets. However, a low current ratio could also mean interrupted production and sales, because of frequent stock out and inability to pay to creditors in time due to restrictive policy.

Thus, it can be said that the inverse relationship between profitability and liquidity is not forever, rather up to a certain level of liquidity, this theory holds good; beyond that level decline in liquidity will cause decline in profitability. A very poor liquidity position in a firm shall create problems in smooth running of business, thereby obstructing the course of business and causing a decline in profitability. Hence, one should strike a balance between liquidity and profitability. It is felt that there is a need to study the impact of liquidity in profit generating process.

Therefore, in this article an effort has also been made to make an empirical study of South Indian private sector Sugar Industry for assessing the impact of liquidity on profitability during the period of study. The impact of liquidity on profitability has been examined by computing co-efficient of correlation and regression analysis of liquidity ratio and profitability ratio. The objective of this attempt is to measure the extent of relationship between liquidity and profitability by using simple correlation co-efficient and also to test the significance of such correlation co-efficient. Further, to study the impact of liquidity on profitability, regression analysis was done individually for all the companies under study.

## SAMPLE DESIGN

Keeping in view of the scope of the study, the private sector sugar companies operated in South India (in the state of Tamilnadu, Kerala, Karnataka, Andhra Pradesh, Maharashtra and Union Territories viz., Pondicherry and Goa) were considered for the study. It is decided to include all the companies working under private sector in the South India working before or from the year 1991-92. But owing to several constraints such as non-availability of financial statements or non-working of the company in particular year etc., it is compelled to restrict the numbers of sample companies to fifteen. Therefore, this study is exposed facto-based on survey method making a survey of 15 private sector sugar companies operated in South India.

There are 324 sugar companies operating in the South India. Out of which seven companies are under public sector, 95 under private sector and 222 companies under co-operative sector. Since majority of the companies under public sector and co-operative sector were inoperative and sick and also due to non-availability of data, it is decided to include only private sector sugar companies in the sample. The Capitaline and CMIE database published key financial data of Indian corporate sector systematically. Hence Capitaline and CMIE databases proved to be complimentary to finalize the sample for the study. The exhaustive list of private sector sugar industry from Capitaline is cross checked with CMIE database to short out industry to make up the sample for the study. The comprehensive list of companies prepared from the database was modified by deleting the firms –

- which were not in operation for any year during the period under study.
- which were in operation but for which financial data were not available for any of the 15-year period under study.
- which were described as sick unit for any year during the period under study.

For the purpose of the study the selected sugar companies were classified as large-sized, medium-sized and small-sized companies based on crushing capacity. The companies having a crushing capacity of 5000 MT (per day) or more have been considered as large-sized, 2501 to 5000 MT (per day) as medium-sized and up to 2500 MT (per day) as small-sized sugar industry. Out of the 95 private sector sugar companies operated in south India, only for 30 companies data are available in the databases. Out of 30 companies, only 15 companies have been included in the study because financial statements for the last 15 continuous years could be obtained for these companies only. The period 1995-96 to 2008-09 is selected for this study of South Indian private sector Sugar Industry. This 14-year period is chosen in order to have a fairly long, cyclically well balanced period, for which reasonably homogeneous, reliable and up-to-date financial data would be available.

## SOURCE OF DATA

The study is mainly based on secondary data. The data analysed and interpreted in this study related to all those companies selected are collected from "Capitaline" and "PROWESS" databases, which are the most reliable on the empowered corporate database of Bombay Stock Exchange and Centre for Monitoring Indian Economy (CMIE) respectively. Beside Capitaline and PROWESS databases, relevant secondary data have also been collected from BSE Stock Exchange Official Directory, CMIE Publications, Annual Survey of Industry, Business newspapers, Reports on Currency and Finance, Libraries of various Research Institutions, through Internet etc. The study required variety of data; therefore, websites like http://indiainfoline.com, www.indiastat.com and www.google.com have been comprehensively searched.

## A. GROWTH AND PROFITABILITY – EMPIRICAL RESULT

In this part of the discussion, the relationship between profitability and growth has been explored by means of regression analysis in the following form.

$$P = a + bG + u$$

Where, P - Profitability

G - growth rate

u - error term

a and b are parameters

For each industry, sector and whole industry, regression equations were estimated, pertaining to alternative measures of profitability and growth. The alternative measures of growth viz., growth rate of total assets, growth rate of fixed assets and growth rate of sales were used. Thus, in all various regression equations were estimated to know how far differences in profit rates could be explained by differences in growth rates. The results of these equations are presented in the Tables 4.1 to 4.3.

Table 4.1 shows the extent to which changes in profitability margin are explained by the changes in the growth of total assets. The co-efficient of determination ($R^2$) is in the case of whole industry i.e. 0.21, this means that 21 per cent change in profitability margin are explained by growth of total assets. The value of regression co-efficient (b) is 0.12 indicating thereby that one per cent increase in growth rate is associated with 0.12 per cent increase in profitability. This co-efficient is statistically significant at 10 per cent level. It is evident from the table that the percentage change in profit margin are explained by the growth of total assets are 52 per cent, 31 per cent and 7 per cent respectively in large-sized sector, medium-sized sector and small-sized sector during the study period.

The value of regression co-efficient is indicated that one per cent increase in growth rate is associated with 0.12 per cent, 0.10 per cent and 0.08 per cent increase in profitability of Large-sized, Medium-sized and Small-sized sectors respectively during the study period. Among the large-sized sector companies except Bannari Amman Sugars Ltd and Jeypore Sugars & Chemicals Ltd showed positive relationship between growth and profitability. Further, values of regression co-efficient are statistically significant only in case of Rajshree Sugars & Chemicals Ltd and Sakthi Sugars Ltd. Similarly, all the selected companies under medium-sized sector and small-sized sector showed positive relationship between growth and profitability. Thus, as expected there is positive relationship between growth rate of total assets and profitability in the selected South Indian private sector Sugar Industry during the study period.

Table 4.2 shows the results of regression of profitability margin on growth of fixed assets. Inter-industry differences regarding relationship between profitability and growth rate are evident from the table. In this table co-efficient of determination ($R^2$) is 0.01 in case of whole industry suggesting that one per cent change in profitability is explained by growth of fixed assets. The value of regression co-efficient is 0.01 indicating thereby that one per cent change in growth rate of fixed assets leads to 0.01 per cent change in profitability in case of these companies. In the cases of large-sized sector, medium-sized sector and small-sized sector, the values of $R^2$ respectively are 0.08, 0.01 and 0.02 suggesting that 8 percent change in profitability of large-sized sector, 1 percent change in profitability of medium-sized sector and 2 percent change in profitability of small-sized sector are explained by the 1 per cent change in growth rate of fixed assets. None of the regression co-efficient of growth rate of fixed assets is significant during the study period. Bannari Amman Sugars Ltd in large-sized sector, Kothari Sugars & Chemicals Ltd and Kakatiya Cements Sugar & Industries Ltd in medium-sized sector and Dharani Sugars & Chemicals Ltd and Empee Sugars & Chemicals Ltd in small-sized sector showed negative relationship between growth rate of fixed assets and profitability. Thus, as expected there is positive, though weak, relationship between growth rate of fixed assets and profitability in the selected sectors and the sample industry as a whole during the study period.

Table 4.3 depicts the results of regression of profitability on growth of net sales of all firms. Regression co-efficient is statistically significant in EID Parry Ltd (large-sized), Kothari Sugars & Chemicals Ltd (medium-sized) and Dharani Sugars & Chemicals Ltd (small-sized). The highest value of $R^2$ (i.e. 0.41) in this industry tells that 41 per cent variations in profitability are explained by variation in growth of sales. Further, in the cases of large-sized sector, medium-sized sector and small-sized sector, 33 per cent, 3 per cent and 25 per cent changes in profitability are due to changes in growth of net sales.

The value of regression co-efficient in this industry (i.e.0.13) indicating that one per cent increase in growth rate of sales is associated with 0.13 per cent increase in profitability. It was 0.06 per cent, 0.03 per cent and 0.13 percent as in the cases of large-sized, medium-sized and small-sized sectors during the study period. It is evident from the result that as expected, there is positive relationship between growth rate of sales and profitability during the study period.

## B. LIQUIDITY AND PROFITABILITY - EMPIRICAL RESULT

The correlations co-efficient of current ratio and return on capital employed ratios of fifteen companies under study are mentioned in Table 4.4. It is evident from the result that there was a positive correlation between profitability and liquidity in the South Indian private sector Sugar Industry during the study period. The correlation co-efficient between current ratio and return on capital employed is 0.634 and it is statistically significant at 5 percent level. Similarly, the correlation co-efficient of large-sized industry and small-sized industry have shown positive correlation between profitability and liquidity and its statistical significance is 1 percent and 5 percent respectively. Further, the medium-sized sugar industry also showed positive correlation between profitability and liquidity but it was not statistically significant.

Among the large-sized industry group, however, five companies depicted negative correlation between current ratio and return on capital employed. These companies are Bannari Amman Sugars Ltd, EID Parry Ltd, Jeypore Sugars & Chemicals Ltd, Sakthi Sugars Ltd and Ugar Sugar Works Ltd. The two companies' viz., Rajshree Sugars & Chemicals Ltd and Thiru Arooran Sugars Ltd showed positive correlation co-efficient between their liquidity and profitability. Among the medium-sized industry, out of four companies two companies viz., Sri Chamundeswari Sugars Ltd and Sri Sarvaraya Sugars Ltd showed negative correlation co-efficient between current ratio and return on capital employed. However, the two companies' viz., Kothari Sugars & Chemicals Ltd and Kakatiya Cements Sugar & Companies Ltd showed positive correlation co-efficient between their liquidity and profitability. Among the four companies under small-sized groups except Ponni Sugars Ltd, the remaining three companies' viz., Dharani Sugars & Chemicals Ltd, Empee Sugars & Chemicals Ltd and India Sugars and Refineries Ltd showed positive correlation co-efficient between their liquidity and profitability. Except Jeypore Sugars & Chemicals Ltd and Kakatiya Cements Sugar & Companies Ltd none of the industry's correlation co-efficient was found to be statistically significant.

The correlation analysis between liquidity and profitability position of the fifteen companies under study indicated a mix of positive and negative correlation co-efficient. However, eight out of fifteen companies revealed negative correlation and seven out of fifteen companies' depicted positive correlation. However, only two companies (Jeypore Sugars & Chemicals Ltd and Kakatiya Cements Sugar & Industries Ltd) out of fifteen companies depicted significant correlation.

## LIQUIDITY AND PROFITABILITY – REGRESSION ANALYSIS

For performing regression analysis current ratio has been taken as independent variable and return on capital employed as dependent variable. The simple regression has been performed to assess the effect of current ratio on return on capital employed. In this regard the following research hypothesis is tested.

$H_0$ - **There is a significantly negative relationship between liquidity and profitability of South Indian private sector Sugar Industry.**

The regression equation to be estimated is:

$$ROCE = a + bCR + e$$

Where,

ROCE stands for Return on Capital Employed

'a' denotes intercept of regression equation

'b' denotes co-efficient of independent variable

'CR' stands for current ratio

'e' denotes error term

In Table 4.4 regression co-efficient for fifteen companies under study are given along with their co-efficient of determination ($R^2$). The analysis of data in the Table 4.3 indicates that there was a positive relationship between liquidity and profitability in the selected South Indian private sector Sugar Industry. The regression equation of selected South Indian private sector Sugar Industry as a whole indicates that an increase of one per cent in current ratio will cause an increase of 24.68 per cent in return on capital employed. Similarly, large-sized industry and small-sized industry showed positive and statistically significant relationship between liquidity and profitability at 1 per cent and 5 per cent level respectively.

Out of fifteen companies, eight companies indicate negative relationships between liquidity and profitability. However, out of the eight industry only one industry viz., Jeypore Sugars & Chemicals Ltd's co-efficient was found to be statistically significant at 10 per cent level. The remaining companies showed positive relationship between liquidity and profitability. Of these seven companies, none of the companies' co-efficient depicted statistically significant relationship between liquidity and profitability. Generally, the theories have revealed that there is inverse relationship between liquidity and profitability. But, on the whole, it may be concluded that no established relationship between liquidity and profitability exists for this industry: the various forms of the companies depicted different type of relationship (both negative and positive) between liquidity and profitability during the study period.

## CONCLUSION

The relationship between profit and growth has been explored by means of regression analysis. The pooled regression results of the model regressing profit rate with growth measured by growth rate of total assets shows that degree of explanation of profitability by growth is 21 per cent in whole industry, 52 per cent in large-sized industry, 31 per cent in medium-sized industry and 7 per cent in small-sized industry. The results also showed the positive relationship between growth and profitability in all the sectors and whole industry. It is also evident from the results that negative relationship between the growth and profitability reported in Bannari Amman Sugars Ltd and Rajshree Sugars & Chemicals Ltd (large-sized) and Kothari Sugars & Chemicals Ltd and Sri Sarvaraya Sugars Ltd (medium-sized). The pooled regression results of the model regressing profit margin with growth measured by rate of gross block and rate of sales shows more or less similar findings to the results of regressing profit margin with growth rate of total assets. However, the explanatory capacity of growth rate of gross block and growth rate of net sales on profit rate has not improved in this model. It can be concluded from the analysis that growth and profit have positive relationship in all the sectors and whole industry.

The relationship between liquidity and profitability has been examined through correlation and regression analysis. It is evident from the results that there is positive correlation between profitability and liquidity in all the three sectors and whole industry during the study period. But, the correlation analysis between liquidity and profitability position of the fifteen companies under study indicated a mix of positive and negative correlation. Eight out of fifteen companies reveal negative correlation and the remaining industry depicted positive correlation. The regression analysis also showed that there is a positive relationship between liquidity and profitability in all the three sectors and whole industry.

It can be concluded from the analysis that growth and profit have positive relationship in all the sectors and whole industry. Further, the theories have revealed that there is inverse relationship between liquidity and profitability. But in the whole, it may be concluded that no established relationship between liquidity and profitability exists for these companies. The various forms of the companies depicted different type of relationship (both negative and positive) between liquidity and profitability during the study period.

## REFERENCES

1. Kumar Prem (1982), "Corporate Growth in India : A case study as 100 largest companies", New Delhi: *Deep and Deep publications.*
2. Bharatwaj, Sundar, G., Varadarajan Rajan P. and Szymanski David, M. (1993). "An analysis of market share and profitability relationship", *Journal of Marketing,* 57, pp. 1-18.
3. Geroski Paul, A., Machin Stephen, J. and Walters Christoper, F. (1997). "Corporate growth and profitability", *The Journal of Industrial Economics,* 45(2), pp. 171-189.
4. Narayan, K. (1998). "Technology Acquisition and growth of firms under changing policies regimes: A study of the Indian Automobiles sector". *http:/ knowledgeforum.tifac.org.in/ indesserver/ tifac/ article/ 13.doc.*

5. Rama Ruth (1998). "Growth in Food and Drink Multinational", *Journal of International Food and Agricultural Marketing*, 10(1), pp. 31-51.

6. Bonn Ingrid (2000). "Staying on Top : Characteristics of long term survival". *Journal of Organizational Change Management*, 13(1), pp. 32-48.

7. Mak, T.Y. and Kusnadi Yuan (2001). "Size really matters: Further evidence on negative relation between firm size and value", *www.Sbacr.uca.edu/ docs/ 200asbe/ ooasbc076.html.*

8. Kakani, Ram Kumar, Biswatosh saha and Reddy, V.N. (2001). "Determinants of Financial Performance of Indian Corporate Sector in the Post – Liberalization Era : An exploratory study", NSE Research Institute, Paper No. 5, Mumbai : National Stock Exchange of India Limited.

9. Shanmugam, K.R. and Bhaduri Saumitra, N. (2002). "Size, Age and Firm growth in the Indian Manufacturing Sector", *Applied Economics Letters*. 9, pp. 607-613.

10. Harabi Najib (2003). "Determinants of Firm Growth : An empirical analysis from Morocco", *http/ / www.erf.org.eg/ grp/ GRP-Sepo3/ morocco-Firms.pdf*.

11. Kalirajan Kaliappa and Bhide Sheshanka (2003). "The post reform performance of manufacturing sector in India", *Asian Economic papers*, 3, pp. 126-157.

12. Liu Wein-Chun and Hsu Chan-min (2004). "Financial structure, corporate finance and growth of Taiwans manufacturing Firm's", *http: / / papers.ssrn.com / sol.3/ papers.cfm? Abstract-id = 415047*.

13. Niskanon, Meri and Niskanen, Jyrki (2005). "The determinants of firms growth in small and micro firms", Evidence on relationship sending effects.

14. Subhash Chander and Priyanka Aggarwal (2007). "Determinants of corporate growth : An empirical study of Indian Drugs and Pharmaceutical Industry", *The Icfaian Journal of Management Research*, VI (10), pp. 50-70.

## TABLE 4.1

## GROWTH AND PROFITABILITY – REGRESSION RESULTS

$(PR = b_0 + b_1 ROG_1)$

| S.No | Industry | Constant | Co-efficient | $R^2$ | F value | D.W |
|---|---|---|---|---|---|---|
| 1 | Bannari Amman Sugars Ltd | 6.99 | -0.04 (-1.623) | 0.17 | 2.64 | 1.46 |
| 2 | EID Parry Ltd | 3.91 | 0.03 (1.171) | 0.10 | 1.37 | 0.99 |
| 3 | Jeypore Sugars & Chemicals Ltd | 1.52 | -0.03 (-0.29) | 0.01 | 0.08 | 1.02 |
| 4 | Rajshree Sugars & Chemicals Ltd | 0.11 | 0.46 (4.591)* | 0.62 | 21.08 | 1.74 |
| 5 | Sakthi Sugars Ltd | -1.89 | 0.10 (2.390)** | 0.31 | 5.71 | 1.10 |
| 6 | Thiru Arooran Sugars Ltd | 0.51 | 0.09 (1.604) | 0.17 | 2.57 | 1.42 |
| 7 | Ugar Sugar Works Ltd | 1.47 | 0.01 (0.241) | 0.01 | 0.06 | 2.00 |
| | **Large-sized industry** | **1.15** | **0.12 (3.721)*** | **0.52** | **13.89** | **1.07** |
| 8 | Kothari Sugars & Chemicals Ltd | 6.99 | -0.04 (-1.623) | 0.17 | 2.64 | 1.46 |
| 9 | Sri Chamundeswari Sugars Ltd | 3.91 | 0.03 (1.171) | 0.10 | 1.37 | 0.99 |
| 10 | Sri Sarvaraya Sugars Ltd | 1.52 | -0.03 (-0.29) | 0.01 | 0.08 | 1.02 |
| 11 | Kakatiya Cements Sugar & Industries Ltd | 0.11 | 0.46 (4.591)* | 0.62 | 21.08 | 1.74 |
| | **Medium-sized industry** | **-1.89** | **0.10 (2.390)**** | **0.31** | **5.71** | **1.10** |
| 12 | Dharani Sugars & Chemicals Ltd | -0.49 | 0.09 (1.959)*** | 0.23 | 3.84 | 0.81 |
| 13 | Empee Sugars & Chemicals Ltd | -6.11 | 0.03 (0.51) | 0.02 | 0.26 | 1.46] |

## TABLE 4.1 (CONTINUED)

## GROWTH AND PROFITABILITY – REGRESSION RESULTS

$(PR = b_0 + b_1 ROG_1)$

| S.No | Industry | Constant | Co-efficient | $R^2$ | F value | D.W |
|---|---|---|---|---|---|---|
| 14 | India Sugars and Refineries Ltd | -.389 | 0.09<br>(0.695) | 0.04 | 0.48 | 0.86 |
| 15 | Ponni Sugars Ltd | -3.19 | 0.09<br>(0.852) | 0.05 | 0.73 | 1.49 |
| | **Small-sized industry** | **-3.55** | **0.08**<br>**(0.952)** | **0.07** | **0.91** | **0.87** |
| | **Whole industry** | **-0.49** | **0.12**<br>**(1.835)***** | **0.21** | **3.37** | **0.82** |

PR - Ratio of Return on Total Assets

$b_0, b_1$ - Regression co-efficient

$ROG_1$ - Growth rate of Total Assets

DW - Durbin – Watson statistics

Figures within parentheses indicate 't' values

* - Significant at 0.01 level

** - Significant at 0.05 level

*** - Significant at 0.10 level

***Source:*** Computed

**TABLE 4.2**

**GROWTH AND PROFITABILITY – REGRESSION RESULTS**

$$PR = b_0 + b_1 ROG_2$$

| S.No | Industry | Constant | Co-efficient | $R^2$ | F value | D.W |
|---|---|---|---|---|---|---|
| 1 | Bannari Amman Sugars Ltd | 6.76 | -0.03<br>(-1.618) | 0.17 | 2.62 | 1.33 |
| 2 | EID Parry Ltd | 3.98 | 0.02<br>(0.843) | 0.02 | 0.20 | 1.00 |
| 3 | Jeypore Sugars & Chemicals Ltd | 0.65 | 0.02<br>(0.447) | 0.02 | 0.20 | 1.00 |
| 4 | Rajshree Sugars & Chemicals Ltd | 7.67 | 0.01<br>(0.012) | 0.01 | 0.01 | 1.07 |
| 5 | Sakthi Sugars Ltd | -0.51 | 0.03<br>(1.02) | 0.07 | 1.04 | 1.07 |
| 6 | Thiru Arooran Sugars Ltd | 1.39 | 0.02<br>(0.603) | 0.03 | 0.36 | 0.80 |
| 7 | Ugar Sugar Works Ltd | 1.44 | 0.01<br>(0.231) | 0.01 | 0.05 | 1.90 |
| | **Large-sized industry** | **2.36** | **0.05<br>(1.089)** | **0.08** | **1.19** | **1.04** |
| 8 | Kothari Sugars & Chemicals Ltd | -2.58 | -0.01<br>(-0.075) | 0.01 | 0.01 | 1.12 |
| 9 | Sri Chamundeswari Sugars Ltd | -2.28 | 0.09<br>(0.90) | 0.06 | 0.81 | 1.08 |
| 10 | Sri Sarvaraya Sugars Ltd | 2.27 | 0.10<br>(1.478) | 0.14 | 2.19 | 1.60 |
| 11 | Kakatiya Cements Sugar & Industries Ltd | 6.91 | -0.01<br>(-0.058) | 0.01 | 0.01 | 0.57 |
| | **Medium-sized industry** | **1.39** | **0.02<br>(0.168)** | **0.01** | **0.03** | **0.86** |
| 12 | Dharani Sugars & Chemicals Ltd | 1.96 | -0.05<br>(-1.160) | 0.09 | 1.35 | 0.77 |
| 13 | Empee Sugars & Chemicals Ltd | -3.63 | -0.01<br>(-2.485) | 0.32 | 6.18 | 1.01 |

## TABLE 4.2 (CONTINUED)

## GROWTH AND PROFITABILITY – REGRESSION RESULTS

$$PR = b_0 + b_1 ROG_2$$

| S.No | Industry | Constant | Co-efficient | $R^2$ | F value | D.W |
|---|---|---|---|---|---|---|
| 14 | India Sugars and Refineries Ltd | -5.99 | 0.27 (1.008) | 0.07 | 1.02 | 0.90 |
| 15 | Ponni Sugars Ltd | -2.84 | 0.01 (0.148) | 0.01 | 0.02 | 1.38 |
| | **Small-sized industry** | **-2.20** | **-0.01 (-0.466)** | **0.02** | **0.22** | **0.80** |
| | **Whole industry** | **1.12** | **0.01 (0.259)** | **0.01** | **0.67** | **0.74** |

PR - Ratio of Return on Total Assets
$b_0$,b - Regression co-efficient
$ROG_2$ - Growth rate of Gross block
DW - Durbin – Watson statistics
Figures within parentheses indicate 't' values
**Source: Computed**

## TABLE 4.3
## GROWTH AND PROFITABILITY – REGRESSION RESULTS

$$PR = b_0 + b_1 ROG_3$$

| S.No | Industry | Constant | Co-efficient | $R^2$ | F value | D.W |
|---|---|---|---|---|---|---|
| 1 | Bannari Amman Sugars Ltd | 5.86 | 0.01 (0.228) | 0.01 | 0.05 | 0.95 |
| 2 | EID Parry Ltd | 3.76 | 0.05 (1.792)*** | 0.20 | 3.21 | 0.74 |
| 3 | Jeypore Sugars & Chemicals Ltd | 1.05 | 0.01 (0.061) | 0.01 | 0.01 | 0.99 |
| 4 | Rajshree Sugars & Chemicals Ltd | 5.85 | 0.06 (1.657) | 0.17 | 2.74 | 1.21 |
| 5 | Sakthi Sugars Ltd | 0.43 | -0.01 (-0.470) | 0.02 | 0.22 | 1.99 |
| 6 | Thiru Arooran Sugars Ltd | 1.30 | 0.02 (0.753) | 0.04 | 0.57 | 0.73 |
| 7 | Ugar Sugar Works Ltd | 1.12 | 0.03 (1.024) | 0.08 | 1.05 | 1.77 |
| | **Large-sized industry** | **2.01** | **0.06 (2.512)**** | **0.33** | **6.31** | **1.42** |
| 8 | Kothari Sugars & Chemicals Ltd | -7.41 | 0.28 (2.407)** | 0.31 | 5.79 | 1.82 |
| 9 | Sri Chamundeswari Sugars Ltd | -1.68 | 0.02 (0.752) | 0.04 | 0.57 | 1.28 |
| 10 | Sri Sarvaraya Sugars Ltd | 3.37 | 0.01 (0.461) | 0.02 | 0.21 | 1.68 |
| 11 | Kakatiya Cements Sugar & Industries Ltd | 6.27 | 0.03 (0.493) | 0.02 | 0.24 | 0.52 |
| | **Medium-sized industry** | **1.00** | **0.03 (0.586)** | **0.03** | **0.34** | **0.98** |
| 12 | Dharani Sugars & Chemicals Ltd | -0.99 | 0.06 (2.567)** | 0.34 | 6.59 | 1.03 |
| 13 | Empee Sugars & Chemicals Ltd | -6.49 | 0.03 (0.72) | 0.04 | 0.52 | 1.48 |

## TABLE 4.3 (CONTINUED)

## GROWTH AND PROFITABILITY – REGRESSION RESULTS

$$PR = b_0 + b_1 \, ROG_3$$

| S.No | Industry | Constant | Co-efficient | $R^2$ | F value | D.W |
|---|---|---|---|---|---|---|
| 14 | India Sugars and Refineries Ltd | -4.12 | 0.09 (0.928) | 0.06 | 0.86 | 1.23 |
| 15 | Ponni Sugars Ltd | -2.85 | 0.01 (0.128) | 0.01 | 0.02 | 1.40 |
| | **Small-sized industry** | **-5.57** | **0.13 (2.062)** | **0.25** | **4.25** | **1.45** |
| | **Whole industry** | **-1.66** | **0.13 (2.978)**** | **0.41** | **8.87** | **1.70** |

PR - Ratio of Return on Total Assets

$b_0, b_1$ - Regression co-efficient

$ROG_3$ - Growth rate of Net Sales

DW - Durbin – Watson statistics

Figures within parentheses indicate 't' values

** - Significant at 0.05 level

*** - Significant at 0.10 level

***Source:*** Computed

## TABLE 4.4
## LIQUIDITY AND PROFITABILITY RELATIONSHIP
ROCE = f(CR)

| Industry | r | Constant | Co-efficient | $R^2$ | F-value | DW |
|---|---|---|---|---|---|---|
| Bannari Amman Sugars Ltd | -0.136 | 23.74 | -2.94 (-0.494) | 0.02 | 0.24 | 1.77 |
| EID Parry Ltd | -0.262 | 28.34 | -8.16 (-0.980) | -0.01 | 0.96 | 0.65 |
| Jeypore Sugars & Chemicals Ltd | -0.512*** | 156.37 | -133.58 (-2.151)*** | 0.21 | 4.63 | 0.74 |
| Rajshree Sugars & Chemicals Ltd | 0.212 | 15.67 | 6.90 (0.783) | 0.05 | 0.61 | 1.34 |
| Sakthi Sugars Ltd | -0.366 | 25.73 | -6.31 (-1.416) | 0.13 | 2.00 | 1.75 |
| Thiru Arooran Sugars Ltd | 0.013 | 10.61 | 0.76 (0.047) | 0.01 | 0.01 | 0.49 |
| Ugar Sugar Works Ltd | -0.409 | 106.45 | -67.31 (-1.614) | 0.17 | 2.60 | 1.61 |
| **Large-sized firms** | **0.711*** | **-24.37** | **39.11 (3.644)*** | **0.51** | **13.28** | **1.45** |
| Kothari Sugars & Chemicals Ltd | 0.312 | -46.70 | 36.05 (1.185) | 0.10 | 1.41 | 2.96 |
| Sri Chamundeswari Sugars Ltd | -0.031 | 20.70 | -1.46 (-0.112) | 0.01 | 0.01 | 1.21 |
| Sri Sarvaraya Sugars Ltd | -0.024 | 26.14 | -1.40 (-0.088) | 0.01 | 0.01 | 1.51 |
| Kakatiya Cements Sugar & Industries Ltd | 0.477*** | 10.80 | 2.07 (1.956)*** | 0.17 | 3.83 | 1.02 |
| **Medium-sized firms** | **0.200** | **-0.17** | **10.01 (0.738)** | **0.04** | **0.54** | **2.86** |
| Dharani Sugars & Chemicals Ltd | 0.055 | 16.26 | 1.10 (0.197) | 0.01 | 0.04 | 1.38 |
| Empee Sugars & Chemicals Ltd | 0.275 | -0.33 | 8.35 (1.03) | 0.08 | 1.06 | 1.20 |

## TABLE 4.4 (CONTINUED)

## LIQUIDITY AND PROFITABILITY RELATIONSHIP

ROCE = f(CR)

| Industry | r | Constant | Co-efficient | $R^2$ | F-value | DW |
|---|---|---|---|---|---|---|
| India Sugars and Refineries Ltd | 0.426 | -33.42 | 67.61 (1.699) | 0.18 | 2.89 | 1.24 |
| Ponni Sugars Ltd | -0.271 | 19.29 | -4.21 (-1.01) | 0.07 | 1.03 | 1.26 |
| **Small-sized firms** | **0.577**** | **-4.84** | **18.42 (2.546)**** | **0.33** | **6.48** | **1.02** |
| **Whole Industry** | **0.634**** | **-12.44** | **24.68 (2.915)**** | **0.40** | **8.5** | **2.00** |

***Note:*** Figures in brackets indicate t-values of co-efficient.

* - Significant at 0.01 level

** - Significant at 0.05 level

*** - Significant at 0.10 level

***Source:*** Computed

# 5

# Productivity and Profitability of the Paper Industry

## A Case Study of Seshasayee Paper and Boards Limited, Tamilnadu

Paper plays a vital role in the cultural development of human beings. Paper constitutes one of the most important segments of India's Industrial Economy and is treated as a basic sector. Its performance is crucial to the economy as much as to the growth of service sectors like education, communication, trade and commerce, banking and insurance, public administration, journalism, all of which greatly depend on supplies of printing and writing paper and newsprint. The industrial sector also requires paper and newsprint, both for packaging and for its service sector. One index for measuring a nation's development and progress is the level of per capita consumption of paper. This is lagging far behind in India. The importance of paper and paper products in modern life is so obvious because no other manufactured product possesses such a diversity of uses. Time importance of the growth of this industry in a developing economy like that of India where the literacy rates are to be considerably improved, school enrolments are increasing newspaper subscriptions are rising and the printing and publishing industry has to make further headway can not be over emphasised.

In India, the tradition of making paper by hand can be traced to the 8$^{th}$ century A.D. The first paper mill was successfully started in 1870 and the second in the 1930's in West Bengal. Today there are about 350 paper mills spread over the country. The industry is providing employment to nearly 300,000 persons. It also provides indirect employment to large numbers. The Indian paper industry at present is best with various problems like raw materials shortage, rising cost of production, and downward trend in capacity utilisation. Moreover, the paper industry is a highly capital intensive industry and has a long gestation period and so suffer in regard to profitability. However, there are a few paper mills which run at full capacity and with comfortable profit margins.

## STATEMENT OF THE PROBLEM

Government interventions in an industry through policy measures aim to influence the structure, the running and the performance of firms so as to achieve specific goals. Since there have been substantial changes in the regulatory framework of the paper industry, one would expect that such policy measures would have impact on the firms operating in this industry. Therefore, the objective of this study was to examine the determinants of productivity and profitability in the paper industry.

Productivity involves a comparison between the quantity of goods or services produced and the quantity of resources employed in turning out these goods and services. When the same resources that were employed in the past now produce more than they did before, we say that productivity has increased. Productivity acts as a barometer to measure the efficiency of an industry. Productivity studies help to estimate the measure of protection to be granted to an industry. They also assist in evaluating the influence of production on employment. In this study, an attempt has been made to measure productivity, by using the Cobb-Douglas production function.

Profitability is determined by structural as well as behavioural variables. The structural factors which have a bearing on profitability are size, growth, barriers to entry of new units degree of vertical integration, diversification and cost conditions. Corporate policies relating to various organizational functions will obviously affect profitability. Some policies are relevant in the short-run while others have an impact in the long run. One has to identify certain specific variables considering the purpose of the study and the relevance of different factors in explaining profitability in this industry during the period of study. Financial ratios are used to measure the variables. Hence, in this study, an attempt has been made to identify the factors influencing profitability by using Multiple Regression Analysis.

## THE PRESENT STUDY

The Cobb-Douglas production function is a type of linearly homogeneous production function which has proved particularly useful for empirical work. The general formula for this function is

$$\mathbf{Y = A\,K^{\alpha}\,L^{\beta}}$$

Where $0 < \alpha < 1$, K is Productive capital and L is Labour. In order to arrive at the estimator of the function, the model parameters are linearised by a log transformation.

$$\mathbf{Log\,Y = Log\,A + \alpha Log\,K + \beta Log\,L}$$

Where Y is Gross output;. K is capital' L is Labour; A is constant term; $\alpha$ is co-efficient of capital; and $\beta$ is coefficient of labour. This function characterises the returns to scale as below:

$\alpha + \beta > 1$ : Increasing returns to scale

$\alpha + \beta = 1$ : Constant returns to scale

$\alpha + \beta < 1$ : Decreasing returns to scale

As, there are a number of factors which explain profitability and the measurement of the variables employed can also be different, it is important to mention the variables and explain how they are measured.

Return pm assets and return on sales are widely used measures of profitability. It is assumed that the management is concerned with the effective utilisation of all resources. These two measures would then be proper. The profit rates measured by sales will give a short-term perspective of profitability because sales are annual flows. On the other hand, the return on assets will give us a long term perspective of profitability. In this sense, return on assets has been used as a dependent variable.

The size of the firm affects its profit. The increase in money capital not only increases the absolute profits of the firm but also increases its earning power per unit of investment. However, this will be true only if large firms are efficient and innovative. Though the positive relationship between size and profitability has been found to be significant, after a certain point, profitability increases at a rate proportional to the increase in size. The size of the firm is sought to be measured in this study by the total sales revenue.

The other variables considered here are Capacity Integration (CI) and Capacity Utilisation (CU). High profitability may be the result of adjustments in capacity which were lagging behind changes in demand and/or improvements in efficiency of operation. Firm-specific vertical integration, motivated by considerations such as avoidance of the costs incurred in using the market to organize production, government policies and also considerations of market power, is an important determinant of profitability. In this study, the degree of vertical integration is sought to be measured by the value—added to the sales ratio.

Another variable which can influence the profitability is the leverage ratio. A firm with high leverage ratio represents a greater financial risk than a firm with relatively lower leverage ratio. If competition equalises earnings, then, high debt should result in higher return on net worth. Another variable which can influence the profitability is the inventory turnover ratio. A low inventory ratio will adversely affect the ability of a firm to meet customer demand and in return will affect its profitability. In inter-firm comparisons, the firm with a higher current ratio has better liquidity. A low inventory ratio may be indicative of slack management practices which affect the profitability.

Apart from the factors discussed above, operating expenses are included as an explanatory variable in this study. The implication of a low operating expenses ratio is that it improves the profitability of the concern.

The model specified for estimating profitability is as follows:

$$\mathbf{PP = b_o + b_1 S + b_2\, CI + b_3\, CU + b_4\, VI + b_5\, DTA + b_6\, ITR + b_7\, CR + b_8\, OPES}$$

Where PP is Measure of Profitability; S is Sales; CI is Capacity Integration; CU is Capacity Utilisation; VI is Vertical Integration; DTA is Debt/Total Assets; ITR is Inventory Turnover Ratio; CR is Current Ratio; and OPES is Operating Expenses to Sales Ratio.

## OBJECTIVES OF THE STUDY

The main objectives of the study were:

i) to analyse the growth in production, employment, sales and profit of Seshasayee Paper and Boards Limited;

ii) to identify the determinant factors of profitability in the company.

## METHODOLOGY

The productivity analyses are done using the Cobb-Douglas production function. Determinants of profitability are analyses using the technique of multiple regressions analysis. Based on the existing theories and on relevant econometric empirical works, variables are selected. While using regression technique, efforts are made to reduce the problem of multicollinearity and auto correlation. Moreover, by using cross-section data in combination with time series data, one can avoid the high intercorrelation between the explanatory variables. Though, in practice, multicollinearity cannot be completely avoided, it can be reduced by using appropriate explanatory variables. The Durbin-Watson test is used to arrive at an idea of the existence of autocorrelation. The Durbin-Watson statistics are reported in regressions results. The period of study was from 1981-1982 to 1993-1994. The recent data available and the relevance of the period were considered in selecting the study period.

## EMPIRICAL FINDINGS

Growth of Production, Labour and Productive Capital. Production is one of the most basic economic relationships, and ideally it expresses the technical relationship between the physical quantity of inputs into the production process and the physical quantity of output produced; this description should be applied at the macro economic level, for a single firm or a single homogeneous product and a few homogeneous inputs. Actual production has been examined by economists to measure the relationship between changes in physical inputs and physical outputs and is naturally given a technical consideration. Therefore, the efficiency of technology, technologically determined economics of scale, the capital intensity of technology and the ease with which factors can be substituted for each other can be expressed in terms of the quantum of production.

The production of paper and boards in Seshasayee Paper and Boards Limited for the period 1981-1982 to 1993-1994 is presented in Table 5.1. It is evident from the table that the production of SPB Ltd fluctuated during the period of study. However, on the whole it increased from Rs.4,174.55 lakhs in 1981-82 to Rs.11,630.38 lakhs in 1993-94. The percentage of increase production over the previous year ranged from 0.74 in 1987-89 to 37.91 in 1993-94. The highest increase in production was noticed in 1983-84, 1984-85, 1985-86, 1989-90, 1991-92 and 1993-94. The table also depicts loss in production ranging from – 15.98 per cent in 1982-83 to – 2.08 per cent in 1988-89 through – 9.05 percent in 1986-87.

Labour cost depends upon the number of workers employed. The labour employed in SPB Ltd are both skilled and unskilled. The total number of labourers employed in SPB Ltd. during the study period is presented in Table 5.1. The table indicates that the total number of labourers employed showed a generally decreasing trend during the study period. The number of workers decreased from 2617 in 1981-82 to 2224 in 1993-94, even though the production had nearly trebled.

The capital structure of a paper industry includes both fixed and working capital. The sum of fixed and working capital is termed productive capital. The productive capital of SPB Ltd during the study period is presented in Table 5.1. The table shows that the total productive capital was increasing over the years. It increased from Rs.5,034.25 lakhs in 81-82 to Rs.10,492.29 lakhs in 1993-94. But the percentage increase over the previous year shows ups and downs over the period.

Thus, it is inferred from this analysis that the production growth and productive capital of SPB Ltd show an increasing trend whereas the total number of labourers registered a decreasing trend during the study period.

## PRODUCTIVITY OF SPB LTD.

A production process can be studied empirically in terms of either the production function or the cost function. Estimates of the parameters of these functions provide valuable insights into the technology of firms and industries. Many actual production functions have been examined by economists to measure the relationship between changes in the physical inputs and the output. The important questions relating to technology are (i) whether the production-process display decreasing, increasing or constant returns to scale, (ii) how technological progress affects the parameters of the production process and (iii) at what rate technological progress has occurred. The Cobbdouglas production function gives an explicit measurement of returns to scale and output elasticities for different factors of production. In the analysis, the Cobb-Douglas production function is used to test the hypothesis that "constant returns to scale" operate in SPB Ltd.

Table 5.2 shows the estimates of the Cobb-Douglas production function fitted for SPB Ltd from 1981-82 to 1993-94. The value of $R^2$ indicates that 90 per cent of the variations in the value of the output could be accounted for by variations in capital (K) and labour (L). As the calculated value of 'F' is greater than the critical table value, the whole model fits perfectly. The value of 'F' is greater than the critical table value, the whole model fits perfectly. The value of 'F' is significant at 5% level. The coefficient of capital reveals that one unit increase in output could be brought in by a 1.28 units increase in the capital of SPB Ltd. The statistical validity of this coefficients is significant at 1 percent level. The coefficient of labour ($\beta$) is not significant and it explains that 0.67 unit decrease in labour would bring about one unit increase in the value of output. This model shows that SPB Ltd experienced a condition of increased return to scale. This is supported by the estimated values of (1.28) and (-0.67). The sum of these values is more than one; therefore the hypothesis is not acceptable. Thus, it is concluded that the law of constant returns to scale is not in operation.

## PROFITABILITY OF SPB LTD

The profitability function was estimated using the lease-square method. While estimating, checks were made for model violations such as multicollinearity and auto correlation with the help of the Correction Matrix and the Durbon-Watson Statistics. It is evident from Table 5.3 that none of the selected variables is highly correlated. This shows there is no multicollinearity between the variables selected for the study. The results of the model are presented in Table 5.4.

The estimated equations are found to be statistically fit and with reasonably high explanatory power. The measure of profitability used was return on assets (net profit/total assets). In the estimated equation for the period 1981-94 all the independent variables such as sales, capacity integration, capacity utilisation, vertical integration, debt to total assets ratio, inventory turnover ratio, current ratio and operating expenses to sales ratio are found to be statistically significant in explaining the profitability of SPB Ltd. The significance of an operating expenses ratio with a negative coefficient is that firms which are operationally efficient are able to earn more than inefficient firms.

The results presented in the table also indicate that the coefficient of sales, capacity utilisation, vertical utilisation, inventory turnover ratio and current ratio are positive while that of capacity integration, debt to total assets ratio, and operating expenses to sales are generally negative. The coefficient of size (sales) is significant at the 0.10 level. Seen in quantitative terms however the size effect is not very strong. It is evident from the coefficient of sales that one unit increase in size would result in an increase of 0.07 percentage points in profitability. The strongest structural determinant of profitability appears to be vertical integration. Its coefficient is significant at 0.01 level of significance. The coefficient also shows that an increase of 515.55 percentage points in the degree of vertical integration can result in a one percentage point increase in profitability.

The inventory turnover ratio is also statistically significant in explaining profitability. The coefficient is positive which indicates that SPB Ltd had good inventory management during the period of study. It is quite possible that firms in the paper industry went in for expansion and modernisation. Regarding, leverage, the negative coefficient explains that the companies which had lower debts were able to produce higher return compared to others. The other structural variable, capacity utilisation is seen to have little effect on profitability. The overall explanatory power of the regressions appears to be high. This may be inferred from the F statistic which is significant at 0.01 levels.

## CONCLUSION

The study demonstrates that the law of constant return to scale was not in operation in SPB Ltd during the period of study. The regression analysis further shows that capacity integration, vertical integration, the debt to total assets ratio, inventory turnover ratio, current ratio and operating expenses ratio are permanent variables in determining the profitability of SPB Ltd. The significance of the operating expenses ratio with a negative coefficient is that SPB Ltd. is operationally efficient and earned more profit. The analysis also demonstrates that under the condition of government price controls the most significant determinant of the profitability of firms like SPB Ltd is vertical integration. Size and capacity utilisation do not appear to be major determinants. In conclusion, there is a strong indication that all the selected variables had a very significant role to play in determining profitability in the Seshasayee Paper and Boards Limited, during the period of study.

## REFERENCES

1. Agarwal, R.N. "Profitability and Growth in Indian Automobile Manufacturing Industry", *Indian Economic Review,* Vol.26, No.1, 1991, p.81.

2. Datta, Kamal Kumar, Dan S S & Datta, Amal Kumar. "Productivity, Profitability and Income Distribution in Capturue Fishery: A study of the Orissa Coast", *Economic & Political Weekly,* Vol.24, o.51, 1989, p.A-181.
3. Ekpenyong, D B. "Operational Performance of Newly Privatised Public Companies in Nigeria: A Financial Appraisal of Selected Companies", *Journal of Financial Management & Analysis,* Vol.6, No.1, 1993, p.13.
4. Nagarajan, Mohan, Barthwal, R'R. "Profitability and Size of Firms in the Indian Pharmaceutical Industry", *Indian Journal of Economics,* Vol.69, No.275, 1989, p.405.
5. Narayanaswamy, N and Banu, V. "Size, Cost and Profitability: An Empirical Study of Pandyan Grama Bank in Tamil Nadu", *Finance India,* Vol.7, No.11, 1993, p.97.
6. Pathak, S. "Production, Productivity & Profitability of Jute in India", *Productivity,* Vol.30, No.2, 1989, P.150.
7. Porwal, K Hamendra and Parwal, Sangeetha. "Risk and Profitability on New Issues – An Empirical Study", *The Chartered Accountant,* Vol.40, No.1, 1991, p.20.

## TABLE 5.1

## GROWTH OF PRODUCTION, CAPITAL AND LABOUR OF SPB LTD.

| Years | Production (Rs. in Lakhs) | Productive Capital (Rs. in Lakhs) | No. of Labourers |
|---|---|---|---|
| 1981-82 | 4174.55 | 5034.25 | 2617 |
| 1982-83 | 3507.80 (-15.98) | 4945.76 (-1.76) | 2567 (-1.92) |
| 1983-84 | 4873.62 (37.91) | 5584.26 (12.91) | 2580 (0.50) |
| 1984-85 | 4425.05 (-8.53) | 5989.74 (7.26) | 2604 (0.93) |
| 1985-86 | 5766.25 (30.31) | 7572.78 (26.43) | 2664 (2.30) |
| 1986-87 | 5244.59 (-9.05) | 7550.69 (-0.29) | 2569 (-3.57) |
| 1987-88 | 5283.16 (0.74) | 6951.63 (-7.93) | 2527 (-1.64) |
| 1988-89 | 5172.90 (-2.08) | 6787.82 (-2.36) | 2195 (-13.14) |
| 1989-90 | 6054.50 (17.04) | 7539.65 (11.08) | 2373 (8.11) |
| 1991-91 | 7426.56 (22.66) | 8211.79 (8.91) | 2335 (-1.61) |
| 1991-92 | 8547.10 (15.09) | 8337.58 (1.53) | 2299 (-1.54) |
| 1992-93 | 9125.18 (6.76) | 9439.32 (13.21) | 2261 (-1.66) |
| 1993-94 | 116063.38 (27.16) | 10492.29 (11.16) | 2224 (-1.64) |

**Note:** Figures in parantheses indicates the percentage change from the previous year.

***Source:*** Computed

## TABLE 5.2

## REGRESSION ESTIMATES OF COBB-DOUGLAS PRODUCTION FUNCTION OF SPB LTD. (1981-82 TO 1993-94)

(Log Q = Log A + Log K + Log L)

| *Name of the Unit* | *Constant term (A)* | *Co-efficient of Capital (K)* | *Co-efficient of Labour (L)* | *$R^2$* | *Adj $R^2$* | *F Ratio* | *D.W.* |
|---|---|---|---|---|---|---|---|
| SPB LTD | 1.138 | 1.277<br>(0.198)<br>t=6.44* | -0.675<br>(0.701)<br>t=0.96 | 0.9019 | 0.8823 | 45.98* | 1.31 |

**Note:** figures given in brackets show the standard errors of the parameter.
* Significant at 1% level. Where Q – output; K – Capital; and L – Labour
***Source:*** Computed

## TABLE 5.3

## PAIRWISE CORRELATION MATRIX OF INDEPENDENT VARIABLES IN SPB LTD.

| **Variables** | **S** | **CI** | **CU** | **VI** | **DTA** | **ITR** | **CR** |
|---|---|---|---|---|---|---|---|
| Sales (S) | 1.000 | | | | | | |
| Capacity Integration (CI) | -0.6578 | 1.000 | | | | | |
| Capacity Utilisation (CU) | -0.1553 | 0.5458 | 1.000 | | | | |
| Vertical Integration (VI) | 0.3630 | 0.2936 | 0.3984 | 1.000 | | | |
| Debt./Total Assets (DTA) | -0.5165 | 0.0288 | -0.4727 | -0.2819 | 1.000 | | |
| TR | 0.4937 | -0.0362 | 0.0898 | 0.4149 | -0.5290 | 1.000 | |
| Current Ratio (CR) | 0.4798 | -0.5413 | -0.5809 | -0.5923 | 0.3655 | 0.0920 | 1.000 |
| Operating Expenses Sales (CPES) | 0.3560 | -0.3327 | -0.4434 | -0.9943 | 0.3177 | -0.4478 | 0.6090 |

***Source:*** computed

## TABLE 5.4

## DETERMINATIONS OF PROFITABILITY OF SPB LTD.

| Variables | Beta Co-efficients | t-Value | |
|---|---|---|---|
| Constant | -612.42 | 4.28 | |
| 1. Sales (S) | 0.068 | 2.05 | Significant *** |
| 2. Capacity Integration (CI) | -66.17 | 2.98 | Significant ** |
| 3. Capacity Utilisation (CU) | 1.069 | 3.78 | Significant ** |
| 4. Vertical Integration (VI) | 515.55 | 4.91 | Significant ** |
| 5. Debt./Total Assets (DTA) | -64.23 | 5.73 | Significant * |
| 6. ITR | 3.76 | 1.88 | Significant *** |
| 7. Current Ratio (CR) | 7.20 | 3.33 | Significant ** |
| 8. Operating Expenses/ Sales (OPES) | -5.58 | 3.93 | Significant ** |
| $R^2$ | 0.9918 | | |
| Ad j $R^2$ | 0.9700 | | |
| F Value | 45.49 | | |
| DW Stat | 2.03 | | |

**Note:** * - Significant at 1 percent level
** - Significant at 5 percent level
*** - Significant at 10 percent level

***Source:*** Computed

# PART - II

# ANALYSIS OF CORPORATE LIQUIDITY

# 6

# Assessment of Corporate Liquidity

## A Discriminant Analysis Approach

Liquidity is defined as the ability to realise value in money, the most liquid of assets. It refers to the ability to pay in cash, the obligations that are due. The corporate liquidity has two dimensions viz., quantitative and utilization concepts. The quantitative concept includes the quantum, structure and utilization of liquid assets and in the qualitative concept, it is the ability to meet all present and potential demands on cash from any source in manner that minimizes of the firm. Thus, corporate liquidity is a vital factor in business. Excess liquidity, though a guarantor of solvency would reflect power profitability, deterioration in managerial efficiency, increased speculation and unjustified expansion, extension of too liberal credit and dividend policies. Too little liquidity then may lead to frustration of business objections, reduced rate of return, business opportunity missed and weakening of morale.

## STATEMENT OF THE PROBLEM

Lack of liquidity implies lack of freedom of choice as well as constraints on management's freedom of movement. If sufficient liquidity is not maintained, freedom of movement. If sufficient liquidity is not maintained, the enterprises are technically insolvent and at least faces the financial embracement of renegotiating its obligations to creditors. The control of liquidity requires active working capital management. Thus, in this paper an attempt has been made to determine the short-term liquidity position in the context of the selected sugar factories of Tamil Nadu during the period 1989-85 to 1993-94.

## SAMPLING DESIGN

There are 28 firms in the sugar industry operating in Tamil Nadu of which 14 are under co-operative sector and 14 under private sector. Most of them are just a few years old for which data for the last ten years are not available. In order to select the units for the purpose of the study, only those units that were established before 1984 and were having a crushing capacity of 2000 MT (per day) or more have been considered. There were 10 such units of Which 5 or under co- operative sector and 5 are under the private sector. Thus, the ten units are available for the study and to represent the sugar industry of Tamil Nadu as a whole. The necessary data have been collected mostly from the annual reports of the selected units for the relevant periods

## LIQUIDITY ASSESSMENT AND DISCRIMINANT ANALYSIS

The use of ratio analysis to judge the liquidity position of the enterprises is not free from limitations. The limitations arise from the fact that the methodology is basically unvaried that is each ratio is examined in isolation. Due to this, the financial analyst has to use his own judgment to assess the combined effects of two or more rations. The applications of discriminate analysis to two category classifications problems in empirical financial research has substantially increased in recent years. The need for use of the discriminant analysis is felt in this study due to the fact that if the selected enterprises approach a bank for loan is credit, the bank may determine their risks with the help of it. Here, the risks refer to good and poor risks indicating good and poor liquidity position respectively.

It is no doubt; the bank manager may evaluate their liquidity or risk on the basis of current and quick ratios. It is difficult particularly when some enterprises have high current ratios but low quick ratios and other enterprises have low current ratios but high quick ratios. In such cases, it is difficult to state which of these enterprises good risks are. A discriminant analysis is useful here because it takes to account the effect of both of the ratios in order to distinguish good risks from the poor ones. In this study, the current ratio ($X_1$) and liquid ratio ($X_2$) as reliable indictors of liquidity behaviour have been considered for the selected units. The object now is to determine weights for $X_1$ and $X_2$, that is the values of 'a' and 'b' in

$$\mathbf{Z = a\,X_1 + b\,X_2}$$

Where, Z is the discriminant index.

## EMPIRICAL FINDINGS

### 1.1 Analysis of liquidity

There are several measures with the help of which the short-term liquidity of an enterprise may be assessed. Among them, networking capital itself provides the one, which indicates a 'margin of safety' of protection provided to creditors. Table 6.1 indicates that almost all the selected units have positive net working capital. The average networking capital is comparatively high in private sector units than the cooperative sector units. The average net working capital is largest to SCS, followed by KCS, NCS, ACS and AMCS in the co-operative sector, whereas in the private sector, it is the highest for SSL followed by ASL, KSL, SISL and TASL. The measure of networking capital does not indicate true ability to pay the current debts when they become due. The networking capital (CA-CL) comprised illiquid inventories; these inventories cannot be easily converted into cash. Therefore, while dealing with liquidity, the measure of quick networking capital has been assumed as more relevant than the measure of networking capital. It is evident from the table 6.1 that the average quick networking capital has been positive only in SCS among co-operative sector and ASL, SSL, and KSL among private sector. Thus, the ability to pay current debts out of quick assets by the selected industries goes much lower. However, nothing concrete can be concluded depending solely upon the networking capital or quick networking capital. While assessing the liquidity position, the extent of margin of safety provided to the current ratio creditors. Due to this, the current ratio (CR) and liquid ratio (LR) are regarded as better measures of liquidity. The current ratio and liquid ratio in the selected sugar industries of Tamil Nadu are presented in Table 6.1 a relatively high value of the recurrent ratio is considered as an indication that the firm is liquid and has the ability to pay its bills. On the other hand, a relatively low value of the current ratio is considered as an indication that the firm will find difficulty in paying its bills. As a conventional rule, a current ratio of 1:1 or more is considered to be satisfactory. But the size of current ratio depends upon many factors; a standard of common current ratio cannot be designated as appropriated for all types of business. Therefore, as regards the industrial firms with larger investment in fixed assets and slower operating cycle, the stand of this ratio may fall around 1:5:1. It is evident from the table that all the selected sugar industries have average current ratios of greater than 1.5 during the study period.

Though the current ratio of 1:1 is generally acceptable, the acceptability of a current ratio is highly dependent of a current ratio is highly dependent on the predictability of the firm's cash flows. The more predictable the cash flows, the lower the current ratio required. The high current ratio need not indicate higher liquidity, because current assets comprise of inventories, which can't be concerted into cash easily. Viewed in this way liquid ratios are considered more relevant than current ratios. If the standard liquid ratios are to be taken as 1:1 the majority ratio is to be taken as 1:1 the majority of the selected sugar industries (7 out of 10) have average liquid ratios of less than 1. It is also evident from the table that the average liquid ratios are less than one for all the selected sugar industries under co-operative sector. But the average liquid ratios are greater than one in ASL, SSL and KSL in the private sector.

While dealing with liquidity, an additional ratio, which measures cash adequacy, should be mentioned. The ratio is to compute the proportion of cash to current liabilities, which shows cash is available to pay current obligations. These ratios computed for the selected sugar industries are presented in Table 6.1. It is evident from the table that the average cash to current liabilities ratio has been excessively high for certain industries particularly SCS and ACS in the co-operative sector and SSL in the private sector. It reveals that the level of cash maintained by these industries is higher than the current liabilities on most of the occasions. In a nutshell, it can thus be concluded that comparatively private sector sugar industries has maintained sound liquidity position than the current liabilities on most of the occasions. In a nutshell, it can thus be concluded that comparatively private sector sugar industries has maintained sound liquidity position than the co-operative sector sugar industries during the study period.

## ASSESSMENT OF LIQUIDITY - DISCRIMINANT ANALYSIS

One should evaluate liquidity on the basis of current and liquid ratios but this is not always possible. It is difficult particularly when some industries have high current ratios but low quick ratios and other enterprises have low current ratios but high quick ratios. In such cases, it is difficult to state which of these enterprises are good risks. The risks refer to good and poor risks indicating good and poor liquidity positions respectively. The need for the use of the discriminant analysis is felt in this study due to the fact that it takes into account the effect of both of the ratios in order to distinguish good risks from the poor ones. The discriminant analysis has been explained in the methodology.

## ESTIMATION OF DISCRIMINANT FUNCTION

First of all, the selected sugar industries have been classified into two groups. The industries which have current and liquid ratios of 2:1 and 1:1 or more respectively have been classified as good risks and the remaining industries as poor risks. As per this rule, the number of industries falling in the good and poor risk groups is presented in Table 6.4. After classifying the selected sugar industries into the good and poor risk classes, the values of 'a' and 'b' in the indiscriminant functions are estimated. The discriminant functions of the selected years are presented in Table 6.2 where the co-efficient for 'a' and 'b' indicate values for current and liquid ratios respectively. It is evident from the table that liquid ratios appeared to be stronger that current ratios from 1984-85 to 1993-94 except in the year 1986-87. In 1986-87, current ratios have turned out to be stronger than liquid ratio.

## ESTIMATION OF DISCRIMINANT SCORES

The discriminant function given in table 1.2 was multiplied with the mean values of each industry ratios in order to obtain the discriminant score of each industry. Table 1.3 presents the data relating to the discriminant score of bother groups. Similarly, those industries, which have higher 'Z' values, are said to be in a good liquidity position. It is evident from the table that among the selected industries, the first three industries with good liquidity position may be indicated as KSL., TASL and ALS in 1984-85; ASI., NCS and SSL in 1985-86; ASL, SSL and AMCS in 1987-89; ASL SSL and ACS in 1989 – 90 ASL, SSL and NCS in 1990-91; ASL and SCS in 1991-92; SSL, KSL and KCS in 1992-93; and KSL, SCS and ASL in 1993-94.

With the help of the discriminant scores given in Table 6.3, the cut off values was calculated as follows.

$$\text{Cut of value} \quad \frac{n_1 z_1 + n_2 z_2}{n_1 + n_2}$$

Where $n_1$ and $n_2$ are the size of sample and $z_1$ and $z_2$ are mean of the discriminant score of Group A and Group B respectively. These cut off values have also been presented in Table 6.3 Actual z scores of the individual industries al z scores of the individual industries were then compared with the discriminating z scores. If the z scores, it can be said that such industries have good liquidity position.

## ASSESSMENT OF CORPORATE LIQUIDITY – A DISCRIMINANT ANALYSIS APPROACH

The good risk industries as indicated by z values are ASL, SSL, KSL, and TASL in 1984-85; NCS, ASL SSI, ASL and KSL in 1985-86; AMCS, NCS ASL and SSL in 1986-87; AMCS, ASL and SSL in 1990-91; SCS, ASL and SSL in 1991-92, SCS, KCS, ACL, SSL and KSL in 1992-93; and SCS, ASL, SSL and KSL in 1993-94. It is also inferred from the table that AMCS in co-operative sector classified as poor risk in all the selected years as per CR and LR, have become good risk in the year 1986-87 and 1987-89 as per discriminating Z score.

## CLASSIFICATION MATRIX

The number of good and poor risk industries as per the criteria of current and liquid ratios and as per the discriminant score are presented in Table 6.4. It is clear from the table that the misclassification does not occur in years 1985-86, 1990-91, 1992-93 and 1993-94 respectively. It means that there is no difference between the criteria of current and liquid ratios and the criteria of discriminant score in these four years. Misclassification of industries is noticed for the remaining years. Generally, the industries with lower current and liquid ratios in the good risk group and the industries with higher current and liquid ratios in the poor risk group have been misclassified under the criteria of discriminant score is more than the number of good risk enterprises as per the criteria of current and liquid ratios. It is also inferred that the poor risk industries under criteria of current and liquid ratios appeared to be good risks under the criteria of discriminant score. Such industries are ASL, SSL and TASL in 1984-85; AMCS and SSL in 1986-87; AMCS and SSL in 1987-89; KSL in 1989-90; and SCS and ASL in 1991-92.

## CONCLUSION

The discriminant analysis discussed above may be of great value to all those who are interested in evaluating liquidity position or credit worthiness. The advantage of discriminant analysis is that it is simple and can be performed even by the junior executives of the enterprise. However, the limitation of the discriminant analysis is that it is still based on the traditional current and liquid ratios. Despite of the above limitations, the way discrimination analysis has been employed is useful exercise to determine the combined effect of two ratios. This is more so at a time when some enterprises have high current ratios but low liquid ratios and other enterprise have low current ratios but high liquid ratios, making it difficult to determine which of these enterprises are good risks.

## REFERENCE


1. Horold Bierman, Jr. and Jerome E, Hass, 1975. An Introduction to Managerial Finance, London; Pitman Publishing Ltd.

2. Maurice Joy, D. and John D. Tollejson, on the Financial Applications of Discriminant Analysis, *The Journal of Financial and Quantitative Analysis*, pp.723-739.

3. Walter, J.E., A Discriminant Function for earnings price ratios of Large Industrial Corporation, *Review of Economics and Statistics*, 1959, pp. 44-52.

4. Altman, E.l., Financial Ratios, Discriminant analysis and Prediction of Corporate Bankruptcy, *The Journal of Finance*, Vol. XXIII, No. 4, pp. 589-609.

5. R.S. Pradhan; Management of Working Capital, National Book Organisation, New Delhi, 1986.

6. ACS – Ambur Coperative Sugar Mills Ltd.
   AMCS – Amaravathi Cooperative Sugar Mills Ltd.
   SCS-Salem Cooperative Sugar Mills Ltd.
   NCS – National Cooperative sugar Mills Ltd.
   KCS – Kallakurichi Cooperative Sugar Mills Ltd.
   ASL – Aruna Suagr Ltd.
   SISL – South India Sugar Ltd.
   KSL – Kothari Sugars Ltd.
   TASL – Thiru Arooran Sugars Ltd.

## TABLE 6.1
## MEAN VALUES OF TRADITIONAL LIQUIDITY INDICATORS (1984-85 TO 1993-94)

| Company | NWC (Rs. in lakhs) | QNWC (Rs. in lakhs) | CR | LR | Cash to Current Liabilities |
|---|---|---|---|---|---|
| ***Co-operative Sector*** | | | | | |
| ACS | 526.03 | -152.7 | 1.94 | 0.72 | 31.67 |
| AMCS | 273.90 | -192.6 | 1.85 | 0.52 | 9.08 |
| SCS | 880.40 | 18.4 | 1.94 | 0.98 | 36.90 |
| NCS | 527.05 | -110.0 | 2.86 | 0.72 | 10.09 |
| KCS | 535.05 | -215.6 | 1.84 | 0.57 | 9.65 |
| ***Private sector*** | | | | | |
| ASL | 1663.98 | 177.5 | 3.85 | 1.34 | 60.80 |
| SISL | 509.00 | -306.7 | 1.78 | 0.47 | 5.08 |
| SSL | 2404.76 | 169.3 | 2.89 | 1.11 | 31.70 |
| KSL | 544.08 | 72.6 | 2.25 | 1.15 | 37.40 |
| TASL | 504.42 | -134.7 | 1.73 | 0.06 | 8.21 |
| Total Industry | 836.99 | -67.49 | 2.25 | 0.82 | 19.08 |

NWC – Networking capital; QNWC – Quick Networking capital
CR- Current Ratio; LR: Liquid Ratio

***Source:*** Computed

## TABLE 6.2

## DISCRIMINANT FUNCTIONS FOR THE PERIOD 1984-85 TO 1993-94

| Year | Function | Remark |
|---|---|---|
| 1984-85 | Z=-1.490 a + 6.585 b | b > a |
| 1985-86 | Z=-0.422 a + 1.078 b | b > a |
| 1986-87 | Z=-0.706 a + 0.172 b | b > a |
| 1987-89 | Z=-1.052 a + 1.185 b | b > a |
| 1989-90 | Z=-0.091 a + 0.456 b | b > a |
| 1990-91 | Z=-1.423 a + 3.638 b | b > a |
| 1991-92 | Z=-0.489b a + 1.315b | b > a |
| 1992-93 | Z=-0.448 a + 3.291 b | b > a |
| 1993-94 | Z=-0.748 a + 4.187 b | b > a |

**Note:** The expression a>b is to be read as 'a' is greater than 'b'.
***Source:*** Computed

## TABLE 6.3

## DISCRIMINATING Z SCORES

| Units | 1984-85 | 85-86 | 86-87 | 87-89 | 89-90 | 90-91 | 91-92 | 92-93 | 93-94 |
|---|---|---|---|---|---|---|---|---|---|
| ACS | -0.89 | 1.86 | 1.29 | 2.23 | 0.75 | 5.09 | 2.03 | 3.32 | 4.65 |
| AMCS | -0.93 | 0.99 | 1.99 | 3.41 | 0.50 | 5.01 | 1.18 | 3.64 | 3.93 |
| SCS | -0.65 | 1.80 | 1.27 | 2.62 | 0.63 | 4.90 | 2.51 | 5.12 | 8.75 |
| NCS | -1.02 | 2.67 | 2.66 | 2.93 | 0.54 | 5.41 | 2.03 | 3.20 | 3.88 |
| KCS | -1.13 | 1.07 | 0.93 | 2.20 | 0.24 | 3.34 | 1.76 | 5.50 | 5.23 |
| ASL | 0.05 | 3.26 | 2.83 | 6.79 | 1.57 | 9.84 | 2.61 | 4.86 | 8.56 |
| SISL | -1.68 | 1.26 | 0.78 | 2.10 | 0.32 | 4.37 | 1.56 | 2.57 | 4.32 |
| SSL | -0.17 | 2.41 | 1.86 | 3.98 | 0.86 | 8.22 | 3.52 | 6.52 | 6.92 |
| KSL | 2.15 | 2.24 | 1.50 | 3.05 | 0.72 | 4.63 | 1.93 | 6.01 | 6.80 |
| TASL | 0.12 | 1.25 | 0.88 | 1.73 | 0.52 | 4.02 | 1.67 | 3.27 | 4.77 |
| Cut of Z Value | -0.41 | 1.88 | 1.60 | 3.10 | 0.66 | 5.48 | 2.08 | 4.40 | 5.98 |

***Source:*** Computed

## TABLE 6.4

## CLASSIFICATIONS MATRIX

| Year | As per CR and LR | | As per discriminant Score | |
|---|---|---|---|---|
| | *Good* | *Poor* | *Good* | *Poor* |
| 1984-85 | 1 | 9 | 4 | 6 |
| 1985-86 | 4 | 6 | 4 | 6 |
| 1986-87 | 2 | 8 | 4 | 6 |
| 1987-89 | 1 | 9 | 3 | 7 |
| 1989-90 | 3 | 7 | 4 | 6 |
| 1990-91 | 2 | 8 | 2 | 8 |
| 1991-92 | 1 | 9 | 3 | 7 |
| 1992-93 | 5 | 5 | 5 | 5 |
| 1993-94 | 4 | 6 | 4 | 6 |

***Source:*** Computed

# 7

# Management of Corporate Liquidity and Profitability

## An Empirical Study

Liquidity management is necessary for all businesses, small, medium or large because it means collecting cash from customers in time so that having no difficulty in paying short-term debts. Therefore, when a business does not manage its liquidity well, it will have cash shortages and will results in difficulty in paying obligations. As a result, in addition to profitability, liquidity management is vital for ongoing concerns. Promoters of capital theory share the axiom that profitability and liquidity comprise the salient (albeit frequently conflicting) goals of working capital management. The conflict arises because the maximization of firm's returns could seriously threaten the liquidity and on the other hand, the pursuit of liquidity has a tendency to dilute returns. The crucial part in managing working capital is required maintaining its liquidity in day-to-day operation to ensure its smooth running and meets its obligation (Eljelly, 2004). Yet, this is not a simple task since managers must make sure that business operation is running in efficient and profitable manner. There are possibilities of mismatch of current assets and current liabilities during this process. If this happens and firm's manager cannot manage it properly then it will affect firm's growth and profitability. This will further lead to financial distress and finally firms can go bankrupt.

Corporate liquidity is examined from two distinct dimensions: static or dynamic view (Lancaster et al., 1999; Farris and Hutchison, 2002: and Moss and Stine, 1993). The static view is based on commonly used traditional ratios, such as current ratio and quick ratio, calculated from the balance sheet accounts. These traditional measures of liquidity are incompetent measures that cannot provide detailed and accurate about liquidity management effectiveness (Jose et al., 1996). These ratios measures liquidity at a given point in time. For example, the current ratio, are simple to apply and have some theoretical merit increases in say, accounts receivables will increase the current ratio, suggesting improved liquidity. However, the ability to match short-term obligations has only improved from a liquidation perspective providing current assets may be liquidated at current market value and not from a going-concern approach (Shulman and Dambolena, 1986). Liquidity for the ongoing firm is not reliant on the liquidation value of its assets, but rather on the operating cash flow generated by these assets (Soenen, 1993).

On the other hand, dynamic view measures ongoing liquidity from the firm's operations. As a dynamic measure of the time it takes a firm to go from cash outflow to cash inflow which is measured by Cash Conversion Cycle (CCC) introduced by Hager (1976) and has been recommended by Largay and Stickney (1980), Kamath (1989) and others. Drawing attention to limitations of traditional liquidity ratios, Richards and Laughlin (1980), Kamath (1989), Gentry et al., (1990), and Schilling (1996) have insisted on using ongoing liquidity measures in working capital management.

Ongoing liquidity refers to the inflows and outflows of cash through the product acquisition, production, sales, payment and collection process takes place overtime. As the firm's ongoing liquidity is a function of its cash (conversion) cycle, it will be more appropriate and evaluate effectiveness of working capital management by cash conversion cycle, rather than traditional liquidity measures.

## CASH CONVERSION CYCLE (CCC)

In text books related to finance, CCC is maintained in the context of working capital management (Keown et al., 2003; and Bodie and Merton, 2000). The cash conversion cycle is used as a comprehensive measure of working capital as it shows the time lag between expenditure for the purchase of raw material and the collection of sales of finished goods (Padachi, 2006; Bodie and Merton, 2009; Keown et al., 2003; Jordon, 2003; and Eljelly, 2004).

**CCC = RCP + ICP - APP**

In the above formula, the three variables to which CCC is dependent are defined as follows;

RCP – Receivables Collection Period (in days)
(Accounts Receivables / Sales) * 365

ICP – Inventory Conversion period (in days)
(Inventory / Cost of goods sold) * 365

APP – Accounts Payable Period (in days)
(Accounts Payables / Cost of goods sold) * 365

There seems to be strong relation between the cash conversion cycle of a firm and its profitability. The three different components of CCC (accounts receivables, inventory and accounts payables) can be managed in different ways in order to maximise profitability. It is an indication of how long a firm can carry on if it was to stop its operations or it indicates the time gap between purchase of goods and collection of sales. The optimum level of inventory will have a direct effect on profitability since it will release working capital resources which in turn will be invested in the business cycle, or will increase inventory levels in order to respond to higher product demand. Similarly both credit policy from suppliers and credit period granted to customers will have an impact on profitability. In order to understand the way working capital is managed, CCC and its components will be statistically analysed.

Cash conversion cycle is likely to be negative as well as positive. A positive result indicates the number of days a company must borrow or tie up capital while awaiting payment from a customer. A negative result indicates the number of days a company has received cash from sales before it must pay its suppliers (Hutchison et al., 2007). Of course the ultimate goal is having low CCC, if possible negative. Because the shorter the CCC, the more efficient the company in managing its cash flow. The purpose of this paper is to investigate the implications of the CCC as an indicator of liquidity on profitability of selected firms in Indian Automobile Industry.

## LITERATURE REVIEW – THEORETICAL UNDERPINNINGS

In a study by Kamath (1989), it has been concluded that there is a reverse relationship between cash conversion cycle and profitability. In another study of Shin and Soenen (1998), a sample consisting of American manufacturing firms for the period of 1974-1995 has been analysed and a statistically negative relationship between cash conversion cycle and profitability has been confirmed. To test the relationship between working capital management and corporate profitability, Deloof (2003) used a sample of 1009 large Belgian non-financial firms for a period of 1992-1996. He discussed possible relationships between cash conversion cycle and profitability by dividing cash conversion cycle into its components (inventory, account receivables and account payables period). Results of the study have concluded that increase in all of these periods affect profitability negatively. Lazaridis and Tryfonidis (2006) conducted a cross sectional study by using a sample of 131 firms listed on the Athens Stock Exchange for the period of 2001-2004 and found cash conversion cycle affects profitability negatively.

Eljelly (2004) empirically examined the relationship between profitability and liquidity as measured by current ratio and cash conversion cycle on a sample of 929 Joint stock companies in Saudi Arabia. It has been concluded that the effect of cash conversion cycle on profitability is stronger than the effect of current ratio on it and found significant negative relationship between the firm's profitability and its liquidity level. Raheman and Nasr (2007) studied the effect of different variables of working capital management including cash conversion cycle on the profitability of 94 Pakistani firm listed on Karachi Stock Exchange for a period between 1999-2004 and found that as cash conversion cycle increases, it leads to decreasing profitability of the firm. Garcia-Teruel and Martinez-Solano (2007) collected data for 8872 SMEs from Spain for the period 1996-2002 and tested the effects of working capital management on profitability. The results demonstrated that shortening cash conversion cycle improves the profitability. Falope and Ajilore (2009) used a sample of 50 Nigerian quoted non-financial firms for the period 1996-2005. They found a significant negative relationship between net operating profitability and the average collection period, inventory turnover in days, average payment period and cash conversion cycle.

Mathuva (2009) examined the influence of working capital management components on corporate profitability by using a sample of 30 listed on the Nairobi-Stock Exchange (NSE) for the periods 1993 to 2008. He found that there exists a highly significant negative relationship between the time it takes for firms to collect cash from their customers and profitability. Amarjit Gill, Nahum Biger and Neil Mathur (2010) studied the relationship between the cash conversion cycle and profitability and found significant relationship between them. The other studies, Ali Uyar (2009), Moss Stine (1993), Jose et al., (1996), Hutchison *et al.*, (2007), Vaidyanathan et al., (1990), Lyroudi and McCarty (1993), Soenen (1993) and Wang (2002) empirically examined the relationship between profitability and liquidity showed that there exists a significant and negative relation between profitability and CCC. However, the study conducted by Katerina Lyroudi and Lazoridis (2000) in the Food Industry of Greece found that there was positive relationship between CCC and return on assets.

Among the studies conducted in the Indian context showed both the positive and negative association between liquidity and profitability. Amit K. Mallik, Debdas Rakshit (2005) studied the relationship between liquidity and profitability in the context of Indian Pharmaceutical industry and concluded that no definite relationship can be established between liquidity and profitability. Narware (2004) in his study of working capital management and profitability of NFL, a fertilizer company disclosed both negative and positive association. Bardia (2004) in his study on steel giant SAIL for the period from 1991-92 to 2001-2002 concluded that there was a positive relationship between liquidity and profitability. D. Sur, J. Biswas and Ganguly, P. (2001) revealed in their study of Indian Aluminium producing industry, a very significant positive association between liquidity and profitability. Vijayakumar and Venkatachalam (1995) in their study on Tamil Nadu Sugar Industry with regard to relationship between liquidity and profitability concluded that liquidity was negatively associated with profitability.

In summary, the literature review indicates that working capital management impacts on the profitability of the firm but there still is ambiguity regarding the appropriate variables that might serve as proxies for working capital management. The present study investigates the relationship between a set of such variables and the profitability of a sample of Indian Automobile firms. Further, most of the Indian studies used traditional liquidity ratios viz., current and quick ratio as a measure of liquidity. Only a very few studies used Cash Conversion Cycle (CCC) as a measure for liquidity. Therefore, to fill this gap in the literature, an attempt has been made in this part to study the relationship between cash conversion cycle and profitability of Indian automobile firms. The present study postulates the following hypothesis: **"Firms liquidity negatively affects profitability"**

## VARIABLES SPECIFICATIONS AND EMPIRICAL MODEL

This study investigates the effects of cash conversion cycle on firm's profitability. The dependent variable of the regression model is return on assets (PR). The Cash Conversion Cycle (CCC) used as a comprehensive measure of liquidity is independent variable, and is measured by adding ARP to ICP and then subtracting the APP. It is expected that there is a negative relationship between profitability and cash conversion cycle. This is consistent with the view that the time lag between expenditure for the purchase of raw materials and the collection of sales of finished goods can be too long, and that decreasing the time lag increases profitability. Along with cash conversion cycle, the present study has taken into considerations some control variables relating to firms such as the size of the firm, the growth in its sales and its financial leverage. The size of the firm (SIZE) has been measured by the natural logarithm of its total sales. The growth of the firm (GROWTH) is measured by variations in its annual sales value with reference to previous year's sales $[(sales_t - sales_{t-1})/sales_{t-1}]$. Moreover, the financial leverage (LEV) was taken as the debt to equity ratio of each firm for the whole sample period. Finally, since good economic conditions tend to be reflected in a firm's profitability (Lamberson, 1995), this phenomenon has been controlled for the evolution of the economic cycle using the GDPGR variable, which measures the real annual

GDP growth. Table 7.1 below summarises the definitions and theoretical predicted signs.

**TABLE 7.1**

**PROXY VARIABLES DEFINITION AND PREDICTED RELATIONSHIPS**

| Proxy Variables | Definitions | Predicted Sign |
|---|---|---|
| ARP | Account receivables divided by sales and multiplied by 365 days | +/- |
| ICP | Inventory divided by cost of goods sold and multiplied by 365 days | +/- |
| APP | Accounts payables divided by cost of goods sold and multiplied by 365 days | +/- |
| CCC | No. of days A/R plus No. of days of IC minus No. of days A/P | +/- |
| Size | Natural logarithm of firm's sales | +/- |
| Growth | Difference between current year sales and previous year sales divided by previous year sales | +/- |
| Leverage | Total debt divided by equity | - |
| GDPGR | Difference between current year GDP and previous year GDP divided by previous year GDP | + |

## EMPIRICAL MODEL

The study uses panel data regression analysis of cross-sectional and time series data. The pooled regression is one where both intercepts and slops are constant, where the cross-section firm data and time series data are pooled together in a single column assuming that there is no significant cross-section or temporal effects.

The general form of model is

$$PR_{it} = \beta_0 + \underset{\alpha_{it}}{\overset{n}{\text{€}}} \beta_i X_{it} + e$$

where

$PR_{it}$ - Return on assets of firm i at time t;

i = 1, 2, 3....., 20 firms

$\beta_0$ - The intercept of equation

$\beta_i$ - Co-efficients of $X_{it}$ variables

$X_{it}$ - The different independent variables for working capital management of firms i at time t

t - Time = 1, 2, 3, ......

e - The error term

To investigate the impact of cash conversion cycle on profitability the model used for the regression analysis is expressed in the general form as given above. Specifically, when convert the above general least squares model into specified variables it becomes:

$$\mathbf{PR_{it} = \beta_0 + \beta_1\, CCC_{it} + \beta_2\, SIZE_{it} + \beta_3\, GROWTH_{it} + \beta_4\, LEV_{it} + \beta_5\, GDPGR_{it} + e_{it}}$$

Where,

| | | |
|---|---|---|
| PR | - | Measures the firm profitability with gross profit as a percentage of total assets for firm (i) in the year (t). |
| CCC | - | Cash Conversion Cycle for firm (i) in the year (t). |
| Size | - | Natural logarithm of firm's sales for firm (i) in the year (t). |
| Growth | - | Growth of firm's sales for firm (i) in the year (t). |
| Leverage | - | Measures the leverage with debt to equity for firm (i) in the year (t). |
| GDPGR | - | Measures the growth of GDP for firm (i) in the year (t). |
| $\beta_0$ | - | Constant term for firm (i) in the year (t). |
| $\beta_1, \beta_2....$ | - | Regression Co-efficient. |
| e | - | disturbance term for firm (i) in the year (t). |

## RESEARCH DESIGN

Keeping in view the scope of the study, it is decided to include all the companies under automobile industry working before or from the year 1996-97 to 2008-09. There are 26 companies operating in the Indian automobile industry. But, owing to several constraints such as non-availability of financial statements or non-working of a company in a particular year etc., it is compelled to restrict the number of sample companies to 20. The companies under automobile industry are classified into three sectors namely; Commercial vehicles, Passenger cars and Multiutility vehicles and Two and three wheelers. For the purpose of the study all the three sectors have been selected. It accounts for 73.23 per cent of the total companies available in the Indian automobile industry. The selected 20 companies include 5 under commercial vehicles, 6 under Passenger cars and Multiutility vehicles and 9 under two and three wheeler sectors. It is inferred that sample company represents 98.74 percentage of market share in commercial vehicles, 89.76 percentage of market share in passenger cars and Multiutility vehicles and 99.81 percentage of market share in two and three wheelers. Thus, the findings based on the occurrence of such representative sample may be presumed to be true representative of automobile industry in the country.

The study is mainly based on secondary data. The major source of data analysed and interpreted in this study related to all those companies selected is collected from "PROWESS" database, which is the most reliable on the empowered corporate database of Centre for Monitoring Indian Economy (CMIE). Besides prowess database, relevant secondary data have also been collected from BSE Stock Exchange Official Directory, CIME Publications, Annual Survey of Industry, Business newspapers, Reports on Currency and Finance, Libraries of various Research Institutions, through Internet etc.

## RESULTS AND DISCUSSION

In Table 7.2, the summary statistics of the variables

included in the regression models are presented. Descriptive statistics shows the mean and standard deviation of the different variables of interest in the study. It also presents the standard error of mean, median, minimum and maximum values, kurtosis and skewness of the variables. Table 7.2 presents descriptive statistics for 20 Indian automobile companies for the period of 13 years from 1996-97 to 2008-09 and for a total 216 companies year observations. Overall, the mean profit rate on total assets is 22.29 per cent with the standard deviation of 105.3 per cent. It means that value of the profitability (profit rate on total assets) can deviate from mean to both sides by 105.3 per cent. The maximum value for the profit rate on total assets is 1638.9 per cent for a company in a year while the minimum is -189.4 per cent. The mean cash conversion cycle is 30 days (approximately one month) with the standard deviation of 66 days, implying that Indian automobile company's turnover their stock on an average of 12 times a year.

**TABLE 7.2**

**DESCRIPTIVE STATISTICS OF INDEPENDENT, DEPENDENT AND CONTROL VARIABLES**

**20 Indian Automobile Firms, 1996 – 2009 – 216 Firm -year observations (N = 216)**

| Variables | Mean ± S.D | Standard Error of mean | Median | Minimum | Maximum | kurtosis | Skewness |
|---|---|---|---|---|---|---|---|
| PR | 22.29 ± 105.3 | 6.62 | 14.58 | -189.39 | 1638.92 | 222.83 | 14.44 |
| CCC | 29.90 ± 65.81 | 4.14 | 19.07 | -255.76 | 312.03 | 5.58 | -0.18 |
| Size | 6.90 ± 1.70 | 0.11 | 6.86 | 0.92 | 10.39 | 0.01 | -0.27 |
| Growth | 10.60 ± 36.83 | 2.32 | 10.13 | -97.62 | 356.66 | 31.46 | 3.48 |
| Leverage | 1.33 ± 3.12 | 0.20 | 0.67 | 0.00 | 41.37 | 110.30 | 9.32 |
| GDPG | 12.73 ± 3.41 | 0.98 | 13.44 | 7.76 | 16.92 | -1.56 | -0.33 |

**Notes** : PR-Profit Rate on total assets; CCC-Cash Conversion Cycle; Size-Natural logarithm of sales (proxy for size);Growth-Sales growth; Leverage-Debt/Equity; GDPG-Gross Domestic Product Growth.

***Source :*** Computed.

To check the size of the company and its relationship with profitability, natural logarithm of sales is used as a control variable. The mean value of log of sales is 6.90 while the standard deviation is 1.70. The maximum value of log of sales for a company in a year is 10.39 and the minimum is 0.92. In the same way to check the growth of the company and its relationship with profitability, sales growth is used as a control variable. The average growth of sales for Indian automobile companies is 10.60 per cent with a standard deviation of 36.83 per cent. The highest growth of sales for a company in a particular year is 356.66 per cent and in the same way the minimum growth of sales for a company in a year is -97.62 per cent.

To check the leverage and its relationship with the profitability, the debt ratio (obtained by dividing the total debt of the company by the equity) is used as a control variable. The results of the descriptive statistics show that the average leverage ratio for the Indian automobile companies is 1.33 with a standard deviation of 3.12. The maximum debt financing used by a company is 41.37, whereas the minimum level of the debt ratio is 0.00 which is unusual but may be possible. To check the GDP growth and its relationship with the profitability, GDP growth rate is used as a control variable. The mean value for this ratio is 12.73 per cent with a standard deviation of 3.41 per cent. The maximum GDP growth during the study period is 16.92 per cent and the minimum is 7.76 per cent.

## PEARSON'S CORRELATION CO-EFFICIENT ANALYSIS

Consistent with Shin and Soenen (1998), Table 3 provides the Pearson correlation for the variables used in the regression model. Pearson's correlation analysis is used for data to see the relationship between variables such as those between liquidity (working capital management) and profitability. Table 7.3 shows the negative relationship between profitability and CCC, is consistent with the view that the time lag between the expenditure for the purchases of raw materials and the collection of sales of finished goods can be too long and that decreasing the time lag increases profitability (Deloof, 2003). Firm size is positively related to profitability. This means that larger firm report higher profits compared to smaller firms. This may be due to larger firm's ability to exploit their economies of scale. Growth, which could be an indicator of a firm's business opportunities, is an important factor allowing firms to enjoy improved profitability, as can be seen in the positive sign for the variable GROWTH. With reference to other control variables, leverage and GDPG, profitability is negatively associated with leverage whereas profitability is positively associated with GDPG. Thus, by analyzing the results it is concluded that if the firm is able to reduce these time periods, then the firm is efficient in managing working capital (liquidity). This efficiency will lead to increasing its profitability. The results of correlation analysis indicate that as far as Indian automobile companies are concerned, the liquidity management very significantly and strongly affects their profitability.

**TABLE 7.3**

**CORRELATION MATRIX**

| | PR | CCC | Size | Growth | Leverage | GDPG |
|---|---|---|---|---|---|---|
| PR | 1.00 | | | | | |
| CCC | -0.09 | 1.00 | | | | |
| Size | 0.04 | -0.11 | 1.00 | | | |
| Growth | 0.03 | -0.13 | 0.18 | 1.00 | | |
| Leverage | -0.20 | 0.14 | -0.22 | 0.02 | 1.00 | |
| GDPG | -0.05 | 0.28 | -0.69 | -0.15 | -0.24 | 1.00 |

**Notes :** PR-Profit Rate on total assets; CCC-Cash Conversion Cycle; Size -Natural logarithm of sales (proxy for size); S.Growth-Sales growth; Leverage-Debt/Equity; GDPG-Gross Domestic Product Growth.

***Sources:*** Computed.

## REGRESSION ANALYSIS

Although, Pearson linear correlations give proof of an inverse relationship between profitability and CCC, these measures do not allow us to identify causes from consequences (Shin and Soenen, 1998). Therefore, the main analysis will be derived from appropriate multivariate models estimated using the overall least squares regression model. The model specifies above is estimated using the regression based framework (pooled OLS) as employed by Deloof (2003), Raheman and Nasr (2007), Garcia Teruel and Martinez-Solano (2007), Padachi (2006), David M. Mathuva (2009) and Amarjit Gill et al., (2010). Table 7.4 report the pooled OLS regression results of the overall relationship which exists between working capital management (liquidity) and profitability.

## CASH CONVERSION CYCLE (CCC) AND PROFITABILITY

The results of the regression model shows that consistent with Deloof (2003), Raheman and Nasr (2007), Shin and Soenen (1998), Garcia-Teruel and Martinez-Solano (2007), Padachi (2006) and David M. Mathuva (2009), a negative relationship exists between the Cash Conversion Cycle (CCC) and profitability. This supports the notion that the CCC is negatively related with profitability. Shin and Soenen (1998) argued that the negative relation between profits and the cash conversion cycle could be explained by the market power or the market share, i.e., a shorter CCC because of bargaining power by the suppliers and/ or the customers as well as higher profitability due to market dominance. The negative relationship between the firm's CCC and profitability can also be explained by the fact that minimizing the investment in current assets can help in boosting profits. This ensures the liquid cash is not maintained in the business for long and that it is used to generate profits for the firm.

**TABLE 7.4**

**REGRESSIONS OF PROFITABILITY ON WORKING CAPITAL VARIABLES**

[20 Indian Automobile Firms, 1996-2009 : 216 Firm year observations]

(Dependent variable : Profit Rate on total assets(PR))

| Independent Variables | Model 4 |
|---|---|
| Intercept | 15.07 |
| CCC | -0.01(2.31) *** |
| Size | 0.55(1.66) |
| Growth | 0.14(2.44)** |
| Leverage | -5.05(1.23) |
| GDPG | 0.36(3.02)** |
| $R^2$ | 0.80 |
| Adjusted $R^2$ | 0.66 |
| F Value | 5.65* |
| Durbin Watson | 1.47 |

Notes : PR-Profit Rate on total assets; CCC-Cash Conversion Cycle; Size-Natural logarithm of sales (proxy for size); Growth-Sales growth; Leverage - Debt / Equity; GDPG-Gross Domestic Product Growth.

* P < 0.01; **P < 0.05; ***P < 0.10

***Source :*** Computed

The model also shows that profitability increases with firm size (as measured by natural logarithm of sales). The results of the regression indicate that the coefficient of growth (as measured by growth of sales) on profitability showed significant and positive relationship with profitability. The study used the debt ratio (measured by debt divided by equity) as a proxy for leverage, it shows a negative relationship with the profitability. This means that, when the leverage of the firm increases, it will adversely affect its profitability. Similarly, GDP growth of the country showed a significant positive relationship with profitability. It reflects that if the country's GDP increases, the profitability of Indian Automobile Industry will also increases. The model's adjusted $R^2$ is 66 per cent with an F-value of 5.65 which is significant ($p<0.05$). The Durbin Watson statistic is 1.49.

## CONCLUSION

The study of empirical relationship between liquidity and profitability is one of the areas of performance of corporate enterprise. This study has shown that Indian automobile industry has been able to achieve high scores on the various components of working capital and this has positive impact on its profitability. Empirical results of the study found a significant negative relationship between profitability and Cash Conversion Cycle (CCC) for a sample of Indian automobile industry. These results suggest that managers can create value for their shareholders by reducing the number of days of accounts receivable and inventories to a reasonable minimum. Further, companies are capable of gaining sustainable competitive advantage by means of effective and efficient utilisation of the resources of the organisation through a careful reduction of the cash conversion cycle to its minimum. In doing so, the profitability of the firm is expected to increase. Therefore, managers can create profits for their companies by handling correctly the cash conversion cycle and keeping each different component (accounts receivables, accounts payables and inventory) to an optimum level.

## REFERENCES

1. Deloof, M. (2003). "Does working capital management affect profitability of firms", *Vikalpa*, Vol.28 (2), pp.537-85.
2. Eljelly, A.M.A. (2004). "Liquidity-profitability trade off: An empirical investigation in an emerging market", *International Journal of Commerce and Management*, Vol. 14 (2), pp.48-61.
3. Raheman, A., and M. Nasr (2007). "Working capital management and profitability: case of Pakistani firms",

*International Review of Business Research,* Vol.3(2), pp.275-96.

4. Lazaridis, I., and D. Tryfonidis (2006). “Relationship between working capital management and profitability of listed companies in the Athens Stock Exchange”, *Journal of Financial Management and Analysis,* Vol.19 (1), pp.26-35.
5. Shin,H.H and Soenen, L. (1998). “Efficiency of working capital and corporate profitability”, *Financial Practice and Education,* Vol.8 (2), pp.37-45.
6. Soenen, L.A (1993). “Cash conversion cycle and profitability”, *Journal of Cash Management,* Vol.13 (4), pp.53-58.
7. Padachi, K. (2006). “Trends in working capital management and its impact on firms performance: an analysis of Mauritian small manufacturing firms”, *International Review of Business Research Papers,* Vol. 2(2), pp.45-58.
8. Ali Uyar (2009). “The relationship of cash conversion cycle with firm size and profitability: an empirical investigation in Turkey”, *International Research Journal of Finance and Economics,* ISSN 1450-2887 (24).
9. Bodie, Z. and Merton, R.C. (2000). Finance, International Edition, Prentice-Hall, New Jersey.
10. Farris II, M.T. and Hutchison, P.D. (2002). “Cash-to cash: the new supply chain management metric”, *International Journal of Physical Distribution & Logistic Management,* Vol.32 (4), pp.288-298.
11. Garcia-Teruel, P.J. and Martinez-Solano, P. (2007). “Effects of working capital management on SME profitability”, *International Journal of Managerial Finance,* Vol.3 (2), pp.164-177.
12. Jordan, R.W. (2003). Fundamentals of Corporate Finance, 6th ed., McGraw-Hill Companies, Boston.
13. Jose, M.L., Lancaster, C. and Stevens, J.L. (1996). “Corporate returns and cash conversion cycles”, *Journal of Economics and Finance,* Vol.20 (1), pp.33-46.

14. Keown, A.J.., Martin, J.D., Petty, J.W. and Scott, D.F. (2003). Foundations of Finance, 4th ed., Pearson Education, New Jersey.

15. Lancaster, C.,Stevens, J.L. and Jennings, J.A. (1999). "Corporate liquidity and the significance of earnings versus cash flow: an examination of industry effects", *The Journal of Applied Business Research*, Vol.15 (3), pp.37-46.

16. Moss, J.D. and Stine, B. (1993). "Cash conversion cycle and firm size: a study of retail firms", *Managerial Finance*, Vol.19 (8), pp.25-34.

17. Schilling, G. (1996). "Working capital's role in maintaining corporate liquidity", *TMA Journal*, Vol.16 (5), pp.4-7.

18. Kamath, R. (1989). "How useful are common liquidity measures?," *Journal of Cash Management*, January/ February.

19. Richards, V.D. and Laughlin, E.J. (1980). "A cash conversion cycle approach to liquidity analysis", *Financial Management*, Spring.

20. Gentry, James A., R. Vaidyanathan and Hei Wai Lee (1990). "A weighted cash conversion cycle", *Financial Management*, Vol.19 (1), pp.90-99.

21. Sur, D., J.Biswas and P. Ganguly (2001). "Liquidity Management in Indian Private Sector Enterprises: a case study of Indian Primary Aluminium Producing Industry", *Indian Journal of Accounting*, pp.8-14.

22. Vijayakumar, A. and A. Venkatachalam (1995)."Working capital and profitability-an empirical analysis", *The Management Accountant*, pp.748-50.

23. Narware, P.C. (2004). "Working capital and profitability-an empirical analysis", *The Management Accountant*, pp.546-555.

24. Bardia, S.C. (2004). "Liquidity management: a case study of Steel Authority of India Ltd", *The Management Accountant*, pp.463-67.

25. Amarjit Gill, Nahum Biger, Neil Mathur (2010)."The

relationship between working capital management and profitability: evidence from the United States", *Business and Economics Journal*, Vol.2010:BEJ-10.

26. Falope OI, Ajilore OT (2009). "Working capital management and corporate profitability: evidence from panel data analysis of selected quoted companies in Nigeria", *Research Journal of Business management*, Vol.3, pp.73-84.
27. Mathuva D. (2009). "The influence of working capital management components on corporate profitability: a survey on Kenyan listed firms", *Research Journal of Business Management*, Vol.3, pp.1-11.
28. Hutchison, P.D., Farris II, M.T. and Anders, S.B. (2007). "Cash-to-cash analysis and management", *The CPA Journal*, Vol.77 (8), pp.42-47.
29. Shulman, J.M. and Dambolena, I.G. (1986). "Analysing corporate liquidity", *Journal of Cash Management*, September/October.
30. Wang, Y.J. (2002). "Liquidity management, operating performance and corporate value: evidence from Japan and Taiwan", *Journal of Multinational Financial Management*, Vol. 12, pp.159-69.
31. Amit K. Mallick and Debasish Sur (1998). "Working capital and profitability: A case study in interrelation", *The Management Accountant*, pp. 805-809.
32. Zelia Serrasqueiro (2009). "Growth and Profitability in Portuguese companies: A dynamic panel data approach", *Economic Interferences*, Vol.XI (26), pp.265-279.
33. Lyroudi, K. and Mc Carty, D. (1993). "An empirical investigation of the Cash Conversion Cycle of small business firms", *The Journal of Small Business Finance*, Vol. 2(2), pp. 465-482.
34. Katerina Lyroudi and Jhon Lazaridis (2000). "The cash conversion cycle and liquidity analysis of the food industry in Greece", *http:/papers.ssrn.com/paper.fat?* abstract-id = 236175.
35. Hager H.C.,(1976). " Cash Management and Cash Cycle",

*Management Accounting*, pp.19-21.

36. Largay,J. and C.Stickney.(1980). Cash flows, ratio analysis and the W.T.Grant company bankruptcy, Financial Analyst Journal, 36(4), pp.51-54.

# PART - III

# ANALYSIS OF EVA AND MVA

# 8

# Determinants of Market Value Added

## Some Empirical Evidence from Indian Automobile Industry

Corporate performance measurement is one of the emerging areas of research in finance among the researchers all over the world. Several studies are carried to find out what influences the share price (market price) of a company. Corporate performance is affected by various factors ranging from company specific, industry specific and economic variables. For long, there had been wide acceptance on the objective of the firm to maximize the value or wealth maximization. While the principle that fundamental objective of the business concerns is to increase the value of its shareholder's investment is widely accepted, there is substantially less agreement about how this is accomplished (Rappaport, 1986). As the lenders (debt and others), can protect themselves contractually, the objective can be narrowed down to maximizing stockholders value or stockholders wealth. When financial markets are efficient, the objective of maximizing stockholder wealth can be narrowed even further – to maximizing stock prices (Damodaran, 1996).

Even through stock price maximization as an objective is the narrowest of the value maximization objectives, it is the most prevalent one. It is argued that the stock prices are the most observable of all measures that can be used to judge the performance of a publicly traded firm. Besides this, the stock price is a real measure of stockholder wealth, since stockholders can sell their stock and receive the price now. While the responsibility of firm value maximization has to be fixed with the managers, using stock prices as a measure of periodic measure of corporate performance throws a serious problem. While many argue that the stock prices are not under the full control of the managers, there are many others who believe that stock price maximization leads to a short-term focus for manager-as the stock prices are determined by traders, short-term investors and analysts, all of whom hold the stock for short-periods and spend their time trying to forecast next quarter's earnings.

According to Rappaport (1986), within a business, there are seven drivers (sales growth rate, operating profit margin, income tax rate, working capital investment, fixed capital investment, cost of capital and forecast duration) that can be managed to create value. The theory suggests that improvement in these value drivers leads to an increase in shareholders' value. So, traditionally periodic corporate performance is most often measured using some variant of historical accounting income (eg. Net Profit, EPS) or some measures based on the accounting income (eg. ROI / ROCE). However, it had long been recognized that accounting income is not a consistent predictor of firm value creation and the traditional measures are not appropriate for evaluation of corporate performance.

An appropriate measure of corporate performance on one hand should be highly correlated to share holder return and on the other hand should be able to signal the extent of periodic wealth creation. A search for such a measure had been the trigger for the rapidly growing literature on Value Based Management (VBM). Among the set of popular VBM systems, a variant of the traditional residual income measure known as Economic Value Added (EVA) is arguably the most prominent. Therefore, the present study examines whether Economic Value Added has got any association with the shareholders wealth creation.

## REVIEW OF LITERATURE

Stern (1990) observed that EVA as a performance measure captures the true economic profit of an organisation. EVA-based financial management and incentive compensation scheme gives managers better-quality information and superior motivation to make decisions that will create the maximum shareholder wealth in an organisation. Stewart (1994) has expanded that adoption of the EVA system by more and more companies throughout the world clearly depicts that it provides an integrated decision - making framework, can reform energies and redirect resources to create sustainable value for companies, customers, employees, shareholders and for management. Grant (1996) found that EVA concept might have everlastingly changed the way real profitability is measured. EVA is a financial tool that focuses on the difference between company's after tax operating profit and its total cost of capital. Luber (1996) confirmed that a positive EVA over a period of time will also have an increasing MVA while negative EVA will bring down MVA as the market loses confidence in the competence of a company to ensure a handsome return on the invested capital.

Banerjee (1997) has conducted an empirical research to find the superiority of EVA over other traditional financial performance measures. ROI and EVA have been calculated for sample companies and a comparison of both showing the superiority of EVA over ROI. KPMG - BS study (1998) assessed top 100 companies on EVA, Sales, PAT and MVA criteria. The Survey has used the BS - 1000 list of companies using a composite index comprising sales, profitability and compounded annual growth rate of those companies covering the period 1996-97. Sixty companies have been found able to create positive Shareholder Value whereas 38 companies have been found to destroy it. Bao and Bao (1999) revealed that the EVA is positively and significantly correlated with the firm value. Vijayakumar (2008) empirically indicated that Net Operating profit After Tax (NOPAT) and Return on Net Worth (RONW) are the most significant variable with MVA followed by EVA and EPS. Vijayakumar (2010), in his study supports the hypothesis of Stern and Stewart's that MVA of firm was largely positively associated with EVA in all the selected sectors of Indian Automobile industry. It appears that the concept of EVA, as an emerging concept of financial management is fairly clear in the minds of almost all these researches whose studies have been reviewed above. In a fast changing business environment, the investor friendly financial performance measures may be the need of hour.

## MARKET VALUE ADDED (MVA)

While EVA measures shareholder value addition of firm in terms of its real economic performance, MVA measures market's assessment of firm's value. MVA thus measures value by the management over and above the capital invested in the company by investors.

**Market Value Added (MVA) = Market value of company - Capital employed**

For a public limited company, its market value is calculated as market value of its equity (number of shares outstanding times their share price) plus book value of debt (since market value of debt is generally not available). Capital employed is effectively the book value of investments in the business made-up of debt and equity. Effectively, the formula becomes

**Market Value Added (MVA) = Market value of equity - Book value of equity**

These items have been obtained from balance sheet statement of companies. Data for the market price existing on the close of financial year has been collected from the Economic Times, CMIE Prowess and Capitaline databases.

## SAMPLING SELECTION

Keeping in view the scope of the study, it is decided to include all the companies under automobile industry working before or from the year 1996-97 to 2008-09. There are 26 companies operating in the Indian automobile industry. But, owing to several constraints such as non-availability of financial statements or non-working of a company in a particular year etc., it is compelled to restrict the number of sample companies to 20. Out of 20 selected companies under Indian Automobile Industry, three Multinational Companies (MNC's) namely Hyundai Motors India Ltd, Honda Siel Cars India Ltd and Ford India Private Ltd were omitted because these companies established their operations in India in different accounting years. The companies under automobile industry are classified into three sectors namely; Commercial vehicles, Passenger cars and Multi-utility vehicles and Two and three wheelers. For the purpose of the study all the three sectors have been selected. It accounts for 73.23 per cent of the total companies available in the Indian automobile industry. The selected 20 companies include 5 under commercial vehicles, 3 under passenger cars and multi-utility vehicles and 9 under two and three wheeler sectors. It is inferred that sample company represents 98.74 percentage of market share in commercial vehicles, 79.76 percentage of market share in passenger cars and Multi-utility vehicles and 99.81 percentage of market share in two and three wheelers. Thus, the findings based on the occurrence of such representative sample may be presumed to be true representative of automobile industry in the country.

The study is mainly based on secondary data. The major source of data analysed and interpreted in this study related to all those companies selected is collected from "PROWESS" database, which is the most reliable on the empowered corporate database of Centre for Monitoring Indian Economy (CMIE). Besides prowess database, relevant secondary data have also been collected from BSE Stock Exchange Official Directory, CMIE Publications, Annual Survey of Industry, Business newspapers, Reports on Currency and Finance, Libraries of various Research Institutions, through Internet etc.

## MVA ANALYSIS

MVA is one of the external indicators which give the utmost satisfaction to the investors. From the investor's perspective, increase of the share price is always desirable. The most reliable measure of a management's long term success in adding value is known as "Market Value Added". Hence, it turns out to be very significant and important to analyse the MVA of selected companies during the study period. The present part of analysis examines in detail the MVA of sample companies. A ranking has been done with respect to MVA. Various statistical measures like mean, standard deviation, range, variance, skewness and kurtosis have been computed to understand the central tendency and dispersion of MVA of sample companies. Further Karl Pearson's correlation model has been adopted to establish the relationship between EVA and MVA. Eight variables have been selected which signify the wealth maximisation. Factor analysis has been done to test which among these variables contribute much towards maximizing shareholders wealth. The regression models were run to investigate the strength of relationship between the market value and each of the independent variables. Multiple regression models have been carried out to find out the extent of relationship between dependent variable (MVA) with the selected financial variables.

MVA based frequency distribution of sample companies has been displayed in Table 8.1. Looking at the

Table 8.1 it is inferred that around 6 per cent to 23.5 per cent of the sample companies have registered negative MVA during the year 1996-97 to 2007-08. However, in the terminal year 2008-09, around 53 per cent of companies (9 out of 17) registered negative MVA. Around 29 per cent to 59 per cent of sample companies are generating positive MVA, but it has been up to 50 crores. About 6 per cent to 35 per cent of the sample companies reported MVA of over Rs.250 crores to Rs.500 crores and around 12 per cent to 41 percent of the sample companies reported MVA of above Rs.1000 crores during the study period.

## TRENDS IN MVA – BASED RANKINGS

Trends in MVA of sample companies (year-wise rankings) and trends in MVA of top five and last five of the sample companies are presented in Table 8.2 and Table 8.4. The top five companies include Tata Motors Ltd (under commercial vehicles sector), Maruti Udyog Ltd, Mahindra and Mahindra Ltd (passenger cars and multiutility vehicles sector), Bajaj Auto Ltd and Hero Honda Motors Ltd (two and three wheelers sector). In eight out of thirteen years, Maruti Udyog Ltd and five out of thirteen years Tata Motors Ltd have been holding the first rank. However, in the terminal year 2008-09, Tata Motors Ltd MVA performance is quite discouraging. Among the last five companies includes Ashok Leyland Ltd belongs to commercial vehicles sector and Majestic Auto Ltd, Scooters India Ltd, Kinetic Engineering Ltd and Kinetic Motor Company Ltd belongs to two and three wheelers sector.

## RESULTS AND DISCUSSION ON STATISTICAL ANALYSIS OF MVA

Different statistical measures have been computed for understanding the central tendency and dispersion of MVA of sample companies. Company-wise statistical analysis of MVA is computed and presented in Table 8.3. It is observed from the table that all the selected companies except Ashok Leyland Ltd (94 per cent) have registered positive mean MVA, whereas Tata Motors Ltd stands first in the list with the higher average followed by Maruti Udyog Ltd, Mahindra and Mahindra Ltd, Bajaj Auto Ltd and Hero Honda Motors Ltd. The values of range show the high volatility in MVA and that of standard deviation and variance display the variation scale from central tendency and dispersion. Sixty five per cent of sample companies (11 out of 17) have their MVA positively skewed and fourty seven per cent of sample companies (8 out of 17) indicate positive kurtosis reflecting that observations cluster more and with longer tails.

## REGRESSION ANALYSIS OF SELECTED FINANCIAL VARIABLES

Multiple Regression Analysis has been carried out to explore the extent of relationship existed among dependent and independent variables in case of Indian automobile industry, and also to find out whether a particular independent variable emerges as the most explanatory variable. MVA is taken as the dependent variable and ROCE, Sales, ROS, EPS, ROTA, MP and PAT are taken as the independent variables. The results of multiple regression analysis are presented in Table 8.5 to Table 8.7.

It is evident from Table 8.5 that the values of correlation co-efficient are coming down and that of the adjusted R-square are going up till the 5$^{th}$ model is reached where the estimated standard error is also minimum. This explains that Sales, EPS and PAT are the best explanation of MVA of Indian automobile industry during the study period. The 6$^{th}$ model reveals that both the coefficients of correlation and adjusted R-Square have bared the sliding trends in their values. The Durbin- Watson model rules out any positive auto-correlation between the dependent and independent variables. The Table 8.6 presents the results of ANOVA analysis. The F- Statistics found that the value of the residual is the minimum in $5^{th}$ model and $6^{th}$ model supporting the observation of Table 8.6 and Table 8.7 the values are tested significant through F-Statistics even at 1 per cent level of significance. Table 8.7 is concerned to come across the most explanatory independent variable or set of variable of MVA in Indian automobile industry. Tested with t-statistics, the table transports that PAT is found significant if tested at 11.8 per cent level where as EPS and sales are observed quite significant even at 1 per cent level of significance. On the whole, Tables 8.5 to 8.6 fling beam on single one most significant variable i.e., EPS, Sales and PAT where in PAT stands third and Sales is the best one.

## CONCLUSION

The results of the study showed that 53 per cent to 76 percent of the sample companies have registered negative EVA during the terminal years of the study period. The top five companies in generating EVA include Bajaj Auto Ltd, Hero Honda Motors Ltd (two and three wheelers sector), Mahindra and Mahindra Ltd (passenger cars and multiutility vehicles sector), Ashok Leyland Ltd and Tata Motors Ltd (commercial vehicles sector). Further, the trends in MVA of sample companies showed Tata Motors Ltd (commercial vehicles sector), Maruti Udyog Ltd, Mahindra and Mahindra Ltd (passengers cars and multiutility vehicles), Bajaj Auto Ltd and Hero Honda Motors Ltd (two and three wheelers sector) are the top in the list. All the selected companies except Ashok Leyland Ltd have registered positive MVA, whereas Tata Motors Ltd stands first in the list with the higher average. Further, correlation analysis showed that EVA and MVA have been associated negatively in 65 per cent companies (11 out of 17) during the study period. The results of multiple regression analysis showed that sales, EPS and PAT are the best explanation of MVA of Indian automobile industry during the study period.

## REFERENCES

1. Stern Stewart (1990). "One way to build value in your firm. Executive compensation", *Financial executive,* pp. 51 -54.
2. Luber, R.B. (1996). "Who are the real wealth creators", *Fortune,* pp. 2 -3.
3. Grant, J. (1996). "Foundation of EVA for Investment Management; Just in Time, EVA", *Journal of Financial Management.* Vol. 23(1), pp. 41 - 45.
4. Banerjee, Ashok (1997). "Economic Value Added (EVA): A Better performance measure". *The Management Accountant,* pp. 886 -88,
5. KPMG-BS (1998). "Corporate India: An Economic value scoreboard". *The Strategy.* PP.22-25.
6. Bao, B.H., and Bao, D.H. (1999). "The Association between Firm value and Economic Value Added", *Indian Accounting Review,* Vol. 3(2), pp.161 -64.
7. Vijayakumar, A. (2008). "Linkage between Market Value Added (MVA) and other Financial variables: An analysis in Indian Automobile Industry", *Management and Labour Studies,* Vol. 33(4), pp. 504-521.
8. Vijayakumar, A. (2010). "Economic Value Added (EVA) and Market Value Added (MVA)-An empirical study of relationship". *College Sadhana,* Vol. 2(2), pp.141-148.

## TABLE 8.1

## MVA – FREQUENCY DISTRIBUTION OF SAMPLE COMPANIES (1996-97 TO 2008-09)

| MVA | 1996-97 | 1997-98 | 1998-99 | 1999-00 | 2000-01 | 2001-02 | 2002-03 | 2003-04 | 2004-05 | 2005-06 | 2006-07 | 2007-08 | 2008-09 |
|---|---|---|---|---|---|---|---|---|---|---|---|---|---|
| Negative | 1 (5.9) | 2 (11.8) | - | 1 (5.9) | 2 (11.8) | 1 (5.9) | 1 (5.9) | - | 1 (5.9) | 3 (17.6) | 3 (17.6) | 4 (23.5) | 9 (52.9) |
| Up to Rs. 250Cr | 7 (41.1) | 7 (41.1) | 10 (58.8) | 8 (47.0) | 8 (47.0) | 9 (52.9) | 7 (41.1) | 7 (41.1) | 7 (41.1) | 5 (29.4) | 7 (41.1) | 9 (52.9) | 6 (35.3) |
| Rs.250 Cr to Rs.500 Cr | 3 (17.6) | 3 (17.6) | 2 (11.8) | 2 (11.8) | 2 (11.8) | 1 (5.9) | 2 (11.8) | 3 (17.6) | 2 (11.8) | 6 (35.3) | 4 (23.5) | 1 (5.9) | - |
| Rs.500 Cr to Rs.1000 Cr | 2 (11.8) | 1 (5.9) | - | 2 (11.8) | 1 (5.9) | - | 2 (11.8) | - | 3 (17.6) | 1 (5.9) | - | 1 (5.9) | - |
| Above Rs.1000 Cr | 4 (23.5) | 4 (23.5) | 5 (29.4) | 4 (23.5) | 4 (23.5) | 6 (35.3) | 5 (29.4) | 7 (41.1) | 4 (23.5) | 2 (11.8) | 3 (17.6) | 2 (11.8) | 2 (11.8) |
| Total | 17 (100) | 17 (100) | 17 (100) | 17 (100) | 17 (100) | 17 (100) | 17 (100) | 17 (100) | 17 (100) | 17 (100) | 17 (100) | 17 (100) | 17 (100) |

Figures in brackets denote percentage to total.

***Source :*** Computed.

## TABLE 8.2

## TRENDS IN MVA (YEAR-WISE)

| Company | 96-97 | 97-98 | 98-99 | 99-00 | 00-01 | 01-02 | 02-03 | 03-04 | 04-05 | 05-06 | 06-07 | 07-08 | 08-09 |
|---|---|---|---|---|---|---|---|---|---|---|---|---|---|
| Ashok Leyland Ltd | 6 | 7 | 5 | 6 | 5 | 5 | 10 | 5 | 17 | 15 | 16 | 15 | 15 |
| Tata Motors Ltd | 1 | 3 | 7 | 4 | 4 | 4 | 6 | 7 | 1 | 1 | 1 | 1 | 17 |
| Bajaj Tempo Ltd | 7 | 9 | 8 | 8 | 8 | 9 | 8 | 8 | 10 | 4 | 8 | 11 | 12 |
| Eicher Motors Ltd | 16 | 14 | 10 | 11 | 11 | 8 | 9 | 9 | 6 | 6 | 6 | 7 | 4 |
| Swaraj Mazda Ltd | 14 | 13 | 12 | 13 | 13 | 12 | 11 | 10 | 9 | 8 | 7 | 6 | 8 |
| Hindustan Motors Ltd | 13 | 16 | 17 | 17 | 17 | 17 | 7 | 13 | 8 | 3 | 4 | 4 | 6 |
| Mahindra and Mahindra Ltd | 4 | 5 | 4 | 5 | 6 | 7 | 5 | 4 | 2 | 2 | 2 | 2 | 2 |
| Maruti Udyog Ltd | 2 | 1 | 1 | 1 | 1 | 1 | 1 | 1 | 3 | 17 | 17 | 16 | 1 |
| Bajaj Auto Ltd | 3 | 2 | 2 | 3 | 3 | 3 | 2 | 3 | 5 | 7 | 5 | 9 | 14 |
| LML Ltd | 8 | 6 | 9 | 9 | 9 | 10 | 12 | 12 | 11 | 10 | 9 | 5 | 3 |
| Maharashtra Scooters Ltd | 12 | 10 | 11 | 12 | 14 | 11 | 13 | 11 | 13 | 9 | 10 | 10 | 11 |
| TVS Motor Company Ltd | 9 | 8 | 6 | 7 | 7 | 6 | 4 | 6 | 7 | 5 | 15 | 3 | 13 |
| Kinetic Motor Company Ltd | 10 | 11 | 13 | 10 | 10 | 13 | 14 | 15 | 12 | 11 | 12 | 8 | 5 |

**TABLE 8.2 (CONTINUED)**

**TRENDS IN MVA (YEAR-WISE)**

| Company | 96-97 | 97-98 | 98-99 | 99-00 | 00-01 | 01-02 | 02-03 | 03-04 | 04-05 | 05-06 | 06-07 | 07-08 | 08-09 |
|---|---|---|---|---|---|---|---|---|---|---|---|---|---|
| Hero Honda Motors Ltd | 5 | 4 | 3 | 2 | 2 | 2 | 3 | 2 | 4 | 16 | 3 | 17 | 16 |
| Kinetic Engineering Ltd | 11 | 12 | 14 | 14 | 12 | 14 | 15 | 16 | 15 | 12 | 13 | 13 | 10 |
| Majestic Auto Ltd | 15 | 15 | 16 | 15 | 15 | 15 | 16 | 14 | 14 | 14 | 14 | 14 | 9 |
| Ashok Leyland Ltd | 17 | 17 | 15 | 16 | 16 | 16 | 17 | 17 | 16 | 13 | 11 | 12 | 7 |

***Source :*** Computed

## TABLE 8.3
## COMPANY-WISE STATISTICAL ANALYSIS OF MVA

| Company | Mean | SD | CV | CAGR | Variance | Skewness | Kurtosis | Max. | Min. |
|---|---|---|---|---|---|---|---|---|---|
| Ashok Leyland Ltd | -84.28 | 1465.73 | -17.39 | 22.07 | 2148356 | -0.53 | 0.64 | 2468.99 | -3234.77 |
| Tata Motors Ltd | 7697.11 | 9728.89 | 1.26 | 4.04 | 94651370 | 1.16 | 0.80 | 29814.51 | -4234.95 |
| Bajaj Tempo Ltd | 231.53 | 159.31 | 0.69 | -9.55 | 25378 | -0.70 | 2.14 | 519.06 | -146.10 |
| Eicher Motors Ltd | 196.44 | 179.53 | 0.91 | 21.58 | 32232.14 | 1.06 | 1.02 | 620.32 | 12.44 |
| Swaraj Mazda Ltd | 141.42 | 125.81 | 0.89 | 0.97 | 15828.99 | 0.36 | -1.99 | 306.09 | 21.88 |
| Hindustan Motors Ltd | 196.96 | 252.26 | 1.28 | 8.71 | 63637.58 | 0.64 | -1.16 | 664.39 | -84.34 |
| Mahindra and Mahindra Ltd | 4604.43 | 5275.99 | 1.15 | 9.99 | 27836041 | 1.28 | 0.05 | 15304.25 | 417.72 |
| Maruti Udyog Ltd | 6420.60 | 6750.5 | 1.05 | -2.34 | 5E+07 | -1.00 | -0.49 | 14145 | -6021 |
| Bajaj Auto Ltd | 3486.52 | 3232.30 | 0.93 | -27.14 | 10447752 | 0.31 | -1.08 | 9212.27 | -786.10 |
| LML Ltd | 183.25 | 86.20 | 0.47 | -1.96 | 7430.24 | 0.20 | -0.52 | 343.08 | 40.16 |
| Maharashtra Scooters Ltd | 77.43 | 86.99 | 1.12 | 8.90 | 7566.73 | -0.09 | 1.55 | 252.59 | -109.97 |
| TVS Motor Company Ltd | 499.57 | 750.65 | 1.50 | 9.59 | 563474.20 | 0.20 | 0.40 | 1800.73 | -755.82 |
| Kinetic Motor Company Ltd | 73.63 | 41.52 | 0.56 | -1.60 | 1723.60 | 0.86 | -0.89 | 146.01 | 33.80 |
| Hero Honda Motors Ltd | 2404.70 | 3831.54 | 1.59 | 13.54 | 14680683 | 0.11 | -0.34 | 9662.88 | -3587.26 |
| Kinetic Engineering Ltd | 29.43 | 27.35 | 0.93 | -5.46 | 748.14 | -1.48 | 5.19 | 74.89 | -45.81 |
| Majestic Auto Ltd | 17.64 | 13.65 | 0.77 | -0.31 | 186.22 | -0.11 | -0.21 | 39.32 | -7.3 |
| Scooters India Ltd | 20.08 | 32.55 | 1.62 | 14.87 | 1059.40 | 0.90 | -0.38 | 86.74 | -17.27 |

***Source :*** Computed

## TABLE 8.4

## RANKING BASED ON THIRTEEN YEARS AVERAGE OF MVA - COMPARISON (Top 5 Companies and Last 5 Companies)

| MARKET VALUE ADDED | | | |
|---|---|---|---|
| **Top Five Companies** | **Mean Value (Rs. in Crores)** | **Last Five Companies** | **Mean Value (Rs. in Crores)** |
| Tata Motors Ltd | 7697.11 | Ashok Leyland Ltd | -84.28 |
| Maruti Udyog Ltd | 6420.60 | Majestic Auto Ltd | 17.64 |
| Mahindra and Mahindra Ltd | 4604.43 | Scooters India Ltd | 20.08 |
| Bajaj Auto Ltd | 3486.52 | Kinetic Engineering Ltd | 29.43 |
| Hero Honda Motors Ltd | 2404.70 | Kinetic Motor Company Ltd | 73.63 |

***Source :*** Computed

## TABLE 8.5

## MVA AND OTHER INDEPENDENT VARIABLES - MODEL SUMMARY (WHOLE INDUSTRY)

| Model | R | R Square | Adjusted R Square | Std. Error of the Estimate | Durbin-Watson |
|---|---|---|---|---|---|
| 1. | .600[a] | .360 | .339 | 3312.12 | |
| 2. | .600[b] | .360 | .342 | 3304.38 | |
| 3. | .600[c] | .360 | .345 | 3296.78 | |
| 4. | .600[d] | .359 | .348 | 3289.43 | |
| 5. | .599[e] | .359 | .350 | 3282.24 | |
| 6. | .593[f] | .352 | .346 | 3293.25 | .940 |

a. Predictors: (Constant), ROCE, SALES, ROS, EPS, ROTA, MP, PAT
b. Predictors: (Constant), SALES, ROS, EPS, ROTA, MP, PAT
c. Predictors: (Constant), SALES, EPS, ROTA, MP, PAT
d. Predictors: (Constant), SALES, EPS, ROTA, PAT
e. Predictors: (Constant), SALES, EPS, PAT
f. Predictors: (Constant), SALES, EPS
g. Dependent Variable: MVA

***Source :*** Computed.

## TABLE 8.6

## MVA AND OTHER INDEPENDENT VARIABLES - ANOVA (WHOLE INDUSTRY)

| Model | | Sum of Squares | df | Mean Square | F | Sig. |
|---|---|---|---|---|---|---|
| 1. | Regression | 1.312E9 | 7 | 1.874E8 | 17.086 | .000[a] |
| | Residual | 2.337E9 | 213 | 1.097E7 | | |
| | Total | 3.649E9 | 220 | | | |
| 2. | Regression | 1.312E9 | 6 | 2.187E8 | 20.027 | .000[b] |
| | Residual | 2.337E9 | 214 | 1.092E7 | | |
| | Total | 3.649E9 | 220 | | | |
| 3. | Regression | 1.312E9 | 5 | 2.624E8 | 24.141 | .000[c] |
| | Residual | 2.337E9 | 215 | 1.087E7 | | |
| | Total | 3.649E9 | 220 | | | |
| 4. | Regression | 1.311E9 | 4 | 3.279E8 | 30.301 | .000[d] |
| | Residual | 2.337E9 | 216 | 1.082E7 | | |
| | Total | 3.649E9 | 220 | | | |
| 5. | Regression | 1.311E9 | 3 | 4.370E8 | 40.561 | .000[e] |
| | Residual | 2.338E9 | 217 | 1.077E7 | | |
| | Total | 3.649E9 | 220 | | | |
| 6. | Regression | 1.284E9 | 2 | 6.422E8 | 59.211 | .000[f] |
| | Residual | 2.364E9 | 218 | 1.085E7 | | |
| | Total | 3.649E9 | 220 | | | |

a. Predictors: (Constant), ROCE, SALES, ROS, EPS, ROTA, MP, PAT
b. Predictors: (Constant), SALES, ROS, EPS, ROTA, MP, PAT
c. Predictors: (Constant), SALES, EPS, ROTA, MP, PAT
d. Predictors: (Constant), SALES, EPS, ROTA, PAT
e. Predictors: (Constant), SALES, EPS, PAT
f. Predictors: (Constant), SALES, EPS
g. Dependent Variable: MVA

***Source:*** Computed

## TABLE 8.7

## MVA AND OTHER INDEPENDENT VARIABLES COEFFICIENTS (WHOLE INDUSTRY)

| Model | | Unstandardized Coefficients | | Standardized Coefficients | t | Sig. |
|---|---|---|---|---|---|---|
| | | B | Std. Error | Beta | | |
| 1 | (Constant) | 124.091 | 293.846 | | .422 | .673 |
| | EPS | 19.065 | 3.910 | .289 | 4.876 | .000 |
| | SALES | .472 | .096 | .606 | 4.910 | .000 |
| | PAT | -1.835 | 1.272 | -.183 | -1.443 | .151 |
| | MP | .264 | 1.322 | .015 | .200 | .842 |
| | ROS | -.664 | 5.939 | -.006 | -.112 | .911 |
| | ROTA | -2.070 | 9.044 | -.015 | -.229 | .819 |
| | ROCE | .069 | 2.266 | .002 | .030 | .976 |
| 2. | (Constant) | 123.714 | 292.896 | | .422 | .673 |
| | EPS | 19.072 | 3.894 | .289 | 4.898 | .000 |
| | SALES | .471 | .096 | .605 | 4.922 | .000 |
| | PAT | -1.835 | 1.269 | -.183 | -1.446 | .150 |
| | MP | .266 | 1.317 | .015 | .202 | .840 |
| | ROS | -.638 | 5.861 | -.006 | -.109 | .913 |
| | ROTA | -1.967 | 8.369 | -.014 | -.235 | .814 |
| 3. | (Constant) | 122.627 | 292.052 | | .420 | .675 |
| | EPS | 19.022 | 3.858 | .288 | 4.930 | .000 |
| | SALES | .473 | .095 | .607 | 4.974 | .000 |
| | PAT | -1.845 | 1.262 | -.184 | -1.461 | .145 |
| | MP | .256 | 1.311 | .014 | .196 | .845 |
| | ROTA | -2.090 | 8.274 | -.015 | -.253 | .801 |
| 4. | (Constant) | 149.254 | 257.820 | | .579 | .563 |
| | EPS | 18.983 | 3.844 | .287 | 4.938 | .000 |
| | SALES | .475 | .094 | .610 | 5.042 | .000 |
| | PAT | -1.778 | 1.213 | -.178 | -1.466 | .144 |
| | ROTA | -1.861 | 8.173 | -.013 | -.228 | .820 |
| 5. | (Constant) | 151.220 | 257.111 | | .588 | .557 |
| | EPS | 18.779 | 3.731 | .284 | 5.034 | .000 |
| | SALES | .478 | .093 | .614 | 5.139 | .000 |
| | PAT | -1.844 | 1.175 | -.184 | -1.570 | .118 |
| 6. | (Constant) | 207.417 | 255.463 | | .812 | .418 |
| | EPS | 19.531 | 3.712 | .296 | 5.261 | .000 |
| | SALES | .349 | .044 | .448 | 7.976 | .000 |

Dependent Variable : MVA

***Source :*** Computed

# 9

# EVA and MVA of Indian Automobile Industry

## An Empirical Study of Relationship

Corporate organizations that are increasingly moving into globalization and towards a perfect market place describe the internationally viable working environment at the very outset. At present, the industry is faced with stiff competition, consolidation, rapid technological advancement and obsolescence, high R&D costs and talent retention. Some strategy – focused organizations are looking at growth beyond competition, defining for their expansion path that would sustain their leadership in a world shaped by continuously evolving market forces. They thus have to think over the operational excellence through product innovation to evolve future projections for long-standing growth framework. Economic Value Added (EVA) appears to provide the modus operandi for this self- propelling growth model. EVA holds a company accountable for the cost of capital it used to expand and operate its business and attempts to show whether a company is creating a real value for its shareholders. Maximising EVA consistently would lead to maximisation of market capitalization.

Market Value Added (MVA) is a measure of shareholder's wealth. If the corporate objective is to enhance shareholder's wealth, it can be achieved by improving MVA. MVA is the difference between the market value of invested capital and book value of invested capital. MVA is the absolute rupee spread between a company's market value and its capital. It represents the stock markets assessment as of a particular time of the net present value of all a company's past and projected capital projects. Therefore, maximizing MVA should be the primary objective for any company that is concerned about its shareholders welfare. A company's EVA is the fuel that fires up its MVA. Thus, EVA is the internal measure of corporate performance and MVA is the external measure of corporate performance.

The evidence of the majority of the empirical studies regarding EVA suggests that there is a positive relationship between EVA and shareholder value creation, measured by Market Value Added (MVA). However, when the explaining power of EVA versus traditional performance measures regarding equity market value or returns is considered, the results are mixed. Thus, an attempt has been made in this paper to find the relevance of Stern and Stewart's claim and the hypothesis that MVA of the firm is largely positive associated with or driven by its EVA generating capacity in Indian context.

A brief review of empirical study related to EVA and MVA is presented in Section I. Section II discusses the methodology on which the empirical analysis is based. Section III gives analysis of EVA and MVA trends for the full sample companies. Section IV comprises of empirical relationship between EVA, MVA and other financial variables. Section V summarises the main findings and policy perspective in the context of the Indian Automobile industry.

## INFERENCE ON EVA AND MVA – RE-VISITING THE EXISTING RESEARCHES

Stern (1990) observed that EVA as a performance measure captures the true economic profit of an organisation. EVA-based financial management and incentive compensation scheme gives manager better – quality information and superior motivation to make decisions that will create the maximum shareholders wealth in an organisation. Stewart (1994) has expanded that adoption of EVA system by more and more companies throughout the world clearly depicts that it provides an integrated decision making framework, can reforms energies and redirect resources to create sustainable value for companies, customers, employees, shareholders and for management. Grant (1996) found that EVA concept may have everlastingly changed the way real profitability is measured. EVA is a financial tool that focuses on the difference between company's after tax operating profit and its total cost of capital. Luber (1996) confirmed that a positive EVA over a period of time will also have an increasing MVA while negative EVA will bring down MVA as the market looses confidence in the competence of a company to ensure a handsome return on the invested capi tal.

Banerjee (1997) has conducted an empirical research to find the superiority of EVA over other traditional financial performance measures. ROI and EVA has been calculated for sample companies and a comparison of both showing the superiority of EVA over ROI. Ethiraj (1998) derived those stock prices moves up as a company adopts EVA as an internal performance criterion. Anand, et al. (1999) revealed that EVA and MVA are better measures of business performance that NOPAT and EPS in terms of shareholders' value creation and competitive advantage of a firm. Bao and Bao (1999) revealed that the EVA is positively and significantly correlated with the firm value. Harihar (1999)[9] highlighted some myths regarding EVA. According to him, EVA calculations are not simple and need a lot of adjustments in the financial books. Further, EVA figures can be manipulated to suit the needs of management. Thenmozhi (1999) compared EVA with some other traditional measure of corporate performance viz. ROI, EPS, RONW, ROE, ROCE etc.. She has referred to some of the shortcomings of the concept of EVA but maintain that EVA is a better measure of corporate performance. Riceman, *et al.* (2002) argued that the EVA is a performance measure that is being used by an increasing number of companies, but academic research on EVA is limited.

Bardia (2002) revealed that in a dynamic environment a common investor finds it increasingly difficult to monitor his investments. EVA guides the investors in evaluating the performance of the company and monitoring their investments. Stern, Joel (2003) presented the results of Stern Stewart's research on Indian companies, which shows considerable need to improve the wealth creation performance and allocation of capital in the Indian economy. He explained how the effective implementation of the EVA framework could be a solution to address this problem. EVA, as an emerging concept of financial management appears that the concept is fairly clear in the minds of almost all these researches whose studies have been reviewed above. In a fast changing business environment, the investor friendly financial performance measures may, perhaps, compose this corridor full of spanking new air.

## METHODOLOGY

### Market Value Added (MVA)

While EVA measures shareholder value addition of firm in terms of its real economic performance, MVA measures market's assessment of firm's value. MVA thus measures value by the management over and above the capital invested in the company by investors.

**Market Value Added (MVA) = Market value of company - Capital employed**

For a public limited company, its market value is calculated as market value of its equity (number of shares outstanding times their share price) plus book value of debt (since market value of debt is generally not available). Capital employed is effectively the book value of investments in the business made-up of debt and equity. Effectively, the formula becomes -

**Market Value Added (MVA) = Market value of equity - Book value of equity**

These items have been obtained from balance sheet statement of companies. Data for the market price existing on the close of financial year has been collected from the Economic Times, CMIE Prowess and Capitaline databases.

**Economic Value Added (EVA)**

EVA introduced by Stern Stewart & company is an incarnation of Residual Income concept. Stewart defined 'EVA as an estimate of true economic profit, the amount by which earnings exceed or fall short of required minimum rate of return investors could get by investing in other securities of comparable risk'. It is the net operating profit minus the appropriate charge for the opportunity cost of capital invested in an enterprise (both debt and equity).

Expressed as a formula, EVA for a given period can be written as:

**EVA = NOPAT - COST OF CAPITAL EMPLOYED**

**= NOPAT – (WACC x CE)**

Where

NOPAT - Net Operating Profit After Taxes but before financing costs

WACC - Weighted Average Cost of Capital; and

CE - Capital Employed

(or)

equivalently, if rate of return is defined as NOPAT / CAPITAL , this turns into a perhaps more revealing formula:

**EVA = (RATE OF RETURN – COST OF CAPITAL) X CAPITAL**

Where

Rate of return - NOPAT / CAPITAL

Capital Employed - Total of balance sheet minus non-interest bearing debt in the beginning of the year.

Cost of Capital - [Cost of equity X proportion of equity from capital] + [(cost of debt X proportion of debt from capital) X (1-tax rate)]

Cost of capital or weighted average cost of capital is the average cost of both equity capital and interest bearing debt.

**Cost of debt ($K_d$)**

Cost of debt refers to the average rate of interest the company pays for its debt obligations. Cost of debt ($K_d$) has been computed as:

$$K_d = \text{Total interest expenses X (1-Effective tax rate) / Beginning total borrowings}$$

While calculating beginning borrowing all short-term as well as long-term borrowings has to be included as all debts are interests bearing. Therefore, interest paid in the financial year has been considered as total interest expenses.

**Cost of equity ($K_e$)**

To find out cost of equity ($K_e$), Capital Assets Pricing Model (CAPM) has been used. This model holds that firms' equity cost is the composition of risk free rate of return for a stock plus premium representing the volatility of share prices. According to this model, $K_e$ is the shareholders' expected rate of return and this expected rate of return ($R_j$) is as follows:

$$R_j = R_f + \beta \text{ X } (R_m - R_f)$$

Where, $R_f$ = Risk free rate of return,

$R_m$ = Market rate of return, and

$\beta$ = Sensitivity of the share price in relation to the market index

The interest rate of Government securities has been considered as a proxy for risk free rate of return. The market rate of return has been calculated by using Index Numbers of Security Prices (Bombay Stock Exchange) from year to year basis. The yearly return of the index numbers has been computed by using the following formula:

**$R_m$ = [(Index number for current year – Index number for previous Year) / (Index number of previous year)] x 100**

Beta ($\beta$) is the risk-free co-efficient which measures the volatility of a given script of a company with respect to volatility of market. It is calculated by comparing return on a share to return in the stock market. Mathematically, beta is the statistical measure of volatility. It is calculated as covariance of daily return on the stock market indices and the return on daily share prices of a particular company, divided by variance of return on daily stock market indices. The Beta co-efficient has been calculated as follows:

$$\beta_j = \mathbf{COV_{im}} / \sigma_m^2$$

where, $\beta_j$ - is the Beta of the security in the question

$COV_{im}$ - stands for co-variance between the return of security and return of market, and

$\sigma_m^2$ - stands for the variance of market return

Keeping in view the scope of the study, it is decided to include all the companies under automobile industry working before or from the year 1991-92 to 2003-04. There are 26 companies operating in the Indian automobile industry. But, owing to several constraints such as non-availability of financial statements or non-working of a company in a particular year etc., it is compelled to restrict the number of sample companies to 18. The companies under automobile industry are classified into three sectors namely; Commercial vehicles, Passenger cars and multiutility vehicles and Two and three wheelers. For the purpose of the study all the three sectors have been selected. It accounts for 69.23 per cent of the total companies available in the Indian automobile industry. The selected 18 companies include 5 under commercial vehicles, 4 under passenger cars and multiutility vehicles and 9 under two and three wheeler sectors. It is inferred that sample company represents 98.74 percentage of market share in commercial vehicles, 89.76 percentage of market share in passenger cars and multiutility vehicles and 99.81 percentage of market share in two and three wheelers. Thus, the findings based on the occurrence of such representative sample may be presumed to be true representative of automobile industry in the country.

The period 1991-92 to 2003-04 is selected for this study. The span chosen for the study is the period of the beginning of liberalization measures introduced by the Government of India. Hence, the period 1991-92 to 2003-04 is an era of growth of corporate performance in the manufacturing sector, particularly automobile industry and has got genuine economic significance of its own. The study is mainly based on secondary data. The major source of data analysed and interpreted in this study related to all those companies selected is collected from "PROWESS" database, which is the most reliable on the empowered corporate database of Centre for Monitoring Indian Economy (CMIE). Besides prowess database, relevant secondary data have also been collected from BSE Stock Exchange Official Directory, CIME Publications, Annual Survey of Industry, Business newspapers, Reports on Currency and Finance, Libraries of various Research Institutions, through Internet etc.

## ANALYSIS OF EVA AND MVA TRENDS

### EVA Trends

EVA - based performance framework not only provides a far more accurate report card on corporate financial performance than conventional measures, but also has considerable implications for companies on how to make strategic decisions and manage the healthier financial performance in their pursuit of shareholder value. EVA created by the selected Automobile industry during the study period. i.e. 1991-92 to 2003-04 is depicted in Table 9.1. The table shows that out of eighteen industry, sixteen industry has generated positive EVA during the study period except in the year 1992-93, 1994-95, 1996-97, 1998-99, 2002-03 and 2003-04 and two companies have destroyed their shareholders' wealth during the same period. In the year 1992-93 the number of companies generating negative EVA went up to sixteen, eleven in the year 1998-99 and ten in the year 2002-03. It would be worthwhile to mention here that during this period the economy of the nation faced showery time. Political instability at Union Government level and Kargil War may be the qualified grounds to such downhill state of affairs in the economy. In the year 2001-02 in which Indian economy revealed the optimistic wind, witnessed that sixteen companies are created wealth for the shareholders and only two have destroyed the same. However the number of companies generates negative EVA increased to ten in the year 2002-03. It may be extrapolated that the year 2003-04 may be able to see the economy in a slightly good health yet again.

It may be observed from Table 9.1 that LML Ltd was the only company out of eighteen companies who have been constantly generating the positive EVA all the way throughout the period of study. On the other hand, Daewoo Motors Indian Ltd was the only company who has been annihilating the wealth of shareholders right through the period under reference except in the year 1993-94 and 1995-96. Ashok Leyland Ltd, Eicher Motors Ltd, TVS Motors India Ltd, Bajaj Auto Ltd and Hero Honda Motors Ltd created positive EVA during the major part of thirteen years period. Rest of the companies displayed high instability on this front. On the whole the Table 9.1 concludes that about one-third (6 out 18), of the sample companies have been able to govern affirmative EVA during period under study whereas remaining companies make feasible to append a very little to the value of shareholders.

Table 9.1 also presents EVA - based ranking of sample companies. It is evident from the table that companies like LML Ltd, Bajaj Auto Ltd, Maruthi Udyog Ltd and Tata Motors Ltd are toping in the list during this study period. On the other pass, companies like Swaraj Mazda Ltd, Daewoo Motors India Ltd, Kinetic Engineering Ltd, Majestic Auto Ltd and Scooter India Ltd has been loosing the grounds. Rest of the companies has indexed unsteady position during the period of study period.

Table 9.2 presents sector - wise EVA of sample companies. It is evident from Table 9.2 that the mean EVA generated for the automobile industry was Rs.79.53 crores during the study period. The mean EVA generated was the highest in two and three wheelers sector followed by commercial vehicles and passenger cars and multiutility vehicles sector. Two and three wheelers sector and commercial vehicles sector should perform well in this regard because their average was more than the industry average. It is also evident from the table that all the selected sectors and whole industry witnessed very high fluctuation in their EVA during the study period. Table 9.2 further reported that the commercial vehicles, passenger cars and multiutility vehicles sectors and whole industry registered negative compound annual growth rate of EVA during the study period.

The economic value added of selected industry under commercial vehicles sector during the study period is also presented in Table 9.2. The mean EVA was the highest in Tata Motors Ltd, followed by Ashok Leyland Ltd, Eicher Motors Ltd, Swaraj Mazda Ltd and Bajaj Tempo Ltd. All the industry under the sector had registered very high fluctuation in their EVA during the study period. It is also evident from the table that two companies namely Tata Motors Ltd and Bajaj Tempo Ltd registered negative compound annual growth rate of EVA during the study period.

Table 9.2 depicts the EVA generated by the selected companies under passenger cars and multiutility vehicles sector during the study period. Table 9.2 portrays that Daewoo Motors India Ltd showed negative EVA throughout the study period except in the year 1993-94 and 1995-96. The mean EVA generated was the highest in Mahindra and Mahindra Ltd followed by Maruthi Udyog Ltd and Hindustan Motors Ltd. All the companies registered very high fluctuation in their EVA during the study period. Only Mahindra and Mahindra Ltd witnessed positive compound annual growth rate of EVA and rest of the company showed negative compound annual growth rate of EVA.

The EVA generated by the companies under two and three wheeler sectors during the study period is presented in Table 9.2. It is evident from the Table 2 that Majestic Auto Ltd generated negative EVA in majority of the years, followed by Scooters India Ltd. The rest of the companies had registered a mixed trend of EVA during the study period. Among the selected companies, Bajaj Auto Ltd, LML Ltd, Hero Honda Motors Ltd and TVS Motors India Ltd had shown improved performance with record to EVA generation during the study period. All the selected companies under this sector had registered very high fluctuation in their EVA during the study period. Kinetic Motors Company Ltd, Kinetic Engineering Ltd and Majestic Auto Ltd had registered negative compound annual growth rate of EVA and the rest of the companies showed positive compound annual growth rate of EVA during the study period.

## MVA TRENDS

Table 9.3 presents MVA calculation of selected companies of Indian Automobile industry. On the base of the table, it may be observed that out of 18 companies 15 companies have registered positive MVA throughout the study period. It indicates that the market value of these companies is dominating over the book value. On the other hand Hindustan Motors Ltd (1997-98, 1999-00, 2000-01 and

2001-02), Daewoo Motors Ltd (1997-98 and 1999-2004) and Scooters India Ltd (except 1998-99, 1999-00, 2001-02 and 2003-04) have registered negative MVA during the study period. It shows that the book value of these companies is dominated over the market value.

Table 9.3 also provides MVA based ranking. Glancing all the way through the table, it is noticed that companies like Maruthi Udyog Ltd, Bajaj Auto Ltd, Tata Motors Ltd, Ashok Leyland Ltd, Mahindra and Mahindra Ltd and TVS Motors India Ltd are topping the list and on the other side companies like Scooters India Ltd, Daewoo Motors India Ltd, Hindustan Motors Ltd, Majestic Auto Ltd and Kinetic Engineering Ltd are struggling in terms of MVA over the period.

Table 9.4 portrays whole automobile industry and sector wise information pertaining to MVA. It is evident from Table 9.4 that among the three sectors, passenger cars and multiutility vehicles sector have been generating highest market value added throughout the study period. This was due to the better market value added of Maruthi Udyog Ltd and Mahindra and Mahindra Ltd. It was followed by commercial vehicles sector and two and three wheelers. Table 9.4 also shows that all the selected sectors of automobile industry have been generating positive aggregate MVA throughout the period. The growth of MVA is more confident in case of passenger cars and multiutility vehicles whereas less consistent in case of commercial vehicles and two and three wheelers sector. Table also brings out that only the commercial vehicles sector had registered negative compound annual growth rate of MVA during the study period.

The market value added of selected companies under commercial vehicles sector during the study period is also presented in Table 9.4. Table 9.4 reveals that the mean MVA of Tata Motors Ltd were the highest followed by Ashok Leyland Ltd, Bajaj Tempo Ltd, Eicher Motors Ltd and Swaraj Mazda Ltd. Table 9.4 brings out that all the selected companies under the commercial vehicles sector had registered very high fluctuations in their MVA except Bajaj Tempo Ltd which registered moderate fluctuations during the study period.

Further, Table 9.4 provided that the two companies namely Tata Motors Ltd and Bajaj Tempo Ltd had registered negative compound annual growth rate of MVA and rest of the companies had positive compound annual growth rate of MVA during the study period.

Table 9.4 presents MVA of selected companies under passenger's cars and multiutility vehicles sector. The table shows that the companies like Maruthi Udyog Ltd and Mahindra and Mahindra Ltd are top in the list and it was followed by Hindustan Motors Ltd and Daewoo Motors Ltd. All the selected companies except Maruthi Udyog Ltd had registered very high fluctuation in their MVA during the study period. Table 9.4 also brings out values relating to compound annual growth rate of MVA of selected companies. It is evident from the table that Hindustan Motors Ltd and Daewoo Motors India Ltd had registered negative growth rate and rest of the companies had registered positive growth rate of MVA during the study period.

Table 9.4 brings out the values relating to MVA of selected companies under two and three wheelers. Table 9.4 showed that Bajaj Auto Ltd, Hero Honda Motors Ltd, TVS Motors India Ltd and LML Ltd comparatively top in the list. On the other hand, Scooters India Ltd and Majestic Auto Ltd are struggling on their front with regard to MVA during the study period. It is also noticed that all the selected companies have registered very high fluctuations in their MVA during the study period. The analysis of compound annual growth rate of MVA showed mixed trend among the selected companies under the sector during the study period.

## EMPIRICAL RELATIONSHIP

### MVA-EVA - Regression Analysis

In this section an attempt to find the relevance of Stern and Stewart's claim that MVA of the firm is largely positive association with or driven by its EVA generating capacity. The result of correlation co-efficient, linear regression, Durbin

- Watson model, F - statistics and t - statistics have been determined between dependent variable (MVA) and independent variable (EVA). The values hence obtained have their particular statistical sense. The regression co-efficient for EVA so worked out portrays the temperament of association between the dependent and particular independent variable. The t - statistics and F - statistics so calculated determine the level of significant or insignificant association between the variables. Durbin - Watson model allows the researcher to establish the auto-correlation, if any between dependent and independent variable (the desirable value is two and any value more than two signifies negative auto-correlation and vice versa); values of adjusted $R^2$ indicate the extent of variation in the dependent variable which may be explicated by independent variable (s) and the standard error speaks about the limits within which the estimated value as the dependent variable is expected to lie.

Table 9.5 offers the explanation about the regression analysis between MVA and EVA during the study period for the whole Automobile industry and its three sectors. Table 9.3 provides the values of R, R-square and adjusted R-square for the whole industry 0.165, 0.03 and – 0.06 respectively. It sounds that there exists poor relationship between MVA and EVA in Automobile industry, as the value of adjusted R-square in negative. Interestingly, the t and F statistics give the identical results but both of them lead to insignificant association between the variables under reference. It is evident from the table that the overall result in passenger cars and multiutility vehicles does not differ from whole industry and statistical association between MVA and EVA is again insignificant. Table 9.5 suggests that EVA is serially correlated in commercial vehicles and two and three wheelers sector and adjusted R-square value is also positive. The t and F statistics are resulting identical values and secure that in commercial vehicles and two and three wheelers sector relationship between MVA and EVA is fairly significant. However, the MVA-EVA analysis supports the hypothesis of Stern and Stewart's that MVA of firm is largely positive associated with EVA in all the selected sectors of Indian Automobile industry.

**Determinants of Market Value Added**

The purpose of this analysis whether a particular independent variable or a set of variables emerges as the most explanatory variable of the MVA during the study period. In order to meet this objective, multiple regression analysis has been considered on sector-wise and whole industry during the study period. The results of multiple regression analysis are presented in this section.

**Whole industry**

Table 9.6 brings out the determinants of market value added for whole Automobile industry during the study period. It is observed from the Table 9.6 that all the selected independent variables exists significant influence on MVA of Automobile industry during the study period. Co-efficient of determination, $R^2$ in the case is 0.90 implying that changes in MVA are predicated by these independent variables to the extent of 90 per cent. It is also evident from the table that ROCE is found in strong association with MVA followed by NOPAT, EPS and EVA. However, RONW is negatively related with MVA during the study period. The value of Adjusted $R^2$ and F value shows the good fitness of the model. From these regression results it can be concluded that all the selected independent variables are well explained by the MVA of Automobile industry during the study period.

**Commercial vehicles**

Table 9.7 portrays the results of multiple regression analysis for commercial vehicles sector. It is revealed from the Table 9.7 that all the selected independent variables that are found statistically significant with MVA of commercial vehicles sector during the study period. Co-efficient of determination, $R^2$ in this case is 0.75 implying that change in MVA is predicted by these independent variables to the extent of 75 per cent only. It is also found that EPS is strongly associated with MVA followed by ROCE, RONW, NOPAT and EVA during the study period. The value of F statistic and adjusted $R^2$ showed the good fitness of the model.

**Passenger cars and Multiutility vehicles**

Table 9.8 gives an account of multiple regression analysis between MVA and other financial variables in respect of passenger cars and multiutility vehicles sector. The result provided by this table witnessed that the variables noticed significantly associated with MVA are EVA, EPS, ROCE and NOPAT. The co-efficient of determination, $R^2$ in this case is 0.83 implying that changes in MVA is predicted by these independent variables to the extent of 83 per cent. Once again the ROCE has emerged as the most important variable in determining MVA of passenger cars and multiutility vehicles sector followed by NOPAT, EVA and EPS. The value of $R^2$ and F shows the good fitness of the model.

**Two and Three Wheelers**

Table 9.9 describes the results of multiple regression for determinants of MVA for two and three wheelers sector during the study period. It is explicit from the table that all the independent variables except ROCE significantly associated with MVA of two and three wheelers sector during the study period. Co-efficient of determination, $R^2$ in this case is 0.97 implying that changes in MVA is predicted by selected independent variables to the extent of 97 per cent. Among the selected independent variables, EPS is strongly associated with MVA followed by RONW, NOPAT, and EVA. However, the ROCE has not emerged as one of the most important variables explaining MVA in case of two and three wheelers sector. The value of t, F and adjusted $R^2$ sounds the good fitness of the model.

## CONCLUSION

EVA analysis has captivated much attention in the western countries both as a management innovation as well as stock market analysis. The recognition of such technique in Indian context shows to some extent diverse trends. Some corporate houses like Infoysis, BPL, HLL, NIIT, TCS, Godrej Soaps, etc. have started publishing EVA in their financial statements. Majority of companies are still not prepared to put in the EVA technique for evaluating their financial performances because of certain inherent difficulties associated with the computation. As the corporate most vital objective at this moment is to maximize shareholder value establishing a relationship between financial variables and the corporate objective is imperative. With this objective in mind, the present study intends to examine the relationship between shareholders wealth and financial variables in the case of Indian Automobile industry. The selected financial measures like EVA, EPS , ROCE, NOPAT and RONW have been compared with MVA. The multiple regression analysis has been carried out and the results revealed ROCM as the most significant related variable with MVA followed by EPS and EVA. This study suggests that the relationship between MVA and EVA is positively associated by supporting Stern Steward claim's and statistically significant. When all is said and done, EVA and MVA itself positions in an appearance as the most outstanding factors in the definitive analysis as having a decisive impact on a firm's value.

## REFERENCES

1. Stern, Joel (1990), "One way to build value in your firm, Executive compensation", *Financial Executive*, pp. 51-54.

2. Stewart, G. Bennet, (1994), "EVATM Fact and Fantasy", Journal of Applied *Corporate Finance*, pp. 71-84.

3. Grant, J (1996). "Foundation of EVA for investment managers: Just in time, EVA", *Journal of Financial Management*, Vol.23, No.1, p.41(8).

4. Luber, R. B. (1996), "Who are the real wealth creators". *Fortune*, pp.2-3.

5. Banerjee, Ashok (1997), "Economic Value Added (EVA): a better performance measure", *The Management Accountant*, pp.86-88.
6. Ethiraj, Govindaraj (1998), 'The EVA feather in the market cap', *The Economic Times*, p. 1.
7. Anand, Manoj, Garg, Ajay, and Arora, Asha (1999), "Economic value added : Business performance measure of shareholder value', *The Management Accountant*, pp.351-56.
8. Bao, B.H. and Bao, D.H., 'The Association between firm Value and Economic Value Added', *Indian Accounting Review*, Vol.3, No.2, pp.161-64.
9. Harihar,T.S.(1999), 'EVA prorating Myths', *Chartered Finance Analyst*, pp.8-9.
10. Thenmozhie. M. (1999), 'Economic value added as a measure of corporate performance', *The Indian Journal of Commerce*, Vol.52, No.4, pp. 72-85.
11. Riceman, S.S. and Cahan, S.F. (2002), "Do Managers Perform Better under EVA Bonus Schemes", Social Science Research Network Electronic Paper Collection, at http://oaoers.ssrb.cin.
12. Bardia, S.C.,(2002) "Economic Value Added: Overall Consideration", *Economic Challenger*, pp. 1-7.
13. Stern, Joel, (2003) " Workshop on Value - based Management," Organised by the ASCI, Hyderabad, pp. 21-22.

## TABLE 9.1
## EVA OF SAMPLE COMPANIES

*(Rs. in crores)*

| Sl.No | Companies | 91-92 | 92-93 | 93-94 | 94-95 | 95-96 | 96-97 | 97-98 | 98-99 | 99-00 | 00-01 | 01-02 | 02-03 | 03-04 |
|---|---|---|---|---|---|---|---|---|---|---|---|---|---|---|
| 1 | Ashok Leyland Ltd | 193.33 | -200.47 | 178.07 | 121.34 | 226.19 | 244.25 | 249.12 | 134.05 | 250.08 | 283.39 | 222.16 | 129.23 | 234.91 |
| | | (5) | (17) | (5) | (5) | (4) | (3) | (6) | (2) | (8) | (4) | (6) | (4) | (4) |
| 2 | Tata Motors Ltd | 272.29 | -343.86 | 467.12 | 477.77 | 777.68 | 433.04 | 961.36 | -900.70 | 1888.03 | 199.99 | 25.98 | -1937.03 | 360.56 |
| | | (1) | (18) | (1) | (1) | (1) | (1) | (1) | (18) | (1) | (6) | (10) | (17) | (3) |
| 3 | Bajaj Tempo Ltd | 30.84 | -14.37 | 20.79 | 13.21 | 28.86 | -4.88 | 11.12 | -53.81 | -14.84 | -4.04 | 1.59 | 30.78 | 24.88 |
| | | (9) | (9) | (11) | (11) | (11) | (15) | (13) | (12) | (17) | (16) | (16) | (6) | (11) |
| 4 | Eicher Motors Ltd | 5.63 | -1.62 | 4.06 | 15.63 | 18.21 | 14.28 | 8.58 | 3.33 | 22.81 | 23.00 | 22.82 | 5.21 | 38.26 |
| | | (15) | (5) | (15) | (10) | (12) | (10) | (16) | (5) | (13) | (9) | (13) | (8) | (8) |
| 5 | Swaraj Mazda Ltd | -2.47 | -0.25 | -0.08 | 4.52 | 11.60 | 10.71 | 10.46 | 4.54 | 7.08 | 8.85 | 12.48 | 7.43 | 18.62 |
| | | (18) | (3) | (17) | (14) | (15) | (11) | (14) | (4) | (16) | (11) | (14) | (7) | (12) |
| 6 | Hindustan Motors Ltd | 98.51 | -82.42 | 120.30 | 78.29 | 116.58 | 47.50 | 134.10 | -66.55 | 138.27 | 6.58 | 68.64 | -167.24 | -44.35 |
| | | (7) | (14) | (7) | (7) | (7) | (7) | (7) | (13) | (9) | (14) | (8) | (14) | (17) |
| 7 | Mahindra and Mahindra Ltd | 122.47 | -77.17 | 195.48 | 125.50 | 216.76 | 113.71 | 423.90 | -178.50 | 961.95 | 307.59 | 395.52 | -104.02 | 139.67 |
| | | (6) | (13) | (4) | (4) | (5) | (6) | (4) | (15) | (4) | (3) | (5) | (16) | (5) |
| 8 | Maruthi Udyog Ltd | 266.56 | -158.32 | 256.63 | 414.49 | 584.49 | 311.83 | 834.13 | -452.34 | 1419.86 | -39.45 | 621.12 | -2852.98 | 30.86 |
| | | (2) | (15) | (2) | (2) | (2) | (2) | (2) | (17) | (3) | (17) | (2) | (18) | (9) |
| 9 | Daewoo Motors India Ltd | -0.86 | -1.21 | 2.45 | -6.80 | 62.03 | -48.81 | -87.12 | -161.33 | -15.29 | -91.12 | -185.09 | -101.02 | -58.01 |
| | | (17) | (4) | (16) | (17) | (8) | (18) | (18) | (14) | (18) | (18) | (18) | (13) | (18) |

**TABLE 9.1 (CONTINUED) : EVA OF SAMPLE COMPANIES**

*(Rs. in crores)*

| Sl.No | Companies | 91-92 | 92-93 | 93-94 | 94-95 | 95-96 | 96-97 | 97-98 | 98-99 | 99-00 | 00-01 | 01-02 | 02-03 | 03-04 |
|---|---|---|---|---|---|---|---|---|---|---|---|---|---|---|
| **10** | **Bajaj Auto Ltd** | 242.82 | -175.98 | 231.55 | 278.45 | 414.44 | 237.60 | 535.21 | -425.16 | 1452.88 | 422.51 | 811.70 | 2223.75 | 87.48 |
| | | (4) | (16) | (3) | (3) | (3) | (4) | (3) | (16) | (2) | (1) | (1) | (1) | (7) |
| **11** | **LML Ltd** | 256.28 | 130.25 | 123.90 | 110.86 | 118.75 | 166.24 | 255.71 | 276.42 | 462.71 | 401.60 | 410.00 | 290.32 | 362.97 |
| | | (3) | (1) | (6) | (6) | (6) | (5) | (5) | (1) | (5) | (2) | (4) | (2) | (2) |
| **12** | **Maharastra Scooters Ltd** | 36.69 | -29.20 | 21.97 | 9.65 | 15.66 | -2.29 | 19.08 | -28.90 | 69.39 | 7.58 | 23.43 | 135.48 | 25.14 |
| | | (8) | (10) | (10) | (12) | (13) | (14) | (10) | (11) | (10) | (12) | (11) | (3) | (10) |
| **13** | **TVS Motors India Ltd** | 22.44 | 0.15 | 31.50 | 39.35 | 43.23 | 38.87 | 103.30 | 3.07 | 252.27 | 112.90 | 129.29 | -304.01 | 117.14 |
| | | (11) | (2) | (8) | (8) | (9) | (8) | (8) | (6) | (7) | (7) | (7) | (15) | (6) |
| **14** | **Kinetic Motors Company Ltd** | 9.14 | -7.98 | 6.57 | 4.14 | 7.01 | -0.15 | 9.10 | -1.65 | 27.00 | 19.09 | 28.47 | -33.18 | -21.16 |
| | | (14) | (8) | (13) | (15) | (16) | (13) | (15) | (9) | (12) | (10) | (9) | (10) | (15) |
| **15** | **Hero Honda Motors Ltd** | 2.31 | -5.59 | 28.46 | 22.32 | 29.46 | 37.81 | 85.38 | 39.97 | 278.14 | 254.86 | 496.11 | -34.30 | 494.32 |
| | | (16) | (7) | (9) | (9) | (10) | (9) | (9) | (3) | (6) | (5) | (3) | (11) | (1) |
| **16** | **Kinetic Engineering Ltd** | 12.78 | -4.96 | 9.09 | 6.83 | 12.15 | 5.98 | 15.03 | -1.09 | 36.60 | 23.11 | 22.93 | -38.55 | -40.10 |
| | | (13) | (6) | (12) | (13) | (14) | (12) | (11) | (8) | (11) | (8) | (12) | (12) | (16) |
| **17** | **Majestic Auto Ltd** | 28.41 | -49.00 | 5.45 | -5.97 | -4.18 | -15.16 | -1.07 | -1.97 | 14.78 | 6.99 | -5.47 | -27.78 | 6.31 |
| | | (10) | (12) | (14) | (16) | (17) | (17) | (17) | (10) | (14) | (13) | (17) | (9) | (13) |
| **18** | **Scooters India Ltd** | 15.46 | -37.27 | -0.38 | -7.88 | -7.27 | -14.68 | 12.05 | 1.05 | 10.24 | 3.72 | 3.55 | 94.98 | -1.90 |
| | | (12) | (11) | (18) | (18) | (18) | (16) | (12) | (7) | (15) | (15) | (15) | (5) | (14) |

**Figures in parenthesis denote EVA based ranking of selected companies.**

***Source:*** Computed

## TABLE 9.2

## EVA – SECTOR – WISE TRENDS (1991-92 - 2003-04)

| S. No | Industry | Mean (Rs.in crores) | CV | CAGR |
|---|---|---|---|---|
| 1. | Ashok Leyland Ltd | 174.28 | 0.71 | 15.70 |
| 2. | Tata Motors Ltd | 206.33 | 4.45 | -9.22 |
| 3. | Bajaj Tempo Ltd | 5.39 | 4.50 | -4.89 |
| 4. | Eicher Motors Ltd | 13.86 | 0.80 | 14.70 |
| 5. | Swaraj Mazda Ltd | 7.19 | 0.82 | 20.80 |
| | **Commercial Vehicles Sectors** | **81.41** | **2.42** | **-3.16** |
| 6. | Hindustan Motors Ltd | 34.48 | 2.82 | -22.40 |
| 7. | Mahindra & Mahindra Ltd | 131.30 | 3.41 | 2.50 |
| 8. | Maruthi Udyog Ltd | 95.14 | 10.55 | -17.30 |
| 9. | Daewoo Motors India Ltd | -53.24 | -1.32 | -8.77 |
| | **Passenger Cars and Multiutility Vehicles Sectors** | **51.92** | **7.42** | **-9.01** |
| 10. | Bajaj Auto Ltd | 487.47 | 1.42 | 19.60 |
| 11. | LML Ltd | 258.92 | 0.48 | 9.88 |
| 12. | Maharastra Scooters Ltd | 23.36 | 1.81 | 13.60 |
| 13. | TVS Motors Company Ltd | 45.35 | 2.77 | 16.00 |
| 14. | Kinetic Motors Co. Ltd | 3.57 | 4.87 | -0.73 |
| 15. | Hero Honda Motors Ltd | 133.02 | 1.40 | 30.50 |
| 16. | Kinetic Engineering Ltd | 4.60 | 4.84 | -4.13 |
| 17. | Majestic Auto Ltd | -3.74 | -5.15 | -2.53 |
| 18. | Scooters India Ltd | 5.51 | 5.46 | 11.00 |
| | **Two and Three Wheelers Sectors** | **105.27** | **0.92** | **20.80** |
| | **Whole Automobile Industry** | **79.53** | **2.45** | **-1.24** |

## TABLE 9.3
## MVA OF SAMPLE COMPANIES

*(Rs. in crores)*

| Companies | 91-92 | 92-93 | 93-94 | 94-95 | 95-96 | 96-97 | 97-98 | 98-99 | 99-00 | 00-01 | 01-02 | 02-03 | 03-04 |
|---|---|---|---|---|---|---|---|---|---|---|---|---|---|
| Ashok Leyland Ltd | 424.31 | 464.71 | 917.28 | 1190.49 | 1233.30 | 611.30 | 328.25 | 1027.56 | 511.40 | 676.71 | 1047.77 | 213.17 | 2468.99 |
| | (4) | (4) | (4) | (4) | (5) | (6) | (7) | (5) | (6) | (5) | (5) | (4) | (5) |
| Tata Motors Ltd | 6283.94 | 3503.05 | 6069.37 | 6444.12 | 10112.67 | 10700.65 | 4334.61 | 295.41 | 2345.58 | 2054.88 | 4359.15 | 727.81 | 1206.66 |
| | (2) | (2) | (2) | (2) | (1) | (1) | (3) | (7) | (4) | (4) | (4) | (4) | (7) |
| Bajaj Tempo Ltd | 305.25 | 159.37 | 350.98 | 344.69 | 356.93 | 282.64 | 184.20 | 228.25 | 340.08 | 219.67 | 122.03 | 371.03 | 340.97 |
| | (7) | (7) | (6) | (6) | (6) | (7) | (9) | (8) | (8) | (8) | (9) | (9) | (9) |
| Eicher Motors Ltd | 39.60 | 16.40 | 67.50 | 55.50 | 57.96 | 12.44 | 29.20 | 55.56 | 39.90 | 31.74 | 128.56 | 317.52 | 293.49 |
| | (16) | (16) | (13) | (14) | (14) | (17) | (14) | (11) | (11) | (11) | (8) | (11) | (10) |
| Swaraj Mazda Ltd | 41.27 | 17.06 | 35.15 | 28.90 | 30.18 | 25.53 | 29.55 | 42.64 | 27.89 | 21.88 | 62.12 | 172.52 | 293.49 |
| | (15) | (15) | (17) | (17) | (17) | (15) | (13) | (13) | (13) | (13) | (12) | (11) | (10) |
| Hindustan Motors Ltd | 110.63 | 47.31 | 181.07 | 142.11 | 150.23 | 43.35 | -8.39 | 9.49 | -28.47 | -84.34 | -23.38 | 664.39 | 101.49 |
| | (10) | (11) | (10) | (11) | (11) | (14) | (16) | (18) | (17) | (17) | (17) | (8) | (13) |
| Mahindra and Mahindra Ltd | 384.56 | 367.86 | 880.37 | 841.78 | 1575.30 | 1685.95 | 928.68 | 1785.92 | 926.04 | 417.72 | 462.88 | 1465.79 | 2643.29 |
| | (5) | (5) | (5) | (5) | (4) | (4) | (5) | (4) | (5) | (5) | (7) | (6) | (4) |
| Maruthi Udyog Ltd | 12099.24 | 6377.44 | 10654.64 | 9175.90 | 9478.58 | 9461.12 | 10979.28 | 10544.05 | 14144.72 | 10156.94 | 9771.41 | 9361.00 | 12219.21 |
| | (1) | (1) | (1) | (1) | (2) | (2) | (1) | (1) | (1) | (1) | (1) | (1) | (1) |
| Daewoo Motors India Ltd | 24.92 | 12.48 | 60.57 | 94.04 | 100.11 | 188.56 | -21.98 | 140.00 | -56.74 | -301.09 | -348.11 | -249.46 | -120.64 |
| | (17) | (17) | (16) | (13) | (12) | (10) | (18) | (10) | (18) | (18) | (18) | (18) | (18) |

## TABLE 9.3 (CONTINUED) : MVA OF SAMPLE COMPANIES

*(Rs. in crores)*

| Companies | 91-92 | 92-93 | 93-94 | 94-95 | 95-96 | 96-97 | 97-98 | 98-99 | 99-00 | 00-01 | 01-02 | 02-03 | 03-04 |
|---|---|---|---|---|---|---|---|---|---|---|---|---|---|
| **Bajaj Auto Ltd** | 2951.28 (3) | 1586.69 (3) | 2598.31 (3) | 4731.38 (3) | 4887.86 (3) | 4552.39 (3) | 6777.89 (2) | 5365.98 (2) | 3180.98 (3) | 3180.98 (3) | 4697.99 (3) | 7714.77 (2) | 9212.27 (3) |
| **LML Ltd** | 105.47 (11) | 78.10 (10) | 234.04 (8) | 167.32 (9) | 187.27 (9) | 274.17 (8) | 343.08 (6) | 190.83 (9) | 84.12 (9) | 40.16 (9) | 114.74 (10) | 150.58 (12) | 124.08 (12) |
| **Maharastra Scooters Ltd** | 71.83 (14) | 35.56 (13) | 62.67 (15) | 53.29 (16) | 55.22 (16) | 46.47 (13) | 64.08 (10) | 54.10 (12) | 27.96 (12) | 17.10 (14) | 70.24 (11) | 120.15 (13) | 156.58 (11) |
| **TVS Motors India Ltd** | 349.27 (6) | 175.10 (6) | 305.15 (7) | 260.11 (7) | 269.35 (7) | 268.88 (9) | 315.08 (8) | 301.92 (6) | 411.64 (7) | 331.72 (7) | 1021.94 (6) | 1778.70 (5) | 1800.73 (6) |
| **Kinetic Motors Company Ltd** | 130.04 (9) | 93.36 (9) | 171.23 (11) | 145.69 (10) | 150.93 (10) | 146.01 (11) | 64.07 (11) | 41.25 (14) | 51.53 (10) | 36.80 (10) | 43.85 (13) | 33.80 (14) | 38.19 (15) |
| **Hero Honda Motors Ltd** | 264.47 (8) | 133.27 (8) | 231.39 (9) | 246.58 (8) | 255.52 (8) | 655.81 (5) | 1117.02 (4) | 4352.66 (3) | 3533.09 (2) | 4312.72 (2) | 5531.69 (2) | 6633.43 (3) | 9662.88 (2) |
| **Kinetic Engineering Ltd** | 88.51 (12) | 45.78 (12) | 94.75 (12) | 94.72 (12) | 98.17 (13) | 57.37 (12) | 34.87 (12) | 32.47 (15) | 25.33 (14) | 24.42 (12) | 29.30 (14) | 31.11 (15) | 24.24 (16) |
| **Majestic Auto Ltd** | 74.99 (13) | 34.84 (14) | 64.86 (14) | 54.48 (15) | 56.61 (15) | 21.68 (16) | 17.16 (15) | 14.86 (17) | 6.42 (15) | 8.78 (15) | 17.20 (15) | 24.62 (16) | 39.32 (14) |
| **Scooters India Ltd** | -36.17 (18) | -26.60 (18) | -18.84 (18) | -21.53 (18) | -21.00 (18) | -17.27 (18) | -11.28 (17) | 14.97 (16) | 3.38 (16) | -7.64 (16) | 3.20 (16) | -0.30 (17) | 12.68 (17) |

Figures in parenthesis denotes MVA based ranking of selected companies.

***Source:*** Computed

**TABLE 9.4**

**MVA – SECTOR – WISE TRENDS (1991-92 - 2003-04)**

| S. No | Industry | Mean (Rs.in crores) | CV | CAGR |
|---|---|---|---|---|
| 1. | Ashok Leyland Ltd | 1003.02 | 0.65 | 8.64 |
| 2. | Tata Motors Ltd | 4495.22 | 0.74 | -16.70 |
| 3. | Bajaj Tempo Ltd | 277.39 | 0.31 | -0.54 |
| 4. | Eicher Motors Ltd | 99.63 | 1.31 | 17.00 |
| 5. | Swaraj Mazda Ltd | 63.71 | 1.25 | 13.80 |
| | **Commercial Vehicles Sectors** | **1187.83** | **0.53** | **-6.34** |
| 6. | Hindustan Motors Ltd | 100.43 | 1.87 | -19.00 |
| 7. | Mahindra & Mahindra Ltd | 1105.09 | 0.62 | 7.03 |
| 8. | Maruthi Udyog Ltd | 10340.26 | 0.18 | 1.58 |
| 9. | Daewoo Motors India Ltd | -36.72 | -4.67 | -39.30 |
| | **Passenger Cars and Multiutility Vehicles Sectors** | **2877.27** | **0.18** | **1.85** |
| 10. | Bajaj Auto Ltd | 4726.06 | 0.46 | 8.36 |
| 11. | LML Ltd | 161.07 | 0.53 | -2.70 |
| 12. | Maharastra Scooters Ltd | 64.25 | 0.58 | 3.59 |
| 13. | TVS Motors Company Ltd | 583.81 | 0.98 | 15.30 |
| 14. | Kinetic Motors Co. Ltd | 88.21 | 0.60 | -14.00 |
| 15. | Hero Honda Motors Ltd | 2840.81 | 1.09 | 38.20 |
| 16. | Kinetic Engineering Ltd | 52.39 | 0.58 | -11.90 |
| 17. | Majestic Auto Ltd | 33.52 | 0.68 | -11.60 |
| 18. | Scooters India Ltd | -9.72 | -1.61 | 13.80 |
| | **Two and Three Wheelers Sectors** | **948.68** | **0.62** | **14.60** |
| | **Whole Automobile Industry** | **1671.26** | **0.20** | **2.41** |

## TABLE 9.5

### MVA - EVA: LINEAR REGRESSION ANALYSIS

**Dependent variable - Market Value Added (MVA)**
**Independent variable - Economic Value Added (EVA)**

| Independent Variable | Co-efficient | t | Multiple R | R Square | Adjusted R Square | Std. Error of the Estimate | Durbin-Watson | F Value |
|---|---|---|---|---|---|---|---|---|
| **Commercial Vehicles :** EVA | 1.041 | 1.138 | 0.325 | 0.11 | 0.03 | 623.52 | 0.83 | 1.30 |
| **Passenger Cars and Multiutility Vehicles:** EVA | 0.321 | 0.796 | 0.233 | 0.06 | -0.03 | 537.98 | 1.78 | 0.63 |
| **Two and Three wheelers:**EVA | 2.602 | 1.562 | 0.426 | 0.18 | 0.11 | 558.29 | 0.86 | 2.44 |
| **Whole Industry:**EVA | 0.280 | 0.556 | 0.165 | 0.03 | -0.06 | 339.76 | 1.23 | 0.31 |

***Source:*** Computed

# 10

# Performance of Indian Automobile Industry

## Economic Value Added (EVA) Approach

Maximizing shareholders value is becoming the new corporate standard in India. The corporate, who gave the lowest preference to the shareholders' inquisitiveness, are now bestowing the utmost inclination to it. Shareholder's wealth is measured in terms of the returns they receive on their investment. The returns can either be in the form of dividends or in the form of capital appreciation or both. Capital appreciation in turn depends on the subsequent changes in the market value of the shares. This market value of shares is influenced by a number of factors, which can be company specific, industry specific and macro-economic in nature.

An important goal of financial management is to maximise the wealth of the organisation highest capital employee's wealth and consequently enhance the value of the firm. Shareholder wealth is traditionally reflected by either standard accounting parameters (such as profits, earnings and cash flow from operations) or financial ratios (including earnings per share, return on capital employed, return on net worth, net profit margin, operating profit margin etc). All these indicators failed to measure the true economic worth due to manipulative accounting techniques to state higher or lower earnings, depending on non meaningful decision on how to record revenues or expenses. Further, financial information is used by managers, shareholders and other interested parties to access their firm's current performance, and also by stakeholders to predict its future performance. The question that then arises is, whether these measures of corporate performance are linked to the expectation of the shareholders or not. To help corporate to generate value for shareholders, value-based management system has been developed.

Over the past several years, an alternative performance measure called Economic Value Added (EVA) has been gaining acceptance around the globe and has also been acknowledged by institutional firms as a credible performance measure. In order to overcome the limitations of accounting based measures of financial performance, Joel M Stern and G. Bennett Stewart & Co., introduced a modified concept of economic profit in 1990, in the name of Economic Value - Added (EVA) as a measure of business performance. Stern Stewart has claimed that EVA, as a tool of financial management, was neither 'just a phenomenon' nor was it limited to 'for profit' organizations. Economic Value - Added has been put to use for management performance evaluation, and more than just a measure of performance, it is the framework for a complete financial management (for improving scarce capital allocation; and valuation of a target company at the time of acquisition).

## EVA - TOOL OF FINANCIAL PERFORMANCE MEASUREMENT

Shareholder value creation is the new buzzword today and Economic Value - Added (EVA) is its most popular measure. In simple terms EVA is nothing but returns generated above cost of capital. It is the Net Operating Profit

After Tax (NOPAT) minus an appropriate change for the opportunity cost of all capital invested (WACC) in an organisation. EVA is an estimate of "economic profit" or the amount by which earnings exceed or fall short of the required minimum rate of return that shareholders and lenders could get by investing capital in other securities of analogous risk.

EVA as a tool of financial measurement enlightens whether the operating profit is enough to cover the cost of capital. Shareholders must earn sufficient returns for the risk they have taken in investing their funds in company's capital. According to Business Standard - KPMG, if a company's EVA is negative, the firm is destroying shareholders' wealth even though it may be reporting a positive and growing earning per share and return on capital employed. The EVA framework, which is becoming more and more admired tool for measuring the financial performance of corporate, offers a consistent approach to set goals and measure performance, communicate with investors, evaluate strategies, allocate capital valuing acquisitions and determine incentive bonuses. It is one of the several ongoing initiatives for a new corporate.

The evaluation and growth of the concept EVA, which may be realistically in young age in the west, has been going through its childhood in country like India. It may be quite emerging concept in the mind of Indian corporate policy makers and managers. Hence, this paper examines in detail the EVA of selected automobile industry. It consists of sub-parts like EVA - based ranking of selected companies, industry - wise and sector - wise trends in EVA - based ranking, results and discussion on statistically established trends.

## ECONOMIC VALUE ADDED (EVA)

EVA introduced by Stern Stewart & company is an incarnation of Residual Income concept. EVA model is based on the hypothesis that rational investor takes into account just two things; the cash to be generated over the life of a business; and the risk of the cash receipts. Stewart defined

'EVA as an estimate of true economic profit, the amount by which earnings exceed or fall short of required minimum rate of return investors could get by investing in other securities of comparable risk'. It is the net operating profit minus the appropriate charge for the opportunity cost of capital invested in an enterprise (both debt and equity).

Expressed as a formula, EVA for a given period can be written as:

**EVA = NOPAT - COST OF CAPITAL EMPLOYED**

= NOPAT – (WACC x CE)

Where

NOPAT - Net Operating Profit After Taxes but before financing costs

WACC - Weighted Average Cost of Capital; and

CE - Capital Employed

(or)

equivalently, if rate of return is defined as NOPAT / CAPITAL EMPLOYED, this turns into a perhaps more revealing formula:

**EVA = (RATE OF RETURN – COST OF CAPITAL) X CAPITAL EMPLOYED**

Where

Rate of Return - NOPAT / CAPITAL EMPLOYED

Capital Employed - Total of balance sheet minus non-interest bearing debt in the beginning of the year.

Cost of Capital - [Cost of equity X proportion of equity from capital] + [cost of debt X proportion of debt from capital X (1-tax rate)]

Cost of capital or Weighted Average Cost of Capital (WACC) is the average cost of both equity capital and interest bearing debt.

## COST OF DEBT ($K_D$)

Cost of debt refers to the average rate of interest the company pays for its debt obligations. Cost of debt ($K_d$) has been computed as:

$K_d$ = **Total interest expenses X (1-Effective tax rate) /Beginning total borrowings**

While calculating beginning borrowing all short-term as well as long-term borrowings has to be included as all debts are interests bearing. Therefore, interest paid in the financial year has been considered as total interest expenses.

## COST OF EQUITY ($K_E$)

To scribble down cost of equity ($K_e$), Capital Assets Pricing Model (CAPM) has been used. This model holds that firms' equity cost is the composition of risk free rate of return for a stock plus premium representing the volatility of share prices. According to this model, $K_e$ is the shareholders' expected rate of return and this expected rate of return ($R_j$) is as follows:

$$R_j = R_f + \beta \times (R_m - R_f)$$

Where, Rf = Risk free rate of return,

$R_m$ = Market rate of return, and

$\beta$ = Sensitivity of the share price in relation to the market index

The interest rate of Government securities has been considered as a proxy for risk free rate of return. The market rate of return has been calculated by using Index Numbers of Security Prices (Bombay Stock Exchange) from year to year (on monthly average basis) base. The yearly return of the index numbers has been computed by using the following formula:

**Rm = [(Index number for current year – Index number for previous year / Index number of previous year)] x 100**

Beta (β) is the risk-free co-efficient which measures the volatility of a given script of a company with respect to volatility of market. It is calculated by comparing return on a share to return in the stock market. Mathematically, beta is the statistical measure of volatility. It is calculated as covariance of daily return on the stock market indices and the return on daily share prices of a particular company, divided by variance of return on daily stock market indices. The Beta co-efficient has been calculated as follows:

$$\beta_j = \mathbf{COV_{im}} \ / \ \sigma^2 \mathbf{m}$$

where, $\beta_j$ = is the Beta of the security in the question

$COV_{im}$ = Stands for co-variance between the return of security and return of market, and

$\sigma^2 m$ = Stands for the variance of market return

## INFERENCES ON EVA – RE-VISITING THE EXISTING RESEARCHES

EVA. Stern (1990) observed that EVA as a performance measure captures the true economic profit of an organisation. EVA-based financial management and incentive compensation scheme gives manager better – quality information and superior motivation to make decisions that will create the maximum share holders wealth in an organisation. Stewart (1994) has expanded that adoption of EVA system by more and more companies throughout the world clearly depicts that it provides an integrated decision making frame work, can reforms energies and redirect resources to create sustainable value for companies, customers, employees, shareholders and for management. Grant (1996) found that EVA concept may have everlastingly changed the way real profitability is measured EVA is a financial tool that focuses on the difference between company's after tax operating profit and its total cost of capital. Luber (1996) confirmed that a positive EVA over a period of time will also have an increasing MVA while negative EVA will bring down MVA as the market looses confidence in the competence of a company to ensure a handsome return on the invested capital.

Banerjee (1997) has conducted an empirical research to find the superiority of EVA over other traditional financial performance measures. ROI and EVA has been calculated for sample companies and a comparison of both showing the superiority of EVA over ROI. Ethiraj (1998) derived those stock prices moves up as a company adopts EVA as an internal performance criterion. Anand, et al. (1999) revealed that EVA and MVA are better measures of business performance that NOPAT and EPS in terms of shareholders' value creation and competitive advantage of a firm. Bao and Bao (1999) revealed that the EVA is positively and significantly correlated with the firm value. Harihar (1999) highlighted some myths regarding EVA. According to him, EVA calculations are not simple and need a lot of adjustments in the financial books. Further, EVA figures can be manipulated to suit the needs of management. Thenmozhi (1999) compared EVA with some other traditional measure of corporate performance viz. ROI, EPS, RONW, ROE, ROCE etc... she has referred to some of the short comings of the concept of EVA but maintain that EVA is a better measure of corporate performance. Riceman, et al. (2002) argued that the EVA is a performance measure that is being used by an increasing number of companies, but academic research on EVA is limited.

Bardia, S.C (2002) revealed that in a dynamic environment a common investor finds it increasingly difficult to monitor his investments. EVA guides the investors in evaluating the performance of the company and monitoring their investments. Stern, Joel (2003) presented the results of Stern Stewart's research on Indian companies, which shows considerable need to improve the wealth creation performance and allocation of capital in the Indian economy. He explained how the effective implementation of the EVA frame work could be a solution to address this problem. EVA, as an emerging concept of financial management appears that the concept is fairly clear in the minds of almost all these researches whose studies have been reviewed above. In a fast changing business environment, the investor friendly financial performance measures may, perhaps, compose this corridor full of spanking new air.

## RESEARCH DESIGN

Keeping in view the scope of the study, it is decided to include all the companies under Automobile Industry working before or from the year 1991-92 to 2003-04. But, owing to several constraints such as non-availability of financial statements or non-working of a company in a particular year etc., it is compelled to restrict the number of sample companies to 18. Therefore, this study is expost facto based on survey method making a survey of eighteen companies in Indian Automobile Industry. There are 26 companies operating in the Indian Automobile Industry. The companies under Automobile Industry are classified into three sectors namely; Commercial Vehicles, Passenger Cars and Multiutility Vehicles and Two and Three wheelers.

For the purpose of the study all the three sectors have been selected. The selected sectors include 26 companies. Out of 26 companies, 5 are under commercial vehicles, 8 under passenger cars and multiutility vehicles and 13 under two and three wheelers sector. Out of 26 companies of the selected sectors, 13 years data is available for 18 companies only. Therefore, all the 18 companies are included in the sample. It accounts for 69.23 per cent of the total companies available in the Indian Automobile Industry. The selected 18 companies include 5 under commercial vehicles, 4 under passenger cars and multiutility vehicles and 9 under two and three wheeler sectors. It is inferred that sample company represents 98.74 percentage of market share in Commercial Vehicles, 89.76 percentage of market share in Passenger Cars and Multiutility Vehicles and 99.81 percentage of market share in Two and Three Wheelers. Thus, the findings based on the occurrence of such representative sample may be presumed to be true representative of Automobile Industry in the country.

## PERIOD OF STUDY

The period 1991-92 to 2003-04 is selected for this study of Indian Automobile Industry. This 13 years period is chosen in order to have a fairly long, cyclically well balanced period, for which reasonably homogeneous, reliable and up to-date financial data would be available. Further, the span chosen for the study is the period of the beginning of liberalization measures introduced by the Government of India. Hence, the period 1991-92 to 2003-04 is an era of growth of corporate performance in the manufacturing sector, particularly Automobile Industry and has got genuine economic significance of its own.

## SOURCE OF DATA

The study is mainly based on secondary data. The major source of data analysed and interpreted in this study related to all those companies selected is collected from "PROWESS" database, which is the most reliable on the empowered corporate database of Centre for Monitoring Indian Economy (CMIE). Besides prowess database, relevant secondary data have also been collected from BSE Stock Exchange Official Directory, CIME Publications, Annual Survey of Industry, Business newspapers, Reports on Currency and Finance, Libraries of various Research Institutions, through Internet etc. The study required variety of data; therefore, websites like http://indiainfoline.com, www.indiastat.com and www.google.com have been comprehensively searched.

## EVA OF SELECTED COMPANIES

EVA - based performance framework not only provides a far more accurate report card on corporate financial performance than conventional measures, but also has considerable implications for companies on how to make strategic decisions and manage the healthier financial performance in their pursuit of shareholder value. EVA created by the selected Automobile industry during the study period is depicted in Table 10.1. The table shows that out of eighteen industry, sixteen industry has generated positive EVA during the study period except in the year 1992-93, 1994-95, 1996-97, 1998-99, 2002-03 and 2003-04 and two companies have destroyed their shareholder wealth during the same period. In the year 1992-93 the number of companies generating negative EVA went up to sixteen, eleven in the year 1998-99 and ten in the year 2002-03. It would be worthwhile to mention here that during this period the economy of the nation faced showery time. Political instability at Union Government level and Kargil War may be the qualified grounds to such downhill state of affairs in the economy. In the year 2001-02 in which Indian economy revealed the optimistic wind, witnessed that sixteen companies are created wealth for the shareholders and only two have destroyed the same. However the number of companies generates negative EVA increased to ten in the year 2002-03. It may be extrapolated that the year 2003-04 may be able to see the economy in a slightly good health yet again.

It may be observed from Table 10.1 that LML Ltd was the only company out of eighteen companies who have been constantly generating the positive EVA all the way throughout the period of study. On the other hand, Daewoo Motors Indian Ltd was the only company who has been annihilating the wealth of shareholders right through the period under reference except in the year 1993-94 and 1995-96. Ashok Leyland Ltd, Eicher Motors Ltd, TVS Motors India Ltd, Bajaj Auto Ltd and Hero Honda Motors Ltd created positive EVA during the major part of thirteen years period. Rest of the companies displayed high instability on this front. On the whole the Table 10.1 concludes that about one-third (6 out 18), of the sample companies have been able to govern affirmative EVA during period under study whereas remaining companies make feasible to append a very little to the value of shareholders.

## EVA BASED RANKING OF SELECTED COMPANIES

Table 10.1 also presents EVA - based ranking of sample companies. It is evident from the table that companies like LML Ltd, Bajaj Auto Ltd, Maruthi Udyog Ltd and Tata Motors Ltd are toping in the list during this study period. On the other pass, companies like Swaraj Mazda Ltd, Daewoo Motors India Ltd, Kinetic Engineering Ltd, Majestic Auto Ltd and Scooter India Ltd has been loosing the grounds. Rest of the companies has indexed unsteady position during the period of study period.

EVA based frequencies distribution of sample companies are shown in Table 10.2. It is clear from the table that 16 companies in 1992-93, 11 in 1998-99 and 10 in 2002-03 are reporting negative EVA and the remaining companies generating positive EVA during the study period. It is also observed that 331/3 per cent of the company have added to the economic value between Rs.100 crores to Rs.500 crores during the study period and only two companies in 1995-96, 3 in 1997-98, 4 in 1999-00, 2 in 2001-02 and 1 in 2002-03 reported an EVA of over Rs.500 crores.

## SECTOR-WISE TRENDS IN EVA

Table 10.3 and Figure 10.1 presents sector - wise EVA of sample companies. It is evident from Table 10.3 that the mean EVA generated for the Automobile industry was Rs.79.53 crores during the study period. The mean EVA generated was the highest in two and three wheelers sector followed by commercial vehicles and passenger cars and multiutility vehicles sector. Two and Three Wheelers sector and commercial vehicles sector should perform well in this regard because their average was more than the industry average. It is also evident from the table that all the selected sectors and whole industry witnessed very high fluctuation in their EVA during the study period. Table 10.3 further reported that the commercial vehicles, passenger cars and multiutility vehicles sectors and whole industry registered negative compound annual growth rate of EVA during the study period.

Table 10.3 depicts the EVA generated by the selected companies under passenger cars and multiutility vehicles sector during the study period. Table 10.3 portrays that Daewoo Motors India Ltd showed negative EVA throughout the study period except in the year 1993-94 and 1995-96. The mean EVA generated was the highest in Mahindra and Mahindra Ltd followed by Maruthi Udyog Ltd and Hindustan Motors Ltd. All the companies registered very high fluctuation in their EVA during the study period. Only Mahindra and Mahindra Ltd witnessed positive compound annual growth rate of EVA and rest of the company showed negative compound annual growth rate of EVA.

The EVA generated by the companies under two and three wheeler sectors during the study period is presented in Table 10.3. It is evident from the Table 10.3 that Majestic Auto Ltd generated negative EVA in majority of the years, followed by Scooters India Ltd. The rest of the companies had registered a mixed trend of EVA during the study period. Among the selected companies, Bajaj Auto Ltd, LML Ltd, Hero Honda Motors Ltd and TVS Motors India Ltd had shown improved performance with record to EVA generation during the study period. All the selected companies under this sector had registered very high fluctuation in their EVA during the study period. Kinetic Motors Company Ltd, Kinetic Engineering Ltd and Majestic Auto Ltd had registered negative compound annual growth rate of EVA and the rest of the companies showed positive compound annual growth rate of EVA during the study period.

The sector wise paired test provided the value of t test in Table 10.4. The table exhibits that there has been significant deviation (at 5% level) in the EVA of respective years except for the year 1994-95 and 2001-02 to 2003-04.

## COMPARISON OF EVA AND CONVENTIONAL METHOD OF FINANCIAL PERFORMANCE

Analysing the corporate performance of Indian Automobile Industry based on Return on Capital Employed (ROCE)- the conventional benchmarks and on the new "trendier" one i.e., EVA, the results can be well exhibited in Table 10.5. From the table, it can be inferred that Indian Automobile Industry depicts a rosy picture in terms of return on capital employed. The mean value of return on capital employed of Automobile Industry during the study period 18.40 per cent i.e. for every Rs.100 investment, the return is Rs. 18.40 whereas EVA as a percentage of capital employed is only 14.07 i.e. for every Rs. 100 investment, the company has added value of Rs. 14.07. The same picture is reflected as in the case of commercial vehicles sector and passenger cars and multiutility vehicles sector during the study period. But in case of two and three wheelers sector, EVA as a percentage of capital employed showed better performance than the return on capital employed. Thus, the comparison shows that divergence exists between the performance results given by traditional measure and EVA. The traditional measures do not reflect the real value addition to shareholders' wealth and thus EVA has to be measured to have an idea about the shareholders value addition.

## CONCLUSION

The company h as been successfully able to create value for its shareholders. On comparing industry-wise composite frequencies for EVA for all years, it was found that there has been a significant increasing trend in EVA of the Automobile Industry firms which means that companies have a positive trend to improve their firm values. The recognition of EVA concept in India shows to some extent, diverse trends. A majority of the companics are still not prepared to employ the EVA technique to evaluate their financial performance because of certain inherent difficulties associated with the computation. In view of the above facts, the competent authorities in India should issue necessary guidelines for the computation of EVA and its practices in financial reporting, to the appropriate bodies in India, so that it becomes obligatory for all companies to disclose their EVA in their financial statement and to meet the expectations of shareholders in the country.

## REFERENCES

1. Mangala, Deepa and Joura Simpy, "Linkage between Economic Value Added and Market Value: An Analysis in Indian context", *Indian Management Studies Journal*, June 2002, pp.55-56.
2. Mc Taggart, James et al., "The Value imperative", published by Free Press, New York, 1994, pp 4-6.
3. Jani Shweta, "Godrej Retools for Value" *Business Standard*, Jan 21, 2003, p. 6.
4. Purikh, Parag, "The Universe of Wealth Creation", PPFAS-Financial Advisory Services Ltd-Online, June 2000, p.2.
5. Stern, Joel (1990), "One way to build value in your firm, Executive compensation", *FinancialExecutive*, pp. 51-54.
6. Stewart, G. Bennet, (1994), "EVATM Fact and Fantasy", *Journal of Applied Corporate Finance*, pp. 71-84.
7. Grant, J (1996). "Foundation of EVA for investment managers: Just in time, EVA", *Journal of Financial Management*, Vol.23, No.1, p.41(8).
8. Luber, R. B. (1996), "Who are the real wealth creators". *Fortune*, pp.2-3.
9. Banerjee, Ashok (1997), "Economic Value Added (EVA): a better performance measure", *The Management Accountant*, pp.86-88.
10. Ethiraj, Govindaraj (1998), 'The EVA feather in the market cap', *The Economic Times*, p. 1.
11. Anand, Manoj, Garg, Ajay, and Arora, Asha (1999), "Economic value adde d : Business performance measure

of shareholder value', *The Management Accountant*, pp.351-56.

12. Bao, B.H. and Bao, D.H., 'The Association between firm Value and Economic Value Added', *Indian Accounting Review*, Vol.3, No.2, pp.161-64.
13. Harihar,T.S.(1999), 'EVA prorating Myths', *Chartered Finance Analyst*, pp.8-9.
14. Thenmozhie. M. (1999), 'Economic value added as a measure of corporate performance', *The Indian Journal of Commerce*, Vol.52, No.4, pp. 72-85.
15. Riceman, S.S. and Cahan, S.F. (2002), "Do Managers Perform Better under EVA Bonus Schemes", Social Science Research Network Electronic Paper Collection, at http://oaoers.ssrb.cin.
16. Bardia, S.C.,(2002) "Economic Value Added: Overall Consideration", *Economic Challenger*, pp. 1-7.
17. Stern, Joel, (2003) " Workshop on Value – based Management," Organised by the ASCI, Hyderabad, pp. 21-22.

## TABLE 10.1

## EVA OF SAMPLE COMPANIES

*(Rs. in crores)*

| Sl.No | Companies | 91-92 | 92-93 | 93-94 | 94-95 | 95-96 | 96-97 | 97-98 | 98-99 | 99-00 | 00-01 | 01-02 | 02-03 | 03-04 |
|---|---|---|---|---|---|---|---|---|---|---|---|---|---|---|
| 1 | Ashok Leyland Ltd | 193.33 (5) | -200.47 (17) | 178.07 (5) | 121.34 (5) | 226.19 (4) | 244.25 (3) | 249.12 (6) | 134.05 (2) | 250.08 (8) | 283.39 (4) | 222.16 (6) | 129.23 (4) | 234.91 (4) |
| 2 | Tata Motors Ltd | 272.29 (1) | -343.86 (18) | 467.12 (1) | 477.77 (1) | 777.68 (1) | 433.04 (1) | 961.36 (1) | -900.70 (18) | 1888.03 (1) | 199.99 (6) | 25.98 (10) | -1937.03 (17) | 360.56 (3) |
| 3 | Bajaj Tempo Ltd | 30.84 (9) | -14.37 (9) | 20.79 (11) | 13.21 (11) | 28.86 (11) | -4.88 (15) | 11.12 (13) | -53.81 (12) | -14.84 (17) | -4.04 (16) | 1.59 (16) | 30.78 (6) | 24.88 (11) |
| 4 | Eicher Motors Ltd | 5.63 (15) | -1.62 (5) | 4.06 (15) | 15.63 (10) | 18.21 (12) | 14.28 (10) | 8.58 (16) | 3.33 (5) | 22.81 (13) | 23.00 (9) | 22.82 (13) | 5.21 (8) | 38.26 (8) |
| 5 | Swaraj Mazda Ltd | -2.47 (18) | -0.25 (3) | -0.08 (17) | 4.52 (14) | 11.60 (15) | 10.71 (11) | 10.46 (14) | 4.54 (4) | 7.08 (16) | 8.85 (11) | 12.48 (14) | 7.43 (7) | 18.62 (12) |
| 6 | Hindustan Motors Ltd | 98.51 (7) | -82.42 (14) | 120.30 (7) | 78.29 (7) | 116.58 (7) | 47.50 (7) | 134.10 (7) | -66.55 (13) | 138.27 (9) | 6.58 (14) | 68.64 (8) | -167.24 (14) | -44.35 (17) |
| 7 | Mahindra and Mahindra Ltd | 122.47 (6) | -77.17 (13) | 195.48 (4) | 125.50 (4) | 216.76 (5) | 113.71 (6) | 423.90 (4) | -178.50 (15) | 961.95 (4) | 307.59 (3) | 395.52 (5) | -104.02 (16) | 139.67 (5) |
| 8 | Maruthi Udyog Ltd | 266.56 (2) | -158.32 (15) | 256.63 (2) | 414.49 (2) | 584.49 (2) | 311.83 (2) | 834.13 (2) | -452.34 (17) | 1419.86 (3) | -39.45 (17) | 621.12 (2) | -2852.98 (18) | 30.86 (9) |
| 9 | Daewoo Motors India Ltd | -0.86 (17) | -1.21 (4) | 2.45 (16) | -6.80 (17) | 62.03 (8) | -48.81 (18) | -87.12 (18) | -161.33 (14) | -15.29 (18) | -91.12 (18) | -185.09 (18) | -101.02 (13) | -58.01 (18) |

**TABLE 10.1 (CONTINUED) : EVA OF SAMPLE COMPANIES**

*(Rs. in crores)*

| Sl.No | Companies | 91-92 | 92-93 | 93-94 | 94-95 | 95-96 | 96-97 | 97-98 | 98-99 | 99-00 | 00-01 | 01-02 | 02-03 | 03-04 |
|---|---|---|---|---|---|---|---|---|---|---|---|---|---|---|
| 10 | Bajaj Auto Ltd | 242.82 | -175.98 | 231.55 | 278.45 | 414.44 | 237.60 | 535.21 | -425.16 | 1452.88 | 422.51 | 811.70 | 2223.75 | 87.48 |
| | | (4) | (16) | (3) | (3) | (3) | (4) | (3) | (16) | (2) | (1) | (1) | (1) | (7) |
| 11 | LML Ltd | 256.28 | 130.25 | 123.90 | 110.86 | 118.75 | 166.24 | 255.71 | 276.42 | 462.71 | 401.60 | 410.00 | 290.32 | 362.97 |
| | | (3) | (1) | (6) | (6) | (6) | (5) | (5) | (1) | (5) | (2) | (4) | (2) | (2) |
| 12 | Maharastra Scooters Ltd | 36.69 | -29.20 | 21.97 | 9.65 | 15.66 | -2.29 | 19.08 | -28.90 | 69.39 | 7.58 | 23.43 | 135.48 | 25.14 |
| | | (8) | (10) | (10) | (12) | (13) | (14) | (10) | (11) | (10) | (12) | (11) | (3) | (10) |
| 13 | TVS Motors India Ltd | 22.44 | 0.15 | 31.50 | 39.35 | 43.23 | 38.87 | 103.30 | 3.07 | 252.27 | 112.90 | 129.29 | -304.01 | 117.14 |
| | | (11) | (2) | (8) | (8) | (9) | (8) | (8) | (6) | (7) | (7) | (7) | (15) | (6) |
| 14 | Kinetic Motors Company Ltd | 9.14 | -7.98 | 6.57 | 4.14 | 7.01 | -0.15 | 9.10 | -1.65 | 27.00 | 19.09 | 28.47 | -33.18 | -21.16 |
| | | (14) | (8) | (13) | (15) | (16) | (13) | (15) | (9) | (12) | (10) | (9) | (10) | (15) |
| 15 | Hero Honda Motors Ltd | 2.31 | -5.59 | 28.46 | 22.32 | 29.46 | 37.81 | 85.38 | 39.97 | 278.14 | 254.86 | 496.11 | -34.30 | 494.32 |
| | | (16) | (7) | (9) | (9) | (10) | (9) | (9) | (3) | (6) | (5) | (3) | (11) | (1) |
| 16 | Kinetic Engineering Ltd | 12.78 | -4.96 | 9.09 | 6.83 | 12.15 | 5.98 | 15.03 | -1.09 | 36.60 | 23.11 | 22.93 | -38.55 | -40.10 |
| | | (13) | (6) | (12) | (13) | (14) | (12) | (11) | (8) | (11) | (8) | (12) | (12) | (16) |
| 17 | Majestic Auto Ltd | 28.41 | -49.00 | 5.45 | -5.97 | -4.18 | -15.16 | -1.07 | -1.97 | 14.78 | 6.99 | -5.47 | -27.78 | 6.31 |
| | | (10) | (12) | (14) | (16) | (17) | (17) | (17) | (10) | (14) | (13) | (17) | (9) | (13) |
| 18 | Scooters India Ltd | 15.46 | -37.27 | -0.38 | -7.88 | -7.27 | -14.68 | 12.05 | 1.05 | 10.24 | 3.72 | 3.55 | 94.98 | -1.90 |
| | | (12) | (11) | (18) | (18) | (18) | (16) | (12) | (7) | (15) | (15) | (15) | (5) | (14) |

**Figures in parenthesis denote EVA based ranking of selected companies.** ***Source:*** Computed

## TABLE 10.2

## EVA - BASED FREQUENCIES DISTRIBUTION OF SAMPLE COMPANIES

| EVA | 91-92 | 92-93 | 93-94 | 94-95 | 95-96 | 96-97 | 97-98 | 98-99 | 99-00 | 00-01 | 01-02 | 02-03 | 03-04 |
|---|---|---|---|---|---|---|---|---|---|---|---|---|---|
| **Negative** | 2 | 16 | 2 | 3 | 2 | 6 | 2 | 11 | 2 | 3 | 2 | 10 | 5 |
| **Up to Rs.10 Crores** | 3 | 1 | 5 | 4 | 1 | 1 | 2 | 4 | 1 | 5 | 2 | 2 | 1 |
| **Rs.10-25 Crores** | 3 | | 2 | 3 | 4 | 2 | 5 | | 3 | 3 | 4 | | 2 |
| **Rs.25-50 Crores** | 3 | | 2 | 1 | 3 | 3 | | 1 | 2 | | 2 | 1 | 3 |
| **Rs.50-100 Crores** | 1 | | | 1 | 1 | | 1 | | 1 | | 1 | 1 | 1 |
| **Rs.100-500 Crores** | 6 | 1 | 7 | 6 | 5 | 6 | 5 | 2 | 5 | 7 | 5 | 3 | 6 |
| **Above Rs. 500 Crores** | | | | | 2 | | 3 | | 4 | | 2 | 1 | |
| **Total** | **18** | **18** | **18** | **18** | **18** | **18** | **18** | **18** | **18** | **18** | **18** | **18** | **18** |

***Source:*** Computed

## TABLE 10.3

## EVA – SECTOR – WISE TRENDS (1991-92 - 2003-04)

| S. No | Industry | Mean (Rs.in crores) | CV | CAGR |
|---|---|---|---|---|
| 1. | Ashok Leyland Ltd | 174.28 | 0.71 | 15.70 |
| 2. | Tata Motors Ltd | 206.33 | 4.45 | -9.22 |
| 3. | Bajaj Tempo Ltd | 5.39 | 4.50 | -4.89 |
| 4. | Eicher Motors Ltd | 13.86 | 0.80 | 14.70 |
| 5. | Swaraj Mazda Ltd | 7.19 | 0.82 | 20.80 |
| | **Commercial Vehicles Sectors** | **81.41** | **2.42** | **-3.16** |
| 6. | Hindustan Motors Ltd | 34.48 | 2.82 | -22.40 |
| 7. | Mahindra & Mahindra Ltd | 131.30 | 3.41 | 2.50 |
| 8. | Maruthi Udyog Ltd | 95.14 | 10.55 | -17.30 |
| 9. | Daewoo Motors India Ltd | -53.24 | -1.32 | -8.77 |
| | **Passenger Cars and Multiutility Vehicles Sectors** | **51.92** | **7.42** | **-9.01** |
| 10. | Bajaj Auto Ltd | 487.47 | 1.42 | 19.60 |
| 11. | LML Ltd | 258.92 | 0.48 | 9.88 |
| 12. | Maharastra Scooters Ltd | 23.36 | 1.81 | 13.60 |
| 13. | TVS Motors Company Ltd | 45.35 | 2.77 | 16.00 |
| 14. | Kinetic Motors Co. Ltd | 3.57 | 4.87 | -0.73 |
| 15. | Hero Honda Motors Ltd | 133.02 | 1.40 | 30.50 |
| 16. | Kinetic Engineering Ltd | 4.60 | 4.84 | -4.13 |
| 17. | Majestic Auto Ltd | -3.74 | -5.15 | -2.53 |
| 18. | Scooters India Ltd | 5.51 | 5.46 | 11.00 |
| | **Two and Three Wheelers Sectors** | **105.27** | **0.92** | **20.80** |
| | **Whole Automobile Industry** | **79.53** | **2.45** | **-1.24** |

## TABLE 10.4

## PAIRED TEST OF SECTOR-WISE EVA OF SAMPLE COMPANIES

| Paired sample test | Paired differences | | | | | t | df | Sig (2-taited) |
|---|---|---|---|---|---|---|---|---|
| | Mean | Std Deviation | Std Error Mean | 95% Confidence Level Lower | 95% Confidence Level Upper | | | |
| EVA 91-92 – EVA 92-93 | 148.49 | 187.69 | 44.24 | 55.10 | 241.78 | 3.36 | 17 | .004 |
| EVA 92-93 – EVA 93-94 | -153.46 | 222.50 | 52.44 | -264.10 | -42.81 | -2.93 | 17 | .009 |
| EVA 93-94 – EVA 94-95 | -6.33 | 47.30 | 11.15 | -23.45 | 23.59 | .016 | 17 | .995 |
| EVA 94-95 – EVA 95-96 | -53.89 | 80.84 | 19.05 | -94.09 | -13.68 | -2.83 | 17 | .012 |
| EVA 95-96 – EVA 96-97 | 60.88 | 105.66 | 24.90 | 8.34 | 113.42 | 2.45 | 17 | .026 |
| EVA 96-97 – EVA 97-98 | -111.31 | 178.05 | 41.97 | -199.85 | -22.77 | -2.65 | 17 | .017 |
| EVA 97-98 – EVA 98-99 | 299.39 | 535.38 | 126.19 | 33.15 | 565.63 | 2.37 | 17 | .030 |
| EVA 98-99 – EVA 99-00 | -503.97 | 832.52 | 196.23 | -917.85 | -89.97 | -2.57 | 17 | .020 |
| EVA 99-00 – EVA 00-01 | 295.27 | 539.71 | 127.21 | 26.88 | 563.66 | 2.32 | 17 | .033 |
| EVA 00-01 – EVA 01-02 | -64.34 | 192.02 | 45.26 | -159.83 | 31.15 | -1.42 | 17 | .173 |
| EVA 01-02 – EVA 02-03 | 373.56 | 1030.43 | 242.88 | -138.86 | 885.99 | 1.54 | 17 | .142 |
| EVA 02-03 – EVA 03-04 | -299.70 | 1041.73 | 245.54 | -817.74 | 218.34 | -1.22 | 17 | .239 |
| EVA 91-92 – EVA 03-04 | -9.05 | 149.57 | 35.25 | -83.43 | 65.33 | -0.26 | 17 | .800 |

***Sources:*** Computed

## TABLE 10.5

## COMPARISON OF EVA $V_S$ CONVENTIONAL METHOD OF FINANCIAL PERFORMANCE

(in percentage)

| Year | Commercial Vehicles | | Passengers cars and Multiutility Vehicles | | Two and Three Wheelers | | Industry Average | |
|---|---|---|---|---|---|---|---|---|
| | ROCE | EVA/CE | ROCE | EVA/CE | ROCE | EVA/CE | ROCE | EVA/CE |
| 1991-92 | 16.09 | 13.12 | 8.13 | 20.18 | 17.94 | 36.67 | 14.05 | 23.32 |
| 1992-93 | 7.78 | -4.10 | 6.82 | -11.82 | 16.82 | 8.67 | 10.47 | -2.42 |
| 1993-94 | 17.63 | 13.40 | 15.33 | 19.07 | 27.88 | 33.78 | 20.28 | 22.08 |
| 1994-95 | 23.47 | 16.98 | 21.96 | 15.96 | 28.36 | 26.62 | 24.60 | 19.85 |
| 1995-96 | 27.15 | 21.55 | 33.75 | 20.40 | 26.90 | 25.89 | 29.27 | 22.61 |
| 1996-97 | 20.18 | 10.49 | 26.30 | 7.72 | 28.74 | 16.72 | 25.28 | 11.64 |
| 1997-98 | 13.43 | 13.64 | 16.61 | 17.21 | 21.77 | 28.18 | 17.27 | 19.68 |
| 1998-99 | 8.72 | 1.56 | 9.48 | -8.52 | 22.94 | 7.98 | 13.71 | 0.34 |
| 1999-00 | 11.23 | 10.86 | 5.53 | 22.56 | 27.29 | 42.45 | 14.68 | 25.29 |
| 2000-01 | 12.90 | 10.48 | -0.67 | 2.31 | 16.55 | 24.98 | 9.59 | 12.59 |
| 2001-02 | 17.63 | 10.98 | 3.72 | 9.98 | 19.09 | 30.18 | 13.48 | 17.05 |
| 2002-03 | 33.07 | 19.65 | 8.72 | -38.25 | 19.57 | 15.73 | 20.45 | -0.96 |
| 2003-04 | 41.31 | 16.26 | 23.33 | 1.60 | 13.47 | 17.69 | 26.04 | 11.85 |
| **Mean** | **19.32** | **11.91** | **13.81** | **6.03** | **22.10** | **24.22** | **18.40** | **14.07** |
| **CV** | **0.51** | **0.58** | **0.73** | **2.88** | **0.24** | **0.43** | **0.35** | **0.69** |
| **CAGR** | **4.65** | **5.09** | **-6.60** | **- 14.00** | **-2.36** | **-0.96** | **0.33** | **-5.37** |

# 11

# Linkage Between Market Value Added (MVA) and Other Financial Variables

## An Analysis in Indian Automobile Industry

The corporate missions have undergone radical changes during last decade. This is mainly due to the economic reforms implemented in most of the developing countries in the world particularly in India that has invited greater competition and mounting transparencies in the financial working, management, and control of corporatism. In such altered circumstances, using conventional accounting measures to elucidate the behaviour of performance is, perhaps, not a suitable built-in approach. But in the shifting economic order, it is now well settled that the aim of every business entity be supposed to maximize the wealth of equity shareholders. Simply with this reason, all economic and non- economic activities of the firm should be aimed at to realize this objective.

The expansion of the capital markets, increased shareholder activism, institutional investors with large equity positions, and more active boards of directors have all contributed to heighten the pressure on companies to consistently maximize shareholder value. IN response, and regarding the shortcomings of traditional Profit – related performance measures, consulting companies such as Stern Stewart, The Alcar Group and Strategic planning Associates have developed "New" Value – based Performance measures. Probably, the most popular periodic value – based Performance measure is stern Stewart's Economic Value Added (EVA).

The evidence of the majority of the empirical studies regarding EVA suggests that there is a Positive relationship between EVA and Shareholder value creation, measured by Market Value Added (MVA). However, when the explaining power of EVA versus traditional performance measures regarding Equity Market Value or Returns is considered, the results are mixed. Hence, an attempt has been made in this article to find out the sector – wise trends as far as the factors affecting MVA are concerned. The purpose of this study was to explore whether any relationship existed between dependent and independent variables and to come across, whether a particular independent variable emerges as the most explanatory variable of MVA during the study period.

## MARKET VALUE ADDED

Market Value Added (MVA) is a measure of shareholder's wealth. If the corporate objective is to enhance shareholder's wealth, it can be achieved by improving MVA. MVA is the difference between the market value of invested capital and book value of invested capital. MVA is the absolute rupee spread between a company's market value and its capital. It represents the stock market's assessment as of a particular time of the net present value of all a company's past and projected capital projects. Therefore, maximizing MVA should be the primary objective for any company that is concerned about its shareholder's welfare. Economic

Value Added (EVA) is net operating profit after tax minus an appropriate change for the opportunity cost of all capital invested in an organization. A company's EVA is the fuel that fires up its MVA. Thus, EVA is the internal measure of corporate performance and MVA is the external measure of corporate performance.

The present article makes an attempt to find the relevance in Indian context of Stern and Stewart's claim that MVA of the firm is largely positively associated with or driven by its EVA generating capacity. The study also portrays the association between MVA and other selected traditional financial variables like Earnings Per Share (EPS), Return on Capital Employed (ROCE), Net Operating Profit After Tax (NOPAT) and Return on Net Worth (RONW).

## REVIEW OF LITERATURE

Stern (1990) observed that EVA as a performance measure captures the true economic profit of an organisation. EVA-based financial management and incentive compensation scheme gives managers better–quality information and superior motivation to make decisions that will create the maximum shareholder wealth in an organisation. Stewart (1994) has expanded that adoption of the EVA system by more and more companies throughout the world clearly depicts that it provides an integrated decision - making framework, can reform energies and redirect resources to create sustainable value for companies, customers, employees, shareholders and for management. Grant (1996) found that EVA concept might have everlastingly changed the way real profitability is measured. EVA is a financial tool that focuses on the difference between company's after tax operating profit and its total cost of capital. Luber (1996) confirmed that a positive EVA over a period of time will also have an increasing MVA while negative EVA will bring down MVA as the market loses confidence in the competence of a company to ensure a handsome return on the invested capital.

Banerjee (1997) has conducted an empirical research to find the superiority of EVA over other traditional financial performance measures. ROI and EVA have been calculated for sample companies and a comparison of both showing the superiority of EVA over ROI. Ethiraj (1998) derived those stock prices moves up as a company adopts EVA as an internal performance criterion. KPMG – BS study (1998) assessed top 100 companies on EVA, Sales, PAT and MVA criteria. The Survey has used the BS – 1000 list of companies using a composite index comprising sales, profitability and compounded annual growth rate of those companies covering the period 1996-97. Sixty companies have been found able to create positive Shareholder Value whereas 38 companies have been found to destroy it. Anand, et al (1999) revealed that EVA and MVA are better measures of business performance that NOPAT and EPS in terms of shareholders' value creation and competitive advantage of a firm. Bao and Bao (1999) revealed that the EVA is positively and significantly correlated with the firm value. Harihar (1999) highlighted some myths regarding EVA. According to him, EVA calculations are not simple and need a lot of adjustments in the financial books. Further, EVA figures can be manipulated to suit the needs of management. Thenmozhi (1999) compared EVA with some other traditional measure of corporate performance viz. ROI, EPS, RONW, ROE, ROCE etc. She has referred to some of the shortcomings of the concept of EVA but maintain that EVA is a better measure of corporate performance. Banerjee (2000) attempted to find out whether Market Value of Firm if the function of current operational Value (COV) and Future Growth Value (FGV). Based on the analysis of his data he comes to the conclusion that in many cases there was a considerable divergence between MVA and the sum total of COA and FGV.

Riceman, et al (2002) argued that EVA is a performance measure that is being used by an increasing number of companies, but academic research on EVA is limited. Mangala and Simpy (2002) discussed the relationship between EVA and Market Value among various companies in India. The results of the analysis confirm stern's hypothesis and concluded that the company's current operational value was more significant in contributing to change in market value of share in Indian context. Bardia (2002) revealed that in a dynamic environment, a common investor finds it increasingly difficult to monitor his investments. EVA guides investors in evaluating the performance of the company and monitoring their investments. Stern, Joel (2003) presented the results of Stern Stewart's research on Indian companies, which shows considerable need to improve the wealth creation performance and allocation of capital in the Indian economy. They explained how the effective implementation of the EVA framework could be a solution to address this problem. Balachandran and Sriram (2005) made an attempt to study the value created for the shareholders of the company. They used to determine the relationship between Economic Value Added and dividend paid to the shareholders. The study revealed that the company had utilized the dividend-paying fund ploughing back into the business. The company was very conservative in declaring dividend and always had long-term objective of creating wealth to the shareholders, which has been achieved. Ali M Ghanbari and Narges Sarlak (2006) empirically reviewed the trend of EVA of Indian Automobile Companies. The results indicate that there was a significant increasing trend in EVA during the period of study and the firms in the automobile industry are moving towards the improvement of their firm's value.

It appears that the concept of EVA, as an emerging concept of financial management is fairly clear in the minds of almost all these researches whose studies have been reviewed above. In a fast changing business environment, the investor friendly financial performance measures may be the need of hour.

## RESEARCH DESIGN

Keeping in view the scope of the study, it is decided to

include all the companies under automobile industry working before or from the year 1991-92 to 2003-04. There are 26 companies operating in the Indian automobile industry. But, owing to several constraints such as non-availability of financial statements or non-working of a company in a particular year etc., it is compelled to restrict the number of sample companies to 18. The companies under automobile industry are classified into three sectors namely; Commercial vehicles, Passenger cars and multiutility vehicles and Two and three wheelers. For the purpose of the study all the three sectors have been selected. It accounts for 69 per cent of the total companies available in the Indian automobile industry. The selected 18 companies include 5 under commercial vehicles, 4 under passenger cars and multiutility vehicles and 9 under two and three wheeler sectors. It is inferred that sample company represents 99 percentage of market share in commercial vehicles, 90 percentage of market share in passenger cars and multiutility vehicles and 99 percentage of market share in two and three wheelers. Thus, the findings based on the occurrence of such representative sample may be presumed to be true representative of automobile industry in the country.

With a view to present the methodological analysis placed in this study, the selected variables like MVA, EVA, EPS, ROCE, NOPAT and RONW constitute the variable base. Out of these, MVA is considered as dependent variable and other are independents. The rationale of this analysis is to examine that which particular independent variable has been able to explain the dependent variable in superior manner throughout the period. The period 1991-92 to 2003-04 is selected for this study. The span chosen for the study is the period of the beginning of liberalization measures introduced by the Government of India. Hence, the period 1991-92 to 2003-04 is an era of growth of corporate performance in the manufacturing sector, particularly automobile industry and has got genuine economic significance of its own.

The study is based on secondary data. The major source of data analysed and interpreted in this study related to all those companies selected is collected from "PROWESS" database, which is the most reliable on the empowered corporate database of Centre for Monitoring Indian Economy (CMIE). Besides prowess database, relevant secondary data have also been collected from BSE Stock Exchange Official Directory, CMIE Publications, Annual Survey of Industry, business newspapers, Reports on Currency and Finance, Libraries of various Research Institutions, through Internet etc.

## SECTOR WISE TRENDS IN MVA

Table 11.1 portrays whole automobile industry and sector wise information pertaining to MVA. It is evident from Table 11.1 that among the three sectors, passenger cars and multiutility vehicles sector have been generating highest market value added throughout the study period. This was due to the better market value added of Maruti Udyog Ltd and Mahindra and Mahindra Ltd. It was followed by commercial vehicles sector and two and three wheelers. Table 11.1 also shows that all the selected sectors of automobile industry have been generating positive aggregate MVA throughout the period. The growth of MVA is more in case of passenger cars and multiutility vehicles whereas less consistent in case of commercial vehicles and two and three wheelers sector. Table also brings out that only the commercial vehicles sector had registered negative compound annual growth rate of MVA during the study period.

The market value added of selected companies under commercial vehicles sector during the study period is also presented in Table 11.1. Table 11.1 reveals that the mean MVA of Tata Motors Ltd were the highest followed by Ashok Leyland Ltd, Bajaj Tempo Ltd, Eicher Motors Ltd and Swaraj Mazda Ltd. Table 11.1 brings out that all the selected companies under the commercial vehicles sector had registered very high fluctuations in their MVA except Bajaj

Tempo Ltd which registered moderate fluctuations during the study period. Further, Table 11.1 provided that the two companies namely Tata Motors Ltd and Bajaj Tempo Ltd had registered negative compound annual growth rate of MVA and rest of the companies had positive compound annual growth rate of MVA during the study period.

Table 11.1 presents MVA of selected companies under passenger's cars and multiutility vehicles sector. The table shows that the companies like Maruti Udyog Ltd and Mahindra and Mahindra Ltd is top in the list and it was followed by Hindustan Motors Ltd and Daewoo Motors Ltd. All the selected companies except Maruti Udyog Ltd had registered very high fluctuation in their MVA during the study period. Table 11.1 also brings out values relating to compound annual growth rate of MVA of selected companies. It is evident from the table that Hindustan Motors Ltd and Daewoo Motors India Ltd had registered negative growth rate and rest of the companies had registered positive growth rate of MVA during the study period.

Table 11.1 brings out the values relating to MVA of selected companies under two and three wheelers. Table 11.1 showed that Bajaj Auto Ltd, Hero Honda Motors Ltd, TVS Motors India Ltd and LML Ltd comparatively top in the list. On the other hand, Scooters India Ltd and Majestic Auto Ltd are struggling on their front with regard to MVA during the study period. It is also noticed that all the selected companies have registered very high fluctuations in their MVA during the study period. The analysis of compound annual growth rate of MVA showed mixed trend among the selected companies under the sector during the study period.

## MVA VIS-À-VIS OTHER FINANCIAL VARIABLES-LINEAR REGRESSION

In this section an attempt to find the relevance of Stern and Stewart's claim that MVA of the firm is largely positive association with or driven by its EVA generating capacity and other financial variables like EPS, ROCE, NOPAT and RONW.

In this section, result of correlation co-efficient, linear regression, Durbin - Watson model, F-statistics and t-statistics have been determined between dependent variable (MVA) and independent variables. The values hence obtained have their particular statistical sense. The regression co-efficient for independent variables like EVA, EPS, ROCE, NOPAT and RONW so worked out portrays the temperament of association between the dependent and particular independent variable. The t - statistics and F - statistics so calculated determine the level of significant or insignificant association between the variables. Durbin - Watson model allows the researcher to establish the auto-correlation, if any between dependent and independent variable (the desirable value is two and any value more than two signifies negative auto-correlation and vice versa); values of adjusted $R^2$ indicate the extent of variation in the dependent variable which may be explicated by independent variable (s) and the standard error speaks about the limits within which the estimated value as the dependent variable is expected to lie.

## MVA-EVA ANALYSIS

Table 11.2 offers the explanation about the regression analysis between MVA and EVA during the study period for the whole automobile industry and its three sectors. Table 11.2 provides the values of R, R-square and adjusted R-square for the whole industry 0.165, 0.03 and – 0.06 respectively. It sounds that there exists poor relationship between MVA and EVA in automobile industry, as the value of adjusted R-square in negative. Interestingly, the t and F statistics give the identical results but both of them lead to insignificant association between the variables under reference. It is evident from the table that the overall result in passenger cars and multiutility vehicles does not differ from whole industry and statistical association between MVA and EVA is again insignificant. Table 11.2 suggests that EVA is serially correlated in commercial vehicles and two and three wheelers sector and adjusted R-square value is also positive.

The t and F statistics are resulting identical values and secure that in commercial vehicles and two and three wheelers sector relationship between MVA and EVA is fairly significant. However, the MVA-EVA analysis supports the hypothesis of Stern and Stewart's that MVA of firm is largely positive associated with EVA in all the selected sectors of Indian automobile industry.

## MVA-EPS ANALYSIS

The linear regression analysis between MVA and EPS is presented by Table 11.3 for the study period. It is evident from the Table 11.3 that the correlation co-efficient between MVA and EPS for the whole industry is 0.306 and value of R-square and adjusted R-square is very low and may not be adequate for the fitness of the model. The t and F statistics suggest that the association between MVA and EPS of automobile industry is not significant and EPS does not suitably explain the MVA. It is evident from the table that the correlation co-efficient between MVA and EPS in passenger cars and multiutility vehicles and two and three wheelers 0.223 and 0.246 respectively and value of adjusted R-square is negative. This shows the poor fitness of the model. Both t statistics and F statistics certify that the association between these two variables is insignificant as presented in the table. It is again noticed from the table that the variables are clearly correlated in commercial vehicles sector and adjusted R-square value is also positive. The t and F statistics are resulting identical values and secured that EPS of commercial vehicles sector has been able to describe MVA in best term than the other sectors. The overall results showed that EPS is positively associated with MVA in all the three sectors and the whole industry during the study period.

## MVA – ROCE ANALYSIS

Table 11.4 offers the explanation about the regression analysis between MVA and ROCE during the study period for the whole automobile industry and its three sectors. Table 11.4 provides the values of R, R – square and adjusted R – square are 0.756, 0.57 and 0.53 respectively. It sounds that the good fitness of the model. Interestingly, t and F statistics give the identical result but both of them lead to significant association between the variable under reference. In two and three wheelers sector the results are just about similar to whole industry. Table 11.4 suggests that the variables are clearly correlated in two and three wheelers sector and adjusted R – square value is also positive. The t and F statistics are resulting identical values and secure that in two and three wheelers sectors the association between MVA and ROCE is fairly significant. However, in case of passenger cars and multiutility vehicles and commercial vehicles sector the values of R, R-square and adjusted R-square showed that there exists poor relationship between MVA and ROCE in these sectors. Interestingly, t and F statistics give the identical results but both of them lead to insignificant association between the variables under reference. The overall results showed that ROCE is positively associated with MVA in all the three sectors and the whole industry during the study period.

## MVA – NOPAT ANALYSIS

Linear regression analysis between MVA and NOPAT is presented in Table 11.5. In Table 11.5 the statistical association between MVA and NOPAT of all the three sectors and the whole industry are provided. The table reveals that the value of R, R-square and adjusted R-square are high and it may be adequate for the fitness of the model in case of whole industry, passenger cars and multiutility vehicles sector and two and three wheelers sector. The t and F statistics also suggest that the association between MVA and NOPAT is significant and NOPAT is suitable to explain in the MVA of these sectors and whole industry during the study period. The results regarding the association of MVA and NOPAT in commercial vehicles sector slightly differ. The table reveals that value of adjusted R-square is very low and it may not be adequate for the fitness of the model, the t and F statistics also suggest that the association between the MVA and NOPAT is not significant and NOPAT do not suitably explain the MVA of commercial vehicles sector during the study period. The overall analysis showed that NOPAT is positively associated with MVA in all the three sectors and whole industry.

## MVA – RONW ANALYSIS

Table 11.6 tenders the elucidation concerning the regression analysis between MVA and RONW during the study period. The Table 11.6 provides the values of R, R-square and adjusted R-square. Table 11.6 suggests that variables are clearly correlated in whole industry, commercial vehicles and two and three wheelers sector and adjusted R-square value is also positive. The t and F statistics are resulting identical values and secured that in these sectors and whole industry the relationship between MVA and RONW is fairly significant. However, in case of passenger cars and multiutility vehicles, Table 11.6 provides the value of R, R-square and adjusted R-square are 0.08, 0.01 and -0.08 respectively. It sounds that there exists poor relationship between MVA and RONW in passenger cars and multiutility vehicles sector. The t and F statistics also give identical results but both of them lead to insignificant association between the variables under reference. The overall analysis showed that RONW is negatively association with MVA only in case of two and three wheelers sector during the study period.

## CONCLUSION

A research idea has been evolved in this study to find out the industry-wise and sector-wise trends in the EVA and traditional financial variables that affect MVA. The regression analysis has been carried out and the succeeding outcomes that have been arrived revealed that NOPAT and RONW are the most significant variable with MVA followed by EVA, ROCE and EPS. In almost all cases, the positive relationship through correlation model has been established between the variables under reference. Thus, revealing the influence of this tool for rummaging the financial potency of Indian corporate comprising an industry and Indian industries comprising the particular sector may be measured as the need of the hour for all such companies that have not started reporting their financial position in terms of EVA and MVA.

## ENDNOTES

**Market Value Added (MVA)**

While EVA measures shareholder value addition of firm in terms of its real economic performance, MVA measures market's assessment of firm's value. MVA thus measures value by the management over and above the capital invested in the company by investors.

**Market Value Added (MVA) = Market value of company - Capital employed**

For a public limited company, its market value is calculated as market value of its equity (number of shares outstanding times their share price) plus book value of debt (since market value of debt is generally not available). Capital employed is effectively the book value of investments in the business made-up of debt and equity. Effectively, the formula becomes

**Market Value Added (MVA) = Market value of equity - Book value of equity**

These items have been obtained from balance sheet statement of companies. Data for the market price existing on the close of financial year has been collected from the Economic Times, CMIE Prowess and capitaline databases.

**Economic Value Added (EVA)**

EVA introduced by Stern Stewart & company is an incarnation of Residual Income concept. Stewart defined

'EVA as an estimate of true economic profit, the amount by which earnings exceed or fall short of required minimum rate of return investors could get by investing in other securities of comparable risk'. It is the net operating profit minus the appropriate charge for the opportunity cost of capital invested in an enterprise (both debt and equity).

Expressed as a formula, EVA for a given period can be written as:

**EVA = NOPAT - COST OF CAPITAL EMPLOYED**

**= NOPAT – (WACC x CE)**

Where

NOPAT - Net Operating Profit After Taxes but before financing costs

WACC - Weighted Average Cost of Capital; and

CE - Capital Employed

(or)

equivalently, if rate of return is defined as NOPAT / CAPITAL , this turns into a perhaps more revealing formula:

**EVA = (RATE OF RETURN – COST OF CAPITAL) X CAPITAL**

Where

Rate of return - NOPAT / CAPITAL

Capital Employed - Total of balance sheet minus non-interest bearing debt in the beginning of the year.

Cost of Capital - [Cost of equity X proportion of equity from capital] + [(cost of debt X proportion of debt from capital) X (1-tax rate)]

Cost of capital or weighted average cost of capital is the average cost of both equity capital and interest bearing debt.

**Cost of debt ($K_d$)**

Cost of debt refers to the average rate of interest the company pays for its debt obligations. Cost of debt ($K_d$) has been computed as:

**$K_d$ = Total interest expenses X (1-Effective tax rate) / Beginning total borrowings**

While calculating beginning borrowing all short-term as well as long-term borrowings has to be included as all debts are interests bearing. Therefore, interest paid in the financial year has been considered as total interest expenses.

**Cost of equity ($K_e$)**

To find out cost of equity ($K_e$), Capital Assets Pricing Model (CAPM) has been used. This model holds that firms' equity cost is the composition of risk free rate of return for a stock plus premium representing the volatility of share prices. According to this model, $K_e$ is the shareholders' expected rate of return and this expected rate of return ($R_j$) is as follows:

$$R_j = R_f + \beta X (R_m - R_f)$$

Where, $R_f$ = Risk free rate of return,

$R_m$ = Market rate of return, and

$\beta$ = Sensitivity of the share price in relation to the market index

The interest rate of Government securities has been considered as a proxy for risk free rate of return. The market rate of return has been calculated by using Index Numbers of Security Prices (Bombay Stock Exchange) from year to year basis. The yearly return of the index numbers has been computed by using the following formula:

**$R_m$ = [(Index number for current year – Index number for previous Year) / (Index number of previous year)] x 100**

Beta (β) is the risk-free co-efficient which measures the volatility of a given script of a company with respect to volatility of market. It is calculated by comparing return on a share to return in the stock market. Mathematically, beta is the statistical measure of volatility. It is calculated as covariance of daily return on the stock market indices and the return on daily share prices of a particular company, divided by variance of return on daily stock market indices. The Beta co-efficient has been calculated as follows:

$$\beta_j = COV_{im} / \sigma_m^2$$

where, $\beta_j$ = is the Beta of the security in the question,

$COV_{im}$ = Stands for co-variance between the return of security and return of market, and

$\sigma_m^2$ = Stands for the variance of market return.

## REFERENCES


1. Stern, Joel (1990), "One way to build value in your firm, Executive compensation", *Financial Executive*, pp. 51-54.
2. Stewart, G. Bennet, (1994), "EVATM Fact and Fantasy", *Journal of Applied Corporate Finance*, pp. 71-84.
3. Grant, J (1996). "Foundation of EVA for investment managers: Just in time, EVA", *Journal of Financial Management*, Vol.23, No.1, p.41(8).
4. Luber, R. B. (1996), "Who are the real wealth creators". *Fortune*, pp.2-3.
5. Banerjee, Ashok (1997), "Economic Value Added (EVA): a better performance measure", *The Management Accountant*, pp.86-88.
6. Ethiraj, Govindaraj (1998), 'The EVA feather in the market cap', *The Economic Times*, p. 1.
7. KPMG- BS, (1998) " Corporate India: An Economic Value Scoreboard", *The Strategy*, Jan-march, 1998, pp.22-25.

8. Anand, Manoj, Garg, Ajay, and Arora, Asha (1999), "Economic value added : Business performance measure of shareholder value', *The Management Accountant*, pp.351-56.
9. Bao, B.H. and Bao, D.H., 'The Association between firm Value and Economic Value Added', *Indian Accounting Review*, Vol.3, No.2, pp.161-64.
10. Harihar,T.S.(1999), 'EVA prorating Myths', *Chartered Finance Analyst*, pp.8-9.
11. Thenmozhie. M. (1999), 'Economic value added as a measure of corporate performance', *The Indian Journal of Commerce*, Vol.52, No.4, pp. 72-85.
12. Banerjee, Ashok (2000), "Linkage between Economic Value Added and Market Value : An Analysis", *Vikalpa*, Vol.25, No.3, July-September, pp.23-36.
13. Riceman, S.S. and Cahan, S.F. (2002), "Do Managers Perform Better under EVA Bonus Schemes", Social Science Research Network Electronic Paper Collection, at http://oaoers.ssrb.cin.
14. Mangala, Deppa and Joura Simpy, "Linkage between Economic Value Added and Market Value: An Alaysis in Indian Context", *Indian Mangement Studies Journal*, June 2002, pp.53-65.
15. Bardia, S.C.,(2002) "Economic Value Added: Overall Consideration", *Economic Challenger*, pp. 1-7.
16. Stern, Joel, (2003) " Workshop on Value - based Management," Organised by the ASCI, Hyderabad, pp. 21-22.
17. Balachandran and Sriram (2005), Economic Value Added: A Case Study of M/S Lakshmi Machine Works Ltd, Coimbatore, Management and Accounting Research, pp. 113-122.
18. Ali. M. Ghanbari and Narges Sarlak, (2006), Economic. Value – Added; An Appropriate performance Measure in the Indian Automobile Industry, *The Icfaian Journal of Management Research*, Vol.V, No. 8, pp.45 – 61.

**TABLE 11.1**

**MVA – SECTOR – WISE TRENDS (1991-92 - 2003-04)**

| S. No | Industry | Mean (Rs.in crores) | CV | CAGR |
|---|---|---|---|---|
| 1. | Ashok Leyland Ltd | 1003.02 | 0.65 | 8.64 |
| 2. | Tata Motors Ltd | 4495.22 | 0.74 | -16.70 |
| 3. | Bajaj Tempo Ltd | 277.39 | 0.31 | -0.54 |
| 4. | Eicher Motors Ltd | 99.63 | 1.31 | 17.00 |
| 5. | Swaraj Mazda Ltd | 63.71 | 1.25 | 13.80 |
| | **Commercial Vehicles Sectors** | **1187.83** | **0.53** | **-6.34** |
| 6. | Hindustan Motors Ltd | 100.43 | 1.87 | -19.00 |
| 7. | Mahindra & Mahindra Ltd | 1105.09 | 0.62 | 7.03 |
| 8. | Maruthi Udyog Ltd | 10340.26 | 0.18 | 1.58 |
| 9. | Daewoo Motors India Ltd | -36.72 | -4.67 | -39.30 |
| | **Passenger Cars and Multiutility Vehicles Sectors** | **2877.27** | **0.18** | **1.85** |
| 10. | Bajaj Auto Ltd | 4726.06 | 0.46 | 8.36 |
| 11. | LML Ltd | 161.07 | 0.53 | -2.70 |
| 12. | Maharastra Scooters Ltd | 64.25 | 0.58 | 3.59 |
| 13. | TVS Motors Company Ltd | 583.81 | 0.98 | 15.30 |
| 14. | Kinetic Motors Co. Ltd | 88.21 | 0.60 | -14.00 |
| 15. | Hero Honda Motors Ltd | 2840.81 | 1.09 | 38.20 |
| 16. | Kinetic Engineering Ltd | 52.39 | 0.58 | -11.90 |
| 17. | Majestic Auto Ltd | 33.52 | 0.68 | -11.60 |
| 18. | Scooters India Ltd | -9.72 | -1.61 | 13.80 |
| | **Two and Three Wheelers Sectors** | **948.68** | **0.62** | **14.60** |
| | **Whole Automobile Industry** | **1671.26** | **0.20** | **2.41** |

**TABLE 11.2**

**MVA - EVA: LINEAR REGRESSION ANALYSIS**

**Dependent variable - Market Value Added (MVA)**
**Independent variable - Economic Value Added (EVA)**

| Independent Variable | Co-efficient | t | Multiple R | R Square | Adjusted R Square | Std. Error of the Estimate | Durbin-Watson | F Value |
|---|---|---|---|---|---|---|---|---|
| **Commercial Vehicles :** EVA | 1.041 | 1.138 | 0.325 | 0.11 | 0.03 | 623.52 | 0.83 | 1.30 |
| **Passenger Cars and Multiutility Vehicles:** EVA | 0.321 | 0.796 | 0.233 | 0.06 | -0.03 | 537.98 | 1.78 | 0.63 |
| **Two and Three wheelers:**EVA | 2.602 | 1.562 | 0.426 | 0.18 | 0.11 | 558.29 | 0.86 | 2.44 |
| **Whole Industry:**EVA | 0.280 | 0.556 | 0.165 | 0.03 | -0.06 | 339.76 | 1.23 | 0.31 |

***Source:*** Computed

**TABLE 11.3**

**MVA - EPS: LINEAR REGRESSION ANALYSIS**

**Dependent variable - Market Value Added (MVA)**
**Independent variable - Earning per Value (EPS)**

| Independent Variable | Co-efficient | t | Multiple R | R Square | Adjusted R Square | Std. Error of the Estimate | Durbin-Watson | F Value |
|---|---|---|---|---|---|---|---|---|
| **Commercial Vehicles:** EPS | 46.84 | 1.566 | 0.427 | 0.18 | 0.11 | 596.11 | 0.84 | 2.45 |
| **Passenger Cars and Multiutility Vehicles:** EPS | 2.67 | 0.760 | 0.223 | 0.05 | -0.04 | 539.28 | 1.99 | 0.58 |
| **Two and Three Wheelers:** EPS | 30.09 | 0.840 | 0.246 | 0.06 | -0.03 | 598.19 | 0.34 | 0.71 |
| **Whole Industry:** EPS | 6.53 | 1.068 | 0.306 | 0.09 | 0.12 | 327.93 | 1.37 | 1.14 |

***Source:*** Computed

**TABLE 11.4**

**MVA – ROCE: LINEAR REGRESSION ANALYSIS**

**Dependent variable - Market Value Added (MVA)**
**Independent variable - Return on Capital Employed (ROCE)**

| Independent Variable | Co-efficient | t | Multiple R | R Square | Adjusted R Square | Std. Error of the Estimate | Durbin-Watson | F Value |
|---|---|---|---|---|---|---|---|---|
| **Commercial Vehicles :** ROCE | 19.587 | 1.061 | 0.305 | 0.09 | 0.01 | 627.87 | 0.78 | 1.13 |
| **Passenger Cars and Multiutility Vehicles:** ROCE | 9.765 | 0.629 | 0.186 | 0.04 | -0.05 | 543.56 | 1.90 | 0.40 |
| **Two and Three Wheelers:** ROCE | 53.56** | 1.804 | 0.478 | 0.23 | 0.16 | 542.08 | 0.53 | 3.26 |
| **Whole Industry:** ROCE | 38.99* | 3.830 | 0.756 | 0.57 | 0.53 | 225.51 | 1.34 | 14.67 |

* * - Significant at 0.10 level ; * - Significant at 0.05 level

***Source:*** Computed

## TABLE 11.5

### MVA – NOPAT: LINEAR REGRESSION ANALYSIS

**Dependent variable - Market Value Added (MVA)**
**Independent variable - Net Operating Profit After Tax (NOPAT)**

| Independent Variable | Co-efficient | t | Multiple R | R Square | Adjusted R Square | Std. Error of the Estimate | Durbin-Watson | F Value |
|---|---|---|---|---|---|---|---|---|
| **Commercial Vehicles :** NOPAT | 3.044 | 1.231 | 0.348 | 0.12 | 0.04 | 618.02 | 0.74 | 1.52 |
| **Passenger Cars and Multiutility Vehicles:** NOPAT | 3.295* | 2.568 | 0.612 | 0.38 | 0.32 | 437.47 | 1.33 | 6.59 |
| **Two and Three Wheelers:** NOPAT | 10.870* | 7.896 | 0.922 | 0.85 | 0.84 | 238.99 | 1.21 | 62.34 |
| **Whole Industry:** NOPAT | 4.034* | 4.698 | 0.817 | 0.67 | 0.64 | 198.68 | 1.52 | 22.08 |

*** - Significant at 0.05 level**

***Source:*** Computed

## TABLE 11.6

### MVA – RONW: LINEAR REGRESSION ANALYSIS

**Dependent variable - Market Value Added (MVA)**
**Independent variable - Return on Net Worth (RONW)**

| Independent Variable | Co-efficient | t | Multiple R | R Square | Adjusted R Square | Std. Error of the Estimate | Durbin-Watson | F Value |
|---|---|---|---|---|---|---|---|---|
| **Commercial Vehicles :** RONW | 29.044* | 2.209 | 0.554 | 0.31 | 0.24 | 548.61 | 1.39 | 4.88 |
| **Passenger Cars and Multiutility Vehicles:** RONW | 3.364 | 0.266 | 0.080 | 0.01 | -0.08 | 551.48 | 1.97 | 0.07 |
| **Two and Three Wheelers:** RONW | -62.75* | 2.943 | 00.664 | 0.44 | 0.39 | 461.56 | 1.19 | 8.66 |
| **Whole Industry:** RONW | 20.59** | 1.874 | 0.492 | 0.24 | 0.17 | 299.95 | 1.48 | 3.51 |

*** * - Significant at 0.10 level**

*** - Significant at 0.05 level**

***Source:*** Computed

# 12

# Economic Value Added (EVA) and Shareholders Wealth Creation

## A Factor Analytic Approach

### INTRODUCTION

Corporate performance measurement is one of the emerging areas of research in finance among the researchers all over the world. Several studies are carried to find out what influences the share price (market price) of a company. Corporate performance is affected by various factors ranging from company specific, industry specific and economic variables. For long, there had been wide acceptance on the objective of the firm to maximize the value or wealth maximization. While the principle that fundamental objective of the business concerns is to increase the value of its shareholder's investment is widely accepted, there is substantially less agreement about how this is accomplished (Rappaport, 1986). As the lenders (debt and others), can protect themselves contractually, the objective can be narrowed down to maximizing stockholders value or stockholders wealth. When financial markets are efficient, the objective of maximizing stockholder wealth can be narrowed even further – to maximizing stock prices (Damodaran, 1996).

Even through stock price maximization as an objective is the narrowest of the value maximization objectives, it is the most prevalent one. It is argued that the stock prices are the most observable of all measures that can be used to judge the performance of a publicly traded firm. Besides this, the stock price is a real measure of stockholder wealth, since stockholders can sell their stock and receive the price now. While the responsibility of firm value maximization has to be fixed with the managers, using stock prices as a measure of periodic measure of corporate performance throws a serious problem. While many argue that the stock prices are not under the full control of the managers, there are many others who believe that stock price maximization leads to a short-term focus for manager-as the stock prices are determined by traders, short-term investors and analysts, all of whom hold the stock for short-periods and spend their time trying to forecast next quarter's earnings.

According to Rappaport (1986), within a business, there are seven drivers (sales growth rate, operating profit margin, income tax rate, working capital investment, fixed capital investment, cost of capital and forecast duration) that can be managed to create value. The theory suggests that improvement in these value drivers leads to an increase in shareholders' value. So, traditionally periodic corporate performance is most often measured using some variant of historical accounting income (eg. Net Profit, EPS) or some measures based on the accounting income (eg. ROI / ROCE). However, it had long been recognized that accounting income is not a consistent predictor of firm value creation and the traditional measures are not appropriate for evaluation of corporate performance.

An appropriate measure of corporate performance on one hand should be highly correlated to share holder return and on the other hand should be able to signal the extent of periodic wealth creation. A search for such a measure had been the trigger for the rapidly growing literature on Value Based Management (VBM). Among the set of popular VBM systems, a variant of the traditional residual income measure known as Economic Value Added (EVA) is arguably the most prominent. Therefore, the present study examines whether Economic Value Added has got any association with the shareholders wealth creation.

## REVIEW OF LITERATURE

Stern (1990) observed that EVA as a performance measure captures the true economic profit of an organization. EVA-based financial management and incentive compensation scheme gives managers better-quality information and superior motivation to make decisions that will create the maximum shareholder wealth in an organization. Grant (1996) found that EVA concept might have everlastingly changed the way real profitability is measured. EVA is a financial tool that focuses on the difference between company's after tax operating profit and its total cost of capital. Luber (1996) confirmed that a positive EVA over a period of time will also have an increasing MVA while negative EVA will bring down MVA as the market loses confidence in the competence of a company to ensure a handsome return on the invested capital.

Banerjee (1997) has conducted an empirical research to find the superiority of EVA over other traditional financial performance measures. ROI and EVA have been calculated for sample companies and a comparison of both showing the superiority of EVA over ROI. KPMG - BS study (1998) assessed top 100 companies on EVA, Sales, PAT and MVA criteria. The Survey has used the BS - 1000 list of companies using a composite index comprising sales, profitability and compounded annual growth rate of those companies covering the period 1996-97. Sixty companies have been found able to create positive Shareholder Value whereas 38 companies have been found to destroy it. Bao and Bao (1999) revealed that the EVA is positively and significantly correlated with the firm value. Banerjee (2000) attempted to find out whether Market Value of firm if the function of Current Operational Value (COV) and Future Growth Value (FGV). Based on the analysis of his data he comes to the conclusion that in many cases there was a considerable divergence between MVA and the sum total of COV and FGV.

Mangala and Simpy (2002) discussed the relationship between EVA and Market Value among various companies in India. The results of the analysis confirm stern's hypothesis and concluded that the company's current operational value was more significant in contributing to change in market value of share in Indian context. Manorselvi and Vijayakumar (2007) in their study revealed that the traditional measures of performance do not reflect the real value addition to shareholders wealth and EVA has to be explained shareholders value addition. Vijayakumar (2008) empirically indicated that Net Operating Profit After Tax (NOPAT) and Return on Net Worth (RONW) are the most significant variable with MVA followed by EVA and EPS. Vijayakumar (2010), in his study supports the hypothesis of Stern and Stewart's that MVA of firm was largely positively associated with EVA in all the selected sectors of Indian Automobile industry. It appears that the concept of EVA, as an emerging concept of financial management is fairly clear in the minds of almost all these researches whose studies have been reviewed above. In a fast changing business environment, the investor friendly financial performance measures may be the need of hour.

## MEASUREMENT OF ECONOMIC VALUE ADDED (EVA)

EVA introduced by Stern Stewart & Company is an incarnation of Residual Income concept. Stewart defined 'EVA as an estimate of true economic profit, the amount by which earnings exceed or fall short of required minimum rate of return investors could get by investing in other securities of comparable risk'. It is the net operating profit minus the appropriate charge for the opportunity cost of capital invested in an enterprise (both debt and equity).

Expressed as a formula, EVA for a given period can be written as:

**EVA = NOPAT - Cost of Capital Employed**

**= NOPAT – (WACC x CE)** (1)

Where

NOPAT - Net Operating Profit After Taxes but before financing costs

WACC - Weighted Average Cost of Capital; and

CE - Capital Employed

(or)

equivalently, if rate of return is defined as NOPAT / Capital, this turns into a perhaps more revealing formula:

**EVA = (Rate of Return – Cost of Capital) X Capital** (2)

Where

Rate of return - NOPAT / Capital

Capital Employed - Total of balance sheet minus non-interest bearing debt in the beginning of the year.

Cost of Capital - [Cost of equity X proportion of equity from capital] + [(cost of debt X proportion of debt from capital) X (1-tax rate)]

Cost of capital or weighted average cost of capital is the average cost of both equity capital and interest bearing debt.

**Cost of debt ($K_d$)**

Cost of debt refers to the average rate of interest the company pays for its debt obligations. Cost of debt ($K_d$) has been computed as:

$K_d$ = Total interest expenses X (1-Effective tax rate) / Beginning total borrowings (3)

While calculating beginning borrowing all short-term as well as long-term borrowings has to be included as all debts are interests bearing. Therefore, interest paid in the financial year has been considered as total interest expenses.

**Cost of equity ($K_e$)**

To find out cost of equity ($K_e$), Capital Assets Pricing Model (CAPM) has been used. This model holds that firms' equity cost is the composition of risk free rate of return for a stock plus premium representing the volatility of share prices. According to this model, $K_e$ is the shareholders' expected rate of return and this expected rate of return ($R_j$) is as follows:

$$R_j = R_f + \beta \text{ X } (R_m - R_f) \quad (4)$$

Where, $R_f$ - Risk free rate of return,

$R_m$ - Market rate of return, and

$\beta$ - Sensitivity of the share price in relation to the market index

The interest rate of Government securities has been considered as a proxy for risk free rate of return. The market rate of return has been calculated by using Index Numbers of Security Prices (Bombay Stock Exchange) from year to year basis. The yearly return of the index numbers has been computed by using the following formula:

$R_m$ = **[(Index number for current year - Index number for previous Year) / (Index number of previous year)] x 100** (5)

Beta ($\beta$) is the risk-free co-efficient which measures the volatility of a given script of a company with respect to volatility of market. It is calculated by comparing return on a share to return in the stock market. Mathematically, beta is the statistical measure of volatility. It is calculated as covariance of daily return on the stock market indices and the return on daily share prices of a particular company, divided by variance of return on daily stock market indices. The Beta co-efficient has been calculated as follows:

$$\beta_j = \mathbf{COV_{im}} / \sigma_m^2 \qquad (6)$$

where, $\beta_j$ - is the Beta of the security in the question

$COV_{im}$ - stands for co-variance between the return of security and return of market, and

$\sigma_m^2$ - stands for the variance of market return

**Market Value Added (MVA)**

While EVA measures shareholder value addition of firm in terms of its real economic performance, MVA measures market's assessment of firm's value. MVA thus measures value by the management over and above the capital invested in the company by investors.

**Market Value Added (MVA)** = **Market value of company - Capital employed** (7)

For a public limited company, its market value is calculated as market value of its equity (number of shares outstanding times their share price) plus book value of debt (since market value of debt is generally not available). Capital employed is effectively the book value of investments in the business made-up of debt and equity. Effectively, the formula becomes

**Market Value Added (MVA)** = **Market value of equity - Book value of equity** (8)

These items have been obtained from balance sheet statement of companies. Data for the market price existing on the close of financial year has been collected from the Economic Times, CMIE Prowess and Capitaline databases.

## SAMPLING SELECTION

Keeping in view the scope of the study, it is decided to

include all the companies under automobile industry working before or from the year 1996-97 to 2008-09. There are 26 companies operating in the Indian automobile industry. But, owing to several constraints such as non-availability of financial statements or non-working of a company in a particular year etc., it is compelled to restrict the number of sample companies to 20. Out of 20 selected companies under Indian Automobile Industry, three Multinational Companies (MNC's) namely Hyundai Motors India Ltd, Honda Siel Cars India Ltd and Ford India Private Ltd were omitted because these companies established their operations in India in different accounting years. The companies under automobile industry are classified into three sectors namely; Commercial vehicles, Passenger cars and Multi-utility vehicles and Two and three wheelers. For the purpose of the study all the three sectors have been selected. It accounts for 73.23 per cent of the total companies available in the Indian automobile industry. The selected 20 companies include 5 under commercial vehicles, 3 under passenger cars and multi-utility vehicles and 9 under two and three wheeler sectors. It is inferred that sample company represents 98.74 percentage of market share in commercial vehicles, 79.76 percentage of market share in passenger cars and Multi-utility vehicles and 99.81 percentage of market share in two and three wheelers. Thus, the findings based on the occurrence of such representative sample may be presumed to be true representative of automobile industry in the country.

The study is mainly based on secondary data. The major source of data analyzed and interpreted in this study related to all those companies selected is collected from "PROWESS" database, which is the most reliable on the empowered corporate database of Centre for Monitoring Indian Economy (CMIE). Besides prowess database, relevant secondary data have also been collected from BSE Stock Exchange Official Directory, CMIE Publications, Annual Survey of Industry, Business newspapers, Reports on Currency and Finance, Libraries of various Research Institutions, through Internet etc.

## ANALYSIS OF EVA

The concept of EVA is well established in financial economics but only recently this term has moved into the main stream of corporate finance, as more and more companies have started adopting it as the base for business planning and financial performance monitoring. There is grouping evidence that EVA, not EBIT, determines the value of a firm. Effective use of capital is the key to value. The present part of analysis examines in detail the EVA of sample companies. A ranking has been done with respect to EVA. Various statistical measures like mean, standard deviation, range, variance, skewness and kurtosis have been computed to understand the central tendency and dispersion of EVA of sample companies. Kendall tau-b has been used to test the association between the selected financial variables. Multiple regressions have been adopted to find out the best predictor from among the independent variables. EVA based frequency distribution of sample companies is shown by Table 12.1. It is clear from the Table 12.1 that during the first six years of the study period, 29.4 per cent in 1996-97, 5.9 percent in 1997-98, 58.9 per cent in 1998-99, 5.9 per cent in 1999-2000, 11.8 per cent in 2000-2001 and 5.9 per cent in 2001-02 have registered negative EVA. Looking at the Table 12.1, it is also inferred that around 53 per cent to 76 per cent of the sample companies have registered negative EVA during the year 2002-03 to 2008-09.

Around 29 per cent to 47 per cent of the companies during the first six years of the study period and around 6 per cent to 35 per cent of the sample companies during the last six years under study are generating positive EVA, but it has been up to 50 crores. About 6 per cent to 12 per cent of the sample companies from 1996-97 to 2001-02 and about the same percentage of the sample companies from 2003-04 to 2008-09 reported an EVA of over Rs. 100 crores to Rs. 200 crores. Table 12.1 reveal that the number of companies generating EVA in the range of above Rs. 200 crores has drastically come down during 2002-03 to 2006-07.

## Trends in EVA-Based Rankings

Trends in EVA of sample companies (year-wise ranking) and Trends in EVA of top 5 and last five of the sample companies are portrayed by Table 12.2 and Table 12.5. The top five companies include Bajaj Auto Ltd, Hero Honda Motors Ltd, Mahindra and Mahindra Ltd, Ashok Leyland Ltd and Tata Motors Ltd. Out of the these five companies, one company namely Mahindra and Mahindra Ltd belongs to passenger cars and multiutility vehicles sector, two companies namely Bajaj Auto Ltd and Hero Honda Motors Ltd belongs to two and three wheelers sector and the remaining two companies namely Ashok Leyland Ltd and Tata Motors Ltd belongs to commercial vehicles sector. In four out of thirteen years Hero Honda Motors Ltd and three out of thirteen years Tata Motors Ltd and Bajaj Auto Ltd have been holding the first rank. However in the terminal years, Tata Motors Ltd and Bajaj Auto Ltd EVA performance is quite discouraging. Among the last five companies namely Maruti Udyog Ltd, Kinetic Motor Company Ltd, Majestic Auto Ltd, Kinetic Engineering Ltd and Scooters India Ltd which all belongs to two and three wheelers sector.

## Results and Discussion on statistical analysis of EVA

Different statistical measures have been computed for understanding the central tendency and dispersion of EVA of sample companies. For this purpose, statistical value of the mean, range, standard deviation, variance, skewness and kurtosis have been computed. Kurtosis and skewness have been calculated to show about the distribution (Symmetric/ Asymmetric). Kurtosis is measures of the "peakedness" or the "flatness" of a distribution. A kurtosis value near zero (o) indicates a shape close to normal. A positive value for the kurtosis indicates a distribution more peaked than normal. Negative kurtosis indicates a shape flatter than normal. An extreme negative kurtosis (eg.<–5.0) indicates a distribution where more of the values are in the tails of the distribution that around the mean. A kurtosis value between ± 1.0 is considered excellent for most psychometric purposes and a value between ± 2.0 in many cases also acceptable. Skewness measures to what extent a distribution of values deviates from symmetry around the mean. A value of zero represents a symmetric or evenly balanced distribution. A positive skewness indicates a greater number of smaller values. A negative skewness indicates a greater number of larger values. A skewness value between ± 1 is considered excellent and a value between ± 2 is in many cases acceptable.

Company-wise statistical analysis of EVA is offered by Table 12.3 where it is observed that out of the selected seventeen companies, twelve companies (71 per cent) have registered positive mean EVA, whereas Bajaj Auto Ltd stands first in the list with the higher average followed by Hero Honda Motors Ltd, Mahindra and Mahindra Ltd, Ashok Leyland Ltd and Tata Motors Ltd. The values of range show the high volatility in EVA and that of standard deviation and variance display the variation scale from central tendency and dispersion. Fourty one per cent companies (7 out of 17) have their EVA positively skewed and 58 per cent companies (10 out of 17) indicate positive kurtosis reflecting that the observations cluster more and with longer tails.

**EVA vis-a-vis selected Financial Variables**

Various statistical tools like mean, standard, deviation, variance, range, skewness and kurtosis show inconsistent results to get a grip over EVA's behaviour. Supplementary information based on statistical analysis is considered necessary to understand the behaviour patterns of the EVA measure. The generic research task of this part is to observe and assess how the EVA measure is related with the long established but traditional measures. In this section, an attempt has been made to bring out the basic analysis of relationship between selected financial measures and EVA of selected companies during the study period. These measures include Turnover, Return on Sales (ROS), Return on Total Assets (ROTA), Return on Capital Employed (ROCE), Earnings Per Share (EPS), Market Price Per Share (MP) and Market Value Added (MVA). These measures are mainly used to appraise the financial performance of a corporate. Kendall's tau-b has been considered appropriate tool to measure the relationship of EVA with selected financial variables, since it is based on the ranked variables.

**Kendall's TAU-B**

It is a non parametric measure of association for ordinal or ranked variables that takes ties into account. The sign of the coefficient indicates the direction of the relationship, and its absolute value indicates the strength, with large absolute values indicating stronger relationships. The relationship of EVA with the selected financial variables has been analyzed and are presented in the Table 12.4. Table 12.4 puts forward the synoptic description of the relationship of EVA with select financial variables for the selected Indian Automobile Companies during the study period. Glancing all the way through the Table 12.4, it is noticed that the correlation between EVA and sales is found at above moderate level in Kinetic Motor Company Ltd and Hero Honda Motors Ltd and significant at 1 per cent level. On the other hand, the correlation between these variables in Maruti Udyog Ltd, Bajaj Auto Ltd and Scooters India Ltd recorded negative trend but significant at 5 per cent level only in Scooters India Ltd. Below moderate level of relationship was found during the study period for the remaining companies with regard to EVA with sales.

The correlation coefficient explaining the relationship between EVA and ROS reveals that below moderate level of relationship was found with regard to EVA with ROS except Kinetic Motor Company Ltd but significant at 1 per cent level. The correlation co-efficient explaining the relationship between EVA with ROTA reveals that below moderate level relationships exists in all the selected companies except Kinetic Motor Company Ltd and Hero Honda Motors Ltd. However, in case of Tata Motors Ltd, Bajaj Auto Ltd, Maharashtra Scooters Ltd and TVS Motor Company Ltd, an adverse relationship is noticed. The table further reveals that there exists below moderate degree but positive correlation in ten out of seventeen companies as regards EVA and ROCE. The degrees of negative correlation observed between EVA and ROCE in Tata Motors Ltd, Mahindra and Mahindra Ltd, Maharashtra Scooters Ltd, TVS Motor Company Ltd and Hero Honda Motors Ltd. It is noticed that the degree of correlation is superior and positive in Kinetic Motor Company Ltd but significant at 1 per cent level. Further, there exists low degree of positive correlation (8 out of 17) and low degree of negative correlation (6 out of 17) between EVA and EPS over the study period. The correlation between EVA and EPS is found at above moderate level only in case of Kinetic Engineering Ltd, Hero Honda Motors Ltd and Scooters India Ltd, with 1 per cent and 5 per cent level of significance.

The relationship between EVA and MP shows that insignificant below moderate level of relationship was found in all the selected companies. Similarly, the correlation between EVA and MVA is though negative in twelve out of seventeen companies, the strength is below moderate level / low in all the companies except LML Ltd during the study period but significant at 5 per cent level. Hence, it is concluded that there exists significant positive relationship between EVA with Sales, ROS, ROTA, ROCE and EPS in the case of Kinetic Motor Company Ltd. Further, EVA is significantly associated with ROS in case of Swaraj Mazda Ltd, with MVA in LML Ltd (but negative), with ROTA in TVS Motor Company Ltd, with ROTA and EPS in Hero Honda Motors Ltd, with ROS and EPS in Kinetic Engineering Ltd and with sales (negative) and EPS in Scooters India Ltd during the study period.

**Factor Analysis**

Eight functional parameters which signify the wealth maximisation of shareholders have been considered for the study viz., Earnings Per Share (EPS), Sales (S), Profit After Tax (PAT), Market Price (MP), Market Value Added (MVA), Return on Sales (ROS), Return on Total Assets (RTA) and Return on Capital Employed (ROCE). In order to disclose which among these factors contribute much towards shareholders wealth maximisation, factor analysis has been done. Factor analysis is a multivariate statistical technique used to condense and simplify. This technique is helpful to identify the underlying factors that determine the relationship between the observed variables and provides an empirical classification scheme of clustering of statements into groups called factors. It is often used in data reduction to identify a small number of factors that explain most of the variance observed in a much larger number of manifest variables.

To test the acceptability of data, the following steps were taken. The correlation matrices were computed. It revealed that there is enough correlation to go ahead for factor analysis. Kaiser-Meyer-Olkin measure of sampling adequacy (KMO) and Bartlett's test of sphericity have been applied, to the resultant correlation matrix to test whether the relationship among the variables has been significant or not. A KMO measure which is more than 0.6 is considered 'mediocre' and is acceptable. A measure $<0.5$ is not acceptable. The overall significance of correlation matrices is tested with Bartlett's Test of Sphericity providing support for the validity of the factor analysis of the data set. It also tests whether the correlation matrix is an identity matrix (factor analysis would be meaningless with an identity matrix). A significance value $<0.05$ indicates that these data do not produce an identity matrix and are thus approximately multivariate normal and acceptable for factor analysis.

Communalities represent the proportion of the variance explained by the component or factor. This is similar to the $R^2$ in regression analysis. The higher the loading, the more important is the factor. However, Comrey (1973) suggested that anything above 0.44 could be considered salient, with increased loading becoming more vital in determining the factor. After the standards indicated that the data are suitable for factor analysis, Principal Component Analysis is employed for extracting the data, which allowed determining the factor underlying the relationship between a numbers of variables. Rotation is necessary when extraction technique suggests that there are two or more factors. The rotation of factors is designed to give an idea of how the factors initially extracted differ from each other and to provide a clear picture of which items loads on which factor. An orthogonal rotation is performed using Varimax with Kaiser Normalisation. Factor analysis has been done in the present part of analysis for the Indian automobile industry as a whole and for the entire three sectors.

*Whole Industry*

Table 12.6 demonstrates that the principal component analysis and rotated factor loading method is used for stimulating factor for whole Indian automobile industry. The result of the test shows that with the significant value of 0.000 there is significant relationship among the variable chosen. KMO test yields a result of 0.709 which state that factor analysis can be carried out appropriately for the eight variables that are taken for the study. Table 12.6 gives the rotated factor loadings, communalities, eigen values and the percentage of variance explained by the factors. Out of the eight variables, three factors have been extracted and these three factors put together explain the total variance of these factors to the extent of 69.902 per cent and total Eigen value of the factors is 5.591. The communalities vary from 46 per cent to 88 per cent suggesting that the extracted factors are sufficient to account for most of the variations existing in the data. This inference is confirmed by the total variation explained by the analysis, which is 69.902 per cent.

The varimax rotation results are also given in the Table 12.6. The three factors were identified as it accounted the maximum percentage variance. The three variables such as sales, profit after tax and market price were grouped together as Factor I and accounts for 38.28 per cent of the total variance. The perusal of factor loadings on Factor I reveals that this factor has clearly brought together different variables relating to wealth maximisation of the enterprises. Factor II explains 18.14 per cent of the total variations in the variable sets. The significant loadings on this factor are return on sales, return on total assets and return on capital employed. An examination of the factor loading reveals that significant loadings on this factor include the elements relating to firm's internal performances. The variables Earnings Per Share and Market Value Added are constituted as factor III and accounted for 13.48 per cent. Thus, the factor analysis condensed and simplified the 8 variables and grouped them into 3 factors explaining 69.90 per cent. Sales and Profit After Tax are found to have a stronger relationship.

*Commercial Vehicles*

Using all the eight variables, factor analysis was performed for commercial vehicles sector and the results are presented in Table 12.7. Table 12.7 gives the rotated factor loadings, communalities, eigen values and the percentage of variance explained by the factors. The results of Bartlett's Test (sig.0.000) and KMO test (0.669) shows that factor analysis can be carried out appropriately for these eight variables that are taken for the study. From the table, it is observed that out of eight variables, two factors are identified by the rotation method. The total percentage of variation in the factors show 79.720 per cent and total Eigen value of the factors is 6.378. Table 12.7 also depicts that clustering of stimulating wealth maximization. Two factors were identified which accounted for the maximum percentage variance. The four variables viz., Earnings per share Return on sales, Return on total assets and Return on capital employed were grouped together as Factor I and accounted for 52.66 per cent of the total variance. The remaining four variables viz., Sales, Profit after tax, Market Price and Market Value Added are constituted as factor II and accounted for 27.06 percent of the total variance. The communalities vary from 68 per cent to 88 per cent suggesting that the extracted factors are sufficient to account for most of the variations existing in the data. Return on total assets, Return on sales and sales are found to have a stronger relationship.

*Passenger Cars and Multiutility Vehicles*

Table 12.8 gives the rotated factor loadings, communalities, eigen values and the percentage of variance explained by the factors for passenger cars and multiutility vehicles sector of Indian automobile industry. The KMO test (0.758) and Bartlett's Test of Sphericity (Sig.0.000) states that factor analysis can be carried out appropriately for these eight variables that are taken for the study. Out of the eight variables, two factors have been extracted and these two factors put together explain the total variance of these variables to the extent of 83.217 per cent. In order to reduce the number of factors and enhance the interpretability, the factors were rotated. The results of varimax rotation are also presented in Table 12.8. Two factors were identified which accounted for the maximum percentage variance. Factor I explains 58.616 per cent of the total variance with eigen value of 4.688. The significant loadings on this factor are sales, profit after tax, market price and return on total assets. The remaining four variables Earnings Per Share, Market Value Added, Return on Sales and Return on Capital Employed constituted the Factor II and accounted for 24.616 per cent of the total variance with eigen value of 1.969. The high value of communality ranging 48 per cent to 96 per cent suggesting that the extracted factors are sufficient to account for most of the variations existing in the data and this is confirmed by the total variation explained by the analysis, which is 83.217 per cent. Profit After Tax, Market Price and Earnings Per Share are found to have stronger relationship.

*Two and Three wheelers*

Table 12.9 demonstrates that principal component analysis and rotated factor loading method is used for stimulating factors for the two and three wheelers sector of the Indian automobile industry. From the table, it is observed that out of eight variables, three factors are identified by the rotation method. The total percentages of variation in the factors show 68. 513 per cent and total eigen value of the factors is 5.481. The results of KMO test (0.638) and Bartlett's Test of Sphericity (sig.0.000) confirms that factor analysis can be carried out appropriately for the variables selected for the study. The varimax rotation results are also given in the Table 12.9. From the table, it is observed that three factors were identified as being maximum per cent variance accounted. The three variables viz., Sales, Profit after tax and Market price were cluster together as Factor I and accounts 38. 398 per cent of the total variance. Variables return on sales, return on total assets and return on capital employed are constituted as Factor II and accounts 16.847 per cent of the total variance. Variables Earnings Per Share and Market Value Added constituted as Factor III and accounts 13.267 per cent of the total variance. The high communality values (49 per cent to 89 per cent) suggesting that extracted factors are sufficient to account for most of the variations existing in the data. Stronger relationships between variables are noticed with regard to Sales, Market Value Added and Market Price.

## CONCLUSION

The results of the study showed that 53 per cent to 76 per cent of the sample companies have registered negative EVA during the terminal years of the study period. The top five companies in generating EVA include Bajaj Auto Ltd, Hero Honda Motors Ltd(two and three wheelers sector), Mahindra and Mahindra Ltd (passenger cars and multiutility vehicles sector), Ashok Leyland Ltd and Tata Motors Ltd(commercial vehicles sector). Below moderate level relationship was found during the study period with regard to EVA with the selected financial variables. The results of factor analysis showed that out of the eight variables, three factors have been extracted and these three factors put together explain 69.902 per cent of the total variance. Further, the results showed that sales and profit after tax are found to have a stronger relationship with EVA.

## REFERENCES

1. Bacidore, J.M., Boquist, J.A., Milboum, T.T., and Thakor, A.V. (1997). "The search for the vest financial performance measure". *Financial Analysis Journal*, Vol. 53(3), pp. 11-20.

2. Banerjee, Ashok (2000). "Linkage between Economic value added and market value: An analysis", *Vikalpa*, Vol. 25(3), pp. 23 -36.

3. Bao, B.H., and Bao, D.H. (1999). "The Association between Firm value and Economic Value Added", *Indian Accounting Review*, Vol. 3(2), pp.161 -64.

4. Comrey, A.L. (1973). "A First Course in Factor Analysis", New York : Academic Press.

5. Grant, J. (1996). "Foundation of EVA for Investment Management; Just in Time, EVA", *Journal of Financial Management*. Vol. 23(1), pp. 41 - 45.

6. KPMG-BS (1998). "Corporate India: An Economic value scoreboard". *The Strategy*. PP.22-25.

7. Luber, R.B. (1996). "Who are the real wealth creators", *Fortune*, pp. 2 -3.

8. Mangala, Deepa and Joura Simpy (2002). "Linkage between economic value added and market value: An analysis in Indian context", *Indian Management Studies Journal*, pp. 55-65.

9. Manor Selvi, A. and Vijayakumar, A. (2007). "Performance of Indian Automobile Industry: Economic Value Added Approach", *Management and Labour Studies*, Vol. 32(4), pp. 451 - 467.

10. Stem Stewart (1990). "One way to build value in your firm. Executive compensation", *Financial Executive*, pp. 51 -54.

11. Vijayakumar, A. (2008). "Linkage between Market Value Added (MVA) and other Financial variables: An analysis in Indian Automobile Industry", *Management and Labour Studies*, Vol. 33(4), pp. 504-521.

12. Vijayakumar, A. (2010). "Economic Value Added (EVA) and Market Value Added (MVA)-An empirical study of relationship". *College Sadhana*, Vol. 2(2), pp.141-148.

## TABLE 12.1

## EVA – FREQUENCY DISTRIBUTION OF SAMPLE COMPANIES (1996-97 TO 2008-09)

| EVA | 96-97 | 97-98 | 98-99 | 99-00 | 00-01 | 01-02 | 02-03 | 03-04 | 04-05 | 05-06 | 06-07 | 07-08 | 08-09 |
|---|---|---|---|---|---|---|---|---|---|---|---|---|---|
| Negative | 5 (29.4) | 1 (5.9) | 10 (58.8) | 1 (5.9) | 2 (11.8) | 1 (5.9) | 9 (52.9) | 4 (23.5) | 10 (58.8) | 13 (76.4) | 8 (47.0) | 4 (23.5) | 8 (47.0) |
| Up to Rs.50 Cr | 6 (35.3) | 7 (41.1) | 5 (29.4) | 6 (35.3) | 8 (47.0) | 8 (47.0) | 3 (17.6) | 6 (35.3) | 3 (17.6) | 1 (5.9) | 3 (17.6) | 3 (17.6) | 2 (11.8) |
| Rs.50 Cr to Rs.100 Cr | – | 1 (5.9) | – | 1 (5.9) | – | 1 (5.9) | 1 (5.9) | 1 (5.9) | 2 (11.8) | – | 1 (5.9) | 2 (11.8) | 1 (5.9) |
| Rs.100 Cr to Rs.200 Cr | 2 (11.8) | 2 (11.8) | 1 (5.9) | 1 (5.9) | 2 (11.8) | 1 (5.9) | 2 (11.8) | 2 (11.8) | – | 2 (11.8) | 2 (11.8) | 1 (5.9) | – |
| Above Rs.200 Cr | 4 (23.5) | 6 (35.3) | 1 (5.9) | 8 (47.0) | 5 (29.4) | 6 (35.3) | 2 (11.8) | 4 (23.5) | 2 (11.8) | 1 (5.9) | 3 (17.6) | 7 (41.1) | 6 (35.3) |
| Total | 17 (100) | 17 (100) | 17 (100) | 17 (100) | 17 (100) | 17 (100) | 17 (100) | 17 (100) | 17 (100) | 17 (100) | 17 (100) | 17 (100) | 17 (100) |

Figures in brackets denote percentage to total.

***Source :*** Computed

**TABLE 12.2**

**TRENDS IN EVA (YEAR—WISE)**

| Company | 96-97 | 97-98 | 98-99 | 99-00 | 00-01 | 01-02 | 02-03 | 03-04 | 04-05 | 05-06 | 06-07 | 07-08 | 08-09 |
|---|---|---|---|---|---|---|---|---|---|---|---|---|---|
| Ashok Leyland Ltd | 3 | 6 | 2 | 8 | 4 | 6 | 4 | 4 | 16 | 16 | 2 | 2 | 6 |
| Tata Motors Ltd | 1 | 1 | 17 | 1 | 6 | 10 | 16 | 3 | 2 | 17 | 17 | 6 | 3 |
| Bajaj Tempo Ltd | 15 | 13 | 12 | 17 | 16 | 16 | 6 | 11 | 13 | 11 | 6 | 9 | 8 |
| Eicher Motors Ltd | 10 | 16 | 5 | 13 | 9 | 13 | 8 | 8 | 11 | 3 | 11 | 8 | 16 |
| Swaraj Mazda Ltd | 11 | 14 | 4 | 16 | 11 | 14 | 7 | 12 | 6 | 5 | 10 | 11 | 14 |
| Hindustan Motors Ltd | 7 | 7 | 13 | 9 | 14 | 8 | 14 | 17 | 3 | 12 | 13 | 10 | 13 |
| Mahindra and Mahindra Ltd | 6 | 4 | 14 | 4 | 3 | 5 | 13 | 5 | 4 | 2 | 3 | 3 | 1 |
| Maruti Udyog Ltd | 2 | 2 | 16 | 3 | 17 | 2 | 17 | 9 | 17 | 15 | 5 | 1 | 17 |
| Bajaj Auto Ltd | 4 | 3 | 15 | 2 | 1 | 1 | 1 | 7 | 8 | 6 | 12 | 5 | 4 |
| LML Ltd | 5 | 5 | 1 | 5 | 2 | 4 | 2 | 2 | 15 | 13 | 9 | 17 | 7 |
| Maharashtra Scooters Ltd | 14 | 10 | 11 | 10 | 12 | 11 | 3 | 10 | 7 | 4 | 7 | 12 | 9 |
| TVS Motor Company Ltd | 8 | 8 | 6 | 7 | 7 | 7 | 15 | 6 | 14 | 14 | 4 | 7 | 5 |
| Kinetic Motor Company Ltd | 13 | 15 | 9 | 12 | 10 | 9 | 10 | 15 | 12 | 10 | 16 | 16 | 15 |
| Hero Honda Motors Ltd | 9 | 9 | 3 | 6 | 5 | 3 | 11 | 1 | 1 | 1 | 1 | 4 | 2 |
| Kinetic Engineering Ltd | 12 | 11 | 8 | 11 | 8 | 12 | 12 | 16 | 5 | 8 | 8 | 15 | 12 |
| Majestic Auto Ltd | 17 | 17 | 10 | 14 | 13 | 17 | 9 | 13 | 9 | 7 | 14 | 13 | 11 |
| Scooters India Ltd | 16 | 12 | 7 | 15 | 15 | 15 | 5 | 14 | 10 | 9 | 15 | 14 | 10 |

***Source :*** Computed

## TABLE 12.3

## COMPANY -WISE STATISTICAL ANALYSIS OF EVA

| Company | Mean | SD | CV | CAGR | Variance | Skewness | Kurtosis | Max. | Min. |
|---|---|---|---|---|---|---|---|---|---|
| Ashok Leyland Ltd | 268.82 | 418.77 | 1.56 | 0.84 | 175367.50 | 2.22 | 7.23 | 1508.58 | -248.60 |
| Tata Motors Ltd | 175.30 | 937.62 | 5.35 | 6.39 | 879136.10 | -0.59 | 1.55 | 1888.03 | -1937.03 |
| Bajaj Tempo Ltd | 5.40 | 44.46 | 8.23 | 11.95 | 1976.64 | 0.10 | -0.67 | 77.82 | -57.77 |
| Eicher Motors Ltd | 4.31 | 111.29 | 25.82 | 24.89 | 12385.71 | -2.08 | 6.97 | 164.59 | -321.69 |
| Swaraj Mazda Ltd | 3.87 | 27.68 | 7.15 | 14.47 | 766.43 | -2.16 | 7.52 | 47.35 | -78.08 |
| Hindustan Motors Ltd | 11.14 | 87.78 | 7.88 | 4.06 | 7706.02 | -0.33 | -0.17 | 138.27 | -167.24 |
| Mahindra and Mahindra Ltd | 412.04 | 511.67 | 1.24 | 23.94 | 261809.40 | 1.12 | 0.38 | 1494.67 | -178.50 |
| Maruti Udyog Ltd | -34.63 | 1635.34 | -47.22 | 23.61 | 2674321 | -0.34 | 1.40 | 3210.54 | -3174.69 |
| Bajaj Auto Ltd | 516.17 | 702.76 | 1.36 | 10.24 | 493873.40 | 1.27 | 1.91 | 2223.75 | -425.16 |
| LML Ltd | 174.89 | 224.62 | 1.28 | -5.15 | 50454.24 | -0.43 | -1.33 | 462.71 | -165.39 |
| Maharashtra Scooters Ltd | 23.52 | 39.88 | 1.70 | -4.95 | 1590.17 | 2.06 | 5.33 | 135.48 | -28.90 |
| TVS Motor Company Ltd | 83.35 | 179.43 | 2.15 | 18.70 | 32196.19 | -0.64 | 0.43 | 341.95 | -304.01 |
| Kinetic Motor Company Ltd | -23.12 | 40.88 | -1.77 | 33.00 | 1671.43 | -0.36 | -1.01 | 28.47 | -95.70 |
| Hero Honda Motors Ltd | 475.80 | 396.09 | 0.83 | 32.03 | 156884 | 0.18 | -1.60 | 1060.65 | -34.30 |
| Kinetic Engineering Ltd | -2.34 | 29.87 | -12.76 | 5.80 | 892.31 | -0.49 | -1.06 | 36.60 | -55.50 |
| Majestic Auto Ltd | -5.70 | 12.38 | -2.17 | -9.55 | 153.26 | -0.06 | -0.77 | 14.78 | -27.78 |
| Scooters India Ltd | -0.97 | 33.43 | -34.46 | 51.12 | 1117.24 | 1.98 | 6.03 | 94.98 | -46.36 |

***Source :*** Computed

## TABLE 12.4

## EVA WITH SELECTED FINANCIAL VARIABLES (WHOLE SAMPLE) – KENDALL'S TAU B

| Company | Sales | ROS | ROTA | ROCM | EPS | MP | MVA |
|---|---|---|---|---|---|---|---|
| Ashok Leyland Ltd | 0.103 | 0.000 | 0.103 | 0.000 | -0.077 | -0.179 | -0.128 |
| Tata Motors Ltd | 0.000 | -0.090 | -0.103 | -0.128 | -0.039 | -0.077 | -0.026 |
| Bajaj Tempo Ltd | 0.256 | 0.179 | 0.205 | 0.256 | 0.142 | -0.256 | -0.205 |
| Eicher Motors Ltd | 0.179 | 0.179 | 0.000 | 0.179 | 0.103 | 0.065 | -0.206 |
| Swaraj Mazda Ltd | 0.026 | 0.436* | 0.359 | 0.308 | 0.333 | -0.154 | 0.206 |
| Hindustan Motors Ltd | 0.410 | 0.231 | 0.128 | 0.179 | 0.116 | 0.090 | -0.385 |
| Mahindra and Mahindra Ltd | 0.282 | -0.051 | 0.000 | -0.103 | 0.179 | 0.179 | 0.051 |
| Maruti Udyog Ltd | -0.103 | 0.245 | 0.179 | 0.179 | 0.333 | - | 0.128 |
| Bajaj Auto Ltd | -0.205 | 0.154 | -0.154 | 0.000 | -0.256 | -0.333 | 0.065 |
| LML Ltd | 0.333 | 0.103 | 0.308 | 0.359 | 0.256 | 0.128 | -0.513* |
| Maharashtra Scooters Ltd | 0.000 | -0.231 | -0.231 | -0.205 | -0.231 | -0.103 | 0.282 |
| TVS Motor Company Ltd | 0.179 | -0.245 | -0.462* | -0.410 | -0.308 | -0.385 | -0.154 |
| Kinetic Motor Company Ltd | 0.718** | 0.821** | 0.727** | 0.818** | 0.718** | 0.385 | -0.256 |
| Hero Honda Motors Ltd | 0.641** | 0.000 | 0.503* | -0.026 | 0.564** | 0.385 | -0.410 |
| Kinetic Engineering Ltd | 0.333 | 0.487* | 0.154 | 0.282 | 0.452* | -0.051 | -0.128 |
| Majestic Auto Ltd | 0.179 | 0.179 | 0.179 | 0.103 | -0.077 | -0.333 | -0.282 |
| Scooters India Ltd | -0.462* | 0.385 | 0.256 | 0.308 | 0.538* | -0.333 | -0.410 |

**** - Significant at 0.01 level; * - Significant at 0.05 level;**

***Source :*** Computed

## TABLE 12.5

## RANKING BASED ON THIRTEEN YEARS AVERAGE OF EVA

| ECONOMIC VALUE ADDED | | | |
|---|---|---|---|
| **Top Five Companies** | **Mean Value (Rs. in Crores)** | **Last Five Companies** | **Mean Value (Rs. in Crores)** |
| Bajaj Auto Ltd | 516.17 | Maruti Udyog Ltd | -34.63 |
| Hero Honda Motors India Ltd | 475.80 | Kinetic Motor Company Ltd | -23.12 |
| Mahindra and Mahindra Ltd | 412.04 | Majestic Auto Ltd | -5.70 |
| Ashok Leyland Ltd | 268.82 | Kinetic Engineering Ltd | -2.34 |
| Tata Motors Ltd | 175.30 | Scooters India Ltd | -0.97 |

## TABLE 12.6

## SUMMARY OF FACTOR ANALYSIS – ROTATED FACTOR LOADINGS (WHOLE INDUSTRY)

| **Parameters** | **Factors 1** | **2** | **3** | **Communality** |
|---|---|---|---|---|
| Earnings Per Share (EPS) | - 0.012 | 0.228 | 0.870 | 0.809 |
| Sales (S) | 0.895 | 0.004 | 0.286 | 0.883 |
| Profit After Tax (PAT) | 0.923 | 0.099 | 0.133 | 0.879 |
| Market Price (MP) | 0.822 | 0.189 | - 0.016 | 0.711 |
| Market Value Added (MVA) | 0.406 | - 0.053 | 0.738 | 0.713 |
| Return on Sales (ROS) | - 0.033 | 0.598 | 0.054 | 0.461 |
| Return on Total Assets (RTA) | 0.219 | 0.740 | 0.100 | 0.606 |
| Return on Capital Employed (ROCE) | 0.094 | 0.788 | 0.035 | 0.631 |
| Eigen value | 3.062 | 1.451 | 1.078 | 5.591 |
| % of Variance | 38.279 | 18.141 | 13.481 | 69.902 |
| Cum. % variance | 38.279 | 56.420 | 69.902 | |
| **Kaiser-Meyer-Olkin measure of Sampling Adequacy -** | | | | **0.709** |
| **Bartlett's Test of Sphericity -** | | | | **669.906 (Sig. 0.000)** |

## TABLE 12.7

## COMMERCIAL VEHICLES

| Parameters | Factors 1 | Factors 2 | Communality |
|---|---|---|---|
| Earnings Per Share (EPS) | 0.846 | 0.286 | 0.797 |
| Sales (S) | 0.141 | 0.918 | 0.862 |
| Profit After Tax (PAT) | 0.266 | 0.854 | 0.800 |
| Market Price (MP) | 0.023 | 0.823 | 0.677 |
| Market Value Added (MVA) | 0.130 | 0.863 | 0.761 |
| Return on Sales (ROS) | 0.911 | 0.205 | 0.872 |
| Return on Total Assets (RTA) | 0.918 | 0.195 | 0.880 |
| Return on Capital Employed (ROCE) | 0.849 | - 0.084 | 0.728 |
| Eigen value | 4.213 | 2.165 | 6.378 |
| % of Variance | 52.660 | 27.060 | 79.720 |
| Cum. % variance | 52.660 | 79.720 | |
| **Kaiser-Meyer-Olkin measure of Sampling Adequacy -** | | | **0.669** |
| **Bartlett's Test of Sphericity -** | | | **464.323 (Sig. 0.000)** |

## TABLE 12.8

## PASSENGER CARS AND MULTIUTILITY VEHICLES

| Parameters | Factors 1 | Factors 2 | Communality |
|---|---|---|---|
| Earnings Per Share (EPS) | - 0.116 | 0.899 | 0.821 |
| Sales (S) | 0.889 | 0.183 | 0.824 |
| Profit After Tax (PAT) | 0.976 | - 0.080 | 0.960 |
| Market Price (MP) | 0.964 | - 0.059 | 0.932 |
| Market Value Added (MVA) | - 0.012 | 0.694 | 0.482 |
| Return on Sales (ROS) | 0.642 | 0.657 | 0.844 |
| Return on Total Assets (RTA) | 0.772 | 0.581 | 0.934 |
| Return on Capital Employed (ROCE) | 0.536 | 0.758 | 0.861 |
| Eigen value | 4.688 | 1.969 | 6.657 |
| % of Variance | 58.616 | 24.616 | 83.217 |
| Cum. % variance | 58.616 | 83.217 | |
| **Kaiser-Meyer-Olkin measure of Sampling Adequacy -** | | | **0.758** |
| **Bartlett's Test of Sphericity -** | | | **374.138 (Sig.0.000)** |

**TABLE 12.9**

**TWO AND THREE WHEELERS**

| Parameters | Factors 1 | 2 | 3 | Communality |
|---|---|---|---|---|
| Earnings Per Share (EPS) | 0.314 | 0.367 | 0.512 | 0.496 |
| Sales (S) | 0.946 | 0.027 | 0.005 | 0.896 |
| Profit After Tax (PAT) | 0.819 | 0.142 | 0.425 | 0.871 |
| Market Price (MP) | 0.842 | 0.168 | - 0.014 | 0.737 |
| Market Value Added (MVA) | - 0.016 | 0.002 | 0.938 | 0.880 |
| Return on Sales (ROS) | - 0.055 | 0.707 | - 0.048 | 0.505 |
| Return on Total Assets (RTA) | 0.257 | 0.648 | 0.206 | 0.529 |
| Return on Capital Employed (ROCE) | 0.126 | 0.736 | 0.095 | 0.566 |
| Eigen value | 3.072 | 1.348 | 1.061 | 5.481 |
| % of Variance | 38.398 | 16.847 | 13.267 | 68.513 |
| Cum. % variance | 38.398 | 55.246 | 68.513 | |
| **Kaiser-Meyer-Olkin measure of Sampling Adequacy -** | | | | **0.638** |
| **Bartlett's Test of Sphericity -** | | | | **337.060 (Sig.0.000)** |

***Source :*** Compiled from Annual Reports.

# PART - IV

# ANALYSIS OF PRODUCTION

# 13

# Comparative Study of Linear Trend Regression, Holt and Winter Models, with Application to Production of Indian Automobiles

## INTRODUCTION

The need for quick, reliable, simple and medium term forecasts of various time series is often encountered in economies and business environments. Linear Trend Regression, Holt and Winter models trend provide a comprehensive, simple, accurate and applicable solution to this question. However their computational techniques differs, but their accuracy, simplicity and stability on any time series data can be compared via the behaviour of their forecasts, statistics of forecast error and comparision statistics as shown on Table 13.2-13.4. It is observed that the Holt and winter parameter estimates are recursively obtained, while the linear trend regression model, have their parameters obtained via the least square method. Their accuracy and stability can be deducted from their forecast errors and other forecast criteria, referred to as comparison statistics.

But, the choice of method to use on any time series data depends on factors such, as simplicity, accuracy and stability on the series data. The importance of the automobile industry in India cannot be underestimated as it contributes arround 5 per cent of GDP at present, offering employment to a large number of people in our country as well as contributing significantly to the country's export. Keeping in view the importance of the sector to Indian Economy, it is therefore becomes a matter of immense importance to forecast the production of automobiles. In this study, three forecasting methods considered are used to forecast the production of Indian Automobile and their forecast are compared using forecast criteria.

## OBJECTIVES

The objectives of this study are

(1) To forecast the production of Indian Automobiles using various forecasting techniques.

(2) To choose the best forecasting technique based on the forecasting accuracy of various techniques as judged by hold – out sample performance.

## DATA

The above said objectives are pursued with the help of data on production of Automobiles for the period 1996-97 to 2007-08. The data for the study are collected from the PROWESS database of CMIE (Centre for Monitoring Indian Economy) various journals and from the website www.Indiastat.com. To estimate model parameters QSB package has been used.

## AUTOMOBILES PRODUCTIONS IN INDIA

The production data pertaining to commercial vehicles, passenger cars and multi-utility vehicles, two and three wheelers and total automobiles during 1995-96 to 2007-08 is listed in Table 13.1. The total Indian automobiles production has increased from 3504.2 thousands in 1995-96 to 10685.5 thousands in 2007-08 which accounts for 3 times rise during the study period. The production of automobiles in India had registered an increasing trend except in the year 2000-01 and 2007-08. The compound annual growth rate of Indian automobiles is 9.74 per cent during the study period. It is also evident from the table that the production of commercial vehicles, passenger cars and multi-utility vehicles and two and three wheelers registered fluctuating trend upto 2000-01 and afterwards registered increasing trend.

The commercial vehicles have increased from 217.5 thousands in 1995-96 to 549.2 thousands in 2007-08 i.e., 2.52 times. Passenger cars and multi-utility vehicles during the same period rose from 454.4 thousands to 1646.2 thousands; the rise comes to 3.62 times. Two wheelers production have increased from 2655.9 thousands to 7995.1 thousands during the same period i.e, 3.01 times. The three wheelers during the study period rose from 176.4 thousands to 495 thousands; the rise comes to 2.80 times. On comparing the changes that have taken place in the production of various sectors of automobiles, it is observed that increases in production are more in passenger cars and multi-utility vehicles followed by two wheelers, three wheelers and commercial vehicles. The compound annual growth rate of commercial vehicles, passenger cars and multi-utility vehicles, two wheelers and three wheelers are 8.04 per cent, 11.32 per cent, 9.62 per cent, 8.99 per cent respectively during the study period. The co-efficient of variation (CV) also confirms that the production of Indian Automobiles registered high fluctuations during the study period.

## ESTIMATION OF FORECASTING MODELS AND ANALYSIS

Before choosing a technique for forecasting, it is essential to analyse the data pattern to determine the appropriateness of the technique for forecasting. A simple plot of data indicates that there is both seasonality and trend in the data as evident from Figure 13.1 and 13.2. In this paper, the following – methods would be briefly explained and used for forecasting.

1. Trend Method
2. Holt's Method
3. Winter's Method

### TREND METHOD

In the trend method of forecasting, the linear trend model is a hypothetical curve that shows the direction of movement of a time series over a period of time. It is simply a linear function of time.

$$X_t = B_0 + B_1 t + R_t$$

Where $B_0$, $B_1$ are constants and $R_t$ is an error term. The mean square error of forecast, MSE is defined by.

$$\text{MSE} = \sum_{r=1}^{t} R_t^2 = \sum_{r=1}^{t} (X_r - \hat{B}_0 - \hat{B}_1 r)^2$$

Where $R_t$ is the forecast error for period t, with the associated normal equation as:

$$\sum_{r=1}^{t} X_r - \hat{B}_0 t - \hat{B}_1 \sum_{r=1}^{t} r = 0 \sum_{r=1}^{t} X_r - \hat{B}_0 \sum_{r=1}^{t} r - \hat{B}_1 \sum_{r=1}^{t} r^2 = 0$$

The estimates of the trend parameters are obtained as

$$\hat{B}_0 = \frac{1}{t} \sum_{r=1}^{t} X_r \quad \text{and} \quad \hat{B}_1 = \sum_{r=1}^{t} r x_r / \sum_{r=1}^{t} r^2$$

The estimates of the forecasts are obtained as

$$\hat{X}_{t,h} = \hat{B}_0 + \hat{B}_1 h.$$

Where h is the lead time in future.

The linear trend equation for the production of Indian Automobiles were estimated using ordinary least square method and shown as below.

| | | | | |
|---|---|---|---|---|
| **Linear Trend** | **Y** | **= 2114.04** | **+ 709.27 t** | |
| **Equation** | **t value** | **(4.376)** | **(10.81)*** | **$R^2$=0.91** |

* - Significant at 0.01 level

The above trend equation showed that t – variable is statistically significant at 0.01 level of significance as indicated by t – statistic. Using linear trend equation, forecast for 2009-10, 2010-11, and so on are obtained by substituting t = 14, t = 15 ...... and t = 18 respectively and the results were presented in Table 13.2. An estimate of the Mean Absolute Percentage Error (MAPE) was found to be 9.955 per cent. This was done to examine the accuracy of the forecast for those periods for which actual production was available. The forecast were extended for the period 2009-10 to 2013-14. The results are reported in Table 13.2. The results indicate that absolute percentage errors for the years 1996-97, 1997-98, 2000-01 to 2002-03 and 2006-07, varying 10.78 per cent to 29.19 per cent. Further forecast exhibit an increasing trend, with the estimated forecast for the year 2013-14 being 14880.9 thousands.

## HOLT'S METHOD

Holt's method is used when there is a trend in the time series. It has already obtained time series (Y) on production of Indian Automobiles which has a trend. Therefore, Holt's method is used. The technique smoothes the level and slope directly by using smoothing constants. These smoothing constants provide estimates of level and slope that adopt over time as new observations become available. The equations of Holt's method (Hanke et al 2003) are:

1. The exponentially smoothed series or current level estimate.

$$L_t = \alpha Y_t + (1-\alpha)(L_{t-1} + T_{t-1})$$

2. The trend estimate

$$T_t = \beta(L_t - L_{t-1}) + (1-\beta)T_{t-1}$$

3. Forecast m periods in to future

$$\hat{Y}_{t+m} = L_t + mT_t$$

Where

$L_t$ = New smoothed value

$\alpha$ = Soothing constant for data ($0 \leq \alpha \leq 1$)

$Y_t$ = New observation or actual value of series in period t.

$\beta$ = Smoothing constant for trend estimate ($0 \leq \beta \leq 1$)

$T_t$ = Trend estimate

m = Periods to be forecasted in future

$\hat{Y}_{t+m}$ = Forecast for m periods into future.

To use this method, it is to initialize the values of $L_t$ and $T_t$ The value of $L_t$ is taken as equal to $Y_t$ and the value of $T_t$ is taken as $Y_2 - Y_1$. The values of $\alpha$ and $\beta$ are so chosen as to minimize the error sum of squares. In our case, $\alpha$ (=0.10) and $\beta$ (=0.10) minimized the error sum of square which was obtained by using QSB package. The seasonalised forecast upto 2013-14 and the actual production of Indian automobiles, the last period for which actual data were available, and estimate of forecast error from 1996-97 to 2007-08 are presented in Table 13.3.

It is observed by examining the data in Table 13.3 that the forecast error are high during the year 1997-98 to 2002-03, 2005-06 and 2006-07 and varying between 11.091 per cent to 33.323 per cent. It is also seen that there is an increase in the forecasted trend of Indian Automobiles production with estimated for 2013-14 being 14,920.1 thousands. It is seen that Holt's method gives a MAPE of 16.015 per cent which is higher than what is obtained by using linear trend equation method.

## WINTER'S METHOD

This method is used when there is not only trend but also seasonality in the data. The Holt's model could be modified as given below to take into account the effect of seasonality. The equations of winter's model are given below.

1. The exponentially smoothed series:

$$L_t = \alpha \frac{x_t}{s_t - s} + (1-\alpha)(L_{t-1} + T_{t-1})$$

2. The trend estimate

$$T_t = \beta(L_t - L_{t-1}) + (1-\beta)T_{t-1}$$

3. The seasonal estimate

$$S_t = \gamma \frac{x_t}{L_t} + (1-\gamma)S_{t-s}$$

4. Forecast p periods into future:

$$\hat{X}_{t+p} = (L_t + P^t{}_t)\ S_{t-s+p}$$

Where,

$L_t$ = New smoothed value or current level estimate

$\alpha$ = Soothing constant for the level ($0 \le a \le 1$)

$X_t$ = New observation or actual value in period t.

$\beta$ = Smoothing constant for trend estimate ($0 \le b \le 1$)

$T_t$ = Trend estimate

$\gamma_t$ = Smoothing constant for seasonality estimate ($0 \le \gamma \le 1$)

$S_t$ = Seasonal estimate

P = Periods to be forecast into the future

S = Length of seasonality

$\hat{X}_{t+p}$ = Forecast for m periods into future.

To use this method, it is necessary to initialize the values of $L_t$, $T_t$ and $S_t$. The parameters $\alpha$, $\beta$ and $\gamma$ can be chosen to minimize Mean Square Error (MSE). Using this method, the values of $\alpha, \beta$ and $\gamma$ which minimize the mean square error were obtained by using QSB packages as 0.8, 0.2 and 0.5 respectively.

The forecast upto 2013-14, actual production from 1996-97 to 2007-08 and the error estimates are reported in the Table 4. The forecast errors are high during the year 1999-2000, 2002-03, 2004-05 to 2007-08 varying from 6.638 per cent to 13.519 per cent. It is also observed that forecast exhibit an increasing trend with production for 2013-14 being estimated at 14631 thousands. It is estimated that the MAPE using this method is 7.49 per cent which is the least among all the methods discussed so far.

## COMPARISON OF VARIOUS FORECASTING METHODS

The accuracy of forecasts of production of Indian Automobiles as obtained by various methods are shown in Table 13.2 to 13.4 by presenting the absolute percentage error for the period 1996-97 to 2007-08. The mean absolute percentage error as obtained by various methods is also presented. The mean absolute percentage errors are 9.955 per cent, 16.015 per cent and 7.49 per cent respectively for linear trend equation, Holt's model and Winter's model. On the basis of MAPE, it could be conclude that Winter's model is the best, followed by Linear Trend equation and by Holt's model.

## CONCLUSION

It is very clear that one could recommend winter's model for forecasting the production of Indian Automobiles. This is because the MAPE for this method is the minimum. This is followed by Linear Trend equation and Holt's model where the mean absolute percentage error are 9.955 per cent and 16.015 per cent respectively. It is very essential that the forecast need to be updated as and when more data becomes available as the difference in the accuracy of the three methods is not much. These forecasts could be very useful for the producers and users of automobiles while deciding the price. These are also useful for the policy makers engaged in the welfare of the Indian Automobile Industry.

## REFERENCES


1. Gilchrist, W., (1976). Statistical Forecasting, New york: John Wiley and Sons, pp.221-273
2. Fildes, (1980). Quantitative Forecasting, Great Britain *J.operational Res. Soc.*, 20,pp.705-715.
3. Deepak Chawla and Vidhu Shekhar Jha(2009), Forecasting production of Natural Rubber in Indian, *Paradigam*, Vol.X111,No.1pp.39-55.
4. Hanke, Jonh E., Dean W. Wichern ,and Arthur G. Reitsch (2003), Business forecasting, 7th ed., New Delhi: Pearson Education.
5. Panda, Ajay Kumar,(2007), Forecasting Nominal Exchange Rate of Indian Rupee Vs US Dollar, *The ICFAI Journal of Applied Finance*,13(6), pp.66.79.
6. Gupta, G.S., (1993), ARIMA Model for and forecasts on Tea production in India, *Indian Economic journal*, 41(2), pp.88-110.

## TABLE 13.1

## INDIAN AUTOMOBILES PRODUCTION TRENDS

*(in 000's)*

| Category | 95-96 | 96-97 | 97-98 | 98-99 | 99-2k | 2k-01 | 01-02 | 02-03 | 03-04 | 04-05 | 05-06 | 06-07 | 07-08 | Mean | CV | CAGR |
|---|---|---|---|---|---|---|---|---|---|---|---|---|---|---|---|---|
| Ms HCVs | 129.7 | 155.7 | 95.9 | 80.5 | 112.3 | 88.2 | 96.7 | 120.0 | 166.1 | 214.8 | 219.3 | 294.3 | 304.4 | 159.8 | 0.477 | 7.38 |
| | - | (20.05) | (-38.4) | (-16.05) | (39.5) | (-21.4) | (9.6) | (24.1) | (38.4) | (29.3) | (2.1) | (34.2) | (3.4) | | | |
| LCVs | 87.8 | 84.9 | 65.0 | 55.3 | 61.2 | 63.8 | 65.7 | 82.9 | 108.9 | 138.9 | 171.7 | 275.7 | 244.8 | 115.9 | 0.626 | 8.93 |
| | - | (-3.3) | (-23.4) | (-14.9) | (10.7) | (4.2) | (3.0) | (26.2) | (31.4) | (27.5) | (23.6) | (60.6) | (-11.2) | | | |
| **CVs** | **217.5** | **240.6** | **160.9** | **135.8** | **173.5** | **152** | **162.4** | **202.9** | **275** | **353.7** | **391** | **570** | **549.2** | **275.7** | **0.536** | **8.04** |
| | **-** | **(10.6)** | **(-33.1)** | **(-15.6)** | **(27.8)** | **(-12.4)** | **(6.8)** | **(24.9)** | **(35.5)** | **(28.6)** | **(10.5)** | **(45.8)** | **(-3.6)** | | | |
| Passenger Cars | 348.2 | 411.1 | 104.0 | 390.7 | 577.2 | 504.6 | 500.3 | 557.7 | 782.6 | 960.4 | 1046.1 | 1238.0 | 1401.5 | 701.5 | 0.51 | 12.29 |
| | - | (18.1) | (-2.5) | (-2.6) | (47.7) | (-12.6) | (-0.9) | (11.5) | (40.3) | (22.7) | (8.9) | (18.3) | (13.2) | | | |
| MPUVs | 106.2 | 134.6 | 134.6 | 113.3 | 124.3 | 125.9 | 169.3 | 163.2 | 206.9 | 249.4 | 263.2 | 306.8 | 244.7 | 180.2 | 0.369 | 7.19 |
| | - | (26.7) | - | (-15.8) | (9.7) | (1.3) | (34.5) | (-3.6) | (26.8) | (20.5) | (5.5) | (16.6) | (-20.2) | | | |
| **PVs** | **454.4** | **545.7** | **535.6** | **504** | **701.5** | **630.5** | **669.6** | **720.9** | **989.5** | **1209.8** | **1309.3** | **1544.8** | **1646.2** | **881.7** | **0.469** | **11.32** |
| | **-** | **(20.1)** | **(-1.9)** | **(-5.9)** | **(39.2)** | **(-10.1)** | **(6.2)** | **(7.7)** | **(37.3)** | **(22.3)** | **(8.2)** | **(18)** | **(6.6)** | | | |
| Scooters | 1224.8 | 1312.9 | 1279.5 | 1315.0 | 1259.4 | 879.7 | 937.5 | 850.1 | 935.3 | 987.4 | 1021.0 | 943.9 | 1091.4 | 1079.8 | 0.162 | -0.97 |
| | - | (7.2) | (-2.5) | (2.8) | (-4.2) | (-30.1) | (6.6) | (-9.3) | (10.0) | (5.6) | (3.4) | (-7.6) | (15.6) | | | |
| Motorcycle | 809.1 | 988.2 | 1125.9 | 1387.3 | 1794.1 | 2183.8 | 2906.3 | 3914.6 | 4355.1 | 5193.9 | 6207.7 | 7112.2 | 6465.1 | 3418.7 | 0.662 | 18.91 |
| | - | (22.1) | (13.9) | (23.2) | (29.3) | (21.7) | (33.1) | (34.7) | (11.3) | (19.3) | (19.5) | (14.6) | (-9.1) | | | |

## TABLE 13.1 (CONTINUED)

## INDIAN AUTOMOBILES PRODUCTION TRENDS

*(in 000's)*

| Category | 95-96 | 96-97 | 97-98 | 98-99 | 99-2k | 2k-01 | 01-02 | 02-03 | 03-04 | 04-05 | 05-06 | 06-07 | 07-08 | Mean | CV | CAGR |
|---|---|---|---|---|---|---|---|---|---|---|---|---|---|---|---|---|
| Mopeds | 622 | 678.1 | 667.2 | 672.2 | 724.5 | 694.9 | 427.5 | 344.6 | 332.3 | 348.4 | 379.9 | 379.9 | 420.3 | 514.8 | 0.310 | -3.16 |
| | - | (9.0) | (-1.6) | (0.7) | (7.8) | (-4.1) | (-38.5) | (-19.4) | (-3.6) | (4.8) | (9.0) | - | (10.6) | | | |
| Ele. Two Wheelers | | | | | | | | | | | | 7.9 | 18.3 | 13.1 | 0.561 | |
| | | | | | | | | | | | | - | (131.6) | | | |
| **Two Wheelers** | **2655.9** | **2979.2** | **3072.6** | **3374.5** | **3778** | **3758.4** | **4271.3** | **5109.3** | **5622.7** | **6529.7** | **7608.6** | **8443.9** | **7995.1** | **5015.3** | **0.406** | **9.62** |
| | **-** | **(12.2)** | **(3.1)** | **(9.8)** | **(12)** | **(-0.5)** | **(13.6)** | **(19.6)** | **(10.0)** | **(16.1)** | **(16.5)** | **(11.0)** | **(-5.3)** | | | |
| **Three Wheelers** | **176.4** | **221.6** | **234.8** | **209.0** | **205.5** | **203.2** | **212.7** | **271.2** | **356.2** | **374.4** | **434.4** | **556.1** | **495.0** | **303.9** | **0.415** | **8.99** |
| | **-** | **(25.6)** | **(6)** | **(-11)** | **(-1.7)** | **(-1.1)** | **(4.7)** | **(27.5)** | **(31.3)** | **(5.1)** | **(16.0)** | **(28.0)** | **(-11.0)** | | | |
| **Grand total** | **3504.2** | **3987.1** | **4003.9** | **4223.3** | **4858.5** | **4744.1** | **5316** | **6304.3** | **7243.4** | **8467.6** | **9743.3** | **11,114.8** | **10685.5** | **6476.6** | **0.417** | **9.74** |
| | | **(13.8)** | **(0.4)** | **(5.5)** | **(15.0)** | **(-2.4)** | **(12.0)** | **(18.6)** | **(14.9)** | **(16.9)** | **(15.1)** | **(14.1)** | **(-3.9)** | | | |

***Source :*** Society of Indian Automobile manufacturers (SIAM)

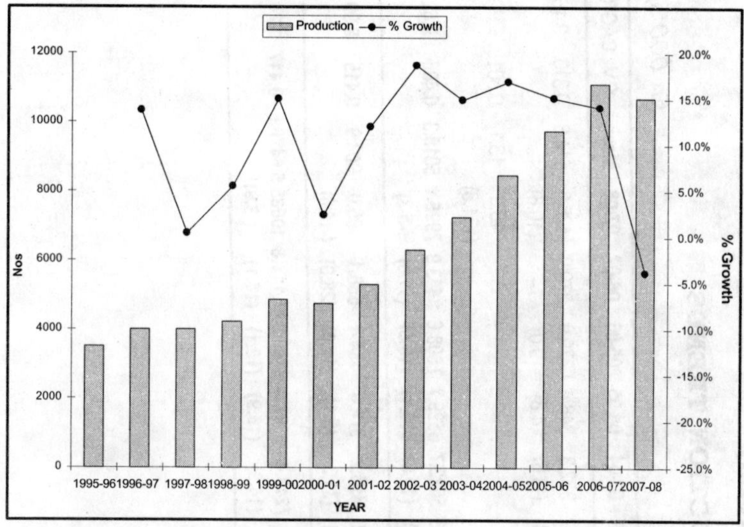


**Figure 13.1 : Total production of Indian Automobiles (1995 - 96 to 2007 - 08)**

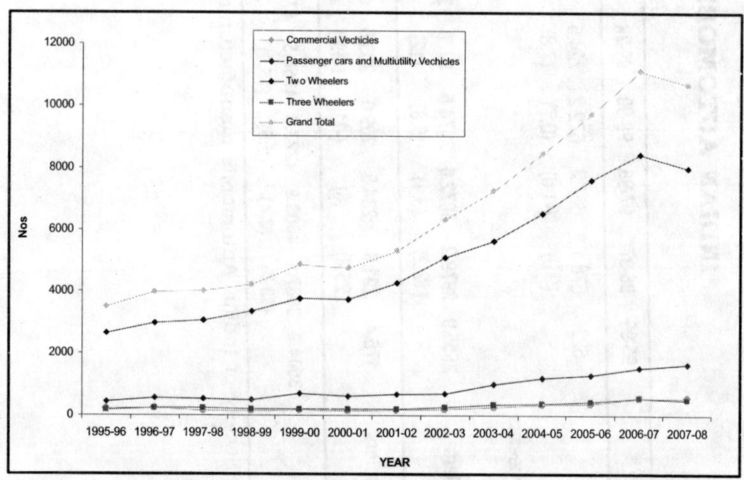


**Figure 13.2 : Total production of different sectors of Indian Automobiles (1995 - 96 to 2007 - 08)**

## TABLE 13.2

## ACTUAL PRODUCTION, SEASONALIZED FORECAST AND ERRORS OF FORECAST USING LINEAR TREND EQUATION

| Period | Actual Production (000[1]) | Seasonalized Forecast | Error | Error (%) | Absolute Error (%) |
|---|---|---|---|---|---|
| 1996-97 | 3987.1 | 2823.3 | 1163.8 | 29.189 | 29.189 |
| 1997-98 | 4003.9 | 3532.6 | 471.3 | 11.771 | 11.771 |
| 1998-99 | 4223.3 | 4241.9 | -18.6 | -0.440 | 0.440 |
| 1999-00 | 4858.5 | 4951.1 | -92.6 | -1.906 | 1.906 |
| 2000-01 | 4744.1 | 5660.4 | -916.3 | -19.315 | 19.315 |
| 2001-02 | 5316.0 | 6369.7 | -1053.7 | -19.821 | 19.821 |
| 2002-03 | 6304.3 | 7078.9 | -774.7 | -12.289 | 12.289 |
| 2003-04 | 7243.4 | 7788.2 | -544.8 | -7.521 | 7.521 |
| 2004-05 | 8467.6 | 8497.5 | -29.9 | -0.353 | 0.353 |
| 2005-06 | 9743.3 | 9206.8 | 536.5 | 5.506 | 5.506 |
| 2006-07 | 11.114.8 | 9916.0 | 1198.8 | 10.786 | 10.786 |
| 2007-08 | 10.685.5 | 10.625.3 | 60.2 | 0.563 | 0.563 |
| 2009-10 | | 12043.9 | | | MAPE= 9.955% |
| 2010-11 | | 12753.1 | | | |
| 2011-12 | | 13462.4 | | | |
| 2012-13 | | 14171.7 | | | |
| 2013-14 | | 14880.9 | | | |

***Source:*** Computed

## TABLE 13.3

## ACTUAL PRODUCTION, SEASONALIZED FORECAST AND ERRORS OF FORECAST USING HOLT'S METHODS

| Period | Actual Production (000[1]) | Seasonalized Forecast | Error | Error (%) | Absolute Error (%) |
|---|---|---|---|---|---|
| 1996-97 | 3987.1 | 4291.6 | -304.5 | -7.637 | 7.637 |
| 1997-98 | 4003.9 | 4867.0 | -863.1 | -21.556 | 21.556 |
| 1998-99 | 4223.3 | 5377.9 | -1154.7 | -27.341 | 27.341 |
| 1999-00 | 4858.5 | 5848.2 | -989.7 | -20.370 | 20.370 |
| 2000-01 | 4744.1 | 6325.1 | -1580.9 | -33.323 | 33.323 |
| 2001-02 | 5316.0 | 6727.0 | -1411.0 | -26.543 | 26.543 |
| 2002-03 | 6304.3 | 7131.8 | -827.5 | -13.126 | 13.126 |
| 2003-04 | 7243.4 | 7586.7 | -343.3 | -4.739 | 4.739 |
| 2004-05 | 8467.6 | 8086.6 | 381.0 | 4.500 | 4.500 |
| 2005-06 | 9743.3 | 8662.7 | 1080.6 | 11.091 | 11.091 |
| 2006-07 | 11114.8 | 9319.5 | 1795.3 | 16.152 | 16.152 |
| 2007-08 | 10685.5 | 10065.8 | 619.7 | 5.799 | 5.799 |
| 2009-10 | | 12245.2 | | | MAPE=16.015% |
| 2010-11 | | 12816.4 | | | |
| 2011-12 | | 13486.6 | | | |
| 2012-13 | | 14148.3 | | | |
| 2013-14 | | 14920.1 | | | |

***Source:*** Computed

## TABLE 13.4

## ACTUAL PRODUCTION, SEASONALIZED FORECAST AND ERRORS OF FORECAST USING WINTER MODEL

| Period | Actual Production (000[1]) | Seasonalized Forecast | Error | Error (%) | Absolute Error (%) |
|---|---|---|---|---|---|
| 1996-97 | 3987.1 | 3987.0 | - | - | - |
| 1997-98 | 4003.9 | 3987.0 | 16.9 | 0.422 | 0.422 |
| 1998-99 | 4223.3 | 4005.0 | 218.3 | 5.169 | 5.169 |
| 1999-00 | 4858.5 | 4239.0 | 619.0 | 12.741 | 15.741 |
| 2000-01 | 4744.1 | 4935.0 | -190.9 | -4.023 | 4.023 |
| 2001-02 | 5316.0 | 4871.0 | 445.0 | 8.371 | 8.371 |
| 2002-03 | 6304.3 | 5452.0 | 852.3 | 13.519 | 13.519 |
| 2003-04 | 7243.4 | 6540.0 | 703.4 | 9.711 | 9.711 |
| 2004-05 | 8467.6 | 7611.0 | 856.6 | 10.116 | 10.116 |
| 2005-06 | 9743.3 | 8963.0 | 780.3 | 8.008 | 8.008 |
| 2006-07 | 11114.8 | 10377.0 | 737.8 | 6.638 | 6.638 |
| 2007-08 | 10685.5 | 11876.0 | -1190.5 | -11.141 | 11.141 |
| 2009-10 | | 12080.0 | | | MAPE=7.490% |
| 2010-11 | | 12718.0 | | | |
| 2011-12 | | 13355.0 | | | |
| 2012-13 | | 13993.0 | | | |
| 2013-14 | | 14631.0 | | | |

***Source:*** Computed

# PART - V

# ANALYSIS OF WORKING CAPITAL MANAGEMENT

# 14

# Working Capital Efficiency and Corporate Profitability

## An Empirical Evidence from Indian Automobile Industry

## INTRODUCTION

Developing economies are confronted with the problem of inefficient utilization of resources available to them. Capital is the limited productive resources promotes the rate of growth, cuts down the cost of production and above all improves the efficiency of the productive system. Total capital of a country comprises fixed capital and working capital. Fixed capital investment generates production capacity where as working capital makes the utilization of that capacity where as working capital makes the utilization of that capacity possible. Thus, the study of working capital occupies an important place in financial management. Funds are needed in every business for carrying on day-to-day operations. Working capital funds are regarded as the life-blood of business units. A firm can exist and survive without making profit but can't survive without working capital funds. If a firm is not earning profit it may be termed as 'sick', but not having working capital may cause it bankruptcy and closure over a period of time. In addition, working capital has acquired great significance and sound positions for the twin objects of 'profitability and liquidity'. It consumes great deal of time to increase profitability as well as to maintain proper liquidity at minimum risk. Leslie R.Howard rightly pointed out that a deeper understanding of the importance of working capital and its satisfactory provision can lead not only to material savings in the economical use of capital but can also assist in furthering the ultimate aim of a business, namely, that of maximizing financial returns on the minimum amount of capital which need to be employed. Viewed in this perspective, the analysis of working capital efficiency may be a very rewarding one.

## PROBLEM STATEMENT

Importance of working capital management stems from two reasons viz., a substantial portion of total invested in current assets and level of current assets and current liabilities will change quickly with the variation in sales. Hence, the purpose of the present part of analysis is to examine the issues how large is the investment in working capital and its various components, how the quality of current assets has evolved over time, and whether working capital and its various components have been utilized efficiently by the selected Indian automobile companies during the period under study. The working capital efficiency of an enterprise should be evaluated by comparison of holding period of different components of working capital. The holding period of different components of working capital of the selected three sectors, individual companies and the whole automobile industry during the study period has been computed and presented in Table 14.1 to Table 14.4.

## SAMPLING SELECTION

Keeping in view the scope of the study, it is decided to include all the companies under automobile industry working before or from the year 1996-97 to 2008-09. There are 26 companies operating in the Indian automobile industry. But, owing to several constraints such as non-availability of financial statements or non-working of a company in a particular year etc., it is compelled to restrict the number of sample companies to 20. Out of 20 selected companies under Indian Automobile Industry, three Multinational Companies (MNC's) namely Hyundai Motors India Ltd, Honda Siel Cars India Ltd and Ford India Private Ltd were omitted because these companies established their operations in India in different accounting years. The companies under automobile industry are classified into three sectors namely; Commercial vehicles, Passenger cars and Multi-utility vehicles and Two and three wheelers. For the purpose of the study all the three sectors have been selected. It accounts for 73.23 per cent of the total companies available in the Indian automobile industry. The selected 20 companies include 5 under commercial vehicles, 3 under passenger cars and multi-utility vehicles and 9 under two and three wheeler sectors. It is inferred that sample company represents 98.74 percentage of market share in commercial vehicles, 79.76 percentage of market share in passenger cars and Multi-utility vehicles and 99.81 percentage of market share in two and three wheelers. Thus, the findings based on the occurrence of such representative sample may be presumed to be true representative of automobile industry in the country.

## METHODS OF DATA COLLECTION

The study is mainly based on secondary data. The major source of data analyzed and interpreted in this study related to all those companies selected is collected from "PROWESS" database, which is the most reliable on the empowered corporate database of Centre for Monitoring Indian Economy (CMIE). Besides prowess database, relevant secondary data have also been collected from BSE Stock Exchange Official Directory, CMIE Publications, Annual Survey of Industry, Business newspapers, Reports on Currency and Finance, Libraries of various Research Institutions, through Internet etc.

## DATA ANALYSIS

The financial and statistical analysis approach plays a vital role in the financial environment. To enjoy the benefit of financial and statistical analysis researcher has collected, assembled and correlated the data, classified the data appropriately and condensed them into a related data series; stated the resultant information in a comprehensive form, text, tables and analyzed and interpreted the reported data. It is well known that management is concerned with assets utilization towards profitability performance. For this purpose it has to study certain specific ratios which are concerned with working capital of the enterprises. For the purpose of this study, ratios namely, Raw material period, work-in-holding period, finished goods holding period, inventory holding period, receivables holding period, payables holding period and cash conversion cycle has been used. The role of statistical tools is important in analyzing the data and drawing inferences therefrom. In order to derive the open handed results from the information collected through secondary data, various statistical tools like mean, standard deviation, variance, compound annual growth rate, t-test ANOVA, and factor analysis have been used to interpret the sense of mathematical relationship amongst values of different variables so computed in the study.

## RAW MATERIALS HOLDING PERIOD

It is evident from the Table 14.1 that the lowest average raw material holding period was 26 days for two and three wheelers sector, followed by commercial vehicles (34 days) and passenger cars and multiutility vehicles (38 days), as against 53 days for whole automobile industry. Further, this period registered very high fluctuations throughout the study period. Further, all selected sectors and whole automobile industry registered negative growth rate which showed efficient utilization of raw materials by the selected companies. It varies from 26 days to 83 days for commercial vehicles sector companies, 18 days to 75 days for passenger cars and multiutility vehicles sector companies and 18 days to 141 days for two and three wheelers sectors. All the selected companies except LML Ltd, Maharashtra Scooters Ltd, TVS Motor Company Ltd, Kinetic Motor Company Ltd and Kinetic Engineering Ltd under two and three wheelers sector showed improved performance in this regard (Table 14.2 to Table 14.4).

The results of analysis of variance presented in Table 14.5 showed that differences in the mean raw materials holding period were significant between the companies and between the years in commercial vehicle sector as the calculated value of F were more than the table value of F at 5 per cent level of significance. Hence, the null hypothesis was rejected. However, no such significant difference was observed between the years in the case of passenger cars and multiutility vehicles sector and two and three wheelers sector.

## WORKING-IN-PROGRESS HOLDING PERIOD

Table 14.1 demonstrated that the average work-in-progress holding period was lowest in two and three wheelers sector and passenger cars and multiutility vehicles sector (4 days) followed by commercial vehicles sector (10 days), as against 30 days for whole Indian automobile industry. WIP holding period registered very high fluctuations and negative compound annual growth rate in all the three sectors of Indian automobile industry. Among the commercial vehicles sector companies, it ranged between 3 days to 16 days, 1 day to 11 days for passenger cars and multiutility vehicles sector and 2 days to 17 days for two and three wheelers sector companies during the study period. Majority of the selected companies WIP holding period were significantly differ from sector mean and industry mean. All the selected companies except Bajaj Tempo Ltd, Eicher Motors Ltd and Swaraj Mazda Ltd under commercial vehicles, Ford India Private Ltd under passenger cars and multiutility vehicles sector and LML Ltd, Maharashtra Scooters Ltd, Kinetic Motors Company Ltd, Kinetic Engineering Ltd, Majestic Auto Ltd and Scooters India Ltd under two and three wheelers sector registered improved performance with regard to WIP holding period.

Table 14.5 represents that the differences in the WIP holding period were significant in between the sectors and the years during the study period. It is also evident from the table that WIP holding period were significant in between the companies and the years in commercial vehicles and two and three wheelers sector. However, in case of passenger cars and multiutility vehicles sector, these holding period were insignificant between the years.

## FINISHED GOODS HOLDING PERIOD

This indicates how quickly a company is turning over its finished goods. When deciding the appropriate level of finished goods, a company should strike a balance between the cost of tying up capital and the demands from the customers. Generally, short finished goods holding period is preferred. An unreasonably long inventory holding period may indicate an economic recession, obsolete inventory, poor sales and marketing, a change of customer taste or bad inventory management. It is evident from the Table 14.1 that two and three wheeler sector had shorter mean finished goods holding period (8 days), followed by passenger cars and multiutility vehicles sector (11 days), commercial vehicles sector (19 days), as against 14 days for whole Indian automobile industry. It ranged between 11 days to 30 days for commercial vehicles sector, 5 days to 29 days for passenger cars and multiutility vehicles sector and 3 days to 33 days for two and three wheelers sector during the study period. The finished goods holding period of all the selected companies registered very high fluctuations during the study period. Majority of the selected passenger cars and multiutility vehicles companies and two and three wheeler sector companies showed better performance in this regard when compared to commercial vehicle sector companies.

The results of analysis of variance presented in Table 14.5 showed that the differences between finished goods holding period were significant in between the companies and the years in case of commercial vehicles and two and three wheelers sector as the calculated value of F exceeds the table value of F at 5 per cent level of significance. However, such a significant differences was not observed in between the years in passenger cars and multiutility vehicles sector during the study period.

## RECEIVABLES HOLDING PERIOD

This ratio measures a company's ability to collect cash from its credit customers. Most companies offer their customers credit in order to boost their sales. However, there are opportunity costs in holding cash for financing receivables and there is also the risk of bad debts. A long receivables collection period may be an indication of worsening credit control. Receivables holding period of all three selected sectors, individual companies and the whole automobile industry were computed and presented in Table 14.1 to Table 14.4. Table 14.1 indicated that the mean receivables collection period was the lowest in two and three wheelers sector (16 days), when compared to 22 days for passenger cars and multiutility vehicles sector and 45 days for commercial vehicles sector as against 35 days for whole Indian automobile industry. It ranged between 28 days to 74 days for commercial vehicles sector companies (Table 14.2), 8 days to 35 days for passenger cars and multiutiltiy vehicles sector companies (Table 14.3) and 7 days to 107 days for two and three wheelers sector companies (Table 14.4) during the study period. All the selected companies registered very high fluctuations in this ratio during the study period. This was due to the differences among the credit and collection policy adopted by the respective companies.

Table 14.5 refers that the differences in the receivables holding period was significant in between the companies and insignificant between the years in commercial vehicles and two and three wheelers sector as per the calculated value of F. However, in case of passenger cars and multiutility vehicles sector, these ratio were significant both between the companies and between the years as the calculated value of F exceeds the table value of F at 5 per cent level of significance.

## PAYABLES PAYMENT PERIOD

This ratio links the value of accounts payables with the amount of goods and services that a company is purchasing on credit. If the payables payment period is short, creditors are being paid relatively early. However, if the payables payment period is too long, the company may have liquidity problems; this can also be harmful to its relationship with suppliers. The payables payment period were computed for all the selected companies, sectors and whole Indian automobile industry and presented in Table 14.1 to Table 14.4. Table 14.1 explaining a fluctuating trend in the payables payment period of the selected sectors and individual companies of the Indian automobile industry. The average payables payment period was the lowest in passenger cars and multiutility vehicles sector (59 days), followed by two and three wheelers (61 days) and commercial vehicles sector (96 days), as against 158 days for whole Indian automobile industry. The company wise analysis revealed that the mean payables payment period ranged between 61 days to 104 days in commercial vehicles sector, 21 days to 86 days in passenger cars and multiutility vehicles and 40 days to 210 days in two and three wheelers sector companies during the study period. Majority of the selected companies mean payables payment periods were significantly different from the sector mean and industry mean.

Table 14.5 showed that the differences in the payables payment period between the sector, between the companies under commercial vehicles sector and two and three wheelers sector were significant and insignificant between the years. However, the payables holding period between the companies and the year were insignificant in passenger cars and multiutility vehicles sector because the calculated value of F is lower than the table value of F.

## CASH CONVERSION CYCLE (CCC)

The cash conversion cycle period of all the selected companies, three sectors and the whole automobile industry were computed and presented in Table 14.1 to Table 14.4. It is evident from the Table 14.1 that the lowest mean value of the CCC is found in the two and three wheelers sector with an average of 7 days, followed by the commercial vehicles sector (13 days ) and two and three wheelers sector (17 days), as against 28 days for whole Indian automobile industry. Considering all the average periods together, it can be seen that the cash conversion cycle is negative in two and three wheelers sector and the whole Indian automobile industry. This is explained by the short storage times of its inventory and receivables. Further, cash conversion cycle period ranged between – 8 days to 95 days in commercial vehicles sector companies, 13 days to 48 days in passenger cars and multiutility vehicles sector companies and – 4 days to 125 days in two and three wheelers sector companies during the study period. Further, tables reveal that there was an erratic fluctuation noticed in cash conversion cycle period in all the selected companies. Further, all the companies mean cash conversion cycle period was significantly different from the sector mean and industry mean.

It can be seen from the results of analysis of variance presented in Table 14.5 that the differences in the cash conversion cycle period in between the companies and between the years were significant in commercial vehicles sector and two and three wheelers sector. But such significant differences were not found between the companies and between the years in passenger cars and multiutility vehicles sector during the study period.

On the whole it can be concluded that two and three wheelers sector was efficient in utilization of working capital components as compared to commercial vehicles sector and passenger cars and multiutility vehicles sector. Among the individual companies, Tata Motors Ltd under commercial vehicles sector and LML Ltd, Maharastra Scooters Ltd, TVS Motor Company Ltd and Hero Honda Motors Ltd under two and three wheelers sector were efficient in managing their working capital during the study period.

## WORKING CAPITAL- FACTOR ANALYSIS

Holding period of different components of working capital such as raw materials, work-in-Progress, finished goods, receivables and payables have been considered for the study to analyze the working capital management efficiency to selected Indian automobile companies during the period under study. In order to disclose which among these factors contribute much towards working capital efficiency, factor analysis has been done. Table 14.6 showed that the principal component analysis and varimax rotation results for whole industry and all the three sectors. In whole industry, raw materials, WIP, finished goods and receivables holding period were cluster together as Factor I and accounts 40.818 per cent of the total variations and payables holding period describes as Factor II which accounts 21.065 per cent of the total variations. Both these factor explain 61.883 per cent of the total variations. WIP holding period and payables holding period are found to have a stronger relationship.

In commercial vehicles sector, two factors are identified by the rotation method and explained 71.175 per cent of total variations. Factor I consists of four variables such as raw materials, WIP, finished goods and receivables holding period and accounted for 49.722 per cent of total variations.

The remaining variable such as payables holding period constituted as Factor II which accounts 21.453 per cent of the total variations. Raw materials holding period and finished goods holding period are found to have a stronger relationship. The same picture was reflected in passenger cars and multiutility vehicles sector, where by Factor I account 46.042 per cent and Factor II accounts 25.510 per cent of the total variations. Both these factors explained 71.552 per cent of the total variations. Further, raw materials holding period and WIP holding period are found to have a stronger relationship in passenger cars and multiutility vehicles sector.

In two and three wheelers sector also two factors are identified by the rotation method and accounts 78.844 per cent of the total variations. Raw materials WIP and payables holding period were clustered together as Factor I and accounts 54.329 percent of the total variations. Variables viz., finished goods and receivables holding periods are constituted as Factor II and accounts 24.515 per cent of the total variations. Stronger relationships between variables are noticed with regard to raw materials and payables holding period. Further, the results of KMO test and Bartlett's Test of sphericity (sig.0.000) confirms that factor analysis can be carried out appropriately for the variables selected for the study.

## CONCLUSION

The working capital efficiency of the selected companies in the Indian automobile industry should be evaluated by comparison of holding period of different components of working capital. The analysis showed that two and three wheeler sectors were efficient in utilization of working capital components as compared to commercial vehicles sectors and passenger cars and multiutility vehicles sector. Among the individual companies, Tata Motors Ltd under commercial vehicles sector and LML Ltd, Maharastra Scooters Ltd, TVS Motor Company Ltd and Hero Honda Motors

Ltd under two and three wheeler sector were efficient in managing their working capital during the study period. The results of analysis of variance showed that there were significant differences in the different holding period between the companies during the study period. This was due to the differences among the inventory and credit and collection policy adopted by the respective companies. Considering all the average periods together, it can be seen that cash conversion cycle is negative in the whole Indian automobile industry. This is explained by short storage times of its inventory and receivables. Factor analysis demonstrated that all the components of working capital contributed much towards the efficiency of working capital management in all selected companies.

## REFERENCES

1. Vijayakumar, A. (1996). "The Transactions Demand for working capital in Indian PSUs: Some theoretical and empirical results", *Institute of Public Enterprises Journal,* pp. 92-100.
2. Pandey, I.M., and Parera, KLW. (1997). "Determinants of effective working capital management – A Discriminant Analysis Approach". IIMA, Working Paper No. 1934. Research and Publication Department, Indian Institute of Management, Ahmedabad, India.
3. Amit K. Mallick and Debasish Sur (1998). "Working capital and profitability: A case study in interrelation", *The Management Accountant,* pp. 805-809.
4. Shin, H.H. and Soenen, L. (1998). "Efficiency of working capital management and corporate profitability", *Financial Practice and Education.* 8(2): 37-45.
5. Govindan Rao, D. and Mohana Rao, P. (1999). "Impact of working capital on profitability in cement industry-A Correlation analysis", New Delhi: Deep and Deep Publishers. .
6. Katerina Lyroudi and Jhon Lazaridis (2000). "The cash conversion cycle and liquidity analysis of the food

industry in Greece", *http:/papers.ssrn.com/paper.fat?* abstract-id = 236175.

7. Rabiul Alam, S.M. and Syed Zabid Hossain, (2001). "Aspects of Inventory Management in Ship Building industry in Bangladesh", *The Management Accountant*, pp. 699-706.
8. Narasimhan, M.S. and Murty, L.S. (2001). "Emerging Manufacturing Industry: A Financial Percept of Management Review", pp. 105-112.
9. Debasish Sur, Joydeep Biswas and Prasenjit Ganguly (2001). "Liquidity Management in Indian Private Sector Enterprises- A case study of Indian Primary Aluminium Industry", *Indian Journal of Accounting,* XXXII: 8-14.
10. Manoj Anand (2001). "Working capital performance of corporate India; An Empirical study", *Management and Accounting Research,* 4(4): 35-65.
11. Marc Deloof (2003). "Does working capital management affect profitability of Belgian Firms?", *Journal of Business Finance and Accounting,* 30(3-4): 573-88.
12. Howorth, C. and Westhead, P. (2003). "The focus of working capital management in UK Small firms", *Management Accounting Research,* 14 (2): 94-111.
13. Santony Kumar Ghosh and Santi Gopal Maji (2003). "Utilization of current assets and operating profitability: An Empirical study on Cement and Tea industries in India", *Indian Journal of Accounting,* XXXIV: 52-60.
14. Khatik, S.K. and Pradeep Kumar Singh (2003). "Liquidity Management in EICHER Ltd – A case study", *The Management Accountant,* pp. 217-220.
15. Narware, P.C. (2004). "Working capital and profitability- An empirical analysis", *The Management Accountant,* pp. 491-495.
16. Singh, P.K. (2004). "Working Capital Management in Lupin Laboratories Ltd - A case study", *The Management Accountant,* pp. 534-539.
17. Eljelly, A. (2004). "Liquidity-Profitability Trade off: An

empirical investigation in an emerging market", *International Journal of Commerce and Management,* 14 (2): 48-61.

18. Bardia, S.C. (2004). "Liquidity Management: A case study of Steel Authority of India Ltd", *The Management Accountant,* pp. 463-67.
19. Chandar, Subbash and Rajan Kumar (2004). "An Empirical Analysis of some aspects of working capital requirements in small scale textile industry in Punjab", *The Management Accountant,* pp. 542-549.
20. Chakraborthy, P.K. (2004). "Managing corporate liquidity and financial flexibility - Different Approach", *The Management Accountant,* 39 (8): 653-655.
21. Sudarsana Reddy, G., Sivarami Reddy, C., and Mohan Reddy, P. (2004). "Debtors Management: A case study of Andra Pradesh Paper Industry", *The Management Accountant,* pp. 265-274.
22. Amit K. Mallick, Debasish Sur and Debdas Rakshit (2005). "Working capital and profitability, A study on their relationship with reference to selected companies in Indian Pharmaceutical Industry", *GITAM Journal of Management,* 3 (2): 51-62.
23. Sushma Vishnani and Bhupesh Kr Shah (2006). "Liquidity Vs Profitability – A detailed study in perspective of Indian Consumer Electronics Industry", *Prajana,* 9 (2): 3-20.
24. Garcia – Teruel P.J., and Martinez – Solano P.M. (2007). "Effects of working capital management on SME Profitability", *International Journal of Managerial Finance,* 3: 164-177.
25. Manoj Anand and Keshav Malhothra (2007). "Working Capital Performance of Corporate India; An empirical study", *ICFAI Journal of Applied Finance,* 13 (1): 46-81.
26. Abdul Raheman and Mohamad Nasr (2007). "Working Capital Management and profitability in case of Pakistani firms", *International Review of Business Research papers,* 3 (1): 279-300.

27. Azhagaiah, R. and Gejalakshmi (2007). "Working capital management-efficiency", *UDYOG PRAGAN*, 31(3): 15-20.

28. Kannadhasan, M. (2007). "Working Capital Management in a Public Limited Company - A case study". *The ICFAI Journal of Management Research*, VI (5): 20-33.

29. Arindam Ghosh (2007). "Working Capital Management practices in some selected industries in India", *The Management Accountant*, pp.60-68.

30. Murthy, E.N. (2007). "Working Capital Performance of Corporate India; An Empirical Study", *Journal of Applied Finance*, 13 (1): 47-60.

31. Adolphus J. Toby (2008). "Liquidity performance relationship in Nigerian manufacturing companies", *Finance India*, XXII: 117-131.

32. Das, P.K. (2008). "A study on liquidity management in Ranboxy Laboratories Ltd.," *The Journal of Accounting and Finance*, 122(1): 135-154.

33. Kesevan Padachi, Narasimhan, M.S., Durbassy, R., and Carole Howrth (2008). "An Analysis of Working Capital Structure and Financing Pattern of Mauritian Small Manufacturing Firms", *ICFAI Journal of Applied Finance*, 14(7): 41-62.

34. Afza, T. and Nazir, M.S. (2008). "Working Capital Management Policies of Firms - Empirical evidence from Pakistan", *Pakistan Journal of Commerce and Social Sciences*, (1): 25-36.

35. Samiloglu, F and Demirgunes, K. (2008). "The effect of working capital management on firm profitability: Evidence from Turkey", *The International Journal of Applied Economics and Finance*, 2 (1): 44-50.

36. Sathyamoorthi, C.R. and Wally-Dima, L.B. (2008). "Working Capital Management: The case of Listed Domestic Companies in Botswana", *The ICFAI Journal of Management Research*, VII (5): 7-24.

37. Ali Uyar (2009). "The relationship of Cash conversion cycle with firm size and profitability: An Empirical investigation in Turkey", *International Research Journal*

*of Finance and Economics*, 24: 1-8.

38. Falope,O.I., and Ajilore,O.I . (2009). "Working capital management and corporate profitability: Evidence from panel data analysis of selected quoted companies in Nigeria", *Research Journal of Business Management*, 3: 73-84.
39. Mathuva,D.(2009). "The influence of working capital management components on profitability: A Survey on Kenyan Listed Firms", *Research Journal of Business Management* , 3: 1-11.
40. Amarjit Gill., Nahum Biger., and Neil Mathur (2010). "The Relationship between Working capital management and Profitability: Evidence from the United States", *Business and Economics Journal*, 10: 1-9.
41. Raja, J and Kalyanasundaram, M. (2010). "Liquidity in Malaysian Public Listed Companies", *SMART Journal of Business Management Studies*, 6 (2): 24-35.

## TABLE 14.1

## STATISTICAL VALUES OF RATIOS RELATING TO THE WORKING CAPITAL

**(For the period 1996-97 to 2008-2009)**

| Particulars | Statistics | Commercial Vehicles | Passenger Cars and Multiutility Vehicles | Two and Three Wheelers | Industry Average |
|---|---|---|---|---|---|
| Raw Materials Holding period (in days) | Mean | 34.37 | 38.19 | 25.58 | 52.67 |
| | CV | 0.38 | 0.42 | 0.36 | 0.32 |
| | CAGR | -3.35 | -10.13 | -8.87 | -2.63 |
| | t Value | **10.61*** | **5.71*** | **9.60*** | |
| Work-In-Progress Holding Period (in days) | Mean | 9.73 | 3.98 | 3.97 | 29.63 |
| | CV | 0.42 | 0.51 | 0.42 | 0.43 |
| | CAGR | -6.93 | -10.88 | -10.54 | -4.72 |
| | t Value | **7.30*** | **8.31*** | **8.16*** | |
| Finished Goods Holding Period (in days) | Mean | 19.00 | 11.04 | 8.13 | 14.04 |
| | CV | 0.29 | 0.10 | 0.15 | 0.18 |
| | CAGR | 4.07 | 0.86 | -1.17 | 3.27 |
| | t Value | **3.58*** | **4.02*** | **9.00*** | |
| Receivables Holding Period (in days) | Mean | 45.27 | 22.34 | 16.39 | 34.66 |
| | CV | 0.77 | 0.29 | 0.34 | 0.42 |
| | CAGR | –9.61 | –0.48 | –4.52 | –6.61 |
| | t Value | **1.82**** | **3.61*** | **6.63*** | |
| Payables Payment Period (in days) | Mean | 95.59 | 58.99 | 60.64 | 158.34 |
| | CV | 0.18 | 0.13 | 0.15 | 0.13 |
| | CAGR | 3.80 | -0.37 | -3.59 | 2.61 |
| | t Value | **12.45*** | **16.93*** | **13.75*** | |
| Cash Conversion Cycle (CCC) (in days) | Mean | 12.79 | 16.57 | -6.57 | -27.34 |
| | CV | 4.40 | 1.19 | 1.60 | 1.72 |
| | CAGR | - | - | 11.92 | - |
| | t Value | **6.00*** | **4.81*** | **1.94**** | |

*** - Significant at 5 per cent level**

**** - Significant at 10 per cent level**

***Source :*** Computed from the Annual Reports of the respective units

## TABLE 14.2

## STATISTICAL VALUES OF RATIOS RELATING TO THE WORKING CAPITAL (COMMERCIAL VEHICLES)

**(For the period 1996-97 to 2008-2009)**

| Particulars | Statistics | ALL | TML | BTL | EML | SML | Sector Average | Industry Average |
|---|---|---|---|---|---|---|---|---|
| Raw Materials | Mean | 51.95 | 25.80 | 82.85 | 27.14 | 51.43 | 34.37 | 52.67 |
| Holding period | CV | 0.53 | 0.33 | 0.37 | 0.35 | 0.48 | 0.38 | 0.32 |
| (in days) | CAGR | -3.74 | -3.84 | -2.87 | -1.58 | -2.83 | -3.35 | -2.63 |
| | t Value[1] | **4.33*** | **6.14*** | **9.07*** | **2.82*** | **4.64*** | | |
| | t Value[2] | **0.20** | **9.75*** | **6.88*** | **7.40*** | **0.42** | | |
| Work-In-Progress | Mean | 11.18 | 8.01 | 15.54 | 2.90 | 5.25 | 9.73 | 29.63 |
| Holding Period | CV | 0.34 | 0.43 | 0.17 | 0.44 | 0.39 | 0.42 | 0.43 |
| (in days) | CAGR | -4.52 | -7.53 | 2.15 | 1.09 | 7.25 | -6.93 | -4.72 |
| | t Value[1] | **4.50*** | **5.50*** | **5.34*** | **6.60*** | **3.61*** | | |
| | t Value[2] | **6.64*** | **7.39*** | **4.56*** | **7.68*** | **6.94*** | | |
| Finished Goods | Mean | 29.54 | 19.45 | 27.24 | 11.02 | 29.13 | 19.00 | 14.04 |
| Holding Period | CV | 0.34 | 0.40 | 0.42 | 0.53 | 0.43 | 0.29 | 0.18 |
| (in days) | CAGR | 3.77 | 1.81 | 3.39 | 11.07 | -3.72 | 4.07 | 3.27 |
| | t Value[1] | **6.19*** | **0.48** | **4.07*** | **3.40*** | **2.92*** | | |
| | t Value[2] | **5.98*** | **2.82*** | **4.23*** | **1.71** | **4.12*** | | |
| Receivables | Mean | 73.28 | 37.31 | 28.20 | 31.16 | 74.24 | 45.27 | 34.66 |
| Holding Period | CV | 0.69 | 0.95 | 0.46 | 0.26 | 0.32 | 0.77 | 0.42 |
| (in days) | CAGR | -10.05 | -11.45 | 15.83 | -2.14 | 6.52 | -9.61 | -6.61 |
| | t Value[1] | **5.58*** | **11.28*** | **1.33** | **1.81**** | **1.96**** | | |
| | t Value[2] | **3.77*** | **0.44** | **0.89** | **1.44** | **3.98*** | | |
| Payables | Mean | 70.92 | 98.23 | 94.68 | 60.82 | 103.97 | 95.59 | 158.34 |
| Payment Period | CV | 0.18 | 0.18 | 0.17 | 0.19 | 0.11 | 0.18 | 0.13 |
| (in days) | CAGR | 3.48 | 4.75 | 2.40 | -6.40 | -3.26 | 3.80 | 2.61 |
| | t Value[1] | **4.84*** | **0.55** | **0.17** | **5.01*** | **1.28** | | |
| | t Value[2] | **15.05*** | **8.52*** | **9.05*** | **12.91*** | **7.57*** | | |
| Cash | Mean | 95.02 | -7.66 | 59.14 | 11.41 | 56.07 | 12.79 | -27.34 |
| Conversion | CV | 0.94 | 7.99 | 0.40 | 1.84 | 0.65 | 4.40 | -1.72 |
| Cycle(CCC) | CAGR | -15.93 | - | -1.44 | 10.33 | 5.53 | - | - |
| (in days) | t Value[1] | **7.28*** | **4.66*** | **3.76*** | **0.09** | **2.99*** | | |
| | t Value[2] | **8.94*** | **2.51*** | **10.07*** | **2.77*** | **5.70*** | | |

***- Significant at 5 per cent level** ***- Significant at 10 per cent level**
**t value[1]**- With the sector average **t value[2]**- With the Industry average
**ALL** - Ashok Leyland Ltd; **TML**- Tata Motors Ltd; **BTL**- Bajaj Tempo Ltd; **EML**- Eicher Motors Ltd; **SML**- Swaraj Mazda Ltd

**Source :** Computed from the Annual Reports of the respective units.

## TABLE 14.3
## STATISTICAL VALUES OF RATIOS RELATING TO THE WORKING CAPITAL (PASSENGER CARS AND MULTIUTILITY VEHICLES)
### (For the period 1996-97 to 2008-2009)

| Particulars | Statistics | HML | MML | MUL | HYML | HSL | FIL | Sector Average | Industry Average |
|---|---|---|---|---|---|---|---|---|---|
| Raw Materials Holding period (in days) | Mean | 74.81 | 28.70 | 28.80 | 23.56 | 17.89 | 25.18 | 38.19 | 52.67 |
| | CV | 0.44 | 0.29 | 0.52 | 0.76 | 0.86 | 0.89 | 0.42 | 0.32 |
| | CAGR | -6.27 | -6.67 | -9.82 | -6.82 | -6.99 | -10.31 | -10.13 | -2.63 |
| | t Value[1] | **6.49*** | **4.10*** | **6.12*** | **1.04** | **2.12**** | **1.78** | | |
| | t Value[2] | **3.49*** | **7.23*** | **7.80*** | **4.85*** | **4.73*** | **1.37** | | |
| Work-In-Progress Holding Period (in days) | Mean | 11.43 | 3.28 | 1.47 | 2.97 | 1.13 | 0.96 | 3.98 | 29.63 |
| | CV | 0.40 | 0.43 | 0.29 | 0.88 | 0.86 | 0.89 | 0.51 | 0.43 |
| | CAGR | -3.94 | -5.47 | -6.40 | -6.89 | -6.92 | 14.13 | -10.88 | -4.72 |
| | t Value[1] | 17.23* | 2.72* | 5.41* | 1.37 | 4.07* | 3.36* | | |
| | t Value[2] | 5.44* | 8.16* | 8.21* | 6.06* | 7.21* | 7.01* | | |
| Finished Goods Holding Period (in days) | Mean | 12.37 | 28.51 | 5.47 | 23.56 | 17.89 | 25.18 | 11.04 | 14.04 |
| | CV | 0.40 | 0.30 | 0.45 | 0.76 | 0.86 | 0.89 | 0.10 | 0.18 |
| | CAGR | -4.44 | -7.85 | 4.48 | -6.82 | -6.99 | -10.31 | 0.86 | 3.27 |
| | t Value[1] | **1.98**** | **7.35*** | **8.64*** | **7.80*** | **8.61*** | **7.71*** | | |
| | t Value[2] | **0.79** | **5.61*** | **9.49*** | **5.92*** | **5.86*** | **5.82*** | | |

## TABLE 14.3 (CONTINUED)

## STATISTICAL VALUES OF RATIOS RELATING TO THE WORKING CAPITAL

| Particulars | Statistics | HML | MML | MUL | HYML | HSL | FIL | Sector Average | Industry Average |
|---|---|---|---|---|---|---|---|---|---|
| Receivables Holding Period (in days) | Mean | 35.37 | 34.74 | 17.40 | 8.73 | 8.21 | 8.79 | 22.34 | 34.66 |
| | CV | 0.45 | 0.37 | 0.40 | 1.73 | 1.47 | 0.88 | 0.29 | 0.42 |
| | CAGR | -7.65 | 2.60 | 2.60 | -16.25 | -36.71 | 2.87 | -0.48 | -6.61 |
| | t Value[1] | **6.43*** | **6.25*** | **3.12*** | **2.15**** | **4.43*** | **4.10*** | | |
| | t Value[2] | **0.71** | **0.02** | **3.60*** | **5.03*** | **5.07*** | **6.22*** | | |
| Payables Payment Period (in days) | Mean | 85.93 | 79.77 | 30.09 | 46.63 | 21.24 | 47.01 | 58.99 | 158.34 |
| | CV | 0.37 | 0.13 | 0.40 | 3.52 | 0.78 | 0.88 | 0.13 | 0.13 |
| | CAGR | -0.50 | 1.24 | 6.76 | -47.84 | 2.48 | -4.99 | 3.80 | 2.61 |
| | t Value[1] | **4.82*** | **7.04*** | **6.33*** | **0.99** | **6.39*** | **3.13*** | | |
| | t Value[2] | **8.18*** | **11.50*** | **23.03*** | **0.94** | **15.24*** | **10.30*** | | |
| Cash Conversion Cycle (CCC) (in days) | Mean | 48.06 | 15.46 | 23.08 | 12.19 | 23.88 | 13.10 | 16.57 | -27.34 |
| | CV | 0.83 | 1.96 | 1.14 | 3.62 | 1.95 | 4.74 | 1.19 | -1.72 |
| | CAGR | -24.72 | - | - | -14.17 | - | 10.26 | - | - |
| | t Value[1] | **4.54*** | **3.69*** | **2.98*** | **1.01** | **0.36** | **5.55*** | | |
| | t Value[2] | **8.68*** | **3.74*** | **5.96*** | **0.98** | **2.83*** | **2.74*** | | |

* - **Significant at 5 per cent level**     ** - **Significant at 10 per cent level**

**t value[1]** - With the sector average     **t value[2]**- With the Industry average

**HML** - Hindustan Motors Ltd; **MML** - Mahindra and Mahindra Ltd; **MUL** - Maruti Udyog Ltd;

**HYML** - Hyundai Motors India Ltd **HSL**- Honda Siel Cars India Ltd; **FIL**- Ford India Private Ltd

***Source :*** Computed from the Annual Reports of the respective units

## TABLE 14.4

### STATISTICAL VALUES OF RATIOS RELATING TO THE WORKING CAPITAL (TWO AND THREE WHEELERS) (For the period 1996-97 to 2008-2009)

| Particulars | Statistics | BAL | LML | MSC | TVS | KMC | HHM | KEL | MAL | SIL | Sector Ave. | Industry Ave. |
|---|---|---|---|---|---|---|---|---|---|---|---|---|
| Raw Materials Holding period (in days) | Mean | 20.81 | 141.11 | 25.36 | 18.79 | 41.10 | 18.03 | 43.15 | 37.51 | 73.45 | 25.58 | 52.67 |
| | CV | 0.57 | 1.29 | 1.17 | 0.26 | 0.48 | 0.49 | 0.56 | 0.45 | 0.34 | 0.36 | 0.32 |
| | CAGR | -13.67 | 15.01 | 11.38 | 1.19 | 0.02 | -9.69 | 2.45 | -4.06 | -4.89 | -8.87 | -2.63 |
| | t Value[1] | 1.75 | 2.42* | 0.02 | 2.02** | 6.06* | 11.71* | 3.70* | 2.84* | 9.91* | | |
| | t Value[2] | 7.78* | 1.91** | 2.53* | 6.34* | 1.19 | 12.58* | 0.38 | 1.81** | 5.05* | | |
| Work-In-Progress Holding Period (in days) | Mean | 4.81 | 14.31 | 10.87 | 3.98 | 5.06 | 1.54 | 14.02 | 11.25 | 16.68 | 3.97 | 29.63 |
| | CV | 1.02 | 1.27 | 0.97 | 0.36 | 0.76 | 0.68 | 0.68 | 0.97 | 0.31 | 0.42 | 0.43 |
| | CAGR | -11.13 | 12.22 | 21.89 | -6.04 | 10.53 | -11.42 | 8.42 | 4.28 | 0.93 | -10.54 | -4.72 |
| | t Value[1] | 0.31 | 2.15** | 2.10** | 0.11 | 1.24 | 11.47* | 4.36* | 2.37* | 9.06* | | |
| | t Value[2] | 6.18* | 1.69 | 3.23* | 8.13* | 5.65* | 8.56* | 2.49* | 3.18* | 3.76* | | |
| Finished Goods Holding Period(in days) | Mean | 6.80 | 13.59 | 15.97 | 12.31 | 19.59 | 2.98 | 22.51 | 6.44 | 32.70 | 8.13 | 14.04 |
| | CV | 0.62 | 0.63 | 0.80 | 0.31 | 0.75 | 0.37 | 0.75 | 0.59 | 0.50 | 0.15 | 0.18 |
| | CAGR | 2.23 | -0.07 | 20.64 | 7.65 | -0.90 | -9.67 | -12.51 | -6.80 | 15.49 | -1.17 | 3.27 |
| | t Value[1] | 0.89 | 4.56* | 2.19* | 3.72* | 4.02* | 18.93* | 4.20* | 1.44 | 5.59* | | |
| | t Value[2] | 6.43* | 1.11 | 0.51 | 1.76** | 2.70* | 14.68* | 3.10* | 6.30* | 4.21* | | |
| Receivables Holding Period (in days) | Mean | 14.85 | 17.20 | 31.31 | 11.82 | 39.35 | 6.67 | 106.93 | 59.49 | 26.92 | 16.39 | 34.66 |
| | CV | 0.37 | 0.69 | 0.68 | 0.45 | 0.55 | 0.36 | 0.79 | 0.50 | 0.46 | 0.34 | 0.42 |

## TABLE 14.4 (CONTINUED)
## STATISTICAL VALUES OF RATIOS RELATING TO THE WORKING CAPITAL

| Particulars | Statistics | BAL | LML | MSC | TVS | KMC | HHM | KEL | MAL | SIL | Sector Ave. | Industry Ave. |
|---|---|---|---|---|---|---|---|---|---|---|---|---|
| CAGR | -1.67 | 2.59 | 7.15 | -0.82 | 8.12 | -4.92 | 20.93 | 0.48 | 15.69 | -4.52 | -6.61 | |
| | t Value[1] | 0.30 | 1.00 | 2.15* | 5.80* | 5.25* | 6.79* | 4.50* | 5.90* | 2.39* | | |
| | t Value[2] | 4.68* | 2.63* | 0.38 | 7.16* | 1.23 | 7.41* | 3.38* | 2.98* | 1.15 | | |
| Payables Payment Period (in days) | Mean | 36.99 | 210.29 | 141.09 | 51.30 | 66.95 | 40.13 | 61.99 | 64.65 | 59.25 | 60.64 | 158.34 |
| | CV | 0.40 | 1.45 | 0.94 | 0.08 | 0.73 | 0.13 | 0.80 | 0.63 | 0.33 | 0.15 | 0.13 |
| | CAGR | 2.57 | 18.14 | 17.05 | -0.58 | 12.87 | -0.28 | 10.18 | 0.05 | 2.28 | -3.59 | 2.61 |
| | t Value[1] | 6.43* | 1.92** | 2.08** | 3.60* | 1.13 | 7.09* | 0.72 | 0.83 | 0.20 | | |
| | t Value[2] | 16.72* | 0.99 | 0.49 | 18.07* | 6.98* | 21.94* | 6.11* | 6.77* | 14.00* | | |
| Cash Conversion Cycle (CCC) (in days) | Mean | 10.28 | -24.08 | -57.59 | -4.43 | 38.15 | -10.90 | 124.61 | 50.07 | 90.50 | -6.57 | -27.34 |
| | CV | 2.05 | 4.23 | -1.55 | 1.94 | 1.05 | 1.26 | 0.69 | 0.63 | 0.36 | 1.60 | 1.72 |
| | CAGR | - | - | 25.96 | - | - | - | 12.04 | -3.59 | -4.88 | 11.92 | - |
| | t Value[1] | 3.08* | 0.72 | 2.13* | 0.76 | 4.28* | 2.13 | 6.61* | 5.92* | 13.85* | | |
| | t Value[2] | 2.55* | 0.34 | 1.48 | 1.80** | 4.38* | 1.67 | 5.22* | 4.08* | 15.13* | | |

*** - Significant at 5 per cent level**    **** - Significant at 10 per cent level**

**t value[1]** - With the sector average    **t value[2]** - With the Industry average

**BAL**- Bajaj Auto Ltd **LML**- LML Ltd **MSC**- Maharashtra Scooters Ltd **TVS**- TVS Motor Company Ltd
**KMC**- Kinetic Motor Company Ltd **HHM**- Hero Honda Motors Ltd **KEL**- Kinetic Engineering Ltd
**MAL**- Majestic Auto Ltd **SIL**- Scooters India Ltd

***Source :*** Computed from the Annual Reports of the respective units

## TABLE 14.5

## ANOVA RESULTS- RATIOS RELATING TO WORKING CAPITAL – COMPARISON

| S. No. | Working capital ratios | Between the sectors F ratio | $H_o$ | Between the years F ratio | $H_o$ |
|---|---|---|---|---|---|
| 1. | Raw materials Holding Period | 19.25 | Rejected | 16.31 | Rejected |
| 2. | WIP Holding period | 73.94 | Rejected | 10.20 | Rejected |
| 3. | Finished Goods Holding Period | 47.06 | Rejected | 1.79 | Accepted |
| 4. | Receivables Holding Period | 9.07 | Rejected | 1.89 | Accepted |
| 5. | Payables Payment Period | 39.72 | Rejected | 1.05 | Accepted |
| 6. | Cash Conversion Cycle (CCC) | 2.68 | Accepted | 2.90 | Rejected |

**Critical Value of 'F' at 5 per cent level: 3.40 and 2.18**

## Commercial Vehicles

| S. No. | Working capital ratios | Between the companies F ratio | $H_o$ | Between the years F ratio | $H_o$ |
|---|---|---|---|---|---|
| 1. | Raw materials Holding Period | 42.20 | Rejected | 10.65 | Rejected |
| 2. | WIP Holding period | 64.03 | Rejected | 3.72 | Rejected |
| 3. | Finished Goods Holding Period | 11.78 | Rejected | 2.87 | Rejected |
| 4. | Receivables Holding Period | 7.46 | Rejected | 1.05 | Accepted |
| 5. | Payables Payment Period | 20.22 | Rejected | 0.40 | Accepted |
| 6. | Cash Conversion Cycle (CCC) | 13.04 | Rejected | 4.35 | Rejected |

**Critical Value of 'F' at 5 per cent level: 2.57 and 1.96**

## Passenger Cars and Multiutility Vehicles

| S. No. | Working capital ratios | Between the companies F ratio | $H_o$ | Between the years F ratio | $H_o$ |
|---|---|---|---|---|---|
| 1. | Raw materials Holding Period | 25.57 | Rejected | 1.64 | Accepted |
| 2. | WIP Holding period | 61.81 | Rejected | 0.53 | Accepted |
| 3. | Finished Goods Holding Period | 10.29 | Rejected | 1.79 | Accepted |
| 4. | Receivables Holding Period | 21.73 | Rejected | 2.44 | Rejected |
| 5. | Payables Payment Period | 0.98 | Accepted | 0.98 | Accepted |
| 6. | Cash Conversion Cycle (CCC) | 1.01 | Accepted | 0.99 | Accepted |

**Critical Value of 'F' at 5 per cent level: 2.37 and 1.92**

### Two and Three Wheelers

| S. No. | Working capital ratios | Between the companies F ratio | $H_o$ | Between the years F ratio | $H_o$ |
|---|---|---|---|---|---|
| 1. | Raw materials Holding Period | 7.24 | Rejected | 1.26 | Accepted |
| 2. | WIP Holding period | 8.17 | Rejected | 2.93 | Rejected |
| 3. | Finished Goods Holding Period | 13.38 | Rejected | 2.23 | Rejected |
| 4. | Receivables Holding Period | 28.51 | Rejected | 1.63 | Accepted |
| 5. | Payables Payment Period | 4.65 | Rejected | 2.47 | Rejected |
| 6. | Cash Conversion Cycle (CCC) | 20.12 | Rejected | 2.32 | Rejected |

**Critical Value 'F' at 5 per cent level: 2.04 and 1.85**
*Source:* Computed

## TABLE 14.6

## WORKING CAPITAL-SUMMARY OF FACTOR ANALYSIS RESULTS-ROTATED FACTOR LOADINGS (Whole Industry)

| Variables | Factors 1 | Factors 2 | Communality |
|---|---|---|---|
| Raw Materials Holding period | **0.807** | - 0.067 | 0.656 |
| WIP Holding period | **0.923** | - 0.075 | 0.858 |
| Finished Goods Holding Period | **0.284** | - 0.580 | 0.417 |
| Receivables Holding period | **0.634** | - 0.026 | 0.402 |
| Payables Holding period | 0.153 | **0.859** | 0.761 |
| **Eigen Value** | **2.041** | **1.053** | **2.094** |
| **% of Variance** | **40.818** | **21.065** | **61.883** |
| **Cum.% variance** | **40.818** | **61.883** | |
| **Kaiser-Meyer-Olkin Measure of Sampling Adequacy -** | | | **0.464** |
| **Bartlett's Test of Sphericity -** | | | **310.688 (Sig.0.000)** |

## (Commercial Vehicles)

| Variables(as % of Gross Sales) | Factors 1 | 2 | Communality |
|---|---|---|---|
| Raw Materials Holding period | **0.895** | 0.052 | 0.803 |
| WIP Holding period | **0.822** | -0.113 | 0.688 |
| Finished Goods Holding Period | **0.823** | 0.116 | 0.691 |
| Receivables Holding period | **0.439** | -0.664 | 0.633 |
| Payables Holding period | 0.373 | **0.778** | 0.744 |
| **Eigen Value** | **2.486** | **1.073** | **3.559** |
| **% of Variance** | **49.722** | **21.453** | **71.175** |
| **Cum.% variance** | **49.722** | **71.175** | |

**Kaiser-Meyer-Olkin Measure of Sampling Adequacy - 0.669**
**Bartlett's Test of Sphericity - 97.738 (Sig.0.000)**

## (Passenger Cars and Multiutility vehicles)

| Variables(as % of Gross Sales) | Factors 1 | 2 | Communality |
|---|---|---|---|
| Raw Materials Holding period | **0.914** | - 0.250 | 0.898 |
| WIP Holding period | **0.899** | - 0.143 | 0.829 |
| Finished Goods Holding Period | **0.102** | - 0.603 | 0.374 |
| Receivables Holding period | **0.795** | 0.339 | 0.749 |
| Payables Holding period | 0.049 | **0.852** | 0.728 |
| **Eigen Value** | **2.302** | **1.276** | **3.578** |
| **% of Variance** | **46.042** | **25.510** | **71.552** |
| **Cum.% variance** | **46.042** | **71.552** | |

**Kaiser-Meyer-Olkin Measure of Sampling Adequacy - 0.580**
**Bartlett's Test of Sphericity - 142.403 (Sig.0.000)**

**(Two and Three Wheelers Sector)**

| Variables(as % of Gross Sales) | Factors 1 | Factors 2 | Communality |
|---|---|---|---|
| Raw Materials Holding period | **0.952** | 0.025 | 0.906 |
| WIP Holding period | **0.815** | 0.460 | 0.876 |
| Finished Goods Holding Period | 0.003 | **0.752** | 0.566 |
| Receivables Holding period | 0.145 | **0.806** | 0.671 |
| Payables Holding period | **0.961** | - 0.008 | 0.924 |
| **Eigen Value** | **2.716** | **1.226** | **3.942** |
| **% of Variance** | **54.329** | **24.515** | **78.844** |
| **Cum.% variance** | **54.329** | **78.844** | |
| **Kaiser-Meyer-Olkin Measure of Sampling Adequacy** | | - | **0.646** |
| **Bartlett's Test of Sphericity** | | - | **340.412 (Sig.0.000)** |

***Source :*** Computed from the Annual Reports

# 15

# Cash Conversion Cycle and Corporate Profitability

## An Empirical Enquiry in Indian Automobile Firms

In general, it is possible to discuss finance theory under three main threads as capital budgeting, capital structure and working capital management. The first two of them are mostly related with financing and managing long-term investments. However, financial decisions about working capital are mostly related with financing and managing short-term investments and undertake both current assets and current liabilities simultaneously. So, most of the time, it is reasonable to term short-term financial management as working capital management (Ross et al., 2003). A great deal of controversy has always been persisting over whether the working capital of a firm, as determined by its investment and financing decisions, affects its profitability. On this issue academicians are sharply divided into two schools of thought.

One school of thought argues that working capital is not a factor of enhancing profitability. Only fixed capital plays a very significant role in profit generating process. Moreover, they also opine that there may be a negative influence of working capital on profitability. The other school of thought considers the extent of fund invested in working capital as relevant to the profitability of the firm. They suggest that unless there is a minimum level of investment in the working capital, which provides a promising vehicle for improving profitability, output and sales can't be maintained. The inadequacy of working capital renders fixed assets inoperative, which results in reduction in profitability. In this sense, working capital acts as an explanatory variable in the profit function (Mallick & Sur, 1998).

Working capital management, which deals with the management of current assets and current liabilities, is very important in corporate finance because it directly affects the liquidity and profitability of the firm (Deloof, 2003; Eljelly, 2004; Raheman and Nasr, 2007; Appuhami, 2008; Dash and Ravipathi, 2009). The current assets of a typical manufacturing firm or even a distributing firm account for more than half of the firm's total assets. Deloof (2003) held that same proposition that the accounts receivables and inventories comprise a substantial percentage of the total assets of a firm. Excessive levels of current assets can easily result in a firm's realizing a substandard return on investment. However, firms with too few current assets may incur shortages and difficulties in maintaining smooth operations (Van Horne and Wachowicz, 2005).

Profitability is the rate of return on firm's investment. An unwarranted high investment in current assets would reduce this rate of return (Vishnani, 2007). The purpose of working capital management is to manage the firm's current accounts so as to attain a desired balance between profitability and risk (Ricci and Vito, 2000). Shin and Soenen (1998) found that efficient working capital management is an integral component of the overall corporate strategy towards creating shareholder value. Efficient working capital management involves planning and controlling the current assets and current liabilities in a manner that eliminates the risk of inability of a firm to meet due short term obligations and to avoid excessive investment in these assets on the other hand (Eljelly, 2004). Smith (1980) and Raheman and Nasr (2007) also observed that working capital management is important because of its effects on the firm's profitability and risk and consequently its value.

The way in which working capital is managed can have a significant impact on both the liquidity and profitability of the firm (Deloof, 2003). The decisions that tend to maximise profitability tend to minimize the chances of adequate liquidity. Conversely, focusing almost entirely on liquidity will tend to reduce the potential profitability of the firm. A firm can have larger sales with a generous credit policy, which extends the cash cycle. In this case, the longer cash conversion cycle may result in higher profitability. However, the traditional view of the relationship between cash conversion cycle and corporate profitability is that, ceteris paribus, a longer cash conversion cycle hurts the profitability of a firm (Deloof, 2003; Smith, 1980). This part of the study aimed at examining the influence of working capital management (liquidity) on corporate profitability in Indian Automobile Industry.

## CONJECTURAL FRAME WORK

Liquidity management is necessary for all businesses, small, medium or large because it means collecting cash from customers in time so that having no difficulty in paying short-term debts. Therefore, when a business does not manage its liquidity well, it will have cash shortages and will results in difficulty in paying obligations. As a result, in addition to profitability, liquidity management is vital for ongoing concerns. Promoters of capital theory share the axiom that profitability and liquidity comprise the salient (albeit frequently conflicting) goals of working capital management. The conflict arises because the maximization of firm's returns could seriously threaten the liquidity and on the other hand, the pursuit of liquidity has a tendency to dilute returns. The crucial part in managing working capital is required maintaining its liquidity in day-to-day operation to ensure its smooth running and meets its obligation (Eljelly, 2004). Yet, this is not a simple task since managers must make sure that business operation is running in efficient and profitable manner. There are possibilities of mismatch of current assets and current liabilities during this process. If this happens and firm's manager cannot manage it properly then it will affect firm's growth and profitability. This will further lead to financial distress and finally firms can go bankrupt.

Corporate liquidity is examined from two distinct dimensions: static or dynamic view (Lancaster et al., 1999; Farris and Hutchison, 2002: and Moss and Stine, 1993). The static view is based on commonly used traditional ratios, such as current ratio and quick ratio, calculated from the balance sheet accounts. These traditional measures of liquidity are incompetent measures that cannot provide detailed and accurate about liquidity management effectiveness (Jose et al., 1996). These ratios measures liquidity at a given point in time. For example, the current ratio, are simple to apply and have some theoretical merit increases in say, accounts receivables will increase the current ratio, suggesting improved liquidity. However, the ability to match short-term obligations has only improved from a liquidation perspective providing current assets may be liquidated at current market value and not from a going-concern approach (Shulman and Dambolena, 1986). Liquidity for the ongoing firm is not reliant on the liquidation value of its assets, but rather on the operating cash flow generated by these assets (Soenen, 1993).

On the other hand, dynamic view measures ongoing liquidity from the firm's operations. As a dynamic measure of the time it takes a firm to go from cash outflow to cash inflow which is measured by Cash Conversion Cycle (CCC) introduced by Hager (1976) and has been recommended by Largay and Stickney (1980), Kamath (1989) and others. Drawing attention to limitations of traditional liquidity ratios, Richards and Laughlin (1980), Kamath (1989), Gentry et al., (1990), and Schilling (1996) have insisted on using ongoing liquidity measures in working capital management. Ongoing liquidity refers to the inflows and outflows of cash through the product acquisition, production, sales, payment and collection process takes place overtime. As the firm's ongoing liquidity is a function of its cash (conversion) cycle, it will be more appropriate and evaluate effectiveness of working capital management by cash conversion cycle, rather than traditional liquidity measures.

## CASH CONVERSION CYCLE (CCC)

In text books related to finance, CCC is maintained in the context of working capital management (Keown et al., 2003; and Bodie and Merton, 2000). The cash conversion cycle is used as a comprehensive measure of working capital as it shows the time lag between expenditure for the purchase of raw material and the collection of sales of finished goods (Padachi, 2006; Bodie and Merton, 2009; Keown et al., 2003; Jordon, 2003; and Eljelly, 2004).

$$CCC = RCP + ICP - APP$$

In the above formula, the three variables to which CCC is dependent are defined as follows;

RCP – Receivables Collection Period (in days)

(Accounts Receivables / Sales) * 365

ICP – Inventory Conversion period (in days)

(Inventory / Cost of goods sold) * 365

APP – Accounts Payable Period (in days)

(Accounts Payables / Cost of goods sold) * 365

There seems to be strong relation between the cash conversion cycle of a firm and its profitability. The three different components of CCC (accounts receivables, inventory and accounts payables) can be managed in different ways in order to maximise profitability. It is an indication of how long a firm can carry on if it was to stop its operations or it indicates the time gap between purchase of goods and collection of sales. The optimum level of inventory will have a direct effect on profitability since it will release working capital resources which in turn will be invested in the business cycle, or will increase inventory levels in order to respond to higher product demand. Similarly both credit policy from suppliers and credit period granted to customers will have an impact on profitability. In order to understand the way working capital is managed, CCC and its components will be statistically analysed.

Cash conversion cycle is likely to be negative as well as positive. A positive result indicates the number of days a company must borrow or tie up capital while awaiting payment from a customer. A negative result indicates the number of days a company has received cash from sales before it must pay its suppliers (Hutchison et al., 2007). Of course the ultimate goal is having low CCC, if possible negative. Because the shorter the CCC, the more efficient the company in managing its cash flow. The purpose of this part of analysis is to investigate the implications of the CCC as an indicator of liquidity on profitability of selected firms in Indian Automobile Industry.

## LITERATURE REVIEW – THEORETICAL UNDERPINNINGS

Before embarking with the empirical study, a quick glance at the existing literature on the relationship between liquidity management and profitability is desirable. Literature review consisting some of previous studies regarding with the relationship between profitability and liquidity (working capital management) is given below.

In a study by Kamath (1989), it has been concluded that there is a reverse relationship between cash conversion cycle and profitability. In another study of Shin and Soenen (1998), a sample consisting of American manufacturing firms for the period of 1974-1995 has been analysed and a statistically negative relationship between cash conversion cycle and profitability has been confirmed. To test the relationship between working capital management and corporate profitability, Deloof (2003) used a sample of 1009 large Belgian non-financial firms for a period of 1992-1996. He discussed possible relationships between cash conversion cycle and profitability by dividing cash conversion cycle into its components (inventory, account receivables and account payables period). Results of the study have concluded that increase in all of these periods affect profitability negatively. Lazaridis and Tryfonidis (2006) conducted a cross sectional study by using a sample of 131 firms listed on the Athens Stock Exchange for the period of 2001-2004 and found cash conversion cycle affects profitability negatively.

Eljelly (2004) empirically examined the relationship between profitability and liquidity as measured by current ratio and cash conversion cycle on a sample of 929 Joint stock companies in Saudi Arabia. It has been concluded that the effect of cash conversion cycle on profitability is stronger than the effect of current ratio on it and found significant negative relationship between the firm's profitability and its liquidity level. Raheman and Nasr (2007) studied the effect of different variables of working capital management including cash conversion cycle on the profitability of 94 Pakistani firm listed on Karachi Stock Exchange for a period between 1999-2004 and found that as cash conversion cycle increases, it leads to decreasing profitability of the firm. Garcia-Teruel and Martinez-Solano (2007) collected data for 8872 SMEs from Spain for the period 1996-2002 and tested the effects of working capital management on profitability. The results demonstrated that shortening cash conversion cycle improves the profitability. Falope and Ajilore (2009) used a sample of 50 Nigerian quoted non-financial firms for the period 1996-2005. They found a significant negative relationship between net operating profitability and the average collection period, inventory turnover in days, average payment period and cash conversion cycle.

Mathuva (2009) examined the influence of working capital management components on corporate profitability by using a sample of 30 listed on the Nairobi-Stock Exchange (NSE) for the periods 1993 to 2008. He found that there exists a highly significant negative relationship between the time it takes for firms to collect cash from their customers and profitability. Amarjit Gill, Nahum Biger and Neil Mathur (2010) studied the relationship between the cash conversion cycle and profitability and found significant relationship between them. The other studies, Ali Uyar (2009), Moss Stine (1993), Jose et al., (1996), Hutchison et al., (2007), Vaidyanathan et al., (1990), Lyroudi and McCarty (1993), Soenen (1993) and Wang (2002) empirically examined the relationship between profitability and liquidity showed that there exists a significant and negative relation between profitability and CCC. However, the study conducted by Katerina Lyroudi and Lazoridis (2000) in the Food Industry of Greece found that there was positive relationship between CCC and return on assets.

Among the studies conducted in the Indian context showed both the positive and negative association between liquidity and profitability. Amit K. Mallik, Debdas Rakshit (2005) studied the relationship between liquidity and profitability in the context of Indian Pharmaceutical industry and concluded that no definite relationship can be established between liquidity and profitability. Narware (2004) in his study of working capital management and profitability of NFL, a fertilizer company disclosed both negative and positive association. Bardia (2004) in his study on steel giant SAIL for the period from 1991-92 to 2001-2002 concluded that there was a positive relationship between liquidity and profitability. D. Sur, J. Biswas and Ganguly, P. (2001) revealed in their study of Indian Aluminium producing industry, a very significant positive association between liquidity and profitability. Vijayakumar and Venkatachalam (1995) in their study on Tamil Nadu Sugar Industry with regard to relationship between liquidity and profitability concluded that liquidity was negatively associated with profitability.

In summary, the literature review indicates that working capital management impacts on the profitability of the firm but there still is ambiguity regarding the appropriate variables that might serve as proxies for working capital management. The present study investigates the relationship between a set of such variables and the profitability of a sample of Indian Automobile firms. Further, most of the Indian studies used traditional liquidity ratios viz., current and quick ratio as a measure of liquidity. Only a very few studies used Cash Conversion Cycle (CCC) as a measure for liquidity. Therefore, to fill this gap in the literature, as attempt has been made in this part to study the relationship between cash conversion cycle and profitability of Indian automobile firms. Thus, all the above studies provided a solid base and gave an idea regarding working capital management (liquidity) and profitability. They also gave the results and conclusions of those researches already conducted on the same area for different countries and environment from different aspects. On the basis of these researches done in different countries, methodology has been formulated.

From the above reviews, the researcher concludes most of the studies support the general notion that there is a negative relationship between liquidity and profitability. In order to test this general notion, the researcher postulates the following hypothesis

**"Firms liquidity negatively affects profitability"**

## VARIABLES SPECIFICATIONS AND EMPIRICAL MODEL

The primary aim of this part of analysis is to investigate the impact of working capital management (liquidity) on corporate profitability of Indian automobile firms. This is achieved by developing a similar empirical framework first used by Shin and Soenen (1998) and the subsequent work of Deloof (2003). The analysis of data employs the use of correlation and a multiple regression model that consists of both liquidity and profitability. For this purpose, four different models using the various components of liquidity and profitability are considered. This helps analyzing changes in the results due to different measures of liquidity and profitability.

## THE EXPLANATORY VARIABLES

This study investigates the effects of accounts receivables period, inventory conversion period, accounts payables period and cash conversion cycle on firms profitability. The dependent variable of the regression model is return on assets (PR). Many researchers use different measures of firm profitability in their analysis. Among, return on assets (Zelia Serrasqueiro, 2009; Kuldip Kaur and Kushwinder Kaur, 2008) and return on sales (Samuels and Smyth, 1968; Vijayakumar, 2002) are widely used measure of profitability. Among these two measures the return on assets is a better measure since it relates the profitability of the business to the asset base. There are many ways of managing return on assets but, in principle, key levers are, of course, profit increase and assets reduction. The later has become important to many businesses as the former becomes more elusive.

Accounts Receivables Period (ARP) used as proxy for the collection policy is an independent variable obtained as accounts receivables/sales*365. Inventory Conversion Period (ICP) used as proxy for the inventory policy is also an independent variable derived as inventory/cost of sales*365.

Average Payment Period (APP) used as proxy for the payment policy is also an independent variable. It is calculated by dividing accounts payable by purchases and multiplying the result by 365. The Cash Conversion Cycle (CCC) used as a comprehensive measure of liquidity is another independent variable, and is measured by adding ARP to ICP and then subtracting the APP. All the above variables have relationship that ultimately affects liquidity of the firm. It is expected that there is a negative relationship between profitability on the one hand and the measures of liquidity (number of days accounts receivables, inventory and accounts payables and cash conversion cycle) on the other hand. This is consistent with the view that the time lag between expenditure for the purchase of raw materials and the collection of sales of finished goods can be too long, and that decreasing the time lag increases profitability.

## CONTROL VARIABLES

In various literature reviews, various studies have used the control variables along with the main variables of liquidity (working capital) in order to have an opposite analysis of working capital management on the profitability of firms (Lamberson, 1995; Smith and Begemann, 1997; Deloof, 2003; Eljelly, 2004; Teruel and Solano, 2005 and Lazaridis and Tryfonidis, 2006). On the same lines, along with working capital variables, the present study has taken into considerations some control variables relating to firms such as the size of the firm, the growth in its sales and its financial leverage. The size of the firm (SIZE) has been measured by the natural logarithm of its total sales. The growth of the firm (GROWTH) is measured by variations in its annual sales value with reference to previous year's sales $[(sales_t - sales_{t-1}) / sales_{t-1}]$. Moreover, the financial leverage (LEV) was taken as the debt to equity ratio of each firm for the whole sample period. Finally, since good economic conditions tend to be reflected in a firm's profitability (Lamberson, 1995), this phenomenon has been controlled for the evolution of the economic cycle using the GDPGR variable, which measures the real annual GDP growth.

Table 15.1 below summarises the definitions and theoretical predicted signs.

**TABLE 15.1**

**PROXY VARIABLES DEFINITION AND PREDICTED RELATIONSHIPS**

| Proxy variables | Definitions | Predicted Sign |
|---|---|---|
| ARP | Account receivables divided by sales and multiplied by 365 days | +/- |
| ICP | Inventory divided by cost of goods sold and multiplied by 365 days | +/- |
| APP | Accounts payables divided by cost of goods sold and multiplied by 365 days | +/- |
| CCC | No. of days A/R plus No. of days of IC minus No. of days A/P | +/- |
| Size | Natural logarithm of firm's sales | +/- |
| Growth | Difference between current year sales and previous year sales divided by previous year sales | +/- |
| Leverage | Total debt divided by equity | - |
| GDPGR | Difference between current year GDP and previous year GDP divided by previous year GDP | + |

## EMPIRICAL MODELS:

The study uses panel data regression analysis of cross-sectional and time series data. The pooled regression is one where both intercepts and slops are constant, where the cross-section firm data and time series data are pooled together in a single column assuming that there is no significant cross-section or temporal effects.

The general form of model is

$$PR_{it} = \beta_0 + \underset{a_{it}}{\overset{n}{\text{€}}} \beta_i X_{it} + e$$

where $PR_{it}$ - Return on assets of firm i at time t;

$i$ = 1, 2, 3....., 20 firms

$\beta_0$ - The intercept of equation

$\beta_i$ - Co-efficients of $X_{it}$ variables

$X_{it}$ - The different independent variables for working capital management of firms i at time t

t - Time = 1, 2, 3, ......

e - The error term

To investigate the impact of working capital management (liquidity) on profitability the model used for the regression analysis is expressed in the general form as given above and the variable ARP will be replaced in turn by the other explanatory variables: ICP, APP and CCC. Specifically, when convert the above general least squares model into specified variables it becomes:

$$\mathbf{PR_{it} = \beta_0 + \beta_1\, ARP_{it} + \beta_2\, SIZE_{it} + \beta_3\, GROWTH_{it} + \beta_4\, LEV_{it} + \beta_5\, GDPGR_{it} + e_{it}}$$

[Model 1]

$$\mathbf{PR_{it} = \beta_0 + \beta_1\, ICP_{it} + \beta_2\, SIZE_{it} + \beta_3\, GROWTH_{it} + \beta_4\, LEV_{it} + \beta_5\, GDPGR_{it} + e_{it}}$$

[Model 2]

$$\mathbf{PR_{it} = \beta_0 + \beta_1\, APP_{it} + \beta_2\, SIZE_{it} + \beta_3\, GROWTH_{it} + \beta_4\, LEV_{it} + \beta_5\, GDPGR_{it} + e_{it}}$$

[Model 3]

$$\mathbf{PR_{it} = \beta_0 + \beta_1\, CCC_{it} + \beta_2\, SIZE_{it} + \beta_3\, GROWTH_{it} + \beta_4\, LEV_{it} + \beta_5\, GDPGR_{it} + e_{it}}$$

[Model 4]

$$\mathbf{PR_{it} = \beta_0 + \beta_1\, ARP_{it} + \beta_2\, ICP_{it} + \beta_3\, APP_{it} + \beta_4\, SIZE_{it} + \beta_5\, GROWTH_{it} + \beta_6\, LEV_{it} + \beta_7\, GDPGR_{it} + e_{it}}$$

[Model 5]

Where,

| | | |
|---|---|---|
| PR | – | Measures the firm profitability with gross profit as a percentage of total assets for firm (i) in the year (t). |
| ARP | – | Accounts Receivables Period for firm (i) in the year (t). |
| ICP | – | Inventory Conversion Period for firm (i) in the year (t). |
| APP | – | Accounts Payable Period for firm (i) in the year (t). |
| CCC | – | Cash Conversion Cycle for firm (i) in the year (t). |
| Size | – | Natural logarithm of firm's sales for firm (i) in the year (t). |
| Growth | – | Growth of firm's sales for firm (i) in the year (t). |
| Leverage | – | Measures the leverage with debt to equity for firm (i) in the year (t). |
| GDPGR | – | Measures the growth of GDP for firm (i) in the year (t). |
| $\beta_0$ | – | Constant term for firm (i) in the year (t). |
| $\beta_1, \beta_2....$ | – | Regression Co |
| e | – | disturbance term for firm (i) in the year (t). |

## RESEARCH DESIGN

Keeping in view the scope of the study, it is decided to include all the companies under automobile industry working before or from the year 1996-97 to 2008-09. There are 26 companies operating in the Indian automobile industry. But, owing to several constraints such as non-availability of financial statements or non-working of a company in a particular year etc., it is compelled to restrict the number of sample companies to 20. The companies under automobile industry are classified into three sectors namely; Commercial vehicles, Passenger cars and Multiutility vehicles and Two and three wheelers. For the purpose of the study all the three sectors have been selected. It accounts for 73.23 per cent of the total companies available in the Indian automobile industry. The selected 20 companies include 5 under commercial vehicles, 6 under Passenger cars and Multiutility vehicles and 9 under two and three wheeler sectors. It is inferred that sample company represents 98.74 percentage of market share in commercial vehicles, 89.76 percentage of market share in passenger cars and Multiutility vehicles and 99.81 percentage of market share in two and three wheelers. Thus, the findings based on the occurrence of such representative sample may be presumed to be true representative of automobile industry in the country.

The study is mainly based on secondary data. The major source of data analysed and interpreted in this study related to all those companies selected is collected from "PROWESS" database, which is the most reliable on the empowered corporate database of Centre for Monitoring Indian Economy (CMIE). Besides prowess database, relevant secondary data have also been collected from BSE Stock Exchange Official Directory, CIME Publications, Annual Survey of Industry, Business newspapers, Reports on Currency and Finance, Libraries of various Research Institutions, through Internet etc.

## RESULTS AND DISCUSSION

In Table 15.2, the summary statistics of the variables included in the regression models are presented. All the variables were calculated using balance sheet (book) values. The book values are used because the companies did not provide any market value related to the variables used in this study. In addition, the measurement of profitability could only be based on income statement values, not on so-called market values. The explanatory variables are all firm specific quantities and there is no way to measure these variables in terms of their 'market value'. Furthermore, when market values are considered in such studies, there is always a rather legitimate question of the date for which the 'market values' refer. This is rather arbitrary. Hence, the study relied on 'book values' as of the date of the financial reports.

Descriptive statistics shows the mean and standard deviation of the different variables of interest in the study. It also presents the standard error of mean, median, minimum and maximum values, kurtosis and skewness of the variables. Table 15.2 presents descriptive statistics for 20 Indian automobile companies for the period of 13 years from 1996-97 to 2008-09 and for a total 216 companies year observations. Overall, the mean profit rate on total assets is 22.29 per cent with the standard deviation of 105.3 per cent. It means that value of the profitability (profit rate on total assets) can deviate from mean to both sides by 105.3 per cent. The maximum value for the profit rate on total assets is 1638.9 per cent for a company in a year while the minimum is -189.4 per cent.

Indian automobile companies receive payment against sales after an average of 37 days (approximately more than one month) and standard deviation is 38 days. Minimum time taken by a company to collect cash from receivables is 0.31 days which is unusual, and maximum time taken for this purpose is 326 days (approximately ten months). On average, Indian automobile companies takes 75 days (approximately two and half months) to convert their inventories into sales with standard deviation of 62 days. Here, maximum time taken by a company is 730 days, which is a very large time period to convert inventory in to sales. Companies wait on average 80 days to pay their purchases with standard deviation of 85 days. Here, minimum time taken by a company is 0.00 days which is unusual, and maximum time taken for this purpose is 1018 days. The mean cash conversion cycle is 30 days (approximately one month) with the standard deviation of 66 days, implying that Indian automobile companies turnover their stock on an average of 12 times a year.

To check the size of the company and its relationship with profitability, natural logarithm of sales is used as a control variable. The mean value of log of sales is 6.90 while the standard deviation is 1.70. The maximum value of log of sales for a company in a year is 10.39 and the minimum is 0.92. In the same way to check the growth of the company and its relationship with profitability, sales growth is used as a control variable. The average growth of sales for Indian automobile companies is 10.60 per cent with a standard deviation of 36.83 per cent. The highest growth of sales for a company in a particular year is 356.66 per cent and in the same way the minimum growth of sales for a company in a year is -97.62 per cent.

To check the leverage and its relationship with the profitability, the debt ratio (obtained by dividing the total debt of the company by the equity) is used as a control variable. The results of the descriptive statistics show that the average leverage ratio for the Indian automobile companies is 1.33 with a standard deviation of 3.12. The maximum debt financing used by a company is 41.37, whereas the minimum level of the debt ratio is 0.00 which is unusual but may be possible. To check the GDP growth and its relationship with the profitability, GDP growth rate is used as a control variable. The mean value for this ratio is 12.73 per cent with a standard deviation of 3.41 per cent. The maximum GDP growth during the study period is 16.92 per cent and the minimum is 7.76 per cent.

## PEARSON'S CORRELATION CO-EFFICIENT ANALYSIS

Consistent with Shin and Soenen (1998), Table 15.3 provides the Pearson correlation for the variables used in the regression model. Pearson's correlation analysis is used for data to see the relationship between variables such as those between liquidity (working capital management) and profitability. If efficient working capital management increases profitability, one should expect a negative relationship between the measures of working capital management and profitability variable. There is a negative relationship between gross profitability on the one hand and the measures of working capital management on the other hand. This consists with the view that the time lag between expenditure for purchases of raw material and the collection of sales of finished goods can be too long, and that decreasing this time lag increases profitability.

Table 15.3 shows that the profitability is negatively related to ARP. The negative relationship of profitability and ARP is consistent with the view that the less time taken by the customer to pay their bills, the more cash is available to replenish the inventory hence leading to more sales which results to an increase in profitability. The table also shows that the profitability is negatively related to ICP. The negative relationship between profitability and ICP can be explained by the fact that firms takes more time in selling inventory, it will adversely affect its profitability due high amount of holding cost. The positive relationship between profitability and APP can be explained by the fact that lagging payments to suppliers ensures that the firm has some cash to purchase more inventory for sales thus increasing its sales levels hence boosting its profits. The negative relationship between profitability and CCC is consistent with the view that the time lag between the expenditure for the purchases of raw materials and the collection of sales of finished goods can be too long and that decreasing the time lag increases profitability (Deloof, 2003).

Firm size is positively related to profitability. This means that larger firm report higher profits compared to smaller firms. This may be due to larger firm's ability to exploit their economies of scale. Growth, which could be an indicator of a firm's business opportunities, is an important factor allowing firms to enjoy improved profitability, as can be seen in the positive sign for the variable SGROWTH. With reference to other control variables, leverage and GDPG, profitability is negatively associated with leverage whereas profitability is positively associated with GDPG. Thus, by analyzing the results it is concluded that if the firm is able to reduce these time periods, then the firm is efficient in managing working capital (liquidity). This efficiency will lead to increasing its profitability. The results of correlation analysis indicate that as far as Indian automobile companies are concerned, the liquidity management very significantly and strongly affects their profitability.

## REGRESSION ANALYSIS

Although, Pearson linear correlations give proof of an inverse relationship between profitability and CCC, these measures do not allow us to identify causes from consequences (Shin and Soenen, 1998). It is hard to say whether a shorter accounts collection period leads to higher profitability or a higher profitability is a result of short accounts receivable period. This means therefore that, care must be exercised while interpreting the Pearson correlation co-efficient because they cannot provide a reliable indicator of association in a manner which controls for additional explanatory variables. Examining simple bivariate correlation in a conventional matrix does not take account of each variable's correlation with all other explanatory variables (Padachi, 2006). The main analysis will be derived from appropriate multivariate models estimated using the overall least squares regression models.

To assess the effects of liquidity on the firm's profitability, the firm's profitability is modelled as a function of the four liquidity measures such as ARP, ICP, APP and CCC in addition to other firm characteristics. The model specifies above is estimated using the regression based framework (pooled OLS) as employed by Deloof (2003), Raheman and Nasr (2007), Garcia Teruel and Martinez-Solano (2007), Padachi (2006), David M. Mathuva (2009) and Amarjit Gill *et al.*, (2010). In the first regression model, the ARP has been regressed against the profitability. In the second regression model, the ICP has been regressed against the profitability. The third regression model involves a regression of the APP against the profitability. In the fourth regression model, the CCC is regressed against the profitability. The fifth regression model involves the regression of ARP, ICP and APP against profitability. In all the above said five regression models, firm size, growth, leverage and GDP growth have been incorporated to control for firm characteristics. Table 15.4 report the pooled OLS regression results of the overall relationship which exists between working capital management (liquidity) and profitability.

## RELATIONSHIP BETWEEN ACCOUNTS RECEIVABLE PERIOD (ARP) AND PROFITABILITY

The results of the regression (Model 1) of ARP with profitability along with other control variables presented in Table 15.4. The results of this regression indicate that, consistent with Deloof (2003), Raheman and Nasr (2007), Shin and Soenen (1998), Garcia-Teruel and Martinez-Solano (2007) and David M. Mathuva (2009) a negative and significant relationship exists between the ARP and Profitability in the Indian Automobile Industry. This result suggests that firms can improve their profitability by reducing the number of days accounts receivables are outstanding. The result can also be interpreted as the less the time it takes for customers to pay their bills, the more cash is available to replenish inventory hence the higher the sales realized leading to higher profitability of the firm. The negative coefficient on the ARP suggests that an increase in the number of days accounts receivable by 1 day is associated with a decline in profitability. Consistent with Lazaridis and Tryfonidis (2006), this finding implies that managers can improve profitability by reducing the credit period granted to their customers. This finding implies that a more restrictive credit policy giving customers less time to make their payments improves performance. The model also shows that profitability increases with firm size (as measured by natural logarithm of sales). The results of the regression indicate that the coefficient of growth (as measured by growth of sales) on profitability showed significant and positive relationship with profitability. The study used the debt ratio (measured by debt divided by equity) as a proxy for leverage, it shows a negative relationship with the profitability. This means that, when the leverage of the firm increases, it will adversely affect its profitability. Similarly, GDP growth of the country showed a significant positive relationship with profitability. It reflects that if the country's GDP increases, the profitability of Indian Automobile Industry will also increases. The model's adjusted $R^2$ is 69 per cent with an F-value of 6.24 which is significant($p<0.05$). The Durbin Watson statistic is 1.49.

## RELATIONSHIP BETWEEN INVENTORY CONVERSION PERIOD (ICP) AND PROFITABILITY

In Model 2, regression is run using Inventory Conversion Period (ICP) in days as an independent variable as a replacement for Accounts Receivables Period (ARP). The other variables are the same as they have been in the first regression. The result of the regression model is presented in Table 15.4. It is evident from the table that the co-efficient of inventory conversion period in days is negative in Indian automobile industry. Consistent with Raheman and Nasr (2007) and Lazaridis and Tryfonidis (2006) a negative relationship exist between Inventory Conversion Period (ICP) and profitability. This result suggests that the increase or decrease in the ICP in days affects profitability of the firm. It can be interpreted that if the inventory takes more time to sell, it will adversely affect profitability. The co-efficient on the other control variables are significant as in case of first regression model. The firm size is positively related to profitability and this is significant at 5 per cent level. The results of the regression also showed that growth of sales is positively related to firm's profitability. Similarly, the results showed that use of leverage have negative impact on firm's profitability. Further, the GDP growth of country is positively related to firm's profitability. The model's adjusted $R^2$ is 75 per cent with an F-value of 8.11 which is significant($p<0.01$). The Durbin Watson statistic is 1.79.

## RELATIONSHIP BETWEEN AVERAGE PAYMENT PERIOD (APP) AND PROFITABILITY.

The third regression is run using the Average Payment Period (APP) as an independent variable as a substitute of Inventory Conversion Period (ICP) in days. The other control variables are same as they have been in first and second regression. The results of the regression model are presented in Table 15.4. In model 3, the co-efficient on the average payment period is positive and significant. This suggests that an increase in the number of days accounts payable by 1 day is associated with an increase in profitability. The positive relationship can be explained in two ways. First, contrary to Deloof (2003) and Raheman and Nasr (2007), this finding holds the more profitable firms waits longer to pay their bills. This implies that they withhold their payment to suppliers so as to take advantage of the cash available for their working capital needs. Second, this results makes economic sense in that the longer a firm delays its payments to its creditors, the higher the level of working capital levels it reserves and uses in order to increase profitability. This finding is in line with the working capital management rule that firms should strive to lag their payments to creditors as much as possible, taking care not to spoil their business relationship with them. Consistent with the other models, firm size, growth and GDP growth being positively related to profitability. Whereas an increase in the use of debt decreases profitability. The model's adjusted $R^2$ is 70 per cent with an F-value of 6.66 which is significant($p<0.01$). The Durbin Watson statistic is 1.76.

## RELATIONSHIP BETWEEN CASH CONVERSION CYCLE (CCC) AND PROFITABILITY.

In fourth regression model, cash conversion cycle is used as an independent variable instead of ARP, ICP and APP. The other variables are kept the same as they were in first three regressions. The results of the fourth regression model are presented in Table 15.4. Consistent with Deloof (2003), Raheman and Nasr (2007), Shin and Soenen (1998), Garcia-Teruel and Martinez-Solano (2007), Padachi (2006) and David M. Mathuva (2009), a negative relationship exists between the Cash Conversion Cycle (CCC) and profitability. This supports the notion that the CCC is negatively related with profitability. Shin and Soenen (1998) argued that the negative relation between profits and the cash conversion cycle could be explained by the market power or the market share, i.e., a shorter ccc because of bargaining power by the suppliers and/ or the customers as well as higher profitability due to market dominance. The negative relationship between the firm's ccc and profitability can also be explained by the fact that minimizing the investment in current assets can help in boosting profits. This ensures the liquid cash is not maintained in the business for long and that it is use to generate profits for the firm. The all other control variables showed similar findings as in the case of first three regression equations and significantly affecting profitability. The model's adjusted $R^2$ is 66 per cent with an F-value of 5.65 which is significant($p<0.05$). The Durbin Watson statistic is 1.47.

Model 5 acts as a control model for the variables under study. The model was run so as to provide an indicator as to the most significant variables affecting the study. The model shows that all the variables included are significant. In this model, the ARP, ICP and Leverage are negatively related with firms' profitability while APP, Size, Growth and GDP Growth variables exhibit a positive relationship. The model's adjusted $R^2$ is 80 per cent with an F-value of 7.71 which is significant($p<0.01$). The Durbin Watson statistic is 2.01.

## CONCLUSION

The study of empirical relationship between liquidity and profitability is one of the areas of performance of corporate enterprise. This study has shown that Indian automobile industry has been able to achieve high scores on the various components of working capital and this has positive impact on its profitability. Empirical results of the study found a significant negative relationship between profitability and Accounts Receivable Period (ARP), Inventory Conversion Period (ICP) and Cash Conversion Cycle (CCC) for a sample of Indian automobile industry. These results suggest that managers can create value for their shareholders by reducing the number of days of accounts receivable and inventories to a reasonable minimum. Further, companies are capable of gaining sustainable competitive advantage by means of effective and efficient utilisation of the resources of the organisation through a careful reduction of the cash conversion cycle to its minimum. In doing so, the profitability of the firm is expected to increase. The study also observed that positive relationship between accounts payable period and profitability. This finding holds that more profitable firms wait longer to pay their bills. These conclusions are in confirmation with Deloof (2003), Eljelly (2004), Shin and Soenen (1998), Raheman and Nasr (2007), Lazaridis and Tryfonidis (2006), Padachi (2006), Amarjit et al., (2010) and Garcia-Teruel and Martinez-Solano (2007) who found a strong negative relationship between the measures of working capital management (liquidity) including accounts receivables period, inventory conversion period and cash conversion cycle with corporate profitability. Therefore, managers can create profits for their companies by handling correctly the cash conversion cycle and keeping each different component (accounts receivables, accounts payables and inventory) to an optimum level.

## REFERENCES

1. Ali Uyar (2009). "The relationship of cash conversion cycle with firm size and profitability: an empirical investigation in Turkey", *International Research Journal of Finance and Economics,* ISSN 1450-2887 (24).
2. Amarjit Gill, Nahum Biger, Neil Mathur (2010)."The relationship between working capital management and profitability: evidence from the United States", *Business and Economics Journal,* Vol.2010:BEJ-10.
3. Amit K. Mallick and Debasish Sur(1998). " Working capital and Profitability: A case study in interrelation", *The Management Accountant,* pp.805-809.
4. Amit K. Mallik, Debashish Sur and Debdas Rakshit (2005). "Working capital and profitability: a study on their relationship with reference to selected companies in Indian Pharmaceutical Industry", *GITAM Journal of Management,* Vol. 3, pp.51-62.
5. Appuhami, B.A.R.,(2008). The impact of firms capital expenditure on working capital management: An empirical study across industries in Thailand, *International Management Review,* Vol.4, pp.8-12.
6. Bodie, Z. and Merton, R.C. (2000). Finance, International Edition, Prentice-Hall, New Jersey.
7. Bardia, S.C. (2004). "Liquidity management: a case study of Steel Authority of India Ltd", *The Management Accountant,* pp.463-67.
8. Blinder, A.S. and Maccini, L.J. (1991). "The resurgence of inventory research: what have we learned?", *Journal of Economic Survey,*Vol.5, pp.291-328.
9. Dash, M. and Ravipati(2009). Liquidity-profitability model for working capital management, Working Paper, Alliance Business School. http://papers.ssrn.com/sol3/papers.cfm?abstract_id=1408722.
10. Deloof, M. (2003). "Does working capital management affect profitability of firms", *Vikalpa,* Vol.28 (2), pp.537-85.

11. Dash, M. and Ravipati(2009). Liquidity-profitability model for working capital management, Working Paper, Alliance Business School. http://papers.ssrn.com/sol3/papers.cfm?abstract_id=1408722.

12. Farris II, M.T. and Hutchison, P.D. (2002). "Cash-to cash: the new supply chain management metric", *International Journal of Physical Distribution & Logistic Management*, Vol.32 (4), pp.288-298.

13. Falope OI, Ajilore OT (2009). "Working capital management and corporate profitability: evidence from panel data analysis of selected quoted companies in Nigeria", *Research Journal of Business management*, Vol.3, pp.73-84.

14. Garcia-Teruel, P.J. and Martinez-Solano, P. (2007). "Effects of working capital management on SME profitability", *International Journal of Managerial Finance*, Vol.3 (2), pp.164-177.

15. Gentry, James A., R. Vaidyanathan and Hei Wai Lee (1990). "A weighted cash conversion cycle", *Financial Management*, Vol.19 (1), pp.90-99.

16. Hager H.C.,(1976). " Cash Management and Cash Cycle", *Management Accounting*, pp.19-21.

17. Hutchison, P.D., Farris II, M.T. and Anders, S.B. (2007). "Cash-to-cash analysis and management", *The CPA Journal*, Vol.77 (8), pp.42-47.

18. Jordan, R.W. (2003). Fundamentals of Corporate Finance, 6th ed., McGraw-Hill Companies, Boston.

19. Jose, M.L., Lancaster, C. and Stevens, J.L. (1996). "Corporate returns and cash conversion cycles", *Journal of Economics and Finance*, Vol.20 (1), pp.33-46.

20. Keown, A.J.., Martin, J.D., Petty, J.W. and Scott, D.F. (2003). Foundations of Finance, 4th ed., Pearson Education, New Jersey.

21. Kamath, R. (1989). "How useful are common liquidity measures?," *Journal of Cash Management*, January/February.

22. Katerina Lyroudi and Jhon Lazaridis (2000). "The cash conversion cycle and liquidity analysis of the food industry in Greece", *http:/papers.ssrn.com/paper.fat?* abstract-id = 236175.

23. Kushwinder Kaur and Kuldip Kaur(2008). Growth and Profitability of acquiring firms in India: An analysis, ANVESAK, Vol.38(2).

24. Lazaridis, I., and D. Tryfonidis (2006). "Relationship between working capital management and profitability of listed companies in the Athens Stock Exchange", *Journal of Financial Management and Analysis*, Vol.19 (1), pp.26-35.

25. Lancaster, C.,Stevens, J.L. and Jennings, J.A. (1999). "Corporate liquidity and the significance of earnings versus cash flow: an examination of industry effects", *The Journal of Applied Business Research*, Vol.15 (3), pp.37-46.

26. Lyroudi, K. and Mc Carty, D. (1993). "An empirical investigation of the Cash Conversion Cycle of small business firms", *The Journal of Small Business Finance*, Vol. 2(2), pp. 465-482.

27. Largay,J. and C.Stickney.(1980). Cash flows, ratio analysis and the W.T.Grant company bankruptcy, *Financial Analyst Journal*, 36(4), pp.51-54.

28 Lamberson, M. (1995). "Changes in working capital of small firms in relation to changes in economic activity", *Mid-American Journal of Business*, Vol.10 (2).

29 Moss, J.D. and Stine, B. (1993). "Cash conversion cycle and firm size: a study of retail firms", *Managerial Finance*, Vol.19 (8), pp.25-34.

30 Mathuva D. (2009). "The influence of working capital management components on corporate profitability: a survey on Kenyan listed firms", *Research Journal of Business Management*, Vol.3, pp.1-11.

31 Narware, P.C. (2004). "Working capital and profitability-an empirical analysis", *The Management Accountant*, pp.546-555.

32 Padachi, K. (2006). "Trends in working capital management and its impact on firms performance: an analysis of Mauritian small manufacturing firms", *International Review of Business Research Papers,* Vol. 2(2), pp.45-58.

33 Richards, V.D. and Laughlin, E.J. (1980). "A cash conversion cycle approach to liquidity analysis", *Financial Management,* Spring.

34 Raheman, A., and M. Nasr (2007). "Working capital management and profitability: case of Pakistani firms", *International Review of Business Research,* Vol.3(2), pp.275-96.

35 Ricci, C. and Vito, N.D. (2000). "International working capital practices in the UK", *European Financial Management,* Vol.6 (1), pp.69-84.

36 Ross, S.A., R.W. Westerfield and B.D.Jordan,(2003). Fundamentals of Corporate Finance.6th Edn. McGraw-Hill Irwin Publications, New York.

37 Shin,H.H and Soenen, L. (1998). "Efficiency of working capital and corporate profitability", *Financial Practice and Education,* Vol.8 (2), pp.37-45.

38 Smith,K. (1980). "Profitability versus liquidity trade offs in working capital management, in readings on the management of working capital", West Publishing Company, St. Paul, New York.

39 Smith, M.B., and Begemann, E. (1997). "Measuring association between working capital and return on investment", *South Africa Journal of Business Management,* Vol.28 (1), pp.1-5.

40 Soenen, L.A (1993). "Cash conversion cycle and profitability", *Journal of Cash Management,* Vol.13 (4), pp.53-58.

41 Schilling, G. (1996). "Working capital's role in maintaining corporate liquidity", *TMA Journal,* Vol.16 (5), pp.4-7.

42 Sur, D., J.Biswas and P. Ganguly (2001). "Liquidity Management in Indian Private Sector Enterprises: a

case study of Indian Primary Aluminium Producing Industry", *Indian Journal of Accounting,* pp.8-14.

43 Sushma Vishnani and Bhupesh Kr. Shah (2007). "Impact of working capital management policies on corporate performance an empirical study", *Global Business Review,* 8/2/267.

44 Shulman, J.M. and Dambolena, I.G. (1986). "Analysing corporate liquidity", *Journal of Cash Management,* September/October.

45 Samuels, J. M. and Smyth, D.J. (1968). "Profits, Variability of Profits and Firm size," *Economica,* Vol. 35, pp. 127-139.

46 Van Horne, J C and Wachowicz J.M. (2004). "Fundamentals of Financial Management, 12th edition, Prentice Hall Publishers, New York.

47 Vijayakumar, A. and A. Venkatachalam (1995)."Working capital and profitability-an empirical analysis", *The Management Accountant,* pp.748-50.

48 Vijayakumar, A. (2002). "Determinants of Profitability-A firm level study of the sugar industry of Tamil Nadu", *The Management Accountant,* pp. 458-465.

49 Wang, Y.J. (2002). "Liquidity management, operating performance and corporate value: evidence from Japan and Taiwan", *Journal of Multinational Financial Management,* Vol. 12, pp.159-69.

50 Zelia Serrasqueiro (2009). "Growth and Profitability in Portuguese companies: A dynamic panel data approach", *Economic Interferences,* Vol.XI (26), pp.265-279.

## TABLE 15.2

## DESCRIPTIVE STATISTICS OF INDEPENDENT, DEPENDENT AND CONTROL VARIABLES

**20 Indian Automobile Firms, 1996 – 2009 – 216 Firm -year observations (N = 216)**

| *Variables* | *Mean ± S.D* | *Standard Error of mean* | *Median* | *Minimum* | *Maximum* | *kurtosis* | *Skewness* |
|---|---|---|---|---|---|---|---|
| PR | 22.29 ± 105.3 | 6.62 | 14.58 | -189.39 | 1638.92 | 222.83 | 14.44 |
| ARP | 37.22 ± 38.18 | 2.40 | 25.83 | 0.31 | 326.84 | 14.46 | 2.97 |
| ICP | 75.36 ± 61.78 | 3.88 | 62.47 | 0.00 | 730.44 | 54.21 | 5.78 |
| APP | 79.89 ± 85.41 | 5.37 | 63.42 | 0.00 | 1018.11 | 71.52 | 7.51 |
| CCC | 29.90 ± 65.81 | 4.14 | 19.07 | -255.76 | 312.03 | 5.58 | -0.18 |
| Size | 6.90 ± 1.70 | 0.11 | 6.86 | 0.92 | 10.39 | 0.01 | -0.27 |
| Growth | 10.60 ± 36.83 | 2.32 | 10.13 | -97.62 | 356.66 | 31.46 | 3.48 |
| Leverage | 1.33 ± 3.12 | 0.20 | 0.67 | 0.00 | 41.37 | 110.30 | 9.32 |
| GDPG | 12.73 ± 3.41 | 0.98 | 13.44 | 7.76 | 16.92 | -1.56 | -0.33 |

**Notes:** PR-Profit Rate on total assets; ARP-Accounts Receivables Period; ICP-Inventory Conversion Period; APP-Accounts Payable Period; CCC-Cash Conversion Cycle; Size-Natural logarithm of sales (proxy for size); Growth-Sales growth; Leverage-Debt/Equity; GDPG-Gross Domestic Product Growth.

***Source:*** Computed.

## TABLE 15.3

## CORRELATION MATRIX

| | PR | APR | ICP | APP | CCC | Size | Growth | Leverage | GDPG |
|---|---|---|---|---|---|---|---|---|---|
| PR | 1.00 | | | | | | | | |
| ARP | -0.02 | 1.00 | | | | | | | |
| ICP | -0.08 | 0.23 | 1.00 | | | | | | |
| APP | 0.01 | 0.16 | 0.68 | 1.00 | | | | | |
| CCC | -0.09 | 0.60 | 0.02 | -0.45 | 1.00 | | | | |
| Size | 0.04 | -0.38 | -0.36 | -0.36 | -0.11 | 1.00 | | | |
| Growth | 0.03 | -0.18 | 0.06 | 0.03 | -0.13 | 0.18 | 1.00 | | |
| Leverage | -0.20 | 0.40 | 0.29 | 0.29 | 0.14 | -0.22 | 0.02 | 1.00 | |
| GDPG | -0.05 | -0.04 | 0.66 | 0.25 | 0.28 | -0.69 | -0.15 | -0.24 | 1.00 |

**Notes :** PR-Profit Rate on total assets; ARP-Accounts Receivables Period; ICP-Inventory Conversion Period; APP-Accounts Payable Period; CCC-Cash Conversion Cycle; Size-Natural logarithm of sales (proxy for size); Growth-Sales growth; Leverage-Debt/Equity; GDPG-Gross Domestic Product Growth.

***Sources:*** Computed.

**TABLE 15.4**

**REGRESSIONS OF PROFITABILITY ON WORKING CAPITAL VARIABLES**
**[20 Indian Automobile Firms, 1996-2009 : 216 Firm year observations]**
**(Dependent variable : Profit Rate on total assets(PR))**

| Independent Variables | Model 1 | Model 2 | Model 3 | Model 4 | Model 5 |
|---|---|---|---|---|---|
| Intercept | 11.85 | 15.59 | 17.48 | 15.07 | 12.35 |
| ARP | -0.06<br>(3.85)* | | | | -0.12<br>(3.87)* |
| ICP | | -0.04<br>(3.61)* | | | -0.05<br>(2.79) ** |
| APP | | | 0.02<br>(3.05)** | | 0.01<br>(3.64)* |
| CCC | | | | -0.01<br>(2.31) *** | |
| Size | 0.35<br>(2.86)** | 0.64<br>(2.39)** | 0.58<br>(2.02)*** | 0.55<br>(1.66) | 0.20<br>(2.58)** |
| Growth | 0.07<br>(2.64)** | 0.28<br>(3.47)* | 0.07<br>(2.71)** | 0.14<br>(2.44)** | 0.07<br>(3.06)** |
| Leverage | -6.22<br>(1.86) | -0.36<br>(0.12) | -4.37<br>(2.33)** | -5.05<br>(1.23) | -3.53<br>(1.94)*** |
| GDPG | 0.33<br>(2.83)** | 0.41<br>(3.82)* | 0.39<br>(3.39)* | 0.36<br>(3.02)** | 0.39<br>(4.01)* |
| **$R^2$** | **0.82** | **0.85** | **0.83** | **0.80** | **0.92** |
| **Adjusted $R^2$** | **0.69** | **0.75** | **0.70** | **0.66** | **0.80** |
| **F Value** | **6.24**** | **8.11*** | **6.66*** | **5.65*** | **7.71**** |
| **Durbin Watson** | **1.49** | **1.79** | **1.76** | **1.47** | **2.01** |

**Notes :** PR-Profit Rate on total assets; ARP-Accounts Receivables Period;
ICP-Inventory Conversion Period; APP-Accounts Payable Period;
CCC - Cash Conversion Cycle; Size- Natural logarithm of sales (proxy for size); S.Growth-Sales growth; Leverage - Debt / Equity;
GDPG-Gross Domestic Product Growth.

* P < 0.01; **P < 0.05; ***P < 0.10

***Source :*** Computed

# 16

# Working Capital and Profitability
## An Empirical Analysis

In conventional production function approach for determination of relationship between output and profit, fixed capital is taken into account as explanatory variable amongst others: the role of working capital is ignored. It is therefore felt that there is the need to study the important role of working capital in profit generating process. Sarkar and saha have aptly observed the management of working capital has an important bearing on the profitability of an enterprise. Generally the higher the working capital, the less the rate of return on capital employed while a lower value of working capital yields a higher rate of return. Hence, in this study an attempt is made to study the association of profitability with working capital. The impact of working capital on profitability has been examined by computing coefficients of correlation and regression between profitability ratio and working capital ratio and working capital ratios, Viz., Current ratio (CR), Liquid Ratio (LR), Working capital Turnover Ratio

(WTR), Inventory Turnover Ratio (ITR) Cash Turnover Ratio (CTR), and Receivables Turnover Ratio (RTR).

## SAMPLING DESIGN

There are about 31 sugar industries operating in Tamil Nadu of which 14 are under co–operative sector, 14 are under private sector and 3 are under public sector. Since the study has been directed towards assessing the problem over a period of time, all these sugar industries are not taken because most of them are just a few years old leading to the absence of data for the last ten years. In order to select the industries for the purpose of study first of all the list of those industries which were established before 1975 and having crushing capacity of 2000 MT (per day) or more has been prepared which shows 13 such industries, 6 under co – operative sector and 7 under private sector. Thus, 13 industries selected for the study form the important industries and seem to have represented the sugar industries of Tamil Nadu as a whole.

## WORKING CAPITAL AND PROFITABILITY – CORRELATION ANALYSIS

The co – efficient of correlation between working capital ratios and profitability ratio for the selected sugar industries of Tamil Nadu as a whole are presented in Table 16.1. It is evident from the table that the co – efficient of correlation between profitability ratio and current ratio is [-]0.78. It reveals a moderate degree of negative correlation between the variables. The value is also found to be significant at 5 percent level of significance. Similarly, the co – efficient of correlation between profitability ratio and liquid ratio stands at [-]0.31. It indicates that there is a low degree of negative correlation between these two variables. At 5 percent level of significance, the value of co – efficient of correlation is found to be not significant. Both the ratios, current and liquid ratios confirms with the assumption that larger amount of current and liquid as sets decreases risk as well as profitability.

Thirdly, the co–efficient of correlation between profitability and working capital turnover ratio is +0.72. It shows that there is a high degree of positive correlation between the two variables, as five percent level of significance, the value of co – efficient of correlation is found to be significant. Fourthly, the co – efficient of correlation between profitability ratio and inventory turnover ratio is found to be +0.49 which is found to be significant at 10 percent level of significance. It shows a moderate degree of positive correlation between the variables. Fifthly, the co – efficient of correlation between profitability ratio and debtors turnover ratio indicates positive association of +0.33. It shows low degree of positive correlation is very insignificant. All these three turnover ratio confirms with the assumption that higher the turnover increases the profitability of the selected sugar industry of Tamil Nadu as a whole.

Lastly, the co – efficient of correlation between profitability and cash turnover ratio is [-]0.18. This correlation is very insignificant. Thus the study of the impact of working capital ratios on profitability showed both negative and positive impacts. Out of the six independent working capital components ratio three ratios, namely CR, LR and CTR, have shown negative correlation with profitability ratio. Among these three ratios, the co – efficient of correlation between profitability ratio and current ratio is found to be significant at five percent level of significance, and LR and CTR have no such significant association with profitability. The remaining three ratios, namely WTR, ITR and RTR, have shown positive co – efficient of correlation with profitability ratio. Among these three ratios, the co – efficient of correlation between profitability ratio and WTR and ITR are found to have significant association with profitability ratio, while CTR is not found to have such significant association with the profitability ratio.

## IMPACT OF WORKING CAPITAL RATIOS ON PROFITABILITY – MULTIPLE REGRESSION ANALYSIS

For the purpose of establishing plied. It implies the interdependence of the set of variables upon each other in such a way that changes in the one are in sympathy with changes in the other. In this section, in order to identify that influence on profitability, a linear multiple regression model were used. In the analysis, working capital ratios VIZ, CR, LR, WTR, independent variables and profit before tax to total assets ratio is used as dependent variable.

For the purpose of selection of variables for the model, the co – efficient of correlation between the independent variables can be computed and presented in Table 16.2. It is evident from the table that there is a high degree of correlation between CR and WTR ([-]0.935) and ITR and WTR ([-]0.873). Therefore, current ratio and working capital turnover ratios are omitted for the analysis. The model used in this study is

$$\mathbf{PBT/TA = b_0 + b_1\,IR + b_2\,LTR + b_3\,RTR + b_4\,CTR}$$

Where $b_0$, $b_1$, $b_2$, $b_3$, and $b_4$ are parameters to be estimated.

The pooled regression results of the models showing impact of working capital ratios on profitability for the total industry are presented in Table 16.3. The table indicates that the impact of liquid ratio, inventory turnover ratio, receivables turnover ratio and cash turnover ratio were statistically significant as seen from the values of regression co – efficient. For a unit increase in liquid ratio, profitability decreased by 0.16 unit which was statistically significant at 5 percent level. When inventory turnover ratio increased by one unit, profitability increased by 0.02 unit which was statistically significant at 5 percent level of significance. When receivables turnover ratio increased by one unit, profitability increased by 0.08 unit which was statistically significant at 0.05 level of significance. For a unit increase in cash turnover ratio, profitability decreased by 0.001 unit which was significant at 0.10 level of significance. The four independent variables contribute 85 percent of the variations in the profitability of the selected sugar industries of Tamil Nadu. Thus, the over – all results presented in the table are encouraging. The signs of all the co – efficients are as expected. The co – efficients are also statistically significant.

## CONCLUSION

It is inferred from this study that liquid ratio, Inventory turnover ratio, receivables turnover ratio and cash turnover ratio influenced the profitability of the selected sugar industries of Tamil Nadu.

## REFERENCES

1. Vittorio *et al.*, (1979), "The Translogy Production Function: some Evidence from Establishment Data". *Journal of Econometrics*, Vol.10, pp 193 – 99.
2. Sarkar and Saha, (1987), "Profitability crises and working capital management in the public sector in India." *The management Accountant*, p. 329.

**TABLE 16.3**

**ESTIMATED REGRESSION RESULTS OF IMPACT OF WORKING CAPITAL RATIOS ON PROFITABILITY (Total Industry)**

$$PBT/TA = b_0 + b_1 LR + b_2 ITR + b_3 RTR + b_4 CTR$$

| Variables | Beta Co-efficient | t Value | |
|---|---|---|---|
| Constant | 0.2456 (0.0501) | 4.90 | Significant * |
| Liquid Ratio (LR) | -0.1591 (0.0405) | -3.93 | Significant * |
| Inventory Turnover Ratio (ITR) | 0.0195 (0.0061) | 3.20 | Significant * |
| Receivables Turnover Ratio (RTR) | 0.0075 (0.0025) | 2.94 | Significant * |
| Cash Turnover Ratio (CTR) | -0.0009 (0.0005) | -1.64 | Significant * |

**$R^2$ = 0.8529**
**Adj $R^2$ = 0.7058**

· Significant at 0.05 level
· Significant at 0.10 level

***Source :*** Computed.

## TABLE 16.2

## CORRELATION MATRIX (TOTAL INDUSTRY)

| | CR | LR | WTR | ITR | RTR | CTR | PBT/TA |
|---|---|---|---|---|---|---|---|
| CR | 1.000 | | | | | | |
| LR | 0.399 | 1.000 | | | | | |
| WTR | -0.935 | 0.175 | 1.000 | | | | |
| ITR | -0.702 | 0.292 | 0.873 | 1.000 | | | |
| RTR | -0.658 | -0.776 | 0.613 | 0.252 | 1.000 | | |
| CTR | 0.156 | -0.729 | -0.374 | -0.614 | 0.342 | 1.000 | |
| PBT/TA | -0.779 | -0.305 | 0.716 | 0.489 | 0.330 | -0.181 | 1.000 |

***Source:*** Computed

## TABLE 16.1

## IMPACT OF WORKING CAPITAL RATIOS' ON PROFITABILITY SIMPLE CORRELATION ANALYSIS (Total Industry)

| Year | Working Capital Ratio | | | | | | PBT to Total |
|---|---|---|---|---|---|---|---|
| | ***CR*** | ***LR*** | ***WTR*** | ***ITR*** | ***RTR*** | ***CTR*** | ***Asset Ratio*** |
| 1982 - 83 | 2.24 | 0.43 | 2.87 | 1.97 | 11.88 | 44.32 | 0.087 |
| 1983 - 84 | 2.13 | 0.91 | 3.88 | 3.58 | 10.21 | 10.45 | 0.079 |
| 1984 - 85 | 1.98 | 0.83 | 3.84 | 3.28 | 7.61 | 13.21 | 0.100 |
| 1985 - 86 | 2.18 | 0.66 | 3.62 | 2.81 | 10.35 | 19.28 | 0.100 |
| 1986 - 87 | 2.21 | 1.02 | 4.17 | 4.24 | 8.99 | 11.56 | 0.092 |
| 1987 - 89 | 1.94 | 0.60 | 4.19 | 2.94 | 11.48 | 16.26 | 0.116 |
| 1989 - 90 | 1.97 | 0.96 | 4.03 | 3.87 | 6.03 | 13.19 | 0.115 |
| 1990 - 91 | 2.80 | 0.99 | 1.67 | 1.66 | 3.67 | 18.77 | 0.073 |
| 1991 - 92 | 2.78 | 1.02 | 2.00 | 2.02 | 4.44 | 17.53 | 0.081 |
| | Co – efficient of Correlation | | | | | | |
| (r) | -0.78<br>(3.29) | -0.31<br>(0.86) | 0.72<br>(2.75) | 0.49<br>(1.49) | 0.33<br>(0.93) | -0.18<br>(0.48) | |

Figures in bracket show t value
- Significant at 0.05 level - Significant at 0.10 level

***Source :*** Computed from annual report of the respective units.

# 17

# Financial Structure of Manufacturing Corporations and the Demand for Working Capital

## Some Empirical Findings

### INTRODUCTION

Fixed capital and working capital are the dominant contributors to the total capital of a developing country. Fixed capital investments generate production capacity whereas working capital makes the utilisation of that capacity possible. Especially in small firms, working capital management may be the factor that decides success or failure; in larger firms, efficient working capital management can significantly affect the firms' risk, return and share price. A firm can exist and survive without fixed capital, but cannot survive without working capital. Management of working capital has acquired a great significance and sound position for the twin objects of profitability and liquidity. In a period of rising capital costs and scarce funds, the working capital is one of the most important areas requiring management review. It consumes a great deal of time to increase profitability as well as to maintain proper liquidity at minimum risk. Viewed in this perspective, the study devoted to working capital management may be very rewarding one.

**Review of Literature**

Interest in the study of the demand for working by Indian Automobile Industry has been stimulated by the empirical works on the demand for cash and inventories. A review of the empirical works on the demand for cash showed that the Post – Keynesian revival of interest in the demand function for cash has followed two distinct paths. Frazer, Nadiri and Coates observed economics of scale thereby supporting Baumol and Tobin, while Meltzer, Whalen, De Allessi and Vogel and Maddala observed diseconomies of scale thereby supporting Friedman as far as the transactions demand for cash is concerned. Similarly, there are no unanimous findings as regards the effect of capital costs on the demand for cash. Among others, Selden De Allessi, Nadiri and Coates showed the statistically significant effect of capital costs on the demand for cash.

Like studies on the demand for cash the earlier studies on the demand for inventories also did not present unanimous findings. Albert et al, Liu Kuznets, Lieberman, Irvine and Akhtar observed significant effects of capital costs on the demand for inventories, while Terleckyj, Robinson, McGouldrick, Lovell, Joyee, Burrows and Maccini and Rossana did not observe the same. Similarly, some reported economies of scale with respect to holding inventories, while others did not report the same. Controversy also exists with respect to coefficients of adjustment. Among others, Lovell and Grossman noticed the slow speed of adjustment between actual inventories and target inventories, while Goodwin, Burrows, and Maccini and Rossana did not find the same.

## STATEMENT OF THE PROBLEM

It has therefore become difficult to support one view or another in the context of Indian Automobile Industry. However, investigation in this study is not limited to the study of the demand for cash and inventories only. It has been extended to test whether models similar to those explaining the demand for cash and inventories also explain the demand for receivables, and gross and net working capital. The purpose of this study is that to determine empirically whether transactions working capital balances including cash and inventories vary proportionately or less than in proportion to changes in the volume of sales. It also describes the effect of capital costs on working capital holdings of the enterprises. Further, the study also takes into account a Partial Adjustment Model of working capital behavior. The partial adjustment or flexible accelerator models that explain the speed with which the actual level of working capital balance is adjusted to the desired level.

## METHODOLOGY

### Econometric Model

In this study, econometric models are used to describe the demand for working capital and its various components by Indian automobile companies. The decisions about the aggregate amount of working capital and its various components to be held may be regard as subject to wealth constraint and opportunity cost of working capital. As a first approximation to the theory, the functions may be written as:

$$y_1 = f(s, i) \text{ ——— (i)}$$

$$y_2 = f(s, i) \text{ ——— (ii)}$$

$$y_3 = f(s, i) \text{ ——— (iii)}$$

$$y_4 = f(s, i) \text{ ——— (iv)}$$

$$y_5 = f(s, i) \text{ ——— (v)}$$

Where

$y_1$ = Real Cash
$y_2$ = Real Inventories
$y_3$ = Real Receivables
$y_4$ = Real Gross working capital
$y_5$ = Real Net working capital
S = Real Sales in terms of $S_t - 1$
C = Opportunity cost of working capital measured by short – term interest rates of Indian commercial banks.

In an empirical investigation, it take the form.

$$Y^* = KS^{b_1} i^{b_{21}} e^u \text{ ...................(vi)}$$

where u is assumed to be independently and normally distributed. Taking the natural logarithm

$$\text{Ln } Y^* = K + b_1 \text{Ln } S + b_2 \text{Ln } i_2 + u \text{ ...................(vii)}$$

Where $b_1$ and $b_2$ are elasticity's of $y^*$ with respect to the explanatory variables of the model. The above models assume reasonable a priori hypothesis of

$$\partial y / \partial s > 0 \text{ and } > \partial y / \partial i_2 < 0$$

**Partial – Adjustment model**

In estimating the above equations, the study also takes into account a partial adjustment or flexible accelerator model of working capital behaviour. This model hypothesizes that each enterprise has a desired target level of working capital and that of each enterprise, finding its actual working capital not equal to its optimum, attempts only a partial adjustment towards the optimum level within any one period. The models indicate the speed with which firms adjust their actual working capital balances to the desired working capital balances.

The simplest assumption to make about the adjustment process on working capital balances is that

$$\frac{\bar{y}_t}{y_{t-1}} = \left( \frac{y^*_t}{y_{t-1}} \right)^f e^{ut} \text{ ...................(viii)}$$

Where $\phi$ - rate of adjustment or adjustment coefficient

$$0 < \phi < 1$$

Substituting expression (viii) for desired level of working capital balances into equation (vii) gives

$$\frac{\bar{y}_t}{y_{t-1}} = \left( \frac{KS_t^{b_1} i_2^{b_2}}{y_{t-1}} \right)^f e^u .....................(ix)$$

Taking logs of this equation gives

$$Ln\,\bar{y}_t - Ln\,\bar{y}_{t-1} = f\,Lnb_0 + f\,b_1 Ln\,S_t + f\,b_2 Ln\,i_2 - f\,Ln\,y_{t-1} + U_t ......(x)$$

(or)

$$Ln\,\bar{y}_t = C_0 + C_1 Ln\,S_t - C_2 Ln\,i_2 + (1-f)Ln\,\bar{y}_{t-1} + U_t .........(X)$$

where $C_1$ and $C_2$ are the short – term elasticity's of working capital or its components with respect to sales and their opportunity cost, respectively. The long run elasticity's with respect to sales and cost are $b_1$ and $b_2$

Since $C_1 = f\,b_1$ and $C_2 = f\,b_2$

$$b_1 = \frac{C_1}{f} \text{ and } b_2 = \frac{C_2}{f}$$

$\phi$ - the rate of adjustment coefficient

The long – run elasticity's of cash with respect to sales and the opportunity cost of cash should be approximately equal to 0.5 and – 0.5, respectively if the Baumol model is correct.

## SAMPLE DESIGN

Keeping in view the scope of the study, it is decided to include all the companies under automobile industry working before or from the year 1996-97 to 2008-09. There are 26 companies operating in the Indian automobile industry. But, owing to several constraints such as non-availability of financial statements or non-working of a company in a particular year etc., it is compelled to restrict the number of sample companies to 20. The companies under automobile industry are classified into three sectors namely; Commercial vehicles, Passenger Cars and Multiutility vehicles and Two and Three wheelers. For the purpose of the study all the three sectors have been selected. It accounts for 73.23 per cent of the total companies available in the Indian automobile industry. The selected 20 companies include 5 under commercial vehicles, 6 under Passenger cars and Multiutility vehicles and 9 under two and three wheeler sectors. It is inferred that sample company represents 98.74 percentage of market share in commercial vehicles, 89.76 percentage of market share in Passenger Cars and Multiutility vehicles and 99.81 percentage of market share in two and three wheelers. Thus, the findings based on the occurrence of such representative sample may be presumed to be true representative of automobile industry in the country.

## DATA

The study is m ainly based on secondary data. The major source of data analysed and interpreted in this study related to all those companies selected is collected from "PROWESS" database, which is the most reliable on the empowered corporate database of Centre for Monitoring Indian Economy (CMIE). Besides prowess database, relevant secondary data have also been collected from BSE Stock Exchange Official Directory, CIME Publications, Annual Survey of Industry, Business newspapers, Reports on Currency and Finance, Libraries of various Research Institutions, through Internet etc.

## RESULTS AND DISCUSSION

### Scale and capital cost effects on demand functions of working capital

The pooled regression results of the model showing the scale and capital cost effects on demand functions of working capital and its components of Indian Automobile Industry and its three sectors are presented in Table 17.1 to Table 17.8. The overall results presented in the table are encouraging. The signs of the entire co-efficient are as expected and the goodness of fit of the model is also satisfactory.

**Automobile Industry**

It is evide nt from the Table 17.1 that the co-efficient of sales are highly significant and indicated that higher sales increases working capital and its components. The sales elasticity varies from 0.34 for cash to 0.91 for gross working capital. Thus, the sales elasticity is smallest for cash, followed by net working capital, receivables, inventory and gross working capital. This elasticity's are consistently less than unity in all cases, suggesting economies of scale. This finding seems to support the theoretical propositions of Baumol, Tobin, Frazer, Nadiri and Coates and contradict the propositions of Friedman, Meltzer, Whalen, De Allessi and Vogel and Maddala, as far as the demand for cash by the Indian Automobile Industry is concerned. Similarly, the results, seem to support the findings of Akhtar and Irvine, among others, and contradict unitary or more than unitary sales elasticity noticed in some of the equations of Liberman showing the demand for inventories is concerned.

Table 17.1 also showed that fluctuations in cash and inventory levels depend in a statistically significant manner on fluctuations in their financial carrying costs. This finding is consistent with the results of Seldom, De Allessi, Nadiri, and Coates and contradicts Friedman's so far as the effect of capital costs on cash holding is concerned. Similarly, the finding supports the conclusion of Albert et al., Liu, Kuznets, Lieberman, Irvine and Akhtar and contradicts the results of Terlekyj, Robinson, Lovell, Jon Joyce and Maccini and Rossana as fər as the effect of interest cost on inventory demand is concerned.

The estimated elasticity's of the target levels of working capital and its components with respect to capital costs measure indicate that the target level of cash is much more sensitive to capital cost fluctuations as compared to the target level of inventory, receivables and gross and net working capital. Among these, the target level of gross working capital is least sensitive to fluctuations in capital costs. It all be seen from the interest rate elasticity of 0.78 for cash, 0.30 for net working capital, 0.29 for inventory, 0.17 for receivables and 0.04 for gross working capital.

Holding the sales constant, Table 17.1 indicates that a one percentage point increase interest rate leads on an average to about 0.78 per cent decline in the cash balances. Similarly, this kind of decline is noticed to be about 0.29 per cent for inventory, 0.17 per cent for receivables, 0.04 per cent for gross working capital and 0.30 per cent for net working capital balances when there is a one percentage point increase in interest rate. In the same way, holding the interest rate constant, a one percentage point increase in sales leads on an average to about 0.34 per cent increase in cash balances. This kind of increase is noticed to be about 0.70 per cent for inventory, 0.65 per cent for receivables, 0.91 per cent for gross working capital and 0.64 per cent for net working capital. The increase in target cash, receivables, inventories and gross and net working capital as a whole due to the increase in the capital cost may mean higher production and higher employment.

The estimated regression results of Partial Adjustment Model of Indian Automobile Industry are presented in Table 17.2. The regression results indicated that co-efficient of $y_{t-1}$ are significant in all the cases. The coefficient of the lagged dependent variable has been observed to be 0.27 for cash, 0.46 for inventory, 0.51 for receivables, 0.34 for gross working capital and 0.28 for net working capital. Since the coefficient of lag $L_n y_t$ is equal to 1 minus the adjustment coefficients $(1-\phi)$, the adjustment coefficient is equal to 0.73 for cash, 0.54 for inventory, 0.49 for receivables, 0.66 for gross working capital and 0.72 for net working capital. It seems that 73 per cent of the adjustment of actual to desired real cash balances is completed within one year. Similarly, the adjustment speed of actual to desired balances is 54 per cent for inventory, 49 per cent for receivables, 66 per cent for gross working capital and 72 per cent for net working capital. The speed of adjustment is however highest for cash followed by net working capital, gross working capital, Inventory and receivables.

In the partial adjustment models, the estimated coefficients of the independent variables are equal to the elasticity's of these variables times the adjustment coefficient. These long-run elasticizes are 0.49 for sales and 0.81 for short-term interest rates with respect to cash; 0.63 and 0.80 with respect to inventory; 1.24 and 0.22 with respect to receivables; 0.88 and 0.13 with respect to gross working capital; and 0.32 and 0.51 with respect to net working capital.

**Commercial Vehicles Sector**

The estimated demand function of commercial vehicles sector of Indian Automobile Industry are presented in Table 17.3. The table indicates that higher the sales increases working capital and its components. The sales elasticity's are consistently less than unity in all cases, suggesting economies of scale. This finding seems to support the theoretical propositions of Baumol, Tobin, Frazer, Nadiri and Coates and contradict the propositions of Friedman, Meltzer, Whalen, De Allessi and Vogel and Maddala, as far as the demand for cash by the commercial vehicles sector of Indian Automobile Industry is concerned. The results also support the findings of Akhtar and Irvine and contradict unitary or more than unitary sales elasticity noticed in the some of the equations of Liberman showing the demand for inventories is concerned.

The table also revealed that fluctuations in cash and inventory levels depend in a statistically significant manner on fluctuations in their financial carrying cost supporting the findings of Selden, De Allessi, Nadiri and Coates and contradicts Friedman's result. Similarly, the finding supports the conclusion of Albert et al., Liu, Kuznets, Liberman, Irvine and Akhtar as far as the effect of interest cost on inventory demand is concerned. The estimated elasticity's of the target levels of working capital and its components with respect to capital costs measure indicated that the target level of cash (0.98) is much more sensitive to capital cost fluctuations, followed by Receivables (0.88), Net working capital (0.86), Gross working capital (0.48) and Inventory (0.30). The increase in target cash, inventories, receivables, gross working capital and net working capital as a whole due to the increase in the capital cost may mean higher production and higher employment.

The pooled estimates of the partial adjustment models of commercial vehicles sector of Indian Automobile Industry are presented in Table 17.4. The regression results indicated that coefficients of $S_{t-1}, i \text{ and } y_{t-1}$ are significant in all cases. It is evident from the table that the adjustment coefficient is equal to 0.76 for cash, 0.85 for inventories, 0.60 for receivables, 0.71 for gross working capital and 0.79 for net working capital. In other words, the speed of adjustment implied by these values is much higher. It seems that 76 per cent of the adjustment of actual to desired real cash balances is completed within one year. Similarly, the adjustment speed of actual to desired balance is 85 per cent for inventories, 60 per cent for receivables, 71 per cent for gross working capital and 79 per cent for net working capital. These results supports the high speed of adjustment observed by Coates and Nadiri in the case of cash and by Goodwin, Burrows, Maccini and Rossana and Irvine in the case of inventories.

In the partial adjustment models, the estimated coefficients of the independent variables are equal to the elasticity's of these variables times the adjustment co-efficient. The long-run elasticity's are 0.20 for sales and 1.07 for short-run interest rates with respect to cash; 0.93 for sales and 0.32 for short-term interest rates with respect to inventories; 0.43 for sales and 1.10 for short-term interest rates with respect to receivables; 0.82 for sales and 0.46 for short-term interest rates with respect to gross working capital; and 0.90 for sales and 1.22 for short-term interest rates with respect to net working capital.

**Passenger cars and multiutility vehicles sector**

It is evide nt from the Table 17.5 that the coefficients of sales are highly significant in the case of passenger cars and multiutility vehicles sector of Indian Automobile Industry and indicate that higher sales increase working capital and its component. The sales elasticity is smallest for networking capital (0.43) followed by inventory and receivables (0.53), gross working capital (0.94) and net working capital (0.97). These elasticity's are consistently less than unity in all cases supports the theoretical propositions of Baumol, Tobin, Frazer, Nadiri and Coates and contradict the propositions of Friedman, Meltzer, Whalen, De Allessi and Vogel and Maddala, as far as the demand for cash is concerned. Similarly, the results support the findings of Akhtar and Irvine and contradict unitary or more than unitary sales elasticity noticed in some of the equations of Lieberman as far as the demand for inventories is concerned.

The results also show that fluctuations in cash and inventory levels depend in a statistically significant manner on fluctuations in their financial carrying costs. This finding is consistent with the results of Selden, De Allessi, Nadiri and Coates and contradicts Friedman's so far as the effect of capital costs on cash holding is concerned. The findings supports the conclusion of Albert et al., Liu, Kuznets, Lieberman, Irvine and Akhtar and contradicts the results of Robinson, Lovell, and Maccini and Rossana as far as the effect of interest cost on inventory demand is concerned. The effect of capital costs can be observed for investment in receivables, gross working capital and net working capital. The sign of interest rate co-efficient is not only negative but also statistically significant in all these cases except net working capital.

The regression results of Partial Adjustment Model are presented in Table 17.6 . It is from the table that the coefficient of the lagged dependent variable has been observed to be 0.25 for cash, 0.65 for inventories, 0.37 for receivables, 0.64 for gross working capital and 0.42 for net working capital. The adjustment co-efficient $(1-\phi)$ is equal to 0.75 for cash, 0.35 for inventory, 0.63 for receivables, 0.36 for gross working capital and 0.58 for net working capital. The speed of adjustment is however highest for cash followed by receivables, net working capital, gross working capital and inventory. These results support the high speed of adjustment observed by Coates and Nadiri in case of cash and contradict by Goodwin, Maccini and Rossana and Irvine in the case of inventories. The long-run elasticity's are 1.32 for sales and 0.53 for short-term interest rates with respect to cash; 2.06 and 1.37 with respects to inventories; 0.62 and 0.51 with respect to receivables; 2.56 and 0.50 with respect to gross working capital; and 0.69 and 0.26 with respect to net working capital.

**Two and Three wheeler sector**

Table 17.7 showed the results of estimated demand functions of two and three wheeler sector of Indian Automobile Industry. It is evident from the table that higher the sales increases working capital and its component and sales elasticity's are consistently less than unity in all cases, suggesting economies of scale. This result supports the findings of Baumol, Tobin, Frazer, Nadiri and Coates and contradict the propositions of Friedman, Meltzer, Whalen, De Allessi and Vogel and Maddala, as far as the demand for cash is concerned. The results also showed that short-term interest rate elasticity's are less than unity in all cases, supporting the findings of Akhtar and Irvine and contradict the findings of Lieberman showing the demand for inventory is concerned.

Further, the estimated elasticity's of the target levels of working capital and its components with respects to capital costs measures indicated that target level of cash (0.67) is more sensitive to capital cost fluctuations, followed by net working capital (0.56), gross working capital (0.36), inventory (0.13) and receivables (0.03). The pooled estimates of the partial adjustment models of two and three wheeler sector of Indian automobile industry presented in Table 17.8. It is evident from the table that the speed of adjustment of actual to desired real cash balances is 79 per cent completed within one year. Similarly, the adjustment speed of actual to desired balance is 88 per cent for inventories, 86 per cent for receivables, 82 per cent for gross working capital and 74 per cent for net working capital. These results supports the high speed of adjustment observed by Coates and Nadiri in the case of cash and by Goodwin, Burrows, Maccini and Rossana and Irvine in the case of inventories. The long-run elasticity's are given by $b_1 = c_1/f$ and $b_2 = c_2/f$. These elasticity's are 1.25 for sales and 0.67 for short-term interest rates with respect to cash; 0.49 and 0.09 for inventories; 0.67 and 0.06 for receivables; 0.77 and 0.38 for gross working capital; and 1.34 and 1.09 for net working capital.

## CONCLUSION

The pooled regression results of this analysis contradict unitary or more than unitary sales elasticity hypothesis of Friedman, Meltzer, Whalen, De Allessi and Vogel and Maddala with respect to demand for cash by all the three sectors and the whole Indian automobile industry. The presence of economies of scale in cash holdings is consistent with the conclusion of Baumol, Tobin, Frazer, Nadiri and Coates. The demand for inventory equations showed economies of scale in inventory thereby supporting the findings of Akhtar and Irvine and contradicts the findings of Lieberman. The presence of economies of scale has also been observed for receivables, gross working capital and net working capital. The regression results also show that the levels of working capital and its components of Indian automobile industry and its three sector desires to hold depend not only on sales but on holding costs also. The capital cost coefficients are all statistically significant with the theoretically correct signs. This finding is consistent with the findings of Selden, De Allessi, Nadiri, and Coates and contradicts Friedman's so far the effect of capital costs on cash holdings is concerned. Further, the results supports the conclusion of Albert et al., Liu, Kuznets, Lieberman, Irvine and Akhtar and contradicts the results of Robinson, Lovell and Maccini and Rossana as far as the effect of capital cost on inventory demand is concerned. Besides, the effect of capital costs has also been observed in the case of receivables, and gross and net working capital. The adjustment speed of actual to desired balances has been observed as highest for cash followed by networking capital, gross working capital, inventory and receivables in the Indian Automobile Industry during the study period.

## REFERENCES


1. Richard M. Goodwin (1948). "Secular and Cyclical Aspects of the Multiplier and Accelerator", in Income, Employment and Public Policy : Essays in honour of Alvin H. Hansen, New York : Norton and Company.
2. Baumol, W. (1952). "The Transactions Demand for Cash: An Inventory Theoretic Approach", *The Quarterly Journal of Economics,* pp.545-566.
3. Tobin, J. (1956). "The Interest Elasticity of Transactions Demand for Cash", *The Review of Economics and Statistics,* pp.241 – 247.
4. Friedman, M. (1959). "The Demand for Money; Some Theoretical and Empirical Results", *The Journal of Political Economy,* pp.327 – 351.
5. Newton Y. Robinson (1959). "The Acceleration Principle: Departmental Store Inventories, 1920 - 1956", *The American Economic Review,* pp. 348 - 358.
6. Richard, T. Selden (1961). "The Postwar Rise in the Velocity of Money : A Sectoral Analysis", *The Journal of Finance,* pp.483 – 545.
7. Nestor E. Terleckyj (1961). "Measures of Inventory Conditions", in Inventory Fluctuations and Economic Stablisations, Part II, (Washington : Joint Economic Committee, 87th Congress, First Session)

8. Mc Gouldrick, P.P. (1961). "The Impact of Credit Cost and Availability on Inventory Management" in Inventory Fluctuations and Economic Stabilisation, Part II (Washington : *Joint Economic Committee, 87th Congress*).
9. Michael Lovell (1961). "Manufacturers, Inventories, Sales Expectations and the Acceleration Principle", *Econometrica,* pp. 293 – 314.
10. Allan H. Meltzer (1963). "The Demand for Money : A Cross – Section Study of Business Firms", *The Quarterly Journal of Economics,* p.410.
11. Ablert Ando et al., (1963). "Lags in Fiscal and Monetary Policy" in Stabilisation Policies : Commission on Money and Credit, (Englewood Cliffs).
12. Liu, T.C. (1963). "An Exploratory Quarterly Model of Effective Demand in the Post-War US Economy", *The Econometrica,* pp. 301 – 308.
13. William J. Frazer, Jr. (1964). "Financial Structure of Manufacturing Corporations and the Demand for Money: Some empirical findings", *The Journal of Political Economy,* pp.176 – 183.
14. Paul W. Kuznets (1964). "Financial determinants of Manufacturing Inventory Behaviour : A Quarterly Study Based on United States Estimates, 1947 - 1961", *Yale Economic Essays,* pp. 331 – 369.
15. Lovell, M.C. (1964). "Determinants of Inventory Behaviour", in Models of Income Behaviour, Edward F. Denison and Lawrence R. Klein, eds., New York.
16. Maddala G.S., and Robert C. Vogel (1965). "The Demand for Money : A Cross-Section Study of Business Firms : Comments", *The Quarterly Journal of Economics,* pp.153 – 159.
17. Edward L. Whalen (1965). "A Cross – Section Study of Business Demand for Cash", *The Journal of Finance,* pp. 423 – 443.
18. Louis De Allessi (1966). "The Demand for Money : A Cross-Section Study of British Business Firms", *Economica,* pp. 288 – 302.

19. Nadiri M.I. (1969). "The Determinants of Real Cash Balances in the US Total Manufacturing Sector", *The Quarterly Journal of Economics,* pp.173 - 196.

20. Paul Burrows (1971). "Explanatory and Forecasting Models of Inventory Investment in Britain", *The Applied Economics,* pp. 275 – 289.

21. Jon M. Joyee, "Cost of Capital and Inventory Investment: Further Evidence", *The Southern Economic Journal,* pp. 323-329.

22. Steven D. Grossman (1973) "A Test of Speed of Adjustment in Manufacturing Inventory Management", *The Quarterly Review of Economics and Business,* pp. 21-32.

23. Robert Coates, C. (1976). "The Demand for Money by Firms", New York : Marcel Dekker, Inc.,

24. Charles Lieberman (1980). "Inventory Demand and Cost of Capital Effects", *The Review of Economics and Statistics,* pp. 348 – 356.

25. F.Owen Irvine, Jr., (1981). "Retail Inventory Investment and the Cost of Capital", *The American Economic Review,* p. 633.

26. Louis J. Maccini and Robert J. Rossana (1981) "Investment in Finished Goods Inventories : An Analysis of Adjustment Speeds", *The American Economic Review Papers and Proceedings,* pp. 17 – 22.

27. Akhtar, M.A., (1983). "Effects of Interest Rates and Inflation on Aggregate Inventory Investment in the United States", *The American Economic Review,* pp. 319 - 328.

28. Vijayakumar, A., (1999). "Estimating Demand Functions of Working Capital – Partial Adjustment Model", *The Management Accountant,* pp. 172 – 174.

**TABLE 17.1**

**ESTIMATING DEMAND FOR WORKING CAPITAL – INDIAN AUTOMOBILE INDUSTRY**

**($LnY^* = \beta_0 + \beta_1 L_n S_{t-1} + \beta_2 L_n\ i$)**

| Dependent Variables | Regression Co-efficient $S_{t-1}$ | $i$ | $R^2$ | Adj $R^2$ | F Value | DW |
|---|---|---|---|---|---|---|
| Cash | 0.34<br>(6.75)* | -0.78<br>(2.03)*** | 0.92 | 0.90 | 54.17 | 1.94 |
| Inventory | 0.70<br>(5.85)* | -0.29<br>(4.25)* | 0.81 | 0.78 | 21.71 | 1.52 |
| Receivables | 0.65<br>(8.86)* | -0.17<br>(5.23)* | 0.92 | 0.90 | 54.05 | 1.48 |
| Gross Working Capital | 0.91<br>(7.42)* | -0.04<br>(3.17)* | 0.90 | 0.88 | 43.44 | 1.86 |
| Net Working Capital | 0.64<br>(2.85)** | -0.30<br>(4.45)* | 0.82 | 0.79 | 20.16 | 1.63 |

*- Significant at 0.01 level; ** - Significant at 0.05 level
*** - Significant at 0.10 level; **DW** - Durban-Watson Statistics;
Figures in Parenthesis denotes 't' value. ***Source :*** Computed

## TABLE 17.2

## PARTIAL ADJUSTMENT MODEL – INDIAN AUTOMOBILE INDUSTRY

$$(LnY^* = \beta_0 + \beta_1 L_n S_{t-1} + \beta_2 L_n\, i + (1 - \phi) L_n\, Y_{t-1} + u)$$

| Dependent Variables | Regression Co-efficient $S_{t-1}$ | $i$ | $Y_{t-1}$ | $R^2$ | Adj $R^2$ | F Value | DW |
|---|---|---|---|---|---|---|---|
| Cash | 0.36 (4.77)* | -0.59 (3.16)* | 0.27 (6.81)* | 0.94 | 0.92 | 44.89 | 1.52 |
| Inventory | 0.34 (2.89)** | -0.43 (3.61)* | 0.46 (4.86)* | 0.82 | 0.76 | 13.60 | 1.96 |
| Receivables | 0.61 (4.46)* | -0.11 (2.80)** | 0.51 (6.04)* | 0.91 | 0.88 | 30.82 | 1.64 |
| Gross Working Capital | 0.58 (3.82)* | -0.09 (4.16)* | 0.34 (3.86)* | 0.90 | 0.87 | 27.50 | 1.89 |
| Net Working Capital | 0.23 (2.84)* | -0.37 (4.07)* | 0.28 (4.26)* | 0.81 | 0.79 | 12.96 | 1.19 |

*- Significant at 0.01 level; ** - Significant at 0.05 level
*** - Significant at 0.10 level; **DW** - Durban-Watson Statistics;
Figures in Parenthesis denotes 't' value. ***Source :*** Computed

## TABLE 17.3

## ESTIMATING DEMAND FOR WORKING CAPITAL – COMMERCIAL VEHICLES SECTOR

$$(LnY^* = \beta_0 + \beta_1 L_n S_{t-1} + \beta_2 L_n i)$$

| Dependent Variables | Regression Co-efficient $S_{t-1}$ | $i$ | $R^2$ | Adj $R^2$ | F Value | DW |
|---|---|---|---|---|---|---|
| Cash | 0.18<br>(4.87) * | -0.98<br>(2.80)** | 0.86 | 0.84 | 31.78 | 1.40 |
| Inventory | 0.76<br>(16.96) * | -0.30<br>(3.20)* | 0.97 | 0.96 | 166.61 | 1.28 |
| Receivables | 0.44<br>(4.93) * | -0.88<br>(4.70)* | 0.75 | 0.70 | 15.19 | 1.37 |
| Gross Working Capital | 0.71<br>(10.66)* | -0.48<br>(3.42)* | 0.92 | 0.91 | 60.12 | 1.31 |
| Net Working Capital | 0.65<br>(5.74)* | -0.86<br>(6.23)* | 0.94 | 0.93 | 75.67 | 1.58 |

*- Significant at 0.01 level; ** - Significant at 0.05 level
*** - Significant at 0.10 level; **DW** - Durban-Watson Statistics;
Figures in Parenthesis denotes 't' value.

***Source :*** Computed

**TABLE 17.4**

**PARTIAL ADJUSTMENT MODEL – COMMERCIAL VEHICLES SECTOR**

**$(LnY^* = \beta_0 + \beta_1 L_n S_{t-1} + \beta_2 L_n\, i + (1-\phi)L_n\, Y_{t-1} + u)$**

| Dependent Variables | Regression Co-efficient $S_{t-1}$ | $i$ | $Y_{t-1}$ | $R^2$ | Adj $R^2$ | F Value | DW |
|---|---|---|---|---|---|---|---|
| Cash | 0.15<br>(3.87)* | -0.81<br>(4.71)* | 0.24<br>(3.19)* | 0.87 | 0.84 | 26.92 | 1.48 |
| Inventory | 0.79<br>(4.90)* | -0.27<br>(3.39)* | 0.15<br>(4.59)* | 0.97 | 0.96 | 90.80 | 1.31 |
| Receivables | 0.26<br>(3.90)* | -0.66<br>(2.84)** | 0.40<br>(3.12)* | 0.77 | 0.73 | 17.66 | 1.71 |
| Gross Working Capital | 0.58<br>(3.75)* | -0.33<br>(3.12)* | 0.29<br>(4.30)* | 0.92 | 0.89 | 33.22 | 1.42 |
| Net Working Capital | 0.71<br>(3.64)* | -0.96<br>(4.15)* | 0.21<br>(2.86)** | 0.96 | 0.95 | 70.98 | 1.33 |

*- Significant at 0.01 level; ** - Significant at 0.05 level
*** - Significant at 0.10 level; **DW** - Durban-Watson Statistics;
Figures in Parenthesis denotes 't' value.
***Source :*** Computed

## TABLE 17.5

## ESTIMATING DEMAND FOR WORKING CAPITAL – PASSENGER CARS AND MULTIUTILITY VEHICLES SECTOR

$$(LnY^* = \beta_0 + \beta_1 L_n S_{t-1} + \beta_2 L_n i)$$

| Dependent Variables | Regression Co-efficient $S_{t-1}$ | $i$ | $R^2$ | Adj $R^2$ | F Value | DW |
|---|---|---|---|---|---|---|
| Cash | 0.97<br>(2.84)** | -0.42<br>(3.67)* | 0.84 | 0.77 | 19.06 | 1.98 |
| Inventory | 0.53<br>(4.03)* | -0.23<br>(2.95)** | 0.87 | 0.83 | 10.22 | 1.74 |
| Receivables | 0.53<br>(5.39)* | -0.09<br>(2.47)*** | 0.81 | 0.77 | 21.60 | 1.19 |
| Gross Working Capital | 0.94<br>(11.45)* | -0.27<br>(3.73)* | 0.95 | 0.94 | 90.39 | 2.01 |
| Net Working Capital | 0.43<br>(3.14)* | -0.23<br>(1.32) | 0.75 | 0.69 | 9.12 | 1.83 |

*- Significant at 0.01 level; ** - Significant at 0.05 level

*** - Significant at 0.10 level; **DW** - Durban-Watson Statistics;

Figures in Parenthesis denotes 't' value. ***Source :*** Computed

**TABLE 17.6**

## PARTIAL ADJUSTMENT MODEL – PASSENGER CARS AND MULTIUTILITY VEHICLES SECTOR

$(LnY^* = \beta_0 + \beta_1 L_n S_{t-1} + \beta_2 L_n\, i + (1 - \phi) L_n\, Y_{t-1} + u)$

| Dependent Variables | Regression Co-efficient $S_{t-1}$ | $i$ | $Y_{t-1}$ | $R^2$ | Adj $R^2$ | F Value | DW |
|---|---|---|---|---|---|---|---|
| Cash | 0.99 (3.29)* | -0.40 (4.28)* | 0.25 (3.14)* | 0.78 | 0.74 | 15.62 | 2.05 |
| Inventory | 0.72 (3.72)* | -0.48 (4.71)* | 0.65 (3.61)* | 0.86 | 0.81 | 18.29 | 1.85 |
| Receivables | 0.39 (4.06)* | -0.32 (2.90)** | 0.37 (2.80)** | 0.86 | 0.81 | 18.37 | 1.79 |
| Gross Working Capital | 0.92 (3.14)* | -0.18 (4.30)* | 0.64 (2.86)** | 0.94 | 0.92 | 49.88 | 1.98 |
| Net Working Capital | 0.40 (3.10)* | -0.15 (4.26)* | 0.42 (2.87)** | 0.72 | 0.71 | 9.32 | 1.86 |

*- Significant at 0.01 level; ** - Significant at 0.05 level
*** - Significant at 0.10 level; **DW** - Durban-Watson Statistics;
Figures in Parenthesis denotes 't' value. ***Source :*** Computed

## TABLE 17.7

## ESTIMATING DEMAND FOR WORKING CAPITAL – TWO AND THREE WHEELERS SECTOR

**($LnY^* = \beta_0 + \beta_1 L_n S_{t-1} + \beta_2 L_n i$)**

| Dependent Variables | Regression Co-efficient $S_{t-1}$ | $i$ | $R^2$ | Adj $R^2$ | F Value | DW |
|---|---|---|---|---|---|---|
| Cash | 0.92<br>(7.87)* | -0.61<br>(2.11)*** | 0.90 | 0.88 | 46.44 | 1.45 |
| Inventory | 0.47<br>(5.74)* | -0.13<br>(3.65)* | 0.90 | 0.88 | 43.50 | 1.97 |
| Receivables | 0.47<br>(7.28)* | -0.03<br>(2.18)*** | 0.93 | 0.91 | 61.60 | 1.62 |
| Gross Working Capital | 0.72<br>(8.82)* | -0.36<br>(1.79)*** | 0.93 | 0.91 | 64.31 | 1.43 |
| Net Working Capital | 0.98<br>(2.33)** | -0.56<br>(3.34)* | 0.96 | 0.93 | 68.50 | 1.69 |

*- Significant at 0.01 level; ** - Significant at 0.05 level
*** - Significant at 0.10 level; **DW** - Durban-Watson Statistics;
Figures in Parenthesis denotes 't' value. ***Source :*** Computed

## TABLE 17.8

## PARTIAL ADJUSTMENT MODEL – TWO AND THREE WHEELERS SECTOR

$(LnY^* = \beta_0 + \beta_1 L_n S_{t-1} + \beta_2 L_n\, i + (1 - \phi) L_n\, Y_{t-1} + u)$

| Dependent Variables | Regression Co-efficient $S_{t-1}$ | $i$ | $Y_{t-1}$ | $R^2$ | Adj $R^2$ | F Value | DW |
|---|---|---|---|---|---|---|---|
| Cash | 0.99 (5.07)* | -0.53 (2.78)*** | 0.21 (2.93)** | 0.93 | 0.90 | 37.29 | 1.86 |
| Inventory | 0.43 (4.78)* | -0.08 (3.42)* | 0.12 (2.14)*** | 0.90 | 0.86 | 25.54 | 1.93 |
| Receivables | 0.58 (4.45)* | -0.05 (2.46)** | 0.14 (3.77)* | 0.93 | 0.91 | 40.32 | 1.89 |
| Gross Working Capital | 0.63 (3.31)* | -0.31 (4.22)* | 0.18 (2.88)** | 0.95 | 0.93 | 51.61 | 1.63 |
| Net Working Capital | 0.99 (3.68)* | -0.81 (2.59)** | 0.26 (3.77)* | 0.98 | 0.95 | 55.16 | 2.02 |

*- Significant at 0.01 level; ** - Significant at 0.05 level
*** - Significant at 0.10 level; **DW** - Durban-Watson Statistics;
Figures in Parenthesis denotes 't' value. ***Source :*** Computed

# 18

# Operational Adequacy of Working Capital in Sugar Industry of Tamil Nadu

## A Bivariate Discriminant Analysis Approach

Fixed capital and working capital are the dominant contributors to the total capital of a developing country. Fixed capital investment generates production capacity whereas working capital makes the utilization of that capacity possible. Since the fifties, there has been a concerted effort to analyse the long-term corporate investment and financial decisions, but virtually no research has been conducted in an attempt to apply them to working capital decisions. It shows that earlier the emphasis in financial management was more on long-term financial decisions. Funds are needed in every business for carrying on day-to-day operations. Working capital funds are regarded as the life-blood of a business firm. A firm can exist and survive without making profit but it cannot survive without working capital funds. In addition, it has acquired great significance and sound position for the twin objects of "profitability and liquidity". It consumes a great deal of time to increase profitability as well as to maintain proper liquidity, at minimum risk. Viewed in this perspective, the study devoted to working capital, may be a very recording one.

## STATEMENT OF THE PROBLEM

The problem of working capital management is the most critical problem in financial management. Most of the time financial executives are engaged in managing the current assets and current liabilities, which are the main constituents of working capital. Inefficient management of working capital will lead to loss of profits in the short-run but it will ultimately lead to the downfall of the enterprise in the long- run. Excessive investment in working capital the solvency position and growth thereby affecting the operation of business. The adequacy of working capital together with its efficient handling virtually determines the survival or demise of an enterprise. Hence, in this study an attempt has been made to determine the operational adequacy of working capitals of the sugar industry of Tamil Nadu with the use of Bivariate Discriminant Analysis.

## SAMPLING DESIGN

There are about 31 sugar industries operating in Tamil Nadu, of which 14 are under co-operative sector, 14 are under private sector and 3 are under public sector. Since this study has been directed towards assessing the operational adequacy of working capital, all these sugar industries are not included because most of them are just a few years old leading to the absence of data for the last ten years. In order to select the industries for the purpose of study, first of all a list was made of those industries, which were established before 1975 and have crushing capacity of 2000 MT (per day) or more. We found 10 such industries, 5 under co-operative sector and 5 under private sector. Thus, ten industries selected for the study form the important industries and seem to have represented the sugar industries of Tamil Nadu as a whole.

## ADEQUACY OF WORKING CAPITAL

There is no standard by which to measure the adequacy of working capital. However practice suggests that the adequacy of working capital can be judged in terms of its relation with the firm's debts. In order to establish such relationship generally the current ratio and liquid ratio are studied. The current ratio and liquid ratio of the selected units are presented in Table 18.1 and Table 18.2.

If the conventional liquidity of 2.1 is considered as a norm, following inferences can be drawn from Table 18.1. In industry, the working capital is observed to be excess, in private sector units it is also in excess and in the co-operative sector units only the working capital is found to be adequate. Among the co-operative sector units, in AMCS, the working capital is found to be inadequate, in ACS and KCS it has been adequate and in the remaining cases, it is found to be excess.

The current ratio can be used to indicate high or low level of working capital but they are unable to give an exact clue of the equality of current assets as some current assets, although classified as current, are not easily converted into cash. To offset this weakness liquid ratios are studied. If the conventional 1.1 is considered as a norm, the following inference can be drawn from Table 18.2.

In all the co-operative sector units and the industry as a whole, the working capital is observed to be inadequate. All the co-operative private sector units except SCS have in adequate working capital and in all the private sector units except SISL and TASL, the working capital is found to be excess. On the whole, it can be said that only in a few cases working capital is found to be adequate, it is either inadequate or excessively high.

## OPERATIONAL ADEQUACY OF WORKING CAPITAL – A BIVARIATE DISCRIMINANT ANALYSIS

Current liquid ratios measure the technical solvency working capital but the operational adequacy of working capital can be measured by ascertaining the magnitude of working capital in relation to average months sales turnover and Mont cost of operations. The present study attempts to apply linear discriminant analysis with only two sets of independent variables. The sample units were classified in two categories as per their liquidity ratios. Group A consisted of those units where the current ratio was found to be at least 2:1 and the rest of the units have been classified in Group B. In this study, adequacy of the size of net working capital has been treated as dependent variable and size of networking capital in terms of monthly operational requirements ($X_1$) and sales requirements ($X_2$) has been treated as independent variable.*****

The object is to determine weights for $X_1$ and $X_2$ that is the value of "a" and of "b" in

$$Z = a\,x_1 + b\,x_2$$

Where, A is the discriminant index.

As per the rule, the selected units falling in the good and poor risk group are presented in Table 18.3. It is to be noticed that three units namely NCS, ASL and SSL appeared to be a "good" risk in all the selected years. It is also to be noticed that no units appeared to be a "poor" risk in all the selected years. After classifying the selected units into the good and poor risk class, the values of a and b in the discriminant functions are estimated and presented in Table 18.4 where the coefficient for "a" and "b" indicate the size of net working capital in terms of monthly operational requirements and sales requirement. The table reveals that the size of net working capital in terms of monthly operations requirements appeared to be stronger than sales requirements in all the years accepts in 1983-84 and 1989-90.

The discriminant co-efficient given in Table 18.4 were multiplied with the mean values of each industry ratios in order to obtain the discriminant score of each unit. Table 18.5 presents the data relating to the discriminant score of both groups. With the help of the discriminant scores, the cut-off value was calculated as follows.

$$\textbf{Cut – Off value} = \frac{n_1 z_1 + n_2 z_2}{n_1 + n_2}$$

Where $n_1$ and $n_2$ are the size of samples and $z_1$ and $z_2$ represents the mean of the discriminant score of Group A and Group B respectively. The cut-off values have also been presented in Table 18.5. Actual Z scores of the individual units were then compared with the discriminating Z scores. In case where the Z scores were found to be more than the discriminating Z sores, it can be said that the size of net working capital was more than the operational and sales requirements.

It is evident from the Table 18.5 that in the year 1982-83, the cut off z score was 2.05. In the case of KSL and NCS, the size of working capital was found to be quite satisfactory in terms of operation and sales requirements. In the case of AMCS, SCS and ACS, the Z scores were found to be low which indicate inadequacy of the size of working capital, considering the operational and sale requirement. In rest of the cases, the size of working capital was found to be in excess in scores was 1.02. Considering this is discriminate scores, in the case of SCS, and KSL, z scores were found to be less than 1.02. But were not top low to be inadequate. In the case ACS, AMCS, KCS and SISL, the size of working capital was found to be very low. In rest of the cases it was found that working capital was in excess as Z scores by the individual units were more than the cut off Z scores.

In 1984-85, the cut-off Z scores was 1.16. In the case of ACS, the size of working capital was found to be quite satisfactory. In the case of KCS, SIS, KSL and TASL, the size of working capital was found to be very low. In rest of cases, the size of working capital was found to be excess, in relation to their operational and sales requirement. In 1985-86, cut -off z scores was found to be 2.06 . In the case AMCS, NCL, ASL and SSL the size of working capital was found to be in excess to meet their operational and sales requirement. SCS had satisfactory size of working capital was found to be inadequate in relation to operational and sale requirements.

In 1986-87, he cut off z score was 0.55. Considering this as discriminant score, in the case of SCS and NCS, Z Scores were found to be less than 0.55 but were not too low to tube inadequate. In the cease of KCS, SISL, KSL and TASI, the size of working capital was found to be very low. In rest of the cases it was found that working capital was in excess as z score by the individual units were more than the cut was off z score. In 1987-89, the size of working capital was fund to be quite satisfactory. In the case of AMCS and TASL, working capital impositions were found to be satisfactory. In the case of KCS, SISL and KSL the size of working capital was found to be too low and in rest of the case the size of working capital was in excess to meet their respective operational and sale requirements.

In 1989-90, the cut off Z score was 0.57. Considering it as discrimination Z score, it was found that in the case of NCS, ASL, SISL and SSL, the size of working capital was found to be excess to meet their respective operational and sale requirement and in the rest of the cases the size of working capital was found to be too low.

In 1990-91, the cut off Z score was 0.97. In the case of ACS and SISL, Z score were found to be less than 0.97 but were not too low to be inadequate. In other words the size of working capital was found to be very low. In rest of the cases it was found that working capital was in excess as Z scores by the individual units were more than the cut off Z score. In 1991-92, the cut off score was 1.65. In the case of ACS and SISL, the size of working capital was found to be quite satisfactory. In the case of AMCS and TASL, the size of working capital was found to be very low. In rest of the cases the size of working capital was found to be in excess as Z scored by the individual units was more than the cut off Z score.

In 1992-93, the cut off Z score was 1.78. Considering it as discriminating Z score, it was found that in the case of ACS, NCS, KCS and SSL, scores were more than the cut off Z score, hence in these cases the size of working capital was observed to be quite satisfactory. In the case of AMCS, the size of working capital was found to be too low and in the rest of the cases the size of working capital was in excess to meet their respective operational and sales requirement. In 1993-94, the cut of Z score was found to be 1.08. In the case of NCS, KCS, ASL, SSL, and KSL, the working capital position was found to be satisfactory. In the cases of AMCS and TASL, the size of working capital was very low. In rest of the cases the size of working capital was found to be in excess, in relation to their operational and sale requirements.

## CONCLUSION

To sum up the reanalysis regarding the operational adequacy of working capital, it can be concluded that all the selected units except ANCS and TASL maintained adequate size of working capital in relation to sales and output requirements in the recent years 1990-91 and 1991-92. In addition NCS and SCS in the eco-operative sector and ASL and SSL in private sector maintained adequate size of working capital in relation to sales and output requirements throughout the period under study.

The number of good and poor risk unites as per the current ratio as per the discriminant score presented in Table 18.6. It is clear from the table that the mis-classification does not occur in the year 1985-86, 1987-89 and 1989-90. Mis-classification of unites is noticed for the remaining years. Generally one unit in the good risk group has been mis-classified under the criteria of discriminant score. Such industries are KSL in the years 1982-83 and 1983-84, NCS in 1986-87, ACS in 1990-91 and ACS and TASL in the year 1991-92, SISL in industries appeared to be good risk under the criteria of discriminate score. Such a unit is SCS in the year 1984-85. From this study, it is concluded that Discriminant Analysis is a very useful technique to analyse the adequacy of working capital of the business enterprises.

## REFERENCES


1. A.K. Mukherjee, *Management of working capital in public Enterprises*. Allahabad: Vohra publishers & Distributors, 1988.
2. S.K. Bhattacharya, M. Raghavachari, "Determinants of effective working capital Management – A discriminant Analysis Approach", working paper No. 151, Indian Institute of Management, Ahemdabad, March 1977.
3. ACS- Ambur Co-operative Sugar Ltd
   AMCS – Amaravathi Co-operative Sugars Ltd.
   SCS – Salem Co-operative Sugars Ltd
   NCS – National Co-operative Sugars Ltd
   KCS – Kallakurichi Co-operative Sugars Ltd
   ASL - Aruna Sugars Ltd.
   SISL – South India Sugars Ltd
   SSL - Sakthi Sugars Ltd
   KSL – Kothari Sugars Ltd
   TASL – Thiru Arooran Sugars Ltd.

**TABLE 18.1**

**CURRENT RATIO OF THE SELECTED UNITS**

| Year | Co-operative Sector | | | | | Private Sector | | | | | |
|---|---|---|---|---|---|---|---|---|---|---|---|
| | ACS | AMCS | SCS | NCS | KCS | ASL | SISL | SSL | KSL | TASL | X |
| 1982-83 | 1.79 | 1.11 | 1.94 | 3.47 | 2.66 | 3.59 | 2.45 | 2.19 | 3.02 | 2.35 | 2.46 |
| 1983-84 | 1.64 | 1.38 | 1.68 | 1.41 | 1.48 | 4.53 | 1.66 | 2.45 | 2.22 | 2.11 | 2.26 |
| 1984-85 | 1.64 | 2.70 | 1.57 | 3.47 | 1.19 | 3.71 | 1.02 | 2.40 | 1.78 | 1.31 | 2.08 |
| 1985-86 | 1.79 | 2.86 | 1.62 | 2.12 | 1.80 | 4.71 | 1.51 | 2.72 | 1.90 | 1.27 | 2.23 |
| 1986-87 | 2.44 | 3.17 | 1.67 | 2.13 | 1.21 | 4.90 | 1.08 | 2.69 | 1.80 | 1.91 | 2.30 |
| 1987-88 | 2.25 | 1.68 | 1.63 | 2.19 | 1.25 | 3.49 | 1.79 | 3.12 | 1.21 | 1.42 | 2.00 |
| 1989-90 | 1.65 | 0.89 | 1.93 | 2.56 | 1.52 | 2.72 | 1.55 | 3.43 | 1.17 | 1.05 | 1.85 |
| 1990-91 | 2.19 | 1.44 | 2.39 | 3.32 | 2.80 | 3.51 | 1.85 | 4.19 | 3.65 | 1.94 | 2.73 |
| 1991-92 | 2.07 | 1.39 | 3.02 | 3.11 | 2.63 | 3.49 | 3.04 | 2.81 | 3.54 | 2.23 | 2.74 |
| 1992-93 | 2.16 | 1.60 | 2.95 | 3.01 | 2.70 | 3.25 | 2.95 | 2.92 | 3.16 | 1.98 | 2.67 |
| 1993-94 | 2.24 | 1.75 | 2.85 | 3.05 | 3.10 | 3.15 | 3.10 | 3.18 | 3.25 | 2.54 | 2.82 |
| X | 1.99 | 1.82 | 2.11 | 2.89 | 2.30 | 3.73 | 2.01 | 2.42 | 1.83 | | |

***Source:*** Computed from annual reports of the respective units

**TABLE 18.2**

**LIQUID RATIO OF THE SELECTED UNITS**

| Year | Co-operative Sector | | | | | Private Sector | | | | | |
|---|---|---|---|---|---|---|---|---|---|---|---|
| | ACS | AMCS | SCS | NCS | KCS | ASL | SISL | SSL | KSL | TASL | X |
| 1982-83 | 0.27 | 0.11 | 0.34 | 0.63 | 0.43 | 0.82 | 0.30 | 0.47 | 1.01 | 0.55 | 0.49 |
| 1983-84 | 1.08 | 0.38 | 1.01 | 1.14 | 0.41 | 1.25 | 0.52 | 1.28 | 1.21 | 0.33 | 0.86 |
| 1984-85 | 0.76 | 0.51 | 0.95 | 1.25 | 0.50 | 1.22 | 0.37 | 0.98 | 1.41 | 0.48 | 0.84 |
| 1985-86 | 0.29 | 0.34 | 0.77 | 0.59 | 0.26 | 1.55 | 0.43 | 0.94 | 0.89 | 0.33 | 0.64 |
| 1986-87 | 1.16 | 0.47 | 1.04 | 0.75 | 0.29 | 2.47 | 0.48 | 1.35 | 1.23 | 0.77 | 1.00 |
| 1987-88 | 0.52 | 0.72 | 0.71 | 0.63 | 0.43 | 1.34 | 0.50 | 1.04 | 0.80 | 0.55 | 0.72 |
| 1989-90 | 0.93 | 0.57 | 1.19 | 0.59 | 0.77 | 0.97 | 0.61 | 1.40 | 1.03 | 0.88 | 0.89 |
| 1990-91 | 0.71 | 0.91 | 1.23 | 0.52 | 1.29 | 1.00 | 0.52 | 1.41 | 1.33 | 0.73 | 0.99 |
| 1991-92 | 0.74 | 0.69 | 1.55 | 0.37 | 0.78 | 1.42 | 0.48 | 1.15 | 1.47 | 0.74 | 0.94 |
| 1992-93 | 0.85 | 0.78 | 1.48 | 0.68 | 0.92 | 1.36 | 0.78 | 1.25 | 1.67 | 0.96 | 1.07 |
| 1993-94 | 0.92 | 0.96 | 1.62 | 0.54 | 0.88 | 1.42 | 0.90 | 1.15 | 1.78 | 0.89 | 1.11 |
| X | 0.75. | 0.58 | 1.08 | 0.70 | 0.63 | 1.35 | 0.54 | 1.13 | 1.25 | 0.66 | |

***Source:*** Computed from annual reports of the respective units

## TABLE 18.3

## GOOD AND POOR RISK UNITS IN TERMS OF CURRENT RATIO

**(Group a Consists of Those Units Whose Current ratio is at least 2:1)**

| 1982 -83 | 83-84 | 84-85 | 85-86 | 86-87 | 87-89 | 89-90 | 90-91 | 91-92 | 92-93 | 93-94 |
|---|---|---|---|---|---|---|---|---|---|---|
| **Group A (Good Risk)** | | | | | | | | | | |
| NCS | NCS | AMCS | AMCS | ACS | ACS | NCS | ACS | ACS | ACS | ACS |
| KCS | ASL | NCS | NCS | AMCS | NCS | ASL | SCS | SCS | SCS | SCS |
| ASL | SSL | ASL | ASL | NCS | ASL | SSL | NCS | NCS | NCS | NCS |
| SISL | KSL | SSL | SSL | ASL | SSL | | KCS | KCS | KCS | KCS |
| SSL | TASL | | | SSL | | | ASL | ASL | ASL | ASL |
| KSL | | | | | | | SISL | SISL | SISL | SISL |
| TASL | | | | | | | SSL | SSL | SSL | SSL |
| | | | | | | | KSL | KSL | KSL | KSL |
| | | | | | | | TASL | | | TASL |
| n1=7 | n1=5 | n1=4 | n1=4 | n1=5 | n1=4 | n1=3 | n1=7 | n1=9 | n1=8 | n1=9 |
| **Group B (Good Risk)** | | | | | | | | | | |
| ACS | ACS | ACS | ACS | SCS | AMCS | ACS | AMCS | AMCS | AMCS | AMCS |
| AMCS | AMCS | SCS | SCS | KCS | SCS | AMCS | SISL | | TASL | |
| SCS | SCS | KCS | KCS | SISL | KCS | SCS | TASL | | | |
| | KCS | SISL | SISL | KSL | SISL | KCS | | | | |
| | SISL | KSL | KSL | TASL | KSL | SISL | | | | |
| | | TASL | TASL | | TASL | KSL | | | | |
| | | | | | | TASL | | | | |
| n2=3 | n2=5 | n2=6 | n2=6 | n2=5 | n2=6 | n2=7 | n2=3 | n2=1 | n2=2 | n2=1 |

***Source:*** Computed

## TABLE 18.4

## DISCRIMINANT FUNCTIONS FOR THE PERIOD 1982-83 TO 1993-94

| YEAR | FUNCTIONS | REMARKS |
|---|---|---|
| 1982-83 | Z = 2.654a – 1.892b | a > b |
| 1983-84 | Z = 0.268a – 0.721b | b > a |
| 1984-85 | Z = 0.423a – 0.005b | a > b |
| 1985-86 | Z = 5.443a – 4.196b | a > b |
| 1986-87 | Z = 0.479a – 0.34b | a > b |
| 1987-89 | Z = 0.681a – 0.317b | a > b |
| 1989-90 | Z = 1.935a + 2.235b | b > a |
| 1990-91 | Z = 0.109a + 0.062b | a > b |
| 1991-92 | Z = 0.471a – 0.169b | a > b |
| 1992-93 | Z = 0.652a – 0.156b | a > b |
| 1993-94 | Z = 0.982a – 0.169b | a > b |

***Note:*** The expression a>b is to be read as "a is stronger than b"
***Source:*** Computed

## TABLE 18.5

## DISCRIMINANT Z VALUES FOR SELECTED UNITS IN THE YEAR

| Units | 82-83 | 83-84 | 84-85 | 85-86 | 86-87 | 87-89 | 89-90 | 90-91 | 91-92 |
|---|---|---|---|---|---|---|---|---|---|
| ACS | 1.41 | 0.86 | 1.08 | 0.38 | 0.62 | 0.72 | 0.24 | 0.89 | 1.42 |
| AMCS | 0.59 | 0.47 | 2.24 | 3.78 | 0.88 | 0.64 | -0.05 | 0.07 | 0.31 |
| SCS | 1.14 | 0.91 | 1.24 | 1.58 | 0.51 | 0.67 | 0.50 | 1.09 | 2.51 |
| NCS | 2.06 | 1.53 | 1.85 | 2.78 | 0.48 | 0.83 | 2.18 | 1.08 | 1.71 |
| KCS | 2.72 | 0.64 | 0.42 | 0.42 | 0.14 | 0.27 | 0.35 | 1.32 | 1.80 |
| ASL | 2.44 | 1.84 | 1.70 | 4.08 | 0.81 | 1.27 | 0.91 | 1.10 | 2.12 |
| SISL | 2.41 | 0.63 | 0.03 | 1.17 | 0.04 | 0.59 | 0.74 | 0.90 | 1.65 |
| SSL | 3.14 | 1.16 | 1.82 | 4.49 | 1.34 | 1.43 | 1.81 | 1.59 | 2.05 |
| KSL | 1.90 | 0.91 | 0.83 | 1.30 | 0.32 | 0.22 | 0.15 | 1.03 | 1.94 |
| TASL | 2.77 | 1.26 | 0.37 | 0.63 | 0.32 | 0.64 | -0.09 | 0.63 | 1.01 |
| **Discriminant Z Score** | **2.05** | **1.02** | **1.16** | **2.06** | **0.55** | **0.72** | **0.97** | **0.97** | **1.65** |

***Source:*** Computed.

## TABLE 18.6

## CLASSIFICATION MATRIX

| Year | As per current Ratio | | As per Discriminant Score | |
|---|---|---|---|---|
| | Adequate | Inadequate | Adequate | Inadequate |
| 1982-83 | 7 | 3 | 6 | 4 |
| 1983-84 | 5 | 5 | 4 | 6 |
| 1984-85 | 4 | 6 | 5 | 5 |
| 1985-86 | 4 | 6 | 4 | 6 |
| 1986-87 | 5 | 5 | 4 | 6 |
| 1987-89 | 4 | 6 | 4 | 6 |
| 1989-90 | 3 | 7 | 3 | 7 |
| 1990-91 | 7 | 3 | 6 | 4 |
| 1991-92 | 9 | 1 | 7 | 3 |
| 1992-93 | 8 | 2 | 7 | 3 |
| 1993-94 | 9 | 1 | 8 | 2 |

***Source:*** Computed

# PART - VI

# ANALYSIS OF CAPITAL STRUCTURE

# 19

# An Empirical Investigation of the Trade-off and Pecking Order Hypotheses on Indian Automobile Firms

The pioneering paper published in 1958 by Merton Miller and Franco Modigliani is considered the cornerstone of modern corporate finance and capital structure analysis. The provocative M&M Theorem provides the conditions under which a firm's financing decisions do not affect its value. It states that, in a perfect capital market, in the absence of taxes, transaction costs, bankruptcy costs and asymmetric information, the value of a firm is unaffected by how that firm is financed. It does not matter if the firm's capital raised by issuing stock or selling debt. It does not matter what the firms' dividend policy is. In a subsequent paper (1963), they eased the initial assumptions and stated that under capital market imperfections (if the financial markets are competitive and corporations are taxed) the value of the levered firm equals that of unlevered firm plus the value of debt tax shield, due to the preferential treatment of debt relative to equity. So the firm's optimal capital structure is determined by the trade-off between the tax advantage associated with debt and the increased bankruptcy risk associated with the higher leverage. This statement predicts that financial leverage and economic performance are in a proportional relationship.

Due to the reflections on MM Theorem, the issue of capital structure has generated unforeseen interest among financial researchers. The results of empirical studies suggested over time that the determination of the optimal capital structure should take into consideration a trade-off between benefits and costs derived from debts. Thus, theories suggest that capital structure affects company's value. Although many empirical studies have been done since the Miller and Modigliani Theorem forms the bases for modern thinking on capital structure, no consensus has been reached with regard to the relationship between profitability and leverage. The three most significant theories that aim to explain the correlation between capital structure and the market value of the firm are the Static Trade-off Theory (STT), Pecking Order Theory (POT) and Market timing models.

## STATIC TRADE-OFF THEORY

The essence of the Static Trade-off Theory is that a value maximising firm will consider the trade-off between the tax shelter provided by debt and the cost financial distress. (Brealey and Myers, 2003). The earliest version of this theory was elaborated by Kraus and Litzenberger (1973) and states that the optimal debt-equity ratio balances the corporate tax advantages of debt against the cost disadvantages of bankruptcy. Firm's adopting this theory could be regarded as setting a target debt-to-value ratio, and would continuously and gradually adjust their capital structures toward this target in order to maximise the firm's value. Hence, if firms seek external financing, they should issue equity when their leverage is above the desired target leverage, issue debt when their leverage is below the target or issue debt and equity proportionately to stay close to the target.

Myers (1984), however, suggests that when the firm's equity is under priced in the market, managers are reluctant to issue equity. The consequence is that potential investors tend to react negatively to an equity issue, because they perceive equity issues to only occur if equity is either fairly priced or overpriced, which conjuncture is not a benefit one to buy the firm's securities. As a result, managers are reluctant to issue equity. In conclusion, according to Static-Trade-off Theory (STT), highly profitable corporations with stable, tangible assets tend to have higher target gearing ratios as their assets are relatively safe. In contrast, companies with mostly intangible and risky assets tend to have lower debt-equity ratio and rely more heavily on equity financing. The trade-off theory fails to explain the simple empirical evidence that more profitable firms have lower leverage, and the use of debt decreases with profitability.

## PECKING ORDER THEORY

Although the trade-off theory has dominated corporate finance circles for a long time, interest is also being paid to the pecking order theory. An intriguing approach to studying the optimal capital structure is the so called Pecking Order Theory (POT) (Donaldson, 1961; Myers and Majluf, 1984; Myers, 1984) constructed on the information asymmetry hypothesis, which suggests that there is no optimal capital structure. It states that because of asymmetries of information between insiders (managers) and outside lenders and investors, the companies prioritize their sources of financing, and establish a hierarchical order according to the law of least effort or of least resistance. Myers and Majluf (1984) assumed that a firm is undervalued because managers have, but cannot reveal, information concerning new and existing investment opportunities. Investors are aware of this asymmetric information problem and they discount the firm's new and existing risky securities when stock issues are announced. On the other side, managers avoid issuing undervalued securities by financing projects with retained earnings and with low-risk debt.

Myers (1984) suggested that the costs of issuing risky debt or equity overwhelm the forces that determine optimal leverage in the trade-off model. The result is the pecking order model, which states that firm finance investments first with retained earnings, then with safe debt, then with risky debt and finally with equity. In conclusion, according to Pecking Order Theory, more profitable firms borrow less, because they have more internal financing available and less profitable firms require external financing, and consequently accumulated debt. However, a number of studies reveal that pecking order theories are not sufficient to explain all capital structure choices (Fama and French, 2002).

Thus, POT implies that profitable companies would usually not opt for debt financing for their new projects because of the availability of sizeable amounts of internal funds. However, as per STT, profitable companies would give preference to the use of debt financing in view of the attraction of tax shield benefit available on borrowed funds. Thus, STT predicts that there would be a direct relationship between profitability and leverage, while POT expects the opposite i.e., an inverse relationship between them.

## THE MARKET TIMING THEORY

The third theory, the Market Timing Theory (MTT) **(Baker and Wurgler, 2002)** based on the corporate mispricing, provides a new explanation to the financing decisions of the firm and challenges both the Trade-off and the Pecking Order theories. The model suggests that manager's recourse to equity issuance in time periods during which the company's stock have high market values relative to their book and past market values. This lowers the firm's cost of equity and benefits current shareholders at the expense of new shareholders. According to this theory, the equity issuing decisions is guided by the managers' capability to time the market accordingly to the relative cost of debt and equity.

## LEVERAGE AND PROFITABILITY – LITERATURE REVIEW

Over the past several decades corporate finance researchers have devoted considerable efforts to transform rationalism of capital structure in to empiricism. The problem of developing a definite theory of capital structure and designing empirical tests those are powerful enough to provide a basis for choosing among the various theories is still unresolved.

The available literature on leverage and profitability depicts a great deal of theoretical controversies. The pecking order theorists Myers (1984), Myers and Majluf (1984) and Shyamsunder and Myers (1999) states that firms have a preference of using internal sources of financing first, then debt and finally external equity obtained by stock issues. The preferences are attributed to the cost gap between internal and external funds due to asymmetric information and agency problems. Holding it true profitable firms prefer capitalisation of earnings over debt and new equity issues respectively. This tendency portrays negative association between leverage and profitability of the firm. This association is one of the most systematic findings in the empirical literature. (Kester, 1986; Harris and Raviv, 1991; Rajan and Zingales, 1995; Kester and Kolb, 1991; Larry et al., 1995; Nikolaos P. Eriotis, 2000; Both et al., 2001; Zhang et al., 2002; Bevan and Danbolt, 2004; Tong and Green, 2005; Fraser et al., 2006; Huang and Song, 2006; Martin Hovey, 2007; Mahdi Salehi, 2009; Gabriela Michalea and Raluca Antal, 2009), their findings suggest that firms follow a pecking order. Whenever possible firms raise finance preferably from their internal sources, rather than bank loans and debt issue. The external equity financing is there last resort.

A study of South Arabia by Sulaiman A. Al-Sakran (2001) where debt do not offer any tax shield, also reported a negative relationship between profitability and leverage. Well known Agency Cost theory (Jensen and Meckling, 1976) also tends to support this relationship. Booth, Aivaizian, Kunt and Maksimovik (2001) documented that more profitable is firm, the lower the debt ratio regardless of how debt ratio is defined. Using a large sample of firms from 1979 to 1997, Hovakimian, Opler and Titman (2001) found that profitable firms have a lower leverage than less profitable firms.

On the other hand in accordance with Trade-off theory in opposite relationship may also be envisaged. Various researchers have analysed different types of trade-offs between capital structure and corporate taxes (Modigliani and Miller, 1963; Miller, 1977), personal taxes (De Angelo and Masulis, 1980), bankruptcy costs (Stiglitz, 1972; Titman, 1984), agency costs (Jensen and Meckling, 1976; Myers, 1977), and information asymmetry (Myers and Majluf, 1984). The stated rational is when firms are profitable they prefer debt to benefit from the tax shield [Mseddi and Abid, 2004; Sohail Amjed, 2007 and Mahdi Salehi, 2009). Other way around profitability is a good proxy for low default risk in consequence profitable firms can borrow more funds at cheaper rates as the likelihood of paying back the debt is greater. Firms use debt financing to dilute their cost of capital due to low Weighted Average Cost of Capital (WACC) firms have wider spans of acceptance for capital budgeting choices. Employment of low cost of capital in productive investment avenues enables firms to magnify their profits. The underlying supposition dictates positive relationship between leverage and profitability.

S. Klien, O'Brien and Peters (2002) argued that firms with lower expected cash flows find it more difficult to incur higher level of debt than do firms with higher level of expected cash flows. Companies with large and stable profits should, all else equal, make greater use of debt to take advantage of interest tax shields (Anil and Marc Zenner, 2005). Jensen (1986) reported that profitable firms might signal quality by leveraging up, resulting in a positive relation between leverage and profitability. Joshua Arbor (2005) reported significantly positive relationship between short-term debt and profitability and negative association between long-term debt and profitability. This shows that an increase in the long-term debt position is associated with a decrease in profitability.

Further, the empirical study of Fama and French (2002) realised on a large panel of firms from 1965 to 1999 reveals support for both theories. Long and Malitz (1985) found no relationship between capital structure and profitability. Based on previous literature, it is difficult to make a clear cut prediction of leverage effects on the firms' profitability. Firms may use their debt-to-equity ratio to affect profitability. Some firms choose a high debt-to-equity ratio, whereas others prefer to choose a lower one. The successful selection and use of the debt-to-equity ratio is one of the key elements of the firms' financial strategy. Empirical studies carried out found either a positive or a negative impact of leverage on firms' profitability. Thus, from this theoretical background, the researcher advances the following hypothesis.

## $H_0$-THERE IS POSITIVE RELATIONSHIP BETWEEN LEVERAGE AND PROFITABILITY.

Thus, the purpose of the paper is to determine for Indian automobile firms support one of the theories of capital structure. The remainder of the paper is organized as follows. Section II presents the variables of the designed model, the data used in order to test the model and the empirical results. Section III presents the conclusions of this study.

## VARIABLES OF THE MODEL

### 2.1 The dependent variable

In the regression, the dependent variable is financial leverage, which is the debt to equity ratio of each firm as measured by the book value of total debt divided by the equity. The main differences among leverage proxies concern the use of book values versus market values and total debt versus only long-term debt. Because of data limitations, the study uses the book values rather than market values. Also, because most of the existing studies focus on a single measure of leverage and the most common measure of debt is total debt, the study defines the Financial Leverage ($D_i$) as the ratio between the book value of total debt and the book value of equity (Rajan and Zingales, 1995; De Miguel and Pindado, 2001; Nivorozhkin, 2005)

**2.2 Explanatory variables**

The study select the explanatory variables which affect the target leverage of firms based on the assumptions of trade-off and pecking order theories of capital structure and on previous empirical work in this area.

The first explanatory variable is Tangibility (TANG) calculated as the ratio between tangible fixed assets and total assets. Tangible assets serve as collateral and the importance of collateral is greater for newly established businesses with no close ties to creditors. Indeed, the results for developed countries (Rajan and Zingales, 1995; Titman and Wessels, 1988) confirm this hypothesis. In transitions, economies, the importance of tangible assets as collateral is limited by a number of factors (underdeveloped and inefficient legal systems, illiquid secondary market) and a negative relationship between leverage and tangibility has been found in some previous studies (Cornelli et al., 1998; Nivorozhkin 2002). Based on the aforementioned arguments, the study expects to find a negative relationship between leverage and tangibility.

Another determinant of optimal capital structure used in many studies (Titman and Wessels, 1988; Rajan and Zingales, 1995; Fama and Jensen, 1983; Nivorozhkin, 2005) is the firm's size. Large firms are more likely to be debt-financed in comparison with smaller firms and that is because of several reasons. One of the reasons is mentioned by Rajan and Zingales (1995) who suggested that larger firms tend to be more diversified and thus, less prone to bankruptcy. Another reason is stipulated by the pecking order hypothesis which states that larger firms exhibit lower information asymmetry with financial markets and therefore they are able to issue more equity compared to small companies. The positive relationship between the size of a firm and its leverage may be reinforced in transition economies. The firm size (SIZE) can be measured either through the number of employee or through net sales. Because the net sales are a more appropriate proxy, the study uses the natural logarithm of net sales (Ln sales) and predicts a positive relationship between size and leverage.

The theories of capital structure state that market imperfections lead to the relevance of a firm's profitability (PROF) for its choice of leverage. The pecking order theory predicts that more profitable firms will have a lower debt ratio. In contrast to the pecking order theory, the static trade-off theory predicts a positive relationship between leverage and profitability because higher profitability implies more income to shield. The study uses the Profit rate on total assets (PR) for firm's profitability and expects to find a negative relationship between leverage and profitability.

Mylers (1977) observed that high growth firms may hold more options for future investments than low growth firms. This statement is congruent with the Pecking order theory, which argues that high growth firms should use less debt for financing. Furthermore, according to the trade-off theory, firms with great growth opportunities (GROW) tend to borrow less than firms holding more tangible assets, because growth opportunities cannot serve as tangible assets. The study defines this proxy as sales growth. However, the firm's profitability positively related to sales growth.

A large non-debt tax shield reduces the expected value of interest tax sav'ngs and lessens the advantages of debt financing. Biger, Nguyen and Hoang (2008) consider the tax deduction for depreciation and investment tax credits as non-debt tax shield (NDTS). **De Angelo and Masulis (1980)** also suggest that tax deductions for depreciation and investment tax credits substitute the tax deduction of debt financing. The study use the ratio of depreciation to total assets as a proxy for NDTS and expected leverage negatively correlated with NDTS.

In summary, literature review shows that Tangibility, Size, Profitability, Growth and Non-debt tax shield are the determinants of capital structure. The basic regression model used in order to estimate the co-efficients of the determinants of capital structure is as it follows:

$$\mathbf{D_{it} = \beta_0 + \beta_1\ Tangibility_{it} + \beta_2\ Size_{it} + \beta_3\ Growth_{it} + \beta_4 Profitability_{it} + \beta_5\ Non\text{-}debt\ Tax\ Shield_{it} + e_{it}}$$

Where,

| | |
|---|---|
| $D_{it}$ | – Measures leverage as the ratio of Total debt to Equity for firm (i) in the year (t) |
| Tangibil:'ty | – Measures as the ratio tangible fixed assets and total assets for firm (i) in the year (t) |
| Size | – Natural logarithm of firm's sales for firm (i) in the year (t) |
| Growth | – Growth of firm's sales for firm (i) in the year (t) |
| Profitability | – Measures the firm profitability with gross profit as a percentage of total assets for firm (i) in the year (t) |
| Non-Debt Tax Shield | – The ratio of depreciation to total assets for firm (i) in the year (t) |
| $\beta_0$ | – Constant term for firm (i) in the year (t). |
| $\beta_1, \beta_2$.... | – Regression Co-efficients |
| e | – disturbance term for firm (i) in the year (t). |

Table 19.1 below summarizes the determinants of capital structure, definitions and theoretical predicted signs.

**TABLE 19.1**

**PROXY VARIABLES DEFINITION AND PREDICTED RELATIONSHIPS**

| Proxy variables | Definitions | Predicted sign |
|---|---|---|
| Tangibility | The ratio of tangible fixed assets and total assets | + |
| Size | Natural logarithm of firm's sales | + / - |
| Growth | Differences between current year sales and previous year sales divided by previous year sales | + / - |
| Profitability | Gross Profit as a percentage of total assets | + / - |
| Non-Debt Tax Shield | Ratio of Depreciation to total assets | - |

## HYPOTHESIS

In this part, three capital structure respective hypotheses have been formulated in light of Agency Cost theory, Static Trade-off theory and Pecking order theory. The first hypothesis is formulated for Agency cost theory. Second hypothesis is formulated for Static Trade-off theory. Third Hypothesis is formulated for Pecking Order theory. The hypotheses are tested to find which of those theories are relevant for Indian Automobile firms. Null hypothesis ($H_0$) is rejected if result is significant at 1 per cent or 5 per cent or 10 per cent, otherwise alternative hypothesis ($H_a$) is accepted.

### Hypothesis 1

$H_0$ – There is negative relationship between leverage and size.

$H_a$ – There is positive relationship between leverage and size.

**Hypothesis 2**

***H2a:***

$H_o$- There is negative relationship between leverage and size.

$H_a$ – There is positive relationship between leverage and size.

***H2b:***

$H_o$ – There is negative relationship between leverage and the value of tangible assets.

$H_a$ – There is positive relationship between leverage and the value of tangible assets.

***H2c:***

$H_o$ – There is negative relationship between leverage and non-debt tax shield.

$H_a$ – There is positive relationship between leverage and non-debt tax shield.

**Hypothesis 3**

***H3a:***

$H_o$- There is negative relationship between leverage and growth.

$H_a$ – There is positive relationship between leverage and growth.

***H3b:***

$H_o$ – There is positive relationship between leverage and profitability.

$H_a$ – There is negative relationship between leverage and profitability.

***H3c:***

$H_o$ – There is positive relationship between leverage and value of tangible assets.

$H_a$ – There is negative relationship between leverage and value of tangible assets.

## SAMPLING DESIGN

Keeping in view the scope of the study, it is decided to include all the companies under automobile industry working before or from the year 1996-97 to 2008-09. There are 26 companies operating in the Indian automobile industry. But, owing to several constraints such as non-availability of financial statements or non-working of a company in a particular year etc., it is compelled to restrict the number of sample companies to 20. The companies under automobile industry are classified into three sectors namely; Commercial vehicles, Passenger cars and Multi-utility vehicles and Two and three wheelers. For the purpose of the study all the three sectors have been selected. It accounts for 73.23 per cent of the total companies available in the Indian automobile industry. The selected 20 companies include 5 under commercial vehicles, 6 under passenger cars and multi-utility vehicles and 9 under two and three wheeler sectors. It is inferred that sample company represents 98.74 percentage of market share in commercial vehicles, 89.76 percentage of market share in passenger cars and Multi-utility vehicles and 99.81 percentage of market share in two and three wheelers. Thus, the findings based on the occurrence of such representative sample may be presumed to be true representative of automobile industry in the country.

The study is mainly based on secondary data. The major source of data analysed and interpreted in this study related to all those companies selected is collected from "PROWESS" database, which is the most reliable on the empowered corporate database of Centre for Monitoring Indian Economy (CMIE). Besides prowess database, relevant secondary data have also been collected from BSE Stock Exchange Official Directory, CMIE Publications, Annual Survey of Industry, Business newspapers, Reports on Currency and Finance, Libraries of various Research Institutions, through Internet etc.

## ANALYSIS AND DISCUSSION OF RESULTS

### Descriptive Statistics and Analysis:

The descriptive statistics for the dependent variable and the explanatory variables of the model are presented in Table 19.2. Descriptive statistics includes the mean, standard deviation, standard error of mean, median, minimum and maximum values, kurtosis and skewness for the period 1996-2009 for 20 Indian automobile firms. The table shows that there are negative values at minimum values i.e., some companies have operated with losses during the period 1996-2009. Table 19.2 reveals that leverage ranges between 0 to 41.37, with mean of 1.39 and a standard deviation 3.18. As for PR, it ranges between -189.39 to 1638.92, with a mean of 22.29 and a standard deviation of 105.3. The same applies to Tangibility, Growth and Non-Debt Tax shield, which show that the standard deviation is more than the mean. This implies that there is a high variation in the companies mean. The table also reveals that Leverage, Tangibility, PR, Growth and Non-Debt Tax shield have a positive skewness, which indicates that the scores are clustered to the left at the low values. As for Ln sales have a negative skewness indicating clustering of scores are at the high end. As far the Kurtosis statistic, all variables show a positive kurtosis suggesting that the distribution has peaked or clustered in the centre, with long thin tails.

### Correlation Analysis

A correlation analysis was performed to verify a possible association between and among the variables, in order to test whether there is any linear correlation between and among the variables. Collinearity explains the dependence of one variable to other. When variables are highly correlated they both express essentially the same information. In general, independent variables having collinearity at 0.70 or greater should not include in regression analysis. Table 19.3 reports the Pearson correlation co-efficients of all the variables employed in the study. Simple correlations among the variables that are reported in Table 19.3 are quite low. The largest reported value (-0.32) was between Non-Debt Tax shield and Ln sales (size). In this respect, Kennedy 1985 suggests that correlation values below 0.70 do not pose a potential multicollinearity problem. Hence, colllinearity should not appear problem in our regression analysis.

**Regression Results**

A multiple regression analysis has been performed to estimate the co-efficients and the direction of relationship between the dependent variable and the independent variables in the specified model in the study. Table 4 shows the stepwise regression results for the model estimated in the study. R-square (co-efficient determination) measures the proportion of the variance jointly explained by the explanatory variables. Adjusted R-square attempts to compensate for this automatic upward shift by imposing a penalty for increasing the number of explanatory variables. The maximum value of R-square is 1. This occurs when the regression line fits the observations exactly. The closer the R-square is to 1, the "better" the overall fit of the estimated regression equation to the actual data. With time series data, R-squared are often in excess of 0.9; with the cross – sectional data, 0.5 might be considered a reasonable good fit (Baye 2005).

It can be observed from the table that R-Square explains 85 per cent of the variation in leverage can be captured by independent variables for Indian automobile industry, respectively 87 per cent for Commercial vehicles sector, 94 per cent for Passenger cars and Multiutility vehicles sector and 95 percent for Two and Three wheeler sectors. The rest of leverage's variance is due to factors other than determinants studied in this article. Among the selected automobile firms, R-Square ranges between 68 per cent and 97 per cent for commercial vehicles sector, 55 per cent to 91 per cent for passenger cars and multiutility vehicles sector and 36 per cent to 96 per cent for two and three wheelers sector. F- Statistic provides a measure of the total variations explained by the regression relative to the total unexplained variation. The greater the F – statistic, the better the overall fit of the regression line through the actual data. Regression that has F- statistics with significant values of 10 per cent or less are generally considered significant. In our case, F- statistic shows that overall models are significant except Hindustan Motors Ltd under passenger cars and multi-utility vehicles sector and Bajaj Auto Ltd, Kinetic Engineering Ltd and Majestic Auto Limited under two and three wheelers sector.

First, there seems to be a mixed relationship between the share of tangible assets and leverage. Theoretically, firms with large amounts of tangible assets probably already own a stable source of return that pushes them to resort to internal funds rather than debt. Theoretical research predicts positive relationship between tangibility and leverage. The empirical analysis showed that there is a positive relationship between tangibility and leverage in the Indian automobile industry, commercial vehicle sector and passenger cars and Multi-utility vehicles sector. These finding are consistent with those of Titman and Wessels (1988) as well as with those of Ozkan (2000) who found a positive relationship between the tangibility and leverage. This evidence supports the trade-off hypothesis, which states that tangible assets are used as collateral. However, in case of two and three wheelers sector, this relationship is positive. This finding supports the pecking order prediction which states that the firms with high proportions of tangible assets are more likely to have a lower debt ratio. These findings are consistent with those of Both et al (2001) have found a negative relationship between tangibility and leverage. Among the selected firms, 3 out of 5 firms in commercial vehicles sector (Ashok Leyland Ltd, Tata Motors Ltd and Eicher Motors Ltd), 3 out of 6 firms in passenger cars and multi-utility vehicles sector (Mahindra and Mahindra Ltd, Hyundai India Ltd and Honda Siel Ltd), and 5 out of 9 firms in two and three wheeler sector (Bajaj Auto Ltd, Maharashtra Scooters Ltd, TVS Motor company Ltd,

Kinetic Engineering Ltd and Majestic Auto Ltd) showed the negative relationship between tangibility and leverage which supports Pecking order hypothesis. In the remaining firms, this relationship is positive which supports the trade-off hypothesis.

Second, the relationship between size and leverage appears to be statistically significant but with a negative sign in the Indian automobile industry, commercial vehicles sector, passenger cars and multi-utility vehicles sector and two and three wheelers sector. This estimate indicates that small manufacturing firms are relatively more indebted compared to larger firms. These findings are inconsistent with those of Rajan and Zingales (1995) and Booth et al. (2001) who found a positive relationship between size and leverage. However, among the selected firms, Hindustan Motors Ltd, Hyundai India Ltd and Honda Siel Ltd under passenger cars and multi-utility vehicles sector and LML Ltd, Maharashtra Scooters Ltd and Scooters India Ltd in two and three wheelers sectors, the relationship between the firm size and leverage is positive and statistically significant. One interpretation of this positive relationship is that the banks tend to favour large firms, giving those credits, due to the fact that they seem to be more credible.

As far as profitability is concerned, its relationship with leverage turns out to be negative and statistically significant in Indian automobile industry, commercial vehicles sector, passenger cars and multi-utility vehicles sector and two and three wheelers sector. The negative co-efficient indicates that firms with more profitable projects are prone to use internally generated funds rather than debt. This result is explained by the Pecking order prediction which states that firms prefer internal to external financing and debt to equity. This finding provides evidence supporting "the Pecking order theory" suggested by Myers and Majluf (1984) that firms prefer internal funding and turn to external resources as a secondary option. It should be emphasized that Rajan and Zingales (1995) and Booth et al. (2001) found similar results respectively for OECD countries and listed companies in developed countries. However, among the selected automobile firms, Swaraj Mazda Ltd under commercial vehicles sector and Maharashtra Scooters Ltd, Hero Honda Motors Ltd and Scooters India Ltd under two and three wheelers sector showed its relationship with leverage turns out to be positive. These findings are consistent with the finding of Long and Maltiz (1985) in which they indicate the positive relationship between leverage and the profitability.

Growth potential is another relevant explanatory variable of capital structure choice of Indian automobile industry. The estimates show that the growth potential is positively associated to leverage. The relationship appears to be statistically significant in few cases only. The estimates are in line with the hypothesis according to which firms with promising growth prospects tend to exhaust their internal funds and to resort more intensively to debt.

Finally, the relationship between Non-Debt Tax shield and Leverage appears to be negative in the majority of the selected Indian automobile firms as shown in the regression of Table 19.4. This finding is also in line with those of Biger, Nguyen and Hoang (2008) and De Angelo and Masulis (1980). These studies find that leverage is negatively correlated with Non-Debt Tax Shield. This shows that a large non-debt tax shield reduces the expected value of interest tax savings and lessens the advantage of debt financing.

## DISCUSSION OF RESULTS

In this section, an attempt has been made to discuss obtained results in terms of the signs and statistically significance of the co-efficient for independent variables. Table below show obtained and expected signs for five independent variables at Indian automobile firms.

**TABLE 19.5**

**EXPECTED AND OBSERVED THEORETICAL SIGNS WITH INDEPENDENT VARIABLES**

| Proxy | Static-Trade off | Pecking order | Observed signs |
|---|---|---|---|
| Tangibility | + | -/+ | -/+ |
| Size | + | - | -/+ |
| Profitability | + | - | -/+ |
| Growth | - | + | -/+ |
| Non-Debt Tax Shield | +/- | ? | -/+ |

It is evident from the Table 19.5 that tangibility is negatively and positively associated with leverage and is consistent with implication of Pecking order theory for Indian automobile firms. Further, size is estimated to have both positive and negative impact on leverage. This is consistent with implications of Pecking order theory and Static Trade-off theory. Similarly profitability variable and growth variable also show both positive and negative impact on leverage, which is consistent with implications of Pecking order theory and Static Trade-off theory. Non-Debt tax shield is also showed both positive and negative impact on leverage, which is consistent with implications of Static Trade-off theory for Indian automobile firms.

## CONCLUDING REMARKS

This study examined the trade-off and pecking order hypotheses using a sample of 20 Indian automobile firms. According to trade-off theory, large firms with tangible assets tend to borrow more than small, risky firms with mostly intangible assets and firms with more profitable assets in place, fewer investments, less volatile earnings and net cash-flow have higher leverage. The Pecking order hypothesis predicts a negative correlation between leverage and profitability of the firms. The empirical findings suggest that there is a difference between capital structure choices for companies. The negative relationship between leverage and tangibility might be explained by the lack of long-term debt financing and contradicts the predictions of the trade-off theory. More profitable companies had less debt, because these firms use first of all, internally generated funds and debt as last resort. This result is compatible with the pecking order theory and contradicts the trade-off theory. The relationship between leverage and company size, leverage and profitability and leverage and growth showed both positive and negative impacts, which are compatible with both theories in the sample of Indian automobile firms. To conclude, the Pecking Order theory is more appropriate to explain the capital structure choice of the Indian automobile firms compared to Trade-off theory.

## REFERENCES

1. Anil Marc Zenner (2005). "How to choose a capital structure: Navigating the Debt-Equity Decisions", *Journal of Applied Corporate Finance*, Vol.17.
2. Barker, M. and Wurgler, J. (2002). "Market timing and capital structure", *Journal f Finance*, Vol.57, pp.1-32.
3. Brealey R. and Myers`S. (2003). "Principles of corporate finance", Mc Graw-Hill / Irwin.
4. Booth, L., V. Aivazian, A. Demirgue-Kunt and V. Maksimorie (2001). "Capital structures in developing countries", *Journal of Finance*, Vol.56 (1), pp.87-130.
5. Bevan, A.A. and J. Danbolt (2004). "Testing for inconsistencies in the estimation of UK capital structure determinants", *Applied Financial Economics*, Vol.14 (1), pp.55-56.
6. Bigger N, Nguyen NV and Hoang QX (2008). "The determinants of capital structure: evidence from Vietnam", *International Financial Review*, Vol.8, pp.307-26.
7. Donaldson, Gordon (1961). "Corporate Debt Capacity: a

study of corporate debt policy and the determination of corporate debt capacity", Graduate School of Business Administration, Harvard University.

8. De Angelo and Masulis (1980). "Optimal capital structure under corporate and personal taxation", *Journal of Financial Economics*, Vol.8.
9. Deloof, M. (2003). "Does working capital management affect profitability of firms", *Vikalpa*, Vol.28 (2), pp. 537-85.
10. David M. Mathuva (2009). "The influence of working capital management components on corporate profitability : a survey on Kenyan listed firms", *Research Journal of Business Management*, Vol.3, pp.1-11.
11. Eljelly and Abuzar M.A (2004). "Liquidity-profitability trade-off: an empirical investigation in an emerging market (Liquidity Management)", *International Journal of Commerce and Management.*
12. Fama, E.F. and French, K.R (2002). "Testing trade-off and pecking order predictions about dividends and debt", *Review of Financial Studies*, Vol.15, pp.1-33.
13. Fraser, D.R., H. Zhang and C. Derashid (2006). "Capital structure and political patronage: the case of Malaysia", *Journal of Banking and Finance*, Vol.30 (4), pp.1291-1308.
14. Fischer, E.O., R. Heinkel and J. Zechner (1989). "Dynamic capital structure choice: theory and tests", *Journal of Finance*, Vol.44, pp.19-40.
15. Gabriela Michalca and Raluca Antal (2009). "An empirical investigation of the trade-off and pecking order hypotheses on Romanian Market", The XIII International conference "Applied stochastic and models and data analysis", held at Vilnius, Lithuania on June 2009.
16. Garcia-Teruel, P.J. and Martinez-Solano, P. (2007). "Effects of working capital management on SME profitability", *International Journal of Managerial Finance*, Vol.3 (2), pp.164-177.

17. Harris and Raviv (1991). "The theory of capital structure", *Journal of Finance,* Vol.46.
18. Huang, G. and F.M. Song (2006). "The determinants of capital structure: evidence from China", *China Economic Review,* Vol.17 (1), pp.14-36.
19. Hovakimian, A., Opler, T. and Sheridan, T. (2001). "The debt-equity choice", *Journal of Financial and Quantitative Analysis,* Vol.36, pp.1-24.
20. Hart, O. and J. Moore (1995). "Debt and Seniority: an analysis of the role of hard claims in constraining management", *American Economic Review*, Vol.85, pp.567-585.
21. Jensen, M. and W.Meckling (1976)."Theory of the firm: managerial behaviour, agency costs and ownership structure", *Journal of Financial Economics,* Vol.3
22. Jensen, M. (1986). "Agency costs of free cash flow corporate finance and takeovers", *American Economic Review,* Vol.76.
23. Joshua Arbor (2005). "The effect of capital structure on profitability: an empirical analysis of listed firms in Ghana", *The Journal of Risk Finance,* Vol.6 (5).
24. Kester (1986). "Capital and ownership structure a comparison of US and Japanese manufacturing corporations", *Financial Management,* Vol.15.
25. Kraus and Litzenberger (1973). "A state preference model of optimal financial structure", *Journal of Finance,* Vol.28.
26. Kester,W.C and R.W. Kolb (1991). "Capital and ownership structure: a comparison of US and Japanese manufacturing corporation", Harvard Business School.
27. Klien, S. O'Brien and Peters (2002). "Debt vs. Equity and asymmetric information: a review", *The Financial Review,* Vol.37.
28. Kuldip Kaur and Kushwinder Kaur (2008). "Growth and profitability of acquiring firms in India; an analysis , Paper presented at Guru Nanak Dev University, Punjab.

29. Larry, L., E.Ofek and R. Stulz (1995). "Leverage investment and firm growth", *Journal of Financial Economics,* Vol.40, pp.3-29.

30. Long M, Maltyz E. (1985). "The investment financing nexus: some empirical evidence", *Midland Corporation Finance Journal,* Vol.3, pp.53-9.

31. Myers (1984). "The capital structure puzzel", *Journal of Financial Economics,* Vol.39.

32. Myers, S. and Majluf, N. (1984). "Corporate financing and investment decisions when firm have information investors do not have", *Journal of Financial Economics,* Vol.13, pp.187-222.

33. Martin Hovey (2007). "Leverage, profitability and ownership structures of listed firms in China", Source http://ssrn.com/abstract = 1009432.

34. Mahdi Salehi (2009). "Study of the relationship between capital structure measures and performance: evidence form Iran", *International Journal of Business and Management,* Vol.4 (1), pp.97-103.

35. Modigliani and Miller (1963). "Taxes and the cost of capital: a correction", *American Economic Review,* Vol.53.

36. Miller, Merton H. (1977). "Debt and taxes", *Journal of Finance,* Vol.32, pp.261-275.

37. Mseddi, S. and Abid, F. (2004). "The impact of operating and financial leverages and intrinsic business risk on firm value", International conference AFFI 2004 at Cergy Ponthoise.

38. Nikolaos P. Eriotis (2000). "Profit margin and capital structure: an empirical relationship", *The Journal of Applied Business Research,* Vol.18(2), pp.85-88.

39. Padachi, K. (2006). "Trends in working capital management and its impact on firms performance: an analysis of Mauritian small manufacturing firms", *International Re·iew of Business Research Papers,* Vol. 2(2), pp.45-58.

40. Rajan, R.G. and Zingales, L. (1995). "What do we know

about capital structure? Some evidence from international data", *Journal of Finance*, Vol.50(5), pp.1421-1460.

41. Raheman, A. and M. Nasr (2007). "Working capital management and profitability: case of Pakistani firms", *International Review of Business Research*, Vol.3(2), pp.275-96.
42. Shyam-Sunder, L. and Myers, S.C (1999). "Testing static trade-off against pecking order models of capital structure", *Journal of Financial Economics*, Vol.51, pp.219-244.
43. Sulaiman A.Al-Sahran (2001). "Leverage determinants in the absence of corporate tax system: the case of non-financial publicly traded corporations in Saudi Arabia", *Managerial Finance*, Vol.27.
44. Stiglitz, J.E (1972). "Some aspects of the pure theory of corporate finance: bankruptcies and takeovers", *Bell Journal of Economics and Management Science*, Vol.3(2), pp.458-482.
45. Sohail Amjed (2007). "The impact of financial structure on profitability: study of Pakistan's Textile Sector", MIBES, 2007.
46. Samuels, J. M. and Smyth, D.J. (1968). "Profits, Variability of Profits and Firm size," *Economica*, Vol. 35, pp. 127-139.
47. Strebulaev, I.A (2003). "Do tests of capital structure theory mean what they say?", Working Paper, London Business School.
48. Shin, H.H and Soenen, L. (1998). "Efficiency of working capital and corporate profitability", *Financial Practice and Education*, Vol.8 (2), pp.37-45.
49. Titman, Sheridan (1984). "The effect of capital structure on a firm's liquidation decision", *Journal of Financial Economics*, Vol.13, pp.1371-1375.
50. Tong, G. and C.J. Green (2005). "Pecking order or trade-off hypothesis? Evidence on the capital structure of Chinese companies", *Applied Economics*, Vol.37 (19), pp.2179-2189.

51. Vijayakumar, A. (2002). "Determinants of Profitability- A firm level study of the sugar industry of Tamil Nadu", *The Management Accountant*, pp. 458-465.

52. Zelia Serrasqueiro (2009). "Growth and Profitability in Portuguese companies: A dynamic panel data approach", *Economic Interferences*, Vol.XI (26);, pp.265-279.

**TABLE 19.2**

**DESCRIPTIVE STATISTICS OF INDEPENDENT, DEPENDENT AND CONTROL VARIABLES**

**20 Indian Automobile Firms, 1996 – 2009 – 216 Firm - Year observations (N = 216)**

| *Variables* | *Mean ± S.D* | *Standard Error of mean* | *Median* | *Minimum* | *Maximum* | *kurtosis* | *Skewness* |
|---|---|---|---|---|---|---|---|
| Leverage | 1.39 ± 3.18 | 0.20 | 0.71 | 0 | 41.37 | 106.68 | 9.18 |
| Tangibility | 0.58 ± 1.06 | 0.07 | 0.50 | 0.04 | 16.95 | 226.91 | 14.64 |
| Ln Sales | 6.90 ± 1.70 | 0.11 | 6.86 | 0.92 | 10.39 | 0.01 | -0.27 |
| PR | 22.29 ± 105.3 | 6.62 | 14.58 | -189.39 | 1638.92 | 222.83 | 14.44 |
| Growth | 10.60 ± 36.83 | 2.32 | 10.13 | -97.62 | 356.66 | 31.46 | 3.48 |
| Non – debt Tax shield | 0.35 ± 1.38 | 0.09 | 0.06 | 0.01 | 9.76 | 27.24 | 5.22 |

***Notes :*** Leverage-Total debt to equity ratio; Tangibility- Ratio between tangible fixed assets and total assets ; Ln sales-Natural logarithm of sales (proxy for size); Growth-Sales Growth; PR- Profit rate on total assets ; Non – debt tax shield- Ratio of depreciation total assets

***Source :*** Computed.

## TABLE 19.3

## CORRELATION MATRIX

| | Leverage | Tangibility | Ln sales | PR | Growth | Non-debt Tax Shield |
|---|---|---|---|---|---|---|
| Leverage | 1.00 | | | | | |
| Tangibility | -0.03 | 1.00 | | | | |
| Ln Sales | -0.09 | -0.25 | 1.00 | | | |
| PR | -0.03 | 0.03 | 0.03 | 1.00 | | |
| Growth | -0.01 | 0.05 | 0.05 | 0.01 | 1.00 | |
| Non – Debt Tax Shield | -0.06 | -0.08 | -0.32 | -0.03 | -0.03 | 1.00 |

***Notes :*** Leverage-Total debt to equity ratio; Tangibility- Ratio between tangible fixed assets and tot^l assets ; Ln sales-Natural logarithm of sales (proxy for size); Growth-Sales Growth; PR-Profit rate on total assets ; Non –debt tax shield- Ratio of depreciation total assets

***Source:*** Computed.

## TABLE 19.4

## RESULTS OF REGRESSION ANALYSIS – INDIAN AUTOMOBILE FIRMS

**[LEVERAGE = $\beta_0 + \beta_1$ TANGIBILITY + $\beta_2$ SIZE + $\beta_3$ PROFITABILITY + $\beta_4$ GROWTH + $\beta_5$ NON-DEBT TAX SHIELD]**

| Particulars | Constant | Tangibility | Size | Profitability | Growth | Non-Tax Shield | $R^2$ | Adj$R^2$ | FValue | DW |
|---|---|---|---|---|---|---|---|---|---|---|
| Ashok Leyland Ltd | 3.34 | -0.72<br>(3.16)* | -0.24<br>(2.45)** | -0.01<br>(3.08)** | 0.03<br>(2.26)** | -6.48<br>(0.84) | 0.91 | 0.84 | 13.63* | 1.91 |
| Tata Motors Ltd | 1.79 | - 1.83<br>(3.14)** | -0.03<br>(0.85) | -0.03<br>(6.80)* | 0.01<br>(1.16) | 12.11<br>(2.60)** | 0.97 | 0.96 | 52.52* | 1.82 |
| Bajaj Tempo Ltd | 5.36 | 5.44<br>(6.30)* | -0.89<br>(3.07)** | -0.01<br>(3.63)* | 0.01<br>(1.56) | -9.13<br>(5.15)* | 0.93 | 0.89 | 19.59* | 1.95 |
| Eicher Motors Ltd | 1.39 | - 0.22<br>(0.36) | -0.11<br>(0.95) | -0.01<br>(1.36) | 0.01<br>(2.62)** | 2.48<br>(0.38) | 0.68 | 0.59 | 3.92*** | 1.39 |
| Swaraj Mazder Ltd | 19.65 | 4.83<br>(0.16) | -2.36<br>(3.68)* | 0.04<br>(0.39) | 0.03<br>(2.67)** | -9.74<br>(0.99) | 0.70 | 0.59 | 3.48*** | 1.80 |
| **Commercial Vehicle** | **3.21** | **0.10<br>(3.09)**** | **-0.18<br>(2.44)**** | **-0.04<br>(2.12)**** | **0.01<br>(0.22)** | **-3.50<br>(0.62)** | **0.87** | **0.77** | **9.17*** | **1.48** |
| Hindustan Motors Ltd | -13.32 | 0.77<br>(0.21) | 2.09<br>(1.92)*** | -0.05<br>(1.89)*** | 0.01<br>(0.54) | 16.95<br>(1.22) | 0.55 | 0.49 | 1.73 | 0.85 |
| Mahindra and Mahindra Ltd | 5.33 | - 7.31<br>(2.01)*** | -0.34<br>(2.46)** | -0.04<br>(2.33)** | 0.02<br>(2.02)*** | 34.78<br>(1.60) | 0.76 | 0.63 | 4.32** | 1.98 |

## TABLE 19.4 (CONTINUED)

## RESULTS OF REGRESSION ANALYSIS – INDIAN AUTOMOBILE FIRMS

**[LEVERAGE = $\beta_0 + \beta_1$ TANGIBILITY + $\beta_2$ SIZE + $\beta_3$ PROFITABILITY + $\beta_4$ GROWTH + $\beta_5$ NON-DEBT TAX SHIELD]**

| Particulars | Constant | Tangibility | Size | Profitability | Growth | Non-Tax Shield | $R^2$ | AdjR$^2$ | FValue | DW |
|---|---|---|---|---|---|---|---|---|---|---|
| Maruti Udyog Ltd | 0.33 | 0.26 (2.81)** | -0.02 (2.27)*** | -0.01 (2.24)*** | 0.03 (0.78) | -0.49 (0.43) | 0.79 | 0.63 | 5.11** | 1.93 |
| Hyundai India Ltd | 0.66 | -0.04 (3.24)* | 0.09 (3.59)* | -0.02 (3.13)** | 0.06 (0.26) | -1.66 (0.44) | 0.91 | 0.85 | 14.50* | 1.37 |
| Honda Siel Ltd | 0.02 | -0.03 (3.05)** | 0.04 (2.73)** | -0.01 (2.40)** | 0.03 (0.80) | 2.35 (1.19) | 0.72 | 0.65 | 4.52** | 1.77 |
| Ford India Ltd | 0.02 | 2.10 (5.13)* | -0.16 (3.38)* | -0.04 (1.44) | 0.03 (0.47) | 23.78 (3.09)** | 0.94 | 0.89 | 20.96* | 1.95 |
| **Passenger cars and Multi-utility Vehicles** | **4.98** | **0.23 (3.21)**** | **-0.36 (2.33)**** | **-0.03 (1.84)** | **0.01 (1.73)** | **-9.05 (2.47)**** | **0.94** | **0.89** | **20.56*** | **1.75** |
| Bajaj Auto Ltd | 1.98 | -1.85 (0.84) | -0.11 (1.23) | -0.01 (0.13) | 0.01 (0.74) | 5.71 (0.27) | 0.61 | 0.54 | 1.41 | 1.12 |
| LML Ltd | -5.79 | 0.15 (3.02)** | 1.38 (2.77)** | -0.07 (6.35)* | 0.01 (0.36) | -3.69 (1.86) | 0.88 | 0.80 | 10.32* | 1.80 |
| Maharastra Scooters Ltd | -0.01 | -0.68 (2.90)** | 0.03 (6.92)* | 0.01 (0.66) | 0.08 (2.99)** | 0.02 (4.06)* | 0.96 | 0.93 | 31.30* | 1.98 |

## TABLE 19.4 (CONTINUED)

## RESULTS OF REGRESSION ANALYSIS – INDIAN AUTOMOBILE FIRMS

**[LEVERAGE = $\beta_0 + \beta_1$ TANGIBILITY + $\beta_2$ SIZE + $\beta_3$ PROFITABILITY + $\beta_4$ GROWTH + $\beta_5$ NON-DEBT TAX SHIELD]**

| Particulars | Constant | Tangibility | Size | Profitability | Growth | Non-Tax Shield | $R^2$ | Adj$R^2$ | FValue | DW |
|---|---|---|---|---|---|---|---|---|---|---|
| TVS Motor Company Ltd | 3.09 | -1.17<br>(2.19)*** | -0.22<br>(1.90)*** | -0.03<br>(4.14)* | 0.01<br>(0.03) | 9.83<br>(2.17)*** | 0.90 | 0.82 | 12.13* | 1.60 |
| Kinetic Motor Company Ltd | 0.39 | 1.77<br>(5.37)* | -1.12<br>(0.15) | -0.01<br>(2.11)*** | 0.01<br>(3.11)** | -2.81<br>(1.96)*** | 0.85 | 0.80 | 7.89* | 1.98 |
| Hero Honda Motors Ltd | 3.12 | 0.03<br>(3.07)** | -0.25<br>(5.36)* | 0.03<br>(2.06)*** | 0.03<br>(1.07) | -17.23<br>(4.26)* | 0.96 | 0.93 | 30.54* | 1.99 |
| Kinetic Engineering Ltd | 25.76 | -4.83<br>(0.77) | -1.67<br>(0.13) | -0.13<br>(0.37) | -0.09<br>(0.25) | 8.52<br>(0.34) | 0.36 | 0.25 | 1.46 | 1.82 |
| Majestic Auto Ltd | 8.15 | -5.56<br>(1.17) | -0.63<br>(0.56) | -0.07<br>(2.74)** | -0.01<br>(0.56) | 28.70<br>(0.90) | 0.39 | 0.31 | 1.36 | 1.44 |
| Scooters India Ltd | -0.95 | 0.07<br>(3.18)** | 0.30<br>(3.43)* | 0.01<br>(3.42)* | 0.01<br>(0.72) | -0.07<br>(2.98)** | 0.86 | 0.81 | 9.31* | 1.78 |
| **Two & Three Wheelers** | **6.38** | **-1.42<br>(1.06)** | **-0.47<br>(5.02)*** | **-0.02<br>(1.98)***** | **0.01<br>(2.93)**** | **-16.60<br>(4.08)*** | **0.95** | **0.92** | **27.08*** | **1.72** |
| **Whole Industry** | **-0.03** | **4.79<br>(3.54)*** | **-0.04<br>(2.34)**** | **-0.02<br>(3.64)*** | **0.01<br>(0.51)** | **-20.68<br>(3.30)*** | **0.85** | **0.75** | **8.09*** | **1.83** |

***Source :*** Computed

# 20

# Industry Influence on Financial Structure
## Empirical Evidence from Indian Automobile Firms

## INTRODUCTION

Accounting regarding the "Financial structure of a business consists of three elements: assets, liabilities and capital". The financial structure provides an insight into the various types of sources tapped to finance, the total assets employed in a business enterprise. The part of financial structure which represents long-term sources is known as capital structure. Since the balance sheet is a detailed form of the fundamental, or structure equation, it is set for the financial structure of an enterprise. It states the nature and amount of each of the various assets, liabilities and property interest of the owner or owners. Stating the nature of the assets, liabilities and capital is not as difficult as stating their amounts. The financial structure can be made initially from the point of view of the time for which funds are needed. It includes both the sources of finance, i.e., long - term and short - term. Thus financial structure refers to the makeup of permanent capital of firm.

Over the past, many researchers have tried to establish the factors which influence a firm's financial structure. The association between a firm's financial structure and its size, profitability similar other operating characteristics have gained considerable importance. Some of them have presented affirmative evidences in respect of a particular factor or a group of factors as determinant of corporate financial structure; others have presented dissenting evidences in respect of the same factor or factors to be a clear determinant of financial structure. Scott and Scott et al., presented empirical evidences claiming that industrial class has got influence on the firm's financial structure. Remmers, et al., in their study, however, presented dissenting evidence arguing that neither size nor industry class is a clear determinant of the firm's financial structure. Therefore in this part an attempt has been made to study the corporate financial structure relationship with reference to size, profitability, operating leverage, external financing and income gearing. Attempts are also made here to offer an econometric interpretation to the factors which determine the financial structure of selected Indian automobile companies. In this regard, the following hypotheses are framed and tested.

- Financial Leverage is independent of Industry class.
- Financial Leverage is independent of Industry size.
- Financial Leverage and Profitability are independent of each other.
- Financial Leverage and Operating leverage have got no association between them.
- Financial Leverage and External financing are independent of each other.
- Financial Leverage has got no association with Income gearing.

## SAMPLE DESIGN

Keeping in view the scope of the study, it is decided to include all the companies under automobile industry working before or from the year 1996-97 to 2008-09. There are 26 companies operating in the Indian automobile industry. But, owing to several constraints such as non-availability of financial statements or non-working of a company in a particular year etc., it is compelled to restrict the number of sample companies to 20. The companies under automobile industry are classified into three sectors namely; Commercial vehicles, Passenger Cars and Multiutility vehicles and Two and Three wheelers. For the purpose of the study all the three sectors have been selected. It accounts for 73.23 per cent of the total companies available in the Indian automobile industry. The selected 20 companies include 5 under Commercial vehicles, 6 under Passenger Cars and Multiutility vehicles and 9 under Two and Three wheeler sectors. It is inferred that sample company represents 98.74 percentage of market share in commercial vehicles, 89.76 percentage of market share in Passenger Cars and Multiutility vehicles and 99.81 percentage of market share in two and three wheelers. Thus, the findings based on the occurrence of such representative sample may be presumed to be true representative of automobile industry in the country.

## DATA

The study is mainly based on secondary data. The major source of data analysed and interpreted in this study related to all those companies selected is collected from "PROWESS" database, which is the most reliable on the empowered corporate database of Centre for Monitoring Indian Economy (CMIE). Besides prowess database, relevant secondary data have also been collected from BSE Stock Exchange Official Directory, CIME Publications, Annual Survey of Industry, Business newspapers, Reports on Currency and Finance,

Libraries of various Research Institutions, through Internet etc.

**Financial leverage and industry class**

The first hypothesis relates to the possible association between industry class and financial structure. Firms in the same industry should experience similar amount of business risk because they produce similar products, incur similar set of rules, regulations, guidelines and environment. Since business risk has got relationship with the types of product, and the product with types of industries, there is reason to believe that a firm's financial structure is influenced by its industrial classification. The same logic should also hold good for inter-industry comparison. Since industries deal with different products, operate under different environment, rely on different technology, have different cost structure, their business risks should essentially be different. As such, their financial structures should also be different. To test whether the financial leverage of selected sectors of Indian automobile industry significantly differs, Analysis of Variance (ANOVA) has been applied and result of which is displayed in Table 20.1. It is evident from Table20.1 that F ratio (3.752) is higher than the table value of F (3.40) at 5 per cent level of significance. This indicates that the means of the financial leverages of the selected sectors of Indian automobile industry differ significantly. Thus the null hypothesis that financial leverage is independent of Industrial class is rejected leading to the conclusion that financial leverage depends upon industrial class.

**Financial leverage and size**

Large firms are generally more diversified, enjoy easier access to capital markets, receive higher credit ratings, and pay lower rates of interest on borrowed capital. Moreover as the level of activity increases with size, more debt is expected in the financial structure of large corporations. Hence, size of the firm should be positively related to its financial structure. The same logic should also hold good for inter-industry variations. In order to test the validity of the second null hypothesis that financial leverage and industry size are independent, correlation co-efficient between financial leverage and industry size have been calculated for all the three sectors namely commercial vehicles, passenger cars and multiutility vehicles, two and three wheelers and whole industry during the study period. To test the significance of correlation co-efficient, significance level is also presented in the Table 20.2. Table 20.2 exhibits details of empirical results found in respect of the hypothesis concerning financial leverage and industry size. It is apparent from the Table 20.2 that not only there exists positive correlations between financial leverages and industry size but also the relations are statistically significant at 1 per cent level in case of passenger cars and multiutility vehicles, two and three wheelers and whole industry and at 5 per cent level in case of commercial vehicles sector during the study period. Therefore, the null hypothesis that leverage is independent of industry size is rejected and hence concluded that size has got bearing on financial structure.

**Financial leverage and profitability**

The third hypothesis is pertaining to the relationship between a firm's profitability and its financial structure. A firm's ability to generate internal surpluses for business expansion depends upon its earning capacity. A more profitable firm may be considered to be in a better position to generate internal funds by way of reserves and surpluses. As reserves and surpluses will grow, the firm's dependence on external financing will decline, and consequently its dependence on dept capital too. This is because, a firm going for external funds will certainly prefer low-cost source and debt will be the first choice. Hence, a negative relationship should exist between a firm's financial leverage and its profitability. This phenomenon should also be true for industry level comparison, for profitability differs from industry to industry. In order to test the validity for the null hypothesis that financial leverage and profitability are independent of each other, correlation co-efficient between financial leverage and profitability have been calculated for all the three sectors and whole industry and empirical results are presented in Table 20.2. It is evident from the Table 20.2 that the existence of negative correlation between financial leverage and profitability in all the three sectors and whole industry and also the relationship are statistically significant at 1 per cent level. Thus, the null hypothesis that financial leverage is independent of profitability is rejected and concluded that there exists negative correlation between them.

**Financial leverage and operating leverage**

The fourth hypothesis relates to the suspected influence of operating leverage on financial structure. Ferri and Jones define operating leverage as "the use of fixed costs in the firm's production scheme but is generally associated with the employment of fixed assets". According to them, the use of fixed assets can magnify the variability of the firm's future income and hence, "operating leverage should be negatively related to the firm's financial structure". Determining the validity of this hypothesis in case of Indian automobile industry was thus the purpose of the fourth test. In order to test the validity of the null hypothesis that financial leverage and operating leverage have got no association between them, correlation co-efficient between financial leverages and operating leverages have been calculated for all the three sectors of automobile industry and whole industry and empirical results are presented in Table 20.2. In case of Indian automobile industry, however a definite conclusion could not be reached as far as the relationship between operating leverage and financial leverage is concerned. Empirical evidences from the Table 20.2 show that there exists negative correlation between operating leverages and financial leverage in case of two and three wheeler sector and whole automobile industry. Interestingly in case of commercial vehicles and passenger cars and multiutility vehicles positive correlation between financial leverage and operating leverage. However, in all the cases the relationships are statistically insignificant. Thus, the null hypothesis that operating leverage and financial leverage are independent of each other could not be fully rejected in the sense there exists both negative as well as positive correlation between them in different sectors in the same period.

**Financial leverage and external financing**

The fifth hypothesis relates to the association between the external financing and financial structure. Generally firms prepare internal to external financing and they will prefer the safest security first, i.e., they will choose debt before equity financing, in case they seek external financing to finance real investments with a positive net present value. This implies that when external financing will increase, the proportion of debt in the total financing will also increase. Hence there should exist, a positive relationship between external financing and firm's financial leverage. This logic should also be valid for inter- industry comparison. Empirical evidence from the Table 20.2 shows that there exists a statistically significant positive relationship between financial leverage and external financing in all the three sectors and whole industry. Thus, the null hypothesis that financial leverage and external financing are independent of each other could be fully rejected in the sense there exists positive correlation between them in different companies in the same period.

**Financial leverage and income gearing**

The sixth and the last hypothesis relates to the possible association between income gearing and a firm's financial leverage. Income gearing is considered to be a measure of corporate vulnerability to fluctuations in general economic conditions. Since firms operate under different economic conditions, and economic conditions have bearing on capital as well as debt markets, there should exist relationship between income gearing and a firm's financial leverage.

Empirical evidence from the Table 20.2 shows that there exists a statistically significant positive relationship between income gearing and corporate financial structure in all the three sectors and whole industry. Thus, while rejecting the null hypothesis that there is no association between income gearing and financial leverage, it may conclude that income gearing and financial leverage are positively correlated.

**Determinants of financial structure-Econometric analysis**

In this part an attempt is made to measure the degree of relationship that exists between a firm's financial structure and the different factors which have bearing on the financial structure. The objective of this discussion is to examine the determinants of financial structure in the selected sectors of Indian automobile industry during the study period. Based on earlier empirical studies, the specific factors are chosen for analyzing determinants of financial structure in Indian automobile industry. The specific factors, which have been taken into consideration are Payout Ratio (PR), Operating Leverage (OL), Size (S), Profitability (PROFIT), External Financing (EF) and Income Gearing (IG). These factors have been taken as the independent variables and Financial Leverage (FL) as the dependent variable. Multiple regression analysis has been applied to measure the effects of the independent variables on the dependent variable. The model to be estimated using from specific cross section data proposed is as follows -

$$\mathbf{FL = b_0 + b_1\,PR + b_2\,OL + b_3\,S + b_4\,PROFIT + b_5\,EF + b_6\,IG}$$

The results of the regression analysis in respect of whole industry, commercial vehicles, passenger cars and multiutility vehicles and two and three wheelers have been presented through Table 20.3 to Table 20.6.

**Whole Industry**

Analysis of the regression results of Indian automobile industry (Table 20.3) reveals that the adjusted $R^2$ is 0.96 and the F ratio is significant, which implies that the independent variables collectively explain 98 percentages of the total variations in the dependent variable. The analysis shows that variables like payout ratio, size, profitability, external financing and income gearing which are found to be statistically significant in explaining financial structure of Indian automobile industry. As far as the importance of individual variables are concerned, size, Income gearing and payout ratio are found to be the most important factors explaining variations in the financial structure of Indian automobile industry during the study period. The results thus indicate that the independent variables explaining the dependent variable well during the study period.

**Commercial Vehicles**

Analysis of regression results of the factors determining financial structure of commercial vehicles sector are presented in Table 20.4. It is evident from the table that the independent variables explain about 94 per cent variation in the dependent variable in this sector. The analysis shows that factors like payout ratio, size, profitability, external financing and income gearing are found to be statistically significant in explaining the financial structure of commercial vehicles sector. However, operating leverage is found to be statistically insignificant. It is evident from the results that size is the stronger determinant of financial structure followed by income gearing, profitability, external financing and payout ratio. The overall explanatory power of regression appears to be good. This may be inferred from the co-efficients of determinants ($R^2$). It is 94 per cent and the adjustment explanation is around 87 per cent.

**Passenger cars and Multi-utility vehicles**

The results of analysis of the regression of passenger cars and multi-utility vehicles are presented in Table 20.5. Analysis of the regression results shows that the $R^2$ is 0.94 and the F-ratio is significant, which implies that the independent variables collectively explain 94 percentages of the total variations in the dependent variable. The analysis shows that all the selected independent variables except operating leverage are found to be statistically significant in explaining financial structure of passenger cars and multi-utility vehicles. It also found that payout ratio has been the most important factor influencing the financial leverage of passenger cars and multi-utility vehicles followed by size, income gearing and profitability. The results thus indicate that the independent variables explain dependent variable well during the study period.

**Two and Three Wheelers**

The results of regression analysis of the factor determining the financial structure of two and three wheelers sector are presented in Table 20.6. It is found from the Table 20.6 that the independent variables collectively explain 99 per cent of the total variations in the dependent variable in two and three wheelers sector during the study period. The analysis shows that all the factors are found to be statistically significant in explaining financial structure of two and three wheelers sector. As far as individual variables are concerned, it is found that income gearing, size, payout ratio and profitability are the most significant variables influencing the financial structure of two and three wheelers sectors during the study period. The results also indicate that the independent variables explain the dependent variable well in two and three wheelers sectors during the study period.

## CONCLUSION

The analysis of industry influence on financial structure of Indian automobile industry reveals that the selected variables collectively explain 88 percentages of total variations in whole industry, 90 per cent in commercial vehicles sector, 60 per cent in passengers and multiutility vehicles sector and 89 per cent in two and three wheelers sectors during the study period. As far as the importance of individual variation of concern size followed by external financing, operating leverage, profitability and income gearing are found to be most important factors explaining the variations in the financial structure of Indian automobile industry during the study period.

## REFERENCES


1. Scott, David F. (1972). Evidence on the importance of Financial Structure, *Financial Management*, Summer, pp.45-50.
2. Scott, David F. and Martin, John D., (1975). Industry influence on Financial structure, *Financial Management*, Vol.4, Spring, pp. 67-75.
3. Remmers Lee, Stonenill, Arthur Wright Richard and Bekhuisen Theo (1974). Industry and size as debt ratio determinants in Manufacturing Internationally, *Financial Management*, pp. 24-32.
4. Ferry, Michael, G., and Jones, Wesley H., (1979). Determination of Financial Structure: A New Methodological Approach, *The Journal of Finance*, Vol, XXXIV, No.3. June, pp.331-344.
5. Singh, A and Hamid J, Corporate Financial Structure in Developing countries, IFC Technical paper, No.1, The world Bank, Washington, D.C.
6. Vijayakumar, A. (2004). "Assessment of financial health of Indian public sector manufacturing enterprises – Altman's z score analysis", *The Journal of Institute of Public Enterprises*, Vol. 27(3 & 4), pp. 110 – 119.
7. Beena, P.L. (2004). "An analysis of Mergers in the private corporate sector in India", Working paper No. 301, Centre for Development Studies, Thiruvananthapuram, pp.1-61.
8. Laurent Weill (2004). Leverage and corporate performance – A frontier efficiency university Robert Schuman, Instituted detudes politiques, 47 avenue de la Foret – Noitu, 67082 Strasbourg cedex, France, e-mail : Laurent weill@urs.G-strasbg.fr.

9. Petia Topalova (2004). "Overview of the Indian corporate sector: 1989-2002". IMF Working paper No: WP/04/64, Asia and Pacific Department. pp.1-41.
10. Alovsal Muslumor (2005). "The financial and operating performance of privatized companies in Turkish Cement Industry", Dogus university, METU Studies in Development, Vol. 32(1), pp.59-100.
11. Tomas Buus (2005). "Performance of Quoted and non-Quoted companies in the Europe", University of Economics, Prague.
12. Raghunatha Reddy, D. and Padma, S. (2005). "Pre and post merger financial performance of selected companies", *Indian Journal of Accounting*, Vol.XXXV (2), pp.29-38.
13. Hamsalakshmi and Manickam (2005). "Financial performance analysis of selected software companies", *Finance India*, Vol.XIX (3), pp.915-935.
14. Marina Martynova, Sjoerd, Oosting and Luc Renneboog (2006). "The long term operating performance of European Acquisitions" Working paper No.137, ECG Working paper series in Finance, pp.1-40.
15. Bardia, S.C. (2006). "Liquidity Trends in the Indian Iron and Steel Industry- A comparative study of SAIC and TISCO", University of Rajasthan, *ICFAI Journal of Financial Economics*, Vol.IV (1), pp. 45-53.
16. Truoug Dong Loc, Ger Laniouw and Robert Lensink (2006). "The impact of privatisation on firm performance in a Transaction Economy: The case of Vietnam", *Economics of Transaction*, Vol.14 (2), pp.349-389.
17. Amit K.Mallik, Debarish Sur (2006). "Business and financial risks in Indian corporate sector: An empirical analysis in the post – liberalization Era", *The Icfai Journal of Applied Finance*, Vol.15 (4), pp.53-68.
18. Mansur A. Mulla (2002). "Use of 'z' score analysis for evaluation of financial health of textile mills – A case study", *Abhigyan*, Vol.XIX (4), pp.37-40.
19. Michail, Pazarskis, Manthos Vogiaizoglog, Petros

Christodoulou and George Drogalas (2006). "Exploring the Improvement of corporate performance after Mergers – The case of Greece", *International Research Journal of Finance and Economics*, pp.184-92.

20. Productivity Commission (2007). "Financial Performance of Government Trading Enterprises 2004-05 to 2005-06", Govt of Australia, Commission Research paper.

21. Pramod Mantravadi, and Vidyadhar Reddy, A. (2007). "Relative size in mergers and operating performance; Indian Experience", *Economic and Political Weekly*, pp.52-66.

22. Ramesh Babu Vooka, Rajendra Prasad and Bayineni (2007). "Performance Evaluation of a public Sector Enterprises: A study of APSRTC", *The ICFAI Journal of Public Administration*, Vol.3 (3), pp.81-95.

23. Manor Selvi, A. and Vijayakumar, A. (2007). "Structure of profit rates in Indian Automobile industries-A comparison", *The Management Accountant*, Vol.42 (10), pp.784-789.

24. Vanitha, S., Selvam, M. (2007). "Financial performance of Indian Manufacturing companies during pre and post merger", *International Research Journal of Finance and Economics*.

25. Cuoug Duc Pham and Tyrone M. Carlin (2008). "Financial performance of privatized State Owned Enterprises, (SOEs) in Vietnam", Macquarie Graduate School of Management, Sydney, MGSM Working paper No.2008-2.

26. Giulio Bottazzi, Angelo Secchi, Federico Tamagni (2008). "Productivity, Profitability and Financial performance", *Industrial and Corporate change*, Vol.17 (4), PP-711-751.

27. Sanghoon Lee (2008). "Ownership structure and financial performance – Evidence from panel data of South Korea", University of Utah Economic, Working paper No. 2008 – 17.

28. Siddharth Mahajan and Mainak Sarkar (2008). "How does financial performance of MNC, in the Automobile

sector compare with Indian companies an analysis using financial ratios".

29. Shirshendu Ganguli (2008). "A comparison of group firms and stand alone firms in Indian Iron and Steel industry", ICFAI Institute for Management Teachers, Hyderabad.
30. Rohini, S. (2008). "Steel Industry : A performance analysis", *Economic and Political Weekly,* pp. 1613 – 1620
31. Patricia M. Fairfield et al., (2008). "Do Industry-Level analysis improve forecast of financial performance", *Journal of Accounting Research,* Vol.47(1) pp.147-177
32. Ram Mudambi, Carmela Nicosia (2008). "Ownership structure and firm performance evidence from the UK Financial Services Industry", The University of Buckingham, WINCOTT discussion paper No. 07, pp.2-17.

**TABLE 20.1**

**ANALYSIS OF VARIANCE (ANOVA) FOR FINANCIAL LEVERAGES OF INDIAN AUTOMOBILE INDUSTRY**

| Sectors | Mean | No. of items |
|---|---|---|
| Commercial vehicles | 0.266 | 13 |
| Passenger cars and Multi-utility vehicles | 0.286 | 13 |
| Two and Three wheelers | 0.223 | 13 |

| Source of variations | Sum of squares | df | Mean square | F-ratio | F-value (at 5%) |
|---|---|---|---|---|---|
| Between the years | 0.249 | 12 | 0.020 | 5.771 | 2.18 |
| Between the sectors | 0.027 | 2 | 0.013 | 3.752 | 3.402 |
| Error | 0.086 | 24 | 0.003 | | |
| **Total** | **0.362** | **38** | | | |

**TABLE 20.3**

**FACTORS DETERMINING THE FINANCIAL STRUCTURE OF INDIAN AUTOMOBILE INDUSTRY–REGRESSION ANALYSIS (Dependent variable - Financial Leverage (FL))**

$$\left[FL = b_0 + b_1PR + b_2OL + b_3S + b_4PROFIT + b_5EF + b_6IG\right]$$

| Independent Variables | Regression co-efficients | t-value | Significant/ Not significant |
|---|---|---|---|
| Payout Ratio (PR) | -0.04 | 2.82 | Significant** |
| Operating Leverage (OL) | -0.003 | 0.87 | Not Significant |
| Size (S) | 0.40 | 5.04 | Significant* |
| Profitability (PROFIT) | -0.01 | 3.27 | Significant* |
| External Financing (EF) | 0.005 | 4.63 | Significant* |
| Income Gearing (IG) | 0.10 | 2.88 | Significant** |

**$R^2$ = 0.98, Adj $R^2$ = 0.96; F ratio = 53.69*;**
*** - Significant at 0.01 level; ** - Significant at 0.05 level.**

***Source :*** Computed

## TABLE 20.2

## STATEMENT SHOWING CORRELATION CO-EFFICIENT, T-VALUES AND LEVELS OF SIGNIFICANCE OF FINANCIAL LEVERAGE AND DIFFERENT FACTORS

| Industry class | Correlation between | r-value | Significance level | Significant/ Not significant |
|---|---|---|---|---|
| Commercial vehicles | FL and Size | 0.128 | 0.031 | Significant** |
| | FL and PR | -0.458 | 0.000 | Significant* |
| | FL and OL | 0.038 | 0.763 | Not Significant |
| | FL and EF | 0.091 | 0.041 | Significant** |
| | FL and IG | 0.026 | 0.034 | Significant** |
| Passenger cars and Multi-utility vehicles | FL and Size | 0.327 | 0.003 | Significant* |
| | FL and PR | -0.494 | 0.000 | Significant* |
| | FL and OL | 0.054 | 0.639 | Not significant |
| | FL and EF | 0.077 | 0.018 | Significant** |
| | FL and IG | 0.172 | 0.081 | Significant*** |
| Two and three wheelers | FL and Size | 0.390 | 0.000 | Significant* |
| | FL and PR | -0.892 | 0.000 | Significant* |
| | FL and OL | -0.035 | 0.708 | Not significant |
| | FL and EF | 0.014 | 0.093 | Significant*** |
| | FL and IG | 0.024 | 0.045 | Significant** |
| Whole Industry | FL and Size | 0.218 | 0.000 | Significant* |
| | FL and PR | -0.886 | 0.000 | Significant* |
| | FL and OL | -0.016 | 0.802 | Not significant |
| | FL and EF | 0.023 | 0.056 | Significant*** |
| | FL and IG | 0.020 | 0.031 | Significant** |

**FL** - Financial Leverage; **OL** - Operating Leverage;
**IG** - Income Gearing; **PR** - Profitability; **EF** - External Financing.
* - Significant at 1% level; ** - Significant at 5% level;
*** - Significant at 10% level. ***Source:*** Computed.

## TABLE 20.4

## FACTORS DETERMINING THE FINANCIAL STRUCTURE OF INDIAN COMMERCIAL VEHICLES SECTOR– REGRESSION ANALYSIS

**(Dependent variable - Financial Leverage (FL))**

$$\left[FL = b_0 + b_1 PR + b_2 OL + b_3 S + b_4 PROFIT + b_5 EF + b_6 IG\right]$$

| Independent Variables | Regression co-efficients | t-value | Significant/ Not significant |
|---|---|---|---|
| Payout Ratio (PR) | 0.005 | 3.12 | Significant* |
| Operating Leverage (OL) | 0.001 | 1.05 | Not Significant |
| Size (S) | 0.09 | 4.14 | Significant* |
| Profitability (PROFIT) | -0.02 | 2.22 | Significant*** |
| External Financing (EF) | -0.009 | 5.06 | Significant* |
| Income Gearing (IG) | -0.08 | 1.89 | Significant*** |

**$R^2$ = 0.94; Adj $R^2$ = 0.87; F ratio = 14.90*;**
*** - Significant at 0.01 level; *** - Significant at 0.10 level.**

***Source :*** Computed.

## TABLE 20.5

## FACTORS DETERMINING THE FINANCIAL STRUCTURE OF INDIAN PASSENGER CARS AND MULTI-UTILITY VEHICLES SECTOR – REGRESSION ANALYSIS

**(Dependent variable - Financial Leverage (FL))**

$$\left[FL = b_0 + b_1 PR + b_2 OL + b_3 S + b_4 PROFIT + b_5 EF + b_6 IG\right]$$

| Independent Variables | Regression co-efficients | t-value | Significant/ Not significant |
|---|---|---|---|
| Payout Ratio (PR) | 0.13 | 3.54 | Significant* |
| Operating Leverage (OL) | 0.006 | 0.69 | Not Significant |
| Size (S) | 0.09 | 1.94 | Significant*** |
| Profitability (PROFIT) | -0.01 | 3.77 | Significant* |
| External Financing (EF) | -0.009 | 3.22 | Significant* |
| Income Gearing (IG) | 0.013 | 4.14 | Significant* |

**$R^2$ = 0.97; Adj $R^2$ = 0.94; F ratio = 14.86***
*** - Significant at 0.01 level; *** - Significant at 0.10 level.**

***Source :*** Computed

**TABLE 20.6**

**FACTORS DETERMINING THE FINANCIAL STRUCTURE OF INDIAN TWO AND THREE WHEELER SECTOR – REGRESSION ANALYSIS (Dependent variable - Financial Leverage (FL))**

$$[FL = b_0 + b_1 PR + b_2 OL + b_3 S + b_4 PROFIT + b_5 EF + b_6 IG]$$

| Independent Variables | Regression co-efficients | t-value | Significant/ Not significant |
|---|---|---|---|
| Payout Ratio (PR) | 0.03 | 4.10 | Significant* |
| Operating Leverage (OL) | 0.0092 | 2.04 | Significant*** |
| Size (S) | -0.13 | 3.62 | Significant* |
| Profitability (PROFIT) | -0.01 | 2.89 | Significant** |
| External Finance (EF) | 0.0003 | 5.96 | Significant* |
| Income Gearing (IG) | 0.22 | 5.26 | Significant* |

**$R^2$ = 0.99; Adj $R^2$ = 0.99; F ratio = 160.17*;**
*** - Significant at 0.01 level;**
**** - Significant at 0.05 level;**
***** - Significant at 0.10 level.**

***Source :*** Computed.

# 21

# Effect of Financial Performance on Share Prices in the Indian Corporate Sector

## An Empirical Study

Investment is concerned with the purchase and sale of financial assets and an attempt of the investor to make logical decisions about the various alternatives in order to earn suitable return. The investor has various alternative options for investing savings to flow in accordance with his preference. Savings are generally flow into investment with an expectation of return, but savings kept as cash are unproductive. Savings are invested into return yielding assets depending on their risk and return characteristics. The price of a commodity, the economist makes us to believe, is determined by the forces of demand and supply in a free economy. Even if we accept the economist's view, what factors influence demand and supply behaviour? price? Yes, but not all the time, at least there are some other factors.

The most basic factors that influence price of equity share are demand and supply factors. If most people start buying then prices move up and if people start selling prices go down. Further, in the securities market, whether the primary or the secondary market, the price of equity is significantly influenced by a number of factors. The financial performance of a company, particularly its records of earnings, dividends, growth and future prospects shapes the primary trends of its share prices. Any event or change in policy would affect its share prices. The fluctuation in security prices, which occur due to various reasons, is a known feature in the stock markets. The factors that cause these fluctuations, besides financial performance of a company, are government policies, projects completion, bonus issues, management decisions and of course the manipulations by the security holders.

The health and stability of a company can be analyzed by studying its financial statements. The overall financial performance of a company can be known when the financial data is compared over a period of time. The effect of this financial performance on the share prices can also be ascertained. Analysis of the relationship between financial performance of a company and its share price will be useful to various interested groups like the management, government, share holders, creditors, prospective investors and research scholars.

## CONCEPTUAL FRAMEWORK AND LITERATURE REVIEW

Several attempts have been made to identify or study the factors that affect equity prices. Some researchers have also tried to determine the correlation between selected factors (internal, external, market and non-market factors, economic and non-economic factors) and equity prices. The outcomes of the studies vary depending on the scope of the study, the equity price and factors examined.

Shefali Sharma and Balwinder Singh (2006) examines the empirical relationship of explanatory variables namely, dividend per share, earnings per share, price – earning ratio, return on capital employed and pay out on the market price of the shares and concludes that earnings per share and Book value per share are important determinants of share price as they are the indices of healthy financial position of companies. Niladri Das and Pattanayak (2009) finds that higher earning power, Returns on Investment, growth possibility and favourable valuation have a positive impact on the share price and stock market movement has a negative impact. Monica Singhania (2006) analysis the behaviour and determinants of equity prices in India and finds that book value, DPS and EPS are significant determinants of market price whereas Dividend cover and Yield are negatively related to market price.

Al – Tamimi (2007) identified company fundamental factors (performance of the company, a change in board of directors, appointment of new management and the creation of new assets, dividends, earnings) and external factors (government rules and regulations, inflation and other economic conditions) as influences of equity prices. He discovered that the firm's fundamental factors exercise the most significant impact on stock prices. Somoye *et al.* (2009) studied the extent to which market indices affect stock prices. They find that EPS, DPS, GDP and oil prices have positive correlation to stock prices. The outcomes of this study agree with the earlier studies by Udegbunam and Eriki (2001), Ibrahim (2003) and Chaudhuri and Smiles (2004).

In the study of the impact of dividend and earnings on stock prices, Hartone (2004) argues that a significantly positive impact is made on equity prices if positive earnings information occurs after negative dividend information. Also, a significantly negative impact occurs in equity pricing if positive dividend information is followed by negative earning information. Docking and Koch (2005) discovers that there is a direct relationship between dividend announcement and equity price behaviour. Al – Qenae Li and Wearing (2002) in their study of the effects of earning (micro – economic factor), inflation and interest rate (macro – economic factor) on the stock prices on the Kuwait Stock

Exchange, discovered that macro – economic factors significantly impact stock prices negatively.

Mohammed Belal Uddin (2009) conducted a study to find out the relationship between micro economic factors with the stock price. He found a significant linear relationship among market return and micro economic factors such that net asset value per share, dividend percentage, earning per share of companies. Zhao (1999) shows that inflation as an external factor exerts a very significant negative influence on the stock prices in Nigeria. Bansal (1996) analyzes the behaviour and determinants of equity prices in India and finds that book value, dividend per share, earnings per share and dividend cover were the variables which contributed the most in determining equity share prices followed by price – earnings ratio and dividend yield.

The firm's beta ratios, its market value to book value, its current price to earnings ratio and the historical growth rate in earning per share are identified by Moore and Beltz (2002) as possessing strong influence on the equity price of the firm. They also argue that identified factors have varying effects on the price and the effects vary from time to time, sector to sector and even from firm to firm within the same industry.

Factors affecting equity prices are numerous and inexhaustible. The factors can be categorized into firm, industry, country and International or market and non - market factors and economic and non – economic factors. All the factors can be summarized into two classes – micro and macro factors. Factors in each class of the classification are inexhaustible. For instance, the firm factors include, ownership structure, management quality, labour force quality, earnings ratios, dividend payments, net book value, etc. have impact on the investor's pricing decision. In the light of the preceding literature review, many factors both micro and macro – economics, have impact on equity pricing in the stock market, the impact differs from firm to firm, industry to industry, economy to economy and from time to time, but one comforting conclusion is that most of the factors appear to have the same behaviour regardless of time, industry or firm constraints.

## OBJECTIVES OF THE STUDY

The main aim of the study is to study the impact of selected variables on share price behaviour. The specific objectives of the study are:

i) To establish the relationship among various explanatory variables affecting the market price movement identified through literature review.

ii) To condense the various explanatory variables into few critical factors having a significant bearing.

iii) To examine the impact of factor score coefficients on the market price of securities.

## METHODOLOGY

The Ashok Leyland Ltd, which is one of the leading commercial vehicles sector industries under Indian Automobiles, has been purposively selected for the study. For this purpose, secondary data has been used. The main aim of the study is to measure the impact of the financial performance on the share price of the sample unit. The data relating to the performance of the sample unit for a period of 12 years from 1996 – 97 to 2007-08 and its market prices were obtained from CMIE (Centre for Monitoring Indian Economy) PROWESS Database. The data for the sample companies as obtained from CMIE is supplemented with information from various financial dailies, magazine, reports, annual reports of the company etc. Based on the review of literature, the explanatory variables are identified and used in the present study. The Description of the variables used in the study and data relating to the study period were presented in Table 21.1 and Table 21.2.

## HYPOTHESES

The following research hypotheses are framed and tested for the study.

i) The book value per share significantly affects the stock price.

ii) The dividend per share significantly affects the stock price.

iii) The earnings per share significantly affect the stock price.

iv) The dividend cover and dividend yield significantly affects the stock price.

v) The price earning ratio significantly affects the stock price.

## PLAN OF ANALYSIS

For analyzing the impact of the explanatory variables on the dependent variable, the following statistical techniques are employed in this study.

## CORRELATION

The analysis of the degree of linear association between various variables used was carried out with the help of Karl Pearson's correlation matrix method. The lower the value of 'r', the lower is the degree of linear relationship between the variables. The value of 'r' needs to be interpreted accurately because a low value of 'r' may be due to the non-linear relationship between these variables. Also, a high-degree of correlation does not imply cause and effect relationship between two variables. The significance of the correlation co-efficient is tested with the help of t-test distribution at 1 per cent and 5 per cent level of significance.

## FACTOR ANALYSIS

Factor analysis is a statistical technique that aims to represent a set of variables in terms of a small number of hypothetical variables. In other words, it simplifies the complex and diverse relationship that exists among a set of observed variables by uncovering common dimensions or factors that link together the seemingly unrelated variables and consequently provides insights into the underlying structure of data. In the present study, principal component Varimax Rotated Factor Analysis method has been used to group the variables.

The principal component Analysis Primarily helps in considering all the variables under each set of data and finds a composite index of variation explainable by such an independent variable on dependent set of variables. Further, this analysis considerably reduces the influe.ıces of statistical auto correlation and multi-collinearity problems with independent variables. The procedure presupposes the use of standardised variables in place of actual variables for ensuring their normality. The procedure also involves the estimation of factor loadings for each of the variables in each set of indicators. Subsequently, the first components are ascertained by weightaging each of the variables with its corresponding factor loading. The algebraic sum of such weighted variables in each set represents the value of the first principal component of the given set of criterion. A multiple regression equation is estimated among the principal components to explain the combined influence of each set on the dependent principal component. This procedure is followed in this study.

## REGRESSION

A Linear Multiple Regression model has been employed to measure the combined effects of explanatory variables on the dependent variable. The general form of multiple linear equations is

$$\mathbf{Y = b_0 + b_1F_1 + b_2F_2 + \ldots\ldots + b_nF_n}$$

where, Y – Dependent variable

$b_0$ – Regression constant

$b_1, b_2, \ldots\ldots b_n$ – Regression co-efficient of Independent Variables.

$F_1, F_2, \ldots\ldots F_n$ – Factor score co-efficient of Independent Variables.

The statistical significance of regression coefficient was worked out and tested by applying the 't' test. The coefficient of determination $R^2$ was computed to determine the percentage variation in the dependent variables. Also, with a view to account for the loss of degree of freedom resulting from the inclusion of additional explanatory variables, the adjusted $R^2$ was computed. The F value was also computed to test the significance the $R^2$ with 'F' distribution at 1 per cent and 5 per cent significance level.

## RESULTS AND DISCUSSION

The value of dependent and independent variables for the period ranging from 1996-97 to 2007-08 are given in Table 21.2. Table 21.2 also presents mean, co-efficient of variables and CAGR of the variables. The market price of shares of Ashok Leyland Ltd has been registered very high fluctuating trend during the study period. The market price of share decreased from Rs.86.75 in 1996-97 to Rs. 47.30 in 2000-01 and afterwards constantly increased to the maximum of Rs.248.78 in 2003-04. But in the terminal years of the study period, the market price of the shares of the Ashok Leyland Ltd has been decreased to Rs. 34.68 in 2007-08. The book value of share of Ashok Leyland Ltd had also registered fluctuating trend during the study period and reflected the same pattern of trend as in the case of market price. Dividend Per Share of Ashok Leyland Ltd had registered increasing trend from the year 1999-2000 to 2007-08. It increased from Rs. 3.50 in 1999-2000 to Rs. 15.00 in 2007-08.

The Earning Per Share, Dividend cover, Growth rate, Price – Earning Ratio and Dividend Yield had also registered fluctuating trend during the study period. All the variables have been decreased during the terminal years of the study period. All the dependent and independent variables showed negative compound annual growth rate except Dividend per share and Price – Earning ratio during the study period. The compound annual growth rate of Dividend Per Share and Price

Earnings Ratio is 10.50 and 2.29 per cent during the study period.

Table 21.3 presents the correlation co-efficient for the sample company over the study period. It shows that net profit margin is significantly and positively related to EPS (r = 0.891) and Dividend cover (r = 0.564). It is also noted that the value of the coefficient of correlation with respect to other variables like Book Value, Growth and Dividend Yield is very small, positive and insignificant. It may also be noted that the correlation of the market price with Dividend per share and price – Earning ratio is very small, negative and insignificant. The book – value of share is most highly correlated with dividend cover (r = 0.963) and dividend yield (r = 0.804). There is also significant negative relationship between book value and dividend per share (r = -0.905).

It is interesting to note that the dividend per share are negatively and significantly correlated with dividend cover (r = -0.827) and Dividend Yield (r = -0.653). However, dividend per share is positively correlated with the growth (r = -0.602) and significant. Further, Earnings Per Share is positively correlated with Dividend Cover (r = 0.677) and Dividend Yield (r = 0.551). Similarly dividend cover is most highly correlated with dividend yield and significant.

A few argue that if there is a high correlation among the variables, factor analysis will include less number of factors to represent a large number of variables. Others say that it will not give meaningful results if the variables are uncorrelated. But, such a highly desirable situation may not exist in real life problems. It is inevitable to extract more number of factors to account for large variance. An examination of the correlation matrix indicates that a considerable number of correlations exceed 0.3 and so the matrix is suitable for factoring. In the next stage, an attempt has made to use of principal component analysis for deciding about the number of factors to be derived.

KMO criterion and Barlett's Test of significance gave a rough rule of thumb to choose factor analysis. The significance (0.000) is less than the assumed value (0.05). This means that the factor analysis is valid. Further, KMO coefficient (0.587) is more than 0.5. So this implies that the factor analysis for data reduction is effective (Table 21.4). The Table 21.5 showed the total variance explained at three stages. At the initial stage, it shows the factors and their associated eigen values, the percentage of variance explained and the cumulative percentages. The Eigen value computed for this correlation matrix (Table 21.5) showed that three factors are extracted adopting principal component method. The total variance accounted for by all these three factors was 94.960 per cent and the remaining was explained by other factors.

The principal factors were further orthogonally rotated using varimax rotation, i.e., a method which simplifies the factor structure by maximizing the variable of a column of the pattern matrix. Loadings that are high become higher after the extraction and loadings that are low become lower. Varimax also tends to re-apportion the variables among the factors. So that they become relatively equal in importance; variance is taken from the first factors extracted and distributed among latter ones. A rotated factor is simply a set of linear combinations of variables and will have different patterns of loading on the rotated factors than they have on the original factors. It is important to point that any set of unroated factors exactly explains the same variance as the original factors but the rotated factors slice it up in a way that is more amenable to interpretation. A description of the three factors is shown in Table 21.6.

From the Table 21.6, it is inferred that factor one explains 52.913 per cent of total variation in the variable set and it identifies eight variables whose factor loading values are more than 0.03. It can be inferred that all the selected variables influence the factor one ($F_1$) and these together form one cluster. Book value per share (NPM) was observed to be a unique variable with high loading value of 0.934 in Factor one. Factor 2 ($F_2$) explain 27.944 per cent of the total variation in the variable set and it identifies all the variables whose factor loading values were more than 0.03. NPM was observed to be a unique variable with high loading value of 0.979 in Factor Two. Similarly, Factor 3($F_3$) explain 13.83 per cent of the total variation in the variable set and it was also observed that Price – Earnings ratio was a unique variable with high loading value of 0.979 in Factor Three.

## RESULTS OF MULTIPLE REGRESSION ANALYSIS

Factor scores computed from the rotated factor transformation matrix are taken as independent variables and year end market price was taken as independent variable for multiple regression analysis. The analysis were done on the above are presented in the Table 21.7 and 21.8. The value R-square (0.974), Adjusted R-square (0.964), standard Error (11.546) and F value (99.87) showed the fitness of the regression model. From Table 21.8, it can be inferred that Factor one has a positive association with market price and significant at 10 per cent level. Factor two has a positive association with the market price of share and turn out to be highly significant determinant of the market price of the share. However, Factor three has a negative association with market price, but it did not turnout to be a significant determinant of the market price of the share.

## CONCLUSION

The study uses the correlation analysis, factor analysis and the multiple linear regressions to analyze the impact of financial performance on the market price of the share. The regression results for the study reveals that the variables taken for the study, i.e, Book value, Earnings per share, Dividend cover, Growth rate and Dividend yield have a positive association with market price of Ashok Leyland and Dividend Per Share and Price – Earnings Ratio have a negative association with market price. In this study only industry financial factors were considered for analysis and one company was under consideration. Further research can be conducted considering macro economic factors like money supply, inflation rate, exchange rate, interest rate etc. Time series analysis also can be done in market as a whole or in different industries.

## REFERENCES


1. Shefali Sharma and Balwinder Singh (2006), Determinants of equity share prices in the Indian corporate sector; An empirical study. *The ICFAI Journal of Applied Finance*, Vol.12, No.4. pp. 21-38.
2. Niladri Das and Pattanayak, J.K. (2009), Analysis of the fundamental factors affecting the market price of shares constituting the Indian Index; a study of SENSEX, I*nternational Journal of Accounting and Finance*, Volume 1, No. 3, pp. 323-355.
3. Monica Singhania (2006), Determinants of Equity prices: A study of select Indian companies, *The ICFAI Journal of Applied Finance*, Vol.12, No.9, pp. 39-51.
4. Al – Tamimi, Hussein (2007), Factors Affecting stock prices in the UAE Financial markets, Singapore Economic Review conference, https:// editorial express.com/conference/SERC 2007.
5. Somoye, R.C., Akintoye, I.R. and Oseni, J.E (2009), Determinants of Equity prices in the stock markets, *International Research Journal of Finance and Economics*, Issue 30, Euro Journals publishing, Inc 2009, http://www.eurojournals.com/finance.htm.
6. Udegbunam, R.I. and Eriki, P.O. (2001), Inflation and stock price behaviour : Evidence from Nigerian Stock Market, *Journal of Financial Management and Analysis*, xx (14).
7. Ibrahim, Mansor H. (2003), Macro economic Forces and capital market Integration; A VAR Analysis for Malaysia, *Journal of the Asia pacific Economy*, 8 (1).
8. Chaudhuri, K. and Smiles, S. (2004), stock market and Aggregate Economic Activity : Evidence from Australia, Applied Financial Economics, (14).

9. Hartono, Jogiyanto. (2004), The Recency Effect of Accounting Information, Gadjah Mada *International Journal of Business*, Vol.6, No.1.

10. Docking, Diane, S., and Koch, Paul D. (2005), Sensitivity of Investor Reaction to Market Direction and Volatility; Dividend change Announcements, *Journal of Financial Research.*

11. Al – Qenae, Rashid and Li, C.W Bob (2002), The information content of Earnings on stock prices; The Kuwait Stock Exchange, *Multinational Finance Journal,* 6.

12. Mohammed Belal Uddin (2009), Determinants of market price of stock, *Journal of Modern Accounting and Auditing,* Vol.5, No.7.

13. Zhao, Xing – Qio (1999), stock prices, inflation and output : evidence from China, Applied Economics Letters, 6.

14. Bansal, S.P. (1996), Behaviour and Determinants of Equity prices in India, Research Methodology in Management Theory and Case studies, Deep & Deep publications Pvt. Ltd, New Delhi.

15. Moore,J.S. and Bdtz, J.C. (2002), Share price performance and observable factors : A perspective from Rule Induction, Small Business Advancement National Centre, http://www.sbaer.uca.edu/toc.pdf.

## TABLE 21.1

## VARIABLES USED IN THE STUDY

| Abbreviation | Description |
|---|---|
| Market price (MP) | $MP = \frac{Highprice + Lowprice}{2}$ where High price – Highest market price during the financial year; Low price – Lowest market price during the financial year |
| Book Value per share (BV) | $BV = \frac{\text{Reserves + Equity capital – Revaluation reserves}}{\text{No. of outstanding shares}}$ |
| Dividend Per Share (DPS) | $DPS = \frac{\text{Dividend paid}}{\text{No. of outstanding shares}}$ |
| Earnings Per Share (EPS) | $EPS = \frac{\text{Net profit after Tax – preference Dividend}}{\text{No. of outstanding shares}}$ |
| Dividend Cover (DC) | $DC = \frac{EPS}{DPS}$ |
| Growth (GH) | $G = \frac{S_t - S_{t-1}}{S_{t-1}}$ where $S_t$ = Net sales in the current year. $S_{t-1}$ = Net sales in the immediate previous year |
| Price to Earnings Ratio (P/E) | $P/E \text{ Ratio} = \frac{\text{Net profit after Tax – preference Dividend}}{\text{No. of outstanding shares}}$ |
| Dividend Yield (DY) | $DY = \frac{DPS}{Marketprice} x100$ |
| Net Profit Margin (NPM) | $NPM = \frac{N.P\ after\ Tax}{Net\ Sales} x100$ |

## TABLE 21.2

## VALUES OF DEPENDENT AND INDEPENDENT VARIABLES (1996-97 TO 2007-08)

| *Year* | *Market price (MP)* | *Book value (BV)* | *Dividend Per Share (DPS)* | *Earnings Per Share (EPS)* | *Dividend Cover (DC)* | *Growth (GH)* | *Price to Earnings Ratio (P/E)* | *Dividend Yield (DY)* | *Net Profit Margin (NPM)* |
|---|---|---|---|---|---|---|---|---|---|
| 1996-97 | 86.75 | 89.74 | 5.00 | 10.01 | 2.00 | 0.21 | 8.42 | 59.31 | 5.64 |
| 1997-98 | 41.65 | 90.18 | 1.00 | 1.45 | 1.45 | -0.18 | 28.55 | 24.15 | 0.27 |
| 1998-99 | 41.23 | 90.82 | 1.00 | 1.60 | 1.60 | 0.03 | 26.56 | 23.53 | 0.25 |
| 1999-00 | 67.85 | 93.53 | 3.50 | 6.21 | 1.77 | 0.24 | 10.93 | 51.55 | 3.31 |
| 2000-01 | 47.30 | 94.76 | 4.00 | 7.30 | 1.83 | -0.01 | 6.45 | 84.93 | 4.02 |
| 2001-02 | 79.70 | 98.73 | 4.50 | 7.76 | 1.72 | 0.01 | 10.32 | 56.18 | 4.06 |
| 2002-03 | 100.25 | 78.50 | 5.00 | 9.47 | 1.89 | 0.18 | 10.30 | 51.28 | 4.31 |
| 2003-04 | 248.78 | 86.32 | 7.50 | 15.32 | 2.04 | 0.25 | 16.55 | 29.57 | 5.49 |
| 2004-05 | 20.93 | 9.61 | 10.00 | 2.14 | 0.21 | 0.23 | 9.81 | 4.76 | 6.31 |
| 2005-06 | 39.50 | 11.37 | 13.10 | 2.5 | 0.19 | 0.25 | 16.10 | 2.98 | 5.52 |
| 2006-07 | 38.15 | 12.61 | 15.00 | 3.12 | 0.21 | 0.37 | 12.32 | 3.90 | 4.85 |
| 2007-08 | 34.68 | 15.99 | 15.00 | 3.27 | 0.22 | 0.08 | 10.80 | 4.25 | 5.89 |
| **Mean** | **70.56** | **64.35** | **7.05** | **5.85** | **1.26** | **0.14** | **13.93** | **33.03** | **4.05** |
| **CV** | **0.87** | **0.60** | **0.72** | **0.73** | **0.63** | **1.07** | **0.50** | **0.82** | **0.49** |
| **CAGR** | **-8.00** | **-14.51** | **10.50** | **-9.67** | **-18.18** | **-8.40** | **2.29** | **-21.31** | **5.81** |

***Source :*** Computed from the annual accounts of Ashok Leyland Ltd.

## TABLE 21.4

## KMO AND BARLETT'S TEST

| | | |
|---|---|---|
| **Bartlett's Test of Sphericity** | Kaiser – Meyar – Olkin Measure of Sampling Adequacy | 0.587 |
| | Approx. Chi-square | 121.648 |
| | df | 28 |
| | Sig | 0.000 |

***Source :*** Computed

## TABLE 21.3

## ZERO – ORDER CORRELATION MATRIX FOR GROUPED DATA OVER THE PERIOD (1996-97 to 2007-08)

| | NPM | BV | DPS | EPS | DC | GH | P/E | DY |
|---|---|---|---|---|---|---|---|---|
| NPM | 1.000 | | | | | | | |
| BV | 0.405 | 1.000 | | | | | | |
| DPS | -0.142 | -0.905* | 1.000 | | | | | |
| EPS | 0.891* | 0.496 | -0.181 | 1.000 | | | | |
| DC | 0.564** | 0.963* | -0.827* | 0.677* | 1.000 | | | |
| GH | 0.226 | -0.494 | 0.602** | 0.241 | -0.314 | 1.000 | | |
| PE | -0.015 | 0.163 | -0.358 | -0.387 | 0.037 | -0.453 | 1.000 | |
| DY | 0.227 | 0.804* | -0.653** | 0.551** | 0.822* | -0.298 | -0.387 | 1.000 |

**NP – Net Profit Margin; BV – Book Value Per Share; DPS – Dividend Per Share; EPS – Earnings Per Share; DC – Dividend Cover; GH – Growth; P/E – Price Earnings Ratio; DY – Dividend Yield; * - Correlation is significant at the 0.01 level; ** - Correlation is significant at the 0.05 level**

**Source : Computed.**

## TABLE 21.5

## TOTAL VARIANCE EXPLAINED

| Component | Initial Eigen values | | | Extraction sums of squared loadings | | |
|---|---|---|---|---|---|---|
| | *Total* | *% of variance* | *Cumulative* | *Total* | *% of variance* | *Cumulative %* |
| 1 | 4.233 | 52.913 | 52.913 | 4.233 | 52.913 | 52.913 |
| 2 | 2.236 | 27.944 | 80.857 | 2.236 | 27.944 | 80.857 |
| 3 | 1.107 | 13.832 | 94.690 | 1.107 | 13.832 | 94.690 |
| 4 | 0.340 | 4.249 | 98.939 | | | |
| 5 | 0.049 | 0.608 | 99.546 | | | |
| 6 | 0.021 | 0.264 | 99.811 | | | |
| 7 | 0.013 | 0.166 | 99.977 | | | |
| 8 | 0.002 | 0.023 | 100.00 | | | |

**Note :** Predictors : (Constant) DY, GH, EPS, PE, DPS, BV, DC

## TOTAL VARIANCE EXPLAINED

| Component | Rotation sums of squared loadings | | |
|---|---|---|---|
| 1 | 3.724 | 46.546 | 46.546 |
| 2 | 2.301 | 28.757 | 75.303 |
| 3 | 1.551 | 19.387 | 94.960 |

**Extraction Method :** Principal Component Analysis

## TABLE 21.6

## ROTATED COMPONENT MATRIX

| | Component | | |
|---|---|---|---|
| | 1 | 2 | 3 |
| **NPM** | 0.107 | 0.979 | -0.067 |
| **BV** | 0.934 | 0.319 | -0.064 |
| **DPS** | -0.929 | -0.053 | 0.243 |
| **EPS** | 0.267 | 0.886 | 0.346 |
| **DC** | 0.854 | 0.504 | 0.042 |
| **GH** | -0.679 | 0.402 | 0.390 |
| **PE** | 0.126 | -0.079 | -0.979 |
| **DY** | 0.837 | 0.175 | 0.502 |

**Extraction Method :** Principal Component Analysis
**Rotation Method :** Varimax with Kaiser Normalization

## TABLE 21.7

## MODEL SUMMARY

| Model | R | R Square | Adjusted R Square | Std. Error of the Estimate | Dubin - Watson |
|---|---|---|---|---|---|
| 1 | 0.987[a] | 0.974 | 0.964 | 11.54619 | 2.044 |

### ANOVA[B]

| Model | | Sum of squares | df | Mean square | F | Sig. |
|---|---|---|---|---|---|---|
| 1 | Regression | 39940.18 | 3 | 13313.40 | 99.87 | 0.000 |
| | Residual | 1066.52 | 8 | 133.32 | | |
| | Total | 41006.70 | 11 | | | |

a. **Predictors :** (constant), REGR factor score 3 for analysis 1, REGT factor score 2 for analysis 1, REGR factor score 1 for analysis 1.

b. **Dependent variable :** Year End Market Price

### TABLE 21.8

### CO-EFFICIENTS[A]

| Model | | Unstandardized Coefficients | | Standardized Coefficients | | |
|---|---|---|---|---|---|---|
| | | β | Std. Error | β | t | Sig. |
| 1 | Constant | 70.566 | 3.333 | | 21.17 | 0.000 |
| | REGR factor score 1 for analysis 1 | 6.551 | 3.481 | 0.107 | 1.882** | 0.097 |
| | REGR factor score 2 for analysis 1 | 59.762 | 3.481 | 0.979 | 17.167* | 0.000 |
| | REGR factor score 3 for analysis 1 | -4.065 | 3.481 | -0.067 | -1.168 | 0.277 |

a. **Dependent variable :** Year and Market Price

*** - Significant at 0.01 level;**

**** - Significant at 0.10 level**

***Source :*** Computed

# PART - VII

# ASSESSMENT OF FINANCIAL HEALTH

# 22

# Use of Altman Bankruptcy Model to analyse the performance of Indian Automobile Companies

## INTRODUCTION

Social analysts have traditionally used ratio derived from the balance sheet and the financial statement to measure financial strength. The ratios can be grouped into four categories: liquidity, leverage, activity and ability. Each measures a different aspect of financial condition. Liquidity ratios gauge the ability of a firm to pay its obligations as they come due, while leverage ratios measure the extent to which a firm uses debt in its capital structure. Activity ratios, sometimes called turnover, measure the productive use of assets and profitability ratios indicate a firm's rate of profit on some basis (such as sales, assets or net worth). Many of the individual accounting ratios used frequently to predict the financial performance of an enterprise may only provide warnings when it is too late to take a corrective action. Further, a single ratio does not convey much of the sense. There is no internationally accepted standard for financial ratio against which the results can be compared. Statistical techniques, such as Multiple Discriminant Analysis (MDA), have been used to weight the different ratio types into a multiple regression model that produces an index, or credit score. By combining ratios into a model, it is hoped that the predictive abilities of these ratios can be enhanced. One such example of MDA applied to ratio analysis is the Altman (1968)[1] Z score model, which combined a number of accounting ratios (liquidity, leverage, activity and profitability) to form an index of the profitability, which are effective indicators of corporate performance in predicting bankruptcy well over the years.

In this study, an attempt has been made to have an insight into the financial stability and financial health of selected Indian automobile companies during the study period. The analysis took the approach of assessing the companies in terms of one of the universally accepted indicators of financial health – the Altman Bankruptcy Model.

## REVIEW OF LITERATURE

In this direction a variety of studies have been conducted, over the period, by applying Multiple Discriminant Analysis (MDA) to predict the corporate failure, as for instance, Bevar (1966), Argenti John (1976) Gupta (1979), Ohlson (1980), Etebari (1987), Makridakis (1991), Sastry (1994), James sena and Dennis Williams (1998), Mansur A. Mulla (2002), Selvam et al., (2004), and Vijayakumar (2004). Therefore, this part of analysis measured the Indian automobile companies performance using this barometer, making observations and, in some case, providing explanations and comments about specific companies in the field.

**Z – Score – Financial Analysis tool.**

A common statistical way of understanding data on one scale so a comparison can take place is using a Z – score. The Z – Score is like a common yard stick for all types of data. Each Z-score corresponds to a point in a normal distribution and as such is sometimes called a normal deviate since a Z – score will describe how much a point deviates from a mean or specification point. Z-score mean statistical measures that quantify the distance a data point is from the mean of a data set. In a more financial sense, Z – score is the output from a credit – strength test that gauges the likelihood of bankruptcy. The formula may be used to predict the probability that a firm will go into bankruptcy within two years. Z scores are used to predict corporate defaults and an easy – to – calculate control measure for the financial distress status of companies in academic studies. The Z – score uses multiple corporate income and balance sheet values to measure the financial health of a company.

## ALTMAN MODEL

The Z-score is a linear combination of five or six common business ratios, weighted by coefficients. The coefficients were estimated by identifying a set of firms which had declared bankruptcy and then collecting a matched sample of firms which had survived, with matching by Industry and approximate size. Edward I. Altman was the first researcher to successfully use step – wise multiple discriminate analyses to develop a prediction model with a high degree of accuracy. It can also be called as a company failure or Bankruptcy prediction method. A company's Z -score is a positive function of five factors; (networking capital/total assets ; (retained earnings) / (total assets); (EBIT) / (total assets); (market value of common and preferred shares) / (book value of debt); and (sales / total assets). Although the weights are not equal, the higher each ratio, the higher the Z – score and the lower, the probability of bankruptcy, also called Zeta. Using the sample of 66 companies, 33 failed and 33 successful, Atman's model achieved an accuracy rate of 95 per cent.

Altman's model takes the following form.

$$Z = 1.2\,A + 1.4\,B + 3.3\,C + 0.6\,D + 0.999\,E$$

Where, A = Working capital/ Total assets

B = Retained earnings / Total assets

C = Earnings before interest and taxes / Total assets

D = Market value of Equity / Book value of Total Debt

E = Sales / Total assets.

Working capital/Total assets is considered a measure of liquidity. In Altman model the measure of liquidity ranks fifth in its contribution to the overall discriminating ability. Retained earnings/Total assets are considered a measure of cumulative profitability over time. It ranks fourth in its contribution to the overall discriminating ability of the model. Earnings Before Interest and Taxes (EBIT)/total assets are considered a measure of productivity of a firm's assets. A firm's existence is based on the earning power of its assets. The measure of productivity ranks first in its contribution to the overall discriminating ability of the model. The market value of equity/book value to total debt shows how much the firm's assets can decline in value before the liabilities exceed the assets and the firm becomes insolvent. It ranks third in its contribution to the overall discriminating ability of the model. Sales/Total assets illustrate the sales generating ability of the firm's assets. This is a standard financial ratio considered to be measure of management's capability in dealing with competitive conditions. It ranks second in its contribution to the overall discriminating ability of the model. The actual weights assigned to the various ratios are shown in Figure 22.1.

It is evident from Figure 22.1 that earnings before interest and taxes to total assets ratio accounts for 44 per cent, retained earnings to total assets accounts for 19 per cent, working capital to total assets accounts for 16 per cent, sales to total assets accounts for 13 per cent and market value to book value accounts for 8 per cent of the Altman Z - score.

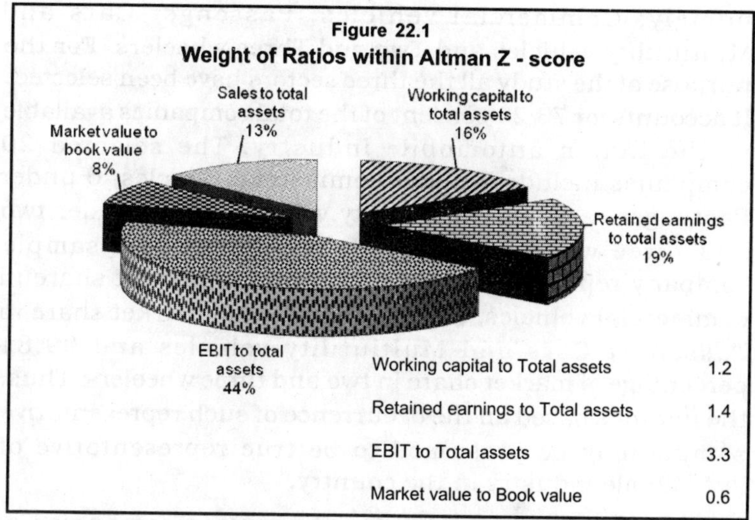


Altman concludes that firms can be classified as non bankrupt, bankrupt or in the "gray area" based on their scores:

| | | |
|---|---|---|
| **Z** | **= > 2.99** | **non bankrupt sector** |
| | **= 1.81 < 2.99** | **gray area** |
| | **= < 1.81** | **bankrupt sector** |

Altman suggests that use of Z scores can aid loan officers in credit evaluation and can help managers predict corporate problems early enough to enable management to realize the gravity of the situation in time to avoid failure.

## METHODOLOGY

Keeping in view the scope of the study, it is decided to include all the companies under automobile industry working before or from the year 1996-97 to 2008-09. There are 26 companies operating in the Indian automobile industry. But, owing to several constraints such as non-availability of financial statements or non-working of a company in a particular year etc., it is compelled to restrict the number of sample companies to 20. The companies under automobile industry are classified into three sectors namely; Commercial vehicles, Passenger Cars and Multiutility vehicles and Two and Three wheelers. For the purpose of the study all the three sectors have been selected. It accounts for 73.23 per cent of the total companies available in the Indian automobile industry. The selected 20 companies include 5 under commercial vehicles, 6 under Passenger cars and Multiutility vehicles and 9 under two and three wheeler sectors. It is inferred that sample company represents 98.74 percentage of market share in commercial vehicles, 89.76 percentage of market share in Passenger Cars and Multiutility vehicles and 99.81 percentage of market share in two and three wheelers. Thus, the findings based on the occurrence of such representative sample may be presumed to be true representative of automobile industry in the country.

The Altman Z - scores for the sixteen companies of Indian automobile industry are shown in Table 22.1. The four companies namely Maruti Udyog Ltd, Hyundai Motors India Ltd, Honda Siel India Ltd, and Ford India Ltd were omitted from this part of analysis because these companies shares were not listed in Stock - Exchanges. The study covers a thirteen years period from 1996 -97 to 2008 -09. Company and overall yearly mean values are computed and shown in Table 22.2. The study also computed the five ratios used by Altman. A summary of these five ratios (mean for all years) is shown in Table 22.5. The summary values are expressed as yearly and company averages. All of the ratios, as presented, include their weightings. The Z - Score for each company is computed, as shown, by summing across the five ratios.

## DATA

The study is mainly based on secondary data. The major source of data analysed and interpreted in this study related to all those companies selected is collected from "PROWESS" database, which is the most reliable on the empowered corporate database of Centre for Monitoring Indian Economy (CMIE). Besides prowess database, relevant secondary data have also been collected from BSE Stock Exchange Official Directory, CIME Publications, Annual Survey of Industry, Business newspapers, Reports on Currency and Finance, Libraries of various Research Institutions, through Internet etc.

## RESULTS AND DISCUSSION

In Table 22.1, the Z- Scores for all the selected companies and all years, it is noted that 62.5 per cent (10 out of 16) of the companies in the study are in the "non - bankrupt" sector. Further, 18.75 per cent (3 out of 16) of the companies in the study are in "gray" sector and the remaining 18.75 percent (3 out of 16) of the companies are in "bankrupt sector". It could infer from this statistic that the majority of the companies (81.25 per cent) in the study are either in the "non bankrupt" or "gray" sectors. This showed the good financial position of selected companies of Indian automobile industry during the study period. It is also obvious from the analysis that mean Z scores for LML Ltd, Kinetic Motor Company Ltd and Kinetic Engineering Ltd (all under two & three wheelers sector) witnessed less than 1.81 during the study period. Excessive use of working capital, failure to earn adequate surplus to meet non - operating activities and failure to achieve the adequate sales are the reasons for this dismal performance of these companies during the study period.

The Z score with respect to each company under commercial vehicles sector for the study period has been computed and presented in Table 22.1. It is evident from the table that Z scores for Eicher Motors Ltd always lie in non - bankrupt zone during the study period. All the remaining companies Z scores lie in the "non - bankrupt" or "gray" area zone during the study period. This shows the better financial performance of all the selected companies under commercial vehicle sector during the study period.

From the analysis of Z scores of passenger cars and multi-utility vehicles sector companies that the Z – score of

Mahindra and Mahindra Ltd witnessed more than 1.81 during the entire period of study. However, the Z – scores of Hindustan Motors Ltd witness more than 1.8 during the entire period of study except in the year 2003-04 and 2008-09. This reveals that financial health of this company is in bankrupt zone during the year 2003-04 and 2008-09. It is imperative from the figures of Z – score with the respect to selected companies under two and three wheelers sector that Bajaj Auto Ltd, Maharashtra Scooters Ltd, TVS Motor Company Ltd and Hero Honda Motors Ltd had never reached the bankruptcy zone during the study period. However, LML Ltd, Kinetic Motor Company Ltd and Kinetic Engineering Ltd showed dismal performance in this regard during the study period 2003-04 to 2008-09. This was attributed to under trading owning to excess working capital, failed to achieve adequate sales and under utilisation of capacity etc. Similarly, Z scores of Majestic Auto Ltd during the study period 2000-01 to 2002 - 03 and 2004 - 05 and Z scores of Scooters India Ltd during the terminal years 2007 - 08 and 2008 - 09 lies in the bankruptcy zone.

In order to test whether there was a downward trend in the Indian automobile companies - a decline to poor performance and insolvency, an yearly mean Z - scores are prepared and presented in Table 22.4. The yearly mean Z scores showed significant shift in to the poor performance. There appears to be a steady decrease from a high in 1997 - 98 (average 8.60 Z-score) through 2008 -09 (Z score of 2.67) with a leveling off and slight increase through 2003 - 04 and 2004 - 05. Given the overall mean, it is noted that none of the selected companies is not in the "bankrupt" sector.

**Examining the weighted Ratios**

To examine the relationship of the weighted ratios to the Z - score in the Altman model, the study computed the correlation of each company's mean weighted ratio and the corresponding company's Z - score and results are shown in Table 22.3. The working capital to total assets ratio ranked fifth in their discriminating ability within Altman model. The Indian automobile companies data confirm these ratings. The ratio of market value to book value was ranked as the highest contributor to the Z - score. The ratio of retained earnings to total assets had only 0.353 correlation, the second best among the five ratios. The ratio of EBIT to total assets was ranked - with a correlation of 0.325, it also appears to confirm in explanatory power to the model. However, the sales to total assets ratio, ranked second in discriminating power in Altman model, had ranked fourth in the Indian automobile companies. Thus, it is concluded that Indian automobile company data conform somewhat to the Altman model - not a perfect fit.

The study also examined the weighted ratios over the thirteen years of the study. Table 22.2 presents a table of yearly averages for the five ratios and the Altman Z - scores. The results are interesting to show that all the five ratios registered a fluctuating trend that parallel the Z - scores. Table 22.5 reflects the results of the four best performers in terms of overall Z - score over the study period (Bajaj Auto Ltd, Swaraj Mazada Ltd, Hero Honda Motors Ltd and Maharashtra Scooters Ltd) with the four lowest performers (Majestic Auto Ltd, Kinetic Engineering Ltd, Kinetic Motor Company Ltd and LML Ltd).

Altman put the greatest weighting on EBIT/ TA (44 per cent) followed by RE/TA (19 per cent) WC/TA (16 per cent), Sales /TA (13 per cent), and MV Equity /BV Equity (8 per cent). It is interesting to note that Bajaj Auto Ltd, ranked first overall, showed poor performance in RE/TA, EBIT/ TA and S/TA. Further, Bajaj Auto Ltd could improve their standings (in terms of overall Z - scores) by addressing only one measure, MV Equity /BV Equity, while Kinetic Motor Company Ltd could potentially improve their position from an overall poor performer by improving only one measure WC/TA. These implications illustrate how close the companies are to making improvements in certain areas.

## CONCLUSION

Financial health plays a significant role in the successful functioning of a firm. Poor financial health threatens the very survival and leads to business failure. The analyses of operational efficiency using Altman Z Score reveals that except few companies, the financial health of Indian automobile companies was good during the study period. The estimated discriminant function could be of great use for the management in attaining the financial health. This study would also be useful to all companies, policy makers and researchers for appraising financial health of corporate sector.

## REFERENCES

1. Altman I. Edward. (1968), " Financial Ratios, Discriminant Analysis and Prediction of corporate Bankruptcy", *Journal of Finance*, Vol.9, pp.589-609.
2. Bevar,W. (1966). "Financial ratios as predictor of failure," *Journal of Accounting Research*, PP.71 – 110.
3. Argenti John (1976). "Corporate collapse – The causes and Symptoms", New Delhi; McGraw Hill, P.91.
4. Gupta, L.C. (1979). "Financial ratios as forwarding predicators of sickness", ICICI, Bombay, PP.65-69.
5. Ohlson, J. (1980). "Financial ratios and the prediction of Bankruptcy, *Journal of Accounting Research*, PP.109 – 131.
6. Etebari, A. (1980). "Financial ratio criteria: A Hypothesis and Empirical testing," Working Paper, University of New Hampshire, PP. 27 – 32.
7. Makridakis (1991), "what can we learn from corporate failure," Long Range planning, Vol 24 (4), PP.115 – 125.
8. Sastry K.S. (1994). "Use of Z score – A note," *Indian Journal of Finance and Research*, PP.85-88.
9. James Sena and Dennis Williams (1998). "Using the Altman Bankruptcy model to Analyse the performance

of oil companies," *Petroleum Accounting and Financial Management Journal*, spring, 17, 1 : pro quest science Journals P.72.

10. Mansur A.Mulla. (2002). " Use of Z-score Analysis for Evaluation of Financial Health of Textile Mill – A case Study", *Abhigyan*, Vol. XIX, No 4, PP.37-41.
11. Selvam,M., Vanitha, S. and Babe (2004) " A study on financial health of cement industry – Z score Analysis," *The Management Accountant*, Vol. 39, No, 7, PP. 591-593.
12. Vijay Kumar, A. (2004)." Assessment of Financial Health of Indian Public Sector Manufacturing Enterprises – Altman's Z-Score Analysis", *The Journal of Institute of Enterprise*, Vol. 27 (384), pp. 112 – 116.

## TABLE 22.1

## ALTMAN Z SCORE FOR INDIAN AUTOMOBILE COMPANIES

| Company Name | 96-97 | 97-98 | 98-99 | 99-00 | 00-01 | 01-02 | 02-03 | 03-04 | 04-05 | 05-06 | 06-07 | 07-08 | 08-09 | Company Mean |
|---|---|---|---|---|---|---|---|---|---|---|---|---|---|---|
| Ashok Leyland Ltd | 3.08 | 2.52 | 2.69 | 3.10 | 2.99 | 3.30 | 3.99 | 5.78 | 4.07 | 4.78 | 5.26 | 4.65 | 2.21 | **3.72** |
| Tata Motors Ltd | 4.54 | 3.22 | 2.34 | 2.60 | 1.95 | 2.77 | 4.12 | 4.56 | 4.53 | 4.76 | 4.69 | 3.53 | 1.78 | **3.49** |
| Bajaj Tempo Ltd | 5.08 | 4.52 | 3.71 | 4.50 | 4.37 | 4.72 | 6.01 | 7.36 | 5.98 | 4.18 | 3.24 | 2.19 | 5.02 | **4.68** |
| Eicher Motors Ltd | 5.02 | 4.60 | 4.42 | 5.37 | 5.40 | 6.46 | 8.19 | 5.66 | 8.03 | 5.93 | 5.45 | 5.63 | 7.92 | **6.01** |
| Swaraj Mazda Ltd | 4.96 | 6.31 | 4.83 | 6.19 | 6.85 | 7.45 | 15.94 | 14.92 | 11.73 | 6.13 | 5.97 | 5.29 | 2.06 | **7.59** |
| Hindustan Motors Ltd | 3.18 | 2.72 | 2.37 | 2.75 | 3.89 | 2.38 | 2.18 | 1.54 | 6.15 | 1.97 | 3.27 | 4.49 | 1.42 | **2.95** |
| Mahindra & Mahindra Ltd | 4.29 | 3.69 | 3.31 | 4.15 | 2.91 | 2.67 | 3.07 | 5.51 | 5.56 | 4.70 | 4.28 | 3.45 | 2.31 | **3.84** |
| Baja Auto Ltd | 32.69 | 74.86 | 37.56 | 35.08 | 16.65 | 8.96 | 4.87 | 15.19 | 14.98 | 25.27 | 21.86 | 14.41 | 10.65 | **24.08** |
| LML Ltd | 2.50 | 2.60 | 3.31 | 2.37 | 1.53 | 0.99 | 2.99 | 1.62 | -0.68 | -4.96 | -6.78 | 2.58 | -2.22 | **0.45** |
| Maharashtra Scooters Ltd | 4.42 | 3.74 | 3.78 | 3.57 | 2.71 | 2.83 | 3.10 | 5.10 | 6.54 | 11.43 | 13.55 | 13.84 | 4.97 | **6.12** |
| TVS Motor Company Ltd | 6.72 | 6.22 | 5.22 | 5.18 | 4.27 | 5.18 | 5.89 | 4.55 | 4.18 | 3.69 | 3.25 | 2.68 | 2.61 | **4.59** |
| Kinetic Motor company Ltd | 4.23 | 4.17 | 3.84 | 4.84 | 5.22 | 4.20 | 3.17 | 1.80 | 1.50 | 1.14 | -2.83 | -11.52 | -3.99 | **1.21** |
| Hero Honda Motors Ltd | 5.89 | 9.70 | 11.96 | 12.93 | 6.61 | 7.94 | 5.69 | 5.43 | 5.63 | 5.71 | 5.42 | 5.00 | 4.95 | **7.14** |

**TABLE 22.1 (CONTINUED)**

**ALTMAN Z SCORE FOR INDIAN AUTOMOBILE COMPANIES**

| Company Name | 96-97 | 97-98 | 98-99 | 99-00 | 00-01 | 01-02 | 02-03 | 03-04 | 04-05 | 05-06 | 06-07 | 07-08 | 08-09 | Company Mean |
|---|---|---|---|---|---|---|---|---|---|---|---|---|---|---|
| Kinetic Engineering Ltd | 3.79 | 3.09 | 2.74 | 2.63 | 2.77 | 2.19 | 1.98 | 0.91 | 0.83 | 0.50 | 0.47 | 0.48 | 0.44 | **1.76** |
| Majestic Auto Ltd | 2.25 | 2.53 | 2.47 | 1.93 | 1.71 | 0.85 | 0.38 | 3.97 | 1.78 | 2.58 | 2.06 | 2.36 | 2.57 | **2.11** |
| Scooters India Ltd | 2.59 | 3.18 | 2.88 | 3.40 | 2.62 | 2.57 | 2.12 | 2.76 | 2.98 | 3.18 | 2.27 | 1.81 | -0.04 | **2.49** |
| **Yearly Mean** | **5.95** | **8.60** | **6.09** | **6.29** | **4.53** | **4.09** | **4.61** | **5.42** | **5.24** | **5.06** | **4.46** | **3.80** | **2.67** | **5.139** |

***Source :*** Computed

## TABLE 22.2

## WEIGHTED RATIOS USED TO COMPUTE ALTMAN Z SCORE

| Company Name | WC/TA* 100 | RE/TA* 100 | EBIT /TA * 100 | MVE/BVD *100 | S/TA | Z Score |
|---|---|---|---|---|---|---|
| **WEIGHTS** | **1.2** | **1.4** | **3.3** | **0.6** | **0.999** | |
| Ashok Leyland Ltd | 0.523 | 0.753 | 0.508 | 0.335 | 1.605 | **3.72** |
| Tata Motors Ltd | 0.118 | 0.750 | 0.546 | 0.400 | 1.674 | **3.49** |
| Bajaj Tempo Ltd | 0.440 | 0.764 | 0.315 | 0.664 | 2.497 | **4.68** |
| Eicher Motors Ltd | 0.331 | 0.745 | 0.772 | 0.818 | 3.338 | **6.01** |
| Swaraj Mazda Ltd | 0.801 | 0.353 | 1.048 | 0.446 | 4.938 | **7.59** |
| Hindustan Motors Ltd | 0.237 | -0.023 | 0.280 | 0.446 | 2.005 | **2.95** |
| Mahindra & Mahindra Ltd | 0.245 | 0.799 | 0.583 | 0.719 | 1.490 | **3.84** |
| Baja Auto Ltd | 0.527 | 0.657 | 0.396 | 21.018 | 1.480 | **24.08** |
| LML Ltd | -0.207 | -0.247 | -0.756 | 0.230 | 1.430 | **0.45** |
| Maharastra Scooters Ltd | -0.007 | 1.250 | 0.270 | 4.072 | 0.537 | **6.12** |
| TVS Motor Company Ltd | 0.178 | 0.778 | 0.691 | 0.861 | 2.078 | **4.59** |
| Kinetic Motor company Ltd | 1.777 | -0.042 | -0.582 | 0.374 | -0.315 | **1.21** |
| Hero Honda Motors Ltd | 0.143 | 1.132 | 1.932 | 1.452 | 2.482 | **7.14** |

## TABLE 22.2 (CONTINUED)

## WEIGHTED RATIOS USED TO COMPUTE ALTMAN Z SCORE

| Company Name | WC/TA* 100 | RE/TA* 100 | EBIT /TA * 100 | MVE/BVD *100 | S/TA | Z Score |
|---|---|---|---|---|---|---|
| Kinetic Engineering Ltd | 0.424 | 0.331 | 0.034 | 0.155 | 0.809 | **1.76** |
| Majestic Auto Ltd | 0.151 | 0.319 | 0.159 | 0.214 | 1.266 | **2.11** |
| Scooters India Ltd | 0.819 | -0.197 | 0.072 | 0.432 | 1.359 | **2.49** |
| **Mean** | **0.406** | **0.507** | **0.391** | **2.039** | **1.792** | |
| **SD** | **0.455** | **0.454** | **0.616** | **5.146** | **1.188** | |

## TABLE 22.3

## CORRELATION OF WEIGHTED FACTORS WITH Z SCORE

| Ranking in Altman's Model | Weighting factor | Correlation |
|---|---|---|
| Working capital to total assets | Fifth | 0.10 |
| Retained Earnings to Total Assets | Fourth | 0.353 |
| EBIT to total assets | First | 0.325 |
| Market value to book value | Third | 0.944 |
| Sales to total assets | Second | 0.197 |

***Source :*** Computed

## TABLE 22.5

## INDIVIDUAL RANKINGS

| Company | Mean Z-score for 13 year period | WC/ TA | RE/ TA | EBIT/ TA | MVE/ BVD | S/ TA |
|---|---|---|---|---|---|---|
| Bajaj Auto Ltd | 24.08 | 4th | 9th | 8th | 1st | 10th |
| Swaraj Mazda Ltd | 7.59 | 3rd | 10th | 2nd | 8th | 1st |
| Hero Honda Motors Ltd | 7.14 | 13th | 2nd | 1st | 3rd | 4th |
| Maharashtra Scooters Ltd | 6.12 | 15th | 1st | 11th | 2nd | 15th |
| Majestic Auto Ltd | 2.11 | 12th | 12th | 12th | 15th | 13th |
| Kinetic Engineering Ltd | 1.76 | 7th | 11th | 14th | 16th | 14th |
| Kinetic Motor Company Ltd | 1.21 | 1st | 14th | 15th | 12th | 16th |
| LML Ltd | 0.45 | 16th | 16th | 16th | 14th | 11th |

***Source :*** Computed

**TABLE 22.4**

**YEARLY AVERAGES OF WEIGHTED RATIOS USED TO COMPUTE THE ALTMAN Z-SCORE**

| | 96-97 | 97-98 | 98-99 | 99-00 | 00-01 | 01-02 | 02-03 | 03-04 | 04-05 | 05-06 | 06-07 | 07-08 | 08-09 |
|---|---|---|---|---|---|---|---|---|---|---|---|---|---|
| Working capital to total assets | 42.61 | 40.67 | 41.68 | 38.37 | 36.08 | 38.98 | 19.21 | 22.24 | 20.24 | 8.28 | 17.36 | 112.33 | 2.27 |
| Retained Earnings to Total Assets | 31.30 | 36.76 | 39.47 | 44.83 | 45.35 | 40.00 | 47.82 | 47.03 | 39.89 | 35.65 | 27.56 | 18.46 | 17.41 |
| EBIT to Total Assets | 19.62 | 16.89 | 14.21 | 17.37 | 13.70 | 14.61 | 21.01 | 19.20 | 12.2 | -0.03 | -7.89 | 11.91 | 1.67 |
| Market value of equity to Book value of equity | 428.5 | 887.63 | 491.81 | 475.25 | 198.06 | 124.88 | 92.06 | 247.38 | 225.5 | 393.5 | 370.75 | 291.19 | 193.81 |
| Sales to total assets | 1.79 | 1.72 | 1.62 | 1.78 | 1.82 | 1.84 | 2.46 | 2.37 | 2.68 | 2.11 | 1.91 | 0.06 | 1.18 |
| Z Score – yearly mean | 5.95 | 8.60 | 6.09 | 6.29 | 4.53 | 4.09 | 4.61 | 5.42 | 5.24 | 5.06 | 4.46 | 3.80 | 2.67 |

***Source :*** Computed

# PART - VIII

# PRODUCTIVITY ANALYSIS

# 23

# Data Envelopment Analysis and Malmquist Total Factor Productivity Indexs

## An Application to Indian Automobile Firms

## INTRODUCTION

Industry has a major role to play in the economic development of a country. Industrial development process should be designed properly to achieve economic development. For any country, which wants to perform in their industrial sector, needs to enhance its cost competitiveness by fostering Total Factor Productivity Growth (TFPG). Naturally, measurement of the total factor productivity changes in manufacturing industries and identifying the factors, which account for productivity changes, are of great interest-both in academic and practical senses. Manufacturing industries in developing countries rely heavily on imported intermediate inputs and sophisticated technology. Availability of both these factors also plays a crucial role in the variation in productivity of concerned industry. In the early phases of industrialization, the productivity in Indian manufacturing sector was limited by the government policies, such as, the reservation of production, high custom tariff – distorting resource allocation and prohibiting Indian Industry's ability to compete in the international market, shutting down industries in response to normal competitive market forces and various types of distortions created by the structure of domestic trade taxes and excise duties. However, the situation is gradually changing since 1970 due to the introduction of economic liberalization process, but at a slow and halting pace.

The first comprehensive economic reform policy statement was formulated for India in July 1991 in the form of industrial and trade sector liberalization. Over the years several measures were undertaken by them for boosting up the industrial productivity. Tariff rates have considerably been brought down; quantitative restrictions on imported goods have been removed to a great extent. These were adopted along with changes in technology-import policy, foreign direct investment policy, to make Indian industrial sector more efficient and productive, technology sounder and an able competitor in the front of world market. Therefore, analysing productivity and efficiency changes during the post reform periods becomes essential for providing strategic inputs to the producers, the government and other stake holders.

## LITERATURE REVIEW

Several studies have attempted to estimate the relationship between economic reforms and productivity growth in Indian manufacturing sector. Estimation of TFPG of Indian manufacturing industries can be seen from Goldar (1986), Ahluwalia (1991), Balakrishnan and Pushpangadan (1994), Fujita (1994), Rao (1996), Majumdar (1996), Joshi and Little (1997), Gangopadhyay and Wadhva (1998), Pradhan and Barik (1998), Krishna and Mitra (1998), Mitra (1999), Trivedi et al., (2000), Balakrishnan et al., (2000), Unni and Rani (2001), Forbes (2001), Srivastava (2001), Chand and Sen (2002), Hasan (2002), Goldar and Kumari (2003), Unel (2003), TSL (2003), Driffield and Kambhampatti (2003), Goldar (2004), Das (2004), Mukherjee (2004), Rani and Unni (2004), Pattnayak and Thangavelu (2005), Banga and Goldar (2007), Madheswaran et al., (2007), Milner *et al.*, (2007), Soo (2008), Jabir Ali et al., (2009). All of them examined the effect of reforms on industrial productivity. Some studies have reported that policies of liberalization improved the productivity of the manfuacturing industry [For example, See Fujita (1994); Majumdar (1996); Krishna and Mitra (1998); Chand and Sen (2002); Unel (2003); TSL (2003); Pattnayak and Thangavelu (2005); Banga and Goldar (2007)], whereas some have detected negative effects, or atleast no significant improvement, in productivity growth since the onset of economic reforms in 1991 [for example, See Trivedi et al., (2000); Balakrishnan et al., (2000); Unni and Rani (2001); Goldar and Kumari (2003); Driffield and Kambhampatti (2003); Goldar (2004); Das (2004)]. Thus, the topic of the effects of economic reforms on productivity growth remains a critical focus of research.

## STATEMENT OF THE PROBLEM

To meet the emerging challenges, there is an urgent need to bring efficiency to the production process, either through maximizing the output or minimizing the cost. While there have been numerous studies conducted on productivity growth, only a relatively few studies have concerned themselves with the sources of productivity growth in the Indian economy. The traditional Tornquist index, which is applied to calculate total factor productivity growth, is incapable of decomposing the productivity change into movements along and changes in frontier, because the Tornquist index assumes that the observed output is the consequences of the best practice frontier. Conversely, the nonparametric Data Envelopment Analysis (DEA) approach is used to compute the Malmquist Total Factor Productivity (TFP) change, which has been further decomposed into efficiency and technical change.

Total Factor Productivity can be increased by using its existing technology and factor inputs more efficiently – this is referred to as "efficiency change". The total factor productivity of an industry can also increase when the industry adopts innovations or technological improvements, and this process is referred to as "technological change". Therefore, changes in TFP from one period to the next are the products of both efficiency change and technological progress. Most previous studies conducted in India have failed to consider the sources of such changes in productivity growth. (Sindhu and Balasubramanyam (2006)). This study has attempted to assess the effects of economic reforms on productivity growth in Indian automobile companies using the Malmquist Productivity Index, decomposes the TFP change into technical and efficiency changes. In particular, this study intends to find the answers to the following question.

***"Has the performance of the automobile companies in India improved since the market liberalization of the 1990s in terms of productivity and efficiency changes"***

## METHODOLOGY

It is widely believed that Total Factor Productivity (TFP) is either measured by an index of outputs divided by an index of inputs, or as the shift in the production function. Technological change is also defined and measured as the shift in the production function and is thus often synonymous with TFP. However, when production is allowed to be inefficient, TFP change also includes technical efficiency change. In the empirical exercise attempted in this study, the study use Malmquist Total Factor Productivity growth, which is estimated using a non-parametric method namely, Data Envelopment Analysis (DEA).

**Data Envelopment Analysis Approach**

The DEA approach was first proposed by Charnes et al., (1978) to construct a production frontier and since then there have been a vast range of applications in the literature using DEA (Fare and Lovell 1978; Banker et al., 1984; Zhang et al., 1998; Ray and Ping 2001; Mahadevan 2004). DEA envelops observed input and output data without requiring a priori specification of functional form which turns out to be its major advantage. A production frontier is empirically constructed using linear programming methods from observed input-output data of sample firms. Efficiency of firms is then measured in terms of how far they are from the frontier. In contrast, different specifications of the production function under the parametric approach provide different results and this remains a methodological problems. Secondly, DEA is more appealing than the econometric model as inefficiency is likely to be correlated with the inputs (Gong and Sickless 1992). However, DEA is not free from drawbacks. These drawbacks include the following. First, measurement error and statistical noise are assumed to be nonexistent. Second, it does not allow for statistical tests typical of the parametric approach.

**The Malmquist Productivity Index**

The study uses the Malmquist Productivity Index approach to analyze changes in the total factor productivity of selected firms in Indian Automobile Industry overtime. The total factor productivity change of a firm has two primary components; the shift in the production frontier over time, representing technical change, and the shift in the firm's efficiency relative to the production frontier over time, representing efficiency change. There are several other ways to measure the productivity change of a firm (such as the Fisher Index or the Tornquist Index), but the Malmquist index is adopt here because it permits the separation of technical change from efficiency change (Fare, Grosskopf, Norris and Zhang, 1994) and is consistent with the DEA efficiency estimation methodology.

The Malmquist index was introduced by Caves et al., (1982 a, b) who dubbed it the (output based) Malmquist index after Sten Malmquist, who earlier proposed constructing quantity indexes as ratios of distance functions (See Malmquist, 1953). The Malmquist index was calculated as follows (as outlined in Fare et al., (1997)).

The measurement of the Malmquist productivity index is predicated on distance functions. For simplicity, $z^t = (x^t, y^t)$ and $z^{t+1} = (x^{t+1}, y^{t+1})$ where $x^t$ is the vector of inputs used in production and $y^t$ is the vector of outputs. Now, for each time period $t = 1, \ldots, T$, the output distance function is defined as follows:

$$D^t(z) = \inf\{\theta : y^t/\theta \in P^t(x)\}$$
$$= [\sup\{\theta : y^t/\theta \in P^t(x)\}]^{-1} \qquad (1)$$

where superscript *t* and $D^t$ denote that technology in period *t* is used as the reference technology. θ is scalar, and its value is the efficiency score for each production activity. It satisfies $0 < \theta \leq 1$ for a non-negative output level, with a value of 1 indicating a point of the frontier, and thus a technically efficient production activity. This output distance function is defined as the reciprocal of the maximal proportional expansion of output vector $y^t$ with the given input vector $x^t$ in relation to the technology at *t*.

The Malmquist productivity index is defined as follows:

$$TFP = M^t = \frac{D^t(z^{t+1})}{D^t(z^t)} \qquad (2)$$

This formulation is called the output-oriented Malmquist productivity index in period *t*, $M^t(z^{t+1}, z)$, where the technology in period *t* is the reference technology for two differing pairs of outputs and inputs. Alternatively, we can define $M^{t+1}$ where the technology in period $t + 1$ is employed as the reference technology.

Consistent with the study of Fare et al., (1994), the output-based Malmquist productivity index is defined as the geometric mean of two output-distance functions, in order to avoid selecting an arbitrary benchmark:

$$M\left(z^{t+1}, z^{t}\right) = \left[M^{t}.M^{t+1}\right]^{1/2} = \left[\left(\frac{D^{t}\left(z^{t+1}\right)}{D^{t}\left(z^{t}\right)}\right)\left(\frac{D^{t+1}\left(z^{t+1}\right)}{D^{t+1}\left(z^{t}\right)}\right)\right]^{1/2} \tag{3}$$

Equation (3) can be rewritten as:

$$M\left(z^{t+1}, z^{t}\right) = \left(\frac{D^{t+1}\left(z^{t+1}\right)}{D^{t}\left(z^{t}\right)}\right) \times \left(\frac{D^{t}\left(z^{t+1}\right)}{D^{t+1}\left(z^{t+1}\right)}\right)\left(\frac{D^{t}\left(z^{t}\right)}{D^{t+1}\left(z^{t}\right)}\right)^{1/2} \tag{3'}$$

where the ratio outside the brackets measures the change in relative efficiency between $t$ and $t +1$, and the geometric mean inside the brackets measures the shift in frontier. That is, the Malmquist productivity index can be decomposed into change in efficiency and change in technical progress.

In a previous empirical work, Fare et al., (1994) utilized non-parametric linear-programming techniques. As can be seen in (3'), it must solve four different linear programming problems: $D^{t}(z^{t}), D^{t}(z^{t+1}), D^{t+1}(z^{t}), and\ D^{t+1}(z^{t+1})$. Calculating the Malmquist index relative to the variable returns to scale technology, $D_{j}^{t}\left(z^{t}\right)$ for each industry, $j \in k = 1,...., K$, one of the four different linear programming problems, can be stated as:

$$\left[D_{j}^{t}\left(z_{j}^{t}\right)^{-1} = \max_{\theta, w} \theta_{j}\right] \tag{4}$$

$$\text{subject to } \theta_{j} y_{m,j}^{t} \leq \sum_{k=1}^{K} w_{k}^{t} y_{m,k}^{t} \quad m = 1,...., M \tag{4a}$$

$$\sum_{k=1}^{K} w_k^t x_{n,j}^t \leq x_{n,j}^t \quad n = 1,\ldots\ldots,N \tag{4b}$$

$$w_k^t \geq 0 \quad k = 1,\ldots\ldots,K \tag{4c}$$

where *n = 1, ....., N* are inputs, *m = 1, ...., M* are outputs, and $w_k^t$ is an intensity variable indicating the production intensity of a particular activity. (Here, each industry is an activity). These intensity variables are used as weights in taking convex combinations of the observed outputs and inputs in both (4a) and (4b). From Equation 4, the reciprocal of the output distance function can be used to find the maximum of $\theta$, which gives the maximal proportional expansion of output given constraints (4a) – (4).

For the other distance functions, the computation of $D^{t+1}(z^{t+1})$ is exactly the same as (4), where *t + 1* is substituted for *t*. Two other distance functions require information from two periods, $D^t(z^{t+1})$ can be computed by replacing $y_{m,j}^t$ and $x_{n,j}^t$ in (4a) and (4b) with $y_{m,j}^{t+1}$ and $x_{n,j}^{t+1}$, respectively and $D^{t+1}(z^t)$ is the same as $D^t(z^{t+1})$ where the *t* and *t + 1* superscripts are exchanged.

**Research Design**

Keeping in view the scope of the study, it is decided to include all the companies under automobile industry working before or from the year 1996-97 to 2008-09. There are 26 companies operating in the Indian automobile industry. But, owing to several constraints such as non-availability of financial statements or non-working of a company in a particular year etc., it is compelled to restrict the number of sample companies to 20. The companies under automobile industry are classified into three sectors namely; Commercial vehicles, Passenger Cars and Multiutility vehicles and Two and Three wheelers. For the purpose of the study all the three sectors have been selected. It accounts for 73.23 per cent of the total companies available in the Indian automobile industry. The selected 20 companies include 5 under commercial vehicles, 6 under Passenger cars and Multiutility vehicles and 9 under two and three wheeler sectors. It is inferred that sample company represents 98.74 percentage of market share in commercial vehicles, 89.76 percentage of market share in Passenger Cars and Multiutility vehicles and 99.81 percentage of market share in two and three wheelers. Thus, the findings based on the occurrence of such representative sample may be presumed to be true representative of automobile industry in the country.

Out of 20 selected companies under Indian Automobile Industry, the productivity performance of three Multinational Companies (MNC's) namely Hyundai Motors India Ltd, Honda Siel Cars India Ltd and Ford India Private Ltd computed separately because these companies established their operations in India in different accounting years. In order to have uniform period, the productivity performance of the three MNC's were computed from the year 2000-01 to 2008-09 (9 years only).

## DATA

The study is mainly based on secondary data. The major source of data analysed and interpreted in this study related to all those companies selected is collected from "PROWESS" database, which is the most reliable on the empowered corporate database of Centre for Monitoring Indian Economy (CMIE). Besides prowess database, relevant secondary data have also been collected from BSE Stock Exchange Official Directory, CIME Publications, Annual Survey of Industry, Business newspapers, Reports on Currency and Finance, Libraries of various Research Institutions, through Internet etc.

## RESULTS AND DISCUSSION

### Malmquist Total Factor Productivity

Table 23.1 shows mean values of change in Malmquist total factor productivity index and its components (efficiency change and technology change) for the period 1996-97 to

2008-09. The malmquist index value greater than one implies positive TFPG and the value less than one indicates TFPG decline. Note that while the product of the efficiency change and technology change components must be definition equal the Malmquist index, those components may be moving in opposite directions. For all the companies put together, the TFP has decreased by 1.05 per cent during the study period. An important question to investigate is whether the TFPG has been achieved by improvement in technical efficiency (catch-up) and / or improvement in technology (shift in production frontier)? The decomposition of TFPG into efficiency change and technical change also reported in the Table 23.1 shows that technological efficiency change has been the main contributor to TFPG. The average technological efficiency was 2.24 per cent, while the average technical efficiency change was negative (-3.20 per cent). This suggests that, in the companies studied, technical efficiency has been the main barrier to achieving high level of TFP during the period under consideration. Further, the analysis of total factor productivity of three sectors revealed that the overall TFP growth is positive in passenger cars and multiutility sector (2.5 per cent) due to improvement in both technical efficiency of 0.6 per cent and technological efficiency of 1.9 per cent.

Another significant results from the Table 23.1 that the efficiency change tends to be a negative contributor to total factor productivity in the commercial vehicles and two and three wheeler sector (i.e, it is less than unity), and technological change tends to be a positive contributor (i.e., it is greater than unity) suggesting that improvement in these sectors is due to their productivity based on production frontier effect. The overall technical efficiency change in these sectors is less than one which is the main cause in dampening the total factor productivity for whole industries.

Technical efficiency change is the result of pure technical efficiency change and scale efficiency change. With regards to pure efficiency change, it is more than one in cars and multiutility vehicles sector only. In case of scale efficiency change, a value close to unity shows that all the sectors are operating at optimum scale. Therefore scale efficiency has only contributed to the improvement in technical efficiency in all the three sectors and the whole Indian automobile industry during the study period.

Another interesting finding is that only 10 out of 17 companies had registered growth in TFP during the period 1996-97 to 2008-09 (Table 23.1). Further, all the companies except LML Ltd under two and three wheeler sector recorded technological efficiency improvement. But only 6 out of 17 companies had recorded technical efficiency improvement. However, not all the companies registered a similar performance during the period. Some companies, for instance, Ashok Leyland Ltd and Tata Motors Ltd (under commercial vehicles sector), Hindustan Motors Ltd (under passenger cars and multiutility vehicles sector) and Bajaj Auto Ltd, Hero Honda Motors Ltd and Majestic Auto Ltd (under two and three wheeler sector) have experienced an increase in overall technical efficiency during the period, while remaining companies experienced a negative growth in technical efficiency. But for technological efficiency is concerned, all the selected companies except LML Ltd have experienced a big increase in overall technological efficiency ranges from 1.002 to 1.048 during the period. Only in case of Ashok Leyland Ltd and Tata Motors Ltd (commercial vehicle sector), Hindustan Motors Ltd (passenger cars and multiutility vehicles sector) and Bajaj Auto Ltd, Hero Honda Motors Ltd and Majestic Auto Ltd (two and three wheeler sector), improvement in these industries is due to their productivity based both catching up effect and production frontier effect.

The technical efficiency change is further decomposed into pure technical efficiency change and scale efficiency change given in the last two columns in Table 23.1. With regards to pure efficiency change, it is one or more than one in Ashok Leyland Ltd, Tata Motors Ltd and Swaraj Mazda

Ltd (Commercial vehicle sector), Hindustan Motors Ltd, Mahindra and Mahindra Ltd and Maruti Udyog Ltd (Passenger cars and Multiutility vehicles sector) and Bajaj Auto Ltd, Hero Honda Motors Ltd and Majestic Auto Ltd (Two and three wheeler sector) during the study period. Scale efficiency indicates whether the firm can increase its productivity by becoming larger. It is evident from the table that incase of scale efficiency change, value close to unity shows that most of the companies are operating at optimum scale. The results of the study show that both the pure and scale efficiency have contributed to the growth of overall efficiency. This suggests that, in achieving high levels of technical performance over time, technical efficiency is not a long-run constraint. From the Table 23.1, the comparison of total factor productivity change in different companies shows that Hero Honda Motors Ltd on average has the highest growth in TFP (12.1 per cent), followed by Majestic Auto Ltd (5.7 per cent) and Bajaj Auto Ltd (4.1 per cent) total factor productivity growth. The worst performers in terms of total factor productivity growth is Maharashtra Scooters Ltd (-28 per cent) followed by Kinetic Motors Ltd (-9 per cent). Both the best and worst performer in terms of total factor productivity growth has been found in two and three wheeler sector of Indian Automobile industry during the study period.

The mean values of changes in Malmquist total factor productivity index and its components (efficiency change and technology change) for the three Multinational companies in Indian automobile industry for the period 1996-97 to 2008-09 were computed and presented in Table 23.2. The analysis of total factor productivity of three MNC revealed that the overall TFP growth is positive in Ford India Private Ltd and Honda Siel Cars India Ltd, but it is negative in Hyundai Motors India Ltd during the study period. The overall TFP growth is highest in Ford India Private Ltd (27 per cent) due to improvement in technical efficiency of 24 per cent and technological efficiency of 2.3 per cent. Similarly, in Honda Siel Cars India Ltd, the productivity growth was 2.7 per cent with technical efficiency growth of 1.2 per cent and technological efficiency change of 1.5 per cent. Another significant result from the Table 23.2 that technological change tends to be a negative contributor to total factor productivity in the Hyundai Motors India Ltd (i.e., it is less than unity) which is the main cause in dampening the total factor productivity in Hyundai Motors India Ltd. The analysis of two components of technical efficiency change presented in the table revealed that pure efficiency change is more than one in Ford India Private Ltd only. In case of scale efficiency change, in all the three MNCs, scale efficiency which is one or more than one, have contributed to the improvement in technical efficiency. The table also revealed that Hyundai Motors India Ltd did not show any change in terms of pure efficiency change and scale efficiency change during 1997-2009.

## CONCLUSION

The empirical estimates on the Indian automobile industry Productivity performance yielded several results that appear striking. The overall automobile industry improved technical (technological) change efficiency by 2.2 per cent while technical efficiency change put a negative effect on the productivity, as a result the overall total factor productivity during 1997-2009 decreased by 1.4 per cent. Among the three sectors, both technical efficiency change and technical change put a positive effect on the productivity only in the case of passenger cars and multiutility vehicles sector. However, in case of commercial vehicles sectors, technical progress leads to an increase of productivity by 0.4 per cent during the study period. The results from individual companies show that TFP growth is mainly contributed by technological change while technical efficiency change is only positive for ten out of twenty companies. It suggests that Indian automobile industry are lacking in terms of managerial efficiency growth. Except few companies which have relatively stable productivity includes Hero Honda Motors Ltd and Ford India Private Ltd, all other companies have a mixed trend over 1997-2009 which affects the productivity and ranking of companies. Ford India Private Ltd is at the top in ranking in terms of TFP followed by Hero Honda Motors Ltd due to highest technical change and technical efficiency. Maharashtra Scooters Ltd and Kinetic Motor Company Ltd are among the worst performer in terms of productivity over 1997-2009. The main reason for this worst performance is less improvement in managerial efficiency.

The research result suggests that Indian Automobile Companies must increase total factor productivity in most of the companies under study and efforts must be made to provide a stable pattern to the productivity growth. The reform process has increased access to superior technology in the manufacturing sector through higher foreign participation, as well as greater access to importation of higher quality of raw materials and capital equipment. However, the benefits of technological progress were not converted into productivity gains, as there was no improvement in efficiency in the reform period. The results of this study suggest the need for the implementation of specific policies to improve technical progress and efficiency change, in order to precipitate a long-run balance in TFP growth. Technological progress should be encouraged in industries with slow technical progress, industries, with slow efficiency change rates should be encourage to use existing technology more effectively via increased training and education.

## REFERENCES

1. Rodrik, D., and Subramanian, A. (2004). "From Hindu growth to productivity surge : The mystery of the Indian growth transition. (NBER Working paper No: W10376). *National Bureau of Economic Research*, Cambridge.
2. Goldar, B.N. (1986). "Productivity growth in Indian industry", New Delhi: *Allied Publishers*.
3. Ahluwalia, Isher Judge (1991). "Productivity and Growth

in Indian Manufacturing – Trends in Productivity and growth", New Delhi: *Oxford University Press.*

4. Balakrishnan, P. and Pushpakandan, K. (1994). "Total Factor Productivity growth in Indian Industry: A fresh look", *Economic and Political Weekly,* No. 29, pp. 2028 – 2035.

5. Fujita, Natsuki (1994). "Liberalization policies and productivity in India", *The Developing Economics,* 32(4): 509 – 524.

6. Rao J. Mohan (1996). "Manufacturing Productivity Growth : Method and Measurement", *Economic and Political Weekly,* 31 (44) : 2927 – 36.

7. Majumdar, Sumit K. (1996). "Fall and Rise of Productivity in Indian Industries : Has Economic Liberalization had an impact?", *Economic and Political Weekly,* 33(9) : M46 – M53.

8. Joshi, Vijay and I.M.D. Little. (1997). "Indian Economic Reforms 1991 – 2001", Clarendon Press, Oxford.

9. Ganagopadhyay, S. and Wadhwa, W. (1998). "Economic Reforms and Labour", *Economic and Political Weekly,* pp. L40 – L48.

10. Krishna, Pravin and Devashish Mitra. (1998). "Trade Liberalization, Market Discipline and Productivity Growth : New Evidence from India", *Journal of Development Economics,* 56(2) : 447 – 62.

11. Pradhan, G. and Barik, K. (1999). "Total Factor Productivity Growth in Developing Economies: A study of selected industries in India", *Economic and Political Weekly,* pp. M92 – M97.

12. Mitra, Arup. (1999). "Total Factor Productivity Growth and Technical Efficiency in Indian Industries", *Economic and Political Weekly,* 31 (31) : M98 – M105.

13. Trivedi, Pushpa, Anand Prakash and David Sinate (2000). "Productivity in Major Manufacturing Industries in India : 1973 – 74 to 1997 - 98", Developing Research Group No: 20, Department of Economic Analysis and

Policy, *Reserve Bank of India,* Mumbai.

14. Balakrishnan, P., and Pushpangadan, K. and Babu, M.S. (2000). "Trade liberalization and productivity growth in manufacturing : Evidence from firm level panel data", *Economic and Political Weekly,* 35 (4) : 3679 – 82.
15. Trivedi, Pushpa; Anand Prakash; and David Sinate (2000). "Productivity in Major Manufacturing Industries in India : 1973 – 74 to 1997 - 98", Developing Research Group No: 20, Department of Economic Analysis and Policy, *Reserve Bank of India,* Mumbai.
16. Jeemol Unni, Lalitha N., and Uma Rani (2001). "Economic reforms and productivity trends in Indian Manufacturing", *Economic and Political Weekly,* pp. 3914 – 3922.
17. Forbes, N. (2001). "Doing business in India : What has liberalization changed? (Working Paper No: 93), Center for Research on Economic Development and Policy Reform, Standard University.
18. Srivastava, V. (2001). "The impact of India's economic reforms on industrial productivity, efficiency and competitiveness: A panel study of Indian companies 1980 – 1997, New Delhi : NCAER.
19. Chand, S., and Sen, K. (2002). "Trade liberalization and Productivity growth: Evidence from Indian manufacturing", *Review of Development Economics,* 6(1) : 120 – 132.
20. Hasan, R. (2002). "The Impact of imported and domestic technologies on the productivity of firms : Panel data evidence from Indian manufacturing firms:, *Journal of Development Economics,* 69(1) : 23 – 49.
21. Unel. Bulent (2003). "Productivity Trends in India's Manufacturing Sectors in the Last Two Decades", *IMF Working Paper No: WP/03/02.*
22. TSL (2003). "Reforms and Productivity Trends in Indian Manufacturing Sector", *Department of Economics and Statistics,* Tata Services, Mumbai.
23. Driffield, N.L., and Kambhampatti, U.S. (2003). "Trade

liberalization and the efficiency of firms in Indian Manufacturing", *Review of Development Economics,* 7(3) : 419 – 30.

24. Deb Kusum Das (2004). "Manufacturing productivity under varying trade regimes, 1980 - 2000", *Economic and Political Weekly,* pp. 423-433.
25. Golder, Bishwanath. (2004). "Indian Manufacturing : Productivity Trends in Pre and Post reform periods", *Economic and Political Weekly,* 39 (46 & 47) : 5033 – 43.
26. Mukherjee, D. (2004). "Productivity in the small manufacturing enterprises: Determinants and policy issues, *Indian Journal of Labour Economics*", 47:913 – 27.
27. Rani, U., Unni, J. (2004). "Unorganised and organised manufacturing in India : Potential for employment generating growth", *Economic and Political Weekly*", 39 : 4568 – 80.
28. Pattnayak, S.S., and Thangavelu, S.M. (2005). "Economies Reform and Productivity growth in Indian Manufacturing Industries : An interaction of technical change and scale economies", *Economic Modelling,* 22 : 601–15.
29. Banga, Rashmi and Goldar, Bishwanath (2007). "Contribution of services to output Growth and Productivity in Indian Manufacturing : Pre and Post Reforms", *Economic and Political Weekly,* 42 (26) : 2769 – 2777.
30. Madheswaran, S., Hailin Liao and Badri Naryan Rath, (2007). "Productivity Growth of Indian Manufacturing Sector : Panel estimation of stochastic production frontier and Technical efficiency", *The Journal of Developing Area,* 40(2) : Spring : 35 – 50.
31. Milner, C., Vencappa, D., and Wright, P. (2007). "Trade Policy and Productivity growth in Indian Manufacturing", *The World Economy,* 30(2); 249 – 66.
32. Soo, Kwok Tong. (2008). "From License Raj to Market Forces: The Determinants of Industrial Structure in India after Reform", *Economica,* 75 : 222 – 43.

33. Jabir Ali., Surendra P. Singh and Enefiok P. KKanem (2009). "Efficiency and Productivity Changes in the Indian Food Processing Industry : Determinants and Policy Implications", *International Food and Agribusiness Management Review*, 12(1) : 43 – 66.
34. Sindhu, J., and Balasubramanyam, V.N. (2006). "India's Growth Performance : The Enigmatic Decade of the Eighties", *The Indian Economic Journal*, 54(3) : 7-24.
35. Charnes A, Cooper WW, Rhodes E (1978). "Measuring the efficiency of decision-making units.", *Europe Journal of Operations Research*, 2 : 429-44.
36. Fare R, Lovell CAK (1978). "Measuring the technical efficiency of Production.", *Journal of Economic Theory*, 19 : 150-162.
37. Banker, R.D., Charnes A., Cooper WW (1984). "Some models for estimating technical and scale inefficiencies in data envelopment analysis", *Management Science*, 30 : 1078-1092.
38. Zhang J, Liu X., Bigsten, A. (1998). "Ownership structure and determinants of technical efficiency; an application of data envelopment analysis to Chinese enterprises, 1986-1990", *Journal of Comparative Economics*, 26: 465-484.
39. Ray S.C., and Ping, Z., (2001). "Technical Efficiency of State owned enterprises in China, 1980-1989 : An assessment of the economic reforms", Working paper 2001-05, Department of Economics, University of Connecticut, C.T.
40. Mahadevan, R. (2004). "The economics of productivity in Asia and Australia", Edward Elgar, Cheltenham.
41. Gong, B.H., and Sickles, R.C. (1992). "Finite Sample Evidence on the performance of stochastic frontiers and data envelopment analysis using panel data", *Journal of Econometrics*, 51 : 259-84.
42. Fare, Rolf, Shawna Grosskopf, Mary Worris and Zhong Yang Zhang (1994). "Productivity Growth, Technical Progress and Efficiency Change in Industrialized

countries", *The American Economic Review*, 84 : 66-83.

43. Caves, Doglas., Christensen, Laurits R. and Diewert, W Ervin (1982a), "Multilateral comparisons of output, input and productivity using Superlative Index Numbers", *Economic Journal*, 92 (365) : 73.
44. ___________., (1982b). "Economic Theory of Index numbers and the measurement of input, output and productivity", *Econometrica*, 50(6) : 1393-1414.
45. Malmquist, Sten (1953). "Index numbers and Indifference curves", Trabajos de Estatistica, 4(1): 209-42.
46. Fare, R., Grosskopf S Grifell – Tatje, and C.A. Knox – Lovell (1997), "Biased Technical Change and the Malmquist Productivity Index", *Scandinavian Journal of Economics*, 99(1) : 119-127.

## TABLE 23.1

## CHANGES IN TOTAL FACTOR PRODUCTIVITY AND ITS COMPONENTS OF SELECTED INDIAN AUTOMOBILE COMPANIES DURING 1996-97 TO 2008-09

(Malmquist Index Summary of Company Means)

| Company | TFP Change | Components of TFPG | Components of Technical Efficiency Change | | |
|---|---|---|---|---|---|
| | | *Technological Change* | *Technical Efficiency Change* | *Pure Technical Efficiency Change* | *Scale Efficiency Change* |
| Ashok Leyland Ltd | 1.030 | 1.022 | 1.008 | 1.012 | 0.996 |
| Tata Motors Ltd | 1.026 | 1.020 | 1.006 | 1.000 | 1.006 |
| Bajaj Tempo Ltd | 0.975 | 1.009 | 0.966 | 0.965 | 1.001 |
| Eicher Motors Ltd | 0.981 | 1.007 | 0.974 | 0.977 | 0.997 |
| Swaraj Mazda Ltd | 1.007 | 1.026 | 0.981 | 1.000 | 0.981 |
| Hindustan Motors Ltd | 1.026 | 1.002 | 1.024 | 1.025 | 0.999 |
| Mahindra and Mahindra Ltd | 1.034 | 1.039 | 0.995 | 1.022 | 0.974 |
| Maruti Udyog Ltd | 1.015 | 1.015 | 1.000 | 1.000 | 1.000 |
| Bajaj Auto Ltd | 1.041 | 1.017 | 1.024 | 1.000 | 1.024 |
| LML Ltd | 0.937 | 0.990 | 0.946 | 0.964 | 0.981 |
| Maharashtra Scooters Ltd | 0.723 | 1.044 | 0.692 | 0.708 | 0.978 |
| TVS Motor Company Ltd | 1.019 | 1.040 | 0.980 | 0.970 | 1.010 |
| Kinetic Motor Company Ltd | 0.910 | 1.027 | 0.885 | 0.891 | 0.994 |
| Hero Honda Motors Ltd | 1.121 | 1.048 | 1.070 | 1.060 | 1.009 |
| Kinetic Engineering Ltd | 0.953 | 1.011 | 0.943 | 0.961 | 0.981 |
| Majestic Auto Ltd | 1.057 | 1.030 | 1.026 | 1.054 | 0.974 |
| Scooters India Ltd | 0.967 | 1.033 | 0.936 | 0.935 | 1.001 |
| **Commercial Vechicles** | **1.004** | **1.017** | **0.987** | **0.991** | **0.996** |
| **Passenger Cars and Multiutility Vechicles** | **1.025** | **1.019** | **1.006** | **1.016** | **0.991** |
| **Two and Three Wheelers** | **0.963** | **1.027** | **0.938** | **0.943** | **0.995** |
| **Whole Automobile Industry** | **0.986** | **1.022** | **0.964** | **0.970** | **0.994** |

## TABLE 23.2

## CHANGES IN TOTAL FACTOR PRODUCTIVITY AND ITS COMPONENTS OF THREE MNC IN INDIAN AUTOMOBILE COMPANIES DURING 1996-97 TO 2008-09

(Malmquist Index Summary of Company Means)

| Company | TFP Change | Components of TFPG | | Components of Technical Efficiency Change | |
|---|---|---|---|---|---|
| | | *Techno-logical Change* | *Technical Efficiency Change* | *Pure Technical Efficiency Change* | *Scale Efficiency Change* |
| Hyundai Motors India Ltd | 0.976 | 0.976 | 1.000 | 1.000 | 1.000 |
| Honda Siel cars India Ltd | 1.027 | 1.015 | 1.012 | 1.000 | 1.012 |
| Ford India Private Ltd | 1.270 | 1.023 | 1.241 | 1.224 | 1.014 |

## TABLE 23.3

## RANKING OF COMPANIES BASED ON MALMQUIST TFP AND ITS COMPONENTS

| Company | Ranks | | | | |
|---|---|---|---|---|---|
| | TFP Change | Tech. Change | TE Change | PE Change | SE Change |
| Ashok Leyland Ltd | 6 | 10 | 7 | 6 | 13 |
| Tata Motors Ltd | 8 | 11 | 8 | 7 | 6 |
| Bajaj Tempo Ltd | 15 | 16 | 15 | 15 | 7 |
| Eicher Motors Ltd | 13 | 17 | 14 | 13 | 12 |
| Swaraj Mazda Ltd | 12 | 8 | 12 | 8 | 15 |
| Hindustan Motors Ltd | 9 | 18 | 4 | 4 | 11 |
| Mahindra and Mahindra Ltd | 5 | 4 | 11 | 5 | 19 |
| Maruti Udyog Ltd | 11 | 13 | 9 | 9 | 9 |
| Bajaj Auto Ltd | 4 | 12 | 5 | 10 | 1 |
| LML Ltd | 18 | 19 | 16 | 16 | 16 |
| Maharashtra Scooters Ltd | 20 | 2 | 20 | 20 | 18 |
| TVS Motor Company Ltd | 10 | 3 | 13 | 14 | 4 |
| Kinetic Motor Company Ltd | 19 | 7 | 19 | 19 | 14 |
| Hero Honda Motors Ltd | 2 | 1 | 2 | 2 | 5 |
| Kinetic Engineering Ltd | 17 | 15 | 17 | 17 | 17 |
| Majestic Auto Ltd | 3 | 6 | 3 | 3 | 20 |
| Scooters India Ltd | 16 | 5 | 18 | 18 | 8 |
| Hyundai Motors India Ltd | 14 | 20 | 10 | 11 | 10 |
| Honda Siel Cars India Ltd | 7 | 14 | 6 | 12 | 3 |
| Ford India Private Ltd | 1 | 9 | 1 | 1 | 2 |

# 24

# Productivity, Technical Progress and Scale Efficiency in Indian Automobile Industry

## New Evidence using Malmquist Productivity Index

## INTRODUCTION

Industry has a major role to play in the economic development of a country. Industrial development process should be designed properly to achieve economic development. For any country, which wants to perform in their industrial sector, needs to enhance its cost competitiveness by fostering Total Factor Productivity Growth (TFPG). Naturally, measurement of the total factor productivity changes in manufacturing industries and identifying the factors, which account for productivity changes, are of great interest-both in academic and practical senses. Manufacturing industries in developing countries rely heavily on imported intermediate inputs and sophisticated technology. Availability of both these factors also plays a crucial role in the variation in productivity of concerned industry. In the early phases of industrialization, the productivity in Indian manufacturing sector was limited by the government policies, such as, the reservation of production, high custom tariff – distorting resource allocation and prohibiting Indian Industry's ability to compete in the international market, shutting down industries in response to normal competitive market forces and various types of distortions created by the structure of domestic trade taxes and excise duties. However, the situation is gradually changing since 1970 due to the introduction of economic liberalization process, but at a slow and halting pace.

The first comprehensive economic reform policy statement was formulated for India in July 1991 in the form of industrial and trade sector liberalization. Over the years several measures were undertaken by them for boosting up the industrial productivity. Tariff rates have considerably been brought down; quantitative restrictions on imported goods have been removed to a great extent. These were adopted along with changes in technology-import policy, foreign direct investment policy, to make Indian industrial sector more efficient and productive, technology sounder and an able competitor in the front of world market.

Theoretically, favourable effects of import liberalization of TFPG of industrial productivity are supported. The positive effects includes; lowering of tariffs will provide to industrial firms cheaper availability of intermediate inputs, which will enable them to improve their productivity performance; reduction in relative cost of imported capital goods will raise capital-labour ratio and embody sophisticated technology, thus enhancing TFPG; openness to foreign competition may compel the industries to close their less-efficient firms and make existing firms technically more efficient; increase in competitive pressure on industrial units under trade reforms policies will direct the industries to utilize the resources more efficiently; right of entry to imported inputs and reform in real effective exchange rate along with different trade policies under liberalization help industrial sector to compete in export markets more effectively through increase in sales and gain in economies of scale which in turn resulted to growth in TFP. As a result of changes in trade policies, Indian manufacturers find themselves threatened by both domestic and foreign competition.

Rodrik and Subramanian (2004) categories the reforms of 1980s and 1990s as "Pro-business" and "Pro-market", respectively. The eighties' reforms focussed on increasing the profitability of existing firms by easing capacity restrictions and reducing corporate taxes, while the reforms of the nineties allowed more competition and increased provisions for the entry of new domestic firms and Multi-National Companies (MNCs) in the Indian manufacturing sector. Under these circumstances, there emerges a need for measurement of TFP and identification of the factors that account for productivity changes. Specifically, finding out the appropriate relationship between effective exchange rate and the other trade related variables such as, import substitution, effective rate of protection, non-tariff barriers, etc., and factor productivity growth is very important in the context of recent policies of reforms. Therefore, analysing productivity and efficiency changes during the post reform periods becomes essential for providing strategic inputs to the producers, the government and other stake holders.

## LITERATURE REVIEW

Several studies have attempted to estimate the relationship between economic reforms and productivity growth in Indian manufacturing sector. Estimation of TFPG of Indian manufacturing industries can be seen from Goldar (1986), Ahluwalia (1991), Balakrishnan and Pushpangadan (1994), Fujita (1994), Rao (1996), Majumdar (1996), Joshi and Little (1997), Gangopadhyay and Wadhva (1998), Pradhan and Barik (1998), Krishna and Mitra (1998), Mitra (1999),

Trivedi et al., (2000), Balakrishnan et al., (2000), Unni and Rani (2001), Forbes (2001), Srivastava (2001), Chand and Sen (2002), Hasan (2002), Goldar and Kumari (2003), Unel (2003), TSL (2003), Driffield and Kambhampatti (2003), Goldar (2004), Das (2004), Mukherjee (2004), Rani and Unni (2004), Pattnayak and Thangavelu (2005), Banga and Goldar (2007), Madheswaran et al., (2007), Milner et al., (2007), Soo (2008), Jabir Ali et al., (2009). All of them examined the effect of reforms on industrial productivity. Some studies have reported that policies of liberalization improved the productivity of the manfuacturing industry [For example, See Fujita (1994); Majumdar (1996); Krishna and Mitra (1998); Chand and Sen (2002); Unel (2003); TSL (2003); Pattnayak and Thangavelu (2005); Banga and Goldar (2007)], whereas some have detected negative effects, or atleast no significant improvement, in productivity growth since the onset of economic reforms in 1991 [for example, See Trivedi et al., (2000); Balakrishnan et al., (2000); Unni and Rani (2001); Goldar and Kumari (2003); Driffield and Kambhampatti (2003); Goldar (2004); Das (2004)]. Thus, the topic of the effects of economic reforms on productivity growth remains a critical focus of research.

## PROBLEM STATEMENT

To meet the emerging challenges, there is an urgent need to bring efficiency to the production process, either through maximizing the output or minimizing the cost. While there have been numerous studies conducted on productivity growth, only a relatively few studies have concerned themselves with the sources of productivity growth in the Indian economy. The traditional Tornquist index, which is applied to calculate total factor productivity growth, is incapable of decomposing the productivity change into movements along and changes in frontier, because the Tornquist index assumes that the observed output is the consequences of the best practice frontier. Conversely, the nonparametric Data Envelopment Analysis (DEA) approach is used to compute the Malmquist Total Factor Productivity (TFP) change, which has been further decomposed into efficiency and technical change.

Total Factor Productivity can be increased by using its existing technology and factor inputs more efficiently – this is referred to as "efficiency change". The total factor productivity of an industry can also increase when the industry adopts innovations or technological improvements, and this process is referred to as "technological change". Therefore, changes in TFP from one period to the next are the products of both efficiency change and technological progress. Most previous studies conducted in India have failed to consider the sources of such changes in productivity growth. (Sindhu and Balasubramanyam (2006)). This study has attempted to assess the effects of economic reforms on productivity growth in Indian automobile companies using the Malmquist Productivity Index, decomposes the TFP change in to technical and efficiency changes. In particular, this study intends to find the answers to the following question.

> ***"Has the performance of the automobile companies in India improved since the market liberalization of the 1990s in terms of productivity and efficiency changes"***

## METHODOLOGY

It is widely believed that Total Factor Productivity (TFP) is either measured by an index of outputs divided by an index of inputs, or as the shift in the production function. Technological change is also defined and measured as the shift in the production function and is thus often synonymous with TFP. However, when production is allowed to be inefficient, TFP change also includes technical efficiency change. In the empirical exercise attempted in this study, the study use Malmquist Total Factor Productivity growth, which is estimated using a non-parametric method namely, Data Envelopment Analysis (DEA).

**Data Envelopment Analysis Approach**

The DEA approach was first proposed by Charnes et al., (1978) to construct a production frontier and since then there have been a vast range of applications in the literature using DEA (Fare and Lovell 1978; Banker et al., 1984; Zhang et al., 1998; Ray and Ping 2001; Mahadevan 2004). DEA envelops observed input and output data without requiring a priori specification of functional form which turns out to be its major advantage. A production frontier is empirically constructed using linear programming methods from observed input-output data of sample firms. Efficiency of firms is then measured in terms of how far they are from the frontier. In contrast, different specifications of the production function under the parametric approach provide different results and this remains a methodological problems. Secondly, DEA is more appealing than the econometric model as inefficiency is likely to be correlated with the inputs (Gong and Sickless 1992). However, DEA is not free from drawbacks. These drawbacks include the following. First, measurement error and statistical noise are assumed to be nonexistent. Second, it does not allow for statistical tests typical of the parametric approach.

**The Malmquist Productivity Index**

The study uses the Malmquist Productivity Index approach to analyze changes in the total factor productivity of selected firms in Indian Automobile Industry overtime. The total factor productivity change of a firm has two primary components; the shift in the production frontier over time, representing technical change, and the shift in the firm's efficiency relative to the production frontier over time, representing efficiency change. There are several other ways to measure the productivity change of a firm (such as the Fisher Index or the Tornquist Index), but the Malmquist index is adopt here because it permits the separation of technical change from efficiency change (Fare, Grosskopf, Norris and Zhang, 1994) and is consistent with the DEA efficiency estimation methodology.

The Malmquist index was introduced by Caves et al., (1982 a, b) who dubbed it the (output based) Malmquist index after Sten Malmquist, who earlier proposed constructing quantity indexes as ratios of distance functions (See Malmquist, 1953). The Malmquist index was calculated as follows (as outlined in Fare et al., (1997)).

The measurement of the Malmquist productivity index is predicated on distance functions. For simplicity, $z^t = (x^t, y^t)$ and $z^{t+1} = (x^{t+1}, y^{t+1})$, where $x^t$ is the vector of inputs used in production and $y^t$ is the vector of outputs. Now, for each time period $t = 1, \ldots\ldots T$, the output distance function is defined as follows:

$$D^t(z) = \inf\{\theta : y^t/\theta \in P^t(x)\}$$

$$= [\sup\{\theta : y^t/\theta \in P^t(x)\}]^{-1} \quad (1)$$

where superscript *t* and $D^t$ denote that technology in period *t* is used as the reference technology. *q* is scalar, and its value is the efficiency score for each production activity. It satisfies $0 < \theta \leq 1$ for a non-negative output level, with a value of 1 indicating a point of the frontier, and thus a technically efficient production activity. This output distance function is defined as the reciprocal of the maximal proportional expansion of output vector $y^t$ with the given input vector $x^t$ in relation to the technology at *t*.

The Malmquist productivity index is defined as follows:

$$TFP = M^t = \frac{D^t(z^{t+1})}{D^t(z^t)} \quad (2)$$

This formulation is called the output-oriented Malmquist productivity index in period *t*, $M^t(z^{t+1}, z)$, where the technology in period *t* is the reference technology for two differing pairs of outputs and inputs. Alternatively, we can define $M^{t+1}$ where the technology in period $t + 1$ is employed as the reference technology.

Consistent with the study of Fare et al., (1994), the output-based Malmquist productivity index is defined as the geometric mean of two output-distance functions, in order to avoid selecting an arbitrary benchmark:

$$M\left(z^{t+1}, z^{t}\right) = \left[M^{t}.M^{t+1}\right]^{1/2} = \left[\left(\frac{D^{t}\left(z^{t+1}\right)}{D^{t}\left(z^{t}\right)}\right)\left(\frac{D^{t+1}\left(z^{t+1}\right)}{D^{t+1}\left(z^{t}\right)}\right)\right]^{1/2} \quad (3)$$

Equation (3) can be rewritten as:

$$M\left(z^{t+1}, z^{t}\right) = \left(\frac{D^{t+1}\left(z^{t+1}\right)}{D^{t}\left(z^{t}\right)}\right) \times \left(\frac{D^{t}\left(z^{t+1}\right)}{D^{t+1}\left(z^{t+1}\right)}\right)\left(\frac{D^{t}\left(z^{t}\right)}{D^{t+1}\left(z^{t}\right)}\right)^{1/2} \quad (3')$$

where the ratio outside the brackets measures the change in relative efficiency between $t$ and $t+1$, and the geometric mean inside the brackets measures the shift in frontier. That is, the Malmquist productivity index can be decomposed into change in efficiency and change in technical progress.

In a previous empirical work, Fare *et al.*, (1994) utilized non-parametric linear-programming techniques. As can be seen in (3'), it must solve four different linear programming problems: $D^t(z^t)$, $D^t(z^{t+1})$, $D^{t+1}(z^t)$, and $D^{t+1}(z^{t+1})$. Calculating the Malmquist index relative to the variable returns to scale technology, $D_j^t\left(z^t\right)$ for each industry, $j \in k = 1,\ldots., K$, one of the four different linear programming problems, can be stated as:

$$\left[D_j^t\left(z_j^t\right)^{-1} = \max_{\theta, w} \theta_j\right] \quad (4)$$

$$\text{subject to } \theta_j y_{m,j}^t \leq \sum_{k=1}^{K} w_k^t y_{m,k}^t \quad m = 1,\ldots., M \quad (4a)$$

$$\sum_{k=1}^{K} w_k^t x_{n,j}^t \leq x_{n,j}^t \quad n = 1,\ldots\ldots, N \quad (4b)$$

$$w_k^t \geq 0 \quad k = 1,\ldots\ldots, K \quad (4c)$$

where $n = 1, \ldots, N$ are inputs, $m = 1, \ldots, M$ are outputs, and $w_k^t$ is an intensity variable indicating the production intensity of a particular activity. (Here, each industry is an activity). These intensity variables are used as weights in taking convex combinations of the observed outputs and inputs in both (4a) and (4b). From Equation 4, the reciprocal of the output distance function can be used to find the maximum of $\theta$, which gives the maximal proportional expansion of output given constraints (4a, – (4).

For the other distance functions, the computation of $D^{t+1}\left(z^{t+1}\right)$ is exactly the same as (4), where $t + 1$ is substituted for $t$. Two other distance functions require information from two periods, $D^t\left(z^{t+1}\right)$ can be computed by replacing $y_{m,j}^t$ and $x_{n,j}^t$ in (4a) and (4b) with $y_{m,j}^{t+1}$ and $x_{n,j}^{t+1}$, respectively and $D^{t+1}\left(z^t\right)$ is the same as $D^t\left(z^{t+1}\right)$ where the $t$ and $t + 1$ superscripts are exchanged.

**Research Design**

Keeping in view the scope of the study, it is decided to include all the companies under automobile industry working before or from the year 1996-97 to 2008-09. There are 26 companies operating in the Indian automobile industry. But, owing to several constraints such as non-availability of financial statements or non-working of a company in a particular year etc., it is compelled to restrict the number of sample companies to 20. The companies under automobile industry are classified into three sectors namely; Commercial vehicles, Passenger Cars and Multiutility vehicles and Two and Three wheelers. For the purpose of the study all the three sectors have been selected. It accounts for 73.23 per cent of the total companies available in the Indian automobile industry. The selected 20 companies include 5 under commercial vehicles, 6 under Passenger cars and Multiutility vehicles and 9 under two and three wheeler sectors. It is inferred that sample company represents 98.74 percentage of market share in commercial vehicles, 89.76 percentage of market share in Passenger Cars and Multiutility vehicles and 99.81 percentage of market share in two and three wheelers. Thus, the findings based on the occurrence of such representative sample may be presumed to be true representative of automobile industry in the country.

Out of 20 selected companies under Indian Automobile Industry, the productivity performance of three Multinational Companies (MNC's) namely Hyundai Motors India Ltd, Honda Siel Cars India Ltd and Ford India Private Ltd computed separately because these companies established their operations in India in different accounting years. In order to have uniform period, the productivity performance of the three MNC's were computed from the year 2000-01 to 2008-09 (9 years only).

## DATA

The study is mainly based on secondary data. The major source of data analysed and interpreted in this study related to all those companies selected is collected from "PROWESS" database, which is the most reliable on the empowered corporate database of Centre for Monitoring Indian Economy (CMIE). Besides prowess database, relevant secondary data have also been collected from BSE Stock Exchange Official Directory, CIME Publications, Annual Survey of Industry, Business newspapers, Reports on Currency and Finance, Libraries of various Research Institutions, through Internet etc.

## RESULTS AND DISCUSSION

### Malmquist Total Factor Productivity

Table 24.1 shows mean values of change in Malmquist total factor productivity index and its components (efficiency change and technology change) for the period 1996-97 to 2008-09. The malmquist index value greater than one implies positive TFPG and the value less than one indicates TFPG decline. Note that while the product of the efficiency change and technology change components must be definition equal the Malmquist index, those components may be moving in opposite directions. For all the companies put together, the TFP has decreased by 1.05 per cent during the study period. An important question to investigate is whether the TFPG has been achieved by improvement in technical efficiency (catch-up) and / or improvement in technology (shift in production frontier)?. The decomposition of TFPG in to efficiency change and technical change also reported in the Table 24.1 shows that technological efficiency change has been the main contributor to TFPG. The average technological efficiency was 2.24 per cent, while the average technical efficiency change was negative (-3.20 per cent). This suggests that, in the companies studied, technical efficiency has been the main barrier to achieving high level of TFP during the period under consideration. Further, the analysis of total factor productivity of three sectors revealed that the overall TFP growth is positive in passenger cars and multiutility sector (2.5 per cent) due to improvement in both technical efficiency of 0.6 per cent and technological efficiency of 1.9 per cent.

Another significant results from the Table 24.1 that the efficiency change tends to be a negative contributor to total factor productivity in the commercial vehicles and two and three wheeler sector (i.e, it is less than unity), and technological change tends to be a positive contributor (i.e., it is greater than unity) suggesting that improvement in these sectors is due to their productivity based on production frontier effect. The overall technical efficiency change in these sectors is less than one which is the main cause in dampening the total factor productivity for whole industries.

Technical efficiency change is the result of pure technical efficiency change and scale efficiency change. With regards to pure efficiency change, it is more than one in cars and multiutility vehicles sector only. In case of scale efficiency change, a value close to unity shows that all the sectors are operating at optimum scale. Therefore scale efficiency has only contributed to the improvement in technical efficiency in all the three sectors and the whole Indian automobile industry during the study period.

Another interesting finding is that only 10 out of 17 companies had registered growth in TFP during the period 1996-97 to 2008-09 (Table 24.1). Further, all the companies except LML Ltd under two and three wheeler sector recorded technological efficiency improvement. But only 6 out of 17 companies had recorded technical efficiency improvement. However, not all the companies registered a similar performance during the period. Some companies, for instance, Ashok Leyland Ltd and Tata Motors Ltd (under commercial vehicles sector), Hindustan Motors Ltd (under passenger cars and multiutility vehicles sector) and Bajaj Auto Ltd, Hero Honda Motors Ltd and Majestic Auto Ltd (under two and three wheeler sector) have experienced an increase in overall technical efficiency during the period, while remaining companies experienced a negative growth in technical efficiency. But for technological efficiency is concerned, all the selected companies except LML Ltd have experienced a big increase in overall technological efficiency ranges from 1.002 to 1.048 during the period. Only in case of Ashok Leyland Ltd and Tata Motors Ltd (commercial vehicle sector), Hindustan Motors Ltd (passenger cars and multiutility vehicles sector) and Bajaj Auto Ltd, Hero Honda Motors Ltd and Majestic Auto Ltd (two and three wheeler sector), improvement in these industries is due to their productivity based both catching up effect and production frontier effect.

The technical efficiency change is further decomposed into pure technical efficiency change and scale efficiency change given in the last two columns in Table 24.1. With regards to pure efficiency change, it is one or more than one in Ashok Leyland Ltd, Tata Motors Ltd and Swaraj Mazda Ltd (Commercial vehicle sector), Hindustan Motors Ltd, Mahindra and Mahindra Ltd and Maruti Udyog Ltd

(Passenger cars and Multiutility vehicles sector) and Bajaj Auto Ltd, Hero Honda Motors Ltd and Majestic Auto Ltd (Two and three wheeler sector) during the study period. Scale efficiency indicates whether the firm can increase its productivity by becoming larger. It is evident from the table that incase of scale efficiency change, value close to unity shows that most of the companies are operating at optimum scale. The results of the study show that both the pure and scale efficiency have contributed to the growth of overall efficiency. This suggests that, in achieving high levels of technical performance over time, technical efficiency is not a long-run constraint. From the Table 24.1, the comparison of total factor productivity change in different companies shows that Hero Honda Motors Ltd on average has the highest growth in TFP (12.1 per cent), followed by Majestic Auto Ltd (5.7 per cent) and Bajaj Auto Ltd (4.1 per cent) total factor productivity growth. The worst performers in terms of total factor productivity growth is Maharashtra Scooters Ltd (-28 per cent) followed by Kinetic Motors Ltd (-9 per cent). Both the best and worst performer in terms of total factor productivity growth has been found in two and three wheeler sector of Indian Automobile industry during the study period.

The mean values of changes in Malmquist total factor productivity index and its components (efficiency change and technology change) for the three Multinational companies in Indian automobile industry for the period 1996-97 to 2008-09 were computed and presented in Table 24.2. The analysis of total factor productivity of three MNC revealed that the overall TFP growth is positive in Ford India Private Ltd and Honda Siel Cars India Ltd, but it is negative in Hyundai Motors India Ltd during the study period. The overall TFP growth is highest in Ford India Private Ltd (27 per cent) due to improvement in technical efficiency of 24 per cent and technological efficiency of 2.3 per cent. Similarly, in Honda Siel Cars India Ltd, the productivity growth was 2.7 per cent with technical efficiency growth of 1.2 per cent and technological efficiency change of 1.5 per cent. Another significant result from the Table 24.2 that technological change tends to be a negative contributor to total factor productivity in the Hyundai Motors India Ltd (i.e., it is less than unity) which is the main cause in dampening the total factor productivity in Hyundai Motors India Ltd. The analysis of two components of technical efficiency change presented in the table revealed that pure efficiency change is more than one in Ford India Private Ltd only. In case of scale efficiency change, in all the three MNCs, scale efficiency which is one or more than one, have contributed to the improvement in technical efficiency. The table also revealed that Hyundai Motors India Ltd did not show any change in terms of pure efficiency change and scale efficiency change during 1997-2009.

**Total Factor Productivity Growth**

The comparative results of individual companies in terms of productivity for each year during 1997-98 to 2008-09 are presented in Table 24.3, which explains the total factor productivity change for all the selected companies on yearly basis and provide a comprehensive understanding about the performance of different companies.

In the first year of analysis (1997-98), Hero Honda Motors Ltd (two and three wheelers sector) is the best performer among all the companies with TFP growth of 30.9 per cent followed by TVS Motor Company Ltd and LML Ltd (two and three wheelers sector) where the productivity increased by 19.9 per cent and 11.5 per cent respectively. Tata Motors Ltd (commercial vehicles) is the worst performer (-27.6 per cent) with Ashok Leyland Ltd (-18.7 per cent). During the year 1998-99, total factor productivity of all the companies except Tata Motors Ltd, Swaraj Mazda Ltd and Bajaj Tempo Ltd (commercial vehicles), Mahindra and Mahindra Ltd (passenger cars and multiutility vehicles) and Scooters India Ltd (two and three wheelers) increased with LML Ltd, Kinetic Engineering Ltd and Majestic Auto Ltd top in ranking with productivity change of 55.4 per cent, 40.2 per cent and 27.9 per cent respectively. In the next year 1999-2000, again the TFP change for all companies except LML Ltd,

Maharashtra Scooters Ltd and Majestic Auto Ltd (all under two and three wheelers sector) increased. This year was also the most favourable for overall automobile industry where the total factor productivity increased by 9.3 per cent i.e second highest for the overall automobile industry during 1997-2009.

In the year 2000-01, downward trend in TFP changes can be seen where only five companies (Eicher Motors Ltd and Swaraj Mazda Ltd under commercial vehicles and Kinetic Motor Company Ltd, Hero Honda Motors Ltd and Kinetic Engineering Ltd under two and three wheelers) has their TFP more than one and Eicher Motors Ltd is top in ranking with 12.4 per cent growth. In the next year 2001-02, TFP changes for all the selected companies except Hindustan Motors Ltd and Mahindra and Mahindra Ltd under Passenger Cars and Multiutility vehicles sector and LML Ltd, Maharashtra Scooters Ltd, Kinetic Motor Company Ltd, Kinetic Engineering Ltd, Majestic Auto Ltd and Scooters India Ltd under two and three wheelers sector are in positive. In this year, TVS Motor Company Ltd under two and three wheelers sector has highest TFP growth of 41.9 per cent. The year 2002-03 was the most favourable for overall automobile industry where the total factor productivity increased by 21.8 per cent i.e., highest during 1997-2009. All the selected companies except Maharashtra Scooters Ltd, Kinetic Motor Company Ltd and Kinetic Engineering Ltd performed during 2002-03 where the TFP for LML Ltd and Bajaj Auto Ltd is top in ranking with growth of 79.9 per cent and 53.5 per cent respectively.

Hero Honda Motors Ltd and Majestic Auto Ltd under two and three wheelers sector played a leading role in total factor productivity growth with 48.9 per cent and 25.6 per cent respectively during 2003-04. Similarly, Maruti Udyog Ltd played a leading role in total factor productivity growth of all the selected companies with the highest (best performance) 92.5 per cent during 2004-05. Year 2005-06 is only suitable for Ashok Leyland Ltd and Tata Motors Ltd (commercial vehicles), Mahindra and Mahindra Ltd and Maruti Udyog Ltd (passenger cars and multiutility vehicles) and Hero Honda Ltd, Majestic Auto Ltd and Scooters India Ltd (under two and three wheelers) in terms of total factor productivity, while all other companies have their productivity growth in negative. In this year, Ashok Leyland Ltd under commercial vehicles productivity increased by 14.5 per cent and Tata Motors Ltd by 7.3 per cent.

Year 2006-07 was a crucial year for overall automobile industry where the productivity change for all the companies declined except for Eicher Motors Ltd and Kinetic Motors Ltd where it increased 2.5 per cent and 5.3 per cent respectively. This year was also the most unfavourable for automobile industry where the TFP decreased by 25.3 per cent, i.e., the highest during 1997-2009. In the year 2007-08, again a tangle up trend similar to the year 2006-07 can be seen only three companies (Swaraj Mazda Ltd, LML Ltd and Majestic Auto Ltd) has their TFP more than 1. During the year 2008-09 where 6 out of 17 companies have their TFP growth more than 1. Kinetic Motor Company Ltd has the highest total factor productivity change 92 per cent and Kinetic Engineering Ltd next in ranking with 48.4 per cent change. Majestic Auto Ltd has 42.3 per cent TFP change in this year. In terms of total factor productivity change Hero Honda Motors Ltd under two and three wheelers sectors has relatively more stable results because TFP change in 9 out of 12 years is greater than unity. Due to this reason this company is top in ranking in terms of total factor productivity.

The comparative results of year-wise productivity performance of MNC are presented in Table 24.4. The results presented in Table 24.4 revealed that Ford India Ltd is the best performer with the mean TFP growth of 27 per cent during 2000-01 to 2008-09. This company TFP growth was more than one in all the study period except 2001-02 and 2005-06. Similarly, the productivity was increased by 2.7 per cent in Honda Siel Cars India Ltd. This company TFP growth was also more than one in all the study period except 2005-06, 2007-08 and 2008-09. Further, the downward trend of productivity of Hyundai Motors India Ltd was observed during the terminal years (2004-2009) of the study period. It is also observed that the productivity performance of all the three MNCs was good during 2000-01, 2002-03 and 2003-04. Comparatively, Ford India Private Ltd has relatively more stable results because TFP change in 7 out of 9 years is greater than unity, which makes it top in ranking in terms of total factor productivity.

The indices of total factor productivity have been decomposed into technical efficiency change also called managerial efficiency and technical (technological adoption) change. These two sources of productivity are presented in Table 24.5 and 24.6 and Table 24.7 and 24.8.

**Managerial Efficiency Growth**

Technical efficiency change can make use of existing input to produce more of same product. As one gets more experience in producing some product, it becomes more and more efficient in it. Labour finds new ways to produce by making minor modifications in the process of manufacturing which contribute to higher productivity. Therefore, to understand the contribution made by technical efficiency in the productivity growth, year-wise technical efficiency movement is presented in Table 24.5.

In general these results suggest that technical efficiency is an important contributor in the total factor productivity. The average efficiency change of whole automobile industry is equal or greater than one in 9 out of 12 years of the study period. During the years 1999-00 and 2000-01, the technical efficiency change for majority of the selected companies are positive and overall automobile industry efficiency increased by 10.2 per cent during 1999-00, being the second highest efficiency growth in entire period. The year 2008-09 was also most favourable for all the selected companies where technical efficiency change increased by 11.2 per cent i.e., highest for the whole automobile industry during 1997-2009. In the year 2004-05, again a tangle up trend can be seen where only two out of seventeen companies has their technical efficiency change more than 1, which was also the most unfavourable for overall automobile industry where the technical efficiency change decreased by 25.1 per cent i.e., highest for the entire period during 1997-98 to 2008-09. The results in the table also explain that Maruti Udyog Ltd did not show any change in terms of efficiency during 1997-2009. The LML Ltd, Hero Honda Motors Ltd and Majestic Auto Ltd under two and three wheelers sector has performed relatively better than all other companies in terms of efficiency change. Other good performing companies in terms of efficiency change are Hindustan Motors Ltd (passenger cars and multiutility vehicles) and Bajaj Auto Ltd and Majestic Auto Ltd (two and three wheelers). These companies have their efficiency change in positive for seven years out of twelve years.

The year wise movement of technical efficiency of three MNC's is presented in Table 24.6. The results presented in Table 24.6 revealed that technical efficiency change of three MNC's is an important contributor in the TFP. The mean efficiency change of all the three companies is greater than one during the study period. During 2002-03 and 2006-07, all the three companies showed positive growth in their technical efficiency change.

**Technology adoption**

The second important source of total factor productivity growth is the change in the technology. Technological change is the development of new technologies or new products to improve and shift production frontier upward. Table 24.7 presents the comparative technical change for all companies during the period 1997-2009. It is observed from the table that the technical change can be seen in whole automobile industry greater than one during 1998-99 and 2001-02 to 2005-06, where technical change increased by 6.2 per cent, 7 per cent, 22.4 per cent, 7.8 per cent 45.8 per cent and 3.1 per cent respectively. Further, during 2001-02, 2002-03, 2004-05 and 2005-06, all the selected companies has performed better in terms of technical change, because their technical change is greater than one. The mean values of technical change of all the selected companies showed that all the companies have a relatively stable and overall technical change. However, in the terminal years 2006-07 and 2008-09 were a dreadful years for all the selected companies where technical change drop for all the companies. Maharashtra Scooters Ltd, TVS Motor Company Ltd, Majestic Auto Ltd and Hero Honda Motors Ltd under two and three wheeler sectors are the most stable companies in terms of technological change as having its change more than unity for seven out of twelve years.

Table 24.8 showed the comparative technical change for all the three MNC's during the study period. It is observed from the table that the mean technical change was more than one in Ford India Private Ltd and Honda Siel Cars India Ltd. Further, Honda Siel Cars India Ltd has a relatively stable in its technical change because it was more than one in six out eight years during the study period. However, technical change growth was decreased in the terminal years of the study period (2005-2009) in case of Hyundai Motors India Ltd.

Table 24.9 presents the ranking of all the selected companies in terms of total factor productivity growth, technical change and technical efficiency change. This table also presents the ranking in terms of pure efficiency change and scale efficiency change being the components of technical efficiency change.

## CONCLUSION

The empirical estimates on the Indian automobile industry Productivity performance yielded several results that appear striking. The overall automobile industry improved technical (technological) change efficiency by 2.2 per cent while technical efficiency change put a negative effect on the productivity, as a result the overall total factor productivity during 1997-2009 decreased by 1.4 per cent. Among the three sectors, both technical efficiency change and technical change put a positive effect on the productivity only in the case of passenger cars and multiutility vehicles sector. However, in case of commercial vehicles sectors, technical progress leads to an increase of productivity by 0.4 per cent during the study period. The results from individual companies show that TFP growth is mainly contributed by technological change while technical efficiency change is only positive for ten out of twenty companies. It suggests that Indian automobile industry are lacking in terms of managerial efficiency growth. Further, year wise analysis highlights that there is divergence in all the companies over 1997-2009 in terms of total factor productivity, technical efficiency and technical change.

Except few companies which have relatively stable productivity includes Hero Honda Motors Ltd and Ford India Private Ltd, all other companies have a mixed trend over 1997-2009 which affects the productivity and ranking of companies. Ford India Private Ltd is at the top in ranking in terms of TFP followed by Hero Honda Motors Ltd due to highest technical change and technical efficiency. Maharashtra Scooters Ltd and Kinetic Motor Company Ltd are among the worst performer in terms of productivity over 1997-2009. The main reason for this worst performance is less improvement in managerial efficiency.

The research result suggests that Indian Automobile Companies must increase total factor productivity in most of the companies under study and efforts must be made to provide a stable pattern to the productivity growth. The reform process has increased access to superior technology in the manufacturing sector through higher foreign participation, as well as greater access to importation of higher quality of raw materials and capital equipment. However, the benefits of technological progress were not converted into productivity gains, as there was no improvement in efficiency in the reform period. Goldar and

Kumari (2003) have presented econometric evidence indicating that slow down in TFP growth in Indian manufacturing in the post reform period is attributable, to a large extent, to deterioration in capacity utilization. It could, therefore, be concluded that there must have been a corresponding increase in efficiency to convert technological progress into productivity growth. The results of this study suggest the need for the implementation of specific policies to improve technical progress and efficiency change, in order to precipitate a long-run balance in TFP growth. Technological progress should be encouraged in industries with slow technical progress, industries, with slow efficiency change rates should be encourage to use existing technology more effectively via increased training and education.

## REFERENCES

1. Rodrik, D. and Subramanian, A. (2004). "From Hindu growth to productivity surge : The mystery of the Indian growth transition. (NBER Working paper No: W10376). *National Bureau of Economic Research*, Cambridge.
2. Goldar, B.N. (1986). "Productivity growth in Indian industry", New Delhi: *Allied Publishers.*
3. Ahluwalia, Isher Judge (1991). "Productivity and Growth in Indian Manufacturing – Trends in Productivity and growth", New Delhi: *Oxford University Press.*
4. Balakrishnan, P. and Pushpakandan, K. (1994). "Total Factor Productivity growth in Indian Industry: A fresh look", *Economic and Political Weekly,* No. 29, pp. 2028 – 2035.
5. Fujita, Natsuki (1994). "Liberalization policies and productivity in India", *The Developing Economics,* 32(4): 509 – 524.
6. Rao J. Mohan (1996). "Manufacturing Productivity Growth : Method and Measurement", *Economic and Political Weekly,* 31 (44) : 2927 – 36.
7. Majumdar, Sumit K. (1996). "Fall and Rise of Productivity

in Indian Industries : Has Economic Liberalization had an impact?", *Economic and Political Weekly,* 33(9) : M46 – M53.

8. Joshi, Vijay and I.M.D. Little. (1997). "Indian Economic Reforms 1991 – 2001", Clarendon Press, Oxford.
9. Ganagopadhyay, S. and Wadhwa, W. (1998). "Economic Reforms and Labour", *Economic and Political Weekly,* pp. L40 – L48.
10. Krishna, Pravin and Devashish Mitra. (1998). "Trade Liberalization, Market Discipline and Productivity Growth : New Evidence from India", *Journal of Development Economics,* 56(2) : 447 – 62.
11. Pradhan, G. and Barik, K. (1999). "Total Factor Productivity Growth in Developing Economies: A study of selected industries in India", *Economic and Political Weekly,* pp. M92 – M97.
12. Mitra, Arup. (1999). "Total Factor Productivity Growth and Technical Efficiency in Indian Industries", *Economic and Political Weekly,* 31 (31) : M98 – M105.
13. Trivedi, Pushpa; Anand Prakash; and David Sinate (2000). "Productivity in Major Manufacturing Industries in India : 1973 – 74 to 1997 - 98", Developing Research Group No: 20, Department of Economic Analysis and Policy, *Reserve Bank of India,* Mumbai.
14. Balakrishnan, P., and Pushpangadan, K. and Babu, M.S. (2000). "Trade liberalization and productivity growth in manufacturing : Evidence from firm level panel data", *Economic and Political Weekly,* 35 (4) : 3679 – 82.
15. Trivedi, Pushpa; Anand Prakash; and David Sinate (2000). "Productivity in Major Manufacturing Industries in India : 1973 – 74 to 1997 - 98", Developing Research Group No: 20, Department of Economic Analysis and Policy, *Reserve Bank of India,* Mumbai.
16. Jeemol Unni, Lalitha N., and Uma Rani (2001). "Economic reforms and productivity trends in Indian Manufacturing", *Economic and Political Weekly,* pp. 3914 – 3922.

17. Forbes, N. (2001). "Doing business in India : What has liberalization changed? (Working Paper No: 93), Center for Research on Economic Development and Policy Reform, Standard University.

18. Srivastava, V. (2001). "The impact of India's economic reforms on industrial productivity, efficiency and competitiveness: A panel study of Indian companies 1980 – 1997, New Delhi : NCAER.

19. Chand, S., and Sen, K. (2002). "Trade liberalization and Productivity growth: Evidence from Indian manufacturing", *Review of Development Economics,* 6(1) : 120 – 132.

20. Hasan, R. (2002). "The Impact of imported and domestic technologies on the productivity of firms : Panel data evidence from Indian manufacturing firms:, *Journal of Development Economics*, 69(1) : 23 – 49.

21. Unel. Bulent (2003). "Productivity Trends in India's Manufacturing Sectors in the Last Two Decades", *IMF Working Paper No: WP/03/02.*

22. TSL (2003). "Reforms and Productivity Trends in Indian Manufacturing Sector", *Department of Economics and Statistics,* Tata Services, Mumbai.

23. Driffield, N.L., and Kambhampatti, U.S. (2003). "Trade liberalization and the efficiency of firms in Indian Manufacturing", *Review of Development Economics,* 7(3): 419 – 30.

24. Deb Kusum Das (2004). "Manufacturing productivity under varying trade regimes, 1980 - 2000", *Economic and Political Weekly,* pp. 423-433.

25. Golder, Bishwanath. (2004). "Indian Manufacturing : Productivity Trends in Pre and Post reform periods", *Economic and Political Weekly,* 39 (46 & 47) : 5033 – 43.

26. Mukherjee, D. (2004). "Productivity in the small manufacturing enterprises: Determinants and policy issues, *Indian Journal of Labour Economics*", 47 : 913 – 27.

27. Rani, U., Unni, J. (2004). "Unorganised and organised manufacturing in India : Potential for employment

generating growth", *Economic and Political Weekly*", 39 : 4568 – 80.

28. Pattnayak, S.S., and Thangavelu, S.M. (2005). "Economies Reform and Productivity growth in Indian Manufacturing Industries : An interaction of technical change and scale economies", *Economic Modelling,* 22 : 601–15.
29. Banga, Rashmi and Goldar, Bishwanath (2007). "Contribution of services to output Growth and Productivity in Indian Manufacturing : Pre and Post Reforms", *Economic and Political Weekly,* 42 (26) : 2769 – 2777.
30. Madheswaran, S., Hailin Liao and Badri Naryan Rath, (2007). "Productivity Growth of Indian Manufacturing Sector : Panel estimation of stochastic production frontier and Techniacl efficiency", *The Journal of Developing Area,* 40(2) : Spring : 35 – 50.
31. Milner, C., Vencappa, D., and Wright, P. (2007). "Trade Policy and Productivity growth in Indian Manufacturing", *The World Economy,* 30(2); 249 – 66.
32. Soo, Kwok Tong. (2008). "From License Raj to Market Forces: The Determinants of Industrial Structure in India after Reform", *Economica,* 75 : 222 – 43.
33. Jabir Ali., Surendra P. Singh and Enefiok P. KKanem (2009). "Efficiency and Productivity Changes in the Indian Food Processing Industry : Determinants and Policy Implications", *International Food and Agribusiness Management Review,* 12(1) : 43 – 66.
34. Sindhu, J., and Balasubramanyam, V.N. (2006). "India's Growth Performance : The Enigmatic Decade of the Eighties", *The Indian Economic Journal,* 54(3) : 7-24.
35. Charnes A, Cooper WW, Rhodes E (1978). "Measuring the efficiency of decision-making units.", *Europe Journal of Operations Research,* 2 : 429-44.
36. Fare R, Lovell CAK (1978). "Measuring the technical efficiency of Production.", *Journal of Economic Theory,* 19 : 150-162.

37. Banker, R.D., Charnes A., Cooper WW (1984). "Some models for estimating technical and scale inefficiencies in data envelopment analysis", *Management Science,* 30 : 1078-1092.

38. Zhang J, Liu X., Bigsten, A. (1998). "Ownership structure and determinants of technical efficiency; an application of data envelopment analysis to Chinese enterprises, 1986-1990", *Journal of Comparative Economics,* 26: 465-484.

39. Ray S.C., and Ping, Z., (2001). "Technical Efficiency of State owned enterprises in China, 1980-1989 : An assessment of the economic reforms", Working paper 2001-05, Department of Economics, University of Connecticut, C.T.

40. Mahadevan, R. (2004). "The economics of productivity in Asia and Australia", Edward Elgar, Cheltenham.

41. Gong, B.H., and Sickles, R.C. (1992). "Finite Sample Evidence on the performance of stochastic frontiers and data envelopment analysis using panel data", *Journal of Econometrics,* 51 : 259-84.

42. Fare, Rolf, Shawna Grosskopf, Mary Worris and Zhong Yang Zhang (1994). "Productivity Growth, Technical Progress and Efficiency Change in Industrialized countries", *The American Economic Review,* 84 : 66-83.

43. Caves, Doglas., Christensen, Laurits R. and Diewert, W Ervin (1982a), "Multilateral comparisons of output, input and productivity using Superlative Index Numbers", *Economic Journal,* 92 (365) : 73.

44. _____________., (1982b). "Economic Theory of Index numbers and the measurement of input, output and productivity", *Econometrica,* 50(6) : 1393-1414.

45. Malmquist, Sten (1953). "Index numbers and Indifference curves", Trabajos de Estatistica, 4(1): 209-42.

46. Fare, R., Grosskopf S Grifell – Tatje, and C.A. Knox – Lovell (1997), "Biased Technical Change and the Malmquist Productivity Index", *Scandinavian Journal of Economics,* 99(1) : 119-127.

**TABLE 24.1**

**CHANGES IN TOTAL FACTOR PRODUCTIVITY AND ITS COMPONENTS OF SELECTED INDIAN AUTOMOBILE COMPANIES DURING 1996-97 TO 2008-09**

(Malmquist Index Summary of Company Means)

| Company | TFP Change | Components of TFPG | | Components of Technical Efficiency Change | |
|---|---|---|---|---|---|
| | | *Techno-logical Change* | *Technical Efficiency Change* | *Pure Technical Efficiency Change* | *Scale Efficiency Change* |
| Ashok Leyland Ltd | 1.030 | 1.022 | 1.008 | 1.012 | 0.996 |
| Tata Motors Ltd | 1.026 | 1.020 | 1.006 | 1.000 | 1.006 |
| Bajaj Tempo Ltd | 0.975 | 1.009 | 0.966 | 0.965 | 1.001 |
| Eicher Motors Ltd | 0.981 | 1.007 | 0.974 | 0.977 | 0.997 |
| Swaraj Mazda Ltd | 1.007 | 1.026 | 0.981 | 1.000 | 0.981 |
| Hindustan Motors Ltd | 1.026 | 1.002 | 1.024 | 1.025 | 0.999 |
| Mahindra and Mahindra Ltd | 1.034 | 1.039 | 0.995 | 1.022 | 0.974 |
| Maruti Udyog Ltd | 1.015 | 1.015 | 1.000 | 1.000 | 1.000 |
| Bajaj Auto Ltd | 1.041 | 1.017 | 1.024 | 1.000 | 1.024 |
| LML Ltd | 0.937 | 0.990 | 0.946 | 0.964 | 0.981 |
| Maharashtra Scooters Ltd | 0.723 | 1.044 | 0.692 | 0.708 | 0.978 |
| TVS Motor Company Ltd | 1.019 | 1.040 | 0.980 | 0.970 | 1.010 |
| Kinetic Motor Company Ltd | 0.910 | 1.027 | 0.885 | 0.891 | 0.994 |
| Hero Honda Motors Ltd | 1.121 | 1.048 | 1.070 | 1.060 | 1.009 |
| Kinetic Engineering Ltd | 0.953 | 1.011 | 0.943 | 0.961 | 0.981 |
| Majestic Auto Ltd | 1.057 | 1.030 | 1.026 | 1.054 | 0.974 |
| Scooters India Ltd | 0.967 | 1.033 | 0.936 | 0.935 | 1.001 |
| **Commercial Vechicles** | **1.004** | **1.017** | **0.987** | **0.991** | **0.996** |
| **Passenger Cars and Multiutility Vechicles** | **1.025** | **1.019** | **1.006** | **1.016** | **0.991** |
| **Two and Three Wheelers** | **0.963** | **1.027** | **0.938** | **0.943** | **0.995** |
| **Whole Automobile Industry** | **0.986** | **1.022** | **0.964** | **0.970** | **0.994** |

## TABLE 24.2

## CHANGES IN TOTAL FACTOR PRODUCTIVITY AND ITS COMPONENTS OF THREE MNC IN INDIAN AUTOMOBILE COMPANIES DURING 1996-97 TO 2008-09

(Malmquist Index Summary of Company Means)

| Company | TFP Change | Components of TFPG | | Components of Technical Efficiency Change | |
|---|---|---|---|---|---|
| | | *Techno-logical Change* | *Technical Efficiency Change* | *Pure Technical Efficiency Change* | *Scale Efficiency Change* |
| Hyundai Motors India Ltd | 0.976 | 0.976 | 1.000 | 1.000 | 1.000 |
| Honda Siel cars India Ltd | 1.027 | 1.015 | 1.012 | 1.000 | 1.012 |
| Ford India Private Ltd | 1.270 | 1.023 | 1.241 | 1.224 | 1.014 |

## TABLE 24.3

## COMPARATIVE TOTAL FACTOR PRODUCTIVITY OF ALL THE SELECTED INDIAN AUTOMOBILE COMPANIES DURING 1996-97 TO 2008-09

| Company | 1997-98 | 1998-99 | 1999-00 | 2000-01 | 2001-02 | 2002-03 | 2003-04 | 2004-05 | 2005-06 | 2006-07 | 2007-08 | 2008-09 | Mean |
|---|---|---|---|---|---|---|---|---|---|---|---|---|---|
| Ashok Leyland Ltd | 0.813 | 1.017 | 1.301 | 0.941 | 1.009 | 1.081 | 1.252 | 1.262 | 1.145 | 0.992 | 0.925 | 0.783 | **1.043** |
| Tata Motors Ltd | 0.724 | 0.877 | 1.353 | 0.845 | 1.090 | 1.420 | 1.188 | 1.290 | 1.073 | 0.993 | 0.917 | 0.808 | **1.048** |
| Bajaj Tempo Ltd | 0.932 | 0.962 | 1.168 | 0.860 | 1.115 | 1.347 | 1.208 | 0.935 | 0.849 | 0.851 | 0.884 | 0.757 | **0.989** |
| Eicher Motors Ltd | 0.858 | 1.061 | 1.281 | 1.124 | 1.031 | 1.406 | 1.171 | 0.833 | 0.745 | 1.025 | 0.943 | 0.598 | **1.006** |
| Swaraj Mazda Ltd | 0.860 | 0.873 | 1.269 | 1.095 | 1.121 | 1.237 | 1.190 | 1.052 | 0.849 | 0.920 | 1.057 | 0.723 | **1.021** |
| Hindustan Motors Ltd | 1.004 | 1.161 | 1.163 | 0.867 | 0.958 | 1.270 | 0.824 | 1.704 | 0.787 | 0.883 | 0.921 | 1.058 | **1.050** |
| Mahindra and Mahindra Ltd | 1.071 | 0.932 | 1.072 | 0.866 | 0.961 | 1.218 | 1.236 | 1.305 | 1.011 | 0.913 | 0.973 | 0.947 | **1.042** |
| Maruti Udyog Ltd | 0.962 | 1.044 | 1.061 | 0.732 | 1.016 | 1.166 | 0.992 | 1.925 | 1.059 | 0.802 | 0.994 | 0.799 | **1.046** |
| Bajaj Auto Ltd | 0.937 | 1.219 | 1.000 | 0.977 | 1.397 | 1.535 | 1.184 | 1.412 | 0.984 | 0.580 | 0.718 | 0.987 | **1.078** |
| LML Ltd | 1.115 | 1.554 | 0.627 | 0.751 | 0.824 | 1.799 | 0.867 | 0.663 | 0.499 | 0.158 | 9.616 | 0.870 | **1.612** |
| Maharashtra Scooters Ltd | 0.916 | 1.178 | 0.936 | 0.534 | 0.591 | 0.730 | 0.660 | 0.947 | 0.931 | 0.259 | 0.482 | 1.204 | **0.781** |
| TVS Motor Company Ltd | 1.199 | 1.036 | 1.123 | 0.806 | 1.419 | 1.324 | 0.944 | 1.076 | 0.948 | 0.877 | 0.754 | 0.932 | **1.037** |
| Kinetic Motor Company Ltd | 1.046 | 1.008 | 1.272 | 1.020 | 0.758 | 0.971 | 0.671 | 0.934 | 0.820 | 1.053 | 0.307 | 1.920 | **0.982** |
| Hero Honda Motors Ltd | 1.309 | 1.218 | 1.274 | 1.086 | 1.160 | 1.133 | 1.489 | 1.185 | 1.016 | 0.877 | 0.939 | 0.920 | **1.134** |
| Kinetic Engineering Ltd | 1.058 | 1.402 | 1.006 | 1.057 | 0.901 | 0.971 | 0.808 | 0.889 | 0.694 | 0.982 | 0.560 | 1.484 | **0.984** |
| Majestic Auto Ltd | 1.061 | 1.279 | 0.917 | 0.929 | 0.905 | 1.418 | 1.256 | 0.894 | 1.024 | 0.745 | 1.078 | 1.423 | **1.077** |

### TABLE 24.3 (CONTINUED)

### COMPARATIVE TOTAL FACTOR PRODUCTIVITY OF ALL THE SELECTED INDIAN AUTOMOBILE COMPANIES DURING 1996-97 TO 2008-09

| Company | 1997-98 | 1998-99 | 1999-00 | 2000-01 | 2001-02 | 2002-03 | 2003-04 | 2004-05 | 2005-06 | 2006-07 | 2007-08 | 2008-09 | Mean |
|---|---|---|---|---|---|---|---|---|---|---|---|---|---|
| Scooters India Ltd | 0.972 | 0.968 | 1.049 | 0.802 | 0.959 | 1.095 | 1.049 | 0.935 | 1.068 | 0.978 | 0.748 | 1.044 | **0.972** |
| **Whole Automobile Industry** | **0.981** | **1.091** | **1.093** | **0.886** | **0.992** | **1.218** | **1.032** | **1.092** | **0.895** | **0.747** | **0.914** | **0.972** | **0.986** |

***Source:*** Computed

### TABLE 24.4

### COMPARATIVE TOTAL FACTOR PRODUCTIVITY OF THREE MNC IN INDIAN AUTOMOBILE COMPANIES DURING 1996-97 TO 2008-09

| Company | 2000-01 | 2001-02 | 2002-03 | 2003-04 | 2004-05 | 2005-06 | 2006-07 | 2007-08 | 2008-09 | Mean |
|---|---|---|---|---|---|---|---|---|---|---|
| Hyundai Motors India Ltd | 1.031 | 0.964 | 1.033 | 1.175 | 0.994 | 0.979 | 0.853 | 0.770 | 1.043 | **0.976** |
| Honda Siel cars India Ltd | 1.03 | 1.134 | 1.216 | 1.120 | 1.509 | 0.952 | 1.045 | 0.959 | 0.556 | **1.027** |
| Ford India Private Ltd | 4.012 | 0.833 | 1.201 | 1.189 | 1.049 | 0.766 | 1.537 | 1.242 | 1.173 | **1.270** |
| | **2.024** | **0.977** | **1.150** | **1.161** | **1.184** | **0.899** | **1.145** | **0.990** | **0.924** | **1.091** |

## TABLE 24.5

## COMPARATIVE TECHNICAL CHANGE OF ALL THE SELECTED INDIAN AUTOMOBILE COMPANIES DURING 1996-97 TO 2008-09

| Company | 1997-98 | 1998-99 | 1999-00 | 2000-01 | 2001-02 | 2002-03 | 2003-04 | 2004-05 | 2005-06 | 2006-07 | 2007-08 | 2008-09 | Mean |
|---|---|---|---|---|---|---|---|---|---|---|---|---|---|
| Ashok Leyland Ltd | 0.995 | 0.992 | 0.978 | 0.824 | 1.055 | 1.234 | 1.051 | 1.475 | 1.029 | 0.85 | 0.999 | 0.928 | 1.034 |
| Tata Motors Ltd | 0.960 | 1.076 | 0.967 | 0.815 | 1.047 | 1.206 | 1.044 | 1.485 | 1.030 | 0.852 | 1.003 | 0.909 | 1.033 |
| Bajaj Tempo Ltd | 1.030 | 0.996 | 0.996 | 0.750 | 1.024 | 1.140 | 1.031 | 1.555 | 1.033 | 0.856 | 1.010 | 0.869 | 1.025 |
| Eicher Motors Ltd | 0.985 | 1.028 | 0.969 | 0.855 | 1.111 | 1.308 | 1.122 | 1.083 | 1.016 | 0.837 | 0.988 | 0.878 | 1.015 |
| Swaraj Mazda Ltd | 0.860 | 1.109 | 0.999 | 1.095 | 1.121 | 1.237 | 1.206 | 1.081 | 1.013 | 0.922 | 0.894 | 0.865 | 1.034 |
| Hindustan Motors Ltd | 0.976 | 1.066 | 1.068 | 0.720 | 1.020 | 1.184 | 0.974 | 1.865 | 1.056 | 0.731 | 0.958 | 0.792 | 1.034 |
| Mahindra and Mahindra Ltd | 0.863 | 1.120 | 0.952 | 0.923 | 1.127 | 1.305 | 1.064 | 1.428 | 1.026 | 0.845 | 0.994 | 0.964 | 1.051 |
| Maruti Udyog Ltd | 0.962 | 1.044 | 1.061 | 0.732 | 1.016 | 1.166 | 0.992 | 1.925 | 1.059 | 0.802 | 0.994 | 0.799 | 1.046 |
| Bajaj Auto Ltd | 1.015 | 0.987 | 0.980 | 0.789 | 1.047 | 1.219 | 1.048 | 1.458 | 1.026 | 0.842 | 0.992 | 0.945 | 1.029 |
| LML Ltd | 0.963 | 0.944 | 0.982 | 0.751 | 1.027 | 1.182 | 1.050 | 1.481 | 1.033 | 0.866 | 0.990 | 0.792 | 1.005 |
| Maharashtra Scooters Ltd | 0.925 | 1.150 | 0.936 | 0.936 | 1.124 | 1.305 | 1.067 | 1.417 | 1.027 | 0.847 | 0.996 | 0.941 | 1.056 |
| TVS Motor Company Ltd | 0.936 | 1.139 | 0.944 | 0.889 | 1.130 | 1.324 | 1.085 | 1.391 | 1.025 | 0.846 | 1.001 | 0.913 | 1.052 |
| Kinetic Motor Company Ltd | 0.986 | 1.046 | 0.974 | 0.834 | 1.062 | 1.230 | 1.044 | 1.494 | 1.030 | 0.850 | 1.000 | 0.926 | 1.040 |
| Hero Honda Motors Ltd | 0.947 | 1.151 | 0.946 | 0.997 | 1.109 | 1.226 | 1.376 | 1.185 | 1.016 | 0.877 | 0.939 | 0.920 | 1.057 |
| Kinetic Engineering Ltd | 1.037 | 1.022 | 1.018 | 0.731 | 1.026 | 1.159 | 1.010 | 1.624 | 1.036 | 0.867 | 1.027 | 0.800 | 1.030 |

## TABLE 24.5 (CONTINUED)

## COMPARATIVE TECHNICAL CHANGE OF ALL THE SELECTED INDIAN AUTOMOBILE COMPANIES DURING 1996-97 TO 2008-09

| Company | 1997-98 | 1998-99 | 1999-00 | 2000-01 | 2001-02 | 2002-03 | 2003-04 | 2004-05 | 2005-06 | 2006-07 | 2007-08 | 2008-09 | Mean |
|---|---|---|---|---|---|---|---|---|---|---|---|---|---|
| Majestic Auto Ltd | 0.887 | 1.118 | 1.122 | 0.755 | 1.021 | 1.183 | 0.974 | 2.215 | 1.058 | 0.811 | 0.958 | 0.792 | 1.074 |
| Scooters India Ltd | 0.851 | 1.092 | 0.999 | 1.131 | 1.144 | 1.228 | 1.272 | 1.096 | 1.013 | 0.921 | 0.894 | 0.865 | 1.042 |
| **Whole Automobile Industry** | **0.950** | **1.062** | **0.992** | **0.846** | **1.070** | **1.224** | **1.078** | **1.458** | **1.031** | **0.847** | **0.978** | **0.874** | **1.022** |

## TABLE 24.6

## COMPARATIVE TECHNICAL CHANGE OF THREE MNC IN INDIAN AUTOMOBILE COMPANIES DURING 1996-97 TO 2008-09

| Company | 2000-01 | 2001-02 | 2002-03 | 2003-04 | 2004-05 | 2005-06 | 2006-07 | 2007-08 | 2008-09 | Mean |
|---|---|---|---|---|---|---|---|---|---|---|
| Hyundai Motors India Ltd | 1.031 | 0.964 | 1.033 | 1.189 | 1.501 | 0.910 | 0.797 | 0.942 | 0.642 | **0.976** |
| Honda Siel cars India Ltd | 1.148 | 1.029 | 1.076 | 1.120 | 1.509 | 0.952 | 1.045 | 0.959 | 0.556 | **1.015** |
| Ford India Private Ltd | 0.926 | 0.903 | 1.126 | 1.047 | 1.517 | 0.845 | 0.761 | 1.092 | 1.173 | **1.023** |
| | **1.035** | **0.965** | **1.078** | **1.117** | **1.509** | **0.902** | **0.868** | **0.998** | **0.790** | **1.005** |

## TABLE 24.7

## COMPARATIVE TECHNICAL EFFICIENCY CHANGE OF ALL THE SELECTED INDIAN AUTOMOBILE COMPANIES DURING 1996-97 TO 2008-09

| Company | 1997-98 | 1998-99 | 1999-00 | 2000-01 | 2001-02 | 2002-03 | 2003-04 | 2004-05 | 2005-06 | 2006-07 | 2007-08 | 2008-09 | Mean |
|---|---|---|---|---|---|---|---|---|---|---|---|---|---|
| Ashok Leyland Ltd | 0.817 | 1.025 | 1.331 | 1.142 | 0.956 | 0.875 | 1.190 | 0.856 | 1.112 | 1.167 | 0.926 | 0.844 | **1.020** |
| Tata Motors Ltd | 0.754 | 0.815 | 1.400 | 1.036 | 1.042 | 1.178 | 1.138 | 0.869 | 1.042 | 1.166 | 0.914 | 0.889 | **1.020** |
| Bajaj Tempo Ltd | 0.905 | 0.966 | 1.172 | 1.147 | 1.089 | 1.181 | 1.172 | 0.602 | 0.821 | 0.994 | 0.876 | 0.871 | **0.983** |
| Eicher Motors Ltd | 0.871 | 1.032 | 1.322 | 1.316 | 0.928 | 1.075 | 1.043 | 0.770 | 0.733 | 1.225 | 0.954 | 0.681 | **0.996** |
| Swaraj Mazda Ltd | 1.000 | 0.787 | 1.270 | 1.000 | 1.000 | 1.000 | 0.986 | 0.974 | 0.839 | 0.999 | 1.182 | 0.836 | **0.989** |
| Hindustan Motors Ltd | 1.029 | 1.089 | 1.089 | 1.205 | 0.939 | 1.072 | 0.846 | 0.914 | 0.745 | 1.208 | 0.962 | 1.335 | **1.036** |
| Mahindra and Mahindra Ltd | 1.240 | 0.832 | 1.127 | 0.938 | 0.853 | 0.933 | 1.161 | 0.914 | 0.985 | 1.081 | 0.979 | 0.982 | **1.002** |
| Maruti Udyog Ltd | 1.000 | 1.000 | 1.000 | 1.000 | 1.000 | 1.000 | 1.000 | 1.000 | 1.000 | 1.000 | 1.000 | 1.000 | **1.000** |
| Bajaj Auto Ltd | 0.923 | 1.236 | 1.021 | 1.239 | 1.334 | 1.259 | 1.130 | 0.969 | 0.959 | 0.689 | 0.724 | 1.044 | **1.044** |
| LML Ltd | 1.157 | 1.646 | 0.638 | 1.000 | 0.803 | 1.521 | 0.826 | 0.447 | 0.483 | 0.182 | 9.711 | 1.097 | **1.623** |
| Maharashtra Scooters Ltd | 0.990 | 1.024 | 1.000 | 0.571 | 0.526 | 0.560 | 0.618 | 0.669 | 0.907 | 0.306 | 0.484 | 1.279 | **0.745** |
| TVS Motor Company Ltd | 1.281 | 0.909 | 1.190 | 0.906 | 1.256 | 1.000 | 0.870 | 0.773 | 0.924 | 1.036 | 0.754 | 1.021 | **0.993** |
| Kinetic Motor Company Ltd | 1.061 | 0.964 | 1.306 | 1.223 | 0.714 | 0.789 | 0.643 | 0.625 | 0.796 | 1.239 | 0.307 | 2.073 | **0.978** |
| Hero Honda Motors Ltd | 1.381 | 1.058 | 1.347 | 1.089 | 1.046 | 0.924 | 1.082 | 1.000 | 1.000 | 1.000 | 1.000 | 1.000 | **1.077** |
| Kinetic Engineering Ltd | 1.021 | 1.372 | 0.989 | 1.446 | 0.878 | 0.837 | 0.800 | 0.547 | 0.670 | 1.132 | 0.545 | 1.854 | **1.007** |

## TABLE 24.7 (CONTINUED)

## COMPARATIVE TECHNICAL EFFICIENCY CHANGE OF ALL THE SELECTED INDIAN AUTOMOBILE COMPANIES DURING 1996-97 TO 2008-09

| Company | 1997-98 | 1998-99 | 1999-00 | 2000-01 | 2001-02 | 2002-03 | 2003-04 | 2004-05 | 2005-06 | 2006-07 | 2007-08 | 2008-09 | Mean |
|---|---|---|---|---|---|---|---|---|---|---|---|---|---|
| Majestic Auto Ltd | 1.197 | 1.144 | 0.817 | 1.231 | 0.886 | 1.198 | 1.290 | 0.404 | 0.967 | 0.918 | 1.126 | 1.795 | **1.081** |
| Scooters India Ltd | 1.143 | 0.886 | 1.050 | 0.709 | 0.839 | 0.891 | 0.825 | 0.852 | 1.055 | 1.061 | 0.838 | 1.208 | **0.946** |
| **Whole Automobile Industry** | **1.032** | **1.028** | **1.102** | **1.047** | **0.927** | **0.995** | **0.958** | **0.749** | **0.868** | **0.882** | **0.935** | **1.112** | **0.964** |

## TABLE 24.8

## COMPARATIVE TECHNICAL EFFICIENCY CHANGE OF THREE MNC IN INDIAN AUTOMOBILE COMPANIES DURING 1996-97 TO 2008-09

| Company | 2000-01 | 2001-02 | 2002-03 | 2003-04 | 2004-05 | 2005-06 | 2006-07 | 2007-08 | 2008-09 | Mean |
|---|---|---|---|---|---|---|---|---|---|---|
| Hyundai Motors India Ltd | 1.000 | 1.000 | 1.000 | 0.988 | 0.663 | 1.076 | 1.070 | 0.817 | 1.625 | **1.000** |
| Honda Siel cars India Ltd | 0.897 | 1.102 | 1.130 | 1.000 | 1.000 | 1.000 | 1.000 | 1.000 | 1.000 | **1.012** |
| Ford India Private Ltd | 4.332 | 0.923 | 1.067 | 1.136 | 0.692 | 0.907 | 2.019 | 1.137 | 1.000 | **1.241** |
| | **2.076** | **1.008** | **1.067** | **1.041** | **0.785** | **0.994** | **1.363** | **0.985** | **1.208** | **1.084** |

**TABLE 24.9**

**RANKING OF COMPANIES BASED ON MALMQUIST TFP AND ITS COMPONENTS**

| Company | Ranks | | | | |
|---|---|---|---|---|---|
| | TFP Change | Tech. Change | TE Change | PE Change | SE Change |
| Ashok Leyland Ltd | 6 | 10 | 7 | 6 | 13 |
| Tata Motors Ltd | 8 | 11 | 8 | 7 | 6 |
| Bajaj Tempo Ltd | 15 | 16 | 15 | 15 | 7 |
| Eicher Motors Ltd | 13 | 17 | 14 | 13 | 12 |
| Swaraj Mazda Ltd | 12 | 8 | 12 | 8 | 15 |
| Hindustan Motors Ltd | 9 | 18 | 4 | 4 | 11 |
| Mahindra and Mahindra Ltd | 5 | 4 | 11 | 5 | 19 |
| Maruti Udyog Ltd | 11 | 13 | 9 | 9 | 9 |
| Bajaj Auto Ltd | 4 | 12 | 5 | 10 | 1 |
| LML Ltd | 18 | 19 | 16 | 16 | 16 |
| Maharashtra Scooters Ltd | 20 | 2 | 20 | 20 | 18 |
| TVS Motor Company Ltd | 10 | 3 | 13 | 14 | 4 |
| Kinetic Motor Company Ltd | 19 | 7 | 19 | 19 | 14 |
| Hero Honda Motors Ltd | 2 | 1 | 2 | 2 | 5 |
| Kinetic Engineering Ltd | 17 | 15 | 17 | 17 | 17 |
| Majestic Auto Ltd | 3 | 6 | 3 | 3 | 20 |
| Scooters India Ltd | 16 | 5 | 18 | 18 | 8 |
| Hyundai Motors India Ltd | 14 | 20 | 10 | 11 | 10 |
| Honda Siel Cars India Ltd | 7 | 14 | 6 | 12 | 3 |
| Ford India Private Ltd | 1 | 9 | 1 | 1 | 2 |

# 25

# Comparing Efficiency and Productivity of MNC in Indian Automobile Firms

## A Malmquist–Meta Frontier Approach

Manufacturing industries in developing countries rely heavily on imported intermediate inputs and sophisticated technology. Availability of both these factors also plays a crucial role in the variation in productivity of concerned industry. In the early phases of industrialization, the productivity in Indian manufacturing sector was limited by the government policies, such as, the reservation of production, high custom tariff – distorting resource allocation and prohibiting Indian Industry's ability to compete in the international market, shutting down industries in response to normal competitive market forces and various types of distortions created by the structure of domestic trade taxes and excise duties. However, the situation is gradually changing since 1970 due to the introduction of economic liberalization process, but at a slow and halting pace. The first comprehensive economic reform policy statement was formulated for India in July 1991 in the form of industrial and trade sector liberalization. Over the years several measures were undertaken by them for boosting up the industrial productivity. Tariff rates have considerably been brought down; quantitative restrictions on imported goods have been removed to a great extent. These were adopted along with changes in technology-import policy, foreign direct investment policy, to make Indian industrial sector more efficient and productive, technology sounder and an able competitor in the front of world market.

Roderick and Subramanian (2004) categories the reforms of 1980s and 1990s as "Pro-business" and "Pro-market", respectively. The eighties' reforms focussed on increasing the profitability of existing firms by easing capacity restrictions and reducing corporate taxes, while the reforms of the nineties allowed more competition and increased provisions for the entry of new domestic firms and Multi-National Companies (MNCs) in the Indian manufacturing sector. Under these circumstances, there emerges a need for measurement of TFP and identification of the factors that account for productivity changes. Specifically, finding out the appropriate relationship between effective exchange rate and the other trade related variables such as, import substitution, effective rate of protection, non-tariff barriers, etc., and factor productivity growth is very important in the context of recent policies of reforms. Therefore, analyzing productivity and efficiency changes during the post reform periods becomes essential for providing strategic inputs to the producers, the government and other stake holders.

## LITERATURE REVIEW

Several studies have attempted to estimate the relationship between economic reforms and productivity growth in Indian manufacturing sector. Estimation of TFPG of Indian manufacturing industries can be seen from Goldar

(1986), Ahluwalia (1991), Balakrishnan and Pushpangadan (1994), Fujita (1994), Rao (1996), Majumdar (1996), Joshi and Little (1997), Gangopadhyay and Wadhva (1998), Pradhan and Barik (1998), Krishna and Mitra (1998), Mitra (1999), Trivedi et al., (2000), Balakrishnan et al., (2000), Unni and Rani (2001), Forbes (2001), Srivastava (2001), Chand and Sen (2002), Hasan (2002), Goldar and Kumari (2003), Unel (2003), TSL (2003), Driffield and Kambhampatti (2003), Goldar (2004), Das (2004), Mukherjee (2004), Rani and Unni (2004), Pattnayak and Thangavelu (2005), Banga and Goldar (2007), Madheswaran et al., (2007), Milner et al., (2007), Soo (2008), Jabir Ali et al., (2009). All of them examined the effect of reforms on industrial productivity. Some studies have reported that policies of liberalization improved the productivity of the manfuacturing industry [For example, See Fujita (1994); Majumdar (1996); Krishna and Mitra (1998); Chand and Sen (2002); Unel (2003); TSL (2003); Pattnayak and Thangavelu (2005); Banga and Goldar (2007)], whereas some have detected negative effects, or at least no significant improvement, in productivity growth since the onset of economic reforms in 1991 [for example, See Trivedi et al., (2000); Balakrishnan et al., (2000); Unni and Rani (2001); Goldar and Kumari (2003); Driffield and Kambhampatti (2003); Goldar (2004); Das (2004)]. Thus, the topic of the effects of economic reforms on productivity growth remains a critical focus of research.

## PROBLEM STATEMENT

To meet the emerging challenges, there is an urgent need to bring efficiency to the production process, either through maximizing the output or minimizing the cost. While there have been numerous studies conducted on productivity growth, only a relatively few studies have concerned themselves with the sources of productivity growth in the Indian economy. The traditional Tornquist index, which is applied to calculate total factor productivity growth, is incapable of decomposing the productivity change into movements along and changes in frontier, because the Tornquist index assumes that the observed output is the consequences of the best practice frontier. Conversely, the nonparametric Data Envelopment Analysis (DEA) approach is used to compute the Malmquist Total Factor Productivity (TFP) change, which has been further decomposed into efficiency and technical change.

Total Factor Productivity can be increased by using its existing technology and factor inputs more efficiently – this is referred to as "efficiency change". The total factor productivity of an industry can also increase when the industry adopts innovations or technological improvements, and this process is referred to as "technological change". Therefore, changes in TFP from one period to the next are the products of both efficiency change and technological progress. Most previous studies conducted in India have failed to consider the sources of such changes in productivity growth. (Sindhu and Balasubramanyam (2006)). This study has attempted to assess the effects of economic reforms on productivity growth of MNC in Indian automobile industry using the Malmquist Productivity Index, decomposes the TFP change into technical and efficiency changes. In particular, this study intends to find the answers to the following questi on.

***"Has the performance of the MNC in Indian automobile industry improved since the market liberalization of the 1990s in terms of productivity and efficiency changes"***

## METHODOLOGY

The study uses the Malmquist Productivity Index approach to analyze changes in the total factor productivity of selected firms in Indian Automobile Industry overtime. The total factor productivity change of a firm has two primary components; the shift in the production frontier over time, representing technical change, and the shift in the firm's efficiency relative to the production frontier over time, representing efficiency change. There are several other ways to measure the productivity change of a firm (such as the Fisher Index or the Tornquist Index), but the Malmquist index is adopt here because it permits the separation of technical change from efficiency change (Fare, Grosskopf, Norris and Zhang, 1994) and is consistent with the DEA efficiency estimation methodology.

The Malmquist index was introduced by Caves et al., (1982 a, b) who dubbed it the (output based) Malmquist index after Sten Malmquist, who earlier proposed constructing quantity indexes as ratios of distance functions (See Malmquist, 1953). The Malmquist index was calculated as follows (as outlined in Fare et al., (1997)).

The measurement of the Malmquist productivity index is predicated on distance functions. For simplicity, $z^t = (x^t, y^t)$ and $z^{t+1} = (x^{t+1}, y^{t+1})$, where $x^t$ is the vector of inputs used in production and $y^t$ is the vector of outputs. Now, for each time period $t = 1, \ldots\ldots T$, the output distance function is defined as follows:

$$D^t(z) = \inf\{\theta : y^t/\theta \in P^t(x)\}$$

$$= [\sup\{\theta : y^t/\theta \in P^t(x)\}]^{-1} \quad (1)$$

where superscript $t$ and $D^t$ denote that technology in period $t$ is used as the reference technology. $q$ is scalar, and its value is the efficiency score for each production activity. It satisfies $0 < \theta \le 1$ for a non-negative output level, with a value of 1 indicating a point of the frontier, and thus a technically efficient production activity. This output distance function is defined as the reciprocal of the maximal proportional expansion of output vector $y^t$ with the given input vector $x^t$ in relation to the technology at $t$.

The Malmquist productivity index is defined as follows:

$$TFP = M^t = \frac{D^t(z^{t+1})}{D^t(z^t)} \quad (2)$$

This formulation is called the output-oriented Malmquist productivity index in period *t*, $M^t(z^{t+1}, z)$, where the technology in period *t* is the reference technology for two differing pairs of outputs and inputs. Alternatively, we can define $M^{t+1}$ where the technology in period *t + 1* is employed as the reference technology.

Consistent with the study of Fare *et al.*, (1994), the output-based Malmquist productivity index is defined as the geometric mean of two output-distance functions, in order to avoid selecting an arbitrary benchmark:

$$M\left(z^{t+1}, z^t\right) = \left[M^t . M^{t+1}\right]^{\frac{1}{2}} = \left[\left(\frac{D^t\left(z^{t+1}\right)}{D^t\left(z^t\right)}\right)\left(\frac{D^{t+1}\left(z^{t+1}\right)}{D^{t+1}\left(z^t\right)}\right)\right]^{\frac{1}{2}} \tag{3}$$

Equation (3) can be rewritten as:

$$M\left(z^{t+1}, z^t\right) = \left(\frac{D^{t+1}\left(z^{t+1}\right)}{D^t\left(z^t\right)}\right) \times \left(\frac{D^t\left(z^{t+1}\right)}{D^{t+1}\left(z^{t+1}\right)}\right)\left(\frac{D^t\left(z^t\right)}{D^{t+1}\left(z^t\right)}\right)^{\frac{1}{2}} \tag{3'}$$

where the ratio outside the brackets measures the change in relative efficiency between *t* and *t +1*, and the geometric mean inside the brackets measures the shift in frontier. That is, the Malmquist productivity index can be decomposed into change in efficiency and change in technical progress.

In a previous empirical work, Fare *et al.*, (1994) utilized non-parametric linear-programming techniques. As can be seen in (3'), it must solve four different linear programming problems: Calculating the Malmquist index relative to the variable returns to scale technology, $D_j^t\left(z^t\right)$ for each industry, $j \in k = 1, \ldots, K$, one of the four different linear programming problems, can be stated as:

$$\left[D_j^t\left(z_j^t\right)^{-1} = \max_{\theta, w} \theta_j\right] \tag{4}$$

$$\text{subject to } \theta_j y^t_{m,j} \leq \sum_{k=1}^{K} w^t_k y^t_{m,k} \quad m = 1,\ldots., M \tag{4a}$$

$$\sum_{k=1}^{K} w^t_k x^t_{n,j} \leq x^t_{n,j} \quad n = 1,\ldots\ldots, N \tag{4b}$$

$$w^t_k \geq 0 \quad k = 1,\ldots\ldots, K \tag{4c}$$

where $n = 1, \ldots.., N$ are inputs, $m = 1, \ldots., M$ are outputs, and $w^t_k$ is an intensity variable indicating the production intensity of a particular activity. (Here, each industry is an activity). These intensity variables are used as weights in taking convex combinations of the observed outputs and inputs in both (4a) and (4b). From Equation 4, the reciprocal of the output distance function can be used to find the maximum of $\theta$, which gives the maximal proportional expansion of output given constraints (4a) – (4).

For the other distance functions, the computation of $D^{t+1}\left(z^{t+1}\right)$ is exactly the same as (4), where $t + 1$ is substituted for $t$. Two other distance functions require information from two periods, $D^t\left(z^{t+1}\right)$ can be computed by replacing $y^t_{m,j}$ and $x^t_{n,j}$ in (4a) and (4b) with $y^{t+1}_{m,j}$ and $x^{t+1}_{n,j}$, respectively and $D^{t+1}\left(z^t\right)$ is the same as $D^t\left(z^{t+1}\right)$, where the $t$ and $t + 1$ superscripts are exchanged.

**Research Design**

Keeping in view the scope of the study, it is decided to include MNC in the Passenger Cars and Multiutility Vehicles sector under Indian automobile industry. Out of 8 companies under passenger cars and multiutility vehicles sector of Indian Automobile Industry, the productivity performance of three Multinational Companies (MNC's) namely Hyundai Motors India Ltd, Honda Siel Cars India Ltd and Ford India Private Ltd purposively selected for the study. The productivity performance of the three MNC's were computed from the year 2000-01 to 2008-09.

## DATA

The study is mainly based on secondary data. The major source of data analysed and interpreted in this study related to all those companies selected is collected from "PROWESS" database, which is the most reliable on the empowered corporate database of Centre for Monitoring Indian Economy (CMIE). Besides prowess database, relevant secondary data have also been collected from BSE Stock Exchange Official Directory, CIME Publications, Annual Survey of Industry, Business newspapers, Reports on Currency and Finance, Libraries of various Research Institutions, through Internet etc.

## RESULTS AND DISCUSSION

The mean values of changes in Malmquist total factor productivity index and its components (efficiency change and technology change) for the three Multinational companies in Indian automobile industry for the period 1996-97 to 2008-09 were computed and presented in Table 25.1. The analysis of total factor productivity of three MNC revealed that the overall TFP growth is positive in Ford India Private Ltd and Honda Siel Cars India Ltd, but it is negative in Hyundai Motors India Ltd during the study period. The overall TFP growth is highest in Ford India Private Ltd (27 per cent) due to improvement in technical efficiency of 24 per cent and technological efficiency of 2.3 per cent. Similarly, in Honda Siel Cars India Ltd, the productivity growth was 2.7 per cent with technical efficiency growth of 1.2 per cent and technological efficiency change of 1.5 per cent. Another significant result from the Table 25.1 that technological change tends to be a negative contributor to total factor productivity in the Hyundai Motors India Ltd (i.e., it is less than unity) which is the main cause in dampening the total factor productivity in Hyundai Motors India Ltd. The analysis of two components of technical efficiency change presented in the table revealed that pure efficiency change is more than one in Ford India Private Ltd only. In case of scale efficiency change, in all the three MNCs, scale efficiency which is one or more than one, have contributed to the improvement in technical efficiency. The table also revealed that Hyundai Motors India Ltd did not show any change in terms of pure efficiency change and scale efficiency change during the study period.

**Managerial Efficiency Growth**

Technical efficiency change can make use of existing input to produce more of same product. As one gets more experience in producing some product, it becomes more and more efficient in it. Labour finds new ways to produce by making minor modifications in the process of manufacturing which contribute to higher productivity. Therefore, to understand the contribution made by technical efficiency in the productivity growth, year-wise technical efficiency movement is presented in Table 25.2. The results presented in Table 25.2 revealed that technical efficiency change of three MNC's is an important contributor in the TFP. The mean efficiency change of all the three companies is greater than one during the study period. During 2002-03 and 2006-07, all the three companies showed positive growth in their technical efficiency change.

**Technology adoption**

The second important source of total factor productivity growth is the change in the technology. Table 3 showed the comparative technical change for all the three MNC's during the study period. It is observed from the table that the mean technical change was more than one in Ford India Private Ltd and Honda Siel Cars India Ltd. Further, Honda Siel Cars India Ltd has a relatively stable in its technical change because it was more than one in six out eight years during the study period. However, technical change growth was decreased in the terminal years of the study period (2005-2009) in case of Hyundai Motors India Ltd.

## CONCLUSION

The empirical estimates on the Indian automobile industry Productivity performance yielded several results that appear striking. Ford India Private Ltd is at the top in ranking in terms of TFP. The research result suggests that Indian Automobile Companies must increase total factor productivity in most of the companies under study and efforts must be made to provide a stable pattern to the productivity growth. The reform process has increased access to superior technology in the manufacturing sector through higher foreign participation, as well as greater access to importation of higher quality of raw materials and capital equipment. However, the benefits of technological progress were not converted into productivity gains, as there was no improvement in efficiency in the reform period. Goldar and Kumari (2003) have presented econometric evidence indicating that slow down in TFP growth in Indian manufacturing in the post reform period is attributable, to a large extent, to deterioration in capacity utilization. It could, therefore, be concluded that there must have been a corresponding increase in efficiency to convert technological progress into productivity growth. The results of this study suggest the need for the implementation of specific policies to improve technical progress and efficiency change, in order to precipitate a long-run balance in TFP growth. Technological progress should be encouraged in industries with slow technical progress, industries, with slow efficiency change rates should be encourage to use existing technology more effectively via increased training and education.

## REFERENCES

1. Rodrik, D., and Subramanian, A. (2004). “From Hindu growth to productivity surge : The mystery of the Indian growth transition. (NBER Working paper No: W10376). *National Bureau of Economic Research*, Cambridge.
2. Goldar, B.N. (1986). “Productivity growth in Indian industry”, New Delhi: *Allied Publishers*.

3. Ahluwalia, Isher Judge (1991). "Productivity and Growth in Indian Manufacturing – Trends in Productivity and growth", New Delhi: *Oxford University Press.*

4. Balakrishnan, P. and Pushpakandan, K. (1994). "Total Factor Productivity growth in Indian Industry: A fresh look", *Economic and Political Weekly,* No. 29, pp. 2028–2035.

5. Fujita, Natsuki (1994). "Liberalization policies and productivity in India", *The Developing Economics,* 32(4): 509 – 524.

6. Rao J. Mohan (1996). "Manufacturing Productivity Growth : Method and Measurement", *Economic and Political Weekly,* 31 (44) : 2927 – 36.

7. Majumdar, Sumit K. (1996). "Fall and Rise of Productivity in Indian Industries : Has Economic Liberalization had an impact?", *Economic and Political Weekly,* 33(9) : M46 – M53.

8. Joshi, Vijay and I.M.D. Little. (1997). "Indian Economic Reforms 1991 – 2001", Clarendon Press, Oxford.

9. Ganagopadhyay, S. and Wadhwa, W. (1998). "Economic Reforms and Labour", *Economic and Political Weekly,* pp. L40 – L48.

10. Krishna, Pravin and Devashish Mitra. (1998). "Trade Liberalization, Market Discipline and Productivity Growth : New Evidence from India", *Journal of Development Economics,* 56(2) : 447 – 62.

11. Pradhan, G. and Barik, K. (1999). "Total Factor Productivity Growth in Developing Economies: A study of selected industries in India", *Economic and Political Weekly,* pp. M92 – M97.

12. Mitra, Arup. (1999). "Total Factor Productivity Growth and Technical Efficiency in Indian Industries", *Economic and Political Weekly,* 31 (31) : M98 – M105.

13. Trivedi, Pushpa; Anand Prakash; and David Sinate (2000). "Productivity in Major Manufacturing Industries in India : 1973 – 74 to 1997 - 98", Developing Research Group No: 20, Department of Economic Analysis and Policy, *Reserve Bank of India,* Mumbai.

14. Balakrishnan, P., and Pushpangadan, K. and Babu, M.S. (2000). "Trade liberalization and productivity growth in manufacturing : Evidence from firm level panel data", *Economic and Political Weekly,* 35 (4) : 3679 – 82.

15. Trivedi, Pushpa; Anand Prakash; and David Sinate (2000). "Productivity in Major Manufacturing Industries in India : 1973 – 74 to 1997 - 98", Developing Research Group No: 20, Department of Economic Analysis and Policy, *Reserve Bank of India,* Mumbai.

16. Jeemol Unni, Lalitha N., and Uma Rani (2001). "Economic reforms and productivity trends in Indian Manufacturing", *Economic and Political Weekly,* pp. 3914 – 3922.

17. Forbes, N. (2001). "Doing business in India : What has liberalization changed? (Working Paper No: 93), Center for Research on Economic Development and Policy Reform, Standard University.

18. Srivastava, V. (2001). "The impact of India's economic reforms on industrial productivity, efficiency and competitiveness: A panel study of Indian companies 1980 – 1997, New Delhi : NCAER.

19. Chand, S., and Sen, K. (2002). "Trade liberalization and Productivity growth: Evidence from Indian manufacturing", *Review of Development Economics,* 6(1): 120 – 132.

20. Hasan, R. (2002). "The Impact of imported and domestic technologies on the productivity of firms : Panel data evidence from Indian manufacturing firms:, *Journal of Development Economics,* 69(1) : 23 – 49.

21. Unel. Bulent (2003). "Productivity Trends in India's Manufacturing Sectors in the Last Two Decades", *IMF Working Paper No: WP/03/02.*

22. TSL (2003). "Reforms and Productivity Trends in Indian Manufacturing Sector", *Department of Economics and Statistics,* Tata Services, Mumbai.

23. Driffield, N.L., and Kambhampatti, U.S. (2003). "Trade liberalization and the efficiency of firms in Indian

Manufacturing", *Review of Development Economics,* 7(3) : 419 – 30.

24. Deb Kusum Das (2004). "Manufacturing productivity under varying trade regimes, 1980 - 2000", *Economic and Political Weekly,* pp. 423-433.
25. Golder, Bishwanath. (2004). "Indian Manufacturing : Productivity Trends in Pre and Post reform periods", *Economic and Political Weekly,* 39 (46 & 47) : 5033 – 43.
26. Mukherjee, D. (2004). "Productivity in the small manufacturing enterprises: Determinants and policy issues, *Indian Journal of Labour Economics*", 47 : 913 – 27.
27. Rani, U., Unni, J. (2004). "Unorganised and organised manufacturing in India : Potential for employment generating growth", *Economic and Political Weekly*", 39 : 4568 – 80.
28. Pattnayak, S.S., and Thangavelu, S.M. (2005). "Economies Reform and Productivity growth in Indian Manufacturing Industries : An interaction of technical change and scale economies", *Economic Modelling,* 22 : 601–15.
29. Banga, Rashmi and Goldar, Bishwanath (2007). "Contribution of services to output Growth and Productivity in Indian Manufacturing : Pre and Post Reforms", *Economic and Political Weekly,* 42 (26) : 2769 – 2777.
30. Madheswaran, S., Hailin Liao and Badri Naryan Rath, (2007). "Productivity Growth of Indian Manufacturing Sector : Panel estimation of stochastic production frontier and Techniacl efficiency", *The Journal of Developing Area,* 40(2) : Spring : 35 – 50.
31. Milner, C., Vencappa, D., and Wright, P. (2007). "Trade Policy and Productivity growth in Indian Manufacturing", *The World Economy,* 30(2); 249 – 66.
32. Soo, Kwok Tong. (2008). "From License Raj to Market Forces: The Determinants of Industrial Structure in India after Reform", *Economica,* 75 : 222 – 43.

33. Jabir Ali., Surendra P. Singh and Enefiok P. KKanem (2009). "Efficiency and Productivity Changes in the Indian Food Processing Industry : Determinants and Policy Implications", *International Food and Agribusiness Management Review*, 12(1) : 43 – 66.

34. Sindhu, J., and Balasubramanyam, V.N. (2006). "India's Growth Performance : The Enigmatic Decade of the Eighties", *The Indian Economic Journal*, 54(3) : 7-24.

35. Charnes A, Cooper WW, Rhodes E (1978). "Measuring the efficiency of decision-making units.", *Europe Journal of Operations Research*, 2 : 429-44.

36. Fare R, Lovell CAK (1978). "Measuring the technical efficiency of Production.", *Journal of Economic Theory*, 19 : 150-162.

37. Banker, R.D., Charnes A., Cooper WW (1984). "Some models for estimating technical and scale inefficiencies in data envelopment analysis", *Management Science*, 30: 1078-1092.

38. Zhang J, Liu X., Bigsten, A. (1998). "Ownership structure and determinants of technical efficiency; an application of data envelopment analysis to Chinese enterprises, 1986-1990", *Journal of Comparative Economics*, 26: 465-484.

39. Ray S.C., and Ping, Z., (2001). "Technical Efficiency of State owned enterprises in China, 1980-1989 : An assessment of the economic reforms", Working paper 2001-05, Department of Economics, University of Connecticut, C.T.

40. Mahadevan, R. (2004). "The economics of productivity in Asia and Australia", Edward Elgar, Cheltenham.

41. Gong, B.H., and Sickles, R.C. (1992). "Finite Sample Evidence on the performance of stochastic frontiers and data envelopment analysis using panel data", *Journal of Econometrics*, 51 : 259-84.

42. Fare, Rolf, Shawna Grosskopf, Mary Worris and Zhong Yang Zhang (1994). "Productivity Growth, Technical Progress and Efficiency Change in Industrialized

countries", *The American Economic Review*, 84 : 66-83.

43. Caves, Doglas., Christensen, Laurits R. and Diewert, W Ervin (1982a), "Multilateral comparisons of output, input and productivity using Superlative Index Numbers", *Economic Journal*, 92 (365) : 73.
44. _____________., (1982b). "Economic Theory of Index numbers and the measurement of input, output and productivity", *Econometrica*, 50(6) : 1393-1414.
45. Malmquist, Sten (1953). "Index numbers and Indifference curves", Trabajos de Estatistica, 4(1): 209-42.
46. Fare, R., Grosskopf S Grifell – Tatje, and C.A. Knox – Lovell (1997), "Biased Technical Change and the Malmquist Productivity Index", *Scandinavian Journal of Economics*, 99(1) : 119-127.

**TABLE 25.1**

**CHANGES IN TOTAL FACTOR PRODUCTIVITY AND ITS COMPONENTS OF THREE MNC IN INDIAN AUTOMOBILE COMPANIES DURING 2000-01 TO 2008-09**

(Malmquist Index Summary of Company Means)

| Company | TFP Change | Components of TFPG | | Components of Technical Efficiency Change | |
|---|---|---|---|---|---|
| | | *Techno-logical Change* | *Technical Efficiency Change* | *Pure Technical Efficiency Change* | *Scale Efficiency Change* |
| Hyundai Motors India Ltd | 0.976 | 0.976 | 1.000 | 1.000 | 1.000 |
| Honda Siel cars India Ltd | 1.027 | 1.015 | 1.012 | 1.000 | 1.012 |
| Ford India Private Ltd | 1.270 | 1.023 | 1.241 | 1.224 | 1.014 |

## TABLE 25.2

### COMPARATIVE TECHNICAL CHANGE OF THREE MNC IN INDIAN AUTOMOBILE COMPANIES DURING 2000-01 TO 2008-09

| Company | 2000-01 | 2001-02 | 2002-03 | 2003-04 | 2004-05 | 2005-06 | 2006-07 | 2007-08 | 2008-09 | Mean |
|---|---|---|---|---|---|---|---|---|---|---|
| Hyundai Motors India Ltd | 1.031 | 0.964 | 1.033 | 1.189 | 1.501 | 0.910 | 0.797 | 0.942 | 0.642 | **0.976** |
| Honda Siel cars India Ltd | 1.148 | 1.029 | 1.076 | 1.120 | 1.509 | 0.952 | 1.045 | 0.959 | 0.556 | **1.015** |
| Ford India Private Ltd | 0.926 | 0.903 | 1.126 | 1.047 | 1.517 | 0.845 | 0.761 | 1.092 | 1.173 | **1.023** |
| | **1.035** | **0.965** | **1.078** | **1.117** | **1.509** | **0.902** | **0.868** | **0.998** | **0.790** | **1.005** |

## TABLE 25.3

### COMPARATIVE TECHNICAL EFFICIENCY CHANGE OF THREE MNC IN INDIAN AUTOMOBILE COMPANIES DURING 2000-01 TO 2008-09

| Company | 2000-01 | 2001-02 | 2002-03 | 2003-04 | 2004-05 | 2005-06 | 2006-07 | 2007-08 | 2008-09 | Mean |
|---|---|---|---|---|---|---|---|---|---|---|
| Hyundai Motors India Ltd | 1.000 | 1.000 | 1.000 | 0.988 | 0.663 | 1.076 | 1.070 | 0.817 | 1.625 | **1.000** |
| Honda Siel cars India Ltd | 0.897 | 1.102 | 1.130 | 1.000 | 1.000 | 1.000 | 1.000 | 1.000 | 1.000 | **1.012** |
| Ford India Private Ltd | 4.332 | 0.923 | 1.067 | 1.136 | 0.692 | 0.907 | 2.019 | 1.137 | 1.000 | **1.241** |
| | **2.076** | **1.008** | **1.067** | **1.041** | **0.785** | **0.994** | **1.363** | **0.985** | **1.208** | **1.084** |

# 26

# Does The Firm Size Matter? An Empirical Enquiry into the Performance of Indian Automobile Firms

Economic theory prescribes that increasing firm size allows for incremental advantages because the size of the firm enables it to raise the barriers of entry to potential entrants as well as gain leverage on the economies of scale to attain higher profitability. Key features of a large firm are its diverse capabilities, the abilities to exploit economies of scale and scope and the formalization of procedures. These characteristics, by making the implementation of operations more effective, allow larger firms to generate superior performance relative to smaller firms Penrose (1959). Bokmal (1959) suggested that the larger firm may be in a position to earn a higher rate of return on its investment than the smaller firm because it has all the options of a smaller firm open to it and in addition can undertake projects which are of large scale and are denied to smaller firms. A similar argument had earlier been put forward by Steindl (1945).

Besides large firms have an advantage over smaller firms as they can enter variety of product lines which gives them the benefits of both the scale and the size. Also, bigger firms being more efficient in Research & Development (R&D) which together with their ability to spend larger sums on advertising, substantially raise the cost of entry to a new comer. This creates powerful monopoly position, giving large firms a degree of independence in pricing and output decisions. It is, therefore, important to test this hypothesis and to analyze the relationship between the size of the firm and profitability.

**Theoretical background and the Development of Hypotheses**

The issues of whether larger firms are superior in performance to smaller firms, or vice-versa, have generated large amounts of theoretical and empirical research in the economics, management and sociology disciplines. The origin and drivers of the common belief that size matters can be viewed from three categories of theories. These are: (1) Principal-agent theory, (2) Strategic theories, and (3) Institutional theory.

Principal-agent theory applies whenever one party (the agent) is hired by another (the principal) to take actions or make decisions that affect the pay off of the principal (Besanko et al. 2004). The theory suggests that the separation of corporate ownership and control potentially leads to self-interested actions by managers. According to Porter (1980) there are three generic strategies that firms can use. Firms can attempt to attain overall cost leadership, product differentiation, or focus-based domination. When using product differentiation strategy, the firm's products are capable of commanding price premium relative to competitors, due to the perceived extra benefits of the products. The strategic logic is either to match the price of the rival firms and sell more than they do or to charge a price premium and attain higher price-cost margin than they are able to. When pursuing focus, the company configures its value chains so as to create superior economic value within a narrow set of industry segments. Within these segments, the firm may have lower cost per unit than the broader-scope rivals or it may be capable of commanding a price premium relative to them, or both. In order to pursue an overall cost leadership strategy, the firm must be able to produce its products at lower cost per unit than its rivals and either undercut their prices and sell more or match their prices and attain higher price-cost margin than they can (Besanko *et al.* 2004). The Porter's ideas represent a useful starting point when considering strategic options.

There are several ways for firms to produce their products at lower cost than their rivals; the most important ones are based on economics of scale and scope, or scale economics. Informally, they can be referred to as 'bigger is better'. The economics of scale is that over a range of output the average unit cost declines. If average cost increases, however, the production exhibits diseconomies of scale (the average cost curve starts to rise and becomes U-shaped). Economies of scope on the other hand exist if extra cost savings are available as a result of a production process where separate products share some production facilities, usually by increasing the variety of goods and services produced. It is evident that if a manager decides to use a cost leadership strategy, the firm must have some possibilities of utilising economies of scale or scope. Usually it is necessary that the firm is comparatively large for this to be a possibility, preferably larger than its rivals. One of the drawbacks of becoming larger is a diseconomy of scale, that is, administrative cost or bureaucratic cost increases proportionally with increased size. Larger firms may also be less flexible (Besanko *et al.* 2004).

Institutional theory suggests that organizations seek to behave in ways that will not cause them to be noticed as different and consequently singled out for criticism (Meyer and Rowan 1977). Organisations will therefore gradually become more similar in behaviour over time and adopt approaches to businesses that have been legitimized (Powell and DiMaggio 1991). This gives rise to widespread social conceptions of appropriate organisational forms and behaviours that constitute the institutional environment of organisations. As organisations compete for resources, customers, political power and economic and social fitness, institutional theories posit that they face pressures to confirm to these shared notions of appropriate forms and behaviours, since violating them may call into question the legitimacy of the organisations and thus affect its ability to secure resources and social support (Tolbert 1985). It is therefore suggested that the notion of business growth and that larger is better than smaller is embedded in the institutional environment of organisations. Therefore, theory is equivocal on the precise relationship between size and performance.

A good number of researchers had investigated the relationship between firm size and profitability. Among the pioneering studies conducted in this field is attributed to Hall and Weiss (1967). Their empirical analysis of Fortune 500 Industrial Corporations for the years 1956-1962 aimed at testing the relationship between profit rates and other appropriate variables such as firm size, concentration, leverage and growth. Results of the study showed that firm size exhibit a positive relationship with profitability. The Hall and Weiss study, however, considered only firms of optimal size. A comparable study was made by Marcus (1969) who re-evaluated earlier findings against new data within an improved analytical framework. Marcus study included the entire distribution of firms. Results showed that firm size influences profitability in some, but not all industries. Amato and Wilder (1985) conveyed that the relationship between firm size and profitability may be positive for some firm size ranges and negative for others. Again, if the size reached a threshold, additional expansion of firm size may further separate ownership from control. This suggests that the relationship between firm size and profitability can become negative beyond the threshold firm size.

Various studies attempted in the context of size and profitability relate to the developed countries. Most of the results come out with varying opinions. Some studies postulate negative results while some studies have evidence supporting the positive notion. The studies by Stakler (1963), Kamerschen (1968), Samuels and Smyth (1968), Marcus Matityahu (1969), Montgomercy (1979), Prescott and Vischer (1980), Lindsey (1981), Chittenden et al., (1996), Sumit K. Majumdar (1997), Berk (1997), Michaelas et al., (1999), Hall et al., (2000), Cassar and Holmes (2003), Darko Tipuric (2002), and Leledakis et al., (2004), showed the positive relationship between firm size and profitability. On the other hand, studies by Alexander (1949), Singh and Whittington (1968), Radice (1971), Shephered Williams (1972), Smyth David et al., (1975), Whittington (1980), Pomfret, R. and Shapiro, D. (1980), Ravenscraft David (1983), Capon et al., (1990), Schneider et al., (1993), Rajan and Zingales (2000), Dhawan (2001), Goddard Tavakoli and Wilson (2005), Bala Ramasamy et al., (2005), and Abdussalam Mahmound Abu-Tapanjeh (2006) postulated negative relationship between firm size and profitability.

However, there are some studies that concern developing countries in general and India in particular. Efforts to study size and profitability have been made in some of the studies related to Indian industries. The studies by Siddharthan and Das Gupta (1983), Nagarajan and Barthwal (1990), Sidhu and Bhatia (1993), Shanta (1994), Siddharthan et al., (1994), VishnuKanta Purohit (1998), Vijayakumar and Kadirvel (2003), and Renu Luthra and Mishra (2006) observed positive relationship between large size firms and profitability. Further, the studies by Agarwal (1978), Kuldip Kaur (1998), and Abdul Rahman Ammal (2003) found a negative association between firm size and profitability for Indian industries.

Larger firms can lead to increased coordination requirements, which in turn, make the managerial task more difficult leading to organizational inefficiencies and lower profit rates Downs (1976). Further it has been suggested that increased size tends to be associated with higher bureaucratisation Ahuja and Majumdar (1998). Another plausible argument to justify the possibility of a negative firm size - profitability relationship can be found in the concept of x-inefficiency Leibenstein (1976). X-inefficiency is a measure of the degree to which costs are higher than they need to be. Whilst diseconomies of scale refers more to the inadequacy in matching resource requirements to produce more, x-inefficiency reasons that general managerial or technological inefficiency in larger firms cause higher production costs which end up in reductions in the bottom line i.e. profit rates decline.

Based on previous literature, it is difficult to make a clear, let alone a final prediction of the overall effects of the firm size-profitability relationship from the studies carried out, the association appears to differ depending on the industry under analysis. Given this ambiguity, it seems prudent to empirically resolve, independently, the association between firm size and profitability on a case-by-case basis and avoid the tendency to generalise. Thus, from this theoretical background, the researcher advances the following hypothesis.

**$H_O$ : Firm size positively affects profitability**

**Variables specification and Empirical model**

This part of analysis aims to investigate the relationship between firm size and profitability at Indian Automobile Industry. The analysis of data employs the use of a normal linear regression model that consists of both size and profitability. With a view to estimating the relationship between the size and profitability, this study uses semi-logarithmic specifications. For this purpose, three different models using varying concepts of size and profitability are considered. This helps analyzing changes in the results due to different measures of profitability and size.

**Profitability**

Many researchers use different measures of firm profitability in the analysis of the relationship between size and profitability. Among, Return on Assets (Hall andWeiss, 1967; Shephered, 1972; Bothwell et al., 1984; Amato and Wilder, 1990) and Return on Sales (Samuels and Smyth, 1968; Nagarajan and Barthwal, 1990; Vijayakumar, 2002) are widely used measures of profitability. It is assumed that management may be concerned with effective utilization of all resources and these two measures could be proper in this line of arguments. The profit rates measured by sales will give a short-term perspective of profitability because sales are annual flows. On the other hand, the return on assets and return on capital employed will give us long-term perspective of profitability. In this study, ratio of profit margin on sales (PM), ratio of profit on total assets (PR) and return on capital employed (ROCE) are used as dependent variable in the specified models.

**Size**

One of the very important structural characteristics of the industry which is commonly used to explain profitability in applied research is the size of the firm. As discussed earlier, the relationship between firm size and profitability remains unclear. The size-profitability relationship is perhaps best explained as a curvi-linear relationship where beyond a certain point, scale economies cease to exist and the relationship then may reverse owing to the problems associated with size as highlighted by Downs.

The existing literature mentions an array of alternative measures of firm size. Generally, two sizes measures are employed; they are assets (Shephered, 1972; Amato and Wilder, 1990; Sidhu and Bhatia, 1993) and sales turnover (Abdurahman et al., 2003; Vijayakumar, 2002). Assets express amount of resources utilized for producing output whereas sales is an output variable. Sales are an annual flow depending upon output produced and sold in the market. Further sales needs to be adjusted for excise payment to more meaningful comparison. Therefore, in this study, natural logarithm of net sales (Ln NS) has been employed as the measure of firm size.

**The Models**

The study considered the following regression models.

**Model 1: PM as the dependent variable**

$$\mathbf{PM = \infty 0_{f,y} + ß_1 (Ln\ NS_{f,y}) + 1_{fy}}$$

**Model 2: PR as the dependent variable**

$$\mathbf{PR = \infty 0_{f,y} + ß_1 (Ln\ NS_{f,y}) + 1_{fy}}$$

**Model 3: ROCE as the dependent variable**

$$\mathbf{ROCE = \infty 0_{f,y} + ß_1 (Ln\ NS_{f,y}) + 1_{fy}}$$

Where,

**PM** – measures the firms profitability with gross profit as a percentage of sales turnover for firm (f) in year (y).

**PR** – measures the firms profitability with gross profit as a percentage of total assets for the firm (f) in year (y).

**ROCE** – measures the firms profitability with net profit before tax as a percentage of capital employed for firm (f) in year (y).

$\mathbf{\infty 0_{f,y}}$ – constant term for firm (f) in year (y)

**ß** – Regression Co efficient

$\mathbf{Ln\ NS_{f,y}}$ – Natural Logarithm of Net Sales (size) for firm (f) in year (y).

$\mathbf{1_{fy}}$ – disturbance term for firm (f) in year (y).

**Research Design**

Keeping in view the scope of the study, it is decided to include all the companies under automobile industry working before or from the year 1996-97 to 2008-09. There are 26 companies operating in the Indian automobile industry. But, owing to several constraints such as non-availability of financial statements or non-working of a company in a particular year etc., it is compelled to restrict the number of sample companies to 20. The companies under automobile industry are classified into three sectors namely; Commercial vehicles, Passenger cars and Multiutility vehicles and Two and three wheelers. For the purpose of the study all the three sectors have been selected. It accounts for 73.23 per cent of the total companies available in the Indian automobile industry. The selected 20 companies include 5 under commercial vehicles, 6 under Passenger cars and Multiutility vehicles and 9 under two and three wheeler sectors. It is inferred that sample company represents 98.74 percentage of market share in commercial vehicles, 89.76 percentage of market share in passenger cars and Multiutility vehicles and 99.81 percentage of market share in two and three wheelers. Thus, the findings based on the occurrence of such representative sample may be presumed to be true representative of automobile industry in the country.

The study is mainly based on secondary data. The major source of data analysed and interpreted in this study related to all those companies selected is collected from "PROWESS" database, which is the most reliable on the empowered corporate database of Centre for Monitoring Indian Economy (CMIE). Besides prowess database, relevant secondary data have also been collected from BSE Stock Exchange Official Directory, CIME Publications, Annual Survey of Industry, Business newspapers, Reports on Currency and Finance, Libraries of various Research Institutions, through Internet etc.

**Results and Interpretation**

With a view to estimating the relationship between the size and profitability, this study was used semi-logarithmic specification. For this purpose three different models using varying concepts of size and profitability are considered. This helps in analyzing changes in the results due to different measures of profitability and size. The first two measures of profitability [Profit Margin (PM) and Rate of profit on assets

(PR)] are representative of short-term profitability and remaining one measure [Return on Capital Employed (ROCE)] long-term profitability.

Table 26.1 to 26.3 show the results of various regression equations estimated to test the relationship between size and profitability. The overall results presented in the Tables are encouraging. Co-efficient is statistically significant and goodness of fit of the model is also satisfactory. Table 26.1 show that the degree of explanation of profitability and size (represented by $R^2$) is 27 per cent and 62 per cent respectively and only four of these results include very low insignificant values of the regression co-efficient relating size to profitability.

The analysis shows that size has statistically significant effect on profitability in the Indian Automobile Industry. However. in the overall pooled sample, firm size showed significant negative relation with profitability in the Indian Automobile Industry. This is consistent with many other studies, such as that by Singh and Whittington (1968) and Goddard, Tavakoli and Wilson (2005). The result is contradictory to the findings of Samuels and Smith (1968) and Hall et al., (2000), who postulated positive relationship between size and profitability. This could be due to the changes in output either because of increased demand or reduction of costs. The reduction in costs could come directly from more productive capital equipment, while increased demand could stimulate expansion on the part of the firm, hence affect profitability. It is evident from the results that one unit increase in sales had resulted in 0.27 units decrease in profitability. Thus, the study does not support the hypothesis, as the effect of size on profitability measured by profit margin (PM), is significantly negative at the 0.01 level.

The sector-wise analysis showed that the size had a significant positive relationship between firm size and profit margin in case of Commercial Vehicles and Passenger Cars & Multi-utility Vehicles sector, whereas significant negative relationship between size and profitability in the Two and Three Wheelers sector. It is evident from the results that one unit increase in sales had resulted in 1.38 units and 0.79 units increase in profitability which is significant at 0.10 and 0.01 levels respectively in case of Commercial Vehicles and Passenger Cars and Muilti-utility Vehicles sector. On the other hand, in Two and Three Wheelers sectors, one unit increase in sales will lead 0.53 units decrease in profitability which is significant at 0.01 level.

The results of the equation for Commercial Vehicle companies, for which the analysis is attempted for five companies, indicated that except Bajaj Tempo Ltd., all the selected companies have shown positive significant relationship between size and profitability. In these industries more than 24 per cent of profitability is explained by size. In Passenger Cars and Multi-utility Vehicles sector, for which the analysis is made for six companies indicated that except Mahindra and Mahindra Ltd., all the selected companies have shown positive significant relationship between size and profitability. In these industries size explains 27 per cent to 46 per cent of variations in profitability.

Two and Three Wheelers sector comprises nine sample companies. The results of the equation for these companies indicated that Bajaj Auto Ltd., LML Ltd., Hero Honda Ltd., and Kinetic Engineering Ltd., have shown positive relationship. Among them, only three companies (Bajaj Auto Ltd., LML Ltd. and Kinetic Engineering Ltd.,) have shown statistically significant relationship. In these firms more than 38 per cent of variations in profitability are explained by sales size. On the contrary, Maharastra Scooters Ltd., TVS Motor Company Ltd., Kinetic Motor Company Ltd., Majestic Auto Ltd., and Scooters India Ltd. showed negative relationship, however, it was significant in the case of Majestic Auto Ltd.

Table 26.2 shows the results of regression of Profitability Rate (PR) fitted on size in all the selected companies, sectors and whole automobile industry. The regression co-efficient 'b' relating profitability to sales (size) in the linear regression equation varies between companies. Similarly the table also shows that the degree of explanation of profitability ($R^2$) achieved in different industries, also varied to a considerable degree. In the extreme case of Ashok Leyland Ltd., 62 per cent variations in profitability are explained by sales whereas the other extreme is in case of Bajaj Tempo Ltd. and Ford India Ltd., only one per cent variations in profitability are explained by sales. Out of 24 regressions co-efficient in this table, only five are statistically insignificant.

Equations fitted for profitability (Profit Rate) is hardly significant different from the equation fitted for Profit Margin (shown in Table 26.1) as far as the better explanations ($R^2$) is concerned. Only in case of two companies Mahindra and Mahindra Ltd., in Passenger Cars and Multi-utility Vehicles sector and Maharastra Scooters Ltd., in Two and Three Wheelers sector showed positive relationship between profitability and size, while these were negative in the case of regression profit margin with size (shown in Table 26.1).

Table 26.3 again shows the results of regression of long-term profitability (ROCE) fitted on size. The simple linear regression model describing the relationship between long-term profitability and size showed that both positive and negative relationship (shown in Table 26.1 and 26.2). Here, the maximum explanation of profitability (i.e., highest $R^2$) through sales is in case of TVS Motor Company Ltd., as in Table 26.3. Here, 65 per cent of the variations in long-term profitability are explained by sales. As far as the profitability in case of Ford India Ltd is concerned, it is unexplained by sales, as suggested by the zero value of $R^2$. Out of 24 regression co-efficient in this table, only seven are statistically insignificant. Further, the pooled regression results of the model regression long-term profitability with size, measured by sales shows more or less similar findings to the results of regression profit rate with sales. The co-efficient is also statistically significant and goodness of fit of the model is also satisfactory.

Further, the regression analysis showed that size coefficient are insignificant in explaining profitability of Bajaj Tempo Ltd in Commercial Vehicles sector, Mahindra and Mahindra Ltd in Passenger cars and Multi utility Vehicles, and Hero Honda Motors Ltd and Majestic Auto Ltd in Two and Three Wheelers sector of Indian Automobile industry. The reasons for such insignificant relationship between size and profitability is that there is a large possibility that firm's mismanagement may be adding to this problem, that is, taking projects that are too big and that can't be handled well by the firm. Another possibility is that the projects are too big for the company to finance and consequently that financial cost becomes larger. In addition, one of the drawbacks of becoming larger is a diseconomy of scale, that is, administrative cost or bureaucratic cost increases proportionally with increased size.(Besanko, 2006)

## CONCLUSION

It has been often argued that larger firms in an industry are relatively more efficient than the smaller ones. If this is not so, then why does a firm aspire to be larger and larger; and if this is so, then how do smaller and larger firms coexist in the same industry. Every business is normally encountered with risks and uncertainties; bigger the firm it is expected to be stronger to face such risky and uncertain situations. A bigger firm can perhaps devise better ways and means to fight the market risk and uncertainties. A relatively bigger firm is expected to have better chances to offset random losses. Moreover, size brings bargaining power over the suppliers and competitors. When products are standardised and can be produced on a mass scale with longer production runs, a large firm will be more efficient. A big firm because of its control over the market can buy up the best sites with location advantages, the superior technology, R&D and best professional experts.

In conclusion, the findings have an interesting policy implication, which may add to the ongoing debate on the issues of firm size and the firm profitability relations. The micro-econometric study on Indian Automobile Industry firms finds firm size affecting profitability. The "law of proportionate effect" does not hold in the selected Indian automobile companies, see, Table 26.1 to 26.3. The results show mixed evidence; the firm size is positively significant in Commercial Vehicles and Passenger Cars & Multi-utility Vehicles sector and negatively significant in Two and Three Wheelers sector and the Whole Industry. Among the various companies selected for the study, some companies showed positive relationships while others not so. Therefore, while relatively bigger firms perform better in Commercial Vehicles and Passenger Cars & Multi-utility Vehicles sector, the opposite holds true in Two and Three Wheelers sector and the Whole Industry. These findings should be useful to the managerial authorities to decide on the extent to which firm size needs to be monitored and controlled. The validity and the generalization of the conclusion mentioned are pending future research in other industries or sectors that ratifies or refutes them.

## REFERENCES


1. Steindl, J. (1945). "Small and Big Business: Economic problems of the size of firms", Oxford University Press, pp.33-35.
2. Alexander,S.S. (1949). "The effect of size of manufacturing corporation on the distribution of the rate of return", *Review of Economic Statistics*.
3. Penrose, E.T. (1959). "The Theory of Growth of the Firm", Oxford: Basil Blackwell.
4. Baumol, W.J. (1959). "Business Behaviour, Value and Growth", New York: Mac Millan.
5. Stakler, H.O. (1963). "Profitability and Size of Firm", Institute of Business and Economic Research, University of California, Berkeley.

6. Hall, M. and Weiss, L. (1967). "Firms Size and Profitability", *The Review of Economics and Statistics,* Vol. 49, pp.319-331.
7. Samuels, J. M. and Smyth, D.J. (1968). "Profits, Variability of Profits and Firm size," *Economica* , Vol. 35, pp. 127-139
8. Kamerschen, D.R. (1968). "The Influence of Ownership and Control on Profit Rates", *American Economic Review,* Vol.58, pp.319-331.
9. Singh, Ajit and Whittington, G. (1968). "Growth, Profitability and Valuation", Cambridge University Press.
10. Marcus, M. (1969). "Profitability and size of firm: some further evidence", *Review of Economics and Statistics,* Vol. 51, pp. 104-107.
11. Radice, H.K. (1971). "Control Type, Profitability and Growth in Large Firms: An Empirical Study", *Economic Journal,* Vol.81, pp.547-562.
12. Shepherd, W.G. (1972). "The Elements of Market Structure", *Review of Economics and Statistics,* Vol.54, pp.25-38.
13. Smyth David, J., Boyes William, J. and Peseau Bennis, E. (1975). "Size, Growth, Profits and Executive Compensation in the Large Corporation London", Mac Millan Press.
14. Downs, A. (1976). "Inside Bureaucracy", Boston: Little, Brown & Co.,
15. Leibenstein, H. (1976). "Beyond Economic Man", Cambridge, MA: Harward University Press.
16. Meyer, J.W. and Rowan, B. (1977). "Institutionalised Organisation: Formal Structures as Myth and Ceremony", *American Journal of Sociology,* Vol.83 (2), pp.340-363.
17. Agarwal, V.K. (1978). "Size, Profitability and Growth of some Manufacturing Industries", Published Thesis, IIM, Ahmedabad.

18. Montgomercy, C.A. (1979). "Diversification, Market Structure and Firm Performance: An Extension of Rumelt's Model", Ph.D., Dissertation, Purdue University.

19. Whittington, G. (1980). "The Profitability and size of United Kingdom companies 1960-1964", *The Journal of Industrial Economies*, Vol. 28, pp. 335-342.

20. Porter, M.E. (1980). Competitive Strategy, New York: The Free Press.

21. Pomfret, R. and Shapiro, D. (1980). "Firm Size, Diversification and Profitability of Large Corporations in Canada", *Journal of Economic Studies*, Vol.7 (3), pp.140-150.

22. Prescott, E.C. and Vischer, S. (1980). "Organisation Capital", *Journal of Political Economy*, Vol.88, pp.446-461.

23. Lindsey C.W. (1981). "Firm Size and Profit rate in Philippine Manufacturing", *Journal of Developing Areas*, pp. 445-458.

24. Siddharthan, N.S. and Das Gupta, Ajit, K. (1983). "Entry Barriers, Exports and Inter Industry differences in Profitability", *The Developing Economies*, Vol.21 (1), pp.14-23.

25. Ravenscraft David, J. (1983). "Structure Profit Relationship at the Line of Business and Industry Level", *The Review of Economics and Statistics*, Vol.65, pp.22-31.

26. Amato, L. and Wilder, R.P. (1985). "The Effect of Firm Size on Profit Rate in US Manufacturing", *Southern Economics Journal*, Vol.52, pp.181-190.

27. Jol bert, P.S. (1985). "Institutional Environments and Resource Dependence: Sources of Administrative Styructure in Institotions of Higher Education", *Administrative Science Quarterly*, Vol.30 (1), pp.1-13.

28. Nagarajan, M. and Barthwal, R.R. (1990). "Profitability and Structure: A Firm Level Study of Indian Pharmaceutical Industry", *The Indian Economic Journal*, Vol.38 (2), pp.70-84.

29. Capon, N., Farley, J. and Hoenig, H. (1990). "Determinants of Financial Performance: A Meta Analysis", *Management Science*, pp.1143-1159.

30. Powell, W. and Dimaggio, P. (eds.) (1991). "The New Institutionalisation in Organizational Analysis", Chicago: University of Chicago press.

31. Schneider, Friedrich and Lenzelbaurer, Werner (1993), "An inverse relationship between efficiency and profitability according to size of (Upper) Australian Firms? - Some further tentative result", *Small Business Economics*, Springer, Vol.5 (1), pp. 1-22.

32. Sidhu, H.S. and Bhatia, G. (1993). "Factors affecting Profitability in Indian Textile Industry", *The Indian Economic Journal*, Vol.41 (2), pp.137-143.

33. Shanta N. (1994). "Growth of Firms in Indian Manufacturing Industry", Center for Development Study, Monograph Series, Trivandrum, Kerala.

34. Siddharthan, N.S., Pandit, B.L. and Agarwal, R.N. (1994). "Growth and Profit Behaviour of Large Scale Indian Firms", *The Developing Economies*, Vol.32 (2).

35. Chittenden, F., Hall, G. and Hutchinson, P. (1996). "Small Firm Growth, access to Capital Markets and Financial Structure: Review of Issues and Empirical Investigation", *Small Business Economics*, Vol.8 (1), pp.59-67.

36. Sumit K.Majumdar (1997). "The Impact of Size and Age on Firm Level Performance: Some Evidence from India", *Review of Industrial Organization*, Vol.12. pp.231-241.

37. Berk, J.B. (1997). "Does Size Really Matter?", *Financial Analysts Journal*, Vol.53, pp.12-18.

38. Kuldip kaur (1998). "Size, Growth and Profitability of firms in India-An Empirical Investigation", *Finance India*, Vol. XII (2), pp. 455-457.

39. Ahuja, G. and Majumdar, S.K. (1998). "An Assessment of the Performance of Indian State Owned Enterprises", *Journal of Productivity Analysis*, Vol.9, pp.113-132.

40. Vishnukanta Purohit (1998). "Profitability in Indian Industries", New Delhi: *Gayathri Publications*.

41. Michaelas, N., Chittenden, F. and Poutziouris, P. (1999). "Financial Policy and Capital Structure Choice in UK SMEs: Empirical Evidence from Company panel data", *Small Business Economics Journal*, Vol.12 (2), pp.113-130.

42. Hall, G., Hutchinson, P. and Michael, M. (2000). "Industry Effects on the Determinants of Unquoted SME Capital Structure", *International Journal of the Economics of Business*, Vol.7 (3), pp.297-312.

43. Rajan, R. and Zingales, L. (2000). "The Firm as a Dedicated Hierarchy, A Theory of the Origins and Growth of Firms", NBER Working Paper No. W7546.

44. Dhawan, R. (2001). "Firm Size and Productivity Differential: Theory and Evidence from a Panel of US Firms", *Journal of Economic Behaviour and Organisation*, Vol.44, pp.269-293.

45. DarkoTipuric (2002). "Is there relationship between firm size and profitability?", *Journal Zagreb International Review of Economics and Business*, Vol.5, conference issue, pp. 139-154.

46. Vijayakumar, A. and Kadirvel, S. (2003). "Profitability and size of the firm in Indian Minerals and Metals industry", *The Management Accountant*, pp. 816-821.

47. Abdul Rahman Ammal., Hanna, A.S., Nordheim, E.P. and Russell, J.S. (2003). "Indicator variable model of firms size-profitability relationship of Electrical contractors using financial and economic data", *Journal of Construction Engineering and Management* @ASCE

48. Cassar, G. and Holmes (2003). "Capital Structure and Financing of SMEs: Australian Evidence", *Accounting and Finance Journal*, Vol.43 (2), pp.123-147.

49. Leledakis, G., Davidson, I. and Smyth, J. (2004). "Does Firm Size Predict Stock Returns?: Evidence from the London Stock Exchange", EFMA, 2004, Basel Meetings Paper.

50. Besanko, D., Dranove, D., Shanley, M. and Schaefer, S. (2004). "Economics of Strategy", Hoboken, N.J: John Wiley & Sons.

51. Renu Luthra, Vaishampayan and Dheeraj Mishra (2006). "Profitability and Size: A study of small scale industries in Uttar Pradesh", *The Icfaian Journal of Management Research*, pp. 28-37.

52. Bala Ramasamy, Darrylong and Matthew, C.H., Yeung (2005). "Firm Size, Ownership and Performance in the Malaysian Palm Oil Industry", *Accounting and Finance*, Vol.1, pp.81-104.

53. Goddard Tavakoli and Wilson (2005). "Determinants of profitability in European manufacturing and service", Evidence from Dynamic Panel Model, *Applied Financial Economics* , Vol.15, pp.1269-1282.

54. Abdussalam Mahmound Abu- Tapanjeh (2006). "An Empirical Study of Firm Structure and Profitability Relationship: The case of Jordan", *Journal of Economic and Administrative Sciences*, Vol.22 (1), pp.41-59.

## TABLE 26.1

## REGRESSION ANALYSIS FOR FIRM SIZE AND PROFITABILITY

(MODEL I – PM, AS THE DEPENDENT VARIABLE)

| Particulars | Constant | Size Co-efficient | $R^2$ | Adj $R^2$ | F Value | DW |
|---|---|---|---|---|---|---|
| Ashok Leyland Ltd | 30.53 | 2.64<br>(3.69)* | 0.55 | 0.51 | 13.65 | 1.75 |
| Tata Motors Ltd | -3.59 | 1.23<br>(2.71)* | 0.41 | 0.38 | 9.15 | 1.96 |
| Bajaj Tempo Ltd | 21.14 | -2.74<br>(1.32) | 0.08 | 0.03 | 1.26 | 1.42 |
| Eicher Motors Ltd | 14.09 | 1.30<br>(1.87)*** | 0.24 | 0.17 | 3.51 | 1.14 |
| Swaraj Mazda Ltd | 7.91 | 0.38<br>(2.72)* | 0.36 | 0.29 | 8.12 | 1.36 |
| **Commercial Vehicles** | **3.36** | **1.38<br>(2.18)***** | **0.29** | **0.26** | **4.46** | **0.64** |
| Hindustan Motors Ltd | -137.91 | 20.30<br>(3.49)* | 0.53 | 0.48 | 12.20 | 1.18 |
| Mahindra and Mahindra Ltd | 10.95 | -0.10<br>(0.07) | 0.06 | -0.09 | 1.26 | 0.86 |
| Maruti Udyog Ltd | -1.35 | 1.14<br>(3.31)* | 0.47 | 0.38 | 10.23 | 0.69 |
| Hyundai | -23.65 | 27.78<br>(10.41)* | 0.92 | 0.91 | 108.39 | 1.31 |
| Honda Siel | -24.25 | 3.75<br>(2.12)*** | 0.33 | 0.26 | 4.48 | 0.85 |
| Ford India | -17.21 | 2.33<br>(2.33)** | 0.26 | 0.18 | 6.78 | 2.10 |
| **Passenger cars and Multi-utility Vehicles** | **-1.58** | **0.79<br>(3.16)*** | **0.36** | **0.27** | **9.36** | **0.52** |
| Bajaj Auto Ltd | -7.69 | 2.98<br>(2.59)* * | 0.38 | 0.32 | 6.69 | 0.47 |
| LML Ltd | -148.07 | 22.21<br>(4.02)* | 0.60 | 0.56 | 16.18 | 0.51 |

## TABLE 26.1 (CONTINUED)

## REGRESSION ANALYSIS FOR FIRM SIZE AND PROFITABILITY

(MODEL I – PM, AS THE DEPENDENT VARIABLE)

| Particulars | Constant | Size Co-efficient | $R^2$ | Adj $R^2$ | F Value | DW |
|---|---|---|---|---|---|---|
| Maharashtra Scooters Ltd | 338.26 | -69.38 (4.75)* | 0.67 | 0.64 | 22.52 | 0.93 |
| TVS Motor Company Ltd | 48.28 | -5.41 (5.78)* | 0.75 | 0.73 | 33.37 | 1.36 |
| Kinetic Motor Company Ltd | -479.55 | -84.80 (6.78)* | 0.81 | 0.79 | 46.01 | 1.16 |
| Hero Honda Motors Ltd | 10.08 | 0.39 (0.61) | 0.03 | -0.06 | 0.38 | 0.64 |
| Kinetic Engineering Ltd | -231.14 | 42.18 (3.98)* | 0.59 | 0.55 | 15.87 | 0.72 |
| Majestic Auto Ltd | 15.57 | -2.56 (0.63) | 0.03 | -0.05 | 0.39 | 1.60 |
| Scooters India Ltd | 106.33 | -21.60 (-1.88)*** | 0.24 | 0.17 | 3.52 | 0.71 |
| **Two & Three Wheelers** | **12.78** | **-0.53 (3.05)*** | **0.36** | **0.32** | **8.96** | **1.72** |
| **Whole Industry** | **10.35** | **-0.27 (2.58)**** | **0.33** | **0.28** | **7.16** | **0.50** |

*** - P < 0.01, ** - P < 0.05, *** - P < 0.10**

***Source:*** Computed

## TABLE 26.2

## REGRESSION ANALYSIS FOR FIRM SIZE AND PROFITABILITY

(MODEL II – PR, AS THE DEPENDENT VARIABLE)

| Particulars | Constant | Size Co-efficient | $R^2$ | Adj $R^2$ | F Value | DW |
|---|---|---|---|---|---|---|
| Ashok Leyland Ltd | -88.63 | 12.76 (4.20)* | 0.62 | 0.58 | 17.64 | 0.81 |
| Tata Motors Ltd | -97.42 | 12.14 (2.81)* | 0.42 | 0.36 | 7.87 | 0.67 |
| Bajaj Tempo Ltd | 28.77 | -1.45 (0.09) | 0.01 | -0.09 | 0.89 | 1.64 |
| Eicher Motors Ltd | 0.24 | 3.87 (2.96)* | 0 32 | 0.29 | 8.81 | 1.22 |
| Swaraj Mazda Ltd | 7.91 | 8.17 (3.77)* | 0.46 | 0.38 | 9.52 | 0.82 |
| **Commercial Vehicles** | **-4.60** | **1.73 (2.99)*** | **0.42** | **0.40** | **9.78** | **0.93** |
| Hindustan Motors Ltd | -191.67 | 29.16 (3.63)* | 0.46 | 0.38 | 12.16 | 1.84 |
| Mahindra and Mahindra Ltd | -63.78 | 9.66 (2.85)** | 0.43 | 0.37 | 8.12 | 0.71 |
| Maruti Udyog Ltd | 11.57 | 2.15 (4.22)* | 0.45 | 0.39 | 10.16 | 0.46 |
| Hyundai | 0.14 | 2.93 (3.03)* | 0.46 | 0.41 | 9.20 | 0.82 |
| Honda Siel | -6.51 | 4.42 (2.04)*** | 0.27 | 0.21 | 4.16 | 0.88 |
| Ford India | -0.98 | 0.15 (1.28) | 0.01 | -0.08 | 0.08 | 2.11 |
| **Passenger cars and Multi-utility Vehicles** | **-44.65** | **5.76 (2.17)**** | **0.30** | **0.24** | **4.71** | **0.61** |
| Bajaj Auto Ltd | 1.90 | 2.52 (2.39)** | 0.34 | 0.28 | 5.73 | 0.54 |
| LML Ltd | -94.17 | 13.34 (0.66) | 0.04 | -0.05 | 0.44 | 1.65 |

## TABLE 26.2 (CONTINUED)

## REGRESSION ANALYSIS FOR FIRM SIZE AND PROFITABILITY

(MODEL II – PR, AS THE DEPENDENT VARIABLE)

| Particulars | Constant | Size Co-efficient | $R^2$ | Adj $R^2$ | F Value | DW |
|---|---|---|---|---|---|---|
| Maharashtra Scooters Ltd | 0.27 | 2.27<br>(2.10)*** | 0.29 | 0.22 | 4.41 | 0.86 |
| TVS Motor Company Ltd | 89.40 | -8.12<br>(3.15)* | 0.36 | 0.31 | 9.16 | 0.82 |
| Kinetic Motor Company Ltd | 558.73 | -99.30<br>(2.39)** | 0.34 | 0.28 | 5.69 | 2.28 |
| Hero Honda Motors Ltd | -1.02 | 7.70<br>(1.33) | 0.14 | 0.06 | 1.77 | 0.45 |
| Kinetic Engineering Ltd | -61.83 | 11.79<br>(3.25)* | 0.38 | 0.29 | 8.42 | 0.37 |
| Majestic Auto Ltd | 43.97 | -8.16<br>(1.05) | 0.09 | 0.01 | 1.10 | 2.12 |
| Scooters India Ltd | 341.12 | -70.01<br>(2.43)** | 0.35 | 0.29 | 5.90 | 0.78 |
| **Two & Three Wheelers** | **57.58** | **-3.93<br>(3.58)*** | **0.38** | **0.31** | **6.18** | **1.68** |
| **Whole Industry** | **8.79** | **-0.29<br>(3.52)*** | **0.36** | **0.32** | **5.98** | **0.36** |

*** - P < 0.01, ** - P < 0.05, *** - P < 0.10**

***Source:*** Computed

## TABLE 26.3

## REGRESSION ANALYSIS FOR FIRM SIZE AND PROFITABILITY

(MODEL III – ROCE, AS THE DEPENDENT VARIABLE)

| Particulars | Constant | Size Co-efficient | $R^2$ | Adj $R^2$ | F Value | DW |
|---|---|---|---|---|---|---|
| Ashok Leyland Ltd | -59.46 | 9.37 (4.41)* | 0.64 | 0.61 | 19.46 | 1.75 |
| Tata Motors Ltd | -89.84 | 11.66 (2.52)** | 0.37 | 0.31 | 6.33 | 0.76 |
| Bajaj Tempo Ltd | 53.17 | -6.57 (0.33) | 0.01 | -0.08 | 0.11 | 1.40 |
| Eicher Motors Ltd | 35.87 | 1.80 (2.42)** | 0.30 | 0.27 | 5.87 | 1.01 |
| Swaraj Mazda Ltd | -73.49 | 19.91 (2.05)*** | 0.28 | 0.21 | 4.20 | 0.71 |
| **Commercial Vehicles** | **-78.65** | **9.83 (2.54)**** | **0.37** | **0.31** | **6.45** | **0.79** |
| Hindustan Motors Ltd | -239.15 | 35.11 (2.70)** | 0.40 | 0.34 | 7.28 | 0.89 |
| Mahindra and Mahindra Ltd | -52.90 | 8.44 (2.04)*** | 0.28 | 0.21 | 4.16 | 0.72 |
| Maruti Udyog Ltd | 40.39 | 1.44 (3.11)* | 0.36 | 0.32 | 6.78 | 0.53 |
| Hyundai | -0.35 | 2.09 (1.77) | 0.24 | 0.16 | 3.12 | 0.77 |
| Honda Siel | -120.50 | 18.78 (2.44)** | 0.40 | 0.33 | 5.96 | 0.78 |
| Ford India | -3.51 | 0.27 (0.07) | 0.00 | -0.12 | 0.01 | 2.16 |
| **Passenger cars and Multi-utility Vehicles** | **-68.34** | **8.27 (3.42)*** | **0.41** | **0.37** | **8.61** | **0.47** |
| Bajaj Auto Ltd | 15.99 | 1.17 (0.75) | 0.05 | -0.04 | 0.57 | 0.88 |

**TABLE 26.3 (CONTINUED)**

**REGRESSION ANALYSIS FOR FIRM SIZE AND PROFITABILITY**

(MODEL III – ROCE, AS THE DEPENDENT VARIABLE)

| Particulars | Constant | Size Co-efficient | $R^2$ | Adj $R^2$ | F Value | DW |
|---|---|---|---|---|---|---|
| LML Ltd | -413.16 | 60.38 (2.12)*** | 0.29 | 0.23 | 4.49 | 1.49 |
| Maharashtra Scooters Ltd | -0.62 | 2.05 (2.75)* | 0.28 | 0.23 | 4.27 | 0.61 |
| TVS Motor Company Ltd | 232.46 | -26.46 (4.51)* | 0.65 | 0.62 | 20.34 | 1.07 |
| Kinetic Motor Company Ltd | -396.21 | -69.65 (1.79)*** | 0.23 | 0.16 | 3.19 | 1.97 |
| Hero Honda Motors Ltd | 52.07 | 1.96 (0.37) | 0.01 | -0.08 | 0.14 | 0.41 |
| Kinetic Engineering Ltd | -111.43 | 20.11 (3.35)* | 0.36 | 0.30 | 8.12 | 0.75 |
| Majestic Auto Ltd | 15.51 | -2.11 (0.24) | 0.01 | -0.09 | 0.06 | 1.52 |
| Scooters India Ltd | 708.03 | -147.57 (1.23) | 0.12 | 0.04 | 1.52 | 1.37 |
| **Two & Three Wheelers** | **54.85** | **-2.65 (3.79)*** | **0.41** | **0.38** | **0.63** | **0.97** |
| **Whole Industry** | **5.54** | **-1.27 (2.79)*** | **0.29** | **0.27** | **5.62** | **0.52** |

*** - P < 0.01, ** - P < 0.05, *** - P < 0.10**

***Source :*** Computed

# PART - IX

# ANALYSIS OF FINANCIAL COMPETITIVENESS

# 27

# Composite Indicators of Financial Competitiveness

## A Critical Assessment

The Indian Industrial Sector has undergone fundamental regulatory changes in recent times as a consequence of the economic reforms program put together between 1988 and 1991. India moved away from the control era towards the 'open' economy model. The policy changes in the automobile industry took place in two phase i.e. pre-liberalisation (total control and partial de-control) and post-liberalisation periods. The automobile industry in India grew under a highly regulated and protected economic environment over the period 1950 to 1985. The initial changes, introduced in 1985, eased the licensing requirements. Though these measures represented a "domestic liberalisation" the policy environment continued being geared towards imposing trade and investment regulations, constraining the growth of big business houses and regulating exchange rates (Narayanan 2001). Liberalisation of economic policies and outward orientation introduced since 1991 brought about a dramatic change in this industry. Growth trends of key industry indicators such as industry volumes, export performance and domestic sales are improving every year with a steady rate. Domestic manufacturers acting as a global hub for exports is also gaining acceptance. Domestic players maintain capacity utilization at a healthy level. Consolidation of the industry has gained momentum. Foreign automobile firms have arrived and are in queue. There is a long list of foreign companies that are forging alliances with their Indian counterparts. (Burange and Shruthi Yamini, 2008)

**Financial Competitiveness of firms**

The Oxford Dictionary of Economics defines the term competitiveness as "the ability to compete in markets for goods or services". Competitiveness can be observed from different perspectives, through products, firms, industry and branches of the economy. At each level of aggregation, there are different measures or indicators of competitiveness. Another significant discussion on the concept of competitiveness of firms was published by ADB (2003). It states that competitiveness of firms can be defined as a firm's ability to survive under competition and being competitive implies succeeding in an environment where firms try to stay ahead of each other by reducing prices, by increasing the quality of their current products and services, and by creating new ones. A firm's competitiveness can thus be examined as a function of various factors.

As competitiveness is linked to a large number of variables, defining it is in itself a research problem. Keeping this in mind, an effort has been made to build up a competitiveness that can measure a firm's competitive position in the industry which it can sustain in medium to long-run. In this part of analysis, an attempt has been made to bring out the competitive flavour of the Indian automobile industry. Intense competition has gripped the industry in recent years with major world players entering the market bringing better technology and experience. Therefore the study on competitiveness of firms in the industry in domestic market, in the present state is interesting to examine.

**Methodology**

The variables that compose the competitiveness for Indian automobile industry have been identified on the basis of factors related to competitiveness at the firm level, considering the specific issues peculiar to the Indian automobile industry. Competitiveness is concerned with the ability of firms to perform better than rivals, where performance is dependent on both financial and non-financial conditions of the firm. For this purpose, profitability, assets utilization, cost effectiveness, liquidity, working capital efficiency, long-term solvency, market value, foreign trade, productivity performance and value-added performance are grouped under financial indicators and other indicators such as, sales and marketing strategy, consumer satisfaction, technological issues, human resources and growth variables are grouped under non-financial indicators. However, non-financial indicators beyond the scope of the study, an attempt has been made in this study to analysis the financial indicators which help to measures the competitiveness of the firms selected for the study in Indian Automobile Industry. The sub-indicators which are used to construct the financial competitiveness of the firm are listed in Table 27.2. All of these sub-indicators are grouped into ten main indicators that clearly describe its components.

Financial ratios are one of the most common tools of managerial decision making. Financial ratios involve the comparison of various figures from the financial statements in order to gain information about a company's performance. It is the interpretation, rather than the calculations that makes financial ratios a useful tool for business managers. Ratios may serve as indicators, clues or red flags regarding noteworthy relationship be tween variables used to measure the firm's performance in terms of profitability, asset utilization, liquidity, leverage, market valuation etc..

There are basically two uses of financial ratio analysis: to track individual firm performance overtime, and to make comparative judgments regarding firm performance. Firm performance is evaluated using trend analysis- calculating individual ratios on a per-period basis, and tracking their values over time. This analysis can be used to spot trends that may be cause for concern, such as an average collection period for outstanding receivables or a decline in the firm's liquidity status. In this role, ratios serve as a red flag for troublesome issues or as benchmarks for performance measurement. Another common usage of ratios is to make relative performance comparisons. For example, comparing a firm's profitability to that of a major competitor or observing how the firm stacks up versus industry averages enables the user to form judgement concerning key areas such as profitability or management effectiveness.

## SAMPLING DESIGN

Keeping in view the scope of the study, it is decided to include all the companies under automobile industry working before or from the year 1996-97 to 2008-09. There are 26 companies operating in the Indian automobile industry. But, owing to several constraints such as non-availability of financial statements or non-working of a company in a particular year etc., it is compelled to restrict the number of sample companies to 20. The companies under automobile industry are classified into three sectors namely; Commercial vehicles, Passenger cars and Multi-utility vehicles and Two and three wheelers. For the purpose of the study all the three sectors have been selected. It accounts for 73.23 per cent of the total companies available in the Indian automobile industry. The selected 20 companies include 5 under commercial vehicles, 6 under passenger cars and multi-utility vehicles and 9 under two and three wheeler sectors. It is inferred that sample company represents 98.74 percentage of market share in commercial vehicles, 89.76 percentage of market share in passenger cars and Multi-utility vehicles and 99.81 percentage of market share in two and three wheelers. Thus, the findings based on the occurrence of such representative sample may be presumed to be true representative of automobile industry in the country.

The study is mainly based on secondary data. The major source of data analysed and interpreted in this study related to all those companies selected is collected from “PROWESS” database, which is the most reliable on the empowered corporate database of Centre for Monitoring Indian Economy (CMIE). Besides prowess database, relevant secondary data have also been collected from BSE Stock Exchange Official Directory, CMIE Publications, Annual Survey of Industry, Business newspapers, Reports on Currency and Finance, Libraries of various Research Institutions, through Internet etc.

**Financial Competitiveness – Factor Analysis**

In order to analyse the overall financial competitiveness of the selected companies under three sectors of Indian automobile industry. 42 variables are considered under eleven indicators. In order to draw conclusions on the overall financial competitiveness, a statistical technique called Factor Analysis with Principal Component method is applied. Factor analysis is used to reduce a set of ‘n’ variables into another set of ‘K’ (where K<n) hypothetical variables, where each hypothetical variables is a linear combination of ‘n’ variables. The variables that are interrelated to one another are included in each one of the ‘K’ hypothetical variables. Each hypothetical variable comprises of meaningful grouping of original variables; and each new variable can be suitably named based on the variables that are highly loaded in it. In this part of analysis, an attempt is made to identify the factors that are significantly contributing to the data set for the three sectors and whole Indian automobile industry.

The financial competitiveness of the selected companies of Indian automobile industry concentrates on 11 sub-indicators namely profitability, assets utilization, cost effectiveness, liquidity, working capital efficiency, solvency, market values, export performance, value added, productivity and macro economic variables. For this purpose the profitability ratios used for the analysis are Operating Profit Margin Ratio (OPMR), Net Profit Margin Ratio (NPMR), Return On Capital Employed (ROCE), Return On Total Assets (ROTA), and Return On Net worth (RONW). The assets utilization ratios such as Total Assets Turnover Ratio (TATR), Fixed Assets Turnover Ratio (FATR), Working Capital Turnover Ratio (WCTR), Inventory Turnover Ratio (ITR) and Debtors Turnover Ratio (DTR), cost effectiveness ratios such as Raw Material (RMTSR), Wages (WTSR), Factory Overhead (FOTSR), Administration and Selling and Distribution Overhead (ASDTSR), Financial Charges (FCTSR), (all as percentage to total sales) and Total Cost as Percentage to Total Sales (TCTSR), liquidity ratios such as Current Ratio (CR), Quick Ratio (QR) and Cash Position Ratio (CPR), working capital efficiency ratios such as Raw Material Holding Period (RMHP), WIP Holding Period (WIPHP), Finished Goods Holding Period (FGHP), Receivables Holding Period (RHP), Payables Payment Period (PPP) and Cash Conversion Cycle Period (CCCP), solvency ratios such as Debt-Equity Ratio (DER), Interest Coverage Ratio (ICR), Proprietary Ratio (PR), Long-term Debt to Total Debt ratio (LTDTDR) and Capital Gearing Ratio (CGR), Market value ratios such as Earnings Per Share (EPS), Price-Earnings Ratio (PER), Book-Value Per Share (BVPS) and Dividend Yield Ratio (DYR), Export as Percentage to Total Sales (ETSR), Value added ratios such as Economic Value Added (EVA) and Market Value Added (MVA), Total Factor Productivity (TFP) and Macro-Economics variables such as Gross Domestic Product (GDP) Interest Rate (IR), Money Supply (MS) and Whole Sale Price Index (WPI) are used for the analysis. The results of the factor analysis are presented in Table 27.1.

Fourty two ratios pertaining to financial competitiveness of the Indian Automobile Industry used in factor analysis is presented in Table 27.1. Table 27.1 gives the rotated factor loadings, communalities, eigen values and the percentage of variance explained by the factors. Out of 42 ratios, 13 factors have been extracted and these thirteen factors put together explain the total variance of these ratios to the extent of 76.122 per cent. In this industry the shortage information by grouping the data set into factors are of 23.878 per cent during the study period. The communalities vary from 40 per cent to 99 per cent suggesting that the extracted factors are sufficient to account for most of the variations existing in the data. This inference is confirmed by the total variation explained by the analysis. Table 27.1 reveals that the hypothetical variables that are highly loaded in the first factor includes profitability ratio such as NPMR, cost effectiveness ratios such RMTSR, WTSR, ASDTSR and TCSR, working capital efficiency ratios such as PPP and CCCP and export performance ratio ETSR. Since, more cost effectiveness ratios are loaded in the factor, it is termed as Cost factor. This factor totally contributes 14.741 per cent. The Macro- Economic factor such as IR, GDP, MS and WPI are highly loaded in the second factor. Its contribution to the total variance is 12.425 per cent. The profitability ratios such as ROCE, the assets utilization ratios such as TATR and solvency ratio such as PR and LTDTDR are highly loaded in the third factor. So, this factor is termed as Profitability and Solvency factor. This factor totally contributes 8.178 per cent to the total variance.

In the fourth factor the hypothetical variables which are highly loaded includes cost effectiveness ratio FCTSR, working capital efficiency ratios such as RMHP and WIPHP and productivity factor such as TFP and this factor can be termed as Working Capital and Productivity factor. It's contribution is 6.387 per cent to the total variance. The variables which are highly loaded in the fifth factor includes profitability ratio such as RONW and solvency ratios such as DER and CGR. This factor is termed as Profitability and Solvency factor which contributes 5.660 per cent to the total variance. The profitability ratios such as OPMR and cost effectiveness ratio such as FOTSR are highly loaded in the sixth factor and it can be termed as Profitability and Cost factor. Its contribution to the total variance is 5.358 per cent.

The liquidity ratios such as CR, QR and CPR and working capital efficiency ratio such as FGHP are highly loaded in the seventh factor and its contribution to the total variance is 4.605 per cent. It is named as Liquidity factor.

In the eighth factor the hypothetical variables which are highly loaded includes market value ratios such as EPS and BVPS and value added ratio such as MVA and it is called Market value and Value added factor. Its contribution to the total variance is 4.309 per cent. The assets utilization ratios such as FATR and ITR and market value ratio such as PER are highly loaded in the ninth factor and this factor can be termed as Assets utilization and Market value factor. Its contribution to the total variance is 3.606 per cent. The tenth factor is highly loaded with working capital efficiency ratio such as DTR and solvency ratio such as ICR and it can be termed as Working capital and Solvency factor and its contribution to the total variance is 3.094 per cent. Profitability ratio such as ROTA and value added ratio such as EVA are highly loaded in the eleventh factor and it can be named as Profitability and Market Value factor and its contribution to the total variance is 2.786 per cent. Similarly, working capital efficiency ratio such as RHP and Market value ratio such as DYR include in the twelfth factor and it is called a Working capital and Market value factor and its contribution to the total variance is 2.539 per cent. The thirteenth factor is highly loaded with working capital turnover ratio and it can be termed as Working capital factor and its contribution to the total variance is 2.432 per cent.

The results of the test show that with the significant value 0.000, there is significant relationship among the variable chosen. KMO test yields a result of 0.636 which state that factor analysis can be carried out appropriately for the 42 variables that are taken for the study.

Zaltman and Burger (1975) have suggested the following as criteria of factor analysis significance.

(i) The eigen value is greater than 1.

(ii) The loadings of the factors after varimax rotation are

larger than 0.3

(iii) The variance explained of all factors in the factor analysis is greater than 40 per cent.

(iv) No variable loads significantly on more than one factor.

The factor analysis performed above rates satisfactory on all the above said four criteria.

**Overall Financial Competitiveness of the Firm**

In the present study, the ten broad categories of indicators were considered such as profitability, asset utilization, cost effectiveness, liquidity, working capital efficiency, solvency, market value, foreign trade, productivity and value added performance to determine the financial competitiveness of the selected companies in the Indian automobile Industry. The company's performances are ranked according to the sub-indicators. After ranking to each component of sub-indicators, these rank scores are aggregated into a composite score. The aggregation of rankings is an additive nature. The aggregate index for each of the ten broad indicators is derived first using relevant variables (sub-indicators). The formula used for this is given below:

$$V_i = \frac{1}{n}\sum_{i=1}^{n} x_i$$

where, $V_i$ is $i_{th}$ indicator, $x_i$ is the $i_{th}$ sub-indicators, $n$ is the number of sub-indicators with in the indicators. This composite competitive index can be used to measure a firm's competitive position in the industry which it can sustain in medium to long-run. In the context of policy analysis, indicators are useful in identifying trends and drawing attention to particular issues. It can also be helpful in benchmarking or monitoring performance.

**Overall Financial competitiveness of the firm – sector wise analysis:**

The sector wise composite financial competitive index and ranks of the firms for indicators are presented in the

Table 27.2. In the commercial vehicles sector, Eicher Motors Ltd comes first. This result is largely due to its position in profitability, assets utilization and solvency indicators. However the company's performance in productivity and value added is scored on 4$^{th}$ position among the selected companies. Tata Motors Ltd is at the second position in the competitiveness index. It can be noted here that this company has 1$^{st}$ ranks in cost effectiveness, working capital, market value and value added indicators; still it has got second ranking in the overall index mainly because of poor performance in profitability, liquidity and solvency indicators where it stands 4$^{th}$. In the list of competitive performance 3$^{rd}$, 4$^{th}$ and 5$^{th}$ positions are held by Swaraj Mazda Ltd, Ashok Leyland Ltd and Bajaj Tempo Ltd. It is noted that Ashok Leyland Ltd should stand first with regard to liquidity. foreign trade and productivity indicators. However the company's performance in assets utilizations, working capital efficiency and cost effectiveness is very low.

Among the passenger cars and multiutility vehicles sector companies, Honda Siel Cars India Ltd comes first. This may be due to its position in the assets utilization, cost effectiveness and liquidity indicators. The good competitive position it enjoys in productive performance is because of its highest capacity utilization and assets productivity. Maruti Udyog Ltd is at the second position in the competitiveness index. It is noted that this company has 1$^{st}$ rank in two indicators namely profitability and solvency and 2$^{nd}$ ranks in assets utilization, cost effectiveness, market value, foreign trade and value added indicators. The performance wise Mahindra and Mahindra Ltd is doing well as it stands at number 3 position. It is noted that this company has 1$^{st}$ ranks in value added indicator; it has got third ranking in the overall index mainly because of poor performance in assets utilization, working capital and cost effectiveness indicators. In the list of competitive performance, 4$^{th}$, 5$^{th}$ and 6$^{th}$ positions are held by Hyundai Motors India Ltd, Ford India Private Ltd and Hindustan Motors Ltd. Hyundai Motors India Ltd holds 1$^{st}$

position in market value and foreign trade. However, cost effectiveness and productivity have pulled it down to this position. Similarly, Ford India Private Ltd holds 1st position in working capital efficiency and productivity, but profitability and liquidity have pulled it down to this position.

The competitiveness rankings among two and three wheelers sector companies, Hero Honda Motors Ltd is at the first position. It is noted here that this company has 1st ranks six indicators namely profitability, assets utilization, cost effectiveness, working capital, market value and productivity. Bajaj Auto Ltd is at the second position in the competitiveness index. The performance wise TVS Motor Company Ltd hold third positions which may be due to assets utilization, working capital, cost effectiveness and market value indicators. In the list of competitive performance, 4th, 5th, 6th and 7th positions are held by Maharashtra Scooters Ltd, Majestic Auto Ltd, Kinetic Motor Company Ltd and Kinetic Engineering Ltd. Scooters India Ltd and LML Ltd performance in all the indicators is very poor. Hence, this company's are placed in the 8th and 9th position.

**Financial competitiveness of the firm – Individual rankings**

The overall competitiveness rankings for the selected companies of Indian automobile industry presented in Table 27.4. In the overall competitiveness rankings, Hero Honda Motors Ltd comes first. This result is largely due to its position in the productivity performance and working capital efficiency. The good competitive position it enjoys in productive performance is because of its highest capacity utilization and technology up gradation. However the company's performance in foreign trade and liquidity is scored very low and is on 18th position in the list of sample firms. Bajaj Auto Limited is at the second position in the overall competitiveness rankings. The performance wise Honda Siel Cars India Ltd is doing well as it stands at number 3 position. The company holds 1st position in assets utilization, cost effectiveness and liquidity. Maruti Udyog

Ltd stands at the fourth position. It can be noted here that this company has 1st ranks in profitability and solvency indicators; still it has got fourth ranking in the overall index mainly because of poor performance in productivity and working capital indicators. In this list of overall competitive performance, 5th, 6th and 7th positions are held by TVS Motor Company Ltd, Eicher Motors Ltd and Mahindra and Mahindra Ltd, with little difference in the total scores. Nevertheless, strength of TVS Motor Company is its working capital and assets utilization indicators. Eicher Motors Ltd is doing well in assets utilization, solvency, profitability and working capital indicators whereas productivity performance is relatively poor. Value added and profitability indicators are strongest for Mahindra and Mahindra Ltd, which is offset by working capital and assets utilization indicators.

Tata Motors Ltd, Hyundai Motors India Ltd and Swaraj Mazda Ltd are 8th, 9th and 10th in the list of overall competitiveness rankings. All are very close with each other although Tata Motors Ltd is exceptionally good in value added, working capital, assets utilization and cost effectiveness and average in other indicators. Hyundai Motors India Ltd's strength seems to be market value and export where it has 1st position but because of productivity, profitability and cost effectiveness the overall score is low. Whereas Swaraj Mazda Ltd had average performance in all the indicators of competitiveness. Companies such as Maharashtra Scooters Ltd, Ashok Leyland Ltd and Ford India Private Ltd are on the 11th, 12th and 13th rankings respectively in the list of index of competitiveness being very close in scoring. Ashok Leyland Ltd is ranked 1st in productivity and foreign trade indicator and Ford India Private Ltd ranked 1st in productivity performance. In case of other indicators, all these three firms show average performance. Bajaj Tempo Ltd, Hindustan Motors Ltd and Majestic Auto Ltd are 14th, 15th and 16th in the list of competitive rankings. All are very close to each other and very poor performance in all the indicators. Scooters India Ltd, Kinetic Motor Company Ltd, Kinetic Engineering Ltd and LML Ltd had very poor performance in all the indicators of competitiveness and stands 17th, 18th and 19th and 20th rankings respectively in the list of index of competitiveness.

## CONCLUSION

Factor analysis has been applied to identify the factors that are significantly contributing the financial competitiveness. Out of 42 variables, 13 factors have been extracted and these thirteen factors put together explain 76.122 per cent of the total variance. If the industry is classified in segments then it can be seen that passenger cars and multiutility vehicles is dominated followed by two and three wheeler sector and commercial vehicles sector. The commercial vehicles sector is obviously ruled by Eicher Motors Ltd where as the passenger cars and multiutility vehicles sector is dominated by Honda Siel Cars India Ltd and Maruti Udyog Ltd. Further, two and three wheeler sector is dominated by Honda Motors Ltd and Bajaj Auto Ltd.

## REFERENCES

1. Burange L.G. and Shruti Yamini (2008). "Competitiveness of Firms in Indian Automobile Industry", Working Paper UDE(CAS)23/(8)/1/2008, University of Mumbai, JEL Code(s):L62.
2. Booysen, Frederick (2002). "An Overview and Evaluation of Composite Indices of Development, Social Indicators Research 59, pp.115-151.
3. Gooroochum, Nishaal and Guntur Sugiyarto (2004). Measuring Competitiveness in the Travel and Tourism Industry, Dicussion Paper 7, Tourism and Travel Research Institute, Nottingham University, U.K.
4. Khisty, Vasant (2000), "Globalisation and Competitivene ss of Indian Auto Component Industry", Associated with RAHA- World Independent Writers' Home in Exile, World News, Kabul Press.
5. Ministry of Heavy Industries and Public Enterprises

(2006a). Automotive Mission Plan 2006-2016, Government of India, New Delhi.

6. Narayanan, K.(2001), "Liberalisation and the Differential Conduct and Performance of Firms: A Study of the Indian automobile Sector", Discussion Paper Series – A.No.414, The Institute of Economic Research, Hitotsubashi University and United Nations University Instutute of Advanced studies, Japan.
7. Society of Indian Automobile Manufacturers(2007), Market Share Analysis Report, Report VII, SOP 11-F-09/01, New Delhi.
8. Prahalad, C.K. and Hamel,G., (1990). "The core competence of the corporation", Harvard Business Review, 68(3):79-81.
9. Singh, Neelam(2004). "Strategic Approach to strengthening the International Competitiveness in Knowledge Based Industries: The case of Indian Automotive Indutry", RIS Dicussion Paper Series No.82, Research and Information System for the Non-Aligned and other Developing countries, New Delhi.

**TABLE 27.1**

**SUMMARY OF FACTOR ANALYSIS – ROTATED FACTOR LOADINGS (Whole Industry)**

| Variables | Factors | | | | | | | | | | | | | Communality |
|---|---|---|---|---|---|---|---|---|---|---|---|---|---|---|
| | 1 | 2 | 3 | 4 | 5 | 6 | 7 | 8 | 9 | 10 | 11 | 12 | 13 | |
| Operating Margin | -.029 | .057 | .105 | -.017 | -.161 | **.877** | -.018 | .054 | .070 | .032 | .088 | .005 | .027 | .828 |
| Net Profit Margin | **-.967** | .063 | .025 | .018 | -.013 | .163 | .030 | .27 | .036 | .017 | .012 | .004 | .016 | .971 |
| Return on Capital Employed | -.015 | -.201 | **.758** | -.016 | -.031 | .066 | .105 | .002 | .041 | -.008 | .410 | -.115 | .054 | .818 |
| Return on Total Assets | -.019 | -.113 | .186 | -.062 | -.219 | .087 | .083 | .007 | .244 | .087 | **.702** | .030 | .155 | .699 |
| Return on Net worth | -.031 | -.190 | .227 | -.177 | **-.489** | .144 | .075 | -.038 | .262 | .011 | .376 | .266 | .098 | .677 |
| Total Assets Turnover | -.045 | .047 | **.827** | .039 | -.038 | -.148 | -.128 | .051 | .228 | .119 | -.128 | .051 | .040 | .820 |
| Fixed Assets Turnover | -.054 | .026 | .155 | -.078 | .014 | -.253 | -.054 | .028 | **.663** | .161 | .152 | .108 | -.058 | .605 |
| Working Capital Turnover | -.010 | -.050 | -.007 | -.042 | .023 | .011 | -.105 | -.003 | -.149 | .030 | .027 | .075 | **.809** | .700 |
| Inventory Turnover | -.055 | .233 | .064 | -.250 | -.140 | -.169 | .096 | .215 | **.466** | .142 | .427 | -.218 | .108 | .706 |
| Debtors Turnover | -.010 | .007 | .026 | -.085 | .063 | -.014 | .134 | -.034 | -.024 | **.856** | .017 | -.097 | -.011 | .775 |
| RM as % of Total Cost | **.568** | .022 | .018 | .088 | .078 | -.357 | .143 | .104 | .286 | .155 | -.006 | .098 | .119 | .626 |
| Wages as % of Total Cost | **.750** | .064 | -.024 | -.012 | -.022 | .617 | -.027 | -.020 | -.015 | -.012 | -.052 | .002 | -.023 | .954 |
| Factory Overhead as % to Total Cost | -.030 | .098 | -.105 | .328 | .338 | **.722** | .035 | -.011 | -.199 | -.049 | -.111 | -.010 | -.043 | .822 |

## TABLE 27.1 (CONTINUED)

## SUMMARY OF FACTOR ANALYSIS – ROTATED FACTOR LOADINGS (Whole Industry)

| Variables | Factors | | | | | | | | | | | | | Communality |
|---|---|---|---|---|---|---|---|---|---|---|---|---|---|---|
| | 1 | 2 | 3 | 4 | 5 | 6 | 7 | 8 | 9 | 10 | 11 | 12 | 13 | |
| Administration and selling and Distribution Overhead to Total Cost | **.985** | -.037 | -.003 | -.057 | -.005 | -.007 | -.033 | -.025 | -.038 | -.021 | -.004 | -.007 | -.011 | .978 |
| Financial Charges to Total Cost | .004 | -.017 | -.218 | **.548** | .338 | -.104 | .072 | -.091 | -.415 | -.040 | -029 | -.009 | -.079 | .668 |
| Total Cost as % on Sales | **.979** | .012 | -.020 | -.028 | .007 | .181 | -.023 | -.011 | -.005 | -.004 | -.026 | .006 | -.009 | .995 |
| Current Ratio | -.088 | -.122 | .127 | .010 | -.078 | -.053 | **.739** | .005 | -.040 | .219 | -.056 | .313 | -.137 | .763 |
| Quick Ratio | -.037 | .111 | .077 | -.007 | .084 | .058 | **.783** | .008 | .164 | .034 | .078 | .118 | -.132 | .708 |
| Cash Position Ratio | -.009 | .001 | -.188 | -.126 | .004 | -.012 | **.723** | -.006 | -.012 | -.025 | -.019 | -.279 | .175 | .683 |
| Raw Material Holding Period | -.018 | -.032 | -.128 | **.885** | -.006 | .029 | -.039 | -.081 | -.151 | .019 | -.115 | -.047 | -.075 | .853 |
| Work – in – Progress Holding Period | -.031 | .118 | -.115 | **.744** | .205 | .271 | .026 | -.139 | -.154 | -.087 | -.129 | .135 | -.090 | .792 |
| Finished Goods Holding Period | -.080 | -.052 | .133 | .077 | .034 | -127 | **.404** | -.328 | -.323 | .010 | -.190 | .329 | .087 | .578 |
| Receivables Holding Period | .059 | .033 | -.071 | .304 | .562 | .095 | .189 | -.069 | .019 | -.186 | .000 | **.470** | -.072 | .728 |

**TABLE 27.1 (CONTINUED)**

**SUMMARY OF FACTOR ANALYSIS – ROTATED FACTOR LOADINGS (Whole Industry)**

| Variables | Factors | | | | | | | | | | | | | Communality |
|---|---|---|---|---|---|---|---|---|---|---|---|---|---|---|
| | 1 | 2 | 3 | 4 | 5 | 6 | 7 | 8 | 9 | 10 | 11 | 12 | 13 | |
| Payables Payment Period Cash Conversion Cycle Period | **.991** | -.039 | -.011 | .004 | -.017 | .013 | -.043 | -.026 | -.018 | -.014 | -.003 | -.004 | -.010 | .986 |
| | **-.989** | .039 | .004 | .056 | .039 | -.007 | .050 | .015 | .008 | .006 | -.006 | .023 | .004 | .988 |
| Debt Equity Ratio | -.008 | .021 | .042 | .005 | **.851** | -.031 | -.089 | -.012 | -.027 | .002 | -.186 | -.026 | -.017 | .771 |
| Interest Coverage Ratio | -.005 | .094 | .025 | -.050 | -.025 | .002 | .008 | -.026 | .034 | **.837** | .041 | -.006 | .020 | .718 |
| Proprietary Ratio | -.013 | -.043 | **.812** | -.251 | -.064 | .112 | .036 | .069 | .130 | .047 | .005 | .153 | 4.100E-5 | .790 |
| Long – Term Debt to Total Debt | -.008 | -.115 | **.838** | -.152 | .160 | .009 | .063 | -.036 | -.155 | -.078 | .078 | -.091 | -.045 | .815 |
| Capital Gearing Ratio | -.001 | .002 | .074 | .018 | **.884** | .022 | .080 | -.038 | -.035 | -.036 | .037 | -.045 | .086 | .810 |
| Earnings Per Share | -.021 | -.062 | -.033 | .001 | .241 | .006 | -.032 | **.795** | .009 | .014 | .150 | .002 | -.050 | .721 |
| Price Earnings Ratio. | -.016 | -.026 | .016 | -.029 | -.068 | .120 | .133 | -.066 | **.519** | -.173 | -.117 | 080 | -.137 | .381 |
| Book Value per Share | -.015 | -.043 | .046 | -.063 | -.110 | .004 | -.028 | **.853** | -.022 | -.020 | .051 | .080 | -.050 | .762 |
| Dividend Yield Ratio | -.018 | -.116 | -.003 | -.015 | -.064 | -.018 | .058 | .007 | -.009 | -.066 | -89 | **.704** | .060 | .533 |
| Export as % to Total Sales | **.539** | .208 | -.065 | .385 | .147 | -.197 | -.053 | .032 | -.289 | -.076 | .25 | -.171 | -.056 | .673 |
| Economic Value Added | -.021 | .103 | -.008 | -.080 | -.013 | -.067 | -.118 | .140 | -.171 | -.018 | **.570** | .104 | -.185 | .455 |

## TABLE 27.1 (CONTINUED)

## SUMMARY OF FACTOR ANALYSIS – ROTATED FACTOR LOADINGS (Whole Industry)

| Variables | Factors | | | | | | | | | | | | | Communality |
|---|---|---|---|---|---|---|---|---|---|---|---|---|---|---|
| | 1 | 2 | 3 | 4 | 5 | 6 | 7 | 8 | 9 | 10 | 11 | 12 | 13 | |
| Market Value Added | -.017 | -.019 | .055 | -.018 | -.145 | .004 | .036 | **.708** | .026 | -.047 | -.045 | -.086 | .093 | .548 |
| Total Factor Productivity | -.043 | .118 | -.030 | **.746** | -.099 | -.008 | -.119 | .137 | .280 | -.116 | .031 | .017 | .174 | .740 |
| Interest Rate | .041 | **-.476** | -.140 | -.015 | .020 | .104 | -.265 | -.012 | -.135 | .091 | .239 | .086 | -.456 | .629 |
| Gross Domestic Product | -.016 | **.967** | -.100 | .052 | .027 | .063 | -.025 | -.046 | -.007 | 0.52 | .030 | -.043 | -.045 | .963 |
| Money Supply | -.013 | **.963** | -.102 | .052 | .036 | .064 | -.033 | -.045 | -.006 | .059 | .035 | -.053 | -.052 | .959 |
| Whole Sale Price Index | -.022 | **.983** | -.064 | .048 | .027 | .036 | .020 | -.041 | .013 | .034 | -.015 | -.052 | .039 | .983 |
| **Eigen Value** | **6.191** | **5.218** | **3.435** | **2.683** | **2.377** | **2.250** | **1.935** | **1.810** | **1.514** | **1.299** | **1.170** | **1.066** | **1.021** | |
| **% of Variance** | **14.741** | **12.425** | **8.178** | **6.387** | **5.660** | **5.358** | **4.605** | **4.309** | **3.606** | **3.094** | **2.786** | **2.539** | **2.432** | **76.122** |
| **Cum. % Variance** | **14.741** | **27.166** | **35.343** | **41.731** | **47.391** | **52.749** | **57.356** | **61.666** | **65.272** | **68.365** | **71.151** | **73.690** | **76.122** | |

**Kaiser – Meyer – Olkin Measure of Sampling Adequacy** **- 0.636**
**Bartlett's Test of Shericity** **- 6.848 E 3 (Sigx.000)**

**Extraction Method : Principal Component Analysis** **Rotation Method : Varimax with Kaiser Normalization**

***Source:*** Computed from the Annual Reports

**TABLE 27.2**

**FINANCIAL COMPETITIVENESS – SCORES AND RANKS OF THE FIRMS FOR INDICATORS (SECTOR WISE)**

| Companies | Overall Index | | Profitability Index | | Assets Utilisation Index | | Cost Effectiveness | | Liquidity Index | | Working capital Efficiency Index | | Solvency Index | | Market Value Index | | Foreign Trade Index | | Productivity Performance Index | | Value Added Performance Index | |
|---|---|---|---|---|---|---|---|---|---|---|---|---|---|---|---|---|---|---|---|---|---|---|
| | Score | Rank | Score | Rank | Score | Rank | Score | Rank | Score | Rank | Score | Rank | Score | Rank | Score | Rank | Score | Rank | Score | Rank | Score | Rank |
| Ashok Leyland Ltd | 10.47 | 4 | 2.40 | 2 | 4.40 | 5 | 3.00 | 4 | 1.30 | 1 | 4.30 | 5 | 2.20 | 2 | 3.00 | 3 | 1.00 | 1 | 1.00 | 1 | 3.00 | 3 |
| Tata Motors Ltd | 9.50 | 2 | 3.00 | 4 | 2.20 | 2 | 2.60 | 1 | 4.00 | 4 | 2.00 | 1 | 3.40 | 4 | 2.70 | 1 | 2.00 | 2 | 2.00 | 2 | 1.50 | 1 |
| Bajaj Tempo Ltd | 12.26 | 5 | 4.60 | 5 | 3.60 | 4 | 3.60 | 5 | 4.30 | 5 | 3.50 | 4 | 3.00 | 3 | 3.25 | 5 | 5.00 | 5 | 5.00 | 5 | 2.50 | 2 |
| Eicher Motors Ltd | 8.32 | 1 | 2.20 | 1 | 2.00 | 1 | 2.85 | 3 | 1.60 | 2 | 2.16 | 2 | 1.80 | 1 | 2.75 | 2 | 3.00 | 3 | 4.00 | 4 | 3.50 | 4 |
| Swaraj Mazda Ltd | 9.92 | 3 | 2.80 | 3 | 2.80 | 3 | 2.80 | 2 | 3.60 | 3 | 3.00 | 3 | 4.60 | 5 | 3.20 | 4 | 4.00 | 4 | 3.00 | 3 | 4.50 | 5 |
| Hindustan Motors Ltd | 12.63 | 6 | 5.60 | 5 | 4.40 | 5 | 4.60 | 5 | 5.30 | 5 | 4.50 | 6 | 5.80 | 6 | 4.00 | 6 | 5.00 | 5 | 4.00 | 4 | 2.50 | 3 |
| Mahindra and Mahindra Ltd | 8.58 | 3 | 2.20 | 2 | 4.60 | 6 | 3.80 | 4 | 3.00 | 3 | 4.16 | 5 | 3.80 | 4 | 2.25 | 4 | 4.00 | 4 | 2.00 | 2 | 1.50 | 1 |
| Maruti Udyog Ltd | 7.82 | 2 | 1.60 | 1 | 2.20 | 2 | 2.80 | 2 | 3.33 | 4 | 3.66 | 4 | 1.40 | 1 | 2.00 | 2 | 2.00 | 2 | 5.00 | 5 | 2.00 | 2 |
| Hyundai Motors India Ltd | 9.70 | 4 | 3.60 | 4 | 3.80 | 3 | 5.00 | 6 | 2.60 | 2 | 2.83 | 2 | 2.80 | 3 | 0.50 | 1 | 1.00 | 1 | 6.00 | 6 | - | - |
| Honda Siel Cars India Ltd | 7.41 | 1 | 2.60 | 3 | 1.80 | 1 | 1.60 | 1 | 1.00 | 1 | 3.00 | 3 | 2.00 | 2 | 2.20 | 3 | 6.00 | 6 | 3.00 | 3 | - | - |

**TABLE 27.2 (CONTINUED)**

**FINANCIAL COMPETITIVENESS – SCORES AND RANKS OF THE FIRMS FOR INDICATORS (SECTOR WISE)**

| Companies | Overall Index | | Profitability Index | | Assets Utilisation Index | | Cost Effectiveness | | Liquidity Index | | Working capital Efficiency Index | | Solvency Index | | Market Value Index | | Foreign Trade Index | | Productivity Performance Index | | Value Added Performance Index | |
|---|---|---|---|---|---|---|---|---|---|---|---|---|---|---|---|---|---|---|---|---|---|---|
| | Score | Rank | Score | Rank | Score | Rank | Score | Rank | Score | Rank | Score | Rank | Score | Rank | Score | Rank | Score | Rank | Score | Rank | Score | Rank |
| Ford India Private Ltd | 10.88 | 5 | 5.40 | 6 | 4.20 | 4 | 3.00 | 3 | 5.60 | 6 | 2.80 | 1 | 5.20 | 5 | 2.50 | 5 | 3.00 | 3 | 1.00 | 1 | - | - |
| Bajaj Auto Ltd | 6.84 | 2 | 2.40 | 2 | 3.60 | 3 | 2.60 | 2 | 3.33 | 3 | 3.00 | 3 | 3.00 | 3 | 3.00 | 4 | 4.00 | 4 | 3.00 | 3 | 1.00 | 1 |
| LML Ltd | 14.29 | 9 | 8.20 | 8 | 6.80 | 8 | 7.00 | 8 | 7.33 | 8 | 6.33 | 7 | 6.45 | 7 | 6.75 | 8 | 1.00 | 1 | 7.00 | 7 | 3.50 | 3 |
| Maharastra Scooters Ltd | 10.03 | 4 | 2.80 | 3 | 4.80 | 4 | 5.50 | 6 | 4.33 | 4 | 5.00 | 4 | 2.20 | 1 | 2.70 | 2 | - | - | 9.00 | 9 | 5.00 | 5 |
| TVS Motor Company Ltd | 8.03 | 3 | 3.00 | 4 | 2.65 | 2 | 4.00 | 3 | 6.33 | 6 | 2.83 | 2 | 4.80 | 5 | 2.75 | 3 | 6.00 | 6 | 4.00 | 4 | 3.55 | 4 |
| Kinetic Motor Company Ltd | 13.82 | 6 | 8.40 | 9 | 6.20 | 7 | 7.50 | 9 | 4.66 | 5 | 6.16 | 6 | 6.40 | 6 | 5.75 | 6 | 5.00 | 5 | 8.00 | 8 | 7.50 | 7 |
| Hero Honda Motors Ltd | 6.61 | 1 | 1.80 | 1 | 2.60 | 1 | 2.50 | 1 | 7.00 | 7 | 1.50 | 1 | 2.60 | 2 | 2.50 | 1 | 7.00 | 7 | 1.00 | 1 | 2.00 | 2 |
| Kinetic Engineering Ltd | 13.89 | 7 | 7.20 | 7 | 7.40 | 9 | 6.00 | 7 | 3.30 | 2 | 7.50 | 9 | 8.20 | 9 | 7.00 | 9 | 3.00 | 3 | 6.00 | 6 | 7.00 | 6 |
| Majestic Auto Ltd | 12.65 | 5 | 5.40 | 5 | 5.60 | 6 | 5.16 | 4 | 7.66 | 9 | 5.66 | 5 | 7.00 | 8 | 6.70 | 7 | 2.00 | 2 | 2.00 | 2 | 8.00 | 9 |
| Scooters India Ltd | 13.24 | 8 | 5.80 | 6 | 5.40 | 5 | 5.18 | 5 | 1.33 | 1 | 7.16 | 8 | 4.40 | 4 | 5.50 | 5 | 8.00 | 8 | 5.00 | 5 | 7.55 | 8 |

***Source:*** Computed

**TABLE 27.3**

**OVERALL RANKINGS AND SCORES OF AUTOMOBILE FIRMS**

| **Company** | **Rank** | **Score** |
|---|---|---|
| Hero Honda Motors Ltd | 1 | 6.61 |
| Bajaj Auto Ltd | 2 | 6.84 |
| Honda Siel Cars India Ltd | 3 | 7.41 |
| Maruti Udyog Ltd | 4 | 7.82 |
| TVS Motor Company Ltd | 5 | 8.03 |
| Eicher Motors Ltd | 6 | 8.32 |
| Mahindra and Mahindra Ltd | 7 | 8.58 |
| Tata Motors Ltd | 8 | 9.50 |
| Hyundai Motors India Ltd | 9 | 9.70 |
| Swaraj Mazda Ltd | 10 | 9.92 |
| Maharashtra Scooters Ltd | 11 | 10.03 |
| Ashok Leyland Ltd | 12 | 10.47 |
| Ford India Private Ltd | 13 | 10.88 |
| Bajaj Tempo Ltd | 14 | 12.26 |
| Hindustan Motors Ltd | 15 | 12.63 |
| Majestic Auto Ltd | 16 | 12.65 |
| Scooters India Ltd | 17 | 13.24 |
| Kinetic Motor Company Ltd | 18 | 13.82 |
| Kinetic Engineering Ltd | 19 | 13.89 |
| LML Ltd | 20 | 14.29 |
| **Industry Average** | **10.34** | |

***Source:*** Computed

## TABLE 27.4

## FINANCIAL COMPETITIVENESS – OVERALL SCORES AND RANKS OF THE FIRMS FOR INDICATORS

| Companies | Profitability Index | | Assets Utilisation Index | | Cost Effectiveness | | Liquidity Index | | Working capital Efficiency Index | | Solvency Index | | Market Value Index | | Foreign Trade Index | | Productivity Performance Index | | Value Added Performance Index | | Overall Index | |
|---|---|---|---|---|---|---|---|---|---|---|---|---|---|---|---|---|---|---|---|---|---|---|
| | Score | Rank | Score | Rank | Score | Rank | Score | Rank | Score | Rank | Score | Rank | Score | Rank | Score | Rank | Score | Rank | Score | Rank | Score | Rank |
| Ashok Leyland Ltd | 2.40 | 5 | 4.40 | 12 | 3.00 | 8 | 1.30 | 2 | 4.30 | 13 | 2.20 | 4 | 3.00 | 11 | 1.00 | 1 | 1.00 | 1 | 3.00 | 8 | 10.47 | 12 |
| Tata Motors Ltd | 3.00 | 10 | 2.20 | 3 | 2.60 | 3 | 4.00 | 11 | 2.00 | 2 | 3.40 | 10 | 2.70 | 7 | 2.00 | 4 | 2.00 | 4 | 1.50 | 2 | 9.50 | 8 |
| Bajaj Tempo Ltd | 4.60 | 13 | 3.60 | 8 | 3.60 | 10 | 4.30 | 12 | 3.50 | 10 | 3.00 | 8 | 3.25 | 14 | 5.00 | 13 | 5.00 | 13 | 2.50 | 6 | 12.26 | 14 |
| Eicher Motors Ltd | 2.20 | 3 | 2.00 | 2 | 2.85 | 7 | 1.60 | 4 | 2.16 | 3 | 1.80 | 2 | 2.75 | 9 | 3.00 | 7 | 4.00 | 10 | 3.50 | 9 | 8.32 | 6 |
| Swaraj Mazda Ltd | 2.80 | 8 | 2.80 | 7 | 2.80 | 5 | 3.60 | 10 | 3.00 | 7 | 4.60 | 13 | 3.20 | 13 | 4.00 | 10 | 3.00 | 7 | 4.50 | 12 | 9.92 | 10 |
| Hindustan Motors Ltd | 5.60 | 16 | 4.40 | 12 | 4.60 | 13 | 5.30 | 15 | 4.50 | 14 | 5.80 | 16 | 4.00 | 15 | 5.00 | 13 | 4.00 | 10 | 2.50 | 6 | 12.63 | 15 |
| Mahindra and Mahindra Ltd | 2.20 | 3 | 4.60 | 14 | 3.80 | 11 | 3.00 | 6 | 4.16 | 12 | 3.80 | 11 | 2.25 | 4 | 4.00 | 10 | 2.00 | 4 | 1.50 | 2 | 8.58 | 7 |
| Maruti Udyog Ltd | 1.60 | 1 | 2.20 | 3 | 2.80 | 5 | 3.33 | 8 | 3.66 | 11 | 1.40 | 1 | 2.00 | 2 | 2.00 | 4 | 5.00 | 13 | 2.00 | 4 | 7.82 | 4 |
| Hyundai Motors India Ltd | 3.60 | 12 | 3.80 | 10 | 5.00 | 14 | 2.60 | 5 | 2.83 | 5 | 2.80 | 7 | 0.50 | 1 | 1.00 | 1 | 6.00 | 16 | - | - | 9.70 | 9 |
| Honda Siel Cars India Ltd | 2.60 | 7 | 1.80 | 1 | 1.60 | 1 | 1.00 | 1 | 3.00 | 7 | 2.00 | 3 | 2.20 | 3 | 6.00 | 16 | 3.00 | 7 | - | - | 7.41 | 3 |
| Ford India Private Ltd | 5.40 | 14 | 4.20 | 11 | 3.00 | 8 | 5.60 | 16 | 2.80 | 4 | 5.20 | 15 | 2.50 | 5 | 3.00 | 7 | 1.00 | 1 | - | - | 10.88 | 13 |

## TABLE 27.4 (CONTINUED)

## FINANCIAL COMPETITIVENESS – OVERALL SCORES AND RANKS OF THE FIRMS FOR INDICATORS

| Companies | Profitability Index | | Assets Utilisation Index | | Cost Effectiveness | | Liquidity Index | | Working capital Efficiency Index | | Solvency Index | | Market Value Index | | Foreign Trade Index | | Productivity Performance Index | | Value Added Performance Index | | Overall Index | |
|---|---|---|---|---|---|---|---|---|---|---|---|---|---|---|---|---|---|---|---|---|---|---|
| | Score | Rank | Score | Rank | Score | Rank | Score | Rank | Score | Rank | Score | Rank | Score | Rank | Score | Rank | Score | Rank | Score | Rank | Score | Rank |
| Bajaj Auto Ltd | 2.40 | 5 | 3.60 | 8 | 2.60 | 3 | 3.33 | 8 | 3.00 | 7 | 3.00 | 8 | 3.00 | 11 | 4.00 | 10 | 3.00 | 7 | 1.00 | 1 | 6.84 | 2 |
| LML Ltd | 8.20 | 19 | 6.80 | 19 | 7.00 | 19 | 7.33 | 19 | 6.33 | 18 | 6.45 | 18 | 6.75 | 19 | 1.00 | 1 | 7.00 | 18 | 3.50 | 9 | 14.29 | 20 |
| Maharastra Scooters Ltd | 2.80 | 8 | 4.80 | 15 | 5.50 | 17 | 4.33 | 13 | 5.00 | 15 | 2.20 | 4 | 2.70 | 7 | - | - | 9.00 | 20 | 5.00 | 13 | 10.03 | 11 |
| TVS Motor Company Ltd | 3.00 | 10 | 2.65 | 6 | 4.00 | 12 | 6.33 | 17 | 2.83 | 5 | 4.80 | 14 | 2.75 | 9 | 6.00 | 16 | 4.00 | 10 | 3.55 | 11 | 8.03 | 5 |
| Kinetic Motor Company Ltd | 8.40 | 20 | 6.20 | 18 | 7.50 | 20 | 4.66 | 14 | 6.16 | 17 | 6.40 | 17 | 5.75 | 17 | 5.00 | 13 | 8.00 | 19 | 7.50 | 15 | 13.82 | 18 |
| Hero Honda Motors Ltd | 1.80 | 2 | 2.60 | 5 | 2.50 | 2 | 7.00 | 18 | 1.50 | 1 | 2.60 | 6 | 2.50 | 5 | 7.00 | 18 | 1.00 | 1 | 2.00 | 4 | 6.61 | 1 |
| Kinetic Engineering Ltd | 7.20 | 18 | 7.40 | 20 | 6.00 | 18 | 3.30 | 7 | 7.50 | 20 | 8.20 | 20 | 7.00 | 20 | 3.00 | 7 | 6.00 | 16 | 7.00 | 14 | 13.89 | 19 |
| Majestic Auto Ltd | 5.40 | 14 | 5.60 | 17 | 5.16 | 15 | 7.66 | 20 | 5.66 | 16 | 7.00 | 19 | 6.70 | 18 | 2.00 | 4 | 2.00 | 4 | 8.00 | 17 | 12.65 | 16 |
| Scooters India Ltd | 5.80 | 17 | 5.40 | 16 | 5.18 | 16 | 1.33 | 3 | 7.16 | 19 | 4.40 | 12 | 5.50 | 16 | 8.00 | 19 | 5.00 | 13 | 7.55 | 16 | 13.24 | 17 |
| **Industry Average** | **4.05** | | **4.05** | | **4.00** | | **4.01** | | **4.20** | | **4.05** | | **3.55** | | **3.78** | | **3.80** | | **3.88** | | **10.34** | |

***Source:*** Computed